2e Managing Organizations

Principles & Guidelines

Second Edition

Thomas N. Duening, Ph.D.

Director, Entrepreneurial Programs Office
Arizona State University

John M. Ivancevich, DBA

Cullen Research Professor of Organizational
Behavior and Management
C.T. Bauer College of Business
University of Houston

ATOMIC**dog**PUBLISHING

Cincinnati, Ohio
www.atomicdog.com

Book Team

Vice President, Publisher Steve Scoble
Managing Editor Kendra Leonard
Director of Interactive Media and Design Joe Devine
Director of Quality Assurance Tim Bair
Production Coordinator Kathy Davis
Web Production Editor Joyce Powers
Quality Assurance Editor Dan Horton
Marketing Manager Mikka Baker
Cover Designer Zach Hicks

When ordering this title, use ISBN 1-59260-207-X

ISBN 1-59260-205-3

Library of Congress Control Number: 2005929458

Printed in the United States of America by Atomic Dog Publishing,
35 East Seventh Street, Fourth Floor, Cincinnati, OH 45202

10 9 8 7 6 5 4 3 2 1

This book is dedicated to our families who inspire and support the entire process of developing a teachable book.

Brief Contents

Contents

Preface

Over the course of our careers we have learned a number of things about the work of managers. A few of these factors have influenced how we teach, study, and write about managers. First, the work of managers is challenging and ranges from routine to dramatic uncertainty.

Second, managers are needed to plan, organize, control, and direct, but to also encourage, facilitate, develop, and motivate human assets. It is managers who can play the most noticeable role in protecting and nurturing human assets.

Third, much of the work of managers can be referred to as art. However, as more sound theoretical frameworks and empirical studies are aggregated and disseminated, more science is starting to impact human assets and organizational operations.

Fourth, managers need to learn more about different cultures, global alliance building, and legal facts. The education of managers is certainly continuous.

Finally, for students of management to learn the content of this book, it must be meaningful, relevant, realistic, interesting, and accurate. These five lessons learned served as the "core" in revising the book. This revision is based on the core lessons and feedback received on the first edition.

Managing Organizations: Principles & Guidelines, Second Edition, is written in a style that will invite interest, continuous learning, and attention to managerial tasks, responsibilities, and functions. In the 21st century, managers will play a crucial role in operating organizations in every industry classification, geographical location, and of every conceivable size. As teachers of management we know that managerial concepts that fit so well in one setting are often misaligned in other settings. The practice of management is challenging, simple, mysterious, rewarding, and frustrating all at the same time.

The revised book clearly illustrates the following:

1. There is no one best way to manage
2. Organizations are currently encouraging more self-management and empowerment than in any era.
3. Managerial applications and efficient leadership styles are needed in developing countries to enhance and/or sustain the quality of life and standard of living.
4. Effective management requires knowledge, practice, persistence, and a commitment to learn by doing.
5. Managers need to manage change or they will inevitably be consumed by totally unpredictable events and circumstances.
6. The manager in the 21st century must have knowledge and some background in economics, writing, history, sociology, psychology, political science, law, organizational behavior, finance, the social sciences, mathematics and statistics, ethical principles, marketing, and international relations and transactions. There is no short cut in acquiring knowledge and experience for managers to take to improve their effectiveness.

7. Managers must do more than talk about the importance of "human capital assets." They must apply the best available principles and guidelines to manage, coach, support, and lead the people they are responsible for in organizations.

8. Each generation has a different mindset in terms of what they want from their work, organization, colleagues, and managers. Learning and being sensitive about generational mind-sets and differences across generations is a part of the manager's responsibility.

9. Managers must accept the fact that they will be continuously learning. The learning lessons apply to individuals, teams, groups, communities, processes, procedures, techniques, and style. The learning should and will never cease.

These few lessons should come alive as you progress through this revised edition. Being engaged and involved with the book will help students (readers) recognize each of these nine lessons as the book's journey unfolds.

The Structure of the Book

Books are organized for the purpose of learning. However, each instructor has his or her perspective of the sequence of chapters or the parts to cover in their course. We respect each instructor's perspective. This book's structure is versatile and can be easily modified by instructors to fit their style, preference, and classroom objectives. The architecture of the book has been rated highly by adopters of the first edition. Thus, we continue to use the preferred layout.

Part 1

Introduction to Management consists of four introductory chapters that present the background for the remainder of the book. Chapters 1 and 2 examine the manager's job, skills, and roles. Chapter 3 explores the important concepts of ethics and social responsibility. Chapter 4 presents globalization and diversity concepts, examples, and issues.

Part 2

Planning includes three chapters. Chapter 5 explores the elements of planning, Chapter 6 examines strategic planning, and Chapter 7 covers decision making and problem solving.

Part 3

Organizing includes three chapters. Chapter 8 examines work design, Chapter 9 explores organizational structure, and Chapter 10 covers the management of human resources.

Part 4

Leading consists of four chapters. Chapter 11 presents leadership, Chapter 12 discusses motivation, Chapter 13 is on communications, and Chapter 14 covers work groups and teams.

Part 5

Controlling includes two chapters on control concepts.

Part 6

Managing Change and Innovation is covered in one chapter that examines change, change strategies, learning, and knowledge management.

Chapter Elements

Learning, understanding, critically evaluating, and comparing are what is intended for the students (readers) using this book. To accomplish these goals a number of chapter elements are incorporated throughout the book. Each chapter in *Managing Organizations: Principles & Guidelines,* Second Edition, includes the following elements:

Learning Objectives—multiple performance objectives to establish the pathways that will be taken in each chapter. These objectives are linked to the "Management Summary" elements.

Opening Vignette—an actual in-company example to introduce the main subject and content of the chapter.

Management Focus on Stories/Examples—a number of themes are covered in the example boxes including diversity, globalization, innovation, customer service, technology, ethics, and leadership. This element focuses on an issue, person, or problem.

Learning Moment—interspersed in the chapter are these "learning moment" review boxes. Brief summaries of key points are highlighted.

Management Summary—a brief bullet point review of some of the main points made in the chapter.

Review and Discussion Questions—short response/essay type questions linked to the chapter's opening objectives are presented.

Practice Quiz—true, false and multiple-choice questions and answers are used for self-testing. Students can test their knowledge acquisition by using these questions. They are a quick way to check progress, find problem spots, and pause and reflect. The quizzes are interactive, which means that the students can take the quiz online and are given feedback on their answers. Errors are explained and students are referred back to appropriate sections for reexamination.

Case Study—a real-world situation facing a manager or managers is presented for review, debate, and analysis. Using these in class will result in discussions and differences of opinions. This type of analysis, debate, and learning is exactly what occurs in organizations when individuals are faced with an issue, problem, or situation.

Internet Exercise—an assignment for students to complete by using the Internet. Each exercise is tied to some aspect of the chapter's content.

Experiential Exercise—an individual or group exercise that asks the student to explore an issue, situation, or incident that pertains to the subjects covered in the chapter.

AACSB/IAME

The Association to Advance Collegiate Schools of Business/International Association for Management Education encourages instructors, schools, and authors to cover globalization, cultural diversity, ethical decision making, and customer and product issues. *Managing Organizations: Principles & Guidelines,* Second Edition, specifically and thoroughly covers each of these subject areas in the chapter content and elements.

Using the Online Edition

Managing Organizations: Principles & Guidelines, Second Edition, is available online as well as in print. The online chapters demonstrate how the interactive media components of the text enhance presentation and understanding. For example,

- Animated illustrations help clarify concepts.
- QuickCheck interactive questions and chapter quizzes test your knowledge of various topics and provide immediate feedback.
- Clickable glossary terms provide immediate definitions of key concepts.
- The search function allows you to quickly locate discussions of specific topics throughout the text.
- Highlighting capabilities allow you to emphasize main ideas. You can also add personal notes in the margin.

You may choose to use just the online version of the text, or both the online and the print versions together. This gives you the flexibility to choose which combination of resources works best for you. To assist those who use the online and print versions together, the primary heads and subheads in each chapter are numbered the same. For example, the first primary head in Chapter 1 is labeled 1-1, the second primary head in this chapter is labeled 1-2, and so on. The subheads build from the designation of their corresponding primary head: 1-1a, 1-1b, etc. This numbering system is designed to make moving between the online and print versions as seamless as possible.

Finally, next to a number of figures in the print version of the text, you will see an icon similar to the one on the left. This icon indicates that these figures in the online version of the text are interactive in a way that applies, illustrates, or reinforces the concept.

The Author Team

Authors come in all varieties, with different backgrounds and experiences, and various knowledge, skill, and talent pools. We (Tom Duening and John Ivancevich) are experienced teachers, researchers, trainers, and consultants. Together we have taught management courses for over 50 years, and we continue to teach. We have authored textbooks, trade books, monographs, technical reports, and refereed professional papers. In addition, we are in constant contact, discussions, problem solving, and analysis with practicing managers from around the world. Throughout the day we talk to, debate with, observe, and learn from managers. This constant contact and continuous learning has helped shape the book's content, elements, style, examples, and presentation.

We both recognize the importance of preparing a student/reader-friendly book. The unity, style, tone, flow, and themes were prepared for the reader and the instructor using the book. In future editions we will use the feedback we receive to further refine and improve the contents and elements. This book is purposefully written for students and instructors. Their satisfaction and acceptance of our work is very important and will be monitored so that the best guided changes and improvements in the book can be made.

Ancillary Materials

Test Bank—Includes more than 2,500 questions, developed by Kathy Hayward of PivotalForce and Suntech Data Systems. Available in ExamView Pro® format, which enables instructors to quickly create printed tests using either a Windows or Macintosh computer. Instructors can enter their own questions and customize the appearance of the tests they create.

PowerPoint® Presentations—Offer over 425 slides created by Dr. Paula E. Brown, Northern Illinois University, and Suntech Data Systems.

Instructors Manual—Contains chapter overview, sample lesson plans, chapter outlines with important topics, key terms, in-class teaching ideas, and suggestions, plus much more.

About the Authors

Thomas N. Duening, Ph.D., Arizona State University

Dr. Tom Duening is Director, Entrepreneurial Programs Office at the Ira A. Fulton School of Engineering, Arizona State University. He has previously served as founder and director of the Entrepreneur & Venture Development Center at the University of Houston Downtown, and as the assistant dean of the C.T. Bauer College of Business at the University of Houston.

Dr. Duening has published numerous trade books and textbooks on management and business. His most recent book, *Essentials of Businesss Process Outsourcing,* was published in March 2005 by John Wiley & Sons. Dr. Duening has published numerous articles in business journals, magazines, and newspapers, and popular media often seeks his views on management, business trends, and other issues. He is president of INSYTE Business Research Group, a business research and advisory firm. Dr. Duening has M.A. and Ph.D. degrees from the University of Minnesota.

John M. Ivancevich, DBA, University of Houston

Dr. John M. Ivancevich is the Hugh Roy and Lillie Cranz Cullen Chair in Organizational Behavior and Management at the University of Houston. As part of a continuing academic career as distinguished professor, dean, provost, and recognized authority in management, John (Jack) Ivancevich is currently working on teaching, textbooks, professional books, field research, and developing Web-enabled courseware products and services.

Jack has a B.S. in Industrial Management from Purdue University, an MBA in Organizational Behavior and a DBA (Doctor of Business Administration) in Administrative Behavior and Organizational Analysis, both from the University of Maryland.

As Dean of the College of Business Administration 1988–1995 and Provost 1995–1997, Jack was recognized for his leadership in academic program building, fundraising, curriculum reform, the development of innovative programs in entrepreneurship, dispute resolution and environmental concerns, and initiating international exchange and degree programs with institutions in Europe and the Far East.

Jack joined the UH faculty in 1974 as professor in the College of Business Administration. Previously, he taught at the University of Maryland and the University of Kentucky. In 1975, he became Chair of the Department of Organizational Behavior and Management and was named Associate Dean for Research in 1976, where he was responsible for stimulating research activities and the creation of the school's first information technology support center. In 1979 Jack was awarded the Hugh Roy and Lillie Cranz Cullen Chair of Organizational Behavior and Management.

He is the author or co-author of 70 textbooks and 150 refereed articles in management, human resource management, and organizational behavior and an increasing library of Web-enabled courses on management and organizational behavior, which are used by educational and corporate institutions around the world. Jack serves on a number of boards and business associations and organizations and is a reviewer and member of editorial boards for a number of academic journals. He has conducted research, training, and consulting in over 100 firms of all sizes.

He is the recipient of numerous awards, among them the Esther Farfel Award, UH's highest faculty award; The Academy of Management's Hall of Fame, as one of the first 33 charter members for recognition of research and productivity; the Presidential Service Award from the UH Alumni Organization; and the University of Houston Law Alumni Association Faculty Award. He is listed in the *Who's Who* registry of Global Business Leaders.

Acknowledgments

We are grateful to Steve Scoble, Kendra Leonard, Victoria Putman, Kathy Davis, Ann Peter, and the entire Atomic Dog Publishing team. They each have, because of their professionalism, made this revised edition's preparation and delivery a pleasant and enjoyable experience.

Peggy Adams of Applied Management Sciences Institute served as the coordinator, manager, and preparer of the book. Her ability to manage and lead the two authors has been exceptional. Schedules, reviews, and changes were ably handled by Peggy. We thank her for everything that you like about this book.

Part 1

Introduction to Management

 1 The Evolution of Management Thought

 2 Management: Skills, Roles, and Modern Challenges

 3 Social Responsibility and Management Ethics

4 Managing Globally

The chapters that compose Part 1 of this text introduce the reader to the study of management. This part conveys the importance of management as a force for achieving the good things of life. Managers are found in any and all organizations that societies create to produce goods and services; to deliver health care, social support, and education; and to provide settings for worship, public service, and government. Managers perform the difficult task of seeing to it that these organizations accomplish the purposes that societies expect of them.

Analyzing and understanding the processes that managers use to achieve organizational performance is the underlying theme of this book. Chapter 1 introduces the concept of "management" and suggests that it can be understood and studied by dealing with four separate functions: planning, organizing, leading, and controlling.

Managers' jobs consist of activities that can be classified according to these four functions. With this classification, we are better able to study, understand, and practice management. The discussion in Chapter 1 demonstrates that management processes have been the subject of considerable theory development and research. Many scholars and practitioners of management have contributed to the growing body of literature in the field. This literature provides a rich source of information for those who wish to learn more about the problems, practices, and promises of management.

What does it take to be an effective manager? This question has been at the heart of the study of management throughout the history of the field. Chapter 2 presents information from studies that have sought answers to this important question. The findings from these studies indicate that managers play particular roles in organizations and that playing these roles requires certain skills. Through the application of managerial skills, the managerial process can be the source of high levels of organizational and individual performance.

Chapter 3 focuses on issues that have been getting increasing attention by the public, business schools, and top executives: the ethical and social responsibility of business. There are widely varying views about the role of business organizations in modern society. You will have a chance to study and think about these views, and discuss them in class.

Finally, Chapter 4 discusses another important issue for modern managers, the globalization of the economy. The term *globalization* is used so often today that we may have become immune to its true meaning and impact. It may seem common to talk about the "global" economy because we are, today, so familiar with news reports, sporting events, and other occurrences around the globe coming to us each night on television. But you must keep in mind that this global communications revolution is only about thirty years old, and the Internet and the withdrawal of communism are less than a decade old. These and other dramatic changes have brought with them new markets, new business opportunities, and new challenges for managers.[1] Chapter 4 will discuss the changes wrought by the global economy.

Management is a discipline in continual evolution. Three well-established approaches—classical, behavioral, and management science—have contributed to our ability to manage different aspects of organizations, namely work and organizations, people, and production and operations. Thus, it would be virtually impossible to write a management book without including contributions from all approaches. In addition, wherever possible, the book encourages "systems thinking" and a "contingency perspective." The plan for this book is outlined in Figure 1-1.

Figure 1-1 indicates that the process of management is the focus of the book. You should know that merely learning the many techniques and concepts that other disciplines have contributed to the field of management will not necessarily produce an effective manager. To be effective you must know which technique is appropriate for which situation. This view is clearly stated by management scholar Peter Drucker:

> Managers practice management. They do not practice economics. They do not practice quantification. They do not practice behavioral science. These are tools for the manager.... As a specific discipline, management has its own basic problems ... specific approaches ... distinct concerns. A man who only knows the skills and techniques, without understanding the fundamentals of management, is not a manager; he is, at best, only a technician.[2]

When you finish this book, you will be equipped with the knowledge, attitudes, and skills that will enable you to evaluate which management practice fits which situation.

The Evolution of Management Thought

Managing Today

Applied Management at Ford Motor Company

CEO Bill Ford, Jr. of the Ford Motor Company touted a new environmentally friendly Ford. Finally, in 2004 the Ford Escape Hybrid made its entrance. The management coordination, planning, organizing, and controlling that went into the development, testing, production, and scheduling could fill an entire book. The Escape contains nine technologies and posed many complex decisions for the Ford team.

The launch of the Ford Escape Hybrid SUV required management expertise, technical problem solving, human resource motivation, leadership, coordination, adaptation to changes, and intense relationship building between Ford and its suppliers around the globe. It took over five years of effective management of the Escape project to bring the SUV to market.

The stakes for Ford are high because Honda and Toyota brought their hybrids to market in the United States in 1999 (Honda) and 2000 (Toyota). In order to gain some market traction, Ford broke a number of its 101-year-old management traditions. Ford did so in order to speed the development to market cycle and to optimize the talents of the team assembled to produce the most environmentally friendly vehicle possible at the time. A few of the unconventional Ford approaches were:

- Integrating teams of engineers and scientists, instead of operating as separate specialties.
- Allowing the Escape team to operate without senior Ford executives poking around, watching, or asking for updates. The typical Ford approach is to closely manage and monitor a new product.
- Requesting help immediately from outside the hybrid team. Ford is notorious for not seeking help outside a project.

The managerial success of the Ford Escape Hybrid SUV is a testament to the faith the company displayed in its managers, engineers, scientists, technicians, operating employees, and marketing experts. The market will be voting over the next few years on the Escape. If the SUV is what Ford believes it is, and if it avoids recalls, then the company can make another addition to its history of successes.

Sources: Chuck Slater, "Ford's Escape Route," *Fast Company,* October 2004, pp. 106–110; Ford Annual Report, 2003; *Preview: 2005 Ford Escape Hybrid,* www.autosite.com/Previews; and James R. Henley, "Test Drive," *USA Today,* May 13, 2004, p. 2D.

1-1 Introduction

This book deals with the functions that managers must perform to be successful. Modern managers must coordinate the efforts of diverse people with complex technology and focused strategies to face global competitive challenges. The primary objective of this text is to provide students with the tools needed to perform more effectively when they become managers. By studying with this book, you will gain an increased understanding of the attributes managers need to help them achieve their mission. The book's thesis is that . . . , to be successful, a manager must use an integrated approach. In other words, successful managers do not rely on a single management skill or principle, favorite technique, or specific model to achieve their goals. They use a combination of existing tools, principles, and approaches.

Today the tools and principles managers need to be successful must be updated and upgraded continuously. Many organizations have beefed up their training and education programs for managers to help them keep pace with the rising competition, information technology, and rapid change that mark the modern business environment. Peter Drucker, a well-known management scholar and philosopher, has identified three major tasks of management:

1. To decide the purpose and mission of the organization
2. To make work productive
3. To manage social impacts and responsibilities[3]

In society, important work is done by individuals with such titles as restaurant manager, production manager, marketing manager, chairperson, college dean, superintendent, ship captain, mayor, governor, and many others. These individuals may work in different types of organizations with different purposes, but they all have one thing in common: They practice management. Our society depends on the goods and services provided by the organizations these individuals manage.

Each of us is influenced by the actions of managers everyday because we come into contact with organizations everyday. Our experiences may be as students in a college, patients in a hospital, customers of a business, or citizens of a state. Whether we are *satisfied* with our experiences, however, depends greatly on the individuals who manage the organization. *All* organizations are guided and directed by the decisions of one or more individuals who are commonly known as *managers*.

1-2 Management Has Different Meanings

The term **management** can have different meanings, and it is important that you understand each. There are four primary views of "management":

1. Management is a process.
2. Management is a discipline.
3. Management is a human activity.
4. Management is a career.

> **management** The process undertaken by one or more persons to coordinate the activities of other persons to achieve results not attainable by any one person acting alone.

None of these views of management is a correct or incorrect view. Each has a different perspective on this important part of modern life. Let's explore each view briefly.

1-2a Management Is a Process

Have you ever said, or heard anyone else say, "That is a well-managed company" or "That organization is mismanaged." What is meant by such statements? They seem to imply that:

1. Management is some type of work or set of activities.
2. Sometimes the activities are performed quite well, and sometimes not so well.

Such statements imply that management is a *process* involving certain functions and activities that managers perform. This book introduces you to the management process, the functions managers perform, and the principles they apply in managing organizations.

1-2b Management Is a Discipline

If you say that you are a student of management or are majoring in management, you are referring to the *discipline* of management. Classifying management as a discipline implies that it is an accumulated body of knowledge that can be learned. Thus, management is a subject with principles, concepts, and theories. A major purpose of studying management is to learn how to apply these principles, concepts, and theories at the right time and under the right circumstances to produce desired results.

1-2c Management Is a Human Activity

Whether you say, "That company has an entirely new management team" or "She is the best manager I've ever worked for," you are referring to the people who guide, direct, and, thus manage organizations. The word *management* used in this manner refers to the *people* who engage in the process of management. Managers are the people primarily responsible for seeing that work gets done in an organization.

The perspective of management as a human activity has another meaning. It refers to and emphasizes the importance of the employees whom managers work with and manage in accomplishing an organization's objectives. People are an organization's most important asset; successful organizations—indeed the well-being of society—require a strong, mutually satisfying partnership between managers and the people they manage.

1-2d Management Is a Career

"Mr. Johnson has held several managerial positions since joining the bank upon his graduation from college." "After receiving her degree in business, Ms. Smith entered the company's management training program." Such statements imply that management is a career. People who devote their working lives to managing often progress through a sequence of activities, jobs, organizations, and challenges that constitute a **career.** More

> **career** An individually perceived sequence of attitudes and behaviors associated with work-related experiences and activities over the span of a person's life.

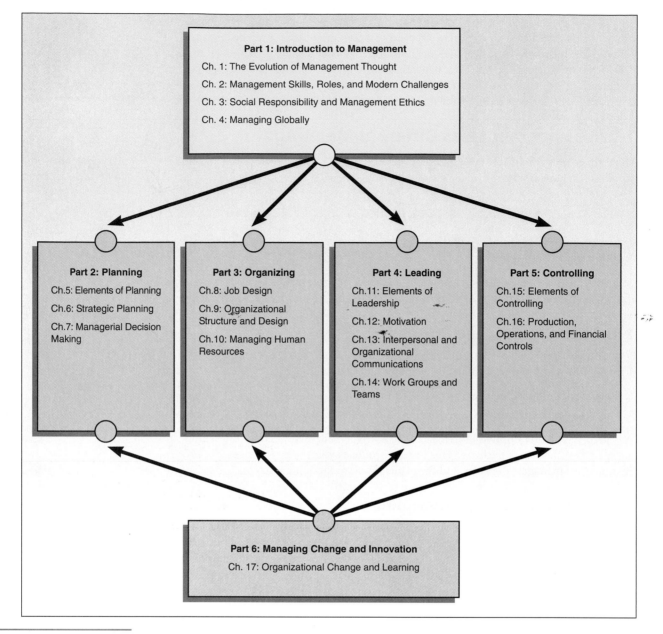

Part 1: Introduction to Management

Ch. 1: The Evolution of Management Thought

Ch. 2: Management Skills, Roles, and Modern Challenges

Ch. 3: Social Responsibility and Management Ethics

Ch. 4: Managing Globally

Part 2: Planning

Ch.5: Elements of Planning

Ch.6: Strategic Planning

Ch.7: Managerial Decision Making

Part 3: Organizing

Ch.8: Job Design

Ch.9: Organizational Structure and Design

Ch.10: Managing Human Resources

Part 4: Leading

Ch.11: Elements of Leadership

Ch.12: Motivation

Ch.13: Interpersonal and Organizational Communications

Ch.14: Work Groups and Teams

Part 5: Controlling

Ch.15: Elements of Controlling

Ch.16: Production, Operations, and Financial Controls

Part 6: Managing Change and Innovation

Ch. 17: Organizational Change and Learning

Figure 1-1
Plan for This Book

▶ **management functions**
The activities that a manager must perform as a result of the position held in the organization. The text identifies planning, organizing, leading, and controlling as the management functions.

than ever before, today's business environment is fast changing and competitive, posing challenges, opportunities, and rewards for individuals pursuing careers in management. To keep up, managers need to constantly learn new skills and update their understanding of their business and their industry.[4]

1-3 The Functions of Management

The process of management consists of certain basic **management functions.** The entire process and the individual management functions are presented in Figure 1-1, which shows the overall plan for this book.

Figure 1-1 indicates that the management process is an integrated whole. However, something as complex as the management process is more easily understood when it is described as a series of separate activities or functions making up the entire process. The model of management used throughout this book identifies the management functions as *planning, organizing,* and *controlling,* linked together by *leadership.* Planning determines *what* results the organization will achieve; organizing specifies *how* it will achieve the

Management Focus on Diversity

Diversity at the Top Provides Different Viewpoints

The United States' workforce is now approximately 40% female and the population now numbers about 15% Hispanic and 13% African American. However, a look at the Fortune 1000 board of directors rosters displays only 15% women, 5% African Americans, and 2% Hispanics serving on these boards.

The Sarbanes-Oxley Act of 2001 requires that boards of publicly traded companies should include truly independent directors. The traditional networks of filling board seats with friends and colleagues will not provide the degree of diversity that boards lack. A more diverse board in many cases has shown that it provides new perspectives on cultures, life experiences, purchasing decisions, needs, and interests. The voices and ideas of women and minorities suggest that opening the boardroom door can be very good for business and considering different approaches to problem solving.

Source: Julie Bennett, "For Women and Minorities, Reaching the Boardroom Remains a Rough Ride," *Wall Street Journal,* October 12, 2004, p. B11.

results; and controlling determines ~~whether~~ results are achieved. Through planning, organizing, and controlling, managers exercise leadership.

1-3a Leading

Leading is the management process that integrates everything else a manager does. No matter if a manager is involved in planning, organizing, or controlling, his or her leadership style and leadership abilities play a significant role. **Leadership** is a difficult concept to define, but essentially means the ability to influence others to pursue a common goal. We all know examples of good leaders: Martin Luther King, Jr., Gandhi, and Winston Churchill, to name just a few. Good leaders typically are driven by an overriding vision or mission. They influence others to pursue that vision by communicating it in captivating ways. Leadership requires courage and commitment. Often, a leader will have a vision of change that others are unable to accept. This can lead to resistance, foot-dragging, and even outright hostility. The Management Focus on Diversity box, "Diversity at the Top Provides Different Viewpoints," discusses how far organizations have to go to capture diverse viewpoints of board members to achieve advantages for their organizations.

> **leadership** In the context of management theory, a person's ability to influence the activities of followers in an organizational setting.

1-3b Planning

The **planning function** is the capstone activity of management. Planning activities determine an organization's objectives and establish the appropriate strategies for achieving those objectives. The organizing, leading, and controlling functions all derive from planning in that these functions carry out the planning decisions.

All managers at every level of the organization engage in planning. Through their plans, managers outline what the organization must do to be successful. Although plans may differ in focus, they are all concerned with achieving organizational goals in the short and long term.

> **planning function** All managerial activities that lead to the definition of objectives and to the determination of appropriate means to achieve those objectives.

1-3c Organizing

After managers develop objectives and plans to achieve them they must design and develop an organization that will be able to accomplish the objectives. The **organizing function** creates a structure of task and authority relationships that serves this purpose.

To ensure that objectives set by planning can be achieved, the organizing function takes the tasks identified during planning and assigns them to individuals and groups within the organization. Organizing, then, can be thought of as turning plans into action. The organizing function also provides an organizational structure that enables the organization to function effectively as a cohesive whole.

> **organizing function** All managerial activity that results in the design of a formal structure of task and authority.

LearningMoment *Becoming a Manager*

Reading a book is not the only way to learn about management. This text can provide you with the *knowledge, attitudes, and skills to apply to your knowledge once you become a manager*. You would probably learn these attitudes and skills on the job, but the process would certainly take longer and not be as tightly organized. The important thing to remember is that you *can* learn to be an effective manager. Though this book may not make you an effective manager by itself, it will help you accomplish this goal.

▶**controlling function** The actions and decisions that managers undertake to ensure that actual results are consistent with desired results.

1-3d Controlling

Finally, managers must make sure that the actual performance of the organization conforms with the performance that was planned for the organization. This is the **controlling function** of management, and it requires three elements:

1. Established standards of performance
2. Information that indicates deviations between actual performance and the established standards
3. Action to correct performance that does not meet the standards

Simply speaking, management control makes sure the organization stays on the path that was planned for it.

At this point, you should note that the management process does not involve four separate or unrelated activities but a group of closely related functions. Also, the four functions do not necessarily occur in the sequence we have presented. In fact, the only time they might do so is when a new organization is being formed. In reality, various combinations of the four activities usually occur simultaneously.

1-4 History of Management Thought

Most of the early management theorists were practicing executives who described their own experiences from which they developed broad principles. They wanted to share with others the practices that seemed to work for them. A great deal of management knowledge comes from the autobiographies and memoirs of people who practiced management.

Many individuals whose interest in management was or is strictly scientific also have contributed knowledge to the field. Management professors, psychologists, sociologists, and anthropologists consider management to be a social phenomenon and managers to be an important social resource. Their interest is strictly scientific—they want to understand and to explain the process of management, and the skills that are required to be an effective manager. Numerous other professions such as mathematics, accounting, economics, law, political science, engineering, and philosophy also have contributed to the understanding of management.

With so many individuals with different purposes and such diverse fields of study contributing to understanding, we face a problem: How can we study the discipline of management in a coherent way? The answer is: The knowledge must be organized so that it becomes meaningful and useful. Management scholars (and textbook writers) have looked back on the history of management thought and have grouped the diverse ideas into three basic approaches:

1. The *classical* approach
2. The *behavioral* approach
3. The *management science* approach

Figure 1-2 shows how these different theories were influential during different times over the past 130 years.

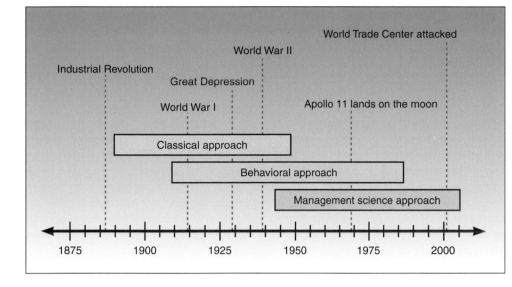

Figure 1-2
The Evolution of Management Thought

1-5 The Classical Approach

Serious study of management began in the late nineteenth century. This was a time when the United States was in the throes of the Industrial Revolution. Automobile plants, steel mills, textile mills, railroad yards, and other major industries were revving up. Immigrants from around the world flocked to U.S. shores to work in the plants and carve out a living for themselves and their families. One of the critical problems facing managers at that time was how to increase the efficiency and productivity of this ready and willing, but unskilled workforce. The effort to understand work, and how workers could be made more productive and efficient, marked the beginning of the study of modern management. This early research produced theories, concepts, and practices that have come to be labeled the *classical approach.*

The **classical approach to management** can be better understood by examining it from two perspectives. These two perspectives are based on the organizational problems each examined. One perspective concentrated on the problems of lower-level managers dealing with the everyday problems of the workforce. This perspective is known as **scientific management.** The other perspective concentrated on the problems top-level managers face in managing the organization as a whole. This perspective is known as **classical organization theory.**

1-5a Scientific Management

At the beginning of the twentieth century, business was expanding and creating new products and new markets, but labor was in short supply. Two solutions were available:

1. Substitute capital for labor, or
2. Use labor more efficiently.

▶ **classical approach to management** An approach that places reliance on such management principles as unity of command, a balance between authority and responsibility, division of labor, and delegation to establish relationships between managers and subordinates.

▶ **scientific management** The practices introduced by Frederick W. Taylor to accomplish the management job. Taylor advocated the use of scientific procedures to find the "one best way" to do a job.

▶ **classical organization theory** A body of ideas that focused on the problem faced by top managers of large organizations; its two major purposes were to develop basic principles that guide the design, creation, and maintenance of large organizations and to identify the basic functions of managing organizations.

LearningMoment   *The Classical Approach Is Fundamental*

Don't think that because many ideas in the classical approach were formulated more than a century ago they are not relevant today. For the student of management, the contributions of the classical approach are critical. These insights, in fact, constitute the core of the discipline of management and the process of management and comprise a major part of this book.

Scientific management concentrated on the second solution. The labor force in America's factories and mills at the beginning of the twentieth century was largely made up of immigrants with little or no formal education. Most were reliable, hardworking individuals, but they didn't have the intellectual skills needed to evaluate the organization's work flow and the communication skills to drive change. Thus, scientific management emerged as a means of studying work processes and finding ways to make them more efficient.

The most well-known contributor to scientific management was Frederick W. Taylor.[5] Taylor joined the American Society of Mechanical Engineers in 1886 (www.asme.org) and used this organization to develop and test the ideas he formulated while working in various steel firms. In one of these firms, Midvale Steel Company, he observed workers producing far less than their capacities. Taylor believed this waste was due to ignorance of what constituted a fair day's work. At that time, no studies had been conducted to determine expected daily output per worker (work standards) and the relationship between work standards and the wage system. Taylor's personal dislike for waste caused him to rebel at what he interpreted as inefficient labor and management practices based solely on hunch, common sense, and experience.

Taylor tried to find a way to combine the interest of both management and labor to avoid the necessity for sweatshop management. He believed that the key to harmony was to

1. Discover the *one best way* to do a job,
2. Determine the optimum work pace,
3. Train people to do the job properly, and
4. Reward successful performance by using an *incentive pay system.*

Taylor believed that cooperation would replace conflict if workers and managers knew what was expected and the positive benefits of achieving mutual expectations. Taylor followed his own teachings when he conducted observations and experiments within organizations, leading to the following four principles of effective management:

Principle 1: Study the way workers perform their tasks, gather all the informal knowledge that workers possess, and experiment with methods of improving the way tasks are performed.

Principle 2: Codify the new methods of performing tasks into written rules and standard operating procedures.

Principle 3: Carefully select workers so that they possess skills and abilities that match the needs of the task, and train them to perform the task according to the established rules and procedures.

Principle 4: Establish a fair or acceptable level of performance for a task, and then develop a pay system that provides a reward for performance above the acceptable level.

Carefully study the preceding four principles. Do they seem logically consistent? Do they seem to make sense? Remember, these principles were developed in the early part of the twentieth century when the average worker was far less educated than today. Nonetheless, Taylor's influence was significant, and many of his ideas have had lasting effects on how organizations are organized and governed.[6]

Taylor isn't the only management thinker associated with the scientific management approach. His ideas and principles were elaborated and extended by the husband and wife team of Frank (1868–1924) and Lillian (1878–1972) Gilbreth. The Gilbreths conducted their work in the early part of the twentieth century. They used the emerging technology of video cameras to capture workers' actions on film. The Gilbreths were interested in breaking down the motions involved in the performance of a job into their elementary components, and then finding better ways to perform each component action.[7] Their work was the beginning of the so-called **time and motion study** that is still used in manufacturing plants today. The Gilbreths' research was depicted in the movie *Cheaper by the Dozen,* which lampoons the Gilbreths trying to use their management techniques at home with their children.

time and motion study The process of analyzing work to determine the most efficient motions for performing tasks and to determine the appropriate elapsed time for the completion of a task or job.

To the modern student of management, Taylor's ideas may not appear to be pioneering. Given the times in which he developed them, however, his ideas were, and continue to be, lasting contributions to the way work is done at the shop floor level. He urged managers to take a more systematic approach in performing their job of coordination. His experiments with stopwatch studies and work methods stimulated many others at that time to undertake similar types of studies.

1-5b Classical Organization Theory

As noted earlier, another body of concepts and approaches developed at the same time as scientific management. These were focused on the problems faced by top managers of large organizations. Since this branch of the classical approach focused on the management of organizations while scientific management focused on the management of work, it was labeled *classical organization theory*. Its two major purposes were:

1. To develop basic principles that could guide the design, creation, and maintenance of large organizations, and
2. To identify the basic functions of managing organizations.

Whereas engineers were the prime contributors to scientific management, practicing executives were the major contributors to classical organization theory. As with scientific management, there were many contributors to classical organization theory. Two of the most influential figures in classical organization theory are Max Weber and Henri Fayol. Weber introduced the Theory of Bureaucracy, while Fayol focused on managers and workers alike.

The Theory of Bureaucracy
Max Weber (1864–1920) was the primary architect of the theory of the organization as a **bureaucracy.**[8] Today, when we use the term *bureaucracy* it is usually used in derision. We think of a bureaucracy as a sort of mindless machine that is inefficient and slow. That's not what Weber had in mind when he advanced his ideas of the organization as a bureaucracy. Quite the contrary, Weber conceived of a bureaucracy as a smooth functioning, highly efficient machine where each part is exquisitely tuned to perform its prescribed function. Weber believed that an efficient organization should be based on five principles:

> *Principle 1:* In a bureaucracy, a manager's formal authority derives from the position held within the organization.
>
> *Principle 2:* In a bureaucracy, people should occupy positions because of their performance, not because of their social standing or personal contacts.
>
> *Principle 3:* The extent of each position's formal authority and task responsibilities, and its relationship to other positions in an organization, should be clearly specified.
>
> *Principle 4:* So that authority can be exercised effectively in an organization, positions should be arranged hierarchically so employees know whom to report to, and who reports to them.
>
> *Principle 5:* Managers must create a well-defined system of rules, standard operating procedures, and norms so that they can effectively control behavior within an organization.

To summarize these principles, Weber's theory called for organizations to be arranged with clear, hierarchical structures where each individual's **role** is well defined. This notion of "role" includes both task and reporting responsibilities. In Weber's bureaucracy, people hold jobs based on their qualifications for its responsibilities. Jobs that managers oversee should be controlled by rules and **standard operating procedures (SOPs).** The latter are specific written instructions about how to perform a certain task.

Weber believed that not only would bureaucratic structure create a more efficient organization, it would also create a more harmonious and joyous workplace. He believed

bureaucracy An organization design that relies on specialization of labor, a specific authority hierarchy, a formal set of rules and procedures, and rigid promotion and selection criteria.

role A set of shared expectations regarding a member's attitude and task behavior within the group.

standard operating procedures (SOPs) Specific, written instructions about how to perform a certain task.

that promotion on merit, and authority based on position would help create opportunities for upwardly mobile managers, on the one hand, and reduce political gamesmanship, on the other hand.

Bureaucracies can achieve the ends Weber envisioned, but they can also become the lumbering giants that led to the derisive use of the term *bureaucracy*. The specialization of tasks that Weber believed in can lead to a sense of isolation for the individual, rather than harmony. In addition, tall organizational hierarchies can lead to a slowing down of internal processes as multiple layers of management get involved in decisions of all types—even routine decisions that should be made quickly when and where they are needed. Modern ideas that are an offshoot of Weber's ideas include total quality management, process specialization, and competency testing.[9]

Fayol's Principles of Management

Henri Fayol (1841–1925) was the CEO of Comambault Mining when he conceived fourteen principles that he thought to be essential to effective management. Writing at the same time as Weber but, as far as is known, wholly independently of him, Fayol devised his principles based on observations of workers and managers at his company.[10] His fourteen principles are as follows:

> *Principle 1: Division of Labor*—Although Fayol believed strongly in job specialization and division of labor, he also realized that too much specialization can lead to workers being bored. Thus, he advocated specialization and increasing workers' responsibilities.
>
> *Principle 2: Management Authority and Responsibility*—Fayol held that managers must have the authority to give orders and they must have the responsibility for the effectiveness of their departments.
>
> *Principle 3: Unity of Command*—This principle states that employees should receive orders from, and report to, only one superior.
>
> *Principle 4: Line of Authority*—This principle points to the importance of limiting the length of the chain of command extending from the top of the organization to the bottom. Restricting the number of levels in the organization enables the organization to act quickly and flexibly.
>
> *Principle 5: Centralization*—Fayol believed that managers must decide how much authority to centralize at the top of the organization and how much to devolve to workers.
>
> *Principle 6: Unity of Direction*—This principle holds that all workers in an organization should be committed to the same plan of action.
>
> *Principle 7: Equity*—This principle points to the fact that workers need to be treated with respect and justice if they are expected to perform at high levels.
>
> *Principle 8: Order*—Fayol regarded order as the methodical arrangement of jobs to provide the organization with the greatest benefits and to provide employees with career opportunities to satisfy their needs.
>
> *Principle 9: Initiative*—Fayol believed that managers must encourage workers to act on their own, to take initiative that benefits the organization.
>
> *Principle 10: Discipline*—Fayol emphasized that employees should be expected to be obedient, energetic, and concerned about the welfare of the organization.
>
> *Principle 11: Remuneration of Personnel*—Fayol proposed that managers should use reward systems, including profit sharing and bonuses, to acknowledge high performance.
>
> *Principle 12: Stability of Tenure of Personnel*—Fayol believed that long-term employment helped employees develop the skills they need to make significant contributions to the organization.
>
> *Principle 13: Coordination of Individual Interest to the Common Interest*—Fayol believed that employees must learn to subordinate their individual interests to those of the firm.

LearningMoment *Assessing Fayol's Fourteen Principles*

Pause for a moment and reflect on Fayol's Fourteen Principles of Effective Management. How many of these principles do you agree with? How many do you disagree with? Are there any that need modification to fit your impression of today's workers? Are there any that need modification to fit your impression of today's managers?

Principle 14: Esprit de Corps—This principle highlights the importance of a sense of shared commitment, comradeship, and enthusiasm in the effective organization.

These fourteen points developed by Fayol have been debated, evaluated, and cited by management scholars and practitioners countless times over the years.[11] Many are "timeless" truths about management. Others have been rejected or modified better to fit the work styles and preferences of modern workers and managers. (See the Learning Moment box, "Assessing Fayol's Fourteen Principles.")

1-5c Contributions and Limitations of the Classical Approach

The greatest contribution of the classical approach was that it identified management as an important element of organized society. Management has, if anything, increased in importance over time as organizations have become a more important part of society and of the lives of most individuals. The fact that management skills must be applied in businesses, schools, government, hospitals, and various other types of organizations is stressed throughout this book. Advocates of the classical approach believed that management, like law, medicine, and other occupations, should be practiced according to principles that managers can learn.

The identification of management functions such as planning, organizing, controlling, and leading provide the basis for training new managers. The manner in which the management functions are presented often differs, depending on who is presenting them. But any listing of management functions acknowledges that managers are concerned with *what* the organization is doing, *how* it is to be done, and *whether* it was done.

The contributions of the classical approach, however, go beyond the important work of identifying the field of management and its process and functions. Many management techniques used today are direct outgrowths of the classical approach. For example, time and motion analysis, work simplification, incentive wage systems, production scheduling, personnel testing and evaluation, and budgeting are all techniques derived from the classical approach. These contributions are summarized in Table 1-1.

TABLE 1-1
The Classical Approach

Scientific Management

- Concentrates on problems of lower-level managers
- Greatest contributor is Frederick W. Taylor
- Sought "one best way" to do a job

Classical Organization Theory

- Concentrates on problems of top level managers
- Greatest contributor is Henri Fayol
- Embodied fourteen principles of management

One major criticism of the classical approach is that the majority of its insights are too simplistic for today's complex organizations. Critics argue that scientific management and classical organization theory are more appropriate for the past, when the environments of most organizations were very stable and predictable. One outgrowth of this criticism is a body of management thought known as the behavioral science approach. This approach begins with the *people* who staff and manage the organization, rather than the organization as a whole, as the starting point for understanding and improving management. It assumes that a deeper understanding of "human nature" and how people interact with one another will lead to more effective management. Let's turn our attention to this approach next.

1-6 The Behavioral Approach

The **behavioral approach to management** developed partly because practicing managers found that following the ideas of the classical approach did not achieve total efficiency and workplace harmony. Although they applied the classical approach in a wide variety of settings, managers still encountered problems because subordinates did not always behave as they were supposed to. Thus, an increased interest in helping managers become more effective began to grow in the middle of the twentieth century.

The behavioral approach to management has two branches. The first branch, the *human relations approach*, became very popular in the 1950s and still receives a great deal of attention today. The second branch, the *behavioral sciences approach*, is more technically rigorous and drawn from the human sciences. We next examine each approach briefly.

1-6a The Human Relations Approach

The term **human relations** refers to the manner in which managers interact with subordinates. To develop good human relations, followers of this approach believe, managers must know why their subordinates behave as they do and what psychological and social factors influence them.

Students of human relations brought to the attention of management the important role individuals play in determining the success or failure of an organization. They tried to show how the process and functions of management are affected by differences in individual behavior and the influence of groups in the workplace. Thus, while scientific management concentrated on the *physical* environment of the job, human relations concentrated on the *social* environment.

Human relations proponents believe that management should recognize employees' need for recognition and social acceptance. They suggest that, since groups provide members with feelings of acceptance and dignity, management should look upon the work group as a positive force that could be utilized productively. Therefore, managers should be trained in human relations skills as well as in technical skills.

1-6b The Behavioral Sciences Approach

Other individuals who were university trained in social sciences such as psychology, sociology, and anthropology began to study people at work. They had advanced training in applying the scientific approach to the study of human behavior. These individuals are known as *behavioral scientists,* and their approach is considered to be distinct from the human relations approach.

The individuals in the behavioral science branch of the behavioral approach believe that humans are much more complex than the "economic man" description of the classical approach and the "social man" description of the human relations approach.[12] The emphasis of the behavioral science approach concentrates more on the nature of work itself, and the degree to which it can fulfill the human need to express skills and abilities. Behavioral scientists believe that an individual is motivated to work for many reasons in addition to making money and forging social relationships. These include recognition, making meaningful contributions to society, or personal fulfillment. The Management Focus on Ethics box suggests a number of behavioral issues have to be weighed in making

---

behavioral approach to management
A management approach that emphasizes people and how the structure of an organization affects their behavior and performance. The advocates of a behavioral orientation to management believe that the classical approach suppresses personal development because it is so rigid and restrictive.

human relations The manner in which managers interact with subordinates.

Management Focus on Ethics

Ethics, Priorities, and Policy

The Centers for Disease Control and Prevention in Atlanta had a problem in the fall of 2004. Faced with a flu vaccine shortage they decided to set up a panel to cope with future epidemics.

The panel had to decide whether babies should have priority over the elderly or whether members of crucial professions should be given priority over others. In the fall of 2004 vaccine shipments were sent to members of the U.S. Congress. Is this ethical and fair?

The panel will help develop a process to decide whether future flu vaccine shipments should go first to pediatricians' offices, nursing homes, or veteran's hospitals.

One ethical argument is that people are supposed to get a certain number of preferential treatments in their lifetime. Thus, when there is a shortage the young should be treated first since the old have already received their share of preferential treatments.

The panel has a lot of hard work to do before establishing a policy for dealing with future flu vaccine shortages.

Source: Adapted from "CDC Ethics Panel to Help Set Flu Vaccine Priorities", *Wall Street Journal,* October 28, 2004, p. 1.

decisions about resource allocations. Different groups must be considered in making the best ethical choice regarding flu vaccine shortages.

The behavioral approach to management theorizing owes much to the work of Mary Parker Follett (1868–1933). Follett was one of the earliest management theorists to recognize that organizations could be viewed from the perspective of individual or group behavior.[13] She was a social philosopher whose writings favored a more people-centered view of the organization than scientific management writing, which still predominated. According to Follet, the manager's job was to harmonize and coordinate group efforts. She believed that managers and workers should view themselves as partners in a common project. Thus, she felt, managers needed to act more from their knowledge of human behavior than from their formal authority.

1-6c The Hawthorne Studies

A well-known series of research studies conducted at the Hawthorne Works of the Western Electric Company helped to lend credence to the behavioral approach to management theory. The studies were conducted between 1924 and 1932 and have come to be known generally as the **Hawthorne Studies.**

The research was initiated as an attempt to determine whether physical characteristics of the work setting, in this case the level of illumination, affect worker performance. The researchers varied lighting levels in the plant's secretarial pool to determine the effects of the different levels on productivity.

The results produced by those experiments were surprising. The researchers found that, regardless of whether they raised or lowered the level of illumination, productivity increased. Productivity only dropped when the level of illumination dropped so low that workers could no longer see well enough to perform their work. The researchers didn't expect these results. Based on their background in scientific management, they expected to see a smooth, linear relationship between illumination and productivity, with a clearly identified optimum level.

To understand the findings of the research, the investigators recruited noted Harvard psychologist Elton Mayo. Mayo proposed another series of experiments to help understand the findings.[14] These next experiments were conducted over a two-year period. They used a different group of female workers and varied different characteristics of the work environment such as the worker and length of rest periods.

Once again, the investigators found that their manipulations of the work environment led to productivity increases. Gradually, the researchers discovered that the results they were obtaining were, to some extent, directly related to the presence of the researchers in

> **Hawthorne Studies**
> Management studies involving teams of researchers studying working conditions and pay plans conducted at the Western Electric Hawthorne plant in a suburb of Chicago; the most famous studies conducted in the field of management.

the workplace. The presence of the researchers was affecting the results because the workers enjoyed the attention and produced the results they believed the researchers wanted.

This effect of increased productivity due to increased attention has come to be known as the **Hawthorne Effect.** Management theorists interpreted the series of studies as indicating that workers' attitudes toward their managers affects the level of their performance.[15] This important work has often been regarded as the beginning of the behavioral approach to management theory.

> **Hawthorne Effect** The tendency of people who are being observed or involved in a research effort to react differently than they otherwise would.

1-6d Contributions and Limitations of the Behavioral Approach

For the student of management, the behavioral approach has contributed a wealth of important ideas and research results on the people-managing aspect of the discipline of management. The basic rationale is that since managers must get work done through others, management is really applied behavioral science, because a manager must motivate, lead, and understand interpersonal relations.

Modern manifestations of the behavioral approach abound. Increased use of teams to accomplish organizational goals, the focus on training and development of employees, and the use of innovation reward and incentive systems are just some examples of how the behavioral approach affects modern managers.

The basic assumption that managers must know how to deal with people appears valid. But management is more than applied behavioral science. For the behavioral approach to be useful to managers, it must make them better practitioners of the process of management. It must help them in problem situations. In many cases, this objective has not been achieved because of the difficulty of translating technical scientific findings about human behavior into useful management tools and policies. Another problem is that, in some situations, one behavioral scientist (a psychologist) may have a different suggestion than another (a sociologist) for the same management problem. Human behavior is complex and is studied from a variety of viewpoints. This complicates the problem for a manager trying to use insights from the behavioral sciences.

As a result of some of the confusion that surrounds translating scientific findings about human behavior into applied management strategies, another body of management thought emerged. This approach, known as the **management science approach,** uses the same rigorous scientific tools as the behavioral science approach but applies them specifically to questions concerning practicing mangers. In this way, the translation problem is avoided, but the rigor of using scientific method is maintained. We review the management science approach next.

> **management science approach** Formerly known as the operations research approach; involves mixed teams of specialists from fields required to address a specific problem.

1-7 The Management Science Approach

The management science approach is in one sense a modern version of the early emphasis on the "management of work" by those interested in scientific management. Its key feature is the *use of mathematics and statistics to aid in resolving production and operations problems.* Thus, the approach focuses on solving technical rather than human behavior problems. The computer has been of tremendous value to this approach because it has enabled analyses of problems that would otherwise be too complex.

The management science approach has only existed formally for approximately fifty years. It began during the early part of World War II when England was confronted with some complex military problems that had never been faced before, such as antisubmarine warfare strategy. To try to solve these kinds of problems, the English formed teams of scientists, mathematicians, and physicists. The units were named *operations research* teams, and they proved to be extremely valuable. When the war was over, American business firms began to use a similar approach to deal with operating issues.

Today the operations research approach has been formalized and renamed the *management science approach.* Basically, it involves mixed teams of specialists from whatever fields the problem being attacked calls for. The team members analyze the problem and often develop a mathematical representation of it. Thus, they can change certain factors in the equations to see what would happen if such a change was actually made in the real world. The results of their work often become useful to management in making a final decision. One of their important purposes is to provide management with *quantitative bases* for decisions.

1-7a Contributions and Limitations of the Management Science Approach

Today, the most important contributions of management science are in the areas of production management and operations management. *Production management* focuses on manufacturing technology and the flow of materials in a manufacturing plant. Here, management science has contributed techniques that help solve production scheduling problems, budgeting problems, and maintenance of optimal inventory levels.

Operations management is very similar to production management except that it focuses on a wide class of problems and includes organizations such as hospitals, banks, government, and the military, which have operations problems but do not manufacture tangible products. For these types of organizations, operations management forces development programs and scheduling.

Management is more than applied behavioral science. At this point, it should be stressed that management science is not a substitute for management. The techniques of the management science approach are especially helpful to the manager performing the management process. However, while it is used in many problem areas, management science does not deal with the people aspect of an organization.

1-8 Integrating the Three Approaches

Some management scholars have attempted to integrate the three approaches to management. One of these attempts, the **systems approach,** stresses that organizations must be viewed as systems with each part linked to every other part. Another effort, the **contingency approach,** stresses that the correctness of a managerial practice is contingent on how it fits the particular situation to which it is applied; in other words, it "depends on the situation." Let's examine each approach.

1-8a The Systems Approach

The systems approach to management is essentially a way of thinking about organizations and management problems. The approach views an organization as interrelated parts with a unified purpose: surviving and ideally thriving in its environment.

From the systems perspective, management should focus on efficiency and effectiveness in each part of the organization, with the understanding that actions taken in one part of the organization affect other parts of the organization.[16] For example, implementing a strategy in the production department of a company will likely affect other aspects of the company such as marketing, finance, and personnel. Each part is tightly linked to other organizational parts; no single part of an organization exists and operates in isolation from the others. Thus, in their day-to-day activities, managers must view the organization as a dynamic whole and try to anticipate the unintended as well as the intended impacts of their decisions.

The systems approach views the elements of an organization as interconnected. The approach also views the organization as linked to its environment. Organizational effectiveness, even survival, depends on the organization's interaction with its environment. To further your understanding of these ideas, let's consider Dell Computer, Inc., as an example. As a computer manufacturer, Dell Computer is an **open system** that actively interacts with its environment. (For now, consider the environment as comprised of such factors as customers, competitors, financial institutions, suppliers, and the government. The environment will be discussed in more detail in Chapter 2.) Basic elements of Dell Computer as an open system are shown in Figure 1-3.

systems approach A way to think about organizations and management problems; views an organization as interrelated parts with a unified purpose: surviving and thriving in its environment.

contingency approach A management approach that considers an organization's objectives, organization and job design, human resources, environment, and managerial skills as interacting and affecting the type of management decisions made about planning, organizing, leading, and controlling.

open system An organization that interacts with its environment and uses the feedback received to make changes and modifications.

Figure 1-3
The Four Parts of an Open System Organization (e.g., Dell Computer, Inc.)

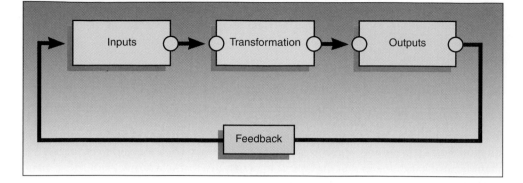

Active interaction means that Dell both obtains resources from and provides resources to its environment. For example, in order to function, Dell must obtain *inputs* from the environment. The company needs motivated and skilled employees with the ability to design and manufacture innovative, high-quality personal and business computers. Dell obtains this resource from the environment—specifically from the graduating classes of universities nationwide, from competitors, and from other organizations.

Financial resources (money) are inputs needed to build manufacturing facilities, to fund Dell's R&D efforts, and to meet any number of other expenses. Dell obtains the funds from the environment—from banks, other lending institutions, and from people who buy shares of Dell's stock. Raw materials (e.g., computer parts) are obtained from outside suppliers in the environment. Information about the latest computer product technology and about the latest products developed by Dell's competitors is also needed. This information substantially influences the design and manufacture of Dell's computers. Information is obtained from the environment; that is, from research journals, computer conferences, and other external contacts.

These inputs are employed, used, coordinated, and managed in a *transformation* process that produces *output*—in this case, personal and business computers. However, the company's task is not complete. Dell provides this resource (output) to the environment by delivering its computers to retail outlets for sale to customers. Does the company survive? Only if the customer reacts to Dell's computers and decides to purchase the product. The customer's decision to buy or look elsewhere (for an IBM or Hewlett-Packard Bell computer, for example) provides Dell with **feedback.**

If the feedback is positive (customers buy Dell computers), the environment provides a critical input to the Dell—cash that the company uses to obtain other inputs from the environment, such as quality employees, materials, and knowledge. Negative feedback (no sales) provides Dell with a problem. Dell Computer must closely monitor feedback and act upon it (e.g., changing a failing product's design or features based on customer responses). As an open system in a dynamic environment Dell cannot afford to ignore the environment. Neglecting developments in the environment (e.g., technological innovations, competitors' moves) will, over time, doom the company.

However, not all organizations are open systems. Some, like a Catholic monastery, are **closed systems.** The organization pays little attention to the environment. A monastery, for example, obtains some resources from the Catholic Church. However, beyond this relationship, the monastery has little need to closely monitor its environment. Its members remain in the monastery for their adult life, with no active interaction with the outside world. Developments in the outside world have little impact on the organization.

Today most organizations must operate as open systems to survive and utilize a systems perspective to management. Managers must think broadly about a problem and not concentrate only on the desired results because these results will impact other problems and parts of the organization and even in the environment beyond the organization. The age-old confrontation between the production objective and the marketing objective of a broad product line (requiring high production costs) is a good example. Both objectives cannot be achieved at the same time. In this situation, a compromise is necessary for the overall system to achieve its objective. And in seeking a compromise, the organization must always be aware of the environment (e.g., will customers accept fewer products?).

feedback The component of a system whereby the effects of the system on its environment influence the future functioning of the system.

closed system An approach that generally ignores environmental forces and conditions.

Management Focus on Innovation

SportsExpress Manages Travelers' Gear

Innovation does not have to mean a new technical invention or electronic gizmo. Innovation comes in a wide variety of forms. Sometimes the most innovative business concepts are those that solve nagging problems. *SportsExpress* was founded by a group of individuals who happen to be golf, ski, and snowboard enthusiasts. These individuals noticed that traveling to great locations to practice their hobbies was something of a challenge. Packing, transporting, and lugging the tools of their trade (golf clubs, skis, etc.) was time consuming and often frustrating, as airlines would notoriously misplace gear. Their innovation was to realize that others must be in the same predicament. They reasoned that outdoor enthusiasts like themselves would pay for a service that would ease the process of moving their gear. *SportsExpress* will pack your outdoor gear and make sure it arrives at your destination. No more hassle with airport check-in, no hassles with packing, and no more hassles at luggage claim. *SportsExpress* picks up your gear at your house and delivers it directly to your final destination—a simple innovation that will surely be welcomed by outdoor enthusiasts, airlines, and travel agents.

The objectives of the individual parts of the organization must be balanced with the objectives of the entire firm.

Today, managers realize that being responsive to their customers is a vital part of organizational success. Systems theory helps managers envision how to integrate feedback from customers into organizational planning and decision making. The Management Focus on Innovation box, "*SportsExpress* Manages Travelers' Gear," highlights a company that helps outdoor enthusiasts transport their gear to their final destination. The idea for the company emerged from listening to sports enthusiasts' frustration with the existing systems for transporting their gear.

1-8b The Contingency Approach

The systems approach to management advocates that managers recognize that organizations are systems composed of interdependent parts and that a change in one part affects others. This insight is important, but not important enough. Beyond recognizing that an organization's parts interact, it's useful for managers to see how the parts fit together. The contingency approach can help in better understanding the interactions of an organization's components.

Our discussion of the contingency approach is presented within the context of the contrasting views on management effectiveness, which is shown in Figure 1-4.

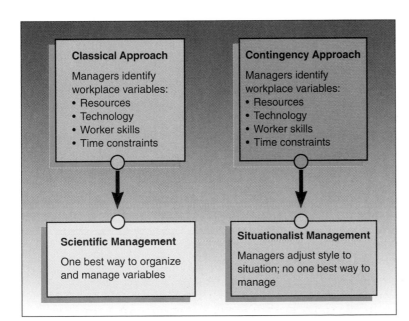

Figure 1-4
Contrasting Views of Management Effectiveness

Recall that the classical approach was based on the assumption that managers could find optimum solutions to organizational problems. Scientific management, for example, was based on the principles of analysis and control. Managers were to analyze the variables associated with a particular job, and then identify the "one best way" to arrange these variables to maximize productivity.

This view can be contrasted with modern contingency theorists who believe a manager's style and approach is contingent on the variables associated with a job. Contingency theorists believe most workplace situations are too complex to analyze and control as in scientific management. Thus, instead of focusing on trying to find the one best way to arrange workplace variables, managers focus on adopting their behavior to match the demands of the situation.[17]

This view, also know as the *situationalist approach,* is popular with many scholars and practicing managers today. For example, Paul Hersey, an organizational scholar, has developed a **situationalist theory of leadership,**[18] and others have used the situationalist approach to develop tools for managing modern, information-rich workplaces.

Contingency theorists do not subscribe to any one best approach to management. In their view, the situations that managers encounter are complex and prohibit any "one best" prescription. However, the contingency theorists stop short of asserting that all managerial situations are totally unique. Rather, they argue that situations can be roughly "classified," allowing for the application of appropriate management principles at appropriate times. However, the appropriate principles must be identified. This is done by first identifying the relevant *contingency variables* in the situation and then evaluating those factors.[19]

In essence, the contingency approach to management involves identifying the important contingency variables in different situations, evaluating the variables, and then applying appropriate management knowledge and principles for the situation.

Both the systems approach and the contingency approach have developed valuable insights for students of management. At this point, however, they are in early stages of development. Thus, it is too soon to know if either or both approaches will add lasting value to the understanding and practice of management.

▶**situationalist theory of leadership** An approach that advocates that leaders understand their own behavior, the behavior of their subordinates, and the situation before they utilize a particular leadership style.

Management Summary

- A successful manager does not rely on a single managerial skill, but rather a combination of skills.

- Management can be thought of as multidimensional in nature. It can be defined as a process, a discipline, a human activity, and a career.

- Four key functions make up the process of management: planning, organizing, leading, and controlling.

- The discipline of management is continually evolving and is addressed through three primary approaches to the subject. They are the classical approach, the behavioral approach, and the management science approach.

- The classical approach focuses on ways to increase workers' efficiency and productivity. The behavioral approach focuses on the human dynamics of the workplace. The management science approach addresses the use of math and statistics in solving production and operations problems.

- More recently, attempts have been made to integrate the three approaches to the study of management. These integrative approaches are known as the systems approach and the contingency approach.

- The systems approach stresses the interrelatedness of all aspects of organizations and the links between the organization and its environment. The contingency approach emphasizes the need to evaluate contingency variables in selecting approaches to managerial situations.

Key Terms

behavioral approach to management (p. 14)
bureaucracy (p. 11)
career (p. 5)
classical approach to management (p. 9)
classical organization theory (p. 9)
closed system (p. 18)
contingency approach (p. 17)
controlling function (p. 8)
feedback (p. 18)

Hawthorne Effect (p. 16)
Hawthorne Studies (p. 15)
human relations (p. 14)
leadership (p. 7)
management (p. 5)
management functions (p. 6)
management science approach (p. 16)
open system (p. 17)
organizing function (p. 7)

planning function (p. 7)
role (p. 11)
scientific management (p. 9)
situationalist theory of leadership (p. 20)
standard operating procedures (SOPs)
   (p. 11)
systems approach (p. 17)
time and motion study (p. 10)

Review and Discussion Questions

1. What does management scholar Peter Drucker mean when he states that "A man who only knows the skills and techniques, without understanding the fundamentals of management, is not a manager; he is, at best, a technician"?

2. Clearly distinguish between the process of management and the functions of management. How are they related?

3. Why does scientific management believe there is "one best way" to manage? Contrast this view with a contingency approach.

4. List several organizations that significantly influence your life. How well are they managed? In what ways do you think they could be managed better? Why do you think the current managers don't correct the problems you identify?

5. Someone has said that managers are a very important global social resource. Do you agree or disagree? State your reasons.

6. Apply systems theory concepts to an organization with which you are familiar. What are the inputs and outputs? How are the outputs transformed? What are the challenges in managing an organization from the systems theory perspective?

7. Weber's theory of bureaucracy appears logical and seems to be a sound way to organize. What are the strengths of Weber's approach? What are the weaknesses? What influences of Weber's thought can you detect in modern organizations?

8. Have you ever been a manager? Can you think of a situation in which you played a managerial role? Outline your planning, organizing, leading, and controlling functions.

9. As the chapter's figure of the management process indicates, planning leads to organizing, which leads to controlling, which leads to performance; and leading activities affect the other three managerial functions. Is it possible that the controlling function can affect the organizing and planning functions? Or that the organizing function can affect the leading function? Explain.

10. Why is the contingency approach becoming more popular and appealing to managers?

Practice Quiz

Note: You can find the correct answers to these questions by taking the quiz and then submitting your answers in the Online Edition. The program will automatically score your submission. If you miss a question, the program will provide the correct answer, a rationale for the answer, and the section number in the chapter where the topic is discussed.

Indicate whether the sentence or statement is true or false.

_____ 1. Managers exercise leadership through **planning, organizing,** and **controlling.**

_____ 2. The purpose of management control is to make sure that the organization stays on the path that was planned for it.

_____ 3. **Scientific management** emerged as a means of studying work processes and finding ways to make them more efficient.

_____ 4. Frederick Taylor believed that workers were producing far less than their capacities because **they did not understand what constituted a fair day's work.**

_____ 5. The behavioral approach to management has two branches: the **human relations approach** and the **behavioral sciences approach.**

_____ 6. Contingency theorists believe most workplace situations are too complex to analyze and control, as in scientific management.

Identify the letter of the choice that best completes the statement or answers the question.

_____ 7. Which of the following is NOT a primary view of "management"?
   a. Management is a **process.**
   b. Management is a **human activity.**
   c. Management is a **career.**
   d. Management is a **product.**

_____ 8. Successful organizations require a strong, mutually satisfying _____ between managers and the people they manage.
   a. contract
   b. friendship
   c. partnership
   d. both *a* and *c*

_____ 9. Management professors, psychologists, sociologists, and anthropologists consider management to be _____.
   a. a social phenomenon.
   b. good for the economy.
   c. nonscientific.
   d. all of the above.

_____ 10. Modern manifestations of the behavioral approach include _____.
   a. increased use of teams.
   b. training and developing employees.
   c. rewards and incentives.
   d. all of the above.

_____ 11. Which is the most accurate statement about a contingency management approach?
   a. There is one best solution to problems.
   b. It is crucial to identify the most important variables in a situation.
   c. It is most similar to the scientific management approach.
   d. It is fully accepted globally because of the long history.

_____ 12. Researchers have discovered what they refer to as the _____. It is used to designate increased productivity because of an increase in attention toward an individual.
   a. spider model
   b. chaos theory
   c. Hawthorne Effect
   d. meta-analysis

_____ 13. Fayol developed his principles of management on the basis of _____.
   a. university study of management.
   b. serving as a union steward.
   c. experimentation in field studies.
   d. observation of workers and managers in his organization.

_____ 14. Weber considered bureaucracy as _____.
   a. inefficient.
   b. anti-worker.
   c. smooth functioning and effective.
   d. outdated.

_____ 15. In the most concise terms possible, control is _____.
   a. the reverse of planning.
   b. a system that makes sure the organization accomplishes its plans.
   c. a method for creating an authority hierarchy.
   d. a bureaucratic approach to set objectives, modify them, and eventually use them for future decision making.

Case Study

Bill Ford Uses Management to Transform Old Company

Bill Ford, Jr. is determined to become a major player in Chinese auto production. He plans to build a second car plant in the eastern region of China in the Jiangsu province. The plant will be located close to the booming port city of Shanghai. Ford will be able to reduce the cost of transporting raw material and shipping out vehicles.

Instead of riding on the successes of his ancestors, he believes that globalization must be a part of Ford's plans, behaviors, and development. He uses his great-grandfather as a role model to help guide his unique and developing style of managing the globalization of Ford Motor Company.

Bill Ford Jr., 45, is a nice guy with a politician's instinct. He is an unapologetic environmentalist. He is a family man who would rather spend Saturday nights eating pizza with his four children than eating hors d'oeuvres with movers and shakers. He is an iconoclast. He prefers ice hockey to golf—he does not do business on the golf course—and he's working on his black belt in tae kwon do. He says what he thinks and does what he thinks he should.

He is that rare corporate executive who says boldly that his company will do best for its shareholders if it takes care of its employees, its community, and the environment—all of which, he says, will enable Ford Motor Company to attract better talent, develop loyal customers, enhance its brand, sell more cars and services, and, over time, boost its share price. When Bill refers to Ford's workers as his "extended family," even some of his union bosses believe that he's sincere.

Bill Ford Jr. is idealistic, but he is not stupid. He has spent two decades carefully earning and consolidating his power, and he holds a lot of cards. He has the solid backing of the Ford family, which controls 40 percent of the voting stock; that alone gives him some protection from Wall Street. He has strong support from the board of directors. History is on his side; his great-grandfather Henry Ford was also an environmentalist, an idealist, and an iconoclast whose notion of mass-producing cars—and paying his workers a generous $5 a day—transformed society.

Finally, Bill Ford is pragmatic, having learned a thing or two about politics and survival during his time at the company. He encountered plenty of people along the way who didn't want to see a Ford family member returned to power. And he knew that Ford Motor historically had, as he puts it, "more intrigue than czarist Russia."

But the real question about Bill Ford Jr. is whether he can create a new kind of leadership to arouse and right embattled old-economy corporations. Their shareholders and their managers have deserted in droves. Their credibility, on matters from genetic engineering to teen smoking to passenger bumping, is about as bad as a used car salesman's. Now, at the very time Wall Street and Main Street are fed up with the Organization Man, here comes Bill Ford Jr., the antithesis of the Organization Man.

Bill Ford could have spent the last twenty years cashing dividend checks and fishing in Patagonia. Instead he set out to "change the face of industry," as he once wrote. His mission seems fraught with more peril than developing the first mass-produced car. Will he be yet another family executive who can't get along with management? Will he lead Ford off course? Will he turn out to be just plain naive? He knows it's a possibility. "That I'm seen as a kind of irrelevant dilettante is the worst case in my mind," he says. Given his intelligence, his vision, and his commitment, Bill Ford could develop a business model as revolutionary for the times as great-grandfather Henry's was for his. But he could also become just another piece of old-economy roadkill.

Questions for Discussion

1. How does Bill Ford's style fit with Frederick Taylor's scientific management approach?

2. Do you think Bill Ford views Ford Motor Company as an open system? Why or why not?

3. Of the different approaches to management studied in this chapter, which do you think most closely resembles Bill Ford's style? Why?

4. In 2001, Ford Motor Company recalled 13 million Firestone/Bridgestone tires on its popular Ford Explorer because they were suspected of being faulty. From Bill Ford's perspective, how does that decision lead to increased shareholder value for the company?

Sources: "Company Spotlight: Ford Motor Company," *Market Watch Automotive*, April 2004, pp. 14–20 (see also www.datamonitor.com); Betsy Norris, Noshua Watson, and Patricia Neerings, "Idealist on Board," *Fortune*, April 3, 2000; Alex Taylor and Ahmad Diba, "The Fight at Ford," *Fortune*, April 3, 2000; JoAnn Muller, "Ford: Why It's Worse Than You Think," *BusinessWeek*, June 25, 2001.

Internet Exercise

The Hawthorne Studies

The Hawthorne Studies are considered "classics" in the annals of management and human behavior research. Although the findings may seem straightforward and unsurprising to us today, they were unique and unexpected at the time. Additionally, the Hawthorne Studies have had enduring effects on management and management research alike.

Use the Internet to find out more about these classic experiments. Answer the following questions:

1. What did the Hawthorne Studies reveal about human behavior in the workplace?

2. What changes in the workplace have been a direct result of the findings of the Hawthorne Studies?

3. What lessons do the Hawthorne Studies convey to modern managers?

4. Why do you think the results found by the Hawthorne Studies were surprising at the time?

Experiential Exercise

The Four Meanings of Management

This exercise is intended to get students thinking about the four different meanings of management. For each meaning, students are asked to go out and find an example in the real world.

Students should complete this exercise during a single class session. Following in-class discussion of the four meanings of "management," students should be organized into four or eight teams. If four teams are chosen, each should investigate one of the meanings of "management." If eight are chosen, two teams will overlap each of the distinct meanings. Students should be asked to prepare brief presentations and/or lead discussion on their topic during the next class period.

1. Management Is a Process

Students should identify a management process. This process should be something that is familiar to them and their fellow students. It could be the process used at local fast-food restaurants. It could be a process used to register for classes. They should identify the process and the process manager and discuss whether the process is optimal or in need of improvement.

2. Management Is a Discipline

Students should identify primary source management research that reflects the science of management. This could involve taking a trip to the business library and looking through management journals. Students should find an article of interest and bring it to class for discussion. Does the article reflect sound research principles? What are the findings? Are the findings believable? Why or why not?

3. Management Is a Human Activity

Students should identify a manager in an organization and have a conversation with him or her about how being a manager affects his or her lives. What are the human rewards of managing? What are the disappointments? What is the most challenging aspect of being a successful manager?

4. Management Is a Career

Students should identify a manager in an organization and speak with him or her about what it takes to build a successful management career. What are the obstacles to success? What special skills do managers need to be successful? What role do other people play in a manager's road to career success?

Management: Skills, Roles, and Modern Challenges

2

Managing Today

Leading Employees Through a Tough Economy

AvantGo Inc., a registered trademark of iAnywhere, Inc., is headquartered in a spiffy office complex in Hayward, California, on the eastern edge of San Francisco Bay. Immediately across the highway from AvantGo is another office complex where another technology company, AllAdvantage.com, prepares for its bankruptcy sale.

"There's a lot of negativity outside these walls," says AvantGo CEO Richard Owen (the now former CEO). "Employees here don't feel that we're in the same business as a Pets.com or an AllAdvantage. But there's a lot of virtual rubbernecking that happens. People talk to each other; they have friends who worked at these companies."

A significant part of Owen's job is to keep AvantGo's 300 employees focused on the opportunities before them, rather than on the misery that surrounds them. That's why Owen considers himself to be the company's chief communicator. "I spend a lot of time talking about the company's prospects." All-hands meetings take place monthly on "AvantBeach," the outdoor deck built in the parking lot behind the company's headquarters. The company fires up its own barbecue grills, and Owen takes questions from all comers.

Owen says that early in his tenure at AvantGo, he was reluctant to send out broadcast e-mails to address rumors that were circulating around the company. Now he doesn't hesitate if he feels the rumor might be distracting enough. "A lot of times, they're related to the stock price, the ups and downs. I've explained to people that we're a small-cap company with a small float. It will be bumpy for a while."

If Owen can quash the rumors and assuage the worries, AvantGo's employees can focus on the company's objectives: Support all of the new handheld computers being introduced, run pilot programs for prospective customers, and double its revenue in two years. But it's important not to ignore the challenges or gloss over the problems, Owen says. "The number-one question that people ask me is how we're doing as a company, and if I were to tell them, 'Wow, we're landing men on the moon. We're going to be the first $10-trillion-cap company,' people would think that I was totally delusional. You have to be candid and honest."

Sources: Scott Kirsner, www.advantgo.com (December 3, 2004); "How to Stay on the Move… When the World Is Slowing Down," *Fast Company,* July 2001, p. 112; Matthew G. Nelson, "AvantGo Lets Users Stay Mobile," *Informationweek,* December 11, 2000, p. 209.

2-1 Organizational Performance

Performance in an organization does not just happen. Dedicated and skillful managers carrying out specific roles help to make it happen. Managers influence performance by defining objectives, recognizing and minimizing obstacles to the achievement of these objectives, and effectively planning, organizing, leading, and controlling all available resources to attain high levels of performance. This chapter focuses on management skills and roles that must be aggressively applied to everyday organizational situations. The skillful manager is able to manage and monitor performance in such a way that objectives are achieved.

To perform means "to do, to accomplish." The term *productivity* is used to refer to what is being accomplished in the organization through the utilization of resources. **Resources** include such things as capital, machinery, labor, and intelligence. **Productivity** is defined as "the relationship between real inputs and real outputs," or as "the measure of how well resources are combined and utilized to produce a result desired by management."

Productivity is a component of performance, not a synonym for it.[1] Managers are responsible for effectively utilizing all the resources of the organization. Managers design and operate technology and work flow; they purchase and use raw materials; and they produce, market, and sell the organization's products or services. How well they utilize the resources of the organization (performance) will have an effect on how much they will be able to get out of those resources (productivity). In the opening Managing Today vignette, a technology-company executive discusses the importance of keeping employees informed to maintain productivity. During uncertain or difficult times in a company, it is important that managers communicate with employees so they don't waste time worrying or spreading rumors about their situation.

Productivity is a term that applies to service businesses as much as it does to manufacturing. Organizations of all types must be concerned about the productivity of the workforce. For example, in the health care industry, productivity of nurses is of great con-

resources An organization's financial, physical, human, time, or other assets.

productivity The relationship between real inputs and real outputs; a measure of how well resources are combined and utilized to produce a result desired by management.

LearningMoment _Organizational Systems and Productivity_

Organizations are systems. Efficiency improvements in one system don't necessarily lead to greater productivity. In fact, it's possible that greater efficiency in one system could lead to _lower_ productivity. Consider a plant that manufactures computers. Now imagine that efficiency in production is increased, leading to a higher rate of output. Unfortunately, the shipping function of the firm is working at capacity. The higher number of computers coming off the assembly line doesn't mean that more are getting shipped to customers. In fact, as the bottleneck of computers in the shipping area grows, the performance of the workers on the shipping dock declines, resulting in fewer shipments going out the door.

Can you envision something like this happening? It happens all the time. Beware of making efficiency improvements without an eye to the overall organizational design and work flow. Think of the organization as an integrated system.

cern as health care organizations continue to struggle to reduce costs. Nurse productivity has been rarely examined because of the complexity of measurement, and the difficulty of determining productivity of individual nurses.[2]

Managers sometimes use the terms _efficiency_ in place of _performance_ and _effectiveness_ in place of _productivity_. Efficiency is generally a measure of how much a manager or an organization is able to produce from each unit of a given resource. You may have heard of the term _efficiency expert_. This is a person who consults with a manager to find ways to cut costs, improve task execution times, and better design work flow. Better efficiency (performance) often leads to higher productivity, but not necessarily. Organizations are made of interlocking and integrated systems. Often, better efficiency in one area does not lead to higher overall productivity. (See the Learning Moment box, "Organizational Systems and Productivity.")

2-2 The Management System

As any organization increases in size and complexity, its managers must adapt by becoming more specialized. This section addresses some results of specialization of the management process. One result of specialization is the categorization of managers into a variety of types: first line (also called front line), middle, and top.

The history of many firms reveals an evolution through which management has grown from one manager with many subordinates to a team of many managers with many subordinates. The development of different types of managers has occurred as a result of this evolution. For example, Figure 2-1 illustrates a one-manager-many-subordinate firm (probably a new venture start-up where the manager is also the founder/entrepreneur). In this situation, the manager performs all of the management functions.

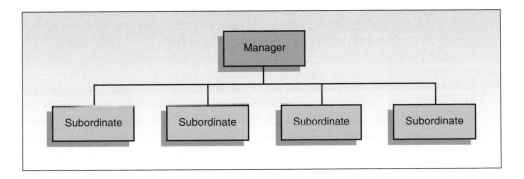

Figure 2-1
**One Manager
and Many Subordinates**

Assume that the firm is successful and the manager decides to add some new products and sell to some new markets. As the manager becomes overworked because of the increased complexity of the job, he or she may decide to specialize *vertically* by assigning the task of supervising subordinates to another person (Figure 2-2) or *horizontally* by assigning certain tasks, such as production or marketing, to another person (Figure 2-3). Whichever method is chosen, the organization's management process has become more complex.

Figure 2-2
Vertical Specialization of the Management Process

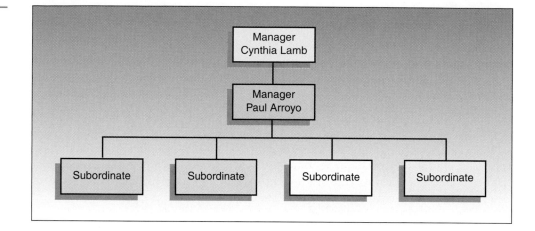

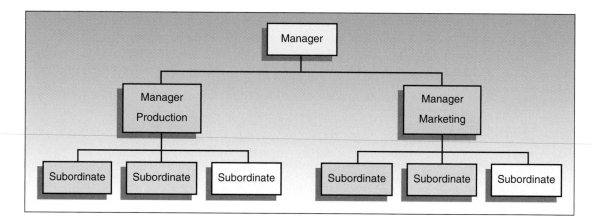

Figure 2-3
Horizontal Specialization of the Management Process

first-line management The lowest level of the hierarchy; a manager at this level coordinates the work of nonmanagers but also reports to a manager. Those involved in front-line management are often called supervisors, office managers, or foremen.

As the management system develops an even higher degree of specialization (Figure 2-4), relationships among the managers and nonmanagers become even more complex. In Figure 2-4, it's clear that the managers in production, marketing, accounting, and research not only manage their own subordinates but also are managed by *their* superiors as well. Figure 2-4 illustrates three types of managers.

2-2a First-Line Management

First-line managers coordinate the work of others who are not themselves managers. Those involved in **first-line management** are often called *supervisors, office managers,* or *foremen.* These are often entry-level positions of recent college graduates, or first-time managerial positions for people who have worked their way up in the organization.

The subordinates of a first-line manager may be blue-collar workers, salespersons, accounting clerks, or scientists, depending on the particular tasks that the subunit performs. First-line managers usually are responsible for the basic work of the organization. They are in daily or near daily contact with their subordinates, and they are ordinarily assigned the job because of their ability to work with people. First-line managers must work with their own subordinates and with other first-line supervisors whose tasks are related to their own.

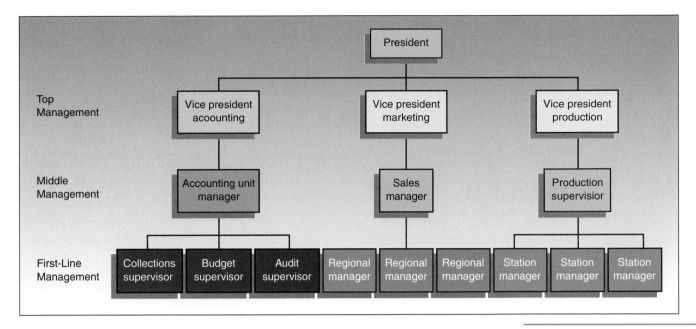

Figure 2-4
Vertical and Horizontal Specialization of the Management Process

Research has determined that the first-line manager's role in retaining key employees is critical. To find out what successful supervisors are doing to address retention challenges, management consulting firm Alignment Strategies interviewed 500 managers from a cross section of industries. Employees identified these managers as having established and sustained quality reporting relationships with younger employees and those from culturally diverse groups. These supervisors were found to engage in similar practices. Steps supervisors can take to create quality relationships with subordinates include:

1. Learn more about employees
2. Learn how likely employees are to leave
3. Set mutual expectations about the supervisory relationship[3]

2-2b Middle Management

The middle manager is known in many organizations as the *departmental manager, plant manager,* or *director of operations.* Unlike first-line managers, those in **middle management** plan, organize, lead, and control the activity of other managers. Yet, like the first-line manager, they are subject to the managerial efforts of a superior. The middle manager coordinates the activity of a subunit of the organization. During the late 1980s and early 1990s, the middle manager was often cast as the villain of productivity. Many organizations went through a cycle of change called "reengineering" that resulted in organizational **downsizing.** What that meant, in reality, was that many organizations slashed middle managers from their payrolls and tried to get by with fewer layers of management.

Today, the middle manager is back in fashion and is regarded as a key implementer of corporate strategy.[4] Research has shown that companies whose middle managers are involved in overall strategy have higher levels of innovation and financial performance. This is due to middle managers' detailed grasp of the inner workings of an organization.[5]

2-2c Top Management

A small cadre of managers, which usually includes a *chief executive officer (CEO), chief financial officer (CFO), chief information officer (CIO), president,* and/or *vice president,* constitutes the **top management** of an organization. Top management is responsible for the performance of the entire organization. Unlike other managers, top managers are accountable to no one other than the owners of the resources used by the organization. These "owners" are the shareholders who usually influence the organization through an elected "board of directors." Most major organizations—those traded on Wall Street—are gov-

middle management The middle level of an administrative hierarchy. Managers at this level coordinate the work of managers but also report to a manager.

downsizing An organizational response to declining revenues and increasing costs that involves reducing the workforce and often closing and /or consolidating operations.

top management The top level of an administrative hierarchy. Managers at this level coordinate the work of other managers but do not report to a manager.

Management Focus on **Diversity**

Are Women Different from Men in Negotiating Preferences?

The good news about women at the executive level in organizations is they are paid every bit as generously as their male counterparts. Both business size and rank within the top five leadership slots affect an individual's compensation level, but gender does not.

Because of a glass ceiling, an informal barrier to advancement, there is some bad news in the reality that more women do not hold key executive positions. Also research shows that men are more likely than women to negotiate pay, promotions, and recognition in the organizational world. Why are women more reluctant than men to negotiate since negotiating pays off? The starting salaries for male graduates are more than 7% higher than those for females.

Perhaps some of the explanation about why women refrain from negotiating may be a result of different attitudes about competition. For example, research has found that competition enhances male performance but does not affect female performance. What are your opinions about the difference in male and female viewpoints about negotiating pay, promotions, and recognition?

Source: Adapted from Laura D'Andrea Tyson, "New Clues to the Pay and Leadership Gap," *Business Week,* October 27, 2003, pp. 16–17.

erned by a board of directors. By law, a board must have a chairperson, and all major corporate decisions must be made by majority vote of the directors. This structure ensures that the company's officers manage resources in a manner that is consistent with the interests of the owners (shareholders).

The Management Focus on Diversity box, "Are Women Different from Men in Negotiating Preferences?" explores the issue of gender among top management with regard to negotiating style. Progress is being made to shatter the glass ceiling, but it is slow relative to negotiating pay and promotions.

The designations "top," "middle," and "first line" classify managers on the basis of their vertical rank in the organization. The completion of a task usually requires the completion of several interrelated activities. As these activities are identified, and as the responsibility for completing each task is assigned, the manager becomes a functional manager.

2-2d Functional Management

As the management process becomes horizontally specialized, a functional manager is responsible for a particular activity. In Figure 2-4 the management process is divided into three functions: production, marketing, and accounting.

Thus, one manager may be a first-line manager in production, while another may be a middle manager in marketing. The function refers to what *activities* the manager actually oversees as a result of horizontal specialization of the management process. The level of the manager refers to the *right to act and use resources* within specified limits as a result of vertical specialization of the management process.

2-2e Management Level and Management Functions

In the last chapter, we noted that all managers perform the management functions of planning, organizing, leading, and controlling. However, the amount of time and effort devoted to each function depends on the manager's level in the organization. Figure 2-5 illustrates this relationship. For example, first-line managers usually spend less time planning than do top managers. However, they spend much more time and effort leading. At high levels in the organization, far more time is spent leading. The amount of time and effort devoted to controlling is usually fairly equal at all levels of management.

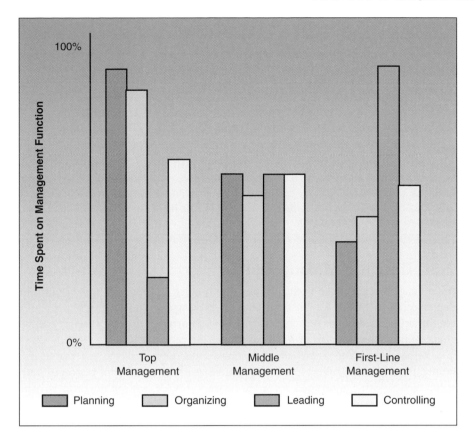

Figure 2-5
Management Level
and the Management Functions

2-3 Managerial Skills

Regardless of the level of management, managers must possess and seek to further develop many critical skills. A **skill** is an ability or proficiency in performing a particular task. Management skills are learned and developed. Various skills classifications have been suggested as being important in performing managerial roles.

> **skill** An ability or proficiency that a person possesses that permits him or her to perform a particular task.

2-3a Technical Skills

Technical skill is the ability to use *specific* knowledge, techniques, and resources in performing work. For example, accounting supervisors, engineering directors, or nursing supervisors must possess the technical skills to perform their management jobs. Technical skills are especially important at the front-line management level, since daily work-related problems must be solved. Managers at this level must be technically proficient, but they must also be able to develop the technical skills of others. Nearly every job today requires some technical competence.

> **technical skill** The skill of working with the resources and having knowledge in a specific area. Such skill is most important to first-level managers.

2-3b Analytical Skills

These skills involve using scientific approaches or techniques to solve management problems. In essence, **analytical skills** are the abilities to identify key factors and understand how they interrelate, and the roles they play in a situation. Analytical skills include the ability to diagnose and evaluate. They're needed to understand problems and to develop plans of action for their resolution.

Analytical skills involve being able to think about how multiple complex variables interact, and to conceive of ways to make them act in a desirable manner. For example, you can test your analytic skills by answering the following question. You have thirty seconds.

> **analytical skills** The abilities to identify key factors, to understand how they interrelate, and to understand the roles they play in a situation as well as to diagnose and evaluate.

TEST YOURSELF

1. Fran is off on a trek across the Sahara desert to see Metallica in concert. It is a six-day hike from the airport to the closest oasis where they are playing. One person is only physically capable of carrying enough supplies (food, water, Metallica CD's) for four days. Obviously, she cannot make the entire trip alone. How many assistants will she need to make it to the oasis while making sure that the assistants have enough supplies to make it back to the airport? (They don't want to see the concert.) Hint: Only Fran needs to actually make it to the oasis.

Answer: Two—*One assistant carries four days' supplies, and after the first day, he gives one day's supplies to the other assistant and one to Fran. This gives them each four days' supplies again. The first assistant, with one day's supplies remaining, returns to the airport. Fran and the other assistant complete another day, and at the end the assistant gives one day's supply to Fran. Fran again has four days' supplies (enough to complete the rest of the trip alone) and the assistant has two days' supplies to get back to the airport.*

2-3c Decision-Making Skills

All managers must make decisions, and the quality of these decisions determines their degree of effectiveness. A manager's decision-making skill in selecting a course of action is greatly influenced by his or her analytical skill. Poor analytical proficiency will inevitably result in inefficient, spotty, or inadequate decision making.

Research indicates that half of managers' decisions fail because managers employ failure-prone tactics. Failure-prone tactics are used for a number of reasons. First, because some tactics with a good track record are commonly known but uncommonly practiced. Second, decision makers take shortcuts when they feel time pressure. Third, there are subtleties in the way problems are framed. So what can you do to improve your chances of making better decisions? Certainly, you should resist pressures for a quick fix, accept uncertainty and ambiguity, and recognize subtleties in what works and what does not. In addition, you should

1. Personally manage your decision making,
2. Search for understanding,
3. Establish your direction with an objective, and
4. Manage the social and political forces that can block you.[6]

2-3d Digital Skills

digital skills Managerial skills comprising the conceptual understanding of and ability to use computers, telecommunications, and digital technology.

Managers who have **digital skills** have a conceptual understanding of computers, telecommunications, and, in particular, know how to use digital technology to perform many aspect of their jobs.

Digital abilities are important because using digital technology substantially increases a manager's productivity. Computers can perform in minutes tasks in financial analysis, human resource planning, and other areas that otherwise take hours, even days to complete. The computer is an especially helpful tool for decision making. The computer instantly places at a manager's fingertips a vast array of information in a flexible and usable form. Software enables managers to manipulate data and perform "what if" scenarios, looking at the projected impact of different decision alternatives. Some managers use technology to improve their self knowledge and managerial performance. The Management Focus on Technology box, "Telecommuting: A Management Perk," illustrates the growing importance of telecommuting to managers today.

2-3e Human Relations Skills

human relations skills The ability to work with, motivate, and counsel people who need help and guidance; most important to middle-level managers.

Since managers must accomplish much of their work through other people, their ability to work with, communicate with, and understand others is most important. **Human relations skills** are essential at every organizational level of management; they are directly related to a manager's leadership abilities. The popularity of team-based management has increased the necessity for strong interpersonal skills for all members of the organiza-

> ## *Management Focus* on Technology

Telecommuting: A Management Perk

Telecommuting (working from home) is becoming a highly desirable perk for a growing number of professionals. Some managers are managing entire departments or major projects from their home offices. Employers are offering telecommuting as a way to recruit and retain managers who are reluctant to relocate. Research indicates that more managers want the same work-at-home opportunities enjoyed by their own employees.

Telecommuting managers have to learn to manage from a distance, and for some jobs this is very difficult. However, a survey conducted by Ladders.com indicated that about 20% of managers looking for high paying jobs (at least $100,000) ranked working from home as an important priority. Nearly 40% said they would take advantage of telecommuting if it were offered.

The demand for telecommuting work is growing annually. The number of employees who performed some part of their work from home grew to 44.4 million in 2004. Technology has enabled telecommuting to grow rapidly. Through technology connections individuals can communicate verbally, view each other, and keep in continuous contact. However, there are problems with motivation, evaluation, and team development that need to be considered and addressed.

Source: Adapted from "Even Bosses Are Getting into the Telecommuting Business," *USA Today,* October 19, 2004, p. A7.

---

tion—managers and employees alike. A key interpersonal attribute is *political skill*—the ability to get things done by understanding and working through others outside of formally prescribed organizational mechanisms. Political skill is a distinct type of social skill that is important for managerial success.[7]

2-3f Communication Skills

Effective **communication**—the written and oral transmission of common understanding—is vital for effective managerial performance. The skill is critical to success in every field, but it is crucial to managers who must achieve results through the efforts of others. Communication skills involve the ability to communicate in ways that other people understand, and to seek and use feedback from employees to ensure that one is understood.

> **communication** The transmission of mutual understanding through the use of symbols.

Recent studies of skills and competencies valued by employers continue to document the need for excellence in writing, speaking, and listening. Equally significant are such interpersonal communication skills as teamwork, working with culturally diverse populations, and adapting to change and the environment while maintaining a positive attitude. If managers are to succeed in the workplace, they must obtain knowledge of soft skills and strengthen their communication skills, including interpersonal negotiations and team skills.[8]

2-3g Conceptual Skills

Conceptual skills consist of the ability to see the big picture, the complexities of the overall organization, and how the various parts fit together. Recall that the systems approach as a way of thinking about organizations stresses the importance of knowing how each part of the organization interrelates and contributes to the overall objectives of the organization. Many CEOs combine analytical and conceptual skills in developing long-range plans for their companies. Both enable a CEO to look forward and project how prospective actions may affect a company five, ten, or even twenty years in the future.

> **conceptual skills** The ability to coordinate and integrate ideas, concepts, and practices. Such skill is most important to top-level managers.

The single most important foundation of business success today is leadership—especially visionary leadership. It is critical that every company develop strategic visioning and process tools to help it reassess and, if necessary, reframe its organizational vision periodically. Visionary companies have a number of things in common, note James Collins and Jerry Porras in their best-selling book, *Built to Last: Successful Habits of Visionary Companies.*[9]

Visionary companies possess a core ideology from which their values spring that is unchanging and that transcends immediate customer demands and market conditions. The unifying ideology of visionary companies guides and inspires people. Coupled with

Figure 2-6
**Managerial Skills
and Management Level**

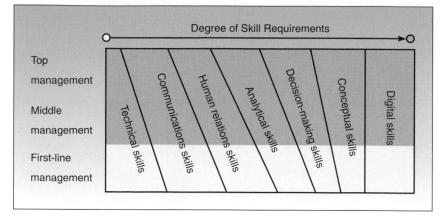

an intense, "cultlike" culture, a unifying ideology creates enormous solidarity and esprit de corps. Last, visionary companies subscribe to what Collins and Porras call "big, hairy, audacious goals" that galvanize people to come together, team, create, and stretch themselves and their companies to achieve greatness over the long haul.[10]

Although the preceding skills are all vital, the relative importance of each will vary according to the level of the manager in the organization. Figure 2-6 illustrates the skills required at each level. For example, note that technical and human relations skills are more important at lower levels of management. These managers have greater contact with the work being done and the people doing the work. Communication and computer skills are equally important at all levels of management. Analytical skills are slightly more important at higher levels of management where the environment is less stable and problems are less predictable. Finally, decision-making and conceptual skills are extremely critical to the performance of top managers. Top management's primary responsibility is to make the key decisions that are executed or implemented at lower levels. This requires that top management see the big picture in order to identify opportunities in the environment and develop strategic plans to capitalize on these opportunities. One reason many individuals find managing to be so challenging is because effective managers must possess such a variety of skills.

2-4 Managerial Roles

We now know that different managers perform at different levels and require different skills. At this point, we want to examine what managers actually do and how they spend their time. One of the most frequently cited studies of **managerial roles** was conducted by Henry Mintzberg. He observed and interviewed chief executives from different industries. He determined that managers serve in ten different but closely related roles.[11] These are illustrated in Figure 2-7. The figure indicates that the ten roles can be separated into three categories: interpersonal roles, informational roles, and decisional roles.[12]

2-4a Interpersonal Roles

The three **interpersonal roles** of figurehead, leader, and liaison grow out of the manager's formal authority and focus on interpersonal relationships. By assuming these roles, the manager also can perform informational roles, which, in turn, lead directly to the performance of decisional roles.

All managerial jobs require some duties that are symbolic or ceremonial in nature. Some examples of the **figurehead role** include a college dean who hands out diplomas at graduation, a shop supervisor who attends the wedding of a subordinate's daughter, and the CEO who cuts the ribbon on a new office building. These roles are largely *symbolic* and have to do more with the manager's position in the company than with who he or she is as a person. For example, the dean hands out diplomas because he or she is *the dean*, not because he or she is Joe or Jane Smith.

managerial roles The organized sets of behavior that belong to the manager's job. The three main types of managerial roles discovered by such researchers as Mintzberg are interpersonal, informational, and decisional roles.

interpersonal roles A manager's interpersonal roles include being a figurehead, providing leadership, and being a liaison both within the company and to stakeholders outside the company.

figurehead role The symbolic or ceremonial role preformed by managers.

CHAPTER 2 Management: Skills, Roles, and Modern Challenges

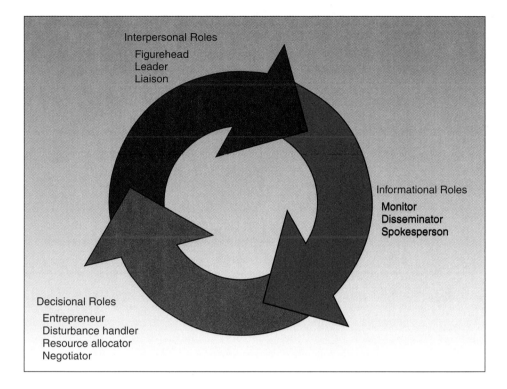

Figure 2-7
Managerial Roles

The manager's **leadership role** involves directing and coordinating the activities of subordinates. This may involve staffing (hiring, training, promoting, dismissing) and motivating subordinates. The leadership role also involves controlling, making sure that things are going according to plan. The manager's leadership role is tied both to the person's role in the company and to who he or she is. Leadership stems from formal position authority, as does the figurehead role, but also draws heavily from a person's history and values. Great leaders imbue their leadership with their own personal style, values, ways of communicating, and personality.

The **liaison role** involves managers in interpersonal relationships outside of their area of authority. This role may involve contacts both inside and outside the organization. Within the organization, managers must interact with numerous other managers and other individuals. They must maintain good relations with the managers who send work to the unit as well as those who receive work from the unit. For example, a marketing manager must interact with both production and distribution managers, a supervisory nurse in the operating room must interact with supervisors of various other groups of nurses, and a production supervisor must interact with engineering supervisors and sales managers. Managers also often have interactions with important people outside of the organization. It is easy to see that the liaison role can often consume a significant amount of a manager's time.

2-4b Informational Roles

The **informational role** establishes the manager as the central point for receiving and sending nonroutine information. As a result of the interpersonal roles already discussed, the manager builds a network of contacts. These contacts aid the manager in gathering and receiving information as the *monitor* and transmitting that information as the *disseminator* and *spokesperson*.

The **monitor role** involves examining the environment to gather information, or to detect changes, opportunities, and problems that may affect the unit. The formal and informal contacts developed in the liaison role are often useful here. The information gathered may be competitive moves that could influence the entire organization or the knowledge of whom to call if the usual supplier of an important part cannot fill an order.

▶**leadership role** A manager's duties that involve directing and coordinating subordinates' activities.

▶**liaison role** A manager's duties that involve interpersonal relationships outside the manager's area of command.

▶**informational role** A manager's duties involved in being the central point for receiving and sending nonroutine information.

▶**monitor role** The aspect of a manager's role that involves examining the environment to gather information or to detect changes, opportunities, and problems that may affect the unit.

disseminator role
A manager's role that involves providing important or privileged information to subordinates.

spokesperson role
A manager's role in representing the unit to other people.

decisional roles A manager's most important duties as entrepreneur, disturbance handler, resource allocator, and negotiator.

entrepreneurial role
A manager's role to change the unit for the better.

disturbance handler role
A manager's role to make decisions or take corrective action in response to pressure from circumstances beyond the manager's control.

resource allocator role
A manager's role that requires allocating resources.

negotiator role A manager's role that involves bargaining with other units and individuals in obtaining advantages for the unit.

The **disseminator role** involves providing important or privileged information to subordinates. The president of a firm may learn during a lunch conversation that a large customer of the firm is on the verge of bankruptcy. Upon returning to the office, the president contacts the vice president of marketing, who in turn instructs the sales force not to sell anything on credit to the troubled company.

In the **spokesperson role** the manager represents the unit to other people. This representation may be internal when a manager makes the case for salary increases to top management. It may also be external when an executive represents the organization's view on a particular issue of public interest to a local civic organization.

2-4c Decisional Roles

Developing interpersonal relationships and gathering information are important, but they are not ends in themselves. They serve as the basic inputs to the process of decision making. Some people believe **decisional roles**—entrepreneur, disturbance handler, resource allocator, and negotiator—are a manager's most important roles.

The **entrepreneurial role** is to change the unit for the better. The effective first-line supervisor is continually looking for new ideas or new methods to improve the unit's performance. The effective marketing manager continually seeks new product ideas.

In the **disturbance handler role** managers make decisions or take corrective action in response to pressure that is beyond their control. Usually the decisions must be made quickly, which means that this role takes priority over other roles. The immediate goal is to bring about stability. When an emergency room supervisor responds quickly to a local disaster, a plant supervisor reacts to a strike, or a first-line manager responds to a breakdown in a key piece of equipment, they are dealing with disturbances in their environments. They must respond quickly and must return the environment to stability.

The **resource allocator role** places a manager in the position of deciding who will get what resources. These resources include, money, people, time, equipment, and information. Invariably there are not enough resources to go around, and managers must allocate scarce resources in many directions. Resource allocation, therefore, is one of the most critical of the manager's decisional roles. A first-line supervisor must decide whether an overtime schedule should be established or whether part-time workers should be hired. A college dean must decide which courses to offer next semester, based on available faculty. The president of the United States must decide whether to allocate more money to defense and less to social programs.

In the **negotiator role,** a manager must bargain with other units and individuals to obtain advantages for her unit. The negotiations may concern work, performance, objectives, resources, or anything else influencing the unit. A sales manager may negotiate with the production department over a special order for a large customer. A front-line supervisor may negotiate for new typewriters, while a top-level manager may negotiate with a labor union representative.

Mintzberg suggests that recognizing these ten roles serves three important functions. First, roles help explain the job of managing while emphasizing that all the roles are interrelated. Neglecting one or more of the roles hinders the total progress of the manager. Second, a team of employees cannot function effectively if any of the roles is neglected. Teamwork in an organizational setting requires that each role be performed consistently. Finally, the magnitude of the ten roles points out the importance of managing time effectively, an essential responsibility of managers if they are to successfully perform each role. (See the Learning Moment box, "Managerial Level and Roles.")

2-5 Modern Challenges for Managers

Thus far, we have examined two important factors—managerial skills and managerial roles—that influence managerial behavior and performance. We know the value of each of these factors will differ from situation to situation and manager to manager. Another factor influencing a manager's ability to perform is the set of challenges posed by the organization's external environment, a set of outside challenges that is difficult to control. These factors may have a profound impact on how well a manager performs.

LearningMoment   *Managerial Level and Roles*

As you might expect, the level in the organization will influence which managerial roles are emphasized, although at every level, each role must be performed to some degree. Obviously, top managers spend much more time in the figurehead role than do front-line supervisors. The liaison role of top and middle managers will involve individuals and groups outside the organization, while at the first-line level, the liaison will be outside the unit but inside the organization. Top managers must monitor the environment for changes likely to influence the particular function (e.g., marketing) that they manage, and the front-line supervisor is concerned about what will influence his unit.

Recall from our discussion of the open-systems concept in the previous chapter that an organization interacts with its external environment and receives feedback. The open-systems view encourages managers to examine the world and events outside the organization. Much of what occurs inside the organization in terms of performance is affected by the external environment. The organization's goals, structure, staffing program, reward and discipline system, and performance evaluation programs reflect external environmental factors. Managers can improve the organization's performance dramatically by providing immediate feedback to employees on key factors in both the internal and external environments.[13]

Organizations must continually scan and evaluate the forces in the external environment. To ensure survival, organizations must respond to environmental developments with speed and effectiveness. It is not possible for us to discuss each of the important environmental influences in detail in these few pages. However, it is necessary to outline the broad impact of environmental influences on the job of managing. Our discussion of environmental effects will focus on the key challenges that managers face. These challenges include information technology, globalization, and intellectual capital.

A challenge that is pointed out in the Management Focus on Globalization box, "Is Work-Life Balance Realistic in a Global World?" suggests that competitive organizations should think again about whether work-life balance is always achievable or desirable.

▸*Management Focus* on Globalization

Is Work-Life Balance Realistic in a Global World?

Sigmund Freud suggested that imbalance is part of the human condition. The father of psychoanalysis observed that some amount of anxiety is a crucial "signal" function, a response to either physical danger or internal psychological danger. Anxiety is a part of who we are. It is a source of creativity and drive; it spurs individuals to stretch themselves and accomplish goals.

Great leaders, innovators, and self-motivated employees need to prove themselves, to achieve, to accomplish excellence. Today, an increasing number of pundits, behavioral scientists, and consultants are driving the notion that balance and self-actualization for everyone is how to proceed. The "balance" movement is mentioned constantly in the media. However, in most organizations success is predicated in most cases on passion, energy, commitment, and time. Can a person be balance driven and achievement driven? This appears to be a contradiction and a false premise.

The global economy is dominated by firms like Accenture and Google who say that they value an environment that allows workers balance. However, they are competing against companies that place a much higher value on achievement. The work ethic around the world is entrepreneurial, competitive, and hard charging. Things taken for granted by those advocating balance are not taken for granted in the developing world.

The "work to live" advocates toil fewer hours than most achievement proponents. If a company is competing against other companies who are working longer, smarter, and more passionately it may be only a matter of time until they are not competitive. Balancing work and life may mean that you can't have everything. In a knowledge-based global world, imbalance may be more realistic and honest.

Source: Adapted from Keith H. Hammonds, "Balance Is Bunk," *Fast Company,* October 2004, pp. 68–76.

While some individuals enjoy balance, others are striving to achieve and/or improve their position and use their competence at the highest level.

2-5a Information Technology

Today's managers are faced with a bewildering array of information technology (IT) choices that promise to change the way work gets done. Computers, the Internet, intranets, telecommunications, and a seemingly infinite range of software applications confront the modern manager with the challenge of using the best technology for his or her workplace. Many managers have a staff of IT specialists to help them decide on the best hardware and software for a job, but no manager should pass all IT decision making to these specialists. Managers must use technology to perform work. If such decisions are left solely in the hands of specialists, IT implementations often do not produce the desired results.[14]

To be truly effective, IT must be selected and implemented with the end user and work to be accomplished firmly in mind. Managers must learn how to work with IT specialists to determine the most effective technologies for the work to be achieved and then consider the best way to implement those technologies.[15] The IT choices available to modern managers far exceed those that were available just a few short years ago. In addition, managers must also determine the best way to network an organization's system, including the crucial decisions about who gets access to what information on the network, how wide the network is, and what types of security are necessary to protect the network.

Besides the choice of which technology to deploy, managers also face the challenge of effectively implementing that technology. Introducing new technology in the workplace can be disastrous if not handled appropriately. Employees who are inadequately prepared to use the new technology will resist its implementation. Effective managers ensure that employees are involved in the new technology implementation process, providing training where necessary. Employees must feel at least as competent to perform their jobs with the new IT as they did before its implementation. In the best situation, IT actually empowers employees to perform at a higher level. Of course, employees should also feel as though their higher level of performance will be rewarded by the organization.[16]

The IT challenge that modern managers face is likely to continue unabated. It has been nearly two decades since the personal computer (PC) burst upon the workplace, and less than a decade since the Internet opened new doors to global interactivity. These relatively recent changes to the workplace are only beginning to be explored. For example, modern telecommunications, coupled with the PC and the Internet, are allowing a new generation of workers to "telecommute." **Telecommuting** means workers either stay at home or travel short distances to "telecenters" to link to the workplace via IT. Management theorists and researchers are working overtime to try to understand the difficulties associated with managing a remote workforce. See the Management Focus on Technology box, "Telecommuting: A Management Perk," set earlier in the chapter that illustrates how managers themselves are attracted toward using telecommuting.

The future surely looks bright for IT-adept managers. Some may soon be able to work for several organizations simultaneously without ever leaving their home office. The aspiring manager today must be immersed in IT and be aware of the opportunities and threats it poses for organizations today and into the future.

2-5b Globalization

The modern economy is said to have been "globalized" by the communications revolution that began shortly after World War II as the Voice of America and other shortwave broadcasters provided information about the Western world to those locked behind the communist "Iron Curtain." Global communication was hastened by the onset of fax machines and has within the past decade accelerated dramatically with the Internet.

A major component of the ongoing **globalization** of business, culture, and economics is the ability and freedom to connect to almost anyone, anytime, and anywhere. Someday, this freedom may be regarded to be as basic a human right and as uncontroversial as are the rights of life, liberty, and the pursuit of happiness. But this freedom has not yet been

telecommuting
Telecommuting means workers either stay at home or travel short distances to "telecenters" to link to the workplace via IT.

globalization The ability and freedom to connect to almost anyone, anytime, anywhere.

firmly established worldwide. In fact, as more nations grapple with the politics of connectivity for their citizens, the liberty to gain access to information content may diminish.

Even the United States, with its self-image as the most wired nation, doesn't provide assurance of freedom of access to any and all. Other nations demand partial content restrictions or limited access only to "qualified" users. A few countries prohibit any connection at all, usually based on a fear of what users might learn. A few remote nations still have no physical means of connection. That problem may soon vanish as all-encompassing satellite systems may provide worldwide wireless access to the Internet, e-mail, and other on-line services.[17]

One offshoot of the communications revolution has been the development of global trading blocks and world trade agreements. Global trading blocks such as the North American Free Trade Agreement (NAFTA), Latin America's MERCOSUR, Asia's ASEAN, and the European Union (EU) have all originated within the past twenty years as old animosities have begun to die away and as the power of free markets has become increasingly evident. The EU provides a good example of how the power of communication has transformed the world. Just five decades earlier, the entire continent was locked in the throes of a devastating war. Now, former bitter enemies, having seen the similarities that underlie their differences, have decided to join under a common banner for the sake of their economic futures.

The growth of regional free trade agreements and the global World Trade Organization (WTO) presents a new set of challenges and opportunities for managers. Free trade allows for firms from anywhere in the world to gain access to local markets. The onset of NAFTA, for example, has been a boon to several U.S. companies such as Wal-Mart who have found the Mexican market to be eager for their products. Another benefit of free trade agreements is the increased labor pool. Manufacturing companies, in particular, have reduced costs by moving some of their production to areas where labor is plentiful and cheap. Many American manufacturers have, at least in part, shifted their production to Mexico to take advantage of its relatively cheap, yet highly skilled, labor. These cost savings are passed on to the consumer, who also benefits from the added competition in the marketplace that is created by foreign goods.

Not everyone agrees that regional trading blocks offer benefits that exceed their costs. Certainly, shifting manufacturing production to foreign locations has cost some American workers, including many American managers, their jobs. In addition, many companies have had to adjust their approach to their domestic markets because of the sudden influx of competitively priced foreign products. The consumer is the one who benefits from this more heated competition. Managers must find ways to beat foreign competition on price and quality as consumer choices widen.

The globalization trend is not likely to change in the coming years. Short of a major world war, the communications revolution and the worldwide shift to free markets are likely to continue. There will always be disagreements regarding acceptable fair trade practices, but the mechanisms are now being put in place that will allow for these disagreements to be handled peacefully.

2-5c Intellectual Capital

In the early part of the last century, most workers were employed in some form of agriculture-related jobs. They either worked directly on farms, or they were involved in service or manufacturing jobs that provided support for the agri-economy. In less than 130 years, agricultural goods have dropped from 40 percent of U.S. gross domestic product to less than 1.4 percent. Today, less than 3 percent of Americans work in agriculture, and that percentage continues to drop.[18]

As the twentieth century moved into its second and third decades, more and more people were shifting from agricultural work to industrial work. Major cities evolved around steel mills and factories that were supporting a world increasingly eager for machines and appliances that were designed to ease some of the burdens of life. The so-called Industrial Revolution was in full swing by World War II as nations around the world shifted production to war material.

Following the war, the roaring 1950s were unprecedented in their demand for consumer goods. A new definition of success in America was exemplified by the suburban family that possessed two cars, washer and dryer, refrigerator, dishwasher, television, and myriad other large and small appliances. Much of the nation was employed in the manufacture of these goods, which helped to create a middle class that was wealthy enough to buy the goods. The cycle of success perpetuated itself. Life was good.

The great promise of the 1950s began to encounter difficulties in the next decade. The 1960s were a time of introspection for many Americans. The difficulties of the Vietnam War, the domestic struggles of civil rights, and the backlash against unfettered factory production by the environmental movement led many to rethink the direction of the Industrial Revolution and its notion of "progress." In part, this introspection was caused by a new generation of Americans who were the most highly educated in the nation's history. This generation wanted more out of life than the daily grind of the factory. They asked questions about the meaning of life and the role of work in creating meaning.

When these ongoing changes in the mood of Americans were coupled with increasing global competition, the typical company had to find a place for the new, more highly educated worker. In essence, these dynamic changes—globalization, a more educated workforce, and employee demands for more meaningful work—signaled the onset of the **Information Revolution.** Like the Industrial Revolution before it, the Information Revolution has redefined work for a large number of people. In 1950, 34 percent of the U.S. workforce was employed in manufacturing. That number today is less than 16 percent and dropping. The best available estimates today are that the information sector of the economy accounts for over 40 percent of GDP.[19]

As worldwide economic competition heated up in the 1970s, managers began to discover that they could gain efficiencies and competitive advantage by implementing information technology throughout the workplace. This was true as much for the growing service economy as well as for traditional manufacturing. Increasing use of IT placed new demands on workers not only to be able to use technology to perform their jobs, but also to improve the organization by using the information provided by the technology. In turn, more highly educated workers placed demands on employers for more responsibility over their work lives.[20]

This new type of worker, the so-called knowledge worker, is vastly different from the worker of Frederick Taylor's day. The **knowledge worker** is someone who expects and is expected to think for themselves in the workplace. Knowledge workers are expected to be able to determine their own "best way" for performing their job. They are also expected to be adaptable and flexible, ready to accept new information technology advances that will help improve overall productivity. Such workers are the **intellectual capital** that is the most important asset of the modern organization.

Intellectual capital is a relatively recent term that has been coined to reflect that the principal assets of many modern organizations lie in the minds of their workers rather than in machinery, bricks, and mortar. Author Thomas Stewart has defined intellectual capital as the "intellectual material—knowledge information, intellectual property, experience—that can be put to use to create wealth." It is the "sum of everything everybody in a company knows that gives it a competitive edge." Old-style companies didn't manage knowledge well. New companies must do so to remain competitive. In addition, the skills managers need to succeed in knowledge-based organizations are different from those of the Industrial Age.[21]

One of the terms that applies to the managing of intellectual capital is "knowledge management." **Knowledge management** refers to the many techniques managers can employ to capture and use the knowledge that is generated within the organization. All organizations have knowledge stored within them. Some of this knowledge is in the minds of workers; this is often called **tacit knowledge.** Some of this knowledge is stored in documents such as manuals; this is often called **explicit knowledge.** Managing knowledge often means converting tacit knowledge into explicit knowledge so that the organization can continue to function if key employees leave.

Knowledge that is vital to the firm's survival is called **mission critical knowledge.** Every manager has a responsibility to see to it that mission critical knowledge is made explicit and available to the organization when and where it's needed. Modern networking

---

Information Revolution
A term used to describe a shift in the focus of Western economies from heavy industry to information and services.

knowledge worker
A modern employee who spends more work time using his or her brain than muscles.

intellectual capital The concept that the principal assets of many modern organizations lie in the heads of their workers rather than in machinery, bricks, and mortar.

knowledge management
Refers to the many techniques managers can employ to capture and use the knowledge that is generated within the organization.

tacit knowledge Knowledge within an organization that is stored in the minds of workers.

explicit knowledge
Knowledge within an organization that is codified and stored in manuals, databases, or handbooks.

mission critical knowledge
Knowledge that is vital to the firm's survival.

and computer applications have enabled effective new approaches to managing this knowledge. The Internet Exercise at the end of this chapter will help you learn more about the practice of knowledge management.

2-5d Measuring Intellectual Capital

It's difficult to measure the impact of intellectual capital on organizations, but many management theorists are giving it a try. **Tobin's Q** is a measure developed by Nobel Prize–winning economist James Tobin. It compares the market value of an asset with its replacement cost. This measure wasn't designed to assess the impact of intellectual capital, but it works well for that purpose. When q is positive, "2" for example, it means an asset is worth twice its replacement cost. In such a situation, a company is getting high returns on a class of assets. Tobin said that q is a measure of what economist call "monopoly rents." This is a company's ability to get unusually high profits because it's got something its competitors don't have. Usually, this is intellectual capital since competitors presumably have, or could have, similar fixed assets. A high q means a company is using its people, systems, and knowledge to squeeze more out of its fixed assets than are competitors.[22]

> **Tobin's Q** A measure developed by Nobel Prize–winning economist James Tobin that compares an asset's market value with its replacement cost.

Modern managers must be concerned that they take care of this intellectual capital. It's not enough any longer simply to provide a paycheck and job security. Knowledge workers want more from their lives than just a job. Many firms that rely heavily upon intellectual capital have opted for lucrative stock options in their compensation plans. These option plans have created a large number of millionaires in Silicon Valley. Other companies ensure that knowledge workers play an important role in deciding the fate of the company. Some firms use a form of full disclosure known as "open book management" so that workers are aware of their direct impact on the company's bottom line.

Management Summary

- Certain managerial skills and roles are essential for performance and to enable a manager to respond to the external environment that influences organizations.

- Management's response to the increasing complexity of an organization as it develops can be discussed in terms of horizontal and vertical specialization.

- Three types of managers are found in most complex organizations. They are first-line management, middle management, and top management.

- Seven skills are central to successful management. They can be classified as technical, analytical, decision making, digital, human relations, communication, and conceptual. The relative importance of most of these skills differs across the three levels of management.

- In his classic study, Henry Mintzberg identifies ten specific roles of management and grouped them into three categories: interpersonal, informational, and decisional.

- Three of the modern challenges that managers face are information technology, globalization, and intellectual capital. Each of these challenges is likely to continue to evolve rapidly over the coming years. Successful managers must be adept at using and implementing information technology, must be comfortable with international competition, and must be flexible to work with a new, more highly educated workforce.

Key Terms

analytical skills (p. 31)
communication (p. 33)
conceptual skills (p. 33)
decisional roles (p. 36)
digital skills (p. 32)
disseminator role (p. 36)
disturbance handler role (p. 36)
downsizing (p. 29)
entrepreneurial role (p. 36)
explicit knowledge (p. 40)
figurehead role (p. 34)
first-line management (p. 28)
globalization (p. 38)

human relations skills (p. 32)
Information Revolution (p. 40)
informational role (p. 35)
intellectual capital (p. 40)
interpersonal roles (p. 34)
knowledge management (p. 40)
knowledge worker (p. 40)
leadership role (p. 35)
liaison role (p. 35)
managerial roles (p. 34)
middle management (p. 29)
mission critical knowledge (p. 40)
monitor role (p. 35)

negotiator role (p. 36)
productivity (p. 26)
resource allocator role (p. 36)
resources (p. 26)
skill (p. 31)
spokesperson role (p. 36)
tacit knowledge (p. 40)
technical skill (p. 31)
telecommuting (p. 38)
Tobin's Q (p. 41)
top management (p. 29)

Review and Discussion Questions

1. Why would it be important for a manager, in discussing performance at any level, to make sure he or she also discusses whether the short or long run is an important issue?

2. A professional football team like the New England Patriots has to be concerned with organizational, managerial (coach), and individual performance. Explain these performance variables in terms of the team.

3. A common misconception is that organizations only wish to have managers with technical, not human relations, skills. Why is this viewpoint incorrect?

4. If quantity, quality, creativity, absenteeism, and lateness are good individual performance measures, why don't all organizations use them?

5. Some management observers assert that Mintzberg's typology of ten managerial roles is incomplete. What other roles do managers assume?

6. Some management experts assert that computer skills aren't relevant to the top-management level because executives rely on others for computer information. Why might this be the case? Explain.

7. Why is telecommuting becoming more popular each year?

8. Discuss the three modern challenges managers face. What changes in traditional managerial behaviors and roles will these challenges require?

9. How would you assess your management skills at this point in your career? What is your plan to improve and keep your skills up-to-date?

10. Some claim that managers are not needed in organizations. Do you agree? Why?

Practice Quiz

Note: You can find the correct answers to these questions by taking the quiz and then submitting your answers in the Online Edition. The program will automatically score your submission. If you miss a question, the program will provide the correct answer, a rationale for the answer, and the section number in the chapter where the topic is discussed.

Indicate whether the sentence or statement is true or false.

_____ 1. Productivity can be defined as "the relationship between real inputs and real outputs."

_____ 2. Workers are responsible for effectively utilizing all the resources of the organization.

_____ 3. During uncertain or difficult times in a company, it's important that managers communicate with employees so they don't waste time worrying or spreading rumors about their situation.

_____ 4. First-line managers coordinate the work of others, who are not themselves managers.

_____ 5. Middle managers are often known as the departmental manager, plant manager, or director.

_____ 6. The amount of time and effort devoted to leading and controlling is fairly equal at all levels of management.

Identify the letter of the choice that best completes the statement or answers the question.

_____ 7. Capital, machinery, labor, and intelligence are all considered _____ .
   a. expenditures.
   b. competitors.
   c. resources.
   d. fixed assets.

_____ 8. Which of the following skills do CEOs usually combine when developing long-range plans for their companies?
   a. analytical and human relations
   b. analytical and communications
   c. analytical and digital
   d. analytical and conceptual

_____ 9. _____ companies possess a core ideology from which their values spring. This ideology is unchanging and transcends immediate customer demands and market conditions.
   a. Established
   b. Visionary
   c. Start-up

_____ 10. Nobel Prize–winning economist James Tobin developed a measure called _____ that compares the **market value** of an asset with its **replacement cost.**
   a. IQ
   b. cost/replacement ratio
   c. Tobin's Q

_____ 11. In performing the spokesman role a manager is _____ .
   a. paid a stipend.
   b. asked to do community programs.
   c. representing the unit to constituents.
   d. required to negotiate with union representatives.

_____ 12. The major conflict resolution work of a manager is referred to in Mintzberg's framework as _____ .
   a. an informational role.
   b. the disturbance handler.
   c. the liaison person.
   d. the facilitator.
   e. the founder.

_____ 13. Collins and Porras in their research found that visionary companies use effectively what they call _____ .
   a. political and impression management.
   b. coaching training programs.
   c. balanced technical q-sorts.
   d. big, hairy, audacious goals.

_____ **14.** Digital skills are considered mandatory and important because _____ .
   a. computers are now faster.
   b. telecommuting is expected to be used by at least 90% of the workforce by 2010.
   c. technology can increase a manager's productivity.
   d. compliance requirements have become laws for digital information.
   e. competitors can access non-digital files easily.

_____ **15.** A measure of how much a manager is able to produce from his or her unit is called _____ .
   a. efficiency.
   b. cost control.
   c. eclectic variance.
   d. output.

Case Study

Herb Kelleher: Managing with a Flair at Southwest Airlines

A few hundred aviation executives are in the midst of a very dull lunch. About halfway through it, Herb Kelleher, famed CEO (now retired) of Southwest Airlines, steps into the room. Instantly the drab banquet hall in the Washington, D.C., convention center is buzzing. "He's here," the whispers sweep across the room. Every neck in the room has turned, straining to follow him as he works his way to the front.

Kelleher is there to deliver a speech on the sober topic of "The Future of Aviation." But his PR man warns in advance: "I have no idea what he'll say—Herb usually just thinks something up minutes before he gets up there." Tanned, relaxed, and beaming at the crowd, Kelleher steps up to the podium. He begins somberly "It is my practice to try to understand how valuable something is by trying to imagine myself without it. Following that practice has brought me to the clear, incontrovertible realization that . . . " Here Kelleher pauses. Looking around the room, he breaks into a broad grin and booms: "Wild Turkey whiskey and Philip Morris cigarettes are essential to the maintenance of human life!" The crowd erupts in cheers and whoops of laughter.

This is vintage Herb, famed for wild partying, impersonating Elvis, and riding a Harley. He once settled a business dispute by arm-wrestling over it rather than going to court. On one occasion Bob Crandall, the formidable ex-CEO of American Airlines, made a snide remark about a Southwest promotion featuring Sea World's Shamu the Killer Whale. Soon afterward at a staff meeting, Crandall received—by special delivery from Kelleher—a massive bowl of chocolate pudding meant to look like whale poop. The card read, "With love, from Shamu."

But of course what makes Kelleher truly legendary is Southwest Airlines. Built from a scrap of an idea on a cocktail napkin in 1966, it is now, bar none, the best-run airline in the country. Since 1973 the company has not lost a dime. No other airline can make that claim. While other carriers have suffered multiple bankruptcies (Continental), crippling strikes (Northwest), and total failure (Pan Am, Eastern), Southwest has thrived. Its margins and balance sheet are the best in the business. Last year the company earned $474 million on $4.7 billion in sales. Its stock price is up 300 percent over the past five years, to a recent $20.

Kelleher was at Southwest since the beginning in 1967 until he stepped down as CEO and president on June 19, 2001. He continues to serve on Southwest's board of directors. He was practicing law in San Antonio when one of his clients, Rollin King (now a board member), came to him with an idea he'd cooked up in a bar. He wanted to start a cut-rate airline to fly between Dallas, San Antonio, and Houston. It took five years of legal wrangling because of fierce opposition from now defunct competitors—but in 1971 the first Southwest flight got off the ground: Dallas to Houston for $20. At the time such cheap fares were revolutionary. Other airlines cost three times as much. To charge such fares and make money, the upstart airline was bent on slashing costs. That meant no frills and a fast turnaround—twenty minutes in and out of the gate. Since then Southwest's business model hasn't changed. Its planes have never served a meal and still take just twenty minutes to turn. As a result, Southwest's costs are 22 percent below the industry average. Its operating margins (16.5%) are triple the industry average. Since 1990 the airline has expanded east and west of its heartland base. It now serves fifty-six cities, up from twenty-nine before 1990.

Southwest's business model has attracted many imitators—US Airways' Metrojet, Continental Lite, Shuttle at United, Delta Express. So far it's not clear that any of them has turned a profit, and one of them—Continental Lite—is out of business. How does Southwest succeed where others fail? "They have a huge competitive advantage," says Brian Harris, airline analyst at Salomon Smith Barney. "Their culture." Kelleher is more emphatic: "Our esprit de corps is the core of our success. That's most difficult for a competitor to imitate. They can [buy] all the physical things. The thing you can't buy is dedication, devotion, loyalty, feeling you are participating in a cause or a crusade."

Kelleher's true gift as a leader is his ability to inspire his troops to be as passionate about Southwest as he is. "Herb makes you feel like you're part of a family" says Andrew Boniface, a stock clerk in Houston. It's a family that, like its patriarch, doesn't let ceremony stand in the way of efficiency—or fun. Pilots, for instance, will help load bags or clean cabins, if necessary, to stay on schedule. Gate agents sometimes restock planes. Flight attendants are famous for popping out of the overhead bins and telling jokes over the speakers. On Halloween employees throw raucous gate parties—complete with costumes, streamers, and cake. Not surprisingly, Southwest has the industry's fewest customer complaints, the fewest lost bags, and the most on-time arrivals.

Southwest's "esprit de corps" can be especially valuable in a crunch. In February 2001 Kelleher sent a letter about the fuel crisis to the home of every employee. Jet fuel, now $1 a gallon, costs three times what it did a year ago. Southwest uses 19 million gallons a week. "Our profitability is in jeopardy," he wrote. In a personal plea, he asked each worker to help out by saving $5 a day. That would, he explained, save Southwest $51 million annually. The response was immediate. One department offered to do its own janitorial work. A group of mechanics figured out how to heat the planes more cheaply. In the first six weeks after the letter went out, Southwest employees saved the company more than $2 million.

But as Southwest grows, sustaining zeal among the troops gets harder. Southwest has 30,000 employees. Over the next five years it will spend $4 billion opening a dozen new destinations. "You have to make sure that they don't become little independent fiefdoms," Kelleher says. Recently tensions broke out between flight attendants and their schedulers (the ones with the sorry job of telling flight attendants they have to work on a day off). The flight attendants believed the schedulers were overworking them; the schedulers claimed the attendants were hostile and uncooperative. The solution was very, well, Southwest: Both sides had to switch jobs for a day and see how difficult the other side had it. For now, at least, the tactic has eased tensions.

Southwest is very careful about who it lets in the door. Only 4 percent of the 90,000 people a year who apply for jobs get in—you've got better odds at Harvard. Essentially, what Southwest is looking for are mini-Herbs. It actually uses a personality test to rate candidates (on a scale from one to five) on seven traits: cheerfulness, optimism, decision-making skills, team spirit, communication, self-confidence, and self-starter skills. Anything less than a three and you're a no-go. This goes for everyone—from pilots to mechanics. "We would rather go short and work overtime than hire one bad apple," says Libby Sartain, vice president of human resources.

Once hired, employees go through rigorous people-skills courses at the University for People, Southwest's training center in Dallas. In one recent class a group of new hires learned to read body language. One demonstrated "negative body language" by stomping past another, head down, hands folded across her chest. In another class a group of mechanics learned the art of positive reinforcement. To protect Southwest's tradition in the field, the company has set up "culture committees" at each airport it goes into. They are responsible for making sure the new site carries on the spirit of Southwest: the gate parties, the jokes, and the games.

Questions for Discussion

1. What managerial roles do you think Kelleher excelled at in his position as CEO of Southwest Airlines?

2. Explain how Kelleher's leadership style and behaviors have helped Southwest Airlines become successful.

3. What role did communication skills play in Kelleher's management style? Analytical skills? Technical skills? Conceptual skills?

4. What are the main challenges that any Herb Kellehers' successor will face in trying to build and sustain on the success of Southwest Airlines?

Sources: "Herb Kelleher," *Business Week Online,* August 24, 2004, www.businessweek.com; Mark Morrison, "Herb Kelleher on the Record," *Business Week Online,* December 23, 2003, www.businessweek.com; Katrina Brooker, "Can Anyone Replace Herb?" *Fortune,* April 17, 2000, pp. 186–192; Joe Queenan, "The Cocktail Napkin as Magna Carta," *Chief Executive,* October 1999, p. 78; and John Huey and Geoffrey Colvin, "The Jack and Herb Show," *Fortune,* January 11, 1999, pp. 163–166.

Internet Exercise

The Hawthorne Studies

As discussed in the text, intellectual capital is one of the modern challenges that managers must learn to contend with. Intellectual capital refers to the "know-how" that a company's workers possess and develop on the job. This increasingly valuable asset has begun to replace traditional, tangible assets as the most important resource companies possess.

Unfortunately, most managers have been trained to manage tangible assets and are finding great difficulty adapting to managing intangible, intellectual assets. A host of management theorists and researchers have turned their attention to this issue and are developing sets of tools to help managers cope with this modern challenge. For example, managers can succeed at "knowledge management."

Take some time outside of class to visit the following website:

http://www.kmresource.com/exp.htm

Browse the website and go to some of the links that are featured there. Be prepared to discuss the following questions during the next class period:

1. What is knowledge management?

2. What are some of the new difficulties managers face now that knowledge has become a primary asset of most organizations?

3. What are some of the techniques managers can use to manage knowledge and knowledge workers?

Experiential Exercise

Test Your Thinking Skills

This exercise is designed to give students the opportunity to match their wits against others through tests of logic and analytic skills. The website that features a simple logic test is:

http://www.queendom.com/mindgames/mindstretching/mindtoys/mt-quiz12.html

Students should take this simple test outside of class and return the following class period to discuss their findings. In addition to the logic test, the general website:

www.queendom.com

features a number of other intelligence, romance, and general skills tests. Students should visit the general site and explore the other challenges there. They should be prepared to discuss the value of analytic and thinking skills in being a successful manager.

Social Responsibility and Management Ethics

3

Managing Today

A View of Some Corporate Citizens

Each year *Business Ethics* publishes a list and a presentation on the 100 Best Corporate Citizens. The objective is to identify firms that excel at serving a variety of stakeholders—shareholders, community, minorities and women, employees, environment, global stakeholders, and customers. A few of the top 100 stories are summarized to capture their strengths:

Modine Manufacturing (Racine, Wisconsin, 7,500 employees with annual auto parts sales of over $1 billion)—Modine's heat and thermal mass transfer systems are helping generate hydrogen for autos of the future. This will help replace the polluting internal combustion engines.

Fannie Mae (number 1)—dedicated to helping Americans become home buyers. The company scores very high in helping those who traditionally have been underserved obtain home loans. Over 1.6 million minority first-time home buyers were helped by Fannie Mae.

Procter & Gamble (P&G)—excels in service to communities in the United States and overseas. Over 2 million children die annually in developing countries from water-borne diarrheal diseases. P&G developed a technology that allows people to clean and disinfect water in their homes at a low cost.

Source: Adapted from "100 Best Corporate Citizens," *Business Ethics,* Spring 2004, pp. 1–4.

3-1 Introduction

The terms *social responsibility, business ethics,* and *management ethics* appear frequently in popular and technical literature. Every day, newspapers report business activities considered by some people to be socially irresponsible and unethical. Yet others think such actions are quite proper, both from a social and ethical standpoint. As the opening Managing Today vignette makes clear, being responsible and a top corporate citizen are important. Earning an award from *Business Ethics* is valued and is recognition of working hard in the community, with stakeholders, and around the world to be a good corporate citizen.

One purpose of this chapter is to provide bases for understanding the meanings and implications of social responsibility and ethics by reviewing (1) society's expectations for organizational and managerial behavior and (2) changing business ethics. Corporate and managerial decisions and actions occur within a dynamic and complex social context. Thus, when you understand the meanings of *social responsibility* and *business ethics,* you recognize that they change with time and circumstance.[1]

3-2 Ethics and Social Responsibility

Many people believe that business ethics is an oxymoron—even a joke. The jokes about business ethics reveal public cynicism about business. Business ethics exists, but it is under siege. As long as people pursue economic ends, business ethics will exist because questions of right and duty will arise.[2] As the Management Focus on Ethics box, "Social Accountability 8000 Guidelines," highlights, companies are interested in exporting their ethics to foreign countries.

Management Focus on Ethics

Social Accountability 8000 Guidelines

Conducting global business requires organizations to practice sound ethical practices wherever negotiations, business, or transactions occurs. A set of guidelines that emphasize ethical practices in any country is found in the Social Accountability 8000 Certification (SA 8000) Practices. These guidelines were developed by the Council on Economic Priorities Accreditation Agency, which is now referred to as Social Accountability International (www.cepaa.org).

The guidelines cover such areas as compensation, disciplinary processes, health and safety, child labor, collective bargaining, and work areas. The process for obtaining SA 8000 certification is similar to those used for ISO 9000 quality certification. An organization agrees to an intensive outside team audit and to a series of unannounced inspections by the team of practices, processes, and documents. A certified organization is provided with written permission to publicize their SA 8000 certification.

In a global marketplace the SA 8000 certification is a mark of complying with acceptable and ethical practices. Organizations that have received SA 8000 certification include Disney, Union Bank in Switzerland, Nissan Electric, Mattel, Indian Oil Company, and British Airways.

Steps	TABLE **3-1**
1. Establish standards, procedures, and processes to be followed.	**Suggested Steps for Compliance with U.S. Sentencing Guidelines**
2. Executive-level managers are responsible and accountable for overseeing compliance.	
3. Be cautious and carry out due diligence to avoid delegating authority to anyone who may have a propensity to engage in illegal activities.	
4. Communicate standards and procedures to all employees and agents.	
5. Take reasonable steps to achieve compliance, including using monitoring and auditing systems.	
6. Enforce standards through fair and prompt disciplinary systems.	
7. Evaluate the effectiveness of the systems used.	
8. Make alterations in compliance based on evaluation results.	

The issue of **ethics** and practicing ethical behavior took on a new meaning with the passage in 1991 of the U.S. Sentencing Commission Guidelines. Historically, if management was not aware of unethical and/or illegal activities they could not be held responsible for their employee's behavior. Under the Guidelines companies and managers could be prosecuted and punished even if they didn't know about the unethical behavior. If an organization (nonprofits included) could be classified as a business it was subject to the Guidelines.[3]

> **ethics** A code of moral principles and values that provides guidance for a person or group in doing what is right.

The U.S. Sentencing Commission Guidelines cover such laws as price fixing, fraud, antitrust violations, civil rights, money laundering, conflict of interest, stolen property, copyrights, and extortion. The Guidelines are intended to not only bring about compliance, but also to encourage preventive steps managers can take to prevent white-collar crime. If a firm is taking preventive steps to encourage ethical behavior or voluntarily disclose illegal activities, the fines imposed are usually much smaller. Fines can be as high as hundreds of millions of dollars. The importance of being in compliance is crucial to managers.

Table 3-1 illustrates a compliance process that could be important in avoiding stiff fines.

3-3 The Meanings of Social Responsibility

A thorough review of literature identifies numerous meanings for **social responsibility.** For the most part, the meanings can be classified in three general categories: *social obligation, social reaction,* and *social responsiveness.*[4]

> **social responsibility** Behavior directed exclusively (but legally) in pursuit of profit.

3-3a Social Responsibility as Social Obligation

The **social obligation** view holds that a corporation engages in socially responsible behavior when it pursues profit only within the constraints of law. Because society supports business by allowing it to exist, business is *obligated* to repay society by making profits. Thus legal behavior in pursuit of profit is socially responsible behavior, and *any behavior that is illegal or not in pursuit of profit is socially irresponsible.*

> **social obligation** The theory that business must repay society by making profits for allowing the business to exist.

This view is particularly associated with economist Milton Friedman and others who believe that society creates firms to pursue one primary purpose—to produce goods and services efficiently and maximize profits.[5] Friedman has stated, "There is one and only one social responsibility of business—to use its resources and engage in activities designed to increase its profits so long as it stays within the rules of the game, which is to say, engages in open and free competition without deception or fraud."[6]

The proponents of social responsibility as social obligation offer four primary arguments in support of their view. First, they assert, businesses are accountable to their shareholders, the owners of the corporation. Thus, management's sole responsibility is to serve the shareholders' interests by managing the company to produce profits from which the shareholders benefit.

Second, socially responsible activities such as social improvement programs should be determined by law, by public policy, and by the actions and contributions of private individuals. As representatives of the people, the government (via legislation and allocation of tax revenues) is best equipped to determine the nature of social improvements and to realize those improvements in society. Businesses contribute in this regard by paying taxes to the government, which rightfully determines how they should be spent.

Third, if management allocates profits to social improvement activities, it is abusing its authority. As Friedman notes, these actions amount to taxation without representation. Management is taxing the shareholders by taking their profits and spending them on activities that have no immediate profitable return to the company. And management is doing so without input from shareholders. Because managers are not elected public officials, they are also taking actions that affect society without being accountable to society. Further, this type of nonprofit-seeking activity may be both unwise and unworkable because managers are not trained to make noneconomic decisions.

Fourth, these actions by management may work to the disadvantage of society. In this sense, the financial costs of social activities may over time cause the price of the company's goods and services to increase, and customers would pay the bill. Managers have acted in a manner contrary to the interests of the customers and ultimately the shareholders. Management theorist Doug Bandow shares the view of social responsibility as social obligation. He summarized his perspective in a scholarly article, stating, "Corporations are specialized institutions created for a specific purpose and are only one form of enterprise in a very diverse society with many different organizations. Business best serves society by satisfying people's desires in an efficient manner. Business people should not be expected to house the homeless, preserve the community, or perform any of many other important tasks for which other institutions have been created. While firms have a duty to respect the rights of others, they are under no obligation to promote the interests of others. In the end, society will benefit most if business concentrates on doing its job well, rather than trying to solve the rest of the world's problems."[7]

In using this meaning, *social responsibility* is the behavior directed exclusively (but legally) toward the pursuit of profit. A manager can, with some justification, state that he or she has discharged an *obligation* to society by creating goods and services in exchange for profit within the limits defined by law.

3-3b Social Responsibility as Social Reaction

▶**social reaction** A theory that views actions that exceed legal requirements as being socially responsible.

A second meaning of social responsibility is behavior that is in reaction to "currently prevailing social norms, values, and performance expectations."[8] The **social reaction** view emphasizes that society is entitled to more than the mere provision of goods and services. At minimum, business must be accountable for the ecological, environmental, and social costs incurred by its actions. At maximum, business must react and contribute to solving society's problems (even those that cannot be directly attributed to business). Thus, this viewpoint would hold that corporate contribution to charity *is* socially responsible.

A somewhat restrictive interpretation of social responsibility as social reaction is that it involves only voluntary actions. This interpretation seeks to separate corporate actions that are *required* by economic or legal imperative from those that are initiated by voluntary, altruistic motives. This narrower view implies that a corporation pursuing only socially obligated behavior is not socially responsible because the behavior is required, not voluntary.

Whether the firm's actions are voluntary or not, a broader interpretation of the social reaction view identifies actions that exceed legal requirements as socially responsible. Typically, these actions are reactions to expectations of specific groups: for example, unions, stockholders, social activists, and consumerists. Because these groups expect more than legal minimums, firms can simply decide not to react. Favorable reaction, however, is considered the socially responsible response. Many organizations achieve their social reaction objectives by voluntarily undertaking an ethics audit. Some will go so far as to place the results of the audit in their annual report for all to see.[9]

The essence of this view of social responsibility is that firms are reactive. Demands are made of them by certain groups, and the firms are socially responsible when they react, voluntarily or involuntarily, to satisfy these demands.

3-3c Social Responsibility as Social Responsiveness

According to this view, socially responsibility behaviors are anticipatory and preventive, rather than reactive and restorative.[10] The term **social responsiveness** has become widely used in recent years to refer to actions that exceed social obligation and social reaction.[11] The characteristics of socially responsive behavior include taking stands on public issues, accounting willingly for actions to any group, anticipating future needs of society and moving toward satisfying them, and communicating with the government about existing and anticipated socially desirable legislation.

A socially responsive corporation actively seeks solutions to social problems. Progressive managers, according to this view, apply corporate skills and resources to every problem—from run-down housing to youth employment, from local schools to small-business job creation. Such behavior reflects the "true" meaning of social responsibility for social responsiveness advocates, and when corporate executives commit their organizations to such endeavors, they are likely to receive substantial public approval. Research has indicated that managers with an "output-oriented" background with a company are more likely to be strong leaders of a socially responsive organization. They are more likely to understand the company's external environment and the needs of its various stakeholders.[12]

The social responsiveness view is the broadest meaning of social responsibility. It places managers and their organizations in a position far removed from the traditional one of singular concern with economic means and ends. This view rests on two premises: (1) corporations *should* be involved in preventing, as well as solving, social problems; and (2) corporations are perhaps the most effective problem-solving organizations in a society.

3-3d A Continuum of Social Responsibility

The three general meanings of social responsibility discussed in the preceding section can be depicted as a continuum, shown in Figure 3-1. At one extreme of the continuum is social obligation—business behavior that reflects only the firm's economic and legal responsibilities. Occupying the middle position is social reaction—behavior demanded by groups with a direct stake in the organization's actions. The furthest extreme, social responsiveness, is behavior that reflects anticipatory, proactive, and preventive expectations.

> **social responsiveness**
> A theory that refers to actions that exceed social obligation and social reaction.

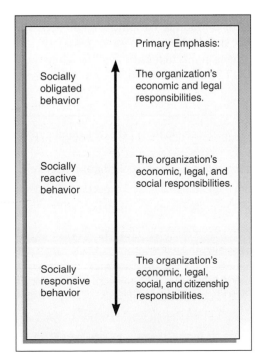

Figure 3-1
A Continuum of Social Responsibility

3-4 Specific Socially Responsible Activities

Socially responsible activities can be classified in different ways. One such classification provides eight categories of socially responsible actions. A business can take socially responsible actions in terms of its *product line* by manufacturing a safe, reliable, and high-quality product and in its *marketing practices* by, for example, being truthful and complete in its product advertising. Concerning *environmental control*, a business may be socially responsible by implementing production technology that reduces the amount of pollutants produced by manufacturing processes. Socially responsible activities in *employee education and training* can include effectively preparing employees to perform jobs well and retraining rather than laying off employees when new technology is implemented. Some argue that it's the organization's responsibility to structure ethics training to help employees clarify both their expectations and the expectations of the organization.[13] Table 3-2 highlights six components of employee training in ethics.

Actions in *employee relations, benefits,* and *satisfaction with work* can include providing benefits that accommodate important but unfulfilled employee needs such as providing an on-site day-care facility for parent employees. In the area of *employment and advancement of minorities or women,* businesses may choose to be socially responsible by focusing efforts on hiring and professionally developing minorities. Efforts to provide a clean, safe, and comfortable working environment are socially responsible activities in the realm of *employee safety and health.*

Some businesses, especially large corporations, focus socially responsible efforts in the area of *corporate philanthropy* by making donations to universities, arts, and cultural foundations, the underprivileged, community development projects, and other groups and causes in society. Today, corporations donate over $6 billion annually to nonprofits through direct contributions and sponsorships of activities.[14] Corporate giving also occurs via donations of volunteered employee time, equipment, loaned facilities, and low-rate loans to nonprofit organizations.[15] Research has determined that over 82 percent of U.S. companies have a volunteer program; 62 percent offer awards and benefits to employees who volunteer; 46 percent loan executives to nonprofit organizations; and 26 percent compensate employees for time off for volunteer work (see Figure 3-2).[16]

Another way to classify socially responsible actions is according to the *beneficiaries* of each action. In some instances, the organization's *customers* benefit; in other instances, the *employees* benefit. Beyond employees and customers are definable interest groups, such as racial and ethnic groups, women's groups, and governmental agencies. In a sense, these groups are organizations that transact business with the corporation. The focus of these transactions is not exchange of economic goods and services, but exchange of concessions based on relative power. In addition to customers, employees, and interest groups, there are abstract beneficiaries, such as future generations, society at large, and the common good. Activities such as giving grants to the arts are directed to these beneficiaries. For simplicity, two general classes of beneficiaries can be identified: *internal* and *external.*

TABLE 3-2 **Six Components of Ethics Training**	1. Provide trainees with an understanding of ethical judgment philosophies and guidelines. 2. Provide industry/profession-specific areas of ethical concern. 3. Provide trainees with organizational ethical expectations and rules. 4. Provide trainees with an understanding of their own ethical tendencies. 5. Take a realistic view—elaborate on the difficulties of ethical decision making. 6. Get the trainees to practice and role-play.

Source: Adapted from Stephen B. Knouse and Robert A. Giacalone, "The Six Components of Successful Ethics Training," *Business & Society Review,* 1997, pp. 10–13. Reprinted with permission of Blackwell Publishing, Ltd.

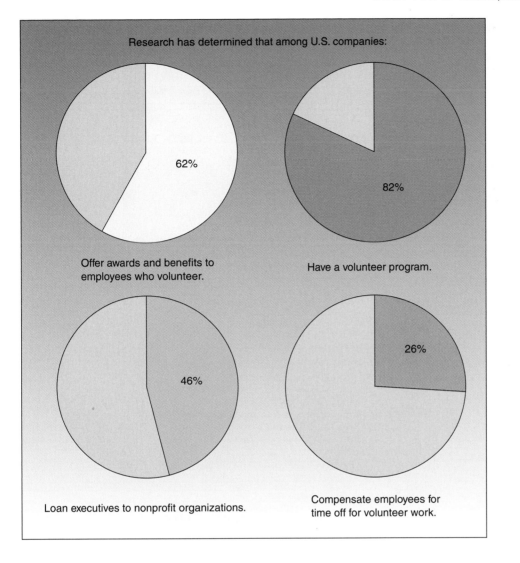

Research has determined that among U.S. companies:

62%

Offer awards and benefits to employees who volunteer.

82%

Have a volunteer program.

46%

Loan executives to nonprofit organizations.

26%

Compensate employees for time off for volunteer work.

Figure 3-2
Types of Corporate Giving

3-4a Internal Beneficiaries

Three groups of internal beneficiaries are apparent: *customers, employees,* and *stockholders* (owners). These groups have immediate and often conflicting stakes in the organization. Corporate activities in response to each group can be classified as obligatory, reactive, or responsive.

Responsibilities to Customers Much of the discussion about the responsibility of business toward its customers is critical. One target of criticism has been the business organization's responsibilities regarding products and marketing.

At Johnson & Johnson, the challenge of being responsible to customers is approached on the basis of a set of principles issued by the company over forty years ago. Since then its Credo (see Figure 3-3) has served as a guide for everyday business and social responsibility decisions, identifying and prioritizing company responsibilities in regard to: (1) all who use company products; (2) employees; (3) the communities of the United States and the world; and (4) the stockholders, who, when the company is operating under the principles of the Credo, should receive a fair return. Johnson & Johnson's actions during the Tylenol crises of 1982 and 1986 provide evidence of how the Credo works in practice. These actions resulted in a solid comeback for that brand just three years after several people died from product tampering at retail outlets. For Johnson & Johnson (www.jnj.com), serving the public interest is both morally responsible and good business.[17]

Laws and regulations establish the bases for judging product safety, but market and competitive forces often set standards for product quality. A case in point is the American

Figure 3-3
Johnson & Johnson Credo

Source: Courtesy of Johnson & Johnson.

Our Credo

We believe our first responsibility is to the doctors, nurses, and patients,
to mothers and fathers and all others who use our products and services.
In meeting their needs everything we do must be of high quality.
We must constantly strive to reduce our costs
in order to maintain reasonable prices.
Customers' orders must be serviced promptly and accurately.
Our suppliers and distributors must have an opportunity
to make a fair profit.

We are responsible to our employees,
the men and women who work with us throughout the world.
Everyone must be considered as an individual.
We must respect their dignity and recognize their merit.
They must have a sense of security in their jobs.
Compensation must be fair and adequate,
and working conditions clean, orderly, and safe.
We must be mindful of ways to help our employees fulfill
their family responsibilities.

Employees must feel free to make suggestions and complaints.
There must be equal opportunity for employment, development,
and advancement for those qualified.
We must provide competent management,
and their actions must be just and ethical.

We are responsible to the communities in which we live and work
and to the world community as well.
We must be good citizens—support good works and charities
and bear our fair share of taxes.
We must encourage civic improvements and better health
and education.
We must maintain in good order
the property we are privileged to use,
protecting the environment and natural resources.

Our final responsibility is to our stockholders.
Business must make a sound profit.
We must experiment with new ideas.
Research must be carried on, innovative programs developed and
mistakes paid for.
New equipment must be purchased, new facilities provided
and new products launched.
Reserves must be created to provide for adverse times.
When we operate according to these principles,
the stockholders should realize a fair return.

Johnson & Johnson

automobile industry. In the early 1980s, this industry faced declining demand for its products, due partly to a recession and high interest rates, but also to competition from Japanese auto manufacturers.

The success of Japanese automobiles rested largely on their superior quality. American consumers believed in the early 1980s that Japanese cars were of better quality than American cars, and they expressed this judgment in their buying decisions. The response of American auto manufacturers has been to implement quality control programs and to publicize those programs in advertisements.

One industry that has had its difficulties in its relations to customers and potential customers is insurance. To help improve its public image, the Insurance Marketplace Standards Association (IMSA) has developed a set of ethical guidelines that go beyond compliance with industry regulations. IMSA's focus is on preparing agents so they have a product and sales knowledge to fully inform their customers. Local offices are seeking IMSA certification as a way of communicating to customers that their agents will deal in an ethical manner.[18]

The issue of social responsibility toward customers is relatively fixed at one extreme (as in instances where specific legal directives define product safety) and quite fluid at the other (as in instances where there are general expectations regarding price/quality relationships). Many firms choose to meet their responsibilities to customers by responding promptly to complaints, by providing complete and accurate product information, and by implementing advertising programs that are completely truthful regarding product performance.

Responsibilities to Employees

Management's responsibilities to employees can be minimally discharged by meeting the legal requirements that relate to employee/employer relationships. Such laws address issues associated with, for example, the physical conditions of work (particularly the safety and health issues), wage and hour provisions, and union and unionization. The thrust of these laws is to encourage management to create safe and productive workplaces within which an employee's civil rights are not violated.

Companies must also create work environments where employees are free from pressures to act in unethical or illegal ways. A survey conducted in the insurance industry found that 56 percent of the workers surveyed are under immense pressure, and 48 percent have decided to act on their stress. These workers had a variety of reactions to their stress: 16 percent cut corners on quality control, 14 percent covered up incidents at work, 11 percent lied about sick days, and 9 percent lied to or deceived customers.[19]

In addition to these responsibilities, the modern corporate practice of providing fringe benefits—retirement funds, health and hospitalization insurance, and accident insurance—has extended the range of socially obligated activity. In some instances, these practices are in response to concerted employee pressure, typically through union activity.

A company may assume other socially responsible activities such as providing comprehensive employee training, career development, counseling, and establishing employee assistance programs (EAPs) to help employees with drug and alcohol problems. Today, over 9,000 U.S. businesses including more than 30 percent of the Fortune 500 companies have established EAPs. A growing number of businesses are also providing day-care assistance for employees; over 3,000 companies now offer day-care services and financial assistance or referral services for child care (a 50% increase in company participation since 1984).[20] Flexibility in human resources strategies was the dominant theme in the 1990s as employees led increasingly complex lives and demanded more time for family commitments. Many firms responded with so-called family friendly policies.[21]

These socially responsible efforts are socially reactive in nature if they are responses to pressures from employees or external parties. The efforts are socially responsive if the organization proactively initiates these activities in the absence of any substantial pressure. However, like many socially responsible actions, activities taken in the interest of employees can also benefit the organization. For example, several companies that have proactively established day-care centers report substantial improvement in attendance and productivity rates among participating parent employees.

Ethical considerations as a part of human resource practice are now linked by an increasing number of managers to profits and return on investment. Human resource programs can be pointed toward creating an ethical culture. A research study found that for an ethical culture to work, its core values must be articulated, communicated, and reinforced. By tying ethical issues to employee perceptions of justice, organizations reap the positive benefits of increased commitment, higher morale, and perceptions of fairness. The researchers contend that an ethical human resource management culture also improves the firm's valuation and image.[22]

Responsibilities to Stockholders

Management has a responsibility to disclose fully and accurately to stockholders its uses of corporate resources and the results of those uses. The law guarantees stockholders the right to financial information and establishes minimum levels of public disclosure. The fundamental right of a stockholder is not to be guaranteed a profit, but to be guaranteed information on which a prudent investment decision can be based. The ultimate action a stockholder can take is to sell the stock.

Many argue that a manager's preeminent responsibility is to the stockholder. In their opinion, any managerial action exceeding socially obligated behavior and benefiting any

LearningMoment _Specific Responsibilities_

Managers have responsibilities to employees and to stakeholders who may have needs that are different. Managers are challenged by attempting to satisfy these needs. In addition, customers, government, and suppliers are also primary stakeholders. What should be obvious is that while employees want fair fringe benefit packages, sound human resource systems, and good treatment, another group such as owners want increased performance and a significant return on their investment. The tug and pull of different responsibilities is complex and difficult.

group other than stockholders is a violation of the stockholder's trust and, therefore, the corporation's social responsibility. We will confront this view later in discussing the origins of the various arguments surrounding corporate involvement in any cause outside of its economic or legal interest.

The internal beneficiaries of corporate actions are the focus of much of management's socially obligated behavior. In their relations with customers, employees, and stockholders, managers are most likely to be judged socially responsible. The relationships between the corporation and its internal beneficiaries are so circumscribed by law, regulation, and custom that the corporation is bound to act out of legal obligation. To do so is no special accomplishment for the corporation. To fail to act within the law, whether intentionally or not, can lead to legal action against the corporation and its management. Therefore, corporations have greater opportunities to be socially reactive and responsive in matters involving _external beneficiaries_. (See the Learning Moment box, "Specific Responsibilities.")

3-4b External Beneficiaries

The external beneficiaries of corporate behavior are of two types, _specific_ and _general_. Both types benefit from the organization's actions, even though they may have no direct or apparent stake in it.

Specific External Beneficiaries   Modern societies consist of a great diversity of special-interest groups working to further the well-being of their members. These groups often represent rather well-defined populations seeking to redress historical grievances: racial and ethnic minorities, women, the handicapped, and the aged. They pursue their interests by bringing political and popular opinion to bear on corporate actions. Some groups succeed in having laws implemented that motivate corporations to support their efforts. For example, equal employment opportunity and affirmative action legislation obligates corporations to recruit, hire, and develop women and members of minority groups. The fundamental contention of these groups is that they have been discriminated against in the past and that corporations have played major roles in that discrimination. Thus, corporations must take some responsibility to erase the vestiges of historical discrimination and to create a new environment of equal access to employment opportunities and economic advancement.

Corporate actions involving specific external beneficiaries can be obligatory, reactive, or responsive. The corporation can be judged irresponsible, both socially and legally, if it violates these laws. But beyond minimal compliance, a corporation has considerable latitude in its implementation of socially beneficial activities. How rapidly it fills its managerial ranks with minorities and women is largely a matter of discretion, as long as good faith can be demonstrated. A corporation can be deemed socially reactive if it goes beyond the letter of the law in implementing such actions. Socially responsive behavior not only seeks solutions to the immediate problems but also attempts to go to the very heart of the causes. Such behavior could include making special efforts to do business with minority-owned businesses, creating programs to train the chronically unemployed, and initiating career development programs for women. When such efforts are not prompted by law or pressure, they are clearly socially responsive.

The most important characteristic of these actions—whether they are obligatory, reactive, or responsive—is that the economic, social, and political well-being of a specific group—and, hence, of all society—is enhanced through the corporation's efforts.

General External Beneficiaries   Programs involving general external beneficiaries often are considered to be practicing social responsibility because they elicit corporate efforts to solve or prevent general social problems. Companies have launched efforts to solve or prevent environmental or ecological problems such as water, air, and noise pollution, and waste and radiation disposal. **Stakeholder management devices (SMDs)** are relatively new mechanisms through which organizations respond to stakeholder concerns.[23] Research suggests that a firm's SMDs affect the perceived moral climates in the firm and affect managers' expectations about the consequences of good corporate social performance, but they do not affect organization members' attitudes about corporate social responsibility.

> **stakeholder management devices (SMDs)**   Relatively new mechanisms through which organizations respond to the concerns of individuals with an interest in the organizations.

The notion that a firm must balance the competing claims of multiple stakeholders in order to sustain their necessary cooperation goes back at least as far as 1938.[24] Currently, the stakeholder concept is the subject of considerable scholarly research and theorizing. Stakeholder management devices provide a means for a firm to meet its responsibilities to various stakeholders.[25] Some examples of SMDs are ethics committees on the board of directors, public affairs offices, written codes of ethics, corporate sponsorship of community functions, and employee newsletters. Given that socially responsive organizations establish such formal structures, processes, and procedures to address the concerns of external stakeholders, most SMDs have an external focus. However, the initial impact of SMDs in an organization must be internal if they are to constrain the behavior of organization members and thereby shape the way the firm conducts its business. Because stakeholders define the individuals and groups to whom the firm must be responsible and responsive, stakeholders are central to the very concept of corporate social performance, which has been defined as: "a business organization's configuration of principles of social responsibility, processes of social responsiveness, and policies, programs, and observable outcomes as they relate to the firm's societal relationships."[26]

Even though the focus of SMDs is primarily external, SMDs impose internal constraints on organization members in their dealings with external stakeholders. Organizational effectiveness and, indeed, survival require dependable behavior on the part of organization members. In pursuit of dependable behavior, the organization establishes (1) formal controls and structures, (2) rewards or instrumental satisfactions, and/or (3) internalized values. SMDs may serve in each of these ways as motivation for organization members to strive for and/or comply with the level of corporate social performance desired by top management.[27]

Corporations have considerable freedom in this area of social responsibility. They can choose which specific problems to become involved with—or they can choose not to become involved at all. But business leaders recognize the growing importance of issues such as the condition of the environment.

But why do corporations engage in behavior that cannot be related, except remotely, to their primary economic and legal responsibilities? It is a matter of fact that they do, and they do so in an atmosphere of controversy.

3-5 Business Ethics Today

The meaning of business ethics is difficult to pin down. Some of the responses received from managers and nonmanagers when asked for a one-sentence definition of business ethics include the following:

- Ethics means complying with law.
- Ethics is a guide to my feelings for making a distinction between right and wrong.
- Ethics reflects my religious beliefs and faith.

Being ethical is not following the law. Laws can deviate from what is ethical. Feelings frequently deviate from what is ethical. Ethics should not be confined to religion since being ethical then would only apply to religious persons.

The diversity of these definitions, expert opinions, and logic suggest that business ethics is two things. First, it refers to standards of right and wrong. Second, ethics refers to the development of one's own ethical standards. Establishing a standard of conduct, belief, values, and sensitivity is what ethics means to people, communities, and institutions.

The proper role of the corporation in American society has reemerged as a topic of national political debate. The contract between business and society has evolved from the traditional view—that economic growth is the source of all progress—to one holding forth an organizational imperative to work for social as well as economic improvement. This latter, expanded meaning of corporate social responsibility includes an implicit, informal social contract between the corporation and its employees. This informal social contract is now breaking apart under the stress of economic transformation.[28]

Many writers are talking about a new social contract between businesses and employees. This new contract will not guarantee lifetime employment for a job well done. However, it will offer employees new responsibilities, new benefits, and new power. Many of today's most effective organizations involve employees in every facet of the business. Managers are consulting employees on everything from strategic insights, to feedback on their (the managers') performance. Such practices would have been unheard of even twenty short years ago.

For their part, employees are benefiting from new compensation schemes such as stock options and gain sharing. These types of compensation systems draw employees into the heart of the business and tie their rewards to its success. A growing number of companies have used stock option plans as a reward. At high-tech companies the value of options have in many cases dwarfed earnings and even revenue. When Silicon Valley lost some of its luster in 2001, most stock option–granting firms reacted to the down market by granting more of them at lower prices. Some critics claim, and research suggests, that a large percentage of stock options actually go to the top executives. At Oracle and Siebel Systems, two giant high-tech firms, more than 30 percent of the options are held by the highest-paid executives. Is this practice fair, ethical, and responsible? Should boards of directors be allowing the few to own so much? These questions are and should be asked so that the cost and impact of options is presented in the light of day.[29]

These changes in the social contract between a business and its employees have led to other major changes in the workplace. For example, it's not uncommon to hear managers talk about employee rights. This has led some companies to develop a process for evaluating how well they protect these rights. The process is known as a "human rights audit."

3-5a The Human Rights Audit

▶ human rights audit
A process for evaluating how well a company protects employee rights.

The concept of the **human rights audit** is not new. Levi Strauss, for example, has a global staff of about fifty people who monitor working conditions in the factories of overseas contractors. "Audits are conducted with any new supplier we may be considering, and suppliers we do business with are audited on a regular basis," says company spokesman Richard Woo (www.levi.com).

The Gap is developing a monitoring mechanism called the Independent Monitoring Working Group. This third-party mechanism hopes to issue standards soon that will define monitoring guidelines. The Gap sources in forty-seven countries from more than 500 factories.

Formulating the codes of conduct on which audits are based is difficult because there are relatively few precedents. Starbucks Coffee consulted with companies including Levi Strauss when it was developing its Framework for a Code of Conduct. It also consulted extensively with workers.

Codes usually allow for several layers of discussion and negotiation before the threat of having to terminate a relationship arises. Commercial incentives to comply can be built into trading relationships. The Code of Business Practices recommended by the International Council of Toy Industries, for example, advises that human rights be part of the conditions of payment on letters of credit.[30]

3-5b The Impact of Technology on Business Ethics

Most technologies existing today were designed to expedite the way we manage, store, handle, analyze, and communicate information. Computers are used routinely to capture transaction data. Devices such as credit card readers, optical scanners, personal digital assistants (PDAs), telephone keypads, and computer terminals collect vast amounts of data daily. Most data is electronically stored in transaction files until they are processed by local or remote computer systems that update organization master transaction files and electronic databases. These systems are then used to create reports that help firms analyze and gauge their performance. This activity in turn provides information for forecasting and strategically planning activities to be communicated to the rest of the organization through diverse communication media, including e-mail, video broadcasts, and other multimedia techniques that combine text, audio, and video information in the same presentation.

Computers and network software help to manage and protect the security and integrity of company data and to monitor and control organizational equipment and processes. Many organizations have used technology to fundamentally change the way work is done, using technology in ways that break traditional rules of doing business. For example, Ford uses database and electronic data interchange technology in efficient and effective ways that eliminate overhead (especially excess inventories) for both Ford and its suppliers—breaking the rule that says that vendors should be treated as adversaries. Wal-Mart and Kmart are using teleconferencing to allow headquarters-based merchandisers to provide store managers in the field with guidance and advice—enabling them to combine local initiatives with corporate advice.

Clearly, nothing has changed communication in organizations more dramatically than advances in technology. Technology has helped organizations overcome the limitations previously imposed by differences in time and place. Computers allow organizations to capture, analyze, and share information from anywhere in the world twenty-four hours a day. These new capabilities have fostered significant changes in organizational processes, decision making, and organizational design.

The value of technological innovations should also be measured by examining them from an ethical perspective. Ethics goes far beyond questions of legality (although the law is clearly an important component). The field of ethics considers what human relationships are and ought to be—between employers, colleagues, subordinates, customers, suppliers, stockholders, distributors, neighbors, and members of the greater community. From a communication perspective, ethical communication facilitates the individual's ability to make sound choices. It might include, for instance, providing complete and accurate information upon which others can base their choices.

While technological advances provide the opportunity to enhance organizational productivity, the real possibility exists that information technology can and will be used in ways that raise ethical questions. In the age of the Internet, many corporations are finding that they have become victims of high-tech crime. Technologies such as e-mail, cellular phones, and the Internet have fostered new types of organizational problems, from employees using their computers to snoop through confidential computer files to criminal theft of trade secrets. In a mail survey of 500 corporate security directors (see Figure 3-4), 98.6 percent reported that their companies had been victims of computer-related crimes. Of those, 43.3 percent said they had been victims at least twenty-five times. The most common crimes reported were credit card fraud, telecommunications fraud, employee use of computers for personal reasons, unauthorized access to confidential files, and unlawful copying of copyrighted or licensed software. Organizations have also had to grapple with problems related to computer-based sexual harassment, pornography, copyright infringement, obscenities, software piracy, and the inadvertent as well as the deliberate communication of trade secrets to external audiences.[31]

Figure 3-4
Survey of 500 Corporate Security Directors

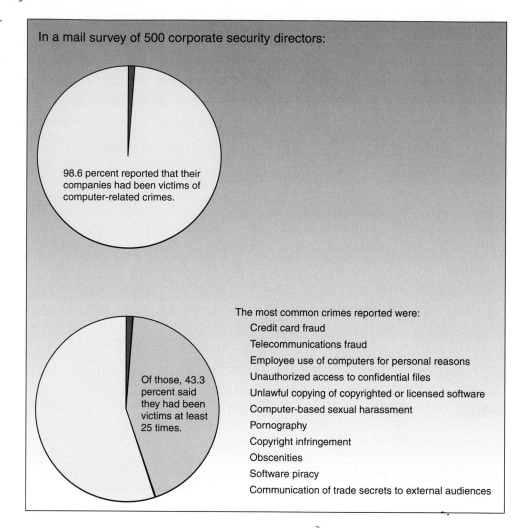

In a mail survey of 500 corporate security directors:

98.6 percent reported that their companies had been victims of computer-related crimes.

Of those, 43.3 percent said they had been victims at least 25 times.

The most common crimes reported were:
  Credit card fraud
  Telecommunications fraud
  Employee use of computers for personal reasons
  Unauthorized access to confidential files
  Unlawful copying of copyrighted or licensed software
  Computer-based sexual harassment
  Pornography
  Copyright infringement
  Obscenities
  Software piracy
  Communication of trade secrets to external audiences

Companies and individuals can be innocent victims of unethical behavior. A few examples on the white-collar crime and unethical behavior blotter are concisely presented in Table 3-3.

The range of scams, fraud, scandals, bribery, and unethical behavior seems endless. Table 3-3 only provides a sample of the violations and the behavior that individuals will use. The widespread use of technology has resulted in many new schemes that people must protect themselves against. The computer, the Internet, and other technology have a wide-reaching impact on business transactions and provide opportunities for unethical behavior. These transactions for the most part are legal, ethical, and crucial for working in a global market. However, occasionally, as illustrated in Table 3-3, some of the transactions are unethical and even illegal. The Management Focus on Ethics box, "The Ten Commandments of Computer Ethics," lists the ten computer-related guidelines developed by the Computer Ethics Institute in Washington, D.C.

The Federal Bureau of Investigations (FBI) and the National White Collar Crime Center (www.nw3c.org) have published a report that presents a picture of computer and Internet fraud. A curious finding was that only one in four victims of crime contacted a law enforcement agency before they contacted the Internet Fraud Complaint Center (IFCC). People who have a problem make their report to the business involved. Most never make any kind of report.

If individuals and organizations are going to gain confidence in using technology to conduct business and other activities, complaints and problems must be quickly and fairly resolved. The most frequent complaints received by the IFCC involve credit and debit card fraud, Internet fraud, and nondeliverable merchandise.

Examples	TABLE **3-3**

Examples

- Eric Stein, founder and managing director of Sterling Group, a company based in Las Vegas, used TV commercials to sell products. He bilked 1,800 investors out of $34 million. He provided them with a scheme to buy stakes in the commercial. He is serving eight years for fraud and money laundering.

- The SEC took action against twenty-three companies and individuals who used the Internet to "pump" the market capitalization of stocks. The perpetrators made false promises, released false financial information, and illustrated inflated performance data.

- Avant, a Fremont, California-based maker of chip design, stole trade secrets from rivals and agreed to pay $35 million in fines.

- Michael Fenne (aka David K. Stanley) promoted phantom technology for broadcasting video over the Internet. He raised $35 million and threw a $16 million launch party that featured headliner entertainers. He received jail time and 2,000 hours of community service.

- John T. Dawson was found guilty of securities fraud and money laundering in connection with creating offshore shell companies in Hong Kong and Europe. These fictitious companies masqueraded as buyers of millions of dollars of software products from his firm.

High-Tech Scams, Scandals, and Unethical Behavior: A Sample

Source: Adapted from Glenn Ruffenach, "Confessions of a Scam Artist," *Wall Street Journal,* August 9, 2004, pp. R1 and R3; and Mike Drumond, "Thinking Out of the Box," *Business 2.0,* July 10, 2001, p. 71.

3-6 Managerial Ethics

The word *ethics* commonly refers to principles of behavior that distinguish between what is good, bad, right, and wrong.[32] Ethics are used by managers as guidelines in making decisions that affect employees, the organization, consumers, and other parties. The importance of ethics increases in proportion to the *consequences* of the outcome of a decision or behavior. As a manager's actions become more consequential for others, the more important are the ethics of that manager.

The role and state of ethics in businesses continue to be a concern among managers and the public. Modern ethical issues are becoming more complex. They involve global transactions and cash flows, as well as individuals of vastly different cultural backgrounds.

A 100-year relationship between Ford Motor Company and Firestone/Bridgestone Tires highlights the complexity of ethics, the law, and global transactions. The U.S.

Management Focus on Ethics

The Ten Commandments of Computer Ethics

1. Thou shalt not use a computer to harm other people.
2. Thou shalt not interfere with other people's computer work.
3. Thou shalt not snoop around in other people's computer files.
4. Thou shalt not use a computer to steal.
5. Thou shalt not use a computer to bear false witness.
6. Thou shalt not copy or use proprietary software for which you have not paid.
7. Thou shalt not use other people's computer resources without authorization or proper compensation.
8. Thou shalt not appropriate other people's intellectual output.
9. Thou shalt think about the social consequences of the program you are writing or the system you are designing.
10. Thou shalt always use a computer in ways that insure consideration and respect for your fellow humans.

Source: From "Ten Commandments of Computer Ethics," by Dr. Ramon C. Barquin, copyright © 1991 by Computer Ethics Institute, reprinted by permission of Dr. Ramon C. Barquin. http://www.cpsr.org/issues/ethics/cei

Congress in 2000 became involved in a faulty auto tire controversy after more than 100 deaths were linked to the tires. In 1997 Ford received reports of tread separations on their SUV Explorers in Saudi Arabia. Also, in 1998 State Farm Insurance notified the federal government about tread failures. At Ford's direction, Firestone/Bridgestone developed a tire in 1999 for countries with hot climates and rough roads.[33]

Who is responsible for the deaths (estimated to be over 200) attributed to the tires? Ford CEO (at the time) Jacques Nasser states that it is a tire problem. Firestone, however, points an accusatory finger at Ford and calls the problem a vehicle design issue. Complaints, lawsuits, and congressional probes have placed this issue in the headlines. The companies are pointing at each other, and there are calls for criminal charges against managers in both companies.[34]

Evidence is unfolding that Ford and Firestone managers knew about the tire tread problems for nearly a decade. Lawmakers are examining the possibility of filing second-degree murder charges against managers who withheld information on defective products (tires or vehicles) that caused deaths. The long-term damage to careers, company image, and business is certain to be significant. As the Ford/Firestone charges and countercharges continue, the concept of ethical behavior will be raised again and again.

Business ethics continues to be a topic of concern because businesses are realizing that ethical misconduct by management can be extremely costly for the company and society as a whole. For example, sweatshop labor, once a low-profile issue, took center stage in 1997 because of allegations that some clothing endorsed by TV personality Kathie Lee Gifford and sold by Wal-Mart stores had been manufactured under grueling conditions.[35] Sensing an opportunity, human rights groups and labor unions stepped up their marketing efforts to reverse the situation. The Union of Needle Trades Industrial & Textile Employees, for example, ran ads that encouraged consumers who believe in human rights, fair wages, and ending child labor to "wear what they believe."

The Wal-Mart debate is picked up in the Management Focus on Ethics box "Is It Ethical to Shop at Wal-Mart?"

As the Wal-Mart controversy grew more heated, President Clinton appointed a task force with representatives of human rights groups, labor unions, and apparel companies to address sweatshop conditions. After eight months of discussion, the group announced a groundbreaking agreement that seeks to end sweatshops by creating a code of conduct on wages and working conditions. Companies that comply with the code will be able to put a label or tag on their clothing assuring consumers that it was not made in a sweatshop.

Despite the seeming appropriateness for national policies on sweatshop labor, it's far from a noncontroversial proposition. For example, some critics suggest that while the task force's code of business conduct may be appropriate for rich nations such as the United States, it's misapplied in Indonesia, Pakistan, Vietnam, and other countries that are the targets of the code. The poor in these countries send children to work because families desperately need their meager earnings. It's a hard life for children, but appalling poverty forces the whole family to struggle with bad nutrition, poor health care, and dismal economic prospects.

Determining what is and isn't ethical is often difficult to do. In some situations, the task is easy. We know, for example, that accepting bribes from a supplier is clearly unethical as is falsifying records or dishonest advertising in promoting a product. However, more often the ethics of a business situation are more complex. Every day, managers face ethical questions that have no easy answers. What for example, is a "fair" profit? What is a "just" price for a product? How "honest" should a company be with the press?

The following Management Focus on Ethics box, "Enron: Plenty of Unethical Behavior," illustrates a case where management failed when faced with ethical decision making.

Because the ethics of a business situation are often complex, managers sometimes differ in their views of what actions are ethical. Currently, several ethical issues are being debated in the business environment. For example, managers are grappling with the ethics of employee surveillance (monitoring their computer work and telephones to measure employee productivity), and with the ethical questions of conducting polygraph tests of job applicants.[36]

Management Focus on Ethics

Is It Ethical to Shop at Wal-Mart?

A question posed at a conference conducted by the Markkula Center for Applied Ethics at Santa Clara University focused on the question: "Is It Ethical to Shop at Wal-Mart?" The name of Wal-Mart shows up each year as one of America's most admired companies. At the same time it is criticized for its poor employment practices and its negative influence on communities.

Two of the panelists offered different views, as follows:

Jeff Seglin (Business Ethics Columnist):

I'm not an apologist for Wal-Mart. I live in the city of Boston and we don't have Wal-Marts. In order to see a Wal-Mart, I had to get my grandson to take me to a Wal-Mart about 40 minutes south of the city last week. My grandson buys his video cards at Wal-Mart. I had to decide whether or not my grandson was ethical in shopping at Wal-Mart. I'd like to look at the question in terms of a couple issues.

First, I had written a column a while ago about Parmalat milk. Parmalat is involved in a terrible scandal right now. The scandal was awful and involved the whole family of products. Parmalat also makes Archway cookies. I used to eat these cookies on my way to the bowling alley as a young person. I really like Archway cookies. I had to decide whether I should boycott Parmalat and not buy and eat Archway cookies. The determination I came to can be used in deciding whether or not to shop at Wal-Mart. It is based on the question of what are my values. If my values are such that I don't care about whether the company has a progressive policy in terms of health care benefits for their employees, then it is perfectly fine to buy the product in question. If my values are such that it is the only product I can afford to buy due the economical class I happen to be in, then, that is a choice I've made based on my values.

If it's a choice that I make because I don't look at those issues, which is the choice many people make when they invest in mutual funds, and have no idea where their mutual funds are invested there may be a problem. Yet, many vocal opponents to shopping at Wal-Mart might discover they hold investments in Wal-Mart. There are 850 mutual funds that are invested in Wal-Mart, some of the largest mutual funds. There are many people who have no idea where their investments lie. If you want to be true to your value against shopping at Wal-Mart, you need to be careful to remove yourself from investments that support Wal-Mart. You have to review your investments and find out where your money is invested. John Kerry's wife, Teresa Heinz was a vocal critic against Wal-Mart, only to find she had one million dollars invested in the company. She held stock in a company of which she was critical. This provides insight into the idea that you have to work hard to consider your values in particular issues and how strongly you do feel.

I once worked with a man named Jerry Useem who now works at *Fortune* magazine. Regardless of what you think of Wal-Mart, Wal-Mart is continually voted as one of the most admired companies in America by *Fortune*.... This is how Jerry began the article he wrote this year in *Fortune:*

There is an evil company in Arkansas, some say. It's a discount store—a very, very big discount store—and it will do just about anything to get bigger. You've seen the headlines. Illegal immigrants mopping its floors. Workers locked inside overnight. A big gender discrimination suit. Wages low enough to make other companies' workers go on strike. And we know what it does to weaker suppliers and competitors. Crushing the dream of the independent proprietor—an ideal as American as Thomas Jefferson—it is the enemy of all that's good and right in our nation.

There is another big discount store in Arkansas, yet this one couldn't be more different from the first. Founded by a folksy entrepreneur whose notions of thrift, industry, and the square deal were pure Ben Franklin, this company is not a tyrant but a servant. Passing along the gains of its brilliant distribution system to consumers, its farsighted managers have done nothing less than democratize the American dream. Its low prices are spurring productivity and helping win the fight against inflation. It is America's most admired company.

Weirdest part is, both these companies are named Wal-Mart Stores Inc.

Bob Browstein (Policy Director of Working Partnership USA):

To answer this question, we have to make some decisions about our values—specifically we have to identify those values on which we will judge an economy and its institutions and actors.

I'm assuming that this audience agrees that economies are human creations. As such they are based on one set of values or another, and we cannot escape from making normative choices about how economies should function. Even supporting laissez-faire represents a value choice.

Wal-Mart pays low wages and appears to aggressively seek to keep wages down. On average, WM workers earn an estimated $8.00/hour with a 32 hour work week. This equals $256 a week or $13,312 a year. The Federal poverty level for a family of three is $14,630. In contrast, union grocery workers earn on average 30% more.

Also, it is alleged that Wal-Mart's personnel policies are aimed at keeping wages low. Charges have been made that older workers are laid off to bring in younger and cheaper employees. Some 40 lawsuits accuse WM of a failure to pay overtime. Accusations have also been made of widespread sex discrimination to keep a class of employees—women—at lower wages.

But Wal-Mart is not just a threat to the standard of living of its own employees. It damages the standard of living of numerous others in the economy.

To begin with, it pulls wages and benefits down in other grocery stores. It lowers area standards. In some cases, it forces the closure of better paying firms. *Business Week* estimates for every WM supercenter that opens, two other supermarkets will close.

It pressures suppliers to make products more cheaply, putting pressure on wages, causing jobs to be moved overseas. Last year, it imported $12 billion in goods from China, 10% of US imports from that nation.

Benefits—Health Care: 2/3's of WM workers can't afford to participate in the company health insurance plan, which costs about 20% of a worker's paycheck. Since 1993 WM has increased the premium cost for its workers by 200%, well above the rise in cost of health insurance.

Again, the effect spreads to competitors. Witness the Safeway strike. The costs of the southern California grocery strike can be considered a response to Wal-Mart.

Wal-Mart doesn't produce new technology or innovations that improve the quality of life. It takes business from existing firms by offering the same merchandise cheaper. That's all it does.

It does increase the wealth of shoppers by allowing them to buy things at lower cost. But the major expenditures of a family aren't for Wal-Mart items; WM doesn't sell houses, cars, or health care.

How much does it help a family economically to shop at WM? Assume a low wage worker earns 20k a year. And let's assume 20% of gross income is spent at WM or places where WM products are sold. WM grocery prices are 14% lower where WM competes. Savings would = $50.00/month. Another approach: Take the figure of $20 billion in savings for consumers from shopping at WM per year. Divide by 110,000,000 households = $180/year. Multiply times 5 to find the effect on WM competitors. The result is 900 divided by 12 = 75.

We're talking about savings of $50.00 to $75.00 per month.

We could do more to improve the economic well-being of low-income WM shoppers, and avoid the negative side-effect by simply increasing the minimum wage by $1.00 an hour.

After reviewing these summarized comments: Do you believe it's unethical to shop at Wal-Mart? Why? Do you shop at Wal-Mart?

Sources: Adapted from "Is It Ethical to Shop at Wal-Mart?" Markkula Center for Applied Ethics, Summer 2004; Jerry Useem, "2004 America's Most Admired Companies," *Fortune,* February 23, 2004, pp. 42-44.

Because the ethics of managerial decision making are often complex and managers often disagree on what comprises an ethical decision, two subjects are particularly relevant: (1) the basis that the individual manager can use in determining which alternative to choose in a decision-making situation, and (2) what organizations can do to ensure that managers follow ethical standards in their decision making. These two topics are addressed in the following section.

Management Focus on Ethics

Enron: Plenty of Unethical Behavior

On December 2, 2001, Enron filed the (at the time) largest bankruptcy in corporate history (World.Com filed a larger bankruptcy in 2002). Enron reported that it was the object of some 22,000 claims by various stakeholders, totaling $400 billion.

The Enron debacle provides lessons about leadership, governance, and regulation. Greed and opportunism at the top were the motive and the modus operandi. Why greed and opportunism got so out of hand, has not yet been well studied. Two self-destructive firms, Enron and Arthur Andersen failed in leadership, governance, and regulation roles. Blame for the Enron failure legally, morally, and ethically points to poor leadership (Lay, Skilling, and Fastow for example), the lack of oversight by the board, the flawed idea of self-enrichment from greedy executives (e.g., Fastow), inadequate audit and oversight controls (e.g., Arthur Andersen), accounting errors, poor implementation, and a culture that encouraged and supported unethical behavior.

The U.S. Senate Committee on The Judiciary in a report stated:

The alleged activity Enron used to mislead investors was not the work of novices. It was the work of highly educated professionals, spinning an intricate spider's web of deceit. The partnerships—with names like Jedi, Chewco, Rawhide, Ponderosa, Sundance—were used essentially to cook the books and trick both the public and federal regulators about how well Enron was doing financially.

The Enron failure and pain it caused illustrates that with an absence of ethics and fiduciary care a disaster can occur. Enron's business model when operated by individuals with character, values, and ethical behavior defects was doomed to fail. It did, and the result has been devastating to ex-employees, suppliers, customers, and societal trust and faith in organizational managers and leaders.

Sources: Adapted from Nancy B. Rapoport and Bala G. Dharan (eds.), *Enron: Corporate Fiascos and Their Implications,* New York: Foundation Press, 2004.

3-7 Ethical Standards

Managers must reconcile competing values in making decisions. They make decisions that have consequences for (1) themselves, (2) the organization that employs them, and (3) the society in which they and the organization exist. For example, managers can be called upon to make decisions that can be good for them, but bad for the organization and society. Figure 3-5 presents an ethics test. By completing it, you can experience firsthand the difficulty of defining ethical standards.

Philosophers, logicians, and theologians have studied ethical issues. Their ideas provide guidelines, but guidelines only, for making value-laden decisions. Figure 3-6 depicts a simplified model of ethical behavior with three different bases for determining ethical guidelines in decision making.[37]

Figure 3-5
An Ethics Test

Indicate the degree to which you agree or disagree with each statement.

Strongly Disagree -0- -1- -2- -3- Strongly Agree

1. Employees should not expect to inform on their peers for wrongdoings.
2. There are times when a manager must overlook contract and safety violations in order to get on with the job.
3. It is not always possible to keep accurate expense account records; therefore, it is sometimes necessary to give approximate figures.
4. There are times when it is necessary to withhold embarrassing information from one's superior.
5. We should do what our managers suggest, though we may have doubts about it being the right thing to do.
6. It is sometimes necessary to conduct personal business on company time.
7. Sometimes it is good psychology to set goals somewhat above normal if it will help to obtain a greater effort from the sales force.
8. I would quote a "hopeful" shipping date in order to get an order.
9. It is proper to use the company 800 line for personal calls as long as it's not in company use.
10. Management must be goal oriented; therefore, the end justifies the means.
11. If it takes heavy entertainment and twisting a bit of company policy to win a large contract, I would authorize it.
12. Exceptions to company policy and procedures are a way of life.
13. Inventory controls should be designed to report "underages" rather than "overages" in goods received.
14. Occasional use of the company's copier for personal or community activities is acceptable.
15. Taking home company property (pens, tape, paper, etc.) for personal use is an accepted fringe benefit.

If your score is:
- 0 Prepare for canonization ceremony
- 1–5 Bishop material
- 6–10 High ethical values
- 11–15 Good ethical values
- 16–25 Average ethical values
- 26–35 Need moral development
- 36–44 Slipping fast
- 45 Leave valuables with warden

Figure 3-6
An Ethical Framework

Source: From *Changing Environment of Business* by Grover Starling, p. 255. Copyright © 1980. Reprinted with permission of South-Western, a division of Thomson Learning.

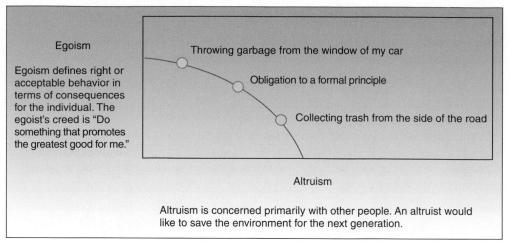

▶**egoism** An ethical standard that places highest value on behavior that is pleasurable and rewarding to the individual.

▶**altruism** An ethical standard that places highest value on behavior that is pleasurable and rewarding to society.

Maximum personal benefits (**egoism**)*,* depicted on the vertical axis in Figure 3-6, can be a manager's sole basis for decision making. A completely selfish manager would always select the alternative that is most personally beneficial. An extreme view of this ethical approach is that one should always seek that which is pleasurable, and conversely, one should avoid pain. A manager driven by egoism would evaluate decision alternatives in terms of personal benefit—salary, prestige, power, or whatever he or she considers valuable. If the action happens to also be beneficial to the organization and society, all is well and good. But these other benefits are incidental; personal welfare is the manager's top priority.

Maximum social benefits (**altruism**)*,* depicted on the horizontal axis in Figure 3-6, also can be the sole consideration in decision making. An altruistic individual will select courses of action that provide maximum social benefit. A manager who follows this ethical guideline would measure right and wrong as the "greatest happiness for the greatest number." As a practical matter, decisions based only on altruistic concerns are particularly difficult to make. For example, altruism provides no means for judging the relative benefits to individuals, unless one is willing to assume that each has the same interest and benefit in a decision.

Obligation to a formal principle is shown in Figure 3-6 between the extremes of egoism and altruism. Egoism holds that an act is good only if the individual benefits from it. Altruism holds that an act is good only if society benefits from it. The criteria for both ethical guidelines are the consequences. In contrast to them, the ethic of adhering to a formal principle is based on the idea that *the rightness or wrongness of an act depends on principle, not consequences.*

Those who adhere to principle in judging their actions could, for example, follow the Golden Rule: "Do unto others what you would have them do unto you." Or they might decide that each action should be judged by the principle: "Act as if the maxim of your action were to become a general law binding on everyone."

But the idea that actions can be judged by one principle is unacceptable to many individuals. Some prefer a *pluralistic* approach comprising several principles arranged in a hierarchy of importance. For example, one writer proposes that the following principles can guide managers in decision making: (1) place the interests of society before the interests of the organization, (2) place the interests of the organization before managers' private interests, (3) reveal the truth in all instances of organizational and personal involvement. These three principles provide guidelines, but not answers. The manager must determine the relative benefits to society, company, and self. The determination of benefits and beneficiaries, however, is seldom simple accounting. But the advantage of a pluralistic approach to ethical decision making is that the decision maker, *with intentions to do right,* has the basis for evaluating decisions.

3-8 The Organization's Role in Ethical Behavior

The approaches to developing guidelines for ethical behavior have so far focused on the individual manager. Many observers assert that the organization should play a major role in ensuring that its managers act ethically in managing the firm. The organization's participation is understandable given that it is the organization that is ultimately responsible for the consequences of the decisions that its managers make.

Although a company is ultimately responsible, surprisingly few organizations have traditionally provided managers with specific guidelines concerning ethics in decision making. However, given the increasing concern about ethics in organizations, a growing number of companies are attempting to provide guidance for their managers.

An organization can do many things to make ethical governance the norm. It helps to have a credo that publicly proclaims its ethical position. In addition, the organization should ensure that top management makes clear that it believes in and personally lives up to those standards. Another tactic is to establish ethics officers. Finally, a firm must establish ongoing education and training programs clearly backed by management, redefine rules for compensation to include ethics as part of performance reviews, and put in place procedures for dealing with those who violate the code of ethics. Next we examine each of these elements of effective governance of ethics in an organization.

3-8a The Credo

The first step is ensuring that the organization has a credo that clearly and forcefully states its ethical values. If employees believe that management takes the credo seriously, they are likely to try to live up to its values.

As discussed earlier, an excellent example of a credo is that of Johnson & Johnson's. Walking into the headquarters of Johnson & Johnson immediately lets you know how seriously the organization takes its credo that "our first responsibility is to those who use our products and services." It is carved into a granite block that sits imposingly in the reception area that every visitor and all new employees pass through. J&J's entire corporate credo is provided in Figure 3-3. You can learn more about the credo, or read it in a variety of languages, at the Johnson & Johnson website (www.jnj.com).

3-8b Walking the Talk

Given that ethical governance is a managerial responsibility, reinforcing the beliefs expressed in the credo is the job of the leaders. Those leaders who are most effective at transmitting their values and beliefs are not embarrassed to speak out. They convey their messages to employees in public speeches and through corporate communications vehicles—as well as through their own actions. They make it clear that they are willing to make hard decisions and will support those in their organizations who do the same.

The actions of Peter Bijur, CEO of Texaco, in response to tapes revealing an atmosphere conducive to discrimination at the company are an example of the kind of leadership that is needed to make a difference. Noting that the recorded statements by a group of senior executives "represent attitudes we hoped and wished had long ago disappeared," he personally—and very quickly and publicly—apologized and laid out a comprehensive, long-term plan of action aimed at making Texaco a "model of workplace opportunity."

To prevent problems such as this from arising in the first place, management must instill a common definition of ethical behavior. Senior management, including the board and key stakeholders, must spend time discussing ethical issues and reaching consensus on the values to be promoted. Everyone must also agree to act in accordance with those precepts. Then, to ensure continued adherence to those ethical values over time, management must hold frequent forums to discuss how well it is adhering to its own standards as well as to examine incidents reported internally or uncovered by outsiders that indicate violations have occurred.

T A B L E 3-4		
Areas of Concern and Interest in Displaying Ethical Behavior	Bribery/improper pressure	Substance abuse
	Conflict of interest	Whistleblowing
	Receiving and giving gifts	Nepotism
	Sexual harassment	Age discrimination
	Safety and health practices	Promotion and evaluation favoritism
	Privacy and confidentiality	Treatment of the environment
	Supplier relations	Use of power and position
	Stealing	Copying of software

Because conflicting realities often are involved in ethical decision making, management must set up mechanisms to ensure that everyone understands the ethical standards in place and management's commitment to them.

3-8c Code of Ethics

Codes of ethics can be simple or complex; what is important is that they not just be sent out. They should be accompanied by materials that explain their purpose and management's commitment to them. Meetings should be held—with members of top management in attendance—to discuss them, and employees should be asked to sign them. The process will serve to convince employees that the codes are to be taken seriously.

Someone skilled in dealing with such issues from both a legal and humanistic perspective should be responsible for these codes and for oversight of the company's training and educational programs in ethics.

Code of ethics statements are not sufficient by themselves to cause people to behave in a socially responsible manner. General Dynamics for years relied on a comprehensive twenty-page ethics policy and conduct document, yet found widespread violations in ethical conduct involving government contracts. Executives and managers are faced with the ongoing challenges of creating, displaying, supporting, and sustaining an environment that develops ethical behavior and a commitment through action of supporting social responsibility. The onus is on managers to show the way to others on a host of behaviors in specific areas. Table 3-4 presents areas that employees need particular guidance in so that ethical behavior becomes a habit.

Texas Instruments emphasized the availability of its ethics director by putting up posters featuring a photo of him looking extremely friendly and approachable, and being quoted as saying, "TI has a long-standing tradition of excellence in the ethical conduct of our business. TI has established the Ethics Office to help TIers understand what is needed to continue this tradition. I'm available to discuss any questions or concerns you have relating to business policies or practices at TI." The poster also contained information on how to reach him directly, promising "confidentiality or anonymity at your request."

3-8d Education and Training

Programs to educate employees about ethics—and to ensure that the values are interpreted in a consistent manner—are essential. These programs must address issues specific to different levels of responsibility. One particularly important step in training is setting up discussion groups that make possible the examination of "gray zone" issues, those ethical questions people confront that require more than a simple yes or no answer.

3-8e Compensation

Part of the process of instilling an ethical culture is setting up mechanisms to ensure that ethical issues are reflected in compensation. Performance reporting must include an evaluation of adherence to codes of ethical behavior, but there must also be provisions that take into account the fact that some employees will have a harder time than others achieving goals while continuing to uphold ethical standards. One way of getting the message across is to be sure that promotion policies publicly reflect the importance of these values.

3-8f Dealing with Violations

Although ethics are determined from the top and must be driven down into the organization, they must also be driven across the organization, with managers at every level aware of and making clear their commitment to these values. Indeed, meetings of management at different levels to discuss these issues is critical to the success of ethics programs.

The most important aspect of the problem is how violations are dealt with. When an organization uncovers clear violations of legal rules of conduct, immediate dismissal should follow. If the lines are not as clear, say, the use of the company car for a pleasure trip at the end of a business trip, penalties must be imposed and rules issued to ensure that such behavior will not be repeated.[38]

3-9 Ethics and Social Responsibility

The relationship between a manager's ethical standards and social responsiveness should be apparent. Ethics serve as bases for assessing the "rightness" of potential actions.[39] In a sense, ethical standards are filters that screen actions according to relative rightness. The ideas that have been developed so far in these discussions of social responsibility, expectations for corporate behavior, and ethics are integrated in Figure 3-7.

Earlier in the chapter Milton Friedman's view about social responsibility as a social obligation was presented. His view resonates with those who believe that organizations are in business to earn profits for their shareholders. It is this stakeholder group who holds the dominant position. As displayed in the chapter, Friedman and his proponents represent one viewpoint. The general public appears to disagree with Friedman's viewpoint. A *Business Week/Harris* poll of over 1,000 Americans found that 95 percent reject the notion that a corporation's main role is profit maximization.[40]

Social responsibility and ethics require serious thinking about right and wrong, good and bad. The onus is placed on managers who play a major role in applying ethical standards and decision making that can meet the test of careful scrutiny, community expectations, and the law.

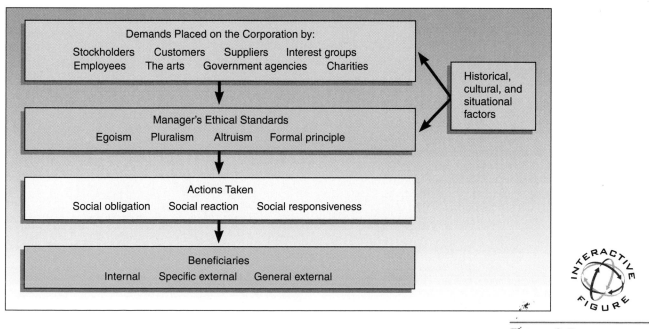

Figure 3-7
The Corporation's Social Responsibility and Managerial Ethics

Management Summary

- The term *social responsibility* has many different meanings. You must keep the differences in mind when discussing the issue. The various meanings can be sorted into three categories.

- One of the three categories defines social responsibility as social obligation. In this sense, business is considered socially responsible when it meets its primary obligation—to pursue, within the law, a profit for owners.

- A second category defines social responsibility as social reaction. From this perspective, business is socially responsible when it reacts to prevailing social norms, values, and expectations. The business must sense, understand, and react to society's expectations.

- A third category defines social responsibility as social responsiveness. This category includes obligatory and reactive behavior, but goes on to state that corporations should be proactive and take action to prevent social problems.

- Socially responsible activities may be categorized by type of activity and by those who benefit from the activities. The beneficiaries may be internal (customers, employees, and shareholders) or external (specific interest groups or more general beneficiaries).

- There is increasing concern about the role and state of ethics in organizations around the world because of the belief that business ethics have declined in recent years. Managers are concerned because of the complexity of ethics in decision making and because the costs of unethical actions can be substantial for the organization and society.

- Managers may use the concepts of egoism, altruism, pluralism, or obligation to a formal principle in their approaches to ethics in decision making. More organizations are also taking steps to ensure their managers make ethical decisions. These actions can include establishing and enforcing a corporate code of ethics, setting realistic performance goals for employees, providing ethics training for decision makers, and creating the position of an ethics officer.

Key Terms

altruism (p. 66)
egoism (p. 66)
ethics (p. 49)
human rights audit (p. 58)

social obligation (p. 49)
social reaction (p. 50)
social responsibility (p. 49)

social responsiveness (p. 51)
stakeholder management devices (SMDs) (p. 57)

Review and Discussion Questions

1. Explain why corporations have "social responsibilities." How does society express its expectations for corporate behavior?

2. Is it possible for a corporate executive to be both unethical personally and ethical professionally? Which is more demanding—the ethics of personal life or the ethics of professional life?

3. Why would organizations believe that earning SA 8000 certification is important?

4. What are the basic arguments for and against each of the three meanings of social responsibility?

5. To which beneficiaries of corporate behavior is management primarily responsible? Explain your answer. Does your answer reflect *your* ethical standards?

6. Some management experts assert that ethics codes are of little value in organizations because a manager's ethics are mostly a product of his or her own individual values, not a written code developed by top management. Do you agree? In your opinion, are there limits to a code's effectiveness in organizations? Explain.

7. Provide an example based on your interactions with an organization that you consider to be very socially responsible. Also, provide an example, based again on personal experience, of a socially irresponsible company.

8. Opponents of the social obligation perspective of social responsibility assert that an organization's socially responsive activities can be directly profitable for the company and thus they don't compromise management's obligations to shareholders. Provide an example that supports this view.

9. Explain how a manager's ethics affect decisions regarding social responsibility.

10. Many observers who believe that business ethics have declined over the last decade also assert that ethics in society overall have declined at the same time. Do you agree? Explain.

Practice Quiz

Note: You can find the correct answers to these questions by taking the quiz and then submitting your answers in the Online Edition. The program will automatically score your submission. If you miss a question, the program will provide the correct answer, a rationale for the answer, and the section number in the chapter where the topic is discussed.

Indicate whether the sentence or statement is true or false.

1. Economist Milton Friedman and others believe that society creates firms to pursue one primary purpose—to produce goods and services efficiently and to maximize profits.

2. Customers and stockholders (owners) are considered **external beneficiaries.**

3. Many firms choose to meet their **governmental reporting obligations** by responding promptly to complaints, by providing complete and accurate product information, and by implementing advertising programs that are completely truthful regarding product performance.

4. From a communications perspective, **ethical communication** facilitates the individual's ability to make sound choices.

5. Companies that comply with a code of conduct on wages and working conditions will be able to put a label or tag on their clothing that assures consumers that it was **made in America.**

6. Although ethics are determined from the top of an organization, they must be driven **up** and **across** the organization.

Identify the letter of the choice that best completes the statement or answers the question.

7. Which of the following is NOT offered by proponents of social responsibility as **social obligation** as an argument in support of their view?
   a. Businesses are accountable to the owners of the corporation. Therefore, management's sole responsibility is to serve the shareholder's interests by maximizing profits.
   b. Social improvement programs should be determined by law, by public policy, and by the actions and contributions of private individuals.
   c. Society is entitled to more than the mere provision of goods and services.
   d. Allocating business profits to social improvement activities amounts to taxation without representation.

8. Laws and regulations establish the basis for judging product safety, but market and competitive forces often set the standard for _____ .
   a. customer preferences.
   b. product quality.
   c. product names.
   d. repeat purchases.

9. The fundamental right of a stockholder is _____ .
   a. to be guaranteed a profit.
   b. to be insured against losses.
   c. to receive information on which a prudent investment decision can be based.
   d. to have a buyer for the stock should they choose to sell.

10. Wal-Mart and Sears are using _____ that allow headquarters-based merchandisers to provide store managers in the field with guidance and advice.
   a. videotapes
   b. CD-based training
   c. teleconferencing
   d. monthly inspections

11. The U.S. Sentencing Guidelines does not cover which law?
   a. antitrust violations
   b. domestic abuse
   c. conflict of interest
   d. money laundering

12. A major force in extending the amount and number of fringe benefits received by employees is _____ .
   a. academic research findings.
   b. union pressure.
   c. dissatisfied workers.
   d. insurance companies.

13. The general opinion is that recently business ethics around the world have _____ .
   a. improved.
   b. been replaced by laws.
   c. become outdated.
   d. declined.

14. In determining a firm's code of ethics it is recommended that they be _____ .
   a. sent out via e-mail.
   b. issued with a memo in pay envelopes.
   c. carefully explained and delivered by top management in meetings.
   d. kept to one or two sentences in length.

15. A necessary step in preparing and disseminating a credo is that the organization has a clearly stated set of _____ .
   a. balance sheets.
   b. cash flow statements.
   c. ethical values.
   d. operating procedures.

Case Study

Pegasus CEO Sets the Tone

Pegasus International Inc. is a leading manufacturer of integrated circuits (chips) and related software for such specialty markets as communications and mass storage, as well as PC-based audio media, video media, and multimedia. With a focus on innovation, Pegasus is committed to "technology leadership in the new millennium." Its long-standing strategy has been to anticipate changes in existing and emerging growth markets and to have hardware and software solutions ready before the market needs them. The company has also made significant strides in wireless communications.

The systems and products of Pegasus's wireless business have been selling well in its already existing markets in the United States, Japan, and Europe. But, like any company, Pegasus is eager to grow the business. At a strategy session with the Wireless Division, Pegasus CEO Tom Oswald and division managers decide to explore the potential of expanding their business to China.

Initial research indicates that China is likely to develop into a huge market for wireless because its people do not currently have this capability and the government has made spending on wireless a priority. Wireless is really the only choice for China because of the high cost of burying the communications cables necessary in wired systems; further, in underdeveloped countries copper wires are often stolen and sold on the black market.

Subsequent research does raise one concern for Pegasus wireless managers. They tell Oswald, "We have this problem. China allocates frequencies and makes franchise decisions city-by-city, district-by-district. A 'payoff' is usually required to get licenses."

The CEO says, "A lot of companies are doing business in China right now. How do they get around the problem?"

His managers have done their homework. "We believe most other companies contract with agents to represent them in the country and to get the licenses. What these contractors do is their own business, but apparently it works pretty well because the CEOs of all those companies are able to sign the disclosure statement required by law saying that they know of no instance where they bribed for their business."

"I wonder if paying someone else to do the crime is the same as our doing the crime," Oswald says. "I'm just not very comfortable with the whole question of payoffs. So, let me ask you, if we don't expand into China, how much business will we lose, potentially?"

His Wireless Division manager responds, "It will be huge not to do business in all the countries expecting payoffs. China alone represents easily $100 million of business per year. It's not life and death, but it is a sizable incremental opportunity for us, not to mention potential Japanese partners who will make significant capital investments. All we have to do is add our already-existing technology. When you consider all that, we have a lot to gain. What will we really lose if our local contractors are forced to make payoffs every now and then?"

Oswald wants his company to succeed, he wants to maximize shareholder value, he wants to keep his job, and he wants to model ethical leadership. He has made an effort to build a corporate culture characterized not only by aggressive R&D and growth but also by integrity, honesty, teamwork, and respect for the individual. As a result, the company enjoys an excellent reputation among its customers and suppliers, employee morale is high, and ethics is a priority at the company.

Questions for Discussion

1. Should Pegasus conclude that doing business in China is a course they will avoid? Explain.

2. How should Oswald proceed?

3. Can U.S. standards of ethical behavior be applied and complied with in other countries? Why?

Source: Adapted from Michael L. Hackworth and Thomas Shank, "The Case of the Million Dollar Decision," Markkula Center for Applied Ethics, Santa Clara University, July 2001.

Internet Exercise

White-collar crime and criminals is serious business. Examine in depth a case involving a white-collar criminal. Report the case and details by using only Internet resources. In specific terms describe:

- The convicted criminal
- The crime
- The victims
- The court process

- The sentence
- The relationship of the crime to social responsibility, fraud, and/or ethics

Do you believe that white-collar crime is punished less severely than what could be called "blue-collar" crime?

Experiential Exercise

Ethical Dilemmas

Purpose: This activity is designed to illustrate the complexity of ethical decision making and how people can differ in their views of what is and is not ethical behavior.

Setting Up the Exercise: Presented below are four situations often encountered in the workplace that pose ethical issues. Read each scenario and place yourself in the position of the respective decision maker. What would you do? Write your decision for each scenario on a sheet of paper.

The Roundabout Raise

When Joe asks for a raise, his boss praises his work but says the company's rigid budget won't allow any further merit raises for the time being. Instead, the boss suggests that the company "won't look too closely at your expense accounts for a while." Should Joe take this as authorization to pad his expense account on grounds that he is simply getting the same money he deserves through a different route, or not take this roundabout "raise"?

Your decision:

The Faked Degree

Bill has done a sound job for more than a year. Bill's boss learns that he got the job by claiming to have a college degree, although he actually never graduated. Should his boss dismiss him for submitting a fraudulent résumé or overlook the false claim since Bill has otherwise proven to be a conscientious and honorable worker, and making an issue of the degree might ruin Bill's career?

Your decision:

Sneaking Phone Calls

Helen discovers that a fellow employee regularly makes about $100 a month worth of personal long-distance telephone calls from an office telephone. Should Helen report the employee to the company or disregard the calls on the grounds that many people make personal calls at the office?

Your decision:

Cover-Up Temptation

Bill discovers that the chemical plant he manages is creating slightly more water pollution in a nearby lake than is legally permitted. Revealing the problem will bring considerable unfavorable publicity to the plant, hurt the lakeside town's resort business, and create a scare in the community. Solving the problem will cost the company well over $100,000. It is unlikely that outsiders will discover the problem. The violation poses no danger whatsoever to people. At most, it will endanger a small number of fish. Should Bill reveal the problem despite the cost to his company, or consider the problem as little more than a technicality and disregard it?

Your decision:

Once everyone has completed the scenarios, your instructor will discuss the class responses to each situation. The instructor will also provide you with the general responses of about 1,500 adults and 400 middle-level managers. They completed the exercise as a part of *The Wall Street Journal/Gallup* poll on ethics in America.

Compare your responses to those of the general public and the executives. What factors account for any differences in how you responded compared to their decisions?

A Learning Note: This exercise aptly demonstrates the complexities of ethical considerations in decision making and the source of the complexities: (1) the differing perspectives among individuals concerning what is ethical; (2) their differing interpretations and assessments of situations; and (3) differing goals, needs, and values.

Source: From *The Wall Street Journal,* November 5, 1983, p. 29. Copyright © 1983 Dow Jones & Co. Reprinted by permission of Dow Jones & Co. via Copyright Clearance Center.

Managing Globally

4

Managing Today

Tele-SalesForce Minimizes Risks Through Extensive Quality Control

Tele-SalesForce (TSF) helps U.S. companies outsource their lead generation processes to a call center in Calcutta, India. Chad Burmeister and Tathagata Dasgupta are co-founders of the Irvine, Calif.-based company. In less than one year of operation, TSF has signed up more than twenty-one clients. Customers range from major companies such as PeopleSoft and Sun Microsystems to small start ups.

TSF was launched with the clear goal of providing value in all aspects of a client's lead generation process. The TSF team works with new clients to identify their needs. Following a carefully designed, step-by-step process TSF helps clients develop a script for the India-based call-center agents to use when talking to prospects. Prior to actually getting on the phone, each call-center agent assigned to the client role-plays the script and potential prospect responses.

For example, an agent was assigned with acquiring leads from Consumer Packaged Goods (CPG) companies who supply products to Wal-Mart. The agent who was assigned to make those calls did not have any idea what Wal-Mart was, what a CPG company was, or how it works in the U.S. Additionally, the agent had no comprehension of how Enterprise Software Application programs could help these companies.

TSF developed a training program for the agent explaining the relationships to the agent in terms of stores and manufacturers she is familiar with in India. The TSF project manager explained the business relationships and chemistry, what an application can do in the middle of all this, and why she is calling the decision makers of those companies. This education and the resulting conviction in her voice turned a campaign from getting two leads per *week* into three leads per *day*. This attention to detail helps minimize errors and enhances the chances for a successful call.

In addition to TSF's careful planning to minimize risks, its call-center partner in Calcutta is equally committed to quality performance. A five-year old company, the India call center used the services of Ernst & Young (E&Y) at its founding to ensure that it installed best practices call-center technologies and procedures. The firm maintains its quality edge by getting regular "check ups" from E&Y.

Tele-SalesForce is anticipating sales in excess of $1 million for 2005, with growth projected to reach over $7 million by 2008. With the risk-mitigation approach the company is taking to call-center outsourcing, it stands a strong chance of meeting and even exceeding its own growth expectations.

Source: Adapted from Ed Taylor, "Entrepreneur Brings Successful Outsourcing Firm to Scottsdale," *East Valley Tribune,* November 10, 2004.

4-1 Introduction

Businesses that aren't directly marketing their products and services internationally are nevertheless involved in international business in the sense that they are competing with foreign companies. Scan the aisles of your local consumer electronics, computer, or even clothing stores and the message is clear: International competitors are a major presence in American markets. Whether a U.S. company like McDonald's, Dell Computer, or Levi Strauss operates at home or abroad, managing a business successfully requires understanding competitors with different outlooks, backgrounds, and strategies.[1]

Why have a growing number of American businesses become so involved in international business? The reason is simple; many international markets provide substantial opportunities and returns for those businesses with the ability and determination to succeed in an often unfamiliar environment. Specifically, many companies venture abroad because of declining markets at home and brighter opportunities overseas. For some companies, the U.S. market for their product may be maturing or even in decline while the market in an overseas country is just taking off. Some businesses venture abroad to use excess manufacturing capacity. Others establish manufacturing facilities worldwide, partly to achieve substantial economies of scale, which provides them with a significant cost advantage over competitors. Other companies go international to alleviate the risk of operating in only one geographical market. Still others, such as Tele-SalesForce (TSF), set up service operations overseas in a practice that is known as "outsourcing." The Managing Today vignette describes how TSF has established procedures to ensure high-quality services delivered by individuals half a world away. Many companies have begun to take advantage of lower-wage service workers in countries around the world. We will examine the outsourcing phenomenon in more detail later in the chapter.

Whatever the specific motive, businesses internationalize to reap potential rewards that are not so readily available at home. However, venturing into an international market is an exceptionally challenging strategy. Once a company decides to do business abroad it confronts an entirely new set of circumstances. In many countries, a business will find that consumer preferences are different. Marketing (i.e., pricing, promotional strategies, advertising, and distribution systems) is unfamiliar as are financial markets and accounting systems. The motivations and perspectives of host country employees may substantially differ along with personnel policies that are typical for doing business. The country's political environment and the relationship between business and government may distinctly differ from the political climate and relationship in the United States. A wide gap may exist between the culture at home and the culture in the international market. In sum, doing business abroad often requires setting aside many of the time-tested assumptions of doing business and building a new set of assumptions for an unfamiliar and often unsettling environment.

4-2 The Multinational Enterprise

A firm doing business in two or more countries is referred to as a **multinational enterprise** (**MNE**). Typically, such firms have sales offices and, in many cases, manufacturing facilities in numerous countries. They view their scope of operation as global in nature. American firms such as Coca-Cola, Chrysler, Nike, and IBM conduct a significant part of their business overseas. Increasingly, small businesses are also finding profits in international markets.[2] For example, MasterWord Services, a Houston-based translation firm with fewer than twenty employees, also has offices in London, Baku, and Moscow.

> **multinational enterprise (MNE)** A firm doing business in two or more countries.

One way to appreciate the truly multinational nature of many business firms is to examine foreign companies that have entered the United States and American firms that are owned by foreign multinationals. Figure 4-1 presents some familiar names in each of these categories.

As competition intensifies, American firms must become more adept in international business. The necessity of avoiding costly mistakes and pressure from experienced competitors requires managers who can direct effective performance in an MNE.

4-2a The MNE Decision

The decision to become an MNE is truly a major one. Although the choice incorporates consideration of many factors, the move to becoming an MNE essentially encompasses three primary decisions:[3] the international market to be served, the products or services to be marketed, and the mode of entry into the international market. The following discussion explores these questions in detail. Note also that companies that decide to go global must involve their entire company in the decision.[4]

US-Owned MNEs	Foreign-Owned MNEs	Nonprofit MNEs
General Motors	Unilever	Red Cross
IBM	Royal Dutch/Shell	Roman Catholic Church
General Electric	Nestlé	United States Army
Nike	Nissan	Salvation Army
Ford Motor	Sony	
Procter & Gamble	Volkswagen	
Boeing	Perrier	
Wal-Mart	Norelco	
	British Petroleum	
	Lukoil	

Figure 4-1
Some Well-Known Multinational Enterprises (MNEs)

The International Market to Be Served   Selecting the country (or countries) as the site for international expansion involves considering many aspects of the country's environment. Many international businesses emphasize the market size in the prospective host country (both current and potential size), the country's consumer wealth (per capita income), and the ease of doing business in the market. In assessing this latter criterion, organizations consider such factors as geographical location, language commonality, governmental relations with business, and the availability of employees with the skills that the business will require. Overall, evaluating the prospective host country's cultural, economic, and political environments are important steps in host country selection. These factors are discussed in more detail later in the chapter.

The Products or Services to Be Marketed   What products or services should an organization establish in an international market? In answering this question, many firms opt for the **shot-in-the-dark method.** They simply select one or more of their products (or services) that have done well in their domestic market and introduce it into the chosen international market. Kellogg's Corn Flakes, Coca-Cola, and McDonald's hamburgers were introduced in this manner.

> **shot-in-the-dark method**
> Method of choosing a product or service for international expansion by selecting a product that is successful in the home country market and introducing it abroad.

A growing number of companies are utilizing more analytical and deliberate approaches to product or service selection. Some firms utilize a **phased internationalization** approach. They travel to the selected host country and conduct product-market research to determine consumer needs in the overall product area in which the company does business. Then the company returns home with the research and designs a product that fits the consumers' needs. The new product (often some variation of the company's product line) is then introduced into the host country. Ferrero's Tic Tac breath mints and IDV's Bailey's Irish Cream liqueur are products that were specifically developed and marketed based on research of multiple international markets.[5]

> **phased internationalization**
> Designing a product or service for international expansion based on product-market research in the prospective host country and identified needs of host country consumers.

Regardless of the approach taken by an organization, a successful international product or service requires that primary attention be given to the needs, preferences, and idiosyncrasies of the consumers in the selected host country. Many hugely successful American products have failed abysmally in international markets because U.S. companies simply ignored international consumer differences.[6]

Other products that initially failed later found success once the manufacturer made some seemingly slight though important changes. Consider S. C. Johnson & Sons Lemon Pledge furniture polish. After the product sold poorly in Japan among older consumers, the company conducted marketing research and found that the polish smelled like a latrine disinfectant used throughout Japan during World War II. Johnson & Sons reduced the lemon scent in the polish and sales boomed.

Mattel's Barbie doll was another faltering product in Japan until marketing research determined that few Japanese identified with the Americanized doll. For the Japanese, Barbie was too tall, too long-legged, and her blue eyes were the wrong color. Mattel produced a Japanized Barbie—shorter with brown eyes and a more Asian figure. Thereafter, two million Barbies were sold in two years.

Even name changes can produce positive results. Pillsbury changed its "Jolly Green Giant" name in Saudi Arabia once it found that the name translated to "intimidating green ogre"; in China, Coca-Cola instituted a name change after it found that in Chinese, "Coca-Cola" means "bite the wax tadpole."[7]

The Mode of Entry into Global Markets   Once the market and product/service for international expansion have been selected, an organization must decide specifically how it will enter its selected market. There are three basic strategies for market entry, which are illustrated in Figure 4-2. Each strategy results in greater commitment to the international venture.

Export   Exporting involves selling a product in the global market without establishing manufacturing facilities there. Exporting encompasses promotion to stimulate demand for the product, collecting revenues, making credit arrangements from sales, and shipping the product to the market.

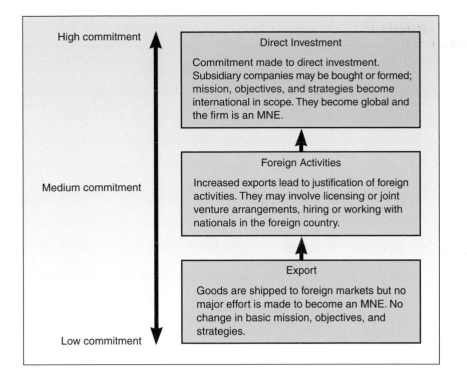

Figure 4-2
Evolving into a
Multinational Corporation

Most companies secure an agent to handle some or all of these tasks. However, once they become accustomed to the exporting business, a number of companies assume most or all of these tasks, often establishing a staff in the host country. The **export entry strategy** is a very popular approach for entering international markets. The U.S. is the world's largest exporter and trading nation. In developed nations such as the U.S., economic growth is tied closely to international trade. Total trade in the U.S. in 2000 was $2 trillion, with exports of $782.4 billion and imports of $1.2 trillion.[8] The 2000 U.S. trade deficit was $428.6 billion.

Table 4-1 shows the top ten international destinations for exports from the United States.

The U.S. Department of Commerce has identified ten so-called Big Emerging Markets that will appear over the next two decades and will provide the greatest commercial opportunities. These markets are the Chinese economic area (including China, Hong Kong, and Taiwan), India, South Korea, Mexico, Brazil, Argentina, South Africa, Poland, Turkey, and the Association of Southeast Asian Nations (ASEAN: including Indonesia, Brunei, Malaysia, Singapore, Thailand, the Philippines, and Vietnam).[9]

Exporting is the least complicated and least risky strategy for entering a foreign market. The strategy involves little or no change in the organization's basic mission, objectives, and strategies since all production continues at home. If problems arise in the host country, an exporting organization can easily exit the market. However, exports are subject to tariffs and other costs imposed by the host country, which can lessen exporting profits and competitive advantage. Moreover, when an agent is used to handle the exporting tasks, the organization has little control over the overall exporting situation, that is, such factors as product price, advertising, and distribution.[10]

Foreign Activities As the importance of exports increases, the firm may decide that it now can justify its own foreign subsidiary. This decision usually involves establishing production and/or marketing facilities in the host country. The **foreign subsidiary entry strategy** differs from direct investment because it entails some type of association with a local firm or individual. This type of association usually takes the form of **licensing** or a **joint venture.**

When a firm negotiates a licensing agreement, it is granting the right to produce the firm's product to an outside company in the host country. A firm may also grant an

▶**export entry strategy** The simplest way for a firm to enter a foreign market. This strategy involves little or no change in the organization's basic mission, objectives, and strategies since it continues to produce all of its products at home. The firm usually secures an *agent* in the particular foreign market who facilitates the transactions with foreign buyers.

▶**foreign subsidiary entry strategy** An approach to entry in a foreign market that involves joining with nationals in the foreign country to establish product and/or marketing facilities.

▶**licensing** The granting by a firm to an outside firm the right to produce and/or market the firm's product in another country.

▶**joint venture** When foreign investors form a group with local investors to begin a local business with each group sharing ownership.

T A B L E 4-1	Leading International Destinations for U.S. Exports, 1997–2003						
Trade Partner	1997	1998	1999	2000	2001	2002	2003
World Total	*$687,597,999*	*$680,474,248*	*$692,820,620*	*$780,418,628*	*$731,025,906*	*$693,257,300*	*$723,743,177*
Canada	$150,124,378	$154,152,162	$163,912,764	$176,429,632	$163,724,462	$160,799,214	$169,480,937
Mexico	$71,378,310	$79,010,087	$87,044,038	$111,720,878	$101,509,075	$97,530,613	$97,457,420
Japan	$65,672,594	$57,887,875	$57,483,535	$65,254,366	$57,639,072	$51,439,625	$52,063,765
United Kingdom	$36,435,090	$39,070,195	$38,337,793	$41,579,356	$40,797,923	$33,253,090	$33,895,379
Germany	$24,466,907	$26,641,872	$26,788,867	$29,243,960	$30,113,948	$26,628,438	$28,847,948
China	$12,805,416	$14,257,953	$13,117,677	$16,253,029	$19,234,827	$22,052,679	$28,418,493
South Korea	$25,066,768	$16,538,271	$22,953,951	$27,901,881	$22,196,592	$22,595,871	$24,098,587
Netherlands	$19,821,580	$19,003,800	$19,412,130	$21,973,675	$19,524,685	$18,334,472	$20,702,905
Taiwan	$20,387,909	$18,157,132	$19,121,126	$24,380,278	$18,151,574	$18,394,301	$17,487,899
France	$15,981,589	$17,727,954	$18,838,451	$20,252,812	$19,895,664	$19,018,869	$17,068,157

Source: TradeStats Express, National Trade Data (http://tse.export.gov/).

outside company the right to use the firm's intangible assets such as patents or technology. In the 1950s, many U.S. firms transferred technology to Japanese companies via licensing agreements. The licensing firm usually receives a flat payment plus royalties from the sale of the goods that are produced using the licensed technology.

Licensing can be an effective way to obtain profits from product sales without establishing and managing facilities in the host country. However, in licensing, a firm loses some control over the asset that is licensed. The company also runs the risk of the outside licensee eventually becoming a competitor. In today's digital environment, everything from published works to music to works of art are susceptible to being used and/or sold by unauthorized parties. Increasingly, firms such as publishers and music distributors are turning to licensing as a means of providing profit-making opportunities for others to distribute intellectual property.[11]

In the joint venture arrangement, a business joins with local investors to create and operate a business in the host country. Each investor is a partner and shares the ownership of the new venture. Joint ventures are a quite popular strategy for launching a business abroad. They are especially popular with U.S. investors in countries such as China and Japan where the business and cultural environment is quite unique to the United States.[12]

The popularity of joint ventures is largely due to the substantial advantages, which the strategy can provide. A joint venture is a lower-cost and lesser-risk approach to establishing production and marketing operations abroad compared to foreign direct investment. Substantial gains can be reaped when partners with complementary abilities pool their skills and resources in making and selling a product.

In Asian markets McDonald's prefers to use joint ventures because entering the market is very difficult. A 50-50 split in ownership encourages local partners to handle all the host country's details. In more politically risky markets (e.g., Yugoslavia, Albania, some parts of Africa), McDonald's limits its risks by not putting up any of its own money. It licenses its name and enforces its worldwide standards for quality. McDonald's retains the right to buy out the license partner at a later date (*McDonald's Annual Report*, 2000).

However, the failure rates of joint ventures are disturbingly high. Approximately 40 percent of these international arrangements fail; most ventures last only from three to four

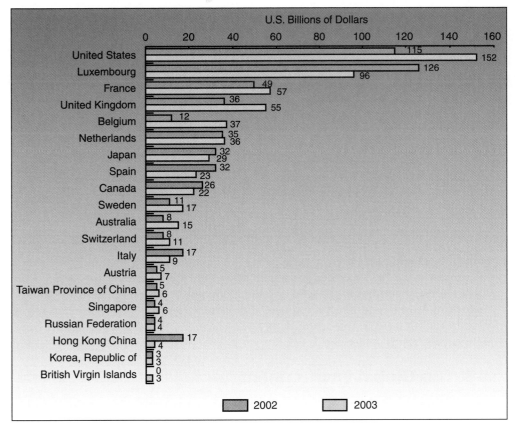

Figure 4-3
Global FDI in U.S.
Billions of Dollars

Source: United Nations Conference on Trade and Development, World Investment Report 2004.

years.[13] At the core of the arrangement's problems are the difficulties of joint ownership and management. Usually two partners from different countries and cultures must work together in setting venture objectives, strategy, and in operating the new business. Differences in management and cultural styles can create major conflicts between the parties, as can differing objectives for the venture.[14]

Given the inherent difficulties with joint ventures, success requires a careful analysis and selection of the joint venture partner. Selection should be based on such factors as compatibility of venture objectives, similar value systems, and mutual respect. Agreements should be reached concerning mechanisms for resolving disagreements and the specific roles of each partner in managing the business.[15]

Direct Investment   The strongest commitment to becoming a global enterprise is made when management decides to begin producing the firm's products abroad with no association with a host country investor. The **direct investment entry strategy** is booming in international business. U.S. firms are the world FDI (foreign direct investment) leaders, placing some $152 billion abroad in 2003.[16] Figure 4-3 includes FDI data from around the world through 2003. Interestingly, the tiny country of Luxembourg is second to the U.S. in foreign direct investment.

Businesses that build and/or buy manufacturing facilities abroad do so for a number of reasons. In some cases, direct investment reduces manufacturing expenses due to lower labor and other costs. This benefit triggered the booming growth of the *maquiladoras* industry along the Mexican border. Direct investment also enables a business to avoid the tariff and other government-imposed costs associated with exporting. The strategy is an effective means for building major national markets and for maintaining total control over international operations. Also, larger benefits can be gained by establishing a local presence via direct investment. By paying taxes in the host country and providing local employment, a foreign business can build confidence among consumers and receive more equitable treatment from the host government.[17] However, direct investment entails a full commitment to an international venture. When problems arise in the host country (e.g.,

▶ **direct investment entry strategy**   A policy to begin producing a firm's products in a foreign country without the association with a host country investor. The strongest commitment to becoming an MNE, it enables the firm to maintain full control over production, marketing, and other key functions.

LearningMoment *Entering Global Markets*

Three specific strategies for entering global markets can be used. Exporting involves selling a product or service in the global market without building plants and facilities. Licensing or a joint venture allows a partner to produce and market the firm's product in a host country. In a joint venture, a business teams up with local investors to create and operate a business in the host country.

The strongest commitment to global business is when a firm produces its products abroad. The direct investment and construction of plants and facilities abroad is a statement that the business is committed to the country and location.

market decline, economic depression, government instability), leaving the country is often quite difficult and costly.

In summary, the exporting, foreign activities, and direct investment strategies for market entry offer different strengths and shortcomings. As one moves along the continuum from exporting to direct investment (depicted in Figure 4-2), commitment to the venture and control over international operations increases. Risk due to this greater commitment also tends to increase.

4-3 The Global Environment

The decision to become an MNE and thereafter effectively managing in a global setting requires careful assessment of the environment. Due appreciation must be given to the differences that exist there relative to an organization's domestic environment.

Environmental factors, which bear great impact on managerial performance in a domestic setting, are magnified many times in global markets. In assessing the global environment, many factors should be evaluated. However, the host country's *culture, economics,* and *politics* should be given special attention. Although other environmental differences may exist, these three have the greatest impact on managerial performance in MNEs. How effectively managers respond to these differences often determines the success or failure of the MNE itself.

4-3a Culture

culture A very complex environmental influence that includes knowledge, beliefs, laws, morals, art, customs, and any other habits and capabilities an individual acquires as a member of society. It is important to be aware that cultures are *learned,* cultures *vary,* and cultures *influence behavior.*

Culture is a very complex environmental influence, encompassing knowledge, beliefs, values, laws, morals, customs, and other habits and capabilities an individual acquires as a member of society. These elements of culture can all vary a great deal across societies. If an MNE is global in nature, management must adapt its managerial practices to the specific and unique aspects of culture in each host country. An MNE's management must be culturally sensitive in its business practices and learn to bridge the cultural gap that exists between its ways of management and business and those of the host country. In making these adjustments, an MNE's management must be aware that cultures are *learned,* cultures *vary,* and cultures *influence behavior.*

Cultures Are Learned Cultures include all types of learning and behavior, the customs that people have developed for living together, their values, and their beliefs of right and wrong. A culture is the sum of what people learn in common with other members of the society to which they belong. That cultures are learned seems to be too obvious to mention, except that it highlights the point that managers of international ventures can learn to adapt to the cultures they are entering. Too often, managers enter new global regions expecting the culture to adapt to them, rather than vice versa. As a student of management, it's important to recognize that you may be called to manage someday in a foreign location. The term for such an assignment is **expatriate.** Many companies offer cultural training for expatriates, both for those going abroad and for those returning home after long

expatriate An MNE employee transferred to a host country from the MNE's home base or from an MNE facility in another country.

stints abroad. Cultures are learned, and they can be learned by managers prior to taking international assignments. Those who prepare for international work by studying the culture before they leave have a higher success rate than those who do not prepare.[18]

Cultures Vary   Different societies have different cultures. Different objectives are prized, and behavior that is valued in one society may be much less important in another. This cultural diversity affects individual perception, and therefore, individual behavior. For example, in Japan and other Asian countries, the culture emphasizes the social relationship as the foundation of business. Consequently, when an American business executive negotiates a joint venture with a prospective Japanese partner, he or she will discover that the Japanese will spend much time asking questions about the American's family and other subjects that seemingly have nothing to do with the joint venture. The American executive seeks to obtain a legal contract that American culture views as the foundation of the business relationship. However, Japanese executives attempt to establish some foundation of a mutual relationship of personal trust and understanding, which they view as the core of the business relationship. The time-consuming questions are an attempt to do so.

While the U.S. business executive seeks the certainty and protection of a legal contract, the Japanese view contracts as a hindrance. As the factors affecting the venture change over time, the Japanese reason, so will the relationship. A legalistic, unchanging contract is an unnecessary obstacle to the venture's natural development. Thus, while American business executives emphasize detail in the contract, Japanese executives work to keep the document as general as possible. American business executives often have difficulty understanding these major cultural differences, which have undone many joint venture relationships.

Cultures Influence Behavior   Diversity in human behavior can be found in almost every human activity. Religious ceremonies, beliefs, values, work habits, food habits, and social activities vary endlessly within the cultural environment. The differences in behavior between peoples of different countries arise from differences in culture rather than differences in people.

Culture can affect behavior in many ways. For example, although human needs may be inherently similar, the cultural environment determines the relative importance of needs and the means through which they are satisfied.[19] Culture influences attitudes of individuals concerning the importance of work, authority, material possessions, competition, time, profit, risk taking, and decision making. Many employees in Israel, Austria, New Zealand, and Scandinavian countries, for example, prefer consultative over unilateral decision making. In some cultures, time is measured in days and years rather than hours, which can substantially affect work scheduling and control. In some countries, especially Muslim societies, the culture does not emphasize self-determination, which is a strong cultural norm in the United States. People believe that fate rather than self-initiative determines the future.[20] This belief has a major impact on business planning, objectives, and work. In some areas of the world hard work is viewed as good, while in other areas it is viewed as something to be avoided. Authority is perceived as a right in some nations but must be earned by demonstrated ability in others such as the United States.[21]

The following Management Focus on Customer Service box, "Reflections of an American Tourist in Europe," illustrates how cultural expectations can influence perceptions of service and the employee-customer relationship.

4-3b Economics

The economic influences of a host country substantially affect MNE performance. Its income levels, economic growth, inflation rates, and the country's balance of payments can significantly affect an MNE's sales, earnings, and business practices. The MNE must constantly be aware of each host country's economic stability. The rate of inflation and currency stability must be closely monitored.

In terms of economic and overall development, countries are classified either as a **developed country (DC)** or a **less-developed country (LDC).** Compared with a DC, an LDC has a lower level of economic development. It usually has a low gross national prod-

▶**developed country (DC)**
A nation in which most workers are employed in the industrial or service economy; has a significant middle class.

▶**less-developed country (LDC)**
Has a very low gross national product, very little industry, or an unequal distribution of income with a very large number of poor.

Management Focus on **Customer Service**

Reflections of an American Tourist in Europe

I used to think it was me. Then I thought poor *service* was a southern culture thing. You know, slower and sweeter because they know how to enjoy life. That was until I moved to Germany and a friend finally explained it to me. "It's your market versus our socialism," she said. "In a market economy," she continued, "the *customer* may be king, but in European socialism, it's the employee who counts most." Which is why "we talk about employee rights and not consumer rights," she added. Since then it made sense. Imagine a world where waiters and sales clerks behave like tenured professors.

Like the time I was in the Austrian town of Zell am, See. In a fine hotel in this idyllic lakeside resort, nestled in the Alps, I rambled in for breakfast and tossed my key and newspaper on an empty table. That was mistake number one. The young waitress in charge signaled that table 52 had already been pre-assigned. It was a nice large table in the corner where, she added, there was an expansive view of the room. I thanked her very much, but gently insisted I would be happy not to move. That was mistake number two.

Five minutes later I was speaking to the supervisor, Frau Kurmugginstein. I made my case persuasively, I thought. You know, I was the *customer*, freedom of choice. The restaurant was barely half-full, after all. That's when I made mistake number three: I escalated. "You mean this is non-negotiable—Ich muss?!" I exclaimed. Of course, table 52 turned out to be just fine, but the moral defeat was a stinging one. And the lesson was clear: the employee is always right.

Source: Jeffrey Gedmin, "Service with a Snarl," *American Spectator*, November 2003, pp. 44–45. Copyright © 2003 *American Spectator*. Reprinted with permission.

uct, little industry, and underdeveloped educational, distribution, and communication systems. Comprising 80 percent of the world's population, LDCs have an unequal distribution of income that keeps many of these people in deep poverty.

Although LDCs comprise most of the world's population, only about 25 percent of the world's international business activity occurs in these countries.[22] However, the amount of international activity is increasing. In particular, a growing number of American companies are establishing direct investments in LDCs to obtain the advantages of much lower labor costs.

Economic relations between MNEs and LDCs often have been the subject of controversy. Many LDCs have strong feelings of nationalism. During the last thirty years, in their drives for political independence and freedom from foreign domination, many developing nations have felt the need to consolidate control of their economies by altering the past pattern of relationships with foreign firms. In some LDCs, extensive government regulations have been adopted with the ultimate purpose of limiting the growth of MNEs. More recently, however, there has been a movement away from this trend. The reasons for the shift are changing attitudes and rising direct investment.[23]

Changing Attitudes   Although charges of exploitation by MNEs still are made quite frequently, attitudes of both host governments and MNEs have changed. This has led to greater mutual understanding and accommodation in relations. Host country fear of foreign domination still exists, but it has eased substantially. Apparently, foreign governments realize that the relationship with MNEs need not be a no-win situation, but rather one of mutual gain.

Globalization offers extensive opportunities for truly worldwide development but it is not progressing evenly. Some countries are becoming integrated into the global economy more quickly than others. Countries that have been able to integrate are seeing faster growth and reduced poverty. Outward-oriented policies brought dynamism and greater prosperity to much of East Asia, transforming it from one of the poorest areas of the world 40 years ago. And as living standards rose, it became possible to make progress on democracy and economic issues such as the environment and work standards.

By contrast, in the 1970s and 1980s when many countries in Latin America and Africa pursued inward-oriented policies, their economies stagnated or declined, poverty increased, and high inflation became the norm. In many cases, especially Africa, adverse external developments made the problems worse. As these regions changed their policies, their incomes have begun to rise. An important transformation is underway. Encouraging this trend, not reversing it, is the best course for promoting growth, development, and poverty reduction.

Rising Direct Investment   Improved relations have given rise to a doubling of direct investment compared to the early 1960s. Apparently, many MNEs believe the possible returns are worth the risk. Also, these direct investments do not reflect the flow of other resources, such as managerial skills, technology, and marketing skills, which may overshadow the MNEs monetary contribution.

Global economic integration is being driven by rising flows of FDI from industrial countries to developing countries. The expansion of manufacturing operations in developing countries is boosting their economic growth and contributing to rising incomes and living standards. As their economic conditions improve, pressures are growing on developing countries to make additional efforts to liberalize their economies, including dismantling barriers to international trade in goods and services and to the mobility of capital. Through this process, international trade is a beneficiary of increasing international capital flows.[24]

Despite greater mutual trust and a greater volume of investment, it would be wrong to assume that MNEs and developing countries have achieved total agreement on the questions of exploitation of resources and threats to sovereignty. These issues have divided them for years and, even today, opinions still diverge widely within each group.

At the heart of the controversy is a basic difference in perceptions and objectives. Many MNEs, though they now are more willing to recognize their social responsibilities, still tend to concentrate on short-run performance criteria. Efficient and profitable operation is regarded as benefiting workers, customers, and suppliers directly, while the rest of the host country benefits indirectly through taxes.

Critics in the host country, on the other hand, point to undesirable political, social, and economic consequences. They charge that MNEs create many problems in developing countries struggling to achieve political and economic autonomy. In fact, similar arguments are made in discussions of the social responsibilities of business firms in the United States.

4-3c Politics

The *political influences* in a host country environment can substantially affect all of the managerial functions of an MNE and can frequently determine the ultimate success of an MNE's global operations. Our discussion of the political environment will focus on two topics: the characteristics of the host country government that most affect an MNE and the concept of *political risk,* including how MNEs forecast and cope with political uncertainty in their global settings.

Concerning the host government, three factors most significantly influence an MNE's operations and performance.

Governmental Attitudes Toward Imports and Direct Investment   Host country governments express their attitudes concerning international imports and investments with actions that can greatly help or hinder an MNE. Governments who encourage investment often provide incentives to persuade foreign companies to establish manufacturing facilities there. Such incentives are often provided by LDCs that want access to the technology, capital, jobs, and educational and managerial skills that an MNE can provide. Singapore, for example, offers low-interest government loans, tax holidays, and accelerated depreciation to foreign investors from certain industries. India provides capital grants to companies that will build manufacturing facilities in certain depressed areas of the country. Malaysia waives taxes for as long as ten years for companies that also locate in certain areas.[25]

Although LDC governments are often eager to attract certain foreign investors, they will also set requirements that seek to obtain as much value from the MNE as possible while not compromising the country's sovereignty. These requirements take on a variety of forms. Many LDCs, for example, require a "fadeout" where the majority ownership of the MNE's facility in the host country is transferred to a host country investor within a certain number of years. Other LDCs such as India set a strict limit on foreign ownership of an MNE facility.

LDCs may also require that an MNE hire a specified number of local citizens for employee and management positions to boost the area's employment. Other LDCs require that the MNE sell its technology to local businesses. Many host countries restrict the amount of funds that an MNE can transfer out of the country. To obtain access to markets in developed countries, some LDCs require that for every good imported by a resident MNE, the MNE must export a local good of equal or higher value.[26]

Both LDC and DC governments often seek to restrict the import of certain goods that compete with host country businesses. In these cases, barriers are established to discourage imports. A government may impose a tariff on certain imported goods, which is a tax calculated as a percentage of the product's value. These tariffs raise the import's sales price, which provides domestic competitors with a competitive advantage.

To further aid domestic competitors, a government may provide them subsidies such as low-cost loans and tax breaks or a quota may be set on a product, which limits the number of goods that can be imported. Another barrier is to require inspection standards that are cost prohibitive for potential imports.

Efficiency of Government

Many American business executives become disillusioned with the inefficient bureaucracies they must deal with in many countries. Often, little assistance is provided by foreign governments to American businesspeople. Customs-handling procedures are inefficient and burdensome, and market information is nonexistent. Systems of law in each country also can be quite different. For example, the United States has developed its legal system by means of English common law. The courts are guided by principles derived from previous cases. In much of Europe and Asia, however, the legal system is one of civil law. In such systems, judges are less important, and the bureaucrat (civil servant) is extremely important.

Unfortunately, American managers have found that many of the inefficiencies and obstacles in local governments tend to disappear when a suitable payment is made to some civil servant. In many nations, such bribes are considered a part of doing business. Culture can also affect the ethics of doing business in a country. Many businesspeople have entered foreign markets with good intentions, only to find that corruption among government officials, businesspeople, and other authorities in the foreign country makes doing business impossible. Some countries, such as Finland, Sweden, and New Zealand, have strong cultural prohibitions against corruption in business. Others, such as Nigeria, Russia, and Pakistan, have a high level of corruption making it exceedingly difficult to conduct business. Table 4-2 displays the rank order of a sample of countries on a scale of "perceived corruption." The rankings are derived from an ongoing survey of businesspeople at the Transparency International website at www.transparency.org.

Based on this tendency to use bribes in foreign countries, the Foreign Corrupt Practices Act was passed into law in 1977. For the first time in U.S. history, it became a crime for corporations to bribe an official of a foreign government to obtain or retain business in another country. More specifically, the law requires publicly held companies to institute internal accounting controls to ensure that all transactions are made in accordance with management's specific authorization and are fairly recorded.

Until 2000 Sweden, Australia, New Zealand, France, and Great Britain allowed payments of bribes abroad in business dealings to be tax deductible. This practice obviously places U.S. managers at a disadvantage in certain areas. The Management Focus on Ethics box, "Bribery in the Real World," discusses this issue in more detail.

Government Stability

The stability of the host country government is perhaps the characteristic that bears the greatest impact on an MNE. Such is the case because highly unstable governments that are subject to volatile change can upend an MNE's operations. The most extreme impact of government instability can occur when an unstable government changes hands. In such cases, the MNE may face **expropriation,** where the new leaders in power seize the MNE's facility without compensation. **Nationalization** may occur where the government forces the MNE to sell its facility to local buyers. Since World War

▶**expropriation** Seizure of an MNE's property in a host country without compensation.

▶**nationalization** A process that occurs when a host country government forces an MNE to sell its facility to local buyers.

TABLE 4-2	Transparency International Corruption Perceptions Index 2004							
Country Rank	Country	2004 CPI Score*	Confidence Range**	Country Rank	Country	2004 CPI Score*	Confidence Range**
1	Finland	9,7	9.5–9.8	11	United Kingdom	8,6	8.4–8.8
2	New Zealand	9,6	9.4–9.6	12	Canada	8,5	8.1–8.9
3	Denmark	9,5	9.3–9.7	13	Austria	8,4	8.1–8.8
4	Iceland	9,5	9.4–9.7	14	Luxembourg	8,4	8.0–8.9
5	Singapore	9,3	9.2–9.4	15	Germany	8,2	8.0–8.5
6	Sweden	9,2	9.1–9.3	16	Hong Kong	8,0	7.1–8.5
7	Switzerland	9,1	8.9–9.2	17	Belgium	7,5	7.1–8.0
8	Norway	8,9	8.6–9.1	18	Ireland	7,5	7.2–7.9
9	Australia	8,8	8.4–9.1	19	USA	7,5	6.9–8.0
10	Netherlands	8,7	8.5–8.9	20	Chile	7,4	7.0–7.8

Source: Transparency International, http://www.transparency.org/cpi/2004/cpi2004.en.html#cpi2004

*CPI score relates to perceptions of the degree of corruption as seen by business people and country analysts and ranges between 10 (highly clean) and 0 (highly corrupt).

**Confidence range provides a range of possible values of the CPI score. This reflects how a country's score may vary, depending on measurement precision. Nominally, with 5 pecent probability the score is above this range and with another 5 percent it is below. However, particularly when only few sources (n) are available an unbiased estimate of the mean coverage probability is lower than the nominal value of 90 percent.

II, most takeovers of MNE facilities have occurred in LDCs, particularly in Latin America. Since the early 1970s, manufacturing facilities have been the most susceptible to government takeover.[27] Beyond these more dramatic events, government instability can render substantial changes in MNE taxation, product pricing, employment of managers from the MNE's corporate headquarters, and other important aspects of doing business.

Government instability and the uncertainty of other elements of the political environment introduce a degree of *political risk* into an MNE's operations in a host country. **Political risk** refers to unanticipated changes in the host country's political environment that affect MNE operations. *Macro risk* involves political changes that affect all MNEs operating in a host country; *micro risk* is changes that affect certain industries or firms.

▶ **political risk** Unanticipated changes in the host country's political environment that affect MNE operations; can be macro (affecting all MNEs in a host country) or micro (affecting only certain industries or firms).

▶ *Management Focus* on **Ethics**

Bribery in the Real World

Wayne Black working out of Miami was contacted by officials of a South American country. The officials said they wanted help with a money laundering investigation. He agreed to terms, but the trouble suddenly started. After Black gave his fee for service proposal an official asked him to double the fees and then pay him the extra as a kickback. Black declined and reported the incident to U.S. authorities.

As the example illustrates, bribery is still an accepted part of conducting business in many markets. Until 2000, a number of countries, including Sweden, Australia, and New Zealand, actually allowed domestic firms that paid bribes overseas to declare them as routine business expenses on their tax returns.

U.S. companies for over twenty-five years have been dissuaded from using bribery by the U.S. Foreign Corrupt Practices Act, which outlaws such activity by any firm based in the United States. The reduction in bribery is important to all firms.

It is estimated that U.S. firms lose as much as $30 billion each year because their competitors pay bribes to receive business contracts and deals.

All U.S. firms are not innocent. One method creative U.S. firms use is to set up a distributor network where a local partner handles the money. For example, some U.S. firms are a guise for building irrigation dams for a country's citizens as a payoff for receiving the business.

Bribery and unethical behavior is a world problem, not just a particular country, company, or industry issue. To combat the temptation, companies prepare clear policy statements and guidelines spelling out that illicit activity of any kind is prohibited.

Source: Adapted from Erika Murphy, "Grease Busting," *Global Business Magazine,* January 2001 (www.globalbusinessmag.com).

Saudi Arabia's nationalization of all foreign operations in the country's oil industry in 1974 is one example of micro political change.[28]

terrorism The use or threat of use of violence for political purposes.

Terrorism is an increasingly important element of political risk abroad and at home. **Terrorism** can be defined as "the use or threat of use, of anxiety inducing . . . violence for political purposes. . . ."[29] International terrorism has assumed many forms such as attacks on military bases, airplane hijackings, crashing airplanes into buildings, the bombing of foreign embassies, and the kidnapping of political officials and business executives.

Although acts of terrorism are usually highly publicized, the actual number of terrorist incidents worldwide is not substantial. In deciding whether to establish operations in a country, few MNEs neglect the presence of political risk. Rather, most conduct **political risk analysis** that involves identifying and assessing the sources of risk and the probabilities that adverse political change will occur in the prospective host country. Several methods of analysis are available. Some MNEs visit the prospect host country and meet with government officials, business executives, and other nationals to obtain their own firsthand assessment of the political environment. There are many services that measure country risk, including:

political risk analysis Identification and assessment of the sources of political risk and the probabilities that adverse political change will occur in a particular location.

- Bank of America World Information Services
- Control Risks Information Services (CRIS)
- Economist Intelligence Unit (EIU)
- Euromoney
- Institutional Investor
- Standard and Poor's Rating Group
- Political Risk Services: International Country Risk Guide (ICRG)
- Political Risk Services: Coplin-O'Leary Rating System
- Moody's Investor Services

Each of the index or rating providers consolidates a range of qualitative and quantitative information into a single index or rating.[30]

Beyond this analysis, MNEs also take actions to hedge against political risk. Some restrict operations to joint ventures where a local partner shares the risk. They may develop the operation by local borrowing, which builds alliances with local banks. MNEs may spread the risk by locating plants in several countries, reducing their dependence on one host country. Many MNEs also obtain insurance policies (available from Lloyd's of London and other companies) that provide coverage against expropriation, damages due to war and terrorism, and other politically related losses.

Companies are also developing strategies for coping with the threat of terrorism. Some MNEs (e.g., IBM and Exxon) are maintaining low profiles in high-risk countries. The U.S. flag is not flown at these facilities. Businesses such as Goodyear Tire and Rubber Co. are reducing the size of corporate signs displayed at their company sites. More companies are boosting security measures at their MNE facilities and hiring counterterrorism consulting firms to train employees in how to deal with a terrorist attack if it occurs.

4-4 Management Functions Applied Globally

The management functions of planning, organizing, leading, and controlling must be applied efficiently (as adapted to the particular situation) in all managerial situations, but particularly globally. How each function can be applied in differing foreign environments is discussed next.

4-4a The Planning Function

The objectives of a multinational enterprise cannot be the same as those of a domestic corporation. There are too many possibilities of conflict between corporate objectives and the economic and political objectives of the countries in which the firm operates. In many

Domestic Setting	Global Setting
Similar culture	Diverse cultures
Limited language differences	Multiple languages
One economic system	Multiple economic systems
One political system	Numerous political systems
One basic legal system	Diverse legal approaches
One monetary system	Multiple monetary systems
Similar markets	Diverse markets

T A B L E 4-3

The Planning Environment in Domestic Versus Global Settings

nations, the role played by government in planning helps heighten the possibility of conflicts with an MNE. For example, Japan's Ministry of International Trade and Industry (MITI) plans the nation's economy to the point of specifying five-year percentage growth rates in exports of specific products.

In certain situations, a country may have objectives—such as a favorable balance of payments or an improved standard of living for its citizens—that do not coincide with the corporate objectives of the MNE. A common source of conflict is that to achieve a profitable objective, some of the foreign subsidiary's earnings must be returned to the MNE's headquarters. This outward flow of earnings could have negative impact on the host country's balance of payments. For this and similar reasons, some nations place restrictions on multinational companies.

Civil servants hold influential positions in foreign bureaucracies. Thus, they often dominate the planning functions of many countries. Managers of multinational companies must become acquainted with the attitudes and practices of these individuals, for an important reason. The civil servants often establish the conditions under which the managers must do their planning.

Table 4-3 presents some of the differences that can complicate the planning environment for a multinational manager. The greater the number of differing factors, the more complex the planning environment.

4-4b The Organizing Function

After a company decides to go multinational and its planning function is well along, it must devise an organizational structure. The structure must provide a network of jobs and authority for achieving the organizational objectives. As with planning, organizational structures in the international arena often must adjust to local conditions. Organizational effectiveness depends greatly on flows of information. And these flows become more difficult to maintain as geographically dispersed decision centers are established. Consequently, an MNE must build effective worldwide communication to transmit information through the organization. Multinational enterprises usually employ the basic organizational structures discussed in Chapter 9.

No organizational structure is suitable in all cases for multinationals or for companies that operate only at home. A multinational company in a high-technology industry, for example, probably would not organize around geographic regions (all functional and operational responsibilities are grouped into geographical areas). More likely, it would use a functional design (major functions such as production, marketing, and finances are managed by an executive team). A company with relatively inexperienced managers, meanwhile, probably would not use a product design (a single unit is assigned the operational responsibilities for a product).

Another factor that influences the organizing function of a multinational company is the degree to which management is home country oriented, host country oriented, or world oriented. How management views itself and the organization will affect how it organizes the firm in foreign countries. Table 4-4 shows how management's particular

T A B L E 4-4

Management Orientation and Impact on the Organization Design

Organization Design	Home Country Oriented	Host Country Oriented	World Oriented
Complexity of organization	Complex in home country, simple in subsidiaries	Varied and independent	Increasingly complex and interdependent
Authority; decision making	High in headquarters	Relatively low in headquarters	Aim for collaborative approach among headquarters and subsidiaries
Evaluation and control	Home standards applied to persons and performance	Determined locally	Find standards that are universal and local
Rewards and punishments; incentives	High in headquarters, low in subsidiaries	Wide variations; can be high or low rewards for subsidiary performance	International and local executives rewarded for reaching local and worldwide objectives
Communication; information flow	High volume to subsidiaries; orders, commands, advice	Little to and from headquarters, little among subsidiaries	Both ways, and among subsidiaries heads of subsidiaries, part of management team
Staffing, recruiting, development	Recruit and develop home country people for key positions everywhere in the world	Develop local people for key positions in their own country	Develop best people everywhere in the world for key positions everywhere in the world

Source: Adapted from Howard V. Perlmutter, "The Tortuous Evolution of the Multinational Corporation," *Columbia Journal of World Business,* January–February 1969, p. 12.

orientation can influence the organizational design. The table also illustrates the impact that the company's orientation can have on decision making, control, performance evaluation, communication, and staffing.

4-4c The Leading Function

Leadership approaches vary in effectiveness from nation to nation because a variety of factors influence styles of leadership and motivation incentives. So effective management of an MNE requires managers to understand the needs and expectations of the people in the nations where the firm operates. Earlier, we noted that attitudes toward work, competition in the workplace, and authority vary greatly among cultures. Thus, leadership styles that might be effective in America, Canada, Great Britain, and parts of Western Europe probably would not work as well in Mexico, Africa, Turkey, Taiwan, or South America.

Because substantial differences can exist between the leadership styles and ways of doing business in many countries, a primary issue in managing the MNE's facility in a host country is whether local or expatriate managers should staff the facility. An expatriate is an MNE employee transferred to the facility from the MNE's home base or from a facility in some other country.

The staffing decision requires evaluating many factors that both favor and disfavor the use of expatriates abroad. Importantly, the use of expatriates ensures that the MNE facility has the necessary managerial skills to oversee the operation. This advantage is noteworthy especially in LDCs where a shortage of managerial skills exists. However, the use of expatriates is much more costly than hiring local managers; many MNEs estimate that expatriates are three times more expensive than are locals. The high costs are due to the double taxing of an expatriate's compensation, and extra costs such as educational and family-related expenses.

Although many MNEs staff a substantial number of management positions with expatriates, the failure rate of U.S. expatriate managers overseas is significant. Experts estimate that on average, 30 percent of all expatriate assignments end in failure, often with the manager returning home sooner than planned.[31] Often the expatriate has a problem adjusting to the cultural and business environment in the host country. Family-related problems are also a frequent factor. Some expatriate managers also lack the special characteristics and abilities that an overseas assignment requires such as communication skills, flexibility, adaptability to change, emotional maturity, and the ability to work with people with different backgrounds, perspectives, and culture. These human relational skills are not emphasized by many MNEs in the selection of individuals for expatriate assignments overseas.[32]

4-4d The Controlling Function

Evaluating and controlling performance is essential to the success of MNEs. Obviously, the more global the operation, the more difficult the controlling function becomes. The control concepts discussed earlier are also applicable to MNEs; however, the control function is not used in some countries to the same degree it is used in the United States because of cultural differences. Such concepts as performance appraisals and quality control may have little meaning in certain countries. But the implementation of control in the international environment requires the same three basic conditions employed domestically: *standards, information,* and *action.*

In establishing **standards** for MNEs, consideration must be given not only to overall corporate objectives but also to local conditions. This often involves bringing local managers into the planning process. As citizens of the country in which they work, these individuals can provide vital input. They can help establish standards of performance that contribute to organizational objectives without causing intercultural conflict.

standards Conditions for control derived from objectives.

Information reporting actual performance and permitting appraisal of that performance against standards is necessary. Problems can occur here that may not appear in domestic organizations. For example, should profitability be measured in local currency or the home currency? The value of different currencies may cause headquarters to arrive at different performance measures than those of local managers. Finally, the long distances involved can cause managers to fill information systems with a great deal of irrelevant information or too much information. Management information systems must be designed or altered to minimize the amount of information necessary for control. New information technologies are providing competitive advantage to those global companies that are able to exploit them.

information Derived from data; essentially, data that are organized for a specific purpose.

Managerial **action** to correct deviations is the final step of the controlling function. The possibilities range from total centralization of decisions (all operating decisions are made at corporate headquarters) to a situation where international units are independent and autonomous. In the majority of cases, most action is taken by international managers with specific guidelines from corporate headquarters.[33] Effective managerial control of a global enterprise is extremely important—and extremely complex.

actions Specified, prescribed means to achieve objectives.

4-5 Global Economic Integration

An important aspect of the expanding global economy is the increased linkages being forged among nations. Regional trade patterns are being influenced by international trading zones or blocs. This pattern of change is most pronounced in Asia and Latin America. Exports among countries in Asia, for example, increased as a percentage of total exports from nearly 45 percent in 1990 to over 56 percent in 2000. Intraregional exports in Latin America rose from 17 percent of all exports in 1990 to 24 percent in 2000.[34]

Formation of the North American Free Trade Agreement (NAFTA), which went into effect in January 1994, has contributed to increased intraregional trade in North America. Merchandise exports among the three NAFTA countries (U.S., Mexico, Canada) increased from 41 percent of total exports in 1990 to over 50 percent in 2000. The U.S. in 2000 exported over $176 billion to Canada and $112 billion to Mexico. The U.S. annually imports about $229 billion from Canada and $135 billion from Mexico.[35] (See Figure 14-3.)

Because the European Union (EU) has been in existence for a longer time than the other regional trading blocs around the world, economic integration through trade in Western Europe is much more advanced. In 1999, the EU exported over $419 billion and imported over $449 billion to and from countries outside the EU.[36]

Global free trade is pursued by countries in a variety of ways, including negotiation of bilateral trade treaties, participation in multilateral trading activities, and formation of a variety of regional trade agreements. Such mechanisms significantly influence the environment within which trade takes place.

4-5a The World Trade Organization

The most broad-based effort to establish a legal and institutional infrastructure for global trade is the World Trade Organization (WTO). The WTO was established in 1995 as the successor to the General Agreement on Tariffs and Trade (GATT). The WTO sets out the principal obligations to be met by governments in implementing domestic trade policies and regulations. The organization also provides a foundation for developing trade relations among countries through negotiations and adjudication.[37]

Two rules form the cornerstone of the WTO. The first is the "most-favored-nation" (MFN) clause. It requires member countries to treat the products of other members no less favorably than they do the products of any other country. The second rule, known as "national treatment," requires that once goods have entered a market, they must be treated no less favorably than the equivalent domestically produced goods.

The WTO has and is dramatically changing the global economy. First, the WTO has a far wider scope than GATT, bringing services, protection of intellectual property rights, and investment into the multilateral trading system. In carrying out its responsibilities, the WTO examines trade polices and member countries' regulations, and reviews proposed measures that could lead to trade conflicts. The organization also provides mechanisms for adjudication of trade disputes that cannot be settled through bilateral negotiations among the affected parties.

4-5b Regional Trade Agreements

Another route to a more open international trade environment is through regional trade agreements (RTAs). The WTO permits RTAs provided that they meet certain strict criteria. RTAs must meet two fundamental criteria. The first is that tariffs or regulations affecting trade of non-RTA member countries with members can be no more restrictive than those that existed before the RTA was established. The second criteria is that RTAs must eliminate barriers between countries on substantially all trade. Today, nearly ninety regional agreements are in place. Five major RTAs are shown in Table 4-5.

A basic question concerning the rapid proliferation of RTAs is whether they will turn out to be building or stumbling blocks in the process of liberalizing trade. Whether an RTA facilitates or impedes global free trade depends in part on how it is designed. Four basic types of regional trade arrangements are:

1. Free trade areas in which member countries reduce or abolish intraregion restrictions on trade while maintaining differential protection against nonmembers—NAFTA is an example.

2. Customs unions, in which the members also establish a common external tariff—MERCOSUR is an example of this type of agreement.

3. Common markets, in which the customs union is extended to free movement of capital, labor, and services—the EU is an example of this type of arrangement.

4. Economic unions, in which national economic policies are also harmonized among members of a common market—such a union does not presently exist, but the EU is moving in this direction.

		TABLE 4-5
Asia-Pacific Economic Cooperation (APEC)	(Australia, Brunei, Canada, Chile, China, Hong Kong, Indonesia, Japan, Malaysia, Mexico, New Zealand, Papua New Guinea, Philippines, Singapore, South Korea, Taiwan, Thailand, United States)	**Major Regional Trade Agreements**
European Union (EU)	(Austria, Belgium, Denmark, Finland, France, Germany, Greece, Ireland, Italy, Luxembourg, Netherlands, Portugal, Spain, Sweden, United Kingdom)	
North American Free Trade Agreement (NAFTA)	(Canada, Mexico, United States)	
Asian Free Trade Area (AFTA)	(Brunei, Indonesia, Malaysia, Philippines, Singapore, Thailand)	
MERCOSUR	(Argentina, Bolivia, Brazil, Chile, Paraguay, Uruguay)	

4-5c Business Process Outsourcing

Business process outsourcing (BPO) is defined simply as the movement of business processes from inside the organization to an external service provider.[38] With the global telecommunications infrastructure now well established and consistently reliable, BPO initiatives often include shifting work to international providers. Five BPO international hot spots have emerged, although firms from many other countries specialize in various business processes and exporting services:

1. *India.* Engineering and technical
2. *China.* Manufacturing and technical
3. *Mexico.* Manufacturing
4. *United States.* Analysis and creative
5. *Philippines.* Administrative

Each of these countries has complex economies that span the range of business activities, but from a BPO perspective, they have comparative advantages in the specific functions cited.

Because of the job shift that accompanies the quest to employ the highest-value talent, BPO has been both hailed and vilified. Business executives and owners praise it as a way to eliminate business processes that are not part of their organization's core competence. Back-office functions, such as payroll and benefits administration, customer service, call center, and technical support, are just a few of the processes that organizations of all sizes have been able to outsource to others who specialize in those areas. Removing these functions from their internal operations enables organizations to reduce payroll and other overhead. In an era when executives have been admonished by business commentators and analysts to focus on core competencies, BPO offers an opportunity to achieve that goal in a dramatic new way.

Like appliance manufacturers that moved production from the Midwest to Mexican *maquiladoras* or apparel firms that moved production to the Far East, businesses of all types and sizes are now shifting back-office jobs to international locations such as China, India, and the Philippines, where labor is inexpensive and highly skilled. In the past several years, companies have turned to these regions for increasingly sophisticated tasks such as financial analysis, software design, tax preparation, and even the creation of content-rich products (e.g., newsletters, PowerPoint presentations, and sales kits).

In the next fifteen years, Forrester Research predicts that 3.3 million service jobs will move to countries such as India, Russia, China, and the Philippines. That is the equivalent of 7.5 percent of all jobs in the United States right now.[39] Estimates from leading research firms more than support this trend. The Gartner Group, a Stamford, Connecticut–based research firm, predicts that:

- One in ten jobs at specialty information technology (IT) firms in the United States will move abroad by 2005, along with one in twenty IT jobs in general businesses—a loss of about 560,000 positions.

- BPO will reach $178 billion in revenues worldwide by 2005, representing a compound annual growth rate of 9.2 percent for the five-year forecast period.[40]

Additionally, market research firm IDC predicts that finance and accounting outsourcing will grow to nearly $65 billion by 2006, up from $36 billion in 2001. Two thirds of U.S. banks already outsource one or more functions.[41]

4-5d Implications for the United States

While the benefits of increased economic integration are widely acknowledged today, a major question concerns the extent to which the United States will participate in further integration activities, especially the formation and development of RTAs.

NAFTA, the development of the Free Trade Area of the Americas, and the Asia-Pacific Economic Cooperation forum are examples of increasing economic integration that will benefit the United States. The recently concluded telecommunications and information technology agreements, under the aegis of the WTO, are examples of other trade agreements that probably wouldn't have been achieved without U.S. leadership.[42]

Regardless of whether the move toward increased economic integration among countries is through regionalization or globalization, the nature of competition for private sector companies is changing. The traditional domestic market is coming to encompass at least those countries in the same regional trade arrangement. Companies within an RTA are becoming, in effect, domestic competitors. U.S. companies must begin to rethink their strategies for the domestic market, since they will not be subject to competition from new companies that are located outside of the country.

Management Summary

- The global enterprise, or multinational enterprise (MNE), presents a challenge to future managers—the challenge to perform the managerial functions effectively in a global environment.

- The decision to become an MNE involves determining the global market to be served, the products or services to be produced and marketed, and the strategy of entry into the selected market.

- The MNE decision requires evaluating the primary characteristics of a global setting—its cultural, economic, and political environments.

- Differences in culture can result in differing attitudes toward the importance of work, competition, authority, material possessions, risk taking, time, profits, and other factors.

- Economic differences in income levels, growth trends, inflation rates, balance of payments, and the stability of the currency and overall economy can significantly affect MNE performance.

- A government's attitude toward imports and direct investment, and government efficiency and stability are important characteristics of a country's political environment.

- Regional trading agreements provide the legal and regulatory infrastructure for free and fair international trade.

Key Terms

actions (p. 91)
culture (p. 82)
developed country (DC) (p. 83)
direct investment entry strategy (p. 81)
expatriate (p. 82)
export entry strategy (p. 79)
expropriation (p. 86)

foreign subsidiary entry strategy (p. 79)
information (p. 91)
joint venture (p. 79)
less-developed country (LDC) (p. 83)
licensing (p. 79)
multinational enterprise (MNE) (p. 77)
nationalization (p. 86)

phased internationalization (p. 78)
political risk (p. 87)
political risk analysis (p. 88)
shot-in-the-dark method (p. 78)
standards (p. 91)
terrorism (p. 88)

Review and Discussion Questions

1. What major factors motivate a company to become a global organization? Discuss and provide examples of firms making this decision.

2. Do you believe you would be effective as an expatriate manager? If so, discuss why. If not, identify and discuss the reasons why.

3. The chapter discusses cultural, economic, and political aspects of the international environment that substantially affect the performance of an MNE. Are there other factors? Discuss.

4. Is it correct to assume that U.S. firms engage in no bribery, less bribery, or more bribery incidents than non-U.S. firms?

5. Do the social responsibilities of managerial actions differ for MNEs in their domestic and international operations? Discuss.

6. Of the four managerial functions (planning, organizing, leading, controlling), which function do you believe is the most challenging to effectively perform as an MNE in different global environments? Explain.

7. Many risk experts assert that accurate political risk analysis is a very difficult task. Why?

8. Has NAFTA been a successful agreement for the United States? Mexico, Canada? Explain your conclusion.

9. "How effective an individual is in international management will be determined by how well he or she can adjust to local conditions." Do you agree? Discuss.

10. What international challenges face companies such as McDonald's, Compaq, and Cisco?

Practice Quiz

Note: You can find the correct answers to these questions by taking the quiz and then submitting your answers in the Online Edition. The program will automatically score your submission. If you miss a question, the program will provide the correct answer, a rationale for the answer, and the section number in the chapter where the topic is discussed.

Indicate whether the sentence or statement is true or false.

_____ 1. A firm doing business in two or more countries is known as **a national market enterprise.**

_____ 2. The United States is the world's largest exporter, but it imports more than it exports.

_____ 3. **Local government** has the greatest influence on the attitudes of individuals concerning the importance of work, authority, material possessions, competition, time, profit, risk taking, and decision making.

_____ 4. Until 2000, Sweden, Australia, New Zealand, France, and Great Britain allowed payment of bribes abroad during business dealings to be tax deductible.

_____ 5. The **World Trade Organization** provides mechanisms for adjudication of trade disputes that cannot be settled though bilateral negotiations among the affected parties.

Identify the letter of the choice that best completes the statement or answers the question.

_____ 6. McDonald's opens nearly 2,000 new restaurants each year, of which _____ are outside the United States.
a. about 250
b. about 500
c. about 900
d. about 1,600

_____ 7. Which of the following is NOT one of the three essential decisions that a company must make before entering the global marketplace?
a. which international market to enter
b. the products or services to be marketed
c. the mode of entry into the international market
d. which currencies to support

_____ 8. As one moves along the continuum from exporting to direct investment, commitment to the venture and control over international operations increases. However, _____ also increases.
a. market share
b. competition
c. risk
d. profit share

_____ 9. _____ hold influential positions in foreign bureaucracies and often dominate the planning functions of many countries.
a. Judges
b. Civil servants
c. Religious leaders
d. Teachers

_____ 10. Leadership approaches vary in effectiveness from nation to nation because leadership styles and motivation incentives are influenced by a variety of factors, including _____.
a. attitudes toward work.
b. competition in the workplace.
c. authority.
d. all of the above.

_____ 11. Which of the following was cited as the least corrupt nation in the 2004 Corruption Perceptions Index?
a. United States
b. Russia
c. Finland
d. Iraq

_____ 12. The _____ provides a foundation for developing trade relations among countries.
a. World Trade Organization
b. General Agreement on Tariffs and Trade
c. Regional Trade Agreement
d. Multinational Enterprise

_____ **13.** _____ is defined as the movement of business processes from inside the business to external service providers.
a. Global free trade
b. Regional trade agreement
c. Business process outsourcing
d. Global economic integration

_____ **14.** Designing a product or service for international expansion based on product and market research in the destination country is termed _____.
a. business process outsourcing.
b. shot-in-the-dark method.
c. exporting.
d. phased internationalization.

_____ **15.** When a firm negotiates a _____ agreement, it is granting the right to produce the firm's product to an outside company.
a. joint venture
b. direct investment
c. licensing
d. outsourcing

Case Study

Metropolitan Life Benefits from Global Outsourcing Strategy

Metropolitan Life Insurance (MetLife) is the largest life insurer in the United States with approximately $2.1 trillion in life insurance policies, nearly 50,000 employees worldwide, and serving 10 million households as well as 88 of the Fortune 100 companies. Despite its size and financial wealth, MetLife had not invested in IT upgrades to its back office processes. As late as 1999, most of its claims processing was paper based and accomplished manually. Its workflow was redundant and its call center operated at less than optimal levels. According to Carlos Creamer, Vice President of Strategic Operations, an average claim took 10 days to process. MetLife decided to look into outsourcing to improve its product offerings and overall claims processing performance.

In 1999 when Creamer interviewed outsourcing candidates, he learned that Affiliated Computer Services, Inc. (ACS) of Dallas, Texas, processes the claims of 8 out of the top 10 healthcare providers in the world, a total of 500 million claims per year. ACS processes claims anywhere from three to nine times faster, from 25 to 75 percent cheaper, and 35 to 40 percent more accurately than MetLife's in-house operations. After interviewing other candidates, MetLife chose ACS because they stood apart from the competition in mail imaging and data capture and were among the leading bids in terms of pricing.

ACS now processes a MetLife claim online in a matter of seconds, not days. MetLife claims arrive at ACS's mailroom in Lexington, Kentucky, where they are opened and prepped for scanning. As an example of how having claims processing as a core competence leads to process innovation, consider that ACS sands the edges off the envelopes it receives instead of slicing them open. Slicing envelopes tends to cut up internal documents which then have to be taped together again before scanning, which adds another step to the workflow.

Once the staff scans the document, the image is almost simultaneously sent offshore for data capture via ACS's proprietary satellite network. ACS has disaster prevention practices in place, including never sending more than 50 percent of a client's work to one offshore location. MetLife preferred this system to other BPO providers who were limited to a single location, or who had no backup or recovery mechanism.

ACS has offshore operations in Ghana, Mexico, Guatemala, and China. When claims arrive at these centers, a single operator keys in the data from the digitized image of the claim and another operator independently keys it in again. The system automatically compares the two versions to verify that there is no difference in the information.

The ACS method has saved MetLife time and money. MetLife did not have imaging technology in-house, so it could not process the claims online. With ACS's imaging system, scanning and image routing happens in seconds. Also, ACS's automated workflow is so precise it drives significant time and cost out of the processing cycle. ACS also pays less for offshore labor and passes on the savings to MetLife. The ACS solution includes a productivity-based compensation model that pays workers on a piece-rate schedule.

To gauge the improvement in processing, MetLife benchmarked its dental claims processing. Prior to outsourcing, the company was processing less than 80 percent of dental claims in 10 days. Now it is well over 95 percent during the same period. As a result, Creamer says MetLife has experienced "a significant improvement in customer satisfaction." What's more, he concludes, "our ROI is huge and we are very pleased."

In this case, MetLife is working with an onshore firm to leverage low-cost offshore labor, reducing overall processing costs. MetLife does not have direct interaction with the offshore team. This distance between the BPO buyer and the offshore vendor can be useful as it relies on the onshore vendor to develop the cultural sensitivities and management techniques appropriate to the offshore labor pool. At the same time, there are additional costs associated with engaging an onshore intermediary. The BPO buyer must assess whether these additional upfront costs are offset by the costs that would be associated with developing the necessary international management expertise. Later, we'll look at a case where the BPO buyer did interact directly with the offshore vendor in an outsourcing deal that didn't work as planned.

Questions for Discussion

1. What do you think of using low-cost foreign labor for service jobs that used to be held by domestic workers? Explain.

2. What are the potential challenges of setting up a business process thousands of miles from the business center?

3. What are the advantages—other than lower costs—of using an outsourcing model to manage claims processing? Explain.

Source: John Harney, "Staking a Claim to Excellence with Offshore Outsourcing," *OutsourcingOffshore.com*, March 2003. Reprinted with permission from Outsourcing Center, www.outsourcing-center.com.

Internet Exercise

Prepare a Short Report

Prepare a two-page report on different issues using only the Internet as the source for writing a few comments on each item.

1. What is the most recent inflation rate in Nigeria, Brazil, and Russia?

2. What is the cost of a McDonald's hamburger in Budapest, Nigeria, and Cancun?

3. What are the largest three companies in the world based on sales revenue?

4. Explain the Berne Convention for the Protection of Literacy and Artistic Works.

Experiential Exercise

Launching an International Business

Purpose: This activity is designed to enhance your understanding of the key elements of the international environment and its impact on expanding a business internationally.

Setting Up the Exercise: The instructor will divide the class into groups comprised of four students each. Each group should complete the following project:

1. Assume that your group is the top-management team of a manufacturing company. Your team's first task is to select a product that your company manufactures. Once you've selected the product, assume that your company makes the product domestically and wants to expand production overseas. Specifically, your company seeks to produce and sell the product in a Latin American, European, or Asian country.

2. Select a country for your international expansion. Once you've identified the nation, conduct an assessment of the country as an international market for your product. Do so by:

   a. Conducting library research on the cultural, economic, and political aspects of the country's environment.

   b. In reviewing your research, answer the following questions:

- What is the level of demand for your product in this potential market?
- In what ways do the cultural, economic, and political aspects of the country's environment facilitate the success of your product in the market?
- In what ways do these environmental aspects hinder the success of your product?
- In your team's opinion, what are the primary challenges in establishing manufacturing facilities and launching your product in this market?

3. Prepare a five- to seven-page typed report that provides an overall profile of your selected market and presents your responses to these questions. Be prepared to discuss your overall findings in class discussion.

A Learning Note: This exercise effectively illustrates the importance of the international environment in launching manufacturing and marketing activities in an international market. Students should quickly realize the complexities involved in expanding business abroad, which is one major reason why a number of overseas ventures fail.

Planning

Part 2 contains three chapters, which are based on the following rationale. The planning function of management involves managers in activities that lead them to identify objectives and to determine strategies for achieving those objectives. Planning has become increasingly important as organizations and their environments have become more complex.

Chapter 5 describes the four elements that are present in any form of planning.

Chapter 6 presents an important planning approach in today's rapidly changing environment—strategic planning. Strategic analysis focuses on the organization's environment and the appropriate responses (strategies) to changes, constraints, and opportunities in that environment.

Chapter 7 discusses planning in the context of decision making. The material in this chapter presents several perspectives on decision making, including the relationship between managerial levels and types of decisions made at each level, and the relationship between degree of uncertainty and decision criteria. Planning requires choices of objectives and decisions. Decision making is, therefore, an inherent feature of planning.

Figure 5-1 presents the four aspects of the planning function. Although these aspects are presented sequentially, it is important to understand that they actually interact.

Elements of Planning

5

Managing Today

News on Planning and Forecasting

In the winter of 2003, swarms of shoppers invaded Restoration Hardware clamoring for one of the holiday season's hottest items: a sleek red cabinet with 25 tiny drawers that counted down the days to December 25—Christmas. But in the middle of the shopping season the cabinet sold out.

Restoration Hardware reported that holiday sales were down by 3.5 percent. The problem was accurately planning for and predicting demand. Demand forecasting is very difficult. Yet with 27 percent of U.S. retail sales occurring in the fourth quarter, the consequences of misguided holiday forecasts are painful. Business planners routinely misread the market.

A growing number of companies are turning to new technology and techniques to improve their planning and forecasting. Warner Home Video, for example, found its sales projections for individual DVDs were off by about 40 percent the previous year. The company purchased enterprise software provider SAS's statistical modeling applications to weigh variables such as genre, stars, box office, and audience demographics when making title specific forecasts.

Companies often blame forecasting gaffes on unseasonable weather. Coca-Cola Bottling, Ann Taylor, and Bob Evans have blamed weather for missing forecasts. Plannbytes is a firm that helps manufacturers and retailers figure out how sales will be impacted by weather. Some firms use forecasting software from Manugistics, SAS, and Steelwedge to plan, anticipate, and predict the future more accurately. As the software is used and evaluated it is expected that more organizations will adopt more refined software in the future. There are even companies such as Best Buy, IBM, and Procter & Gamble who are attempting to work together to create a collaborative planning and forecasting standard. This standard (see www.cpfr.org) provides guidelines for sharing data across the supply chain.

Source: Adapted from Laura Rich, "The Follies of Holiday Forecasting," *Business 2.0,* November 2004, pp. 90–92.

Planning is a vital and necessary management function. This point is made in the Managing Today opening vignette illustrating how some organizations are addressing planning and forecasting problem solving. The functions of organizing, leading, and controlling all carry out the objectives and goals determined through planning. The importance of planning can be seen readily in the great number of executive conferences, workshops, and writings on the subject.

Although some environments are less predictable than others, *all* organizations operate in uncertain environments. For an organization to succeed, management somehow must cope with and adapt to change and uncertainty.[1] Planning is one tool management has to help it adapt to change. If an organization does no planning, its position and fate in the future will mostly be the result of any momentum built up previously and of luck. On its own the organization would follow some kind of course during a specific period of time. If management wishes to have any control over that course, however, it *must* plan. Otherwise, it will have to rely on defensive reactions rather than on planned actions. Management will be forced to respond to current pressures rather than making choices based on the organization's long-run goals.

In one way or another, every manager plans. However, the approach to planning, the manner of arriving at plans, and the completeness of plans can differ greatly from organization to organization. Formal planning (as distinguished from the informal planning that we do in thinking through proposed actions prior to their execution) is an activity that distinguishes managers from nonmanagers. Formal planning also distinguishes effective managers from ineffective ones.

If you want to effectively manage the performance of individuals and organizations you must understand the concept of, and the necessity for, planning. Planning is that part of the management process which attempts to define the organization's future.[2] More formally, *planning includes all the activities that lead to the definition of objectives and to the determination of appropriate courses of action to achieve those objectives.*

To justify the time and resources expended in planning, distinct benefits must accrue to the planner.[3] Three major benefits include:

1. Planning forces managers to think ahead.
2. It leads to the development of performance standards that enable more effective management control.

3. Having to formulate plans forces management to articulate clear objectives.
4. Planning enables an organization to be better prepared for sudden developments.

5-1 Understanding the Need for Planning

You cannot develop a sound plan at any level of an organization without first understanding and appreciating the *necessity* for planning. If a manager does not believe in the value of planning (and some managers do not), it is unlikely that he or she will develop a useful plan.

To better appreciate the need for planning, consider the following four important factors (see Figure 5-1).

5-1a Increasing Time Spans Between Present Decisions and Future Results

The time span separating the beginning of a project and its completion is increasing in most organizations. Managers today must look further into the future than ever before. For example, it took ten years to develop the supersonic jet and ten years for General Foods to develop Maxim, a concentrated instant coffee. Meanwhile, Campbell Soup Company spent twenty years in developing a line of dry soup mixes, and Hills Brothers worked twenty-two years to develop its instant coffee.

Obviously, planning becomes very critical in situations where the results of decisions will occur long after the decisions actually are made. So managers must attempt to consider what *could* happen that might affect the desired outcome. Effective planning can require large commitments of time and money, but management must seek every way possible to minimize uncertainty and its consequences.

5-1b Increasing Organization Complexity

As organizations become larger and more complex, the manager's job also becomes bigger and more complicated by the interdependence among the organization's various parts. It is virtually impossible to find an organization (or even a division of a large organization) in which the decisions of the various functions, such as research and development, production, finance, and marketing, can be made independently of one another. The more products an organization offers and the more markets it competes in, the greater the volume of its decisions. Planning, in these circumstances, becomes even more important for survival.

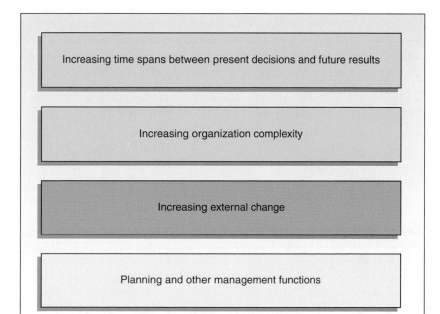

Figure 5-1
Four Important Factors to Appreciate the Need for Planning

Planning enables each unit in the organization to define the job that needs to be done and the way to go about doing it. With such a blueprint of *objectives,* there is less likelihood of changing direction, costly improvising, or making mistakes. Planning should also develop a set of business values. A system that is only driven by business objectives can become dysfunctional if it leads to win-at-all-costs behaviors. Objectives must be tempered by values so that employees know not only what the company intends to achieve but also how it intends to achieve it.[4]

5-1c Increasing External Change

A major role of managers has always been that of change initiator. A manager must be an innovator and doer, someone in constant search of new markets, businesses, and expanded missions. Rapid rates of change in the external environment will force managers at all levels to focus on larger issues rather than solely on solving internal problems. The faster the pace of change becomes, the greater the necessity for organized responses at all levels in the organization.[5] And organized responses spring from well-thought-out plans. Organizational complexity sometimes leaves managers feeling as if things are out of control. However, many practicing managers are finding that that isn't necessarily bad. By using sound planning processes unexpected opportunities can be brought under control and become profitable.

5-1d Planning and Other Management Functions

The need for planning also is illustrated by the relationship between planning and the other management functions. Before a manager can organize, lead, or control, he or she must have a plan. Otherwise, these activities have no purpose or direction. Clearly defined objectives and well-developed strategies set the other management functions into motion.

The effect of planning on the other management functions can be understood by considering its influence on the function of control. Once a plan has been translated from intentions into actions, its relationship to the control function becomes obvious. As time passes, managers can compare actual results with the planned results. The comparisons can lead to corrective action, and this, as we shall see later in the book, is the essence of controlling.

5-2 Types of Planning

Although all effective planning focuses on the customer and on issues of quality and competitiveness, planning activity differs in scope, time frame, and level of detail. **Scope** refers to the range of activities covered by the plan. **Time frame** is the period considered by the plan, ranging from short term to long term. **Level of detail** concerns the specificity of the plan. All plans must be specific enough to direct actual decisions, but multiple contingencies and uncertain futures require some plans to be more general than others.

5-2a Strategic, Operational, and Tactical Planning

Strategic planning is comprehensive, long term, and relatively general (the content of the next chapter). Strategic plans focus on the broad, enduring issues for ensuring a firm's effectiveness over a long period of time. A strategic plan typically states the organization's mission and may describe a set of goals to move a company into the future. For example, it may describe a mission of world leadership in a particular product or service area and set specific goals that are designed to help achieve that mission. Toyota and other Japanese firms are well known for their long-term strategic plans, sometimes looking ahead up to thirty years. Toyota's president, Hiroshi Okuda, expressed his view on the company's strategic outlook, "Everything we are doing today is intended to make Toyota a stronger competitor, a more innovative designer, a more cost-competitive manufacturer, and a more aggressive marketer tomorrow."[6] An example of the work that goes into strategic or long-term planning is presented in the Management Focus on Globalization box, "Planning for the Future."

▶**scope** The range of activities that a plan covers.

▶**time frame** The period considered by a plan, ranging from short term to long term.

▶**level of detail** The amount of specificity in a plan.

▶**strategic planning** The activities that lead to the definition of objectives for the entire organization and to the determination of appropriate strategies for achieving those objectives.

Management Focus on Globalization

Planning for the Future

In India the local subsidiary of Dutch giant Unilever, www.unilever.com, the world's largest consumer-products manufacturer, is Hindustan Lever, (www.hll.com). The local company sells its soaps and detergents to every corner of India. It is now developing plans to use the firm's creativity and infrastructure to market its products to a largely overlooked group of consumers: the rural poor of India.

Venky Venkatesh is a regional sales manager (his region has 200 million people), and he is hard at work on a plan to satisfy customer needs. He talks to merchants, visits stores, and uses his IBM (www.ibm.com) Thinkpad to track the facts and demographics of his region.

Venky believes that the giant Unilever, by developing and executing a sound plan, can be a major force in his region, especially among poor customers. Many companies sell low-quality products at cheap prices to poor customers. This is not in Unilever's plan. Unilever predicts that by 2010, half of it sales will come from the developing world. The rural people of India and other countries offer a vast untapped market.

What Venky and others at Unilever are developing are plans and tactics to reach the rural people. The plan and its execution are considered a crucial growth opportunity. In the plan lower prices is only one part. The key to the plan is to creatively find a way to develop products that do more with less. Venky and Hindustan Lever see opportunities where most companies see only problems.

Source: Adapted from Reicha Balic, "Strategic Innovation: Hindustan Lever," *Fast Company,* June 2001, pp. 120–124.

Operational plans are focused, short term, and specific. **Operational planning** translates the broad concepts of the strategic plan into clear numbers, specific steps, and measurable objectives for the short term. Operational planning requires efficient, cost-effective application of resources to solving problems and meeting objectives. Increasingly, companies are relying on information technology to assist in their operational planning. Heineken U.S.A., for example, installed a system called HOPS (Heineken Operational Planning System) that combines forecasting with real-time replenishment of supplies and allows for secure communications with business partners over the Internet.[7]

Tactical planning falls on the continuum between the strategic and operational planning processes. The tactical planning in an organization is more specific than strategic planning. Tactical plans deal more with issues of efficiency than with long-term effectiveness. Although some theorists counsel a strong distinction between the different levels of planning, research has shown that organizational effectiveness declines for companies that don't integrate, to some extent, the various types of planning. For example, General Motors (www.gm.com) found that its performance declined when it instituted a regimen that called for a strict distinction between strategic and tactical planning.[8]

The type of goals and/or objectives to be achieved by the plan determines the type of planning managers engage in. Not all managers are involved in the three types of planning described (see the Learning Moment box, "Types of Plans"). In general, higher management levels deal with plans with longer time frames, greater scope, and less detail than

> **operational planning**
> Translates the broad concepts of a strategic plan into clear numbers, specific steps, and measurable objectives for the short term.

> **tactical planning** Planning that deals more with issues of efficiency than with long-term effectiveness.

LearningMoment   *Types of Plans*

There are library lists of the types of plans managers need and use. A concise categorization indicates three main plan areas: strategic, operational, and tactical. Strategic planning takes a long-term view and is somewhat predictive. Where will the company be five, six, ten years from now? On the other hand, operational plans are the real-time, now type. Numbers, dates, and amounts are presented and are linked to the long-term view. The tactical plan is more of an intermediary snapshot of needs to be accomplished. Each of the three types of plans should be linked to each other. Showing how the operational and tactical plans can result in the success of the strategic plan is a challenge for managers in their communications with their bosses.

lower level managers. This is changing somewhat today as more and more firms develop participative management where all levels of managers contribute to long-range plans. Participation usually doesn't work in reverse, however. It would be highly unusual, for example, for a company executive to be involved in short-range tactical planning.

5-2b Single-Use and Standing Plans

single-use plans Plans with a clear time frame for their usefulness; includes detailed goals and objectives concerning quality, primary markets, rollout schedule, and so on.

Single-use plans have a clear time frame for their usefulness. For example, a task force may be established to plan the development of a new product. This single-use plan will include detailed goals and objectives concerning quality, primary markets, rollout schedule, and the like. The plan will become obsolete, however, if the firm fails to act to achieve the designated objectives.

standing plan A plan that has ongoing meaning and applications for an organization.

A **standing plan,** in contrast, has ongoing meaning and applications for an organization. A good example is the U.S. Constitution (www.usconstitution.net). This standing plan for the organization of American government and jurisprudence has provided guidance for over 200 years. Management and leadership scholar Burt Nanus wrote, "The Constitution is a written description of the founding fathers' vision for the United States, setting a clear direction and defining values but not specifying how to get there."[9] Although many single-use plans are within the parameters of the Constitution, the Constitution remains as a regulator of the powers and discretion of government.

5-3 The Elements of Planning

The planning function requires managers to make decisions about four fundamental elements of plans:

1. Objectives
2. Actions
3. Resources
4. Implementation

Objectives are integral to plans because they specify future conditions that the planner deems satisfactory. For example, the statement. "The firm's objective is to achieve a 12 percent rate of return on invested capital by the end of 2006" refers to a future, satisfactory condition.

Actions are the specified, preferred means to achieve the objectives. The preferred course of action to lead to a 12 percent return might be to engage in a product development effort so that five new products are introduced in 2006.

Resources are constraints on the courses of action. For example: "The total cost to be incurred in the development of five new products must not exceed $10 million." A plan should specify the kinds and amounts of resources required, as well as the potential sources and allocations of those resources. Specifying resource constraints also involves budgeting—identifying the sources and levels of resources that can be committed to planned courses of action.

Finally, a plan must include ways and means to implement the intended actions. *Implementation* involves the assignment and direction of personnel to carry out the plan.

Establishing objectives and prescribing actions requires *forecasting* the future. Managers cannot plan without explicit consideration of future events and contingencies that could affect what will be possible to accomplish.

Although the four elements of the planning function are discussed separately, they are in fact intertwined. As will be seen, objectives must be set according to what is possible, given the forecasts of the future *and* the budgets of resources. Moreover, availability of resources can be affected by the very actions that management plans. In the previous example, if a 12 percent return is not achieved, $10 million may not be available, because stockholders, bondholders, or other sources of capital will not invest the funds. Then, other action may not be feasible.

In some organizations, planning is the combined effort of managers and staff personnel. In other organizations, planning is done by the top-management group. In still oth-

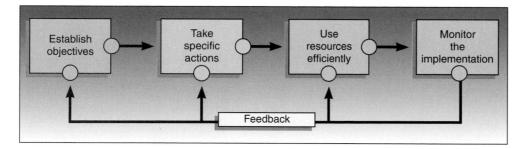

Figure 5-2
The Planning Process

ers, it is done by one individual. Planning activities can range from complex, formal procedures to simple and informal ones. Although the *form* of planning activities varies from organization to organization, the *substance* is the same. Plans and planning inherently involve objectives, actions, resources, and implementation directed toward improving an organization's performance in the future. Figure 5-2 outlines the planning process.

5-3a Objectives

The planning function begins with the determination of future objectives, which must satisfy expectations of the organization's environment. Whether the organization is a business, a university, or a government agency, the environment supplies the resources that sustain it. In exchange for these resources, the organization must supply the environment with goods and services at an acceptable price and quality. Because of the increasing interdependence between organizations and their environments, corporate management in firms like Honda, IBM, and General Mills has turned more and more to formal planning techniques. Moreover, it is clear that organizations that use formal approaches to planning are more profitable than those that do not.[10] Management initiates planning to determine the *priority* and *timing* of objectives. In addition, management also must resolve *conflict* between objectives and provide *measurement* of objectives so results can be evaluated.[11]

Priority of Objectives The phrase *priority of objectives* implies that at a given time, accomplishing one objective is more important than accomplishing any of the others. For example, the objective of maintaining a minimum cash balance may be more important than achieving minimum profitability to a firm struggling to meet payrolls and due dates on accounts. Priority of objectives also reflects the relative importance of certain objectives, regardless of time. For example, survival of the organization is necessary for the realization of all other objectives.

Managers must establish priorities if they want to allocate resources rationally. Alternative objectives must be evaluated and ranked. Managers of nonbusiness organizations are particularly concerned with the ranking of seemingly interdependent objectives. For example, a university president must determine the relative importance of teaching, research, and community service. Determining objectives and priorities is inherently a judgmental decision—and is inherently difficult. British Airways, for example, had to decide it was going to establish globalization as a priority.

To establish appropriate objectives and priorities, many firms use an approach called the **balanced scorecard.** The balanced scorecard provides a balanced picture of current operating performance as well as the drivers of future performance. The scorecard helps managers align their business units, as well as their financial, physical, and human resources, to the company's overall strategy. Companies that use the balanced scorecard approach in this way can strengthen the links between their overall strategy and the programs they implement to attain their goals.[12]

There is a growing consensus that financial indicators on their own are neither an adequate measure of competitiveness nor a guide to future performance. A solution to this is the balanced scorecard. The balanced scorecard still includes the hard financial indicators, but it balances these with other so-called soft measures such as customer acquisition, retention, profitability, and satisfaction; product development cycle times; employee satisfaction; intellectual assets; and organizational learning. Proponents of the balanced

> **balanced scorecard**
> An approach to establishing appropriate objectives and priorities by presenting a balanced picture of current operating performance and the drivers of future performance.

scorecard approach see it as a way of implementing strategy, linking strategy to action, and making strategy understandable to those on the front line as well as to senior managers.[13]

Time Frame of Objectives The role time plays in planning is demonstrated in a practice common to many organizations. They develop different plans for different periods of time. For instance, the long-run objective of a business firm could be stated in terms of a desired rate of return on capital, with intermediate and short-run plans stated in terms of objectives that must be accomplished to realize the ultimate goal. Management is then in a position to know the effectiveness of each year's activities in terms of achieving not only short-run but also long-run objectives.

A bank might consider a long-term loan as one for more than five years and a short-term loan as one for less than one year. Some individuals apply the same logic to planning. In practice, definitions of long-run and short-run plans vary widely. A long-run plan in the aircraft or automobile business could extend to more than five years, while in the volatile world of women's fashion, a long-run plan might extend to only one or two years. In the children's toy business, a production or marketing plan might cover only one selling season. In other words, the organization's product, technology, and market will dictate what long-term and short-term plans are. Here you can see the contingent nature of managerial planning. The major point to remember, however, is that regardless of time spans, all organizations need planning.

In recent years, the increasing pace of change has prompted many organizations to implement strategic planning. *Strategic planning* focuses on all the activities that lead to the definition of long-term objectives and strategies to achieve those objectives. This is in contrast to *functional* or *operational planning*, which is done in the individual units within the organization and focuses on more immediate objectives and problems.

The increasing pace of change is forcing companies to take strong measures to remain viable. In the highly competitive consumer electronics industry, for example, companies have established research and development labs around the world to enable dispersed scientists and technicians to work on projects around the clock. The time frame of bringing new products to market can be reduced using such an approach.[14] There is little doubt that the compression of planning time frames is going to continue into the near future.

Conflicts Among Objectives At any time, stockholders (owners), employees (including unions), customers, suppliers, creditors, and governmental agencies are all concerned with the operation of a firm. The process of setting objectives for an organization must not overlook these interest groups. Managers must instead include and integrate all the groups' interests into corporate plans. The form and weight to be given to any particular interest group, however, is a question that precisely illustrates the nature of management's dilemma. Yet management's responsibility is to make these kinds of judgments. Some of the most common planning tradeoffs faced by managers in business organizations are:

1. Short-term profits versus long-term growth.
2. Profit margin versus competitive position.
3. Direct sales effort versus development effort.
4. Greater penetration of present markets versus developing new markets.
5. Achieving long-term growth through related businesses versus unrelated businesses.
6. Profit objectives versus nonprofit objectives (that is, social responsibilities).
7. Growth versus stability.
8. Low-risk environment versus high-risk environment.

Management must consider the expectations of diverse groups because the firm's ultimate success depends on them. For example, present and potential customers hold ultimate power over the firm. If they are not happy with the price and quality of the firm's product, they will withdraw their support (stop buying), and the firm will fail through lack of sales. Suppliers, too, hold power over firms. They can disrupt the flow of materials to express disagreement with the firm's activities. Government agencies, meanwhile, have the power to enforce the firm's compliance with regulations. Managers must recognize the existence of all these interest groups and their power to affect the objectives of the firm. The organization will exist only as long as it satisfies these diverse groups.[15]

Studies of objectives that business managers set for their organizations attest to the difficulty of balancing the concerns of interest groups. These studies also suggest that the more successful firms consistently emphasize profit-seeking activities that maximize the stockholder's wealth. This is not to say that successful firms seek only profit-oriented objectives, but merely that such objectives are dominant. Evidently, such firms are managed by persons who value pragmatic, dynamic, and achievement-oriented behavior. These individuals, at the same time, recognize that businesses have an increasing responsibility to do what is best for society.[16]

Another source of conflict among objectives in many organizations stems from the serial nature of information flows. One common problem for a manufacturing company such as SONY occurs when there is a change in consumer demand for a product like flat-screen television sets. This change in demand is first noticed at the retail level. The increased retail sales are then fed back to the wholesaler who has change orders. This results in increased production in manufacturing and increased ordering of supplies. You can see from this brief scenario how objectives of one unit can come into conflict with another. Manufacturing, for example, wants to continue its current levels of output, but wholesale has no place to go with its inventory. Thus, the objectives of the wholesaler to reduce input conflict with the objectives of the manufacturer who wants to keep output steady. This conflict of objectives ripples through the system until a new equilibrium is reached.

This type of problem is being circumscribed today through the use of sophisticated supply-chain management software, such as SAP. This software relays the information of reduced consumer demand to every part of the supply chain so that each component can adjust objectives in real time.[17]

Measurement of Objectives   One important reason for having objectives is to help translate the organization's broad social purposes into measurable terms. *Objectives* serve as guides for action and as starting points for more specific and detailed objectives at lower levels in the organization. Well-managed business organizations have at least five categories of objectives: *profitability, competitiveness, efficiency, flexibility,* and *quality.*[18]

Profitability   In business organizations, profitability is one of the most important objectives. Profitability provides the financial resources for future expansion or innovation. The profitability objective usually is expressed in terms of return on investment—net profit divided by the capital invested in the organization or some similar measure. Every profit-seeking organization should establish a profitability objective. Besides competing for customers, business firms also must compete for resources (particular capital). An organization's earnings provide the return on investment, and it is for the sake of this return on investment that a shareholder is willing to supply capital. To compete successfully for this capital, an organization usually must earn a return equivalent to the risk of doing business. The late Roberto C. Goizueta, the former and well-respected CEO of Coca-Cola (www.cocacola.com), said, "What is the mission of business in our society? At the Coca-Cola Company, our stated mission is to create value over time for the owners of our business." He stated that this is so for three reasons:

1. Increasing shareowner value over time is the job the economic system demands of management;

2. Increased shareowner value contributes to society in very meaningful ways; and

3. Focusing on creating value over the long term keeps executives from acting in a shortsighted manner.[19]

Competitiveness   This objective focuses on the prospects for long-term profitability. It measures the competitive strength of the organization.[20] What is the difference between competitive strength and profitability as stated previously? Consider this analogy. Assume that your present normal blood pressure indicates that you are healthy (profitable) today. Assume further that your objective is to remain healthy six months from now. To ensure you will accomplish this profitability objective, you must establish objectives in other areas today (exercise, weight control, proper diet, and so on). Measuring how well you are doing in these other areas will provide you with some idea of your "competitive strength." Each area will be an indicator of how profitable you are likely to be in the long run.

Well-managed organizations establish objectives that concentrate on specific rates of increase in sales and market share. If the economy is expanding at a certain rate, then sales growth objectives should be considerably greater than this percentage. Although the notion of competitiveness lies at the heart of strategy development, its definition is often vague. Nonetheless, there is general agreement that competitiveness depends on a number of factors that are interrelated and cannot be looked at in isolation. These main factors include:

1. Customer values—An organization is competitive in the eyes of its customers if it is able to deliver a better value when compared to its competitors. Superior value results through lower prices for equivalent benefits or differentiated benefits that justify a higher price. This can be expressed in the equation:

$$\text{Customer Value} = \text{Benefit}/\text{Price}$$

2. Shareholder values—An organization is competitive in the eyes of its shareholders if it is able to provide a satisfactory return on investment in the short, medium, and long terms. Shareholder values will influence decisions concerning the dividend policy, growth strategy, and capital structure, which will in turn determine the long-term well-being and profit potential of the organization.

3. The ability to act and react within a competitive environment—This is the ability to retain the competitive position of a company by satisfying the expectations of customers and shareholders while constantly eliminating the threats and exploiting the opportunities that arise in the competitive environment.[21]

Efficiency   An organization must maintain certain types of short-run efficiencies to bring about the prospect of long-run profitability. Measures of efficiency reflect how well the organization's resources are employed. Thus, while it is also a measure of profitability, a ratio such as return on assets (net profit divided by total assets), when compared with that of similar organizations, gives management some indication of how efficient the organization is internally in managing the organization's assets.

Efficiency directly influences performance and involves both the human and nonhuman resources of the organization. Well-managed organizations, regardless of size, establish objectives with respect to the quality of management, the succession of management, the depth of critical personnel, and employee turnover. Nonhuman resources such as the age and condition of the plant and equipment also are important indications of efficiency; objectives should be established in these areas as well. In addition, many of today's most successful firms, such as Nike, Wal-Mart, and Procter & Gamble, are gaining efficiencies in their production systems through teams that work interorganizationally to increase efficiency throughout the value chain.[22]

Flexibility   We noted earlier that managers plan not to predict the future but to uncover important factors in the present that will ensure that there is a future for the organization.[23] One way managers can guard against unforeseen problems is to maintain certain types of flexibilities. For example, a manufacturer of consumer products operating in a volatile market has a flexibility objective that states the maximum percentage of sales, which can be derived from a single product. If this percentage is reached, the firm attempts to introduce a new product. Thus, if customers suddenly change their minds about any one of the organization's products and stop purchasing it, the impact on profitability is minimized. Another organization allows only a certain percentage of sales to be derived from government contracts. This practice ensures that the organization maintains its flexibility and does not become dependent on government contracts. Flexible organizations continually develop new strategies and adapt to new market realities, and then shift all aspects of the organization so that they are congruent with the new strategies. Flexible organizations use their structure as a source of competitive advantage.[24]

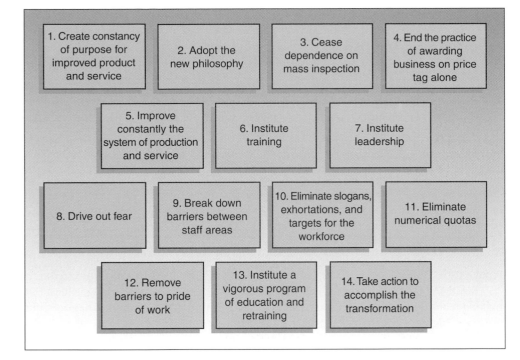

Figure 5-3
Deming's 14 Points of Total Quality Management

Source: Adapted from W. Edwards Deming, *Out of the Crisis,* 2nd ed. (Cambridge, Mass: MIT Center for Advanced Engineering Study, 1986); and Lloyd Dobyns and Clare Crawford-Mason, *Quality or Else* (Boston: Houghton Mifflin, 1991).

Quality   W. Edwards Deming (www.deming.org), Phil Crosby (www.philipcrosby.com), Joseph Juran (www.juran.com), and other noted quality experts have specified fundamental principles or guides for quality management. Deming prepared the list of 14 Points of Quality shown in Figure 5-3 that has been applied in organizations.

Drucker, Deming, Crosby, Juran, and others offer a mix of goals and procedures that provide managers with guidance for planning. When businesses define their objectives in terms of customer satisfaction, planning requires them to translate customer satisfaction into meaningful areas and measures. Table 5-1 lists ten dimensions of service quality that define customer satisfaction. These ten dimensions provide management with key areas on which to concentrate to satisfy customer expectations. Quality derives from meeting or exceeding customer expectations on each dimension.

These dimensions show the planning values that underlie other corporate objectives (e.g., profit, market share, return on assets). *Planning values* are the underlying decision priorities that determine planning objectives and decisions. Five values underlie a quality-based planning process: (1) The firm is customer-driven, not product-driven. (2) All

Concept	How It Is Measured and Demonstrated	TABLE 5-1
1. Access	Availability to customers	**Measures of Service Quality Control**
2. Communication	Providing clear descriptions for customers, answering their questions	
3. Competence	Proven expertise at a task	
4. Courtesy	Friendliness, respect for customer	
5. Credibility	Believability, meeting promises	
6. Reliability	Error reduction	
7. Responsiveness	Speed at meeting customer requests	
8. Security	Maintaining customer safety and privacy	
9. Tangibles	Physical appearance of workplace	
10. Knowing the customer	Demonstrated capacity to listen to, respond to, and satisfy customers	

employees manage, not just the managers. (3) Decisions are fact-based, not based on hunches or tampering. (4) The basic, ongoing work emphasis is on producing quality and continuous improvement, not on short-term profits or fear. (5) Prevention (not detection) of defects is emphasized.

Effective planning also follows from effective strategic thinking and planning in today's turbulent economy. History is not always an effective predictor of future trends.

Regulated standards for products or practices are often used as planning values. But making plans that simply meet standards is a reactive approach to planning that does not motivate higher performance. Proactive, quality-based planning, on the other hand, involves setting objectives that add value by exceeding mandated standards or even setting standards of quality where none had previously existed. For example, innovative hiring or compensation plans, maternity and family leave programs, and financial support for ongoing education of workers at local colleges and technical schools are examples of proactive objectives that display quality-oriented planning values.

Objectives need to emphasize quality over quantity. Harvard business professor David Garvin identified eight planning values that are the basis of a quality-based system: performance (primary operating characteristics, e.g., speed), features (supplements to performance), reliability (no malfunctioning or need for repair), conformance (to established standards), durability (product life), serviceability (speed and ease of repair, if needed), aesthetics (appeal to taste, looks, feel), and perceived quality (customer perception).[25]

Garvin's planning values highlight the difference between traditional and quality-based views. In the traditional view, quality meant the performance characteristics and the number of features available to the customer. These were the primary planning values.

Managers should establish planning values that are responsive to both the internal and external environments of the organization. Internal features are people, processes, and practices that promote quality and continuous improvement. External features relate to external customer satisfaction, such as product attributes that exceed expectations. Noted management thinker Peter Drucker developed a set of eight planning objectives that managers must keep in mind. These are provided in Table 5-2.

5-3b Actions

Actions are specific, prescribed means to achieve objectives. Actions determine success or failure in meeting objectives. Planned courses of action are called strategies and tactics, and are usually differentiated by scope and time frame as we have described. Whatever the name, a planned action is directed toward changing a future condition—that is, achieving an objective.

In some instances, managers simply do not know what action to take. For example, productivity increases can be achieved through a variety of means, including improved technology, employee training, management training, reward systems, and improved working conditions. In such cases, managers must select the most effective alternative. Often several possible courses of action exist for top managers who are planning for the total organization. As the plan becomes more localized to a simple unit in the organization, the number of alternatives tends to become fewer yet more familiar.

The important point is that courses of action and objectives are causally related. That is, the objectives are caused to occur by the courses of action taken. The intellectual effort required in planning involves knowing not only _what_ alternatives will accomplish an

Concept	How It Is Measured and Demonstrated	TABLE 5-2
1. Market standing	Ranking of firm's market share among competitors	**Drucker's Planning Objectives**
2. Innovation	Firm's record in bringing new products and processes onto the market	
3. Productivity	The efficient use of resources	
4. Physical and financial resources	Nonhuman assets the firm owns	
5. Profitability	Earnings, operating income, or net income after taxes	
6. Managerial performance and development	Management's record for achieving objectives over time	
7. Worker performance and attitude	Workers' record for achieving objectives over time	
8. Public responsibility	Firm's record for meeting and exceeding social expectations	

objective but also *which* one is most efficient. Planning is a management process, deductive in nature and designed to produce orderly results.[26]

Forecasting   In some instances managers can test the effects of a course of action by **forecasting** (the process of using past and current information to predict future events). With a forecast, a firm attempts to determine the likely outcome of alternative courses of action. For example, a sales forecast would include past and current information about the firm's product, price, advertising, and cost of goods sold. External conditions to be measured include the price of competing products, the levels of consumer income, consumer credit interest rates, and other measures of local economic activity.

Forecasting models range from the subjective to the sophisticated. Forecasts based on brief, personal, subjective estimates are called hunches. For increasing sophistication, there are statistical studies of predicted consumer purchases (market surveys), historical analyses of past sales to convert into estimates of future sales (time-series analysis), and even more sophisticated models of a wide range of past, current, and predicted economic variables (econometric forecasting). Forecasts are used to predict hiring requirements, factory space needs, employee training expenditures, and health care costs, among other decisions important to the firm.

Scenario Construction   Some firms have successfully established action plans through the use of scenarios. Scenario construction is a technique for combining possible environmental developments in a systematic way to help managers assess possible consequences of alternative courses of action. The process was initiated in the 1950s in classified military studies at the RAND Corporation. Since then the concept of using hypothetical alternative futures for planning purposes has been used by strategic planners.[27]

A typical objective in business planning is to maintain or increase sales volume. Sales volume is a primary source of liquid resources such as cash, accounts receivable, and notes receivable, which managers can use to finance the firm's activities. Courses of action that affect sales include price changes, marketing and sales activities, and new-product development. Factors beyond the control of management also affect sales. Such external factors include the price of competing and substitute products, competitors' marketing/sales activities, and general economic conditions (expansion, recession, inflation). Although managers cannot control many of the factors that determine sales volume, forecasting remains a valuable managerial tool.[28]

5-3c Resources

Resources are defined as the financial, physical, human, time or other assets of an organization. Expenditure of resources is usually controlled by use of a budget. A *budget* is a predetermined amount of resources linked to an activity. For example, as part of the plan to

▶**forecasting** An important element of the planning function that must make two basic determinations: (1) what level of activity can be expected during the planning period and (2) what level of resources will be available to support the projected activity. In a business organization, the critical forecast is the sales forecast.

Figure 5-4
The Budgeting Process

Source: James H. Donnelly, Jr., James L. Gibson, and John M. Ivancevich, *Fundamentals of Management,* 8th ed. (Homewood, ILL: Richard D. Irwin, 1992), p. 157.

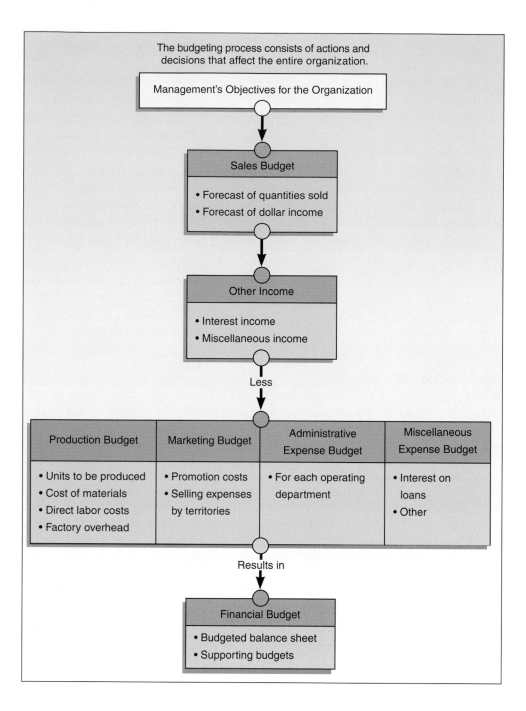

bring a new product to market, a budget is likely to include salaries, materials, facilities, travel, and other resources. A good budget recognizes and allocates the needed resources to ensure implementation.

A close relationship exists between budgeting as a planning technique and budgeting as a control technique.[29] After an organization has been engaged in activities for a time, actual results are compared with the budgeted (planned) results, which may lead to corrective action. This, as we will see in Chapter 15, is the management function of controlling.[30]

The complexity of the budget phase is shown in Figure 5-4. The sales forecast plays a key role, as is evident in its placement at the top of the chart. All other budgets are related to it either directly or indirectly. The production budget, for example, must specify the materials, labor, and other manufacturing expenses required to support the projected sales level. Similarly, the marketing expense budget details the costs associated with the sales level projected for each product in each sales region. Administrative expenses also must be related to the predicted sales volume. The projected sales and expenses are combined in the financial budgets, which consist of formal financial statements, inventory budgets, and the capital additions budget.

Forecast data is based on assumptions about the future. If these assumptions prove wrong, the budgets are inadequate. So financial budgets' usefulness depends mainly on how flexible they are to changes in conditions. Two principal means exist to provide flexibility: variable budgeting and moving budgeting.

5-3d Implementation of Plans

All the planning in the world will not help an organization realize objectives if plans cannot be implemented. (Implementation of plans involves resources and actions as shown in Figure 5-2.) In some instances, the manager can take all the necessary steps to apply resources in planned actions to achieve objectives. In most instances, the manager must implement plans through *other people*, motivating them to accept and carry out the plan. *Authority, persuasion,* and *policy* are the manager's means of implementing plans.

Authority   **Authority** is a legitimate form of power, in the sense that it accompanies the position not the person. That is, the nature of authority in organizations is the right to make decisions and to expect compliance to the implications of these decisions. Thus, a manager can reasonably expect subordinates to carry out a plan so long as it does not require illegal, immoral, or unethical behavior. Authority is often sufficient to implement relatively simple plans that involve no significant change in the status quo. But a complex and comprehensive plan can seldom be implemented through authority alone. Persuasion is another important managerial tool.

> **authority** The legitimate right to use assigned resources to accomplish a delegated task or objective; the right to give orders and to exact obedience.

Persuasion   **Persuasion** is a process of selling a plan to those who must implement it, communicating relevant information so individuals understand all implications. In this sense, it requires convincing others to base acceptance of the plan upon its merits rather than upon the authority of the managers.

Persuasion does present a hazard. What happens if the plan is not implemented after all persuasive efforts have been exhausted? If the plan is crucial and must be implemented, management must resort to authority. Consequently a manager who has failed once at the use of persuasion must limit use of the technique in the future. Individuals who were the objects of unsuccessful attempts at persuasion and who had thought they had the choice of accepting or rejecting a plan would be skeptical of future persuasive efforts.[31]

> **persuasion** A process of selling a plan to those who must implement it and communicating relevant information so individuals understand all implications.

Policy   When plans are intended to be rather permanent fixtures in an organization, management develops policies to implement them. Policies usually are written statements that reflect the basic objectives of the plan and provide guidelines for selecting actions to achieve the objectives. Once plans have been accepted by those who must carry them out policies become important management tools for implementing them. Effective policies have these characteristics (see Figure 5-5):

1. *Flexibility.* A policy must strike a reasonable balance between stability and flexibility. Conditions change, and policies must change accordingly. On the other hand, some degree of stability must prevail if order and a sense of continuity are to be maintained in the organization. A balance of flexibility and stability must exist; only the judgment of management can determine the appropriate balance.

2. *Comprehensiveness.* A policy must be comprehensive enough to cover any contingency if plans are to be followed. The degree depends on the scope of action controlled by the policy itself. If the policy is directed toward very narrow ranges of activity—for example, hiring policies—it need not be as comprehensive as a policy concerned with public relations.

3. *Coordination.* A policy must provide for coordination of the various subunits whose actions are interrelated. Without coordinative direction provided by policies, each subunit is tempted to pursue its own objectives. The ultimate test of any subunit's activity should be its relationship to the policy statement.

Figure 5-5
Characteristics
of Effective Policies

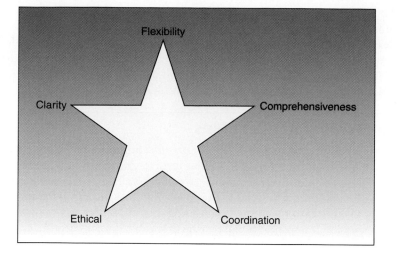

4. *Ethical.* A policy must conform to the canons of ethical behavior that prevail in society. The increasingly complex and interdependent nature of contemporary society has resulted in a great number of problems involving ethical dimensions that are only vaguely understood. The manager is ultimately responsible for the resolution of issues, which involve ethical principles.

5. *Clarity.* A policy must be written clearly and logically. It must specify the intended aim of the action it governs, define the appropriate methods and action, and delineate the limits of freedom of action permitted to those whose actions are to be guided by it.

The ultimate test of the effectiveness of a policy is whether the objective is attained. If the policy does not lead to the objective, the policy should be revised. Thus, policies must be subjected to reexamination continually.

After completing the first five steps in the planning process, management must control the planning decision. The firm must manage ongoing work activities to ensure that the intended objectives are met or, in some cases, adjusted. Controlling includes all managerial activities dedicated to ensuring that actual results conform to planned results.

Managers must provide information that reports actual performance and permits comparison of the performance against standards. Such information is most easily acquired for activities that produce specific and concrete results; for example, production and sales activities have results that are easily identifiable and for which information is readily obtainable.

More will be said about control issues in Chapters 15 and 16. Here you should note that controlling results is a part of the planning function. People responsible for taking corrective steps when actual results are not in line with planned results must know that they are indeed responsible and that they have the authority to take action.

Controlling the implementation means gathering feedback on the effectiveness of the actions that are being taken. Do they meet the objectives of the plan? The Internet has provided companies with an immense challenge as they attempt to tackle what amounts to a new frontier. No one is sure exactly how business will unfold on the net, but there are some ways to gather feedback on how well it works for a firm.

Time-Based Planning Speed can often determine the success or failure of a plan's implementation. General George Patton once remarked that a partial plan, forcefully executed, is better than a complete plan, timidly pursued. This underscores the importance of speed as well as management leadership. The importance of speed and time is illustrated in the Management Focus on Customer Service box, "Saving Customers Time by Planning."

The important period between the time a product is first considered and the time it is sold to the customer is called *concept to customer.* Speed in planning and delivering a product or service can be a strategic competitive advantage. All other things equal, the prize (typically, market share) goes to the fastest firm. Further, paying attention to time

Management Focus on Customer Service

Saving Customers Time by Planning

Wal-Mart, Kmart, Sears, Walgreens, Wells Fargo Bank, and other brick-and-mortar retailers are concerned about congested parking lots, out-of-stock merchandise, endless checkout lines, and indifferent, rude sales clerks. Before e-commerce arrived some of these problems and inconveniences were tolerated. Today, retailers must plan for better customer service if they are to survive. Customers are demanding one-stop superstores and easy, convenient shopping excursions. The retailer that fails to plan properly loses. On the other hand the retailer that minimizes hassles by better planning wins business loyalty and repeat sales.

The same logic that applies to the brick-and-mortar stores applies to Amazon.com, eBay, Travelocity.com, and other e-commerce alternatives. Planning to offer convenience is becoming a must. Customer convenience has driven most innovation in retailing, including department stores, regional malls, supermarkets, and category superstores. The emphasis that customers place on convenience has pushed the need for one-stop shopping and planning in offering service, merchandise on demand, and other services. Consumers want to use their time doing things instead of standing in line, returning merchandise, and looking for merchandise. Retailers know that if they plan to provide more convenience that they will have more satisfied and loyal customers.

Determining what convenience means to customers is an important step in improving customer service. Convenience to the Amazon.com customer is usually different than convenience to the Southwest Airline customer. Assessing these differences in meaning and doing something about the difference is how customers can be served better and retained.

Sources: Adapted from "Customer Service and The Golden Rule," *Christian Science Monitor,* April 2004, p. 19; Chip R. Bell and Bilijack R. Bell, "Leading for Customer Service Ingenuity," *Leader To Leader,* Spring 2004, pp. 12–15; Kerry A. Dolan, "Porcelain and Portals," *Forbes,* April 16, 2001, p. 168; and Kathleen Seiders, Leonard L. Berry, and Larry G. Gresham, "Attention, Retailers! How Convenient Is Your Convenience Strategy?" *Sloan Management Review,* Spring 2000, pp. 79–89.

usually forces the firm to look at other issues (e.g., design, staffing, and inspection) affecting product and service quality. For example, it is not uncommon for a product to lie idle during 90 percent of the time allocated for its assembly. Paying attention to production speed can lead to reductions in these idle periods. Not only are time-sensitive firms likely to deliver products to their customers faster than competitors, they are likely to develop greater customer loyalty and to learn more about improving the production process itself.[32]

Line employees work directly with the product, in contrast to what are designated as overhead employees. The productivity advantage of Japanese-managed companies is often found in their overhead employees' productivity. With one-third the volume and three times the variety, one Japanese company has only one-eighteenth the number of overhead employees of a comparable U.S. firm.[33] More overhead employees lead to slower production.

The pace of innovation varies by industry. The pharmaceutical industry, for example, takes ten years to research, develop, and test drugs prior to bringing them to market. In contrast, the computer software industry is famous for rapid innovation and introduction of new products. Most of you probably have experienced this as you have purchased software labeled something like "Version 5.3" or you may have been frustrated to learn of upgrades in programs that require you to purchase new versions each year just to keep up.[34]

There are also important variations in the pace of innovation within industries. In automotive development time, Honda beats Ford, which beats General Motors. The product design cycle—from concept to customer—turns out to be four to five years for General Motors and European auto firms, three years for Ford, two and a half years for Toyota and about two years for Honda.[35] Those firms that fall behind in the product design cycle can (1) proceed as planned with outdated product or (2) stop the development and restart the cycle.

By examining its product design cycle, a boot manufacturer found that it took seven weeks to complete an order and deliver the product to the customer, although actual production required less than two days of value-added labor. Over 95 percent of the time was spent doing nothing of value to the firm or to the customer. A telecommunications firm found a similar delay in simply converting a customer's order into a work order for the factory. A full 95 percent of the time was wasted.[36] By eliminating the time when a product or process lies idle, speed is added to the planning process. Much improvement stems from simply not wasting time.

5-4 Asking the Right Questions

We have seen that planning, a fundamental activity of managers, can cover any time span from the short run to the long run. We have also surveyed some of the more important forecasting and budgeting techniques. These do not encompass the entire range of problems and issues associated with planning. The discussion, however, emphasizes the fact that planning is the essence of management; all other managerial functions stem from planning.

How does a manager begin the planning process? Many professionals agree that much of the task consists of asking the appropriate questions. Table 5-3 suggests the basic ones. Other, more specific questions might well be posed. Yet the fundamental questions are appropriate regardless of the type and size of the organization.

TABLE 5-3	**Planning Element**	**Key Management Decisions**
Key Planning Questions	*Objectives*	1. What objectives will be sought?
		2. What is the relative importance of each objective?
		3. What are the relationships among the objectives?
		4. When should each objective be achieved?
		5. How can each objective be measured?
		6. Which person or organizational unit should be accountable for achieving the objective?
	Actions	1. What are the important actions that affect the successful achievement of objectives?
		2. What information exists regarding each action?
		3. What is the appropriate technique for forecasting the future state of each important action?
		4. Which person or organizational unit should be accountable for the action?
	Resources	1. What resources should be included in the plan?
		2. What are the interrelationships among the various resources?
		3. What budgeting technique should be used?
		4. Which person or organizational unit should be accountable for the preparation of the budget?
	Implementation	1. Can the plan be implemented through authority or persuasion?
		2. What policy statements are necessary to implement the overall plan?
		3. To what extent are the policy statements flexible, comprehensive, coordinative, ethical, and clearly written?
		4. Which person or organizational unit would be affected by the policy statements?

Management Summary

- The planning function includes those managerial activities that result in predetermined courses of action.

- Planning necessarily focuses on the future, and management's responsibility is to prepare the organization for the future.

- Planning requires managers to make decisions about objectives, actions, resources, and implementation. These four factors are essential to effective planning.

- Through planning, management coordinates efforts, prepares for change, develops performance standards, and manages development.

- Objectives are statements of future conditions that, if realized, are deemed satisfactory or optimal by the planner. All sets of objectives have three characteristics: priority, timing, and measurement. How management responds to priority, timing, and measurement issues in setting objectives reflects individual values and economic considerations.

- To be useful in planning, objectives should be stated in measurable terms and should relate to significant organizational performance determinants. In particular, objectives should be set for profitability, competitiveness, efficiency, and flexibility.

- Courses of action to achieve objectives must be specified. Terms such as *strategies* and *tactics* refer to planned courses of action. An important activity in specifying courses of action is that of forecasting future demand for the organization's output and future availability of resources.

- Resource requirements of a plan must be forecast and specified by budgets. Management can select the type of budget that best suits the planning needs of the organization.

- The fourth part of planning is implementation, a phase that takes into account that plans usually are carried out by other people.

- Implementation by policy has the advantage of continuously reinforcing the plan for those who must implement it. Effective policies are those that produce the planned course of action.

Key Terms

authority (p. 115)
balanced scorecard (p. 107)
forecasting (p. 113)
level of detail (p. 104)

operational planning (p. 105)
persuasion (p. 115)
scope (p. 104)
single-use plans (p. 106)

standing plan (p. 106)
strategic planning (p. 104)
tactical planning (p. 105)
time frame (p. 104)

Review and Discussion Questions

1. What is the relationship between the organization's broad purposes and the objectives that are part of its various plans?

2. What is meant by the request than an objective should be specific and measurable?

3. Has the increase in globalization complicated the planning process for managers? Explain.

4. Most people are not good planners. Why do you think this is the case?

5. Should the manager responsible for the work be involved in planning the work? Explain.

6. Explain the differences between single-use and standing plans. Is the U.S. Constitution a single-use or a standing plan? Explain.

7. Why is forecasting in the retail industry so difficult?

8. What skills do you believe an individual should have to be an effective planner? How do you believe those skills can be acquired?

9. What is the basis for saying that planning is the essential management function? Discuss.

10. A manager was overheard saying, "Plan? I never have time to plan. I live from day to day just trying to survive." Comment on this statement.

Practice Quiz

Note: You can find the correct answers to these questions by taking the quiz and then submitting your answers in the Online Edition. The program will automatically score your submission. If you miss a question, the program will provide the correct answer, a rationale for the answer, and the section number in the chapter where the topic is discussed.

Indicate whether the sentence or statement is true or false.

_____ **1.** Planning leads to the development of performance standards.

_____ **2.** Planning becomes more critical in situations where the results of decisions will occur shortly after the decisions are actually made.

_____ **3.** Planning is usually done by a single individual.

_____ **4.** Speed often determines the success or failure of a plan's implementation.

Identify the letter of the choice that best completes the statement or answers the question.

_____ **5.** _____ is an activity that distinguishes managers from nonmanagers.
    a. Complaining
    b. Decision making
    c. Formal planning
    d. Thinking

_____ **6.** Without a _____, activities have no purpose or direction.
    a. manager
    b. budget
    c. plan
    d. report

_____ **7.** The planning function begins with the determination of _____ .
    a. target markets.
    b. risks.
    c. future objectives.
    d. past mistakes.

_____ **8.** Which equation best expresses customer values (lower prices for equivalent benefits or differentiated benefits that justify a higher price)?
    a. Customer Value = Product/Price
    b. Customer Value = Benefit/Price
    c. Customer Value = Benefit/Value

_____ **9.** The scenario construction process was initiated in the _____ in classified military studies at the RAND corporation.
    a. 1920s
    b. 1950s
    c. 1970s
    d. 1990s

_____ **10.** It is not uncommon for a product to lie idle during _____ of the time allocated for its assembly.
    a. 25 percent
    b. 40 percent
    c. 60 percent
    d. 90 percent

_____ **11.** Most experts suggest that the planning process begins with _____ .
    a. forecasting through the use of five-year look ahead.
    b. asking the appropriate questions.
    c. benchmarking performance against competitor results.
    d. training employees in customer service.

_____ **12.** If a manager could choose, it is best in stating objectives to emphasize _____ .
    a. a financial measurement.
    b. return on investment.
    c. ownership percentages.
    d. quality over quantity.

_____ **13.** In developing an effective plan it is wise for a manager to remember that _____ .
    a. short term planning is the best.
    b. lower level employees are not knowledgeable enough to participate.
    c. history is not an effective predictor of future trends.
    d. international data is not accurate.

_____ **14.** Management must implement plans. This is done by developing _____ .
    a. politics.
    b. action steps.
    c. balanced scorecards.
    d. a matrix design.

_____ **15.** Research on objectives that are established by management indicates that managers have a difficult time balancing _____ .
    a. income and cash flow statements.
    b. the concerns of various interest groups.
    c. short-term growth issues.
    d. international compliance requirements.

Case Study

Nike's Planning and Innovation

When most people think of Nike (www.nike.com) they think of superstar athletes like Tiger Woods, Mia Hamm, and Michael Jordan. When Nike's employees think of their company they think about a retired university track coach and how he created a spirit of innovation. When Coach Bowerman decided that his team needed better running shoes he went to his workshop and tinkered around. After experimenting he poured rubber into the family waffle iron and the famous Nike "waffle sole" was born.

Nike is now a $12.3 billion (2004) world giant that has experienced periods of growth, some new product setbacks, and public backlash because of using labor in poor countries to manufacture shoes. Whatever someone thinks about Nike, it takes its product planning seriously. Planning charts the course for each new generation of shoes.

Nike is into storytelling and passing on the culture from one generation of employees to the next. The stories cover everything, including how innovation and planning work at Nike. Ekins (Nike spelled backward) are tech reps that undergo a nine-day routine training camp at Nike headquarters in Beaverton, Oregon. One of the main stories told to Ekins is how Coach Bowerman, through hard work, planning, and experimenting, set an innovation tone that is still alive at Nike.

Planning a new shoe starts with the ideation process. A Nike line manager might say, "I want an Air Jordan sneaker that costs $165." This idea goes to a designer and then a developer. By the time the first pair rolls off the assembly line in Ecuador or Indonesia, more than 200 data points will have been generated about the shoe. Also, more than seventy-five employees, from the product line manager to the quality assurance inspector, will have worked on the project.

Nike established the Global Product Information Network to produce a seamless flow of information from product ideation to planning to production to distribution. Nike's intranet provides a central, secure place to collect and add information about shoes in development.

Planning for the development and distribution of a new shoe is a major challenge. Marketing, production, engineering, IT, and many other specialties are involved on the project team. Having individuals from different backgrounds collaborate in a timely manner is complex since Nike has no set "how to do it" cookbook. Sharing ideas, changing objectives, communicating plans and schedules, and using the intranet all require patience and understanding.

At Nike planning for a new shoe is serious business. Without a sound plan the project is likely to fail and to cost millions of dollars with no chance of recovering the investment.

Questions for Discussion

1. Why would a sucessful firm like Nike need a sophisticated and efficient planning process?

2. What type of managerial coordination is needed at Nike to develop and distribute a new product (e.g., golf club, shoe)?

3. What role does information technology play in keeping Nike ahead of competitors?

Sources: Adapted from Alex Wong, "Nike: Just Don't Do It," *Newsweek,* September 20, 2004; "Nike's Upward Swoosh," *Business Week Online,* June 25, 2004; Benjamin Chen, "Fancy Footwork," *Darwin,* January 2001, pp. 42–43; Eric Randsdell, "The Nike Story? Just Tell It!," *Fast Company,* January–February 2000, p. 44; and *Nike,* Annual Report 2000.

Internet Exercise

Microsoft is one of the most discussed, analyzed, critiqued, and reviewed companies in the world. Using only the Internet, find statements that represent the firm's strategic, operational, and tactical planning approaches. You should prepare three brief state-ments that indicate what Microsoft is doing in these three different planning areas. Start at www.microsoft.com; also try www.prnewswire.com.

Strategic Planning

6

Managing Today

Kia Strategy Lures in Car Buyers, Moves Them Up-Market

Many American's associate the Kia brand of automobiles with low-end, entry-level vehicles. If they are told about the Amanti, they might think that the Korean car maker has developed a line of Italian suits rather than an upscale car model. But Kia has executed a brilliant strategy since its introduction to the U.S. car market in 1994. Today, Kia outsells BMW, Mercedes Benz, Audi, and Infiniti in the United States, and it will soon pass Mitsubishi.

Kia's strategy is to offer comparable value to car buyers for less money. In the first six years of its presence in the U.S., Kia was a two-model car company. Its base model Spectra was designed to compete with the popular Toyota Corolla and Honda Civic. Its low-priced minivan may be the lowest-priced model in the market, with a six-cylinder version selling for less than $19,000. Kia went from selling 12,000 vehicles in 1994 to more than 237,000 in 2003.

At the same time that Kia is increasing its sales, the company is introducing new, pricier models. The strategy behind the pricier model introduction is that buyer loyalty will be strong from the entry-level model sales. As these original car buyers move up in their careers and salaries they will be able to afford the more expensive models. To demonstrate the success of the Kia strategy, consider that in 2001 the average transaction price for a Kia automobile was just $12,000. Today, that price is approaching $20,000 and it is expected to continue a sharp ascent. There are now over 300 Kia dealers in the United States. In 2004, it introduced the company's top-of-the-line model: The $27,000 Kia Amanti.

In addition to focusing on customer retention throughout their car-buying lifetimes, Kia is also focusing intently on converting used-car shoppers to new car buyers. The company intends to develop a strong Internet advertising campaign, focusing on pop-up ads where people are shopping for used cars. The ads will encourage shoppers to examine the Kia product line as it may be priced to meet their needs. Even more persuasive, perhaps, is the fact that Kia has one of the more generous product warranties in the industry—a 10-year or 100,000-mile warranty.

Sources: Steve Finley, "Kia Slowly Shedding Image of a Cheap Brand," *Ward's Dealer Business,* July 2004, p. 10; Julie Cantwell, "Kia's Strategy: Lure Used-Car Shoppers to Purchase New Kias," *Automotive News,* June 24, 2004, p. 6; and Katherine Zachary, "Kia Banks on Value, Not Price," *Ward's Auto World,* October 2001, p. 46.

strategy A process that results in an outcome, which is the basis for organizational decisions and actions.

strategic thinking The determination of basic long-term goals and objectives of an enterprise and the adoption of courses of action and the allocation of resources necessary for carrying out these goals.

Chapter 5 examined the four phases of planning and introduced important planning terminology. However, before a production manager, marketing manager, human resources manager, or entrepreneur can develop plans for their individual departments or organization, a larger plan—a blueprint—for the entire organization must be developed. Otherwise, on what would the individual departments' or businesses' plans be based?

The larger vision that guides the activities of managers and other employees in an organization is known as a **strategy.** Every organization needs a strategy to help it decide what choices it will make among the myriad that are available to it. Strategies are often based on the historical focus of a company or its founder.

A strategy is built on **strategic thinking,** which is defined as "the determination of the basic long-term goals and objectives of an enterprise, and the adoption of courses of action and the allocation of resources necessary for carrying out these goals."[1] Essentially, strategic thinking is a process that results in an outcome called a strategy that is the basis for organizational decisions and actions. Most companies aren't very good at strategic thinking because managers tend to resist change, and thus don't develop the requisite thinking skills.[2]

Traditionally, strategies have been established by top-level managers. In modern organizations, executives include every level of the organization in the development and implementation of overall strategy.[3] The job of managers is to engage employees, customers, and other organizational stakeholders in meaningful conversations about the organization and its future. Managers need to learn to listen to these diverse voices to take advantage of hidden opportunities and to spot potential threats before they become problems. For example, managers in the food distribution industry have listened to customers and have altered their strategies to focus on the needs of seniors, ethnic shopping preferences, food safety, and satisfying the needs of lower-income customers.[4]

In today's complex, global economy, strategic planning has to account for unexpected events, randomness, and chaos. Managers like to predict the future so they are better able to deal with it. Chaos theory suggests there may be some inherent limitations in their ability to do so with accuracy. On the other hand, chaos theory provides a useful framework for understanding the dynamic evolution of industries and of individual companies.[5] By understanding industries as complex, possibly chaotic systems, managers can build better strategies.[6] Good strategy is uniquely complex, allowing a company to develop a sustainable competitive advantage.[7]

New organizational strategies and structures enable organizations to deal with complexity through constant learning and change. As Harvard Business School professor Rosabeth Moss Kanter stated, "New organizational models offer the best of both worlds—enough structure for continuity, but not so much that creative responses to chaos are stifled."[8] Strategic thinking and strategic planning help organizations create order out of chaos, as Figure 6-1 illustrates.

This chapter focuses on developing and managing strategy in a highly competitive, global economy. First, we explore several important frameworks for strategic thinking. Next, we review a four-step approach to developing a strategic plan. Then we look at some possible strategies and conclude by surveying the different stakeholders who have an interest in a firm's strategic plan.

6-1 The Growth of Strategic Planning

Many of today's most successful business organizations continue to survive because during their organizational history they offered the right product or service at the right time; the same can be said for nonprofit and government organizations. Many critical decisions of the past were made without the benefit of strategic thinking or planning. Whether these decisions were based on wisdom or luck is not important. They resulted in momentum that has carried successful organizations to where they are today. However, present-day managers increasingly recognize that wisdom and intuition alone are not sufficient to guide the destinies of organizations in today's ever-changing environment. These managers are turning to strategic planning to help them chart a course for the future.[9]

In earlier, less dynamic periods in the global economy, the planning systems utilized by most organizations extrapolated current-year sales and other trends for five and ten years into the future. Based on these straight-line extrapolations, managers made plant, product, service, and investment decisions. In most instances, the decisions were fairly accurate because the factors influencing sales were more predictable and the environment was more stable.

In the years after World War II, many of the factors on which earlier planners counted could no longer be taken for granted. Uncertainty, instability, and constantly changing environments became the rule rather than the exception. Managers faced increased inflation and intensifying foreign competition, technological obsolescence, and changing market and population characteristics.

Because changes are occurring so rapidly and in so many different domains today, there is increased pressure on top management to respond. In order to respond more effectively, on a more timely schedule, and with a direction or course of action in mind, managers are increasingly using new approaches to strategic planning. *Strategic planning* is a process that involves the review of market conditions; customer needs; competitive strengths and weaknesses; sociopolitical, legal, and economic conditions; technological developments; and the availability of resources that lead to the specific opportunities or threats facing the organization. In practice, *the development of strategic plans involves taking information from the environment and deciding upon an organizational mission and upon objectives, strategies, and a strategic architecture.* The strategic planning process is depicted in Figure 6-2.

As indicated, to develop a unity of purpose across the organization, the strategic planning process must be tied to objectives and goals at all levels of management. At Matsushita (www.panasonic.co.jp/global/), for example, department managers provide three plans every six months: (1) a five-year plan that incorporates technological and environmental changes; (2) a two-year plan that translates strategies into new products; and (3) a six-month operating plan, developed by department managers, that addresses monthly

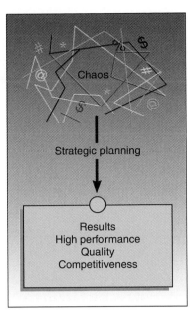

Figure 6-1
Strategic Planning Turns Disorderly Chaos into Orderly Results, High Performance, High Quality, and Competitiveness

Figure 6-2
The Strategic Planning Process

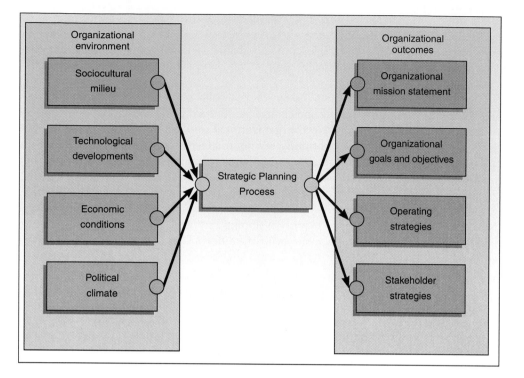

projections for production, sales, profits, inventories, quality control, and personnel requirements. Strategic planning should address strategic and business planning as well as the deployment of plans. This includes effective development, translation, and deployment of overall customer and operational performance requirements derived from the organization's strategy.[10]

Although successful organizations fail in many different ways, most failures share one underlying cause: a failure to reflect on the factors that are most deeply affecting organizational performance. Organizations, particularly successful ones, are so caught up in carrying out their day-to-day work that they rarely, if ever, stop to think objectively about themselves and their business. They don't ask the probing questions that might lead them to challenge their basic assumptions, to refresh their strategies.[11] The basic questions that must be answered when an organization decides to examine and restate its mission are "What is our business?" and "What should it be?" While the questions may appear simple, they are in fact such difficult and critical ones that the major responsibility for answering them must be with top management.

6-2 Strategic Thinking Frameworks

Strategic planning and thinking helps managers prepare for the future. Most organizations can be represented and thought about as a portfolio of businesses. For example, General Motors has several distinct brands under which it sells cars to very different market segments. These brands include entry-level cars (Chevrolet, Saturn), mid-range cars (Buick, Pontiac), and high-end or luxury vehicles (Cadillac). In a similar way, colleges and universities are typically organized around semiautonomous schools or colleges, each with several divisions or departments. These units all compete for resources from the central administration, and they compete for customers (students) in a finite market. Managing such groups of businesses is made a little easier if resources and cash are plentiful and each business unit is experiencing growth and profits. Unfortunately, that is rarely the case.

Today, many firms use merger and acquisition as a means of improving their competitive position.[12] However, the stakes in choosing the right businesses to acquire and integrating them for optimal value and competitive advantage can be daunting. Some experts consider total shareholder return to be the most important performance measure. Others like to look at the trends in the total industry, or begin with customer attitudes.[13]

To more thoroughly examine these differences, some method is needed to help managers make difficult strategic choices about which businesses to add, which to keep, and which to jettison. One of the best-known and most widely used methods is the business portfolio matrix (**BCG matrix**), developed by the Boston Consulting Group (BCG) (www.bcg.com).

6-2a The Business Portfolio Matrix

The first step in BCG's business portfolio matrix approach is to identify each division, product line, and so forth, that can be considered a business. That determination can be made in many different ways. Some organizations focus on so-called profit centers, those parts of the organization most directly attached to revenue generation. Other organizations might use departments, divisions, or other traditional units. In the language of the BCG's framework, these units are called **strategic business units (SBUs).** A SBU is a product or service division within a company that establishes goals and objectives in harmony with the firm's overall mission and is responsible for its own profits and losses. Each SBU has four characteristics:

1. It has a distinct mission.
2. It has its own competitors.
3. It is a single business or collection of businesses.
4. It can be planned for independently of the other businesses of the total organization.

Thus, depending on the organization, an SBU could be a single product, product line, division, department, or agency. Once managers have identified and classified all the SBUs, they need some method of measuring their performance. This is the important contribution of Boston Consulting Group's approach.

Using the BCG approach, an organization would classify SBUs in the business portfolio matrix (Figure 6-3). The business portfolio matrix depends on two business indicators of strategic importance. The vertical indicator, market growth rate, refers to the annual rate of growth of the market in which the product, division, or department is located. The horizontal indicator, relative market share, illustrates an SBU's market share. This indicator ranges from high to low relative share of the market. Based on these two axes, BCG has identified four distinct SBU classifications:

1. *Star.* A star is an SBU that has a high share of a high-growth market. Stars need a great deal of financial resources because of their rapid growth. When growth slows, they become cash cows and important generators of cash for the organization.
2. *Cash cow.* An SBU that has a high share of a low-growth market is labeled a cash cow. They produce a lot of cash for the organization, but, since the market isn't growing, they don't require a great amount of additional financial resources for growth and expansion. As a result, the organization can use the cash they generate to satisfy current debt and to support SBUs in need of cash.

> **BCG matrix** An approach developed by the Boston Consulting Group that evaluates strategic business units with regard to the firm's growth rate and market share.

> **strategic business units (SBUs)** Divisions within an organization by product or service to establish goals and objectives that are in harmony with the firm's overall mission and to assign responsibility for profits and losses.

Figure 6-3
Business Portfolio Matrix

		High	Low
Market Growth Rate	High	Star	Question mark
	Low	Cash cow	Cash trap
		High	Low
		Relative Market Share	

3. *Question mark.*   When an SBU has a low share of a high-growth market, the organization must decide whether to spend more financial resources to build it into a star, to phase it down, or eliminate it altogether. Many times such SBUs require high amounts of resources just to maintain their share, let alone increase it. Any company that makes microchips to compete with Intel necessarily has a question mark on their hands. The world microchip market has learned to rely on Intel technology and will require significant advances in technology to switch to a competing product. Searching for that technology breakthrough will be exceedingly expensive for any company and places their microchip in BCG's question mark category.

4. *Cash trap.*   When an SBU has a low share of a low-growth market, it may generate enough cash to maintain itself or it may drain money from other SBUs. The only certainty is that cash traps are not great sources of cash. Sears made a tough decision in the spring of 1993 to stop publishing its famous catalog. Tradition had been keeping the catalog alive, even though Sears' customers had been using it less. The catalog had become a cash trap. Management finally recognized that reality overcame inertia, built up by tradition, and scrapped the catalog.

Depending on whether SBUs are products, product lines, or entire divisions, an organization can have a number and combination of the preceding classifications. Once the relevant identifications have been made, the organization is faced with strategic choices.

6-2b Strategic Choices

Every organization can be analyzed using the BCG business portfolio matrix. This technique enables managers to put each SBU through some tough questions. Four alternative strategies can be taken with each SBU (Figure 6-4).

1. *Build.*   If an organization has an SBU that it believes has the potential to be a star (probably it's a question mark at present), it would want to build that SBU. The organization may even decide to give up short-term profits to provide the necessary financial resources to achieve this objective. A firm should also build its current stars.

2. *Hold.*   If an SBU is a successful cash cow, a key objective would certainly be to hold or preserve the market share so that the organization can take advantage of the positive cash flow.

3. *Harvest.*   This objective is appropriate for all SBUs except those classified as stars. It focuses on increasing the short-term cash return without too much concern for the long-run impact. It's especially worthwhile when more cash is needed for investment in other businesses.

4. *Divest.*   Getting rid of SBUs with low shares of low-growth markets is often a good move.

Figure 6-4
Alternative Strategies with SBUs

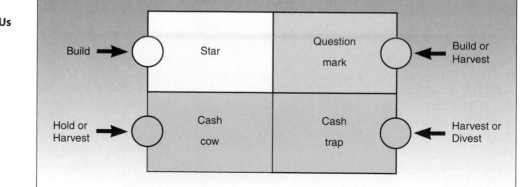

> **LearningMoment** _The BCG Portfolio_
>
> Portfolio analysis can help managers invest scarce resources among competing opportunities. The goal of the BCG matrix is to identify a mix of investments that best serves the accomplishment of objectives.

SBUs can change position in the business portfolio matrix. As time passes, question marks may become stars, stars may become cash cows, and cash cows may become cash traps. In fact, one SBU can move through each category as the market growth rate changes. The industry's technology and competitiveness influence how quickly these changes occur. This underscores (1) the importance and usefulness of viewing an organization in terms of SBUs and (2) the necessity of constantly seeking new ventures as well as managing existing ones.

A major criticism of the business portfolio matrix centers on its focus on market share and market growth as the primary indicators of profitability. One study found that using the BCG matrix actually decreased managers' ability to choose the more profitable project. Looking at managers in six countries over a five-year period, the study found that of those managers who had used the BCG matrix in their analysis of what businesses to invest in, 87 percent selected the less profitable investment.[14] In addition, some critics contend that the BCG matrix tends to lead managers to focus on what to bring to market and to de-emphasize the importance of marketing.[15]

Another caution that should be kept in mind when using the BCG matrix is that many complex concepts in strategic thinking are reduced to 2×2 arrays for the purpose of simplification. The 2×2 is the simplest form of array on which the value of more than one variable can be plotted on each of more than one axis. An important reason for the popularity of the 2×2 seems to be that any concept worth using in the world of business has to be reducible to a fairly stark and simple form. However, the apparent simplicity of the 2×2 is both a strength and a weakness. When it's used to display concepts thoughtfully distilled from the real world, it can be very powerful. When employed to explain a situation whose complexity must fit into four boxes, it can be misleading.[16] Although these criticisms are valid, thanks to the BCG model's power in placing an emphasis on the SBU's strategic position, managers across all industries use it extensively.

It is most appropriately used in addressing strategy in multibusiness, multiproduct, or multiservice situations.

6-2c Porter's Five Forces

Harvard Business School management researcher Michael Porter has developed several useful frameworks for developing an organization's strategy. One of the most popular among managers making strategic decisions is the five competitive forces that determine industry structure. Porter's view is that in any industry the nature of competition is embodied in five competitive forces:

1. Threat of new entrants
2. Bargaining power of suppliers
3. Rivalry among competitors
4. Threat of substitute products or services
5. Bargaining power of buyers

Intel's former CEO Andy Grove stated that Porter neglected a sixth important force: _complementors_. This term refers to the dependence that develops between companies whose products work in conjunction with each other's. For Intel, its vast market for microchips is created in large part by the complementor PC industry or such firms as Hewlett-Packard, Dell, and Gateway.[17]

Figure 6-5
A Value Chain

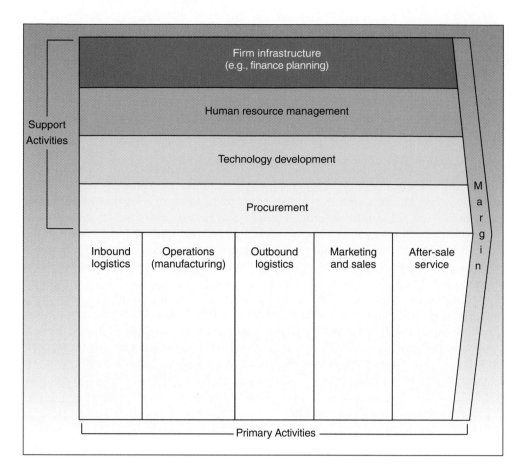

The strength of Porter's five forces varies from industry to industry. However, no matter the industry, these five forces determine profitability because they shape the prices firms can charge, the costs they have to bear, and the investment required to compete in the industry. For example, the threat of new entrants limits the profit potential in an industry because new entrants seek market share by driving down prices, and thus driving down profit margins. Or powerful buyers or suppliers bargain away profits for themselves. Managers should use the five forces framework to determine the competitive structure of an industry prior to making strategic decisions.

6-2d Porter's Value Chain

value chain All activities undertaken by an organization to create value for the customer.

Another concept Porter introduced is known as the **value chain.** The value chain is all the activities an organization undertakes to create value for a customer. Figure 6-5 shows a typical value chain.

According to Porter, competitive advantage grows out of the way firms organize and perform the various activities of their value chain. To gain competitive advantage over rivals, a firm must either provide comparable buyer value but perform the activities of the value chain more efficiently (reducing costs) or perform the activities in a unique way that creates higher value and commands a premium price.

Strategy guides the way a firm organizes its value chain and performs the individual activities. Quality-based organizations understand their value chain not as a set of isolated functions or organizational silos, but as linked activities. Managers in the quality organization view the value chain as a system. Improvements to the system are usually made by teams of individuals representing the various activities.

Value-chain strategy encompasses various elements. In addition to cultivating partnerships and building trust with immediate customers and suppliers, it also includes initiatives that create ripple effects across multiple tiers of a given chain. Among them are:

- Inventory strategies such as JIT delivery, real-time inventory tracking, synchronizing supply/demand planning, and cross-docking of materials at warehouse locations.

- Sharing critical information with suppliers, customers, and other value-chain partners. Providing access to real-time information on production plans, sales orders, and inventory levels can smooth the flow of materials and reduce inventory costs throughout the chain.

- Collaborative product development, specifically, initiatives that involve suppliers and customers in the early stages of the development process.

- Adoption of web technologies, including various e-business solutions that improve the flow of information throughout a value chain, improve logistics management, and reduce cash-to-cash cycle times.

Companies that have implemented effective value-chain strategies tend to perceive a twofold benefit. Not only do they do better individually, but the performance of the overall chain often improves. Among the executives who assess their strategies as highly effective, 57.9 percent rate the overall performance of their primary value chain as "very good" or "excellent." Meanwhile, only 5.6 percent of those with ineffective strategies see their value chains functioning at that level.

Sound value-chain strategies appear to generate better internal results as well. For example, 77.4 percent of the executives who rated their firms' strategies as highly effective reported an increase in the number of immediate customers over the last three years. A considerably lower percentage of firms with "somewhat effective" strategies or ineffective strategies cited growth in their customer base.[18]

Managers use the value chain perspective and other frameworks to engage in strategic thinking. Such frameworks are useful to narrow the range of issues considered, focusing on the forces and sources of competitive advantage. Another phase of strategic development in a firm is the strategic planning process.

6-3 The Strategic Planning Process

Strategic planning is the process of examining the organization's environment, establishing a mission, setting desired goals and objectives, and developing an operating plan. During the strategic planning process, firms will typically ask themselves, "What do we want the future to be?" or "What must we do now to better ensure that the desired future is achieved?"

In high-performance organizations, strategic planning never ends. Either the organization is formulating a new strategy or it's implementing an existing one, assessing progress, and revising processes as needed. For example, a company CEO has the primary task of articulating the firm's strategy on a daily basis to employees, customers, the public, and others. When Ed Zander became the new CEO of technology giant Motorola, he knew that communicating with employees would be a big part of his job if he was going to turn the troubled company around. Five weeks after he arrived, he determined that his job was going to consist of 10 percent technology and 90 percent diplomacy. He began by writing a weekly companywide e-mail message, and inviting top managers to his apartment for pizza.[19] CEOs must be able to communicate a strategy to those in the organization who will be charged with implementing it.

Most managers in an organization don't directly develop the organization's strategic plan. But managers may be involved in this process in two important ways: (1) they usually influence the strategic planning process by providing information and suggestions relating to their particular areas of responsibility, and (2) they must be completely aware of what the process of strategic planning involves as well as the results, because everything their respective departments do and the objectives they establish for their areas of responsibility should all be derived from the strategic plan.

In well-managed organizations, a direct relationship exists between strategic planning and the planning managers do at all levels.[20] The focus of the planning and the time perspectives will, of course, differ. Figure 6-6 illustrates the relationship between the strategic

Figure 6-6
Relationship Between the Organization's Strategic Plan and Operational Plans

Source: Adapted from James H. Donnelly, Jr., James L. Gibson, and John M. Ivancevich, *Fundamentals of Management,* 9th ed. (Burr Ridge, Ill., Richard D. Irwin, 1995), p. 198.

The Strategic Plan

Mission

Contribute to Achievement of → Strategies

Portfolio plan

Objectives

Operational Plans

Production Plan	Marketing Plan	Personnel Plan	Financial Plan	Facilities Plan
Objectives	Objectives	Objectives	Objectives	Objectives
Forecast	Forecast	Forecast	Forecast	Forecast
Budgets	Budgets	Budgets	Budgets	Budgets
Strategies and programs	Strategies and programs	Strategies and programs	Strategies and programs	Strategies and programs
Policies	Policies	Policies	Policies	Policies

At the same time that the strategic plan provides direction for individual departments' plans, they are contributing to the success of the strategic plan.

plan and operational plans. It indicates that all plans should be derived from the strategic plan while at the same time contributing to the achievement of the strategic plan.

Strategic planning is best conceived as a cyclical process that is fueled by strategic thinking. The strategic planning process outlined in this chapter consists of four steps: (1) assessing the organization's internal and external environments; (2) establishing a mission statement; (3) establishing goals and objectives; and (4) establishing an operating plan. Figure 6-7 shows the four major components of strategic planning, each informed by strategic thinking. The cyclical representation is best because it connotes that strategic planning never ends. Competitive organizations are always thinking strategically and are frequently involved in one or more of the components of strategic planning. For example, many firms have five-year strategic plans. If they are competitive, they probably continuously revise and modify the plan. Static, one-year, or five-year plans do not reflect reality. Thus, continuous reviewing, modifying, and evaluating the strategic plan is becoming the preferred approach in most organizations.

6-4 Assessing the Organization's Environment

A strategy, plan, or mission for the future begins with an assessment of the current situation in which the company finds itself. A systematic, thorough analysis requires attention

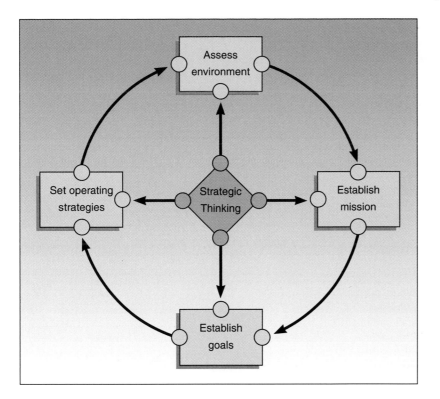

Figure 6-7
The Components of the
Strategic Planning Process

to four things: internal strengths and weaknesses, and external opportunities and threats. Such an analysis is often referred to as a **SWOT analysis** (Strengths, Weaknesses, Opportunities, Threats). Historically, the SWOT analysis has provided managers with useful signals for strategic change.[21] Many organizations, profit and non-profit, use this technique as a starting point for data gathering in their strategic planning process.[22]

A company's strengths are usually derived from its financial, human, and other resources. The firm's financial assets include cash, securities, receivables, and other tangible resources usually presented on its balance sheet and other accounts. Human resources are less easy to evaluate, yet that is a primary component of modern organizations. Human resources include the ideas, ingenuity, patents, and other intangible yet essential bases for competitiveness that only human beings can provide to an organization.

Externally, the company's business environment presents both threats and opportunities. An opportunity is anything that has the potential to increase the firm's strengths. For example, a pending reduction of trade barriers may allow a firm to increase its business in another country. A threat is anything that has the potential to hurt or even destroy a firm. For instance, a change in tax laws may portend ruin for a firm that specializes in using tax breaks that are to be eliminated by the change.

Key components of an organization's environment include the sociocultural milieu, technological developments, economic conditions, and political climate. Each of these is explained in more detail in the following text.

▶**SWOT analysis** A systematic, thorough analysis that requires attention to internal strengths, internal *weaknesses*, internal opportunities, and threats.

LearningMoment   *One More Time on SWOT*

The SWOT analysis of a firm's strengths (S), weaknesses (W), opportunities (O), and threats (T) is important in identifying core competencies. A core competency is the special strength that the firm has or does exceptionally well.

Management Focus on Innovation

Strategy Is the Heart of Innovation and Competitiveness

Successful competitive *strategy* should address the following five critical elements that provide the framework for creating and sustaining competitive advantage:

- **Choosing the future.** A strategic vision is the guiding theme that articulates an organization's intentions for the future. More than a vague expression of hope, it should clearly articulate leadership's beliefs about how the competitive environment is likely to evolve, state its aspirations for what the business can and should become, and establish guiding principles for future success.
- **Redefining competition.** Innovation is the hallmark of competitive strategy. Successful market leaders pursue innovation in products, strategy, and operations as a means to deliver customer expectations and continually redefine the basis for competition in their markets.
- **Turning ideas into action.** The strategic plan is the managerial game plan for how the business intends to

fulfill its mission, realize its vision, and achieve its objectives—how to move from ideas to action.

- **Accelerating competitive performance.** A company's strategy is realized through its leadership structure, operating model, organizational culture, strategic relationships, and competitive capabilities. Organizational structure is aligned to optimize expertise and flexibility. Proprietary sources of advantage are built through innovation, relationships, and resource deployment.
- **Sustaining competitive advantage.** Strategic leadership is the capability to build and strengthen the company's long-term position in the face of emerging market developments, technology advancements, and organizational challenges.

Source: Adapted from Karen Corrigan, "Steps to Competitive Advantage," *Marketing Health Services,* Winter 2004, p. 48.

6-4a Sociocultural Milieu

Change is constant in modern societies. Strategic planners, therefore, must be able to identify the changing cultural and social conditions that will influence the organization. Unfortunately, many organizations still don't consider the impact such changes will have, or they underestimate their impact. Managers need to be aware of developments in the sociocultural milieu. Many organizations use a technique known as **environmental scanning** to stay in touch with developments.[23] This technique provides firms with a framework for examining external trends in business and society in general, to assess the impact of these trends on the industry or profession, and to view the firm's position as part of an interconnected business ecosystem.[24] Research has shown that organizations using this technique focus primarily on the competition, customer, regulatory, and technological sectors of their environment. Information is usually received from multiple, complementary sources.[25] The Management Focus on Innovation box, "Strategy Is the Heart of Innovation and Competitiveness," illustrates how preparing for the next generation's needs and tastes can be organized within a strategic planning process.

environmental scanning
A technique that organizations use to stay in touch with developments in the sociocultural milieu.

Another technique many firms use is called **issues management.** This technique focuses on gathering information about and analyzing issues that are critical to the organization's continued performance. One person is often assigned leadership on a specific issue and is responsible for making and/or recommending strategic decisions on that issue. Issue management must begin with a method for identifying and defining the issues that will be monitored and integrated into the organization's strategic planning.[26] This is not as easy as it sounds as many issues can be complicated and involve multiple interest groups outside of the organization.[27]

issues management
A technique used by many firms that focuses on gathering information about a single issue and analyzing it.

Marketing organizations routinely use measurements of **customer-perceived value**—such as conjoint analysis and focus groups—to develop new products and services and improve existing offerings. Now, an increasing number of innovative companies are relying on techniques such as these to redesign key parts of their organizations. First, they obtain precise information on the needs and values of their internal and external customers. Then, they use this information to, among other things, tailor products and services to meet distinct market segment requirements. As a result, they not only see

customer-perceived value
The need and value of customers identified through the use of techniques such as conjoint analysis and focus groups.

performance improve, but they have also given their customers the opportunity to define what customer satisfaction means. This allows firms to reduce costs and improve customer service, while increasing profitability.[28]

6-4b Technological Developments

Changes in technology can influence an organization's destiny. Technological innovations can create new industries or vastly alter existing ones. Consider the personal computer's impact on management over the last fifteen years. Communication and information technologies are also changing the rules of work.

Telecommuting, for example, has led to "distributed work"—work activity conducted by teams of people separated from each other in time and space. Management of distributed work processes takes place using advanced communications technologies. Strategic thinking helps managers anticipate technological changes, adapt to their implementation in the workplace, and exploit them for competitive advantage.[29]

The Internet's rapid emergence as a business tool also presents a whole new set of challenges to modern managers. They must learn how to use the Internet while avoiding some of the traps that lie hidden there. A new generation of web-based technologies has proven to be more capable than the technologies that were developed during the go-go dot-com years. Managers in companies of all sizes should be careful not to be skeptical of all web-based technologies based on the failures of the past. It is often the case that a first-wave of innovation in a new area of technology produces a high failure rate. Those who are able to learn from the mistakes of others often create a second-wave of innovation that avoids the earlier mistakes and offers real advantages to those willing to adopt the technologies. The Internet and its related technologies will no doubt continue to have a dramatic impact on the way organizations are structured in on the way people work.[30] For example, General Motors has used web-based systems to overhaul its production systems.[31]

6-4c Economic Conditions

The world economy in the first decade of the twenty-first century is increasingly integrated and increasingly competitive. New players enter the worldwide economic game every day. New alliances form, new trading blocs come into existence, and new rules of fair competition are constantly being drafted and debated. The emerging global (digital) economy will create a more complex economic playing field than ever before. Stock markets operate all night around the world. Major investment banks monitor and issue buy and sell orders overnight on the international stock markets. Everywhere, CEOs wake up on some mornings to find a dramatically different economic climate than when they went to sleep the night before. Terrorism shakes investor confidence. Major and respected companies—such as Houston-based Enron—collapse overnight. Long-time bitter competitors such as Compaq and Hewlett-Packard, or K-Mart and Sears, announce a burying of the hatchet and an intent to merge. The world of business never sleeps, and managers need to stay connected to be competitive.

Wired magazine editor Kevin Kelly has tracked the digital revolution for years. He refers to the present situation as the "network economy." Kelly says the new rules governing the network economy revolve around several axes:

1. Wealth in the new economy flows directly from innovation, not optimization; that is, wealth is not gained by perfecting the known, but by imperfectly seizing the unknown.
2. The ideal environment for cultivating the unknown is to nurture the ability and nimbleness of networks.
3. Domestication of the unknown means abandoning the highly successful known— undoing the perfected.
4. In the network economy the cycle of "find, nurture, destroy," happens faster and more intensely than ever before.[32]

Managers will need to make a wide variety of adjustments on a continuous basis if they want their companies to remain competitive. New companies will come into being, and old ones that don't adapt will die. This is an era of instant communication and fast-changing technologies. It's also an era of employee empowerment and changing global relationships and structures. Traditional ways of doing business are gone, along with comfortable relationships. If companies are going to achieve success, they must stay abreast of and adapt to changing economic conditions.[33]

6-4d Political Climate

The political climate that propelled the United States into a world superpower no longer exists. Nations of the world no longer need to align themselves with one of two opposing economic giants. The collapse of the Soviet Union did bring an end to the Cold War that had kept the world on the edge of its nuclear seat since World War II. But the end to this political standoff has thrown the world into disarray as former Soviet satellites struggle for identity, ethnic animosities buried under the weight of the Russian bear rise up again in troubling frequency, and world trade battles rage over differing interpretations of fair play and justice. These and similar complex battles over scarce resources, differing value systems, xenophobia, and long-festering hatreds will be shaping the political climate well into the next century. Business must be prepared for volatile, even revolutionary changes in geographic boundaries, contract and licensure regulations, and limitations on direct investment.

Perhaps the greatest change in the world's political climate is being created in the world's most populous countries: China and India. India's politicians have taken deliberate actions to orient the nation's economy toward the West. India has become a prime destination for outsourcing a wide range of business processes, including technical support, call centers, and software development. This opening of the country to business opportunities linked to exporting services has dramatically altered the country's internal politics, as a rising and prosperous middle class begins to gather influence.

China will present even greater political challenges in the coming years as it continues its path of reform away from strictly communist policies and toward more free-market policies. China's transformation to an economic superpower in the coming years will not only bring a wide range of new products to the U.S.—including the first line of Chinese automobiles expected to arrive in 2005[34]—but also opens up new market opportunities for U.S. firms. The coming decades will surely see dramatic transformations in strategy as firms adjust to the inroads being made by companies located in these two large and highly competitive nations. The Management Focus on Globalization box addresses how consumer products companies in the U.S. are attempting to penetrate the large Chinese market.

6-5 Establishing an Organizational Mission Statement

> **mission** A long-term vision of what an organization is trying to become; the unique aim that differentiates one organization from similar organizations. The basic questions that must be answered to determine an organization's mission are "What is our business? What should it be?"

An organization's **mission** is its raison d'être (French for "reason for being"), the fundamental purpose it's designed to serve. The organizational mission statement answers the question "What is this organization's purpose?" for employees, customers, and other constituents. Whereas a strategy addresses ongoing goals and procedures, the firm's mission statement describes an even more fundamental rationale for its existence.

Some organizational theorists assert that organizational missions should be based on something even more abstract, an organizational vision. In other words, a mission statement should flow out of the vision. A true vision is a snapshot of the future that allows an organization the flexibility of means to build toward it. A vision is important because it helps the firm model strategic plans and provides a kind of touchstone for goal setting. It can be critical in a shifting industry by offering a hedge to reactive decision making. A vision keeps a firm focused on its superordinate, or long-term, goals.

To establish a mission, a firm must take into consideration its history, distinctive competence(s), and environment.

Management Focus on Globalization

Consumer Products Companies Enter the Chinese Market

The world's makers of shampoo, cosmetics, soft drinks, and other consumer goods have long coveted the Chinese market. Now, with rapid economic growth, demand is taking off. Packaged foods already constitute a $47 billion category that is expanding by 8 percent a year—a pace rarely seen these days in developed markets, where sales of some types of consumer goods are stagnating or even shrinking.

In developed markets, consumer goods companies stretch a brand horizontally by offering, say, additional flavors of a brand of carbonated drinks to attract more of the targeted teenage segment. But in China, where the aim is to appeal to a broad range of customers at both high- and low-income levels, foreign consumer goods marketers should consider stretching brands vertically—offering different product benefits aimed at different income levels, all under a brand that has hitherto focused entirely on the premium segment. Such an approach can create a double hazard, however, by diluting the brand image for consumers of the original premium products while the newer, lower-priced ones cannibalize their sales.

Marketers should start by researching the consumers' needs, segmenting them into "premium needs" on the one hand and "generic benefits," on the other—and then establish a clear differentiation between premium products and value-priced variants. Johnson & Johnson, for example, was the first multinational in China to introduce mid-priced sanitary protection products. It identified leakage protection as the core generic benefit and made this the product's focus, restricting claims of comfort and superior absorption to its premium range. Similarly, value-priced variants of Procter & Gamble's Crest toothpaste focus on generic benefits such as cavity protection, leaving claims of teeth-whitening properties to higher-priced versions.

Targeting the middle- and lower-income consumer segments calls for products that are 30 to 50 percent less expensive than premium ones. But unless costs can be brought down proportionately, gross profit margins will quickly turn south. Foreign companies in China can ill afford to increase their costs to launch a new brand aimed at the middle or lower tiers of the market; in fact, they will need to cut their costs substantially to turn a profit. All told, local companies enjoy a cost advantage of as much as 30 percent against their foreign competitors.

Source: Adapted from Yougang Chen and Jacques Penhirin, "Marketing to China's Consumers," *McKinsey Quarterly,* 2004 Special Edition, pp. 62–73; Roger Chen, "Price Wars," *China Business Review,* September/October 2003, pp. 42–46.

6-5a History

For established firms, the mission should be consistent with what is known about the firm's history. This history includes accomplishments and failures, objectives and policies, decisions, employees, and more. An organization must assess its history to determine its current resource base, its image, and its various capacities. Some management consultants help organizations appreciate and use organization stories. Stories tell of experiences and events that transpired where the storyteller works. Within an organization, stories serve to legitimate power, to rationalize group behavior, and to reinforce organizational values, identity, and commitment.[35] Before writing, human cultures relied on stories to convey the history of their culture to the young and to outsiders. Similarly, organizational stories convey the history of the organization to new employees and outsiders. Managers should review organizational stories when establishing a mission statement.

Start-ups and new ventures need a mission, too, but have no history upon which to base a long-term vision. Instead, such firms can look to the history of the industry they are part of, or to the history of the human needs and expectations they hope to satisfy through organized activity.

6-5b Distinctive Competence

Although a firm is likely to be capable of doing many things, strategic success stems from the firm identifying and capitalizing on what it does best and also what customers desire. A **distinctive competence** is a capacity that's unique to the firm and that's valued in the market.

distinctive competence
A factor that gives the organization an advantage over similar organizations; what the organization does well.

6-5c Environment

The business environment contains opportunities, constraints, and threats to the firm. Before a mission is articulated, these conditions must be analyzed and evaluated, as discussed earlier. The mission should be responsive to the organization's environment.

6-6 Characteristics of a Mission Statement

For effective organizations, the mission statement that results from the analysis of history, distinctive competence, and the environment must be (1) customer-focused, (2) achievable, (3) motivational, and (4) specific.

6-6a Customer-Focused

Mission statements in high-performance organizations emphasize a customer focus. Many firms have faltered or failed because they continued to define themselves in terms of what they produced rather than in terms of whom they served.

High-performance organizations formulate strategy based on the premise that customer satisfaction and, better yet, customer delight and loyalty are necessary for enduring success. The reasons are many and fundamental. Finding new customers is far more expensive than keeping current customers. Dissatisfied customers not only fail to return to buy again, they are also likely (1) to decline to express the reasons for their dissatisfaction (which could be a source of learning and growth for the firm) and (2) to share their dissatisfaction with other potential customers. As quality expert W. Edwards Deming noted, "no one can guess the future loss of business from a dissatisfied customer."[36] Customers, not employees, are a firm's best salespeople.

Rubbermaid is a good example of a company that consistently produces customer delight. Virtually every product the company makes is popular, with nine out of ten new products rated a commercial success. In a survey of consumers, Rubbermaid was chosen the second most powerful brand in America in terms of product quality, concern for customer needs, consumer trust, and consumers' willingness to recommend the company. The fundamental new product strategy is to understand the definition of value through the consumer's eyes.[37]

6-6b Achievable

While a mission statement should be challenging, it must also be achievable. Unrealistic ambitions can exceed a firm's capabilities. Although it's important to ensure that goals are achievable, it's equally important to guard against setting your sights too low. Organizational missions should provide future targets that can both be measured and attained, and still provide motivation for even greater achievements. For example, to be a leader in a particular market segment is both measurable and provides a constant challenge to attain and or retain that vaunted position.

6-6c Motivational

The mission must serve as a source of motivation at all levels. Effective mission statements have meaning to every employee, allowing each of them to translate the mission's words into their own motivation, and serving as a guide for decisions and actions.

Motivation affects the enduring effort of employees. Quality and competitiveness consultant Philip Crosby described the three phases involved in getting an organization or a person to be productive: conviction, commitment, and conversion.[38] Conviction means the employee is dedicated to the idea. Commitment describes the behavioral expression of the psychological conviction. Conversion means that the employee has rejected outdated, noncompetitive notions of success and has adopted the company's goals as his/her own.

6-6d Specific

A mission statement must be clear enough to allow employees and customers to know in what business the firm competes as well as in what business it doesn't compete. Being specific in the mission allows employees to focus their energy and to be more productive, making the entire firm more profitable. Broad statements of value or goodness (e.g., "the highest quality at the lowest price") do not make a good mission statement. By attempting to be all things to all people, a firm's energy is scattered, making the firm less able to develop distinctive competence and making it nearly impossible to please anyone.

Most mission statements are directed both inside and outside their respective organizations, providing a message to management, staff, clients, and customers. When writing a mission statement, an organization should step back and reflect on what it's trying to do. It needs to focus on the fundamental elements that both define the organization and make the difference between its success and failure.[39]

6-7 Establishing Organizational Goals and Objectives

A firm's mission must be further translated or reduced into meaningful goals, which specify in more concrete detail the firm's long-term aspirations. Organizational goals are the end points or targets stemming from the organization's mission. Goals define what the organization seeks to accomplish through its ongoing, long-run operations.

Effective goals are capable of being converted into precise actions and shorter-term objectives. Clear goals tell employees where they should direct their efforts, without creating doubt about the firm's intentions. Organizational leaders set the tone by communicating not only what needs to be done, but also how it should be done. All leaders, at whatever level, must focus on the essential flow of the business processes in their area of responsibility. The high-performance organization leader trains the staff so they are able to achieve difficult goals and controls the processes to ensure consistent high quality.

Goals facilitate management control, serving as standards against which the firm's performance will be measured. Clear goals and objectives help employees track progress by providing precise targets and immediate feedback. An employee focused on customer satisfaction as a strategic goal has something to measure as an indicator of success.

6-8 Establishing Operating Strategies

After a mission and goals are specified, they must be put into action through an operating strategy. An **operating strategy** is a broad plan of action for pursuing and achieving the firm's goals and satisfying its mission. The *competitive strategy model* offers several alternative operating strategies. According to the competitive strategy model, organizations can develop distinctive competence in three ways: differentiation, cost leadership, and niche.

> **operating strategy** A broad plan for action for pursuing and achieving a firm's goals and satisfying its mission.

6-8a Differentiation

In an effort to distinguish its products, a firm using the **differentiation strategy** offers a higher-priced product equipped with more product-enhancing features than its competitors' products. Using this strategy, firms seek a premium price for their products and attempt to maintain high levels of customer loyalty. The firm markets and sells the product to a relatively small group of customers who are willing to pay a higher price for the premium features. This strategy (sometimes called a *premium strategy*) leads to relatively high-cost, low-volume production, with a high gross profit margin per item. Often advertising or marketing adds a perception of luxury that creates demand for the product due to the psychological value of buying and using it. Mercedes Benz automobiles, Ben & Jerry's ice cream, and Godiva chocolates are marketed under a differentiation strategy.

> **differentiation strategy** An organization's policy to offer a higher-priced product with more product-enhancing features than those of its competitors.

6-8b Cost Leadership

In contrast to the differentiation strategy, the cost leadership strategy means low costs, low prices, high volume, and low profit margins on each item. With this strategy, a cost leader attempts to attract a large number of customers with low prices, generating a large overall profit by the sheer volume of units sold. Examples of cost leaders are the U.S. Postal Service, McDonald's, and Hyundai. It's difficult, though not impossible, to be both lower cost and differentiated relative to competitors.[40] One company that has managed both is Saturn Corporation. Differentiation is a key competitive strategy that has been built in

Figure 6-8
Competitive Strategy Model

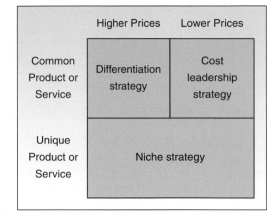

from Saturn's beginnings in 1985. First, Saturn sold the company instead of the car. Second, it developed a relationship with customers. In its first year, Saturn's advertisements centered on employee commitment and low price. Since then, Saturn has focused on the experience of its customers, emphasizing economy and quality at the same time.[41]

6-8c Niche

> **niche strategy** When a firm provides a product or service in a special area.

The **niche strategy** involves offering a unique product or service in a restricted market (usually a geographic region). For example, Dallas-based Southwest Airlines has targeted the point-to-point, low-fare traveler since its beginning. Many airlines have attempted to compete with Southwest in its niche, but usually meet with failure. Continental Airlines, for example, tried to compete with Southwest by introducing a new point-to-point service it called "Continental Lite." However, Continental learned a painful and expensive lesson by trying to compete in this niche at the same time as it maintained its traditional hub-and-spoke system. Continental Lite failed because the company didn't have the infrastructure to compete head to head in Southwest's niche.[42]

Every organization must choose one of these market strategies, summarized in Figure 6-8. Although strategic planning doesn't guarantee success, it can increase the likelihood of achieving success. Integrating quality practice into overall corporate strategy gives firms a powerful source of competitive advantage.

6-9 Stakeholders and Strategy

The renewed emphasis on quality and competitiveness that has occurred among organizations has strong implications for overall strategy. For instance, the drive to grow and expand, so common to businesses for most of the twentieth century, must be tempered by an ability to maintain contact with customers. Many organizations learned the hard way that bigger is not better if all contact with customers is lost. At the same time, companies have learned that customers, or "stakeholders," come in a variety of forms. There are internal and external stakeholders. One important internal stakeholder that has gone through cycles of neglect in American business is the employee. Today, high-performance organizations are focusing on employees as their most vital resource.

6-9a Employees

Whereas the traditional view of strategy suggests that managers and shareholders are a company's most important asset, a modern view directs attention to the customers and non-management employees. These stakeholders are highlighted in modern firms because they are critical in defining and adding value to the product or service.

Employees in the modern workplace are conceived differently from those at the turn of the century, as we have already noted. Increasingly, organizations are relying on their own people as the source of new ideas, energy, and creativity. These employees are frequently finding themselves as members of workplace teams.

A view of employees as a resource has replaced the traditional view of labor as a cost of production. The only sustainable competitive advantage for a firm in the global marketplace is its human resources. Although cash, equipment, facilities, and infrastructure can be quickly transferred, built, or acquired, human resources are not so easily or quickly developed. **Strategic management** of employees requires managers to dedicate time, money, and attention to their training and development. This not only increases workers' value, it also enhances their capacity for continuous improvement. In a global market, allowing a workforce to grow stagnant without ongoing training is to invite failure.[43] Research has shown that training and development offer significant contributions to any organization in enhancing the abilities of employees.[44]

The prudent approach is to adopt a long-term strategy, and then build a sensible training program that helps employees develop skills that can be applied to problems throughout the organization. Employees want training that will help them make progress in their careers, but managers have to recognize that progress in modern organizations has been redefined. Career paths in the modern organization often don't follow the traditional "corporate ladder." In the customer-focused organization, employees spend more time moving along a horizontal ladder, doing projects with people from different departments in their organization, than climbing the vertical ladder.[45]

Much of the work in organizations involves collecting, organizing, and analyzing information. In short, professional work is knowledge work. To help employees succeed requires not only training, but also an organizational structure conducive to continuous learning. The main difference between training and learning is that training is often a group activity; learning is often more effective as an individual activity. Managers who provide both training and a learning environment for employees will create more innovation, better service, and more efficient operations than competitors.

> **strategic management**
> Develops the mission, objectives, and strategies of the entire organization; the top-level decision makers in the organization.

6-9b Customers

Defining organizational strategy in terms of customer expectations is fundamental to the modern approach to strategic management. Customers are defined as the end users of the organization's products and/or services.

For some companies, a variety of customers or groups may use its products and services. For example, a hotel may rent single rooms to walk-up business customers, to tourists in small groups, or to a business manager of a professional organization who secures rooms for thousands of convention goers. Similarly, a household goods moving firm may sell its full range of services to corporate clients at a discount for large volume, and at regular rates to single households that use only some of the firm's services (e.g., shipping but not packing of household goods). Careful identification of the firm's customers is essential.

How does a company find and develop loyal customers? There is no simple answer to this critical question. Happy customers return and refer other customers. Unhappy customers not only fail to return, they are likely to turn away other potential customers. One estimate is that one dissatisfied customer can produce 250 noncustomers (people who are indifferent, perhaps even hostile to a firm's product or service).[46] In a free market economy, where customer choice and freedom are paramount, satisfied customers are the fundamental focus of any strategy.

Customers use the goods and services produced by a firm. Many firms, in turn, are customers of suppliers. Working with suppliers to ensure a steady flow of high-quality raw materials is vital to a firm's overall success.

6-9c Suppliers

Suppliers provide essential raw materials for the firm. The traditional view of suppliers is that a single supplier of any one raw material can threaten a firm's flexibility, especially its capacity to force price concessions by playing off two or more suppliers against one another. This is compounded by a traditional view of purchasing as a low-cost function where the business is awarded to the supplier offering the lowest cost per unit. A more effective strategy focuses on developing long-term relationships with key suppliers, focusing on building partnerships, continuously improving product quality, and driving down costs. Special attention is devoted to eliminating defective parts and to involving the supplier in the design process for the firm's product(s). This type of relationship is the basis of such process innovations as just-in-time manufacturing.

6-9d Stockholders

Publicly traded firms have another set of constituents interested in the firm's performance: stockholders. While many stockholders are interested only in maximizing returns on their investment, most also realize that this is best accomplished through an effective quality strategy.[47] Stockholders are those who own a firm's stock.

The traditional view of business in the United States has placed highest priority on satisfying stockholder expectations, which, because of their exclusively financial interest, usually meant paying close attention to the quarterly report. This focus results in a heavy emphasis on short-term profit improvements, often realized at the expense of long-term investment.

In Japan, by way of contrast, stockholders and senior management are the first to suffer in bad business times. The traditional U.S. approach to a downturn in the business cycle has been to lay off workers first while the firm waits for customer demand to return. A 1980 NBC News White Paper, "If Japan Can, Why Can't We?" showed how Mazda of Japan, during an energy-cost-induced sales crisis, assigned engineers to selling jobs, to learning more about the customer, without layoffs.

A major responsibility of managers is communication with stockholders. Perhaps the most effective communicator is Warren Buffet, chairman of the investment firm Berkshire Hathaway and one of the world's wealthiest people. Buffet is well known for his annual reports to shareholders. In fact, many people purchase Berkshire Hathaway stock just to have an opportunity to read Buffet's message.

6-9e Community

Another stakeholder of most organizations is the community. The community is an important stakeholder in that it defines the rules for legal business activity and is the source of many important resources for the organization's continued success.

The community consists of private citizens plus government and other public or regulatory agencies. Traditionally, the community is dependent on the firm and is grateful for the salaries and taxes it pays and for its use of community suppliers and contractors. Many communities and states offer companies special inducements to bring their production to the community.

Not only must a firm act in a legal, ethical fashion with each stakeholder; the community also expects a strong sense of social responsibility from the firm. Further, most communities view the firm as needing to make a positive contribution to the community, beyond the firm's payroll, purchases, and taxes. The strategic view of the community as a stakeholder must also be long term.

6-9f Relating the Strategic Plan and Operational Plans

Most managers in an organization will not directly develop the organization's strategic plan. However, they may be involved in this process in two important ways: (1) They usually influence the strategic planning process by providing inputs in the form of information and suggestions relating to their particular areas of responsibility. (2) They must be completely aware of what the process of strategic planning involves as well as the results, because everything their respective departments do, the objectives they establish for their areas of responsibility, should all be derived from the strategic plan.

In well-managed organizations, therefore, there is a direct relationship between strategic planning and the planning done by managers at all levels. If planning is done properly, it will result in a clearly defined blueprint for management action *at all levels* in the organization.

Management Summary

- The rapidly changing world that managers face has made the strategic planning process increasingly important. A strategic focus represents management's attempt to anticipate the future and to guard the organization against the effects of change.

- A strategic plan consists of a clearly stated organizational mission, organizational objectives, and an organizational operating plan.

- The organizational mission is a long-term vision of what the organization is trying to become. The basic questions that must be answered are: "What is our business?" and "What should it be?"

- Three important considerations in formulating the organizational mission are the organization's history, its distinctive competencies, and its environment.

- Organizational strategies are the general approaches used to achieve the organizational objectives. These strategies include differentiation, low cost, and niche.

- There is a direct relationship between strategic planning and the planning done by an organization's managers. If the organization's strategic plan is properly executed, the scope, range, issues, and time perspectives will differ from department to department. But all of the organization's plans will be derived from the strategic plan and, after a time, will contribute to its achievement

Key Terms

BCG matrix (p. 127)
customer-perceived value (p. 134)
differentiation strategy (p. 139)
distinctive competence (p. 137)
environmental scanning (p. 134)

issues management (p. 134)
mission (p. 136)
niche strategy (p. 140)
operating strategy (p. 139)
strategic business units (SBUs) (p. 127)

strategic management (p. 141)
strategic thinking (p. 124)
strategy (p. 124)
SWOT analysis (p. 133)
value chain (p. 130)

Review and Discussion Questions

1. "Plans are sometimes useless, but the planning process is generally indispensable." What does this mean?

2. What is meant by the statement, "Every manager plans"?

3. How can components of the environment act as constraints or opportunities?

4. As the U.S. population ages, what impact will it have on the future workforce?

5. Provide examples of businesses that have pursued differentiation, low cost, and niche strategies. In your view, what factors influenced the selection of these strategies?

6. Why would a manager utilize a SWOT analysis?

7. Choose any organization you are familiar with and develop for it a statement of organizational mission.

8. Why is it important to have maximum participation by employees in the strategic planning process?

9. Distinctive competencies distinguish firms from each other. What are the distinctive competencies of Dell Computer, Wal-Mart, and Tyco International?

10. Someone once quoted a well-known cosmetic executive as saying, "In the factory we make cosmetics; in the drugstore we sell hope." What does this statement indicate about the executive?

Practice Quiz

Note: You can find the correct answers to these questions by taking the quiz and then submitting your answers in the Online Edition. The program will automatically score your submission. If you miss a question, the program will provide the correct answer, a rationale for the answer, and the section number in the chapter where the topic is discussed.

Indicate whether the sentence or statement is true or false.

_____ 1. Many of today's most successful business organizations continue to survive because many years ago they offered the right product or service at the right time.

_____ 2. The political climate that propelled the United States into a world superpower still exists.

_____ 3. Many firms have faltered or failed because they continued to define themselves in terms of what they produced rather than in terms of who they served.

_____ 4. While a mission statement should be challenging, it must also be achievable.

Identify the letter of the choice that best completes the statement or answers the question.

_____ 5. Strategies are often based on the_____ of a company or its founder.
   a. lineage
   b. financial needs
   c. historical focus
   d. product line

_____ 6. Many critical decisions were made without the benefit of strategic thinking or planning. Whether these decisions were based on wisdom or luck is not important; they resulted in the _____ that has carried these organizations to where they are today.
   a. intuition
   b. wisdom
   c. momentum
   d. wealth

_____ 7. The U.S. Postal Service, McDonald's, and Hyundai all use the _____ strategy.
   a. differentiation
   b. cost leadership
   c. niche

_____ 8. The drive to grow and expand, so common to businesses for most of the twentieth century, must be tempered by an ability to maintain contact with _____.
   a. suppliers.
   b. employees.
   c. the competition.
   d. customers.

_____ 9. One estimate is that one dissatisfied customer can produce _____ noncustomers (people who are indifferent, perhaps even hostile, to a firm's product or service).
   a. 50
   b. 150
   c. 200
   d. 250

_____ 10. A _____ plan consists of a clearly stated organizational mission, organizational objectives, and an organizational operating plan.
   a. long-term
   b. strategic
   c. logistical
   d. short-term

_____ 11. A _____ is a product or service division within a company that establishes goals and objectives in harmony with the firm's overall mission and is responsible for its own profits and losses.
   a. strategic business unit
   b. cash cow
   c. value chain
   d. competitive advantage

_____ 12. Which of the following is one of the support activities in Michael Porter's value chain model of the organization?
   a. outbound logistics
   b. marketing
   c. human resources
   d. operations

_____ 13. An organization's _____ represents the fundamental purpose it is designed to serve.
   a. goals
   b. objectives
   c. values
   d. mission

_____ 14. Managers should use the _____ to determine the competitive structure of an industry prior to making strategic choices.
   a. SWOT analysis
   b. five forces model
   c. environmental scanning
   d. issues management

_____ 15. Which of the following is a prime candidate for a divest strategy?
   a. cash cow
   b. cash trap
   c. star
   d. question mark

Case Study

Motorola Leverages Technology to Identify Business Trends

Motorola believes that it can serve its customers better by assuring that all employees and partners have access to the same information when making business decisions. This is the focus of the firm's Enterprise Roadmap Management System (ERMS), an effort sponsored by the company's chief technology officer and its Innovation Leadership Team—which is made up of senior technology representatives from across the company.

ERMS provides a common roadmapping process, a common software solution, and a common information architecture for all of Motorola. This gives the company's employees the ability to create, build, and share their technology visions, products, and business strategy roadmaps throughout the organization.

Motorola's former CEO Robert Galvin noted many years ago that "the fundamental purpose of the Technology Review and the Technology Roadmaps is to assure that we put in motion today what is necessary in order to have the right technology, processes, components, and experiences in place to meet the future needs for products and services." ERMS has taken Galvin's vision of roadmapping and infused it into the Motorola culture. Motorola presents roadmaps as snapshots in time during the annual corporate technology reviews and as the main focal point in the continuous process of reviewing what may happen in the future.

An important aspect of the company's strategic planning process is gathering and sharing information globally with respect to customer, supplier, and competitive intelligence. ERMS has created a common roadmap library for the purpose of sharing collaborative roadmaps. These roadmaps include the necessary customer and supplier information as well as competitive intelligence; they capture the whole business environment surrounding an organization's strategies.

The EMRS team is building a strong internal and external library of roadmaps. Included in this library are roadmaps from the various internal organizations as well as industry associations, customers, suppliers, and competitors. This roadmap library allows Motorola associates, managers, and strategists to:

- Create relationships between their own roadmap and a roadmap of interest
- Perform gap analysis between roadmaps
- Improve functional linkage and trend analysis
- Generate representational composites of strategies
- Determine prioritization and level of competitor investments in specific areas

- Monitor industry trends
- Assess technology requirements
- Identify challenges facing Motorola businesses

The practice of building collaborative roadmaps also allows Motorola to identify significant market changes while identifying misalignments between significant strategies. These roadmaps also help prevent executives from being blindsided by disruptive technologies that are emerging quickly and sometimes quietly. The solution of improving the functional linkages and trend analyses has given managers the ability to promote fresh insights about strategic issues and encourage external experts as well as other associates to contribute their strategies. By leveraging this potential strategic intelligence, managers are able to learn more than they could on their own.

Having all these roadmaps in a common repository has given Motorola the ability to form stronger business alignments. It puts the company in a position to provide a system of checks and balances that will reduce misjudgments and market "surprises" through a linkage of technology plans to business strategies and product plans. It is obvious that roadmap collaboration provides a greater potential for communicating information, analyzing data to a greater depth, and formulating more precise business decisions.

Analyzing customer roadmaps allows an organization to determine how certain changes in a customer's business model will impact its own vision. Information such as supplier dependencies and strategic intent will also identify areas of concern that should be addressed in strategic planning.

Questions for Discussion

1. How can having the same information across employees and employee groups lead to better strategic decision making?

2. What is meant by the term "competitive intelligence"? How can this help a company make better strategic decisions?

3. How can roadmaps, such as the ones used by Motorola, help prevent executives from being "blindsided by disruptive technologies"? What is a "trend analysis"? Name two or three trends that are deeply affecting Motorola's business today.

Source: Adapted from James M. Richey and Mary Grinell, "Evolution of Roadmapping at Motorola," *Research—Technology Management,* March–April 2004, pp. 37–41.

Internet Exercise

A Close-Up Look at Michael Porter

In this chapter we spent time covering a number of Michael Porter's views, models, and suggestions on strategic planning and competitive advantages. Use the Internet to examine in more detail who Michael Porter is and what his viewpoints are on strategy and competition. He is spearheading an initiative on urban area competitive advantages. What are the rationale and the results of this initiative?

Take a look at Amazon or Barnes & Noble listings and write-ups on Michael Porter's books. Do you believe that his teaching and research has an impact on what managers think about strategic planning?

Experiential Exercise

Organizational Planning

Purpose: To emphasize the importance of planning in organizations.

Setting Up the Exercise: Follow these instructions:

1. First, every person in the class should be assigned the same organization from the following list.

   Bell & Howell

   Gap

   Crocker National Bank

   Gerber Foods

   JC Penney

   NASA

   Procter & Gamble

   Red Cross

   Nortel

   Shell Oil

   Toyota

   Winnebago

Answer these questions:

a. What events in this organization's environment should be considered in developing short- and long-run plans?

b. How likely are the events to occur? What is the probability of the events (e.g., a gasoline shortage, a change in government regulations, increased foreign competition, a drastic change in consumer demand)?

c. How can planning improve the organization's chances of capitalizing on, or adjusting to, the occurrence of the events cited in your answer to part b?

2. After the members of the class complete part 1 of the exercise individually, the instructor will form groups of five to eight students. Each group will be assigned one of the remaining organizations. The groups should answer a, b, and c in part 1 and report their answers to the class.

Learning Note: This exercise requires some out-of-class homework to prepare the answers. It will show that some organizations need planning more than others because of the forces they must deal with in the environment.

Managerial Decision Making

7

147

Managing Today

Merck's Decision to Pull Vioxx from Store Shelves Begs Many Questions

They burst upon the scene five years ago, grabbing the limelight with an almost shameless display of feel-good ads. A new, kinder generation of painkillers, they were hailed as "super Aspirin"—a boon for arthritis sufferers who literally could not stomach the bleeding and gastrointestinal problems of everyday analgesics. Now *Vioxx*, the big dog in this category, is gone, its spectacular withdrawal in late September still reverberating through Wall Street and about to hit the courts. The line of attack: when did drug giant Merck & Co. Inc. first know *Vioxx* could provoke heart attacks or strokes in a significant number of users? And why didn't it do more in the early stages to follow the clues?

In September 2004, Merck decided to withdraw its Vioxx anti-inflammatory drug from store shelves. Merck had indications of possible heart-related problems with Vioxx almost from the time it started selling it in 1999. But it kept advertising and selling Vioxx to the public while running new tests to make sure it was safe. When tests conclusively showed problems in September 2004, Merck had to make a choice between continuing to sell Vioxx with additional warnings, or to recall the product from circulation. Merck's executive team decided to pull the pills.

As almost anyone outside Merck could have foreseen, that decision left the company open to the financial, legal, and regulatory turmoil that threatens to destroy it. Merck says it pulled Vioxx rather than adopting stronger warnings because the company is run on best-practice medical principles rather than by legal or marketing parameters. However, it is hard to reconcile that position with the fact that Merck sold Vioxx to the public for many years with full knowledge that there might be problems for some people.

Pulling Vioxx is a noble gesture—but it is a tacit admission that the medicine has hurt people. Hanging tough, while restricting Vioxx to people who can tolerate standard anti-inflammatories, would have been a better legal and strategic decision in the eyes of many external observers.

Sources: Adapted from Allan Sloan and David J. Jefferson, "And the Turkey Goes to..." *Newsweek,* November 29, 2004, p. E20; Robert Sheppard and Brian Bergman, "Withdrawal Pain," *MacLean's,* November 29, 2004, pp. 64–65; and "First, Do No Harm," *The Economist,* November 27, 2004, pp. 12–13.

This chapter focuses on management decision making. As you will learn, decision making involves a complex mix of knowledge, experience, creative thinking, and risk taking. Adding to this complexity, today's organizations make many important decisions in groups and teams. The notion of the lone manager controlling all decisions from the top of the corporate hierarchy has gone the way of the dinosaur. As the Managing Today case suggests, decisions made long ago can reverberate for years. Merck will undoubtedly face scrutiny for deciding at one point to sell a flawed product, and then reversing that decision later.

Although the Merck case is one of executive decision making, more and more companies are pushing critical decision making down to the level of the organization most affected by the decision. Although this change provides lower-level managers with a greater degree of autonomy and control, it also carries a higher level of responsibility.

An important measure of the quality of an individual manager or management team is the effectiveness of the decisions reached. Indeed, some have argued that management simply is decision making, and that the essence of managerial behavior can be understood by studying decision making.

decision A conscious choice among alternatives followed by action to implement the choice.

Managers in every type of organization make decisions every day involving competing goals, risk, uncertainty, and alternative courses of action. A **decision** can be defined as a conscious choice among alternatives followed by action to implement the decision. A decision without action is a meaningless concept. Decision making entails a choice and subsequent action. The decision-making process is a series of steps that are followed, either consciously or unconsciously, to make a choice and undertake action.

In today's complex, information-rich organizations, decision making is often a rapid-fire, fragmented process. It's becoming less likely that a single individual can process enough information on his or her own to make the best decision for the organization. Besides the vast amount of data available for most nonroutine decisions, managers often must respond to interruptions, unexpected crises, and important opportunities, and often find that decision making is a process that must occur over time. Managers must learn how

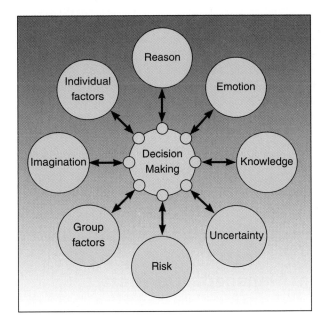

Figure 7-1
The Decision-Making Variables

to deal with a decision-making environment that emphasizes communicating with others inside and outside of the organization, working in groups and teams, with incomplete information, and with decisions often based on impressions, estimates, and personal experience. Decision making often reflects the manager's effort to make sense of the complicated environment, to attain some control over the uncontrollable, and to achieve some sense of order.

Management researchers have studied decision making from many different perspectives and have developed a set of useful concepts to understand the phenomenon. Several of the more important concepts will be explored to increase your awareness of the complexity of this highly social process that involves reason, emotion, risk, and uncertainty. Figure 7-1 shows the many variables that influence a decision maker.

Decision making can be viewed as a series of steps or stages that run from clearly identifying a problem, to implementing and assessing actions, to solving the problem. Using such a systematic approach to decision making ensures that relevant information has been gathered, alternative choices have been considered, and possible consequences of actions are understood. In addition to a systematic component, decision-making research—especially that utilizing artificial intelligence—has determined that human emotions and interest are also important elements of organizational decision making. Managers at all levels are encouraged to recognize this non-systematic or "qualitative" aspect of decision making.[1]

Managers at all levels of organizations make decisions. These decisions may influence the survival of the organization, or the starting salary of a new trainee. All decisions, however, will have some influence—large or small—on performance.[2] Thus, it is important for managers to develop decision-making skills. Like it or not, managers are evaluated and

LearningMoment *Decisions are the Result of a Process*

Remember that a decision is something that happens at a moment in time. Effective managers cultivate an ability to be decisive and to act confidently. This should be clearly distinguished from the decision-making process, which should precede a decision. How a manager conducts the process of gathering relevant information, communicating with others in the organization, and analyzing the information gathered can be equally or more important than the decision itself.

rewarded on the basis of the importance, number, and results of their decisions. The quality of the decisions that managers reach is the yardstick of their effectiveness and of their value to the organization.[3]

Individual decision making differs from group decision making. Each has its own set of strengths and weaknesses that a manager should understand.[4] This chapter discusses both individual and group decision making.

The chapter concludes with an overview of how information technology is being applied to assist managerial and executive decision making. Information technology is a double-edged sword for managerial decision making. On one hand, it has brought forth a bewildering amount of information that is too great for any individual to handle. At the same time, information technology can assist in the analysis and synthesis of information and present it to managers in a way that makes alternative choices and their consequences rather obvious.[5] We'll explore the impact of information technology on managerial decision making later in the chapter. For now, let's consider the types of decisions managers make.

7-1 Types of Managerial Decisions

Given that decision making is an entirely human process, it is fraught with complexities and ambiguities that are reflective of human beings themselves.[6] By gaining an understanding of the different types of decisions commonly confronting managers you can develop skills for handling them. For example, a manager who is used to making routine decisions will have difficulty adjusting to a promotion where many of the decisions are strategic in nature, and far less routine. Prior knowledge of the skills needed for strategic, nonroutine decision making would prepare the manager for the new demands.

7-1a Programmed and Nonprogrammed Decisions

Decision making in organizations occurs during routine operations and in unexpected situations. Management scholar Herbert Simon has distinguished programmed from nonprogrammed decision making to account for these different circumstances. A **programmed decision** is one that would be made if a particular situation occurs and a routine procedure or **policy** has been established to handle it. Decisions are said to be programmed if they are repetitive and routine, and a definite procedure has been developed for determining when the decision should be made and what actions should be taken. Routine decisions become standard operating procedures for an organization. Managers used to making routine decisions under routine circumstances can become highly efficient at recognizing the cues for one choice over another. However, under nonroutine circumstances, their programmed style of decision making may become ineffective. In fact, research has shown that individuals used to making highly routine decisions are prone to fall back on their old ways of thinking even when circumstances have permanently changed.[7]

A **nonprogrammed decision** is one in which there is no preexisting structure or decision-making procedure in place. An example of a nonprogrammed decision might be how to respond to a new and unexpected competitor for a firm's primary market. Such a decision would involve issues of strategy, resource commitments, and long-term returns on investment. It would not be a simple matter of "checking the boxes" on some preexisting form. Managers make nonprogrammed decisions when they purchase new computer equipment or other critical business assets. Research has shown that this decision is often driven by a perception of value that is based on a wide range of subjective and objective factors.[8]

Managers in most organizations are burdened with a large number of programmed decisions in their daily operations. Such decisions should be made with care and concern about effectiveness, but they should be made efficiently without needlessly tying up organizational resources. Nonprogrammed decisions, on the other hand, often have significant implications for the future of the organization and must be made only after careful analysis. Table 7-1 provides examples of each type of decision in different types of organizations.

▶ **programmed decision** Response to repetitive and routine problems, which is handled by a standard procedure that has been developed by management.

▶ **policy** Guidelines for managerial action that must be adhered to at all times. Policymaking is an important management-planning element for ensuring that action is oriented toward objectives. The purpose of policies is to achieve consistency and direction and to protect an organization's reputation.

▶ **nonprogrammed decision** A decision for novel and unstructured problems or for complex or extremely important problems; deserves special attention of top management.

	Programmed Decisions	Nonprogrammed Decisions	**TABLE 7-1**
Type of problem	Frequent, repetitive, routine, much certainty regarding cause-and-effect relationships	Novel, unstructured, much uncertainty regarding cause-and-effect relationships	**Types of Decisions**
Procedure	Dependence on policies, rules, and definite procedures	Necessity for creativity, intuition, tolerance for ambiguity, creative problem solving	
Examples	Business: Periodic reorders of inventory	Business: Diversification into new products and markets	
	University: Necessary grade point average for good academic standing	University: Construction of new classroom facilities	
	Hospital: Procedures for admitting patients	Hospital: Purchase of experimental equipment	
	Government: Merit system for promotion of state employees	Government: Reorganization of state government agencies	

Source: From John M. Ivancevich and Michael J. Matteson, *Organizational Behavior and Management,* 3rd ed. p. 584. Reprinted by permission of the McGraw-Hill Companies.

7-1b Proactive and Reactive Decisions

Recall that "decision" has been defined as a conscious choice among analyzed alternatives. A decision made in anticipation of an external change or other conditions is called a **proactive decision.** Managers who utilize a systematic, proactive approach to decision making can prevent many common problems from affecting their organization.

A **reactive decision** is one made in response to changes that have already occurred. Using a reactive decision-making process, for example, an airline may wait for passengers to complain before changing its food vendor.

Managerial vision or an organizational mission provide the context for proactive decision making. If the vision is strong enough and communicated effectively, many employees will intuitively make decisions in support of that vision.[9] Managers should attempt to create a compelling vision of their organization to empower employees at all levels to make decisions that prevent the common organizational problems from occurring. Southwest Airlines has consistently adhered to a clearly defined purpose—to make a profit, achieve job security for every employee, and make flying affordable for more people. This kind of clarity provides guidance for day-to-day decision making, but allows room for opportunity, flexibility, and agility to enable faster, better *decisions*.

Having too many rules is paralyzing and stifling, but a set of simple rules provides direction, helps define priorities, and shapes how *decisions* get made. Southwest Airlines understands that employees sometimes have to make quick *decisions* that may be outside of the norm. President Colleen Barrett asserts that "You cannot write a scenario for every happening that calls for common sense and good judgment. You have to be there."[10]

7-1c Intuitive and Systematic Decisions

Intuitive decision making involves the use of estimates, guesses, or hunches to decide among alternative courses of action.[11] Most managers will admit that many of their decisions are influenced to a great extent by their "intuitions."[12] The way that term is used here doesn't refer to something mysterious. Instead, intuition is simply the "voice of experience" that speaks to managers when faced with a decision situation. The voice may be no more than a "gut feeling," or it may be loud and clear memories of how a similar situation was handled in the past. Despite the strength of some intuitions, managers must be careful not to rely on their intuition alone when making decisions. It is much wiser to supplement intuition with systematic information gathering and analysis.[13]

In contrast to purely intuitive decision making, **systematic decision making** is an organized, exacting, data-driven process. Systematic decision making requires a clear set of

proactive decision
A decision made in anticipation of an external change or other condition.

reactive decision A decision made in response to changes that have already occurred.

intuitive decision making
Basing decisions on the use of estimates, guesses, or hunches to decide among alternative course of action.

systematic decision making
An organized exacting, data-driven decision-making process that requires a clear set of objectives, a relevant information base, and a sharing of ideas among key managers and other employees.

TABLE 7-2	Intuitive	Systematic
Intuitive Versus Systematic Decision Making	My hunch is that we should improve customer support after we sell them our product.	Customer surveys have indicated that we need to improve postsale support.
	This process is out of control and needs adjustment.	Control charts indicate that this process has been operating beyond the control limits for seven consecutive weeks. Therefore, something needs to be done.
	My feeling is that this firm could benefit from TQM.	Based on successes I've observed with TQM in firms similar to ours, we too could probably benefit from its principles and techniques.

objectives, a relevant information base, and a sharing of ideas among key managers and other employees. Table 7-2 provides lists of intuitive and systematic decisions.

At times, managers must react quickly and intuitively to unexpected situations. Sound intuition, however, is developed primarily from experience and training, as well as from practice in systematic decision making.[14] For example, a service repair manager may have to react to an angry customer who is dissatisfied with a product. If the manager doesn't react quickly and appropriately, the customer may be lost. Yet, the manager's reactive, intuitive decision will be better if it's based on training and experience with similar situations.

7-2 The Decision-Making Process

The decision-making process is a mechanism for seeking a desired result in response to a challenge or opportunity. The nature and structure of the process influence how effective the decision outcome is likely to be. In most decision situations, managers go through a series of steps or stages. In this chapter, we explore a five-step decision-making process:

1. Clarify the problem or opportunity.
2. Develop alternative courses of action.
3. Evaluate and select a course of action.
4. Implement the decision.
5. Monitor its effectiveness.

Figure 7-2 graphically displays the five-step decision-making process.

7-2a Step 1: Clarify the Problem or Opportunity

problem The realization that a discrepancy exists between a desired state and current reality.

Problems are defined as the realization that a discrepancy exists between a desired state and current reality. Thus, problems become apparent when clear goals and objectives have been established for the organization. As we have discussed, goals and objectives are set in the planning and strategic planning processes. Without goals and objectives, there would be no way to make decisions because there would be no way to evaluate their effectiveness. All decisions must be measured by how well they help an organization achieve its goals and objectives.

To clarify a problem, managers must view it from a variety of perspectives. This may seem paradoxical. It would seem that a problem would be clearer if viewed only from a single perspective. This would be a false impression. Most organizational problems have complexities and nuances that only reveal themselves when viewed from several perspectives. For example, most managers deal with employee problems. A common problem is when one employee lodges a complaint about another employee. It would be unwise for a manager to act on that complaint without getting several other perspectives, including the perspective of the employee at the center of the complaint. It will often turn out that the actual problem is much different than it appeared at first.[15]

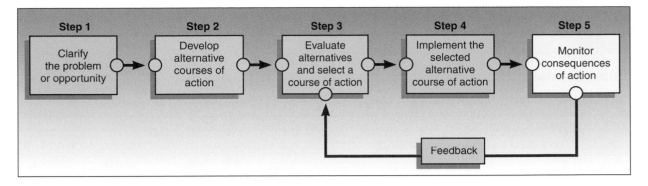

Figure 7-2
The Five-Step Decision-Making Process

Managers make several common biases or mistakes when identifying and clarifying a problem. Three of these are:

1. *Perceptual inaccuracies:* Individual attitudes, feelings, or mental models may prevent individuals from recognizing problems.[16] For example, a common problem is for managers to delay or completely avoid making tough decisions about a problem employee if the manager has personal feelings for the person. It's a difficult situation, but good managers are able to set aside their feelings and attitudes to make decisions that are in the best interest of the organization.

2. *Defining problems in terms of solutions:* This occurs often when someone has a favorite tool or procedure that they like to implement. For example, someone who likes order and exactitude may decide that a time clock is the solution to a problem of employees reporting late to the office. Further investigation may reveal that lateness is due to difficult parking arrangements, or that only one or two employees are violators. Suggesting that lateness is due to lack of a time clock might be counterproductive in this situation.

3. *Identifying symptoms as problems:* This occurs when a manager doesn't look deep enough into a problem to find the larger issue that needs to be addressed. If we again use the example of employee lateness, a manager should realize that such behavior may only be a symptom of a larger morale problem. Solving the lateness issue by instituting strict control measures may only exacerbate the larger problem of declining employee morale.

Clarifying problems means being aware of and avoiding these perceptual biases. It also means seeing an issue from a variety of perspectives. How do managers know when enough perspectives have been used? They can't know. Managers must develop, through experience, a sense of when an adequate set of perspectives have been considered. Usually, this comes through making a lot of mistakes, and learning from them. Knowing that you will make mistakes early in your management career, however, should not stop you from making decisions. In fact, you will make fewer mistakes by consulting various perspectives before you make your decisions. In addition, your superiors will be more lenient on your mistakes if they realize that you did follow a sound information-gathering process prior to your decision. What you should avoid is "paralysis by analysis." This affliction occurs when a manager spends too much time analyzing a decision and delays or never gets around to actually making a decision. In most organizations, it's preferable to make a bad decision than to make none at all.

Opportunities must also be clarified before any decision can be made. Opportunities, like problems, can be clarified by looking at them from a variety of different perspectives. (See the Management Focus on Diversity box, "Research Supports Gathering Multiple Perspectives for Decisions.") Be careful, though. The same perceptual biases that affect managers' perceptions of problems also affect their perceptions of opportunities. Feelings and attitudes could lead a manager to be overly optimistic about the prospects of a certain opportunity, for example. This could lead to a waste of organizational resources. Many venture capitalists injected piles of cash into Internet start-ups over the past few years only to find that the company has no clear way of earning revenues.[17] In 1996, over $6 billion

Management Focus on Diversity

Research Supports Gathering Multiple Perspectives for Decisions

Organizations that populate their employee teams with only the best and brightest workers may be making a big mistake. That suggestion is the result of a study by University of Michigan researcher Scott E. Page and colleague Lu Hong of Loyola University Chicago.

In their study, entitled "Diversity and Optimality," the researchers say that when it comes to solving problems or making good decisions, the best individual people may not be the best collective group of people for the task. In fact, a group of people selected at random is more effective than a collection of the best and the brightest individuals, they claim. This is because the random group is more likely to contain a diversity of approaches.

By using computational and mathematical models, the researchers found that, on average, groups of randomly selected "problem solvers" outperform groups consisting of the best individual problem solvers. "This rather surprising result has an intuitive explanation," says Page. "If the best problem solvers tend to think about a problem similarly, then it stands to reason that as a group they may not be very effective. Random groups may be better, owing to their diversity."

Source: Adapted from Jill Jusko, "Diversity Enhances Decision Making," *Industry Week,* April 2, 2001, p. 9.

in venture capital was directed to high-tech start-ups.[18] The venture capitalists learned to temper their enthusiasm (feelings) with judgment after a few major losses.[19] In the future, Internet start-ups will actually have to demonstrate how they will earn revenue in their business plans before venture capitalists will invest in them.

7-2b Step 2: Develop Alternative Courses of Action

Before a decision is reached, alternative courses of action must be developed. This step involves examining the organization's internal and external environments for information and ideas that may lead to creative solutions to a problem. A popular approach to this is known as **benchmarking.** Benchmarking is used to identify and study firms who are leaders in a given area of business. For example, airlines that want to improve their turnaround time at the gates would benchmark Southwest Airlines, the consistently best performer in this category. Firms that want to improve their customer service might benchmark Walt Disney Corporation or Nordstrom's.

> **benchmarking** A popular approach to identifying and studying firms that are leaders in a given area of business.

Managers should encourage creativity and innovation among employees. Alternative courses of action that lead to higher levels of performance and new moneymaking opportunities for a firm can only arise in an environment where creativity is encouraged.[20] Effective managers realize that individuals have different preferences for problem solving. Encouraging a diversity of approaches to problem solving can lead to better solutions and courses of action.[21] Of course, the ultimate test of any manager is the results he or she produces. An organizational culture that promotes creativity must not lose sight of the fundamental organizational goals and purposes.

7-2c Step 3: Evaluate Alternatives and Select a Course of Action

Once alternatives have been developed, they must be evaluated and compared. In every decision situation, the objective is to select the alternatives that will produce the most favorable outcomes and the least unfavorable outcomes. In selecting among alternatives, the decision maker should be guided by the previously established goals and objectives.

In evaluating alternative courses of action, two cautions should be kept in mind. First, this phase of the decision-making process should be kept distinct from the previous step—especially in a group context. When alternatives are evaluated as they are proposed, this may restrict the number of alternative courses of action identified. If evaluations are positive, there may be a tendency to end the process prematurely by settling on the first positive course of action. On the other hand, negative evaluations make it less likely for someone to risk venturing what may be the best solution.

The second caution is to be wary of solutions that are evaluated as being "perfect"—especially when the decision is being made under conditions of uncertainty. If a course of action appears to have no drawbacks or if, in a group setting, there's unanimous agreement on a course of action, it may be useful to assign someone to take a devil's advocate position. The role of the devil's advocate is to be a thorough critic of the proposed solution.[22]

The purpose of selecting a particular course of action is to solve a problem or take advantage of an opportunity in order to achieve a predetermined goal. In managerial decision making the decision maker usually can't possibly know all of the available alternatives, the consequences of each alternative, and the probability of these consequences occurring. Thus, rather than being an optimizer, the decision maker is said to be a **satisficer.** A satisficer is a person who accepts a reasonable alternative course of action that isn't necessarily the optimum course of action. This shouldn't be construed as an undesirable position.[23] Every decision must be made within a certain time and resource framework. Usually, it would be prohibitive from both a time and resource perspective to gather all pertinent information and to consider all possible alternative courses of action. A satisficer simply acknowledges that reality, and is prepared to act based on a reasonable review of a reasonable set of pertinent information.[24]

> **satisficer** A decision maker who accepts a reasonable alternative course of action that isn't necessarily the optimum course.

7-2d Step 4: Implement the Selected Alternative Course of Action

Any decision is little more than an abstraction if it isn't implemented. And it must be implemented effectively if it is to achieve an objective. It's entirely possible for a good decision to be hurt by poor implementation. In this sense, implementation may be more important than the choice of alternative course of action.

In most situations, implementing a decision involves delegating responsibilities to people. Thus, the effectiveness of a decision is often a function of how well it's put into action by people other than the person who made the decision. A manager's job isn't only to choose sound courses of action, but also to transform these choices into effective actions. This is often accomplished today by empowering employees to make the day-to-day decisions that are needed to carry out the course of action. Figure 7-3 illustrates the following six steps to effective **delegation:**

> **delegation** The process by which authority is distributed downward in an organization.

1. *Clearly define the task.*   When you assign work, don't tell people how to do the job. Instead, describe the results you want. Then let them complete the task on their own. The better you describe the benefits of accomplishing the task, the more they will want to see it through.

2. *Provide guidelines to begin or follow.*   Assuming you match the right task with the right person, you can increase your delegating success by giving guidelines on how to begin. Some people have the skills to accept the task and begin on their own, but are open to suggestions. Others are unsure of how to begin. They are afraid of losing face and won't tell you they don't know how to begin. When you give guidelines, you help everyone perform at a higher level.

3. *Delegate authority to accomplish the task.*   There is nothing worse than being given a job to do but not the authority to get it done. If you don't trust someone, give the job to someone else or assign it in stages so it isn't overwhelming.

4. *Monitor the tasks, but don't hover.*   It is frustrating and discouraging to be given a task and then have someone peering over your shoulder every step of the way. Give people room to operate and the freedom to be creative and use their skills, talents, and abilities.

5. *Provide feedback along the way.*   Ask how things are going, then give people the chance to express themselves. When they feel their opinions count, it is a lot easier to make "course adjustments."

Figure 7-3
Six Steps to Effective Delegation

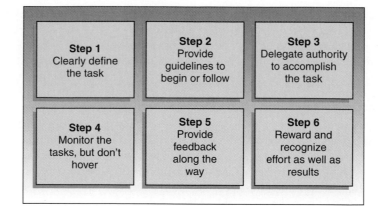

6. *Reward and recognize effort as well as results.*   Some folks need encouragement many times along the way to accomplishing the task. Others are self-starters and self-motivators. When you recognize effort as well as results, you keep people motivated with judicious praise.[25]

7-2e Step 5: Control and Assess the Consequences of the Action

Effective decision making involves periodic assessment of the results of the chosen course of action. If actual results aren't meeting planned results, changes must be made. These changes must be made either in the original objective, the course of action chosen, or in the implementation of the course of action. If the original objective is changed, the entire decision-making process would have to be restarted. The important point is that, once a course of action has been decided upon, a manager can't simply assume that its implementation will match with the objectives. Actions must be monitored and their consequences assessed. Managers use two types of feedback to gather the necessary information: formative and summative.

Formative feedback is that used during the actual implementation process. An example of formative feedback might be to use customer surveys while a new approach to customer service, such as a new telephone system, is being implemented. This feedback can be used to fine-tune the process, or perhaps to extend it further than had originally been intended.[26]

Summative feedback is used at the end of the implementation process. This type of feedback will provide a "bottom line" assessment of the decision's effectiveness by comparing the results to company and industry standards. For example, if the company expects a 12 percent return on assets and your decision resulted in 8 percent ROA, the decision would be deemed ineffective. At this point, the course of action would need to be reevaluated.

▶**formative feedback**
Feedback on job performance while the job is being performed.

▶**summative feedback** Used at the end of the implementation process to provide a "bottom-line" assessment of the effectiveness of a decision by comparing the results to company and industry standards.

7-3 Influences on Individual Decision Makers

Many important factors affect the decision-making process. Some of them affect only certain phases of the process, but others can affect the entire sequence. Each influence, however, will have an impact and therefore must be understood. Although such influences are numerous, we discuss here what we believe are the four major ones: the importance of the decision, time pressures, the manager's values, and the manager's propensity for risk.

7-3a The Importance of the Decision

The mayor of a city may make two decisions in an afternoon, one extending the school year for children because of days missed during bad weather, the other committing $50 million to constructing an expressway around the city. In each case, the steps in the

> ## LearningMoment _Remember the Decision-Making Steps_
>
> You will encounter many decision-making opportunities and challenges as you progress through your managerial career. To deal with such opportunities effectively you should be ready to execute the decision making process without hesitation. You don't want to have to return to this textbook each time to recall the steps involved. Thus, you should commit the following to memory:
>
> **1.** Clarify the problem or opportunity.
> **2.** Develop alternative courses of action.
> **3.** Evaluate and select a course of action.
> **4.** Implement the decision.
> **5.** Monitor its effectiveness.
>
> Or, use the mnemonic CDEIM, to recall the order of _clarify, develop, evaluate, implement,_ and _monitor._

decision-making process were similar, but the time and techniques used were different. Numerous yardsticks are used for measuring the importance of a decision, including the amount of resources involved, the number of people influenced by the decision, and the time required to make the decision. The important point is that managers must allot more time and attention to significant problems. In deciding to extend the school year, the mayor may have considered only a small number of possibilities because the amount of time a public school student must spend in class each year is determined by law. Before deciding to construct an expressway around the city, however, more alternatives were generated, more time and thought were utilized, and more detailed information was required. The importance of the decision in terms of monetary commitments, the number of people affected, and the decision's long-term impact influenced the amount of time and money spent on making the decision.

7-3b Time Pressures

A key influence on the quality of decisions is how much time the decision maker has to make the decisions. Unfortunately, managers must make the most of their decisions in time frames established by others. Obviously, when time pressures are significant, managers may be unable to gather enough information. They may not have enough time to consider additional alternatives.[27] Time management is a priority for most managers today. The pace of business change and the complexity of information has placed a premium on the ability to control and manage time effectively. Today managers must make decisions rapidly in response to an increased pace of competitive challenge. The ability to make decisions rapidly is key to organizational performance.[28]

7-3c The Manager's Values

An individual's values become guidelines when he or she confronts a choice. These values are acquired early in life, and they are a basic, often taken-for-granted part of an individual's thoughts. Because our values are basic to us, we are usually unaware of how they influence us. Their influence on the decision-making process, however, is great.

Many experts consider values to be one of the most important influences on human behavior. Values are the likes, dislikes, shoulds, oughts, judgments, and prejudices that determine how we view the world. Once values become part of an individual, they become (often subconsciously) a standard for guiding his or her actions. Many practicing managers are using an approach called **values-based decision making.** This approach is methodical and ensures that organizational values enter into all major decisions.[29]

▶ **values-based decision making** A methodical decision-making approach that ensures organizational values enter into all major decisions.

The values of managers underlie much of their behavior. How they approach the management functions of planning, organizing, leading, and controlling reflects their values. The decisions managers make in identifying their objectives and strategies, and how managers interpret society's expectations, also reflect their values. Some specific influences of values on the decision-making process include:

1. Value judgments are necessary in the development of objectives and the assignment of priorities.
2. In developing alternatives, you must make value judgments about the various possibilities.
3. When you select an alternative, your value judgments will be reflected in your choice.

To gain insight into your own values, complete the table in Figure 7-4. You may be surprised by the results. In most cases, people don't think consciously about their values and rarely arrange them in any kind of order. Managers, however, should be very aware of their values. It is easy to see that serious conflicts can occur among values. For example, do you

Figure 7-4
Value Survey

Instructions: Study the two lists of values presented here. Then rank the instrumental values in order of importance to you (1 = most important, 18 = least important). Do the same with the list of terminal values.

Instrumental Values	Terminal Values
Rank	Rank
_____ Ambitious (hard-working, aspiring)	_____ A comfortable life (a prosperous life)
_____ Broad-minded (open-minded)	_____ An exciting life (a stimulating, active life)
_____ Capable (competent, effective)	_____ A sense of accomplishment (lasting contribution)
_____ Cheerful (lighthearted, joyful)	_____ A world at peace (free of war and conflict)
_____ Clean (neat, tidy)	_____ A world of beauty (beauty of nature and the arts)
_____ Courageous (standing up for your beliefs)	_____ Equality (brotherhood, equal opportunity for all)
_____ Forgiving (willing to pardon others)	_____ Family security (taking care of loved ones)
_____ Helpful (working for the welfare of others)	_____ Freedom (independence, free choice)
_____ Honest (sincere, truthful)	_____ Happiness (contentedness)
_____ Imaginative (daring, creative)	_____ Inner harmony (freedom from inner conflict)
_____ Independent (self-sufficient)	_____ Mature love (sexual and spiritual intimacy)
_____ Intellectual (intelligent, reflective)	_____ National security (protection from attack)
_____ Logical (consistent, rational)	_____ Pleasure (an enjoyable, leisurely life)
_____ Loving (affectionate, tender)	_____ Salvation (saved, eternal life)
_____ Obedient (dutiful, respectful)	_____ Self-respect (self-esteem)
_____ Polite (courteous, well-mannered)	_____ Social recognition (respect, admiration)
_____ Responsible (dependable, reliable)	_____ True friendship (close companionship)
_____ Self-controlled (restrained, self-disciplined)	_____ Wisdom (a mature understanding of life)

A Memory Device for Making Ethical Decisions

Most people believe it is important that ethics take on a conscious, deliberate role in business decision making. In a nutshell, the issue of ethics boils down to asking yourself, "What price am I willing to pay for this decision, and can I live with that price?" This process can be helped by defining each letter of the word *ethics*.

E = EXPERIENCE. The values we carry with us into adulthood, and into business, are those that were modeled to us, usually by a parent, teacher, or some other significant adult. How people behave and the decisions they make speak much louder and are more convincing than what they say.

T = TRAINING. Training means training yourself to keep the question of ethics fresh in your mind deliberately.

H = HINDSIGHT. Success leaves clues that we need to tap into in order to help us make that tough decision. What if the problem you face was the problem of the person you admire most in life? What would he or she do?

I = INTUITION. What does your "gut" tell you is the right thing to do? Some call it conscience, or insight. How do you know when you've gone against your "gut"? You may feel guilt, shame, remorse, have a restless, sleepless night, etc. Now the decision is what to do about it.

C = COMPANY. How will your decision affect the company, the people who work with and/or for you, your customers, and your family? No matter how big or small your decision is, it affects other people in your life.

S = SELF-ESTEEM. The greatest ethical decision is one that builds one's self-esteem through the accomplishment of goals based on how these goals positively impact those around you.

Sources: Adapted from Frank Bucaro, "Ethical Considerations in Business," *Manage*, August/September 2000, p. 14; Alice Gaudine and Linda Thorne, "Emotion and Ethical Decision Making in Organizations," *Journal of Business Ethics*, May 1, 2001, pp. 175–187.

value both honesty and obedience in the instrumental value column or happiness and accomplishment in the terminal value column? Someone who seeks high levels of accomplishment may have to forgo some happiness. To manage effectively, you must understand your own values. Your values will directly affect the ethics of your decision making. The Management Focus on Ethics box, "A Memory Device for Making Ethical Decisions," discusses how you can ensure that your decisions are informed by your ethical values.

7-3d The Manager's Propensity for Risk

Risk taking is a necessity in most decision situations. From personal experience, you are probably aware that people vary greatly in their propensity to take risks. This aspect of the decision maker's personality has a strong influence on the decision-making process. A manager who is less inclined toward risk taking will establish different objectives, evaluate alternatives differently, and make different choices than will a manager who is more inclined toward risk taking.[30] Understanding this is important because the propensity for risk doesn't enter the picture only when the time comes to make a choice. It influences the entire decision-making process. One manager will be inclined toward situations in which the risk or uncertainty is low or in which the certainty of the outcome is high. Another, because of a greater propensity for risk, will choose the opposite kinds of situations.

Risk is everywhere. It's unavoidable. The issue for managers is not whether to take risks, but how to take reasonable risks. Risk taking can be stressful, but it also fuels creativity and, when met head-on, usually leads to personal development.[31]

7-4 Group Decision Making

The first part of this chapter focused on individuals making decisions. In most organizations, however, a great deal of decision making is achieved through committees, teams, task forces, and other kinds of groups, including "virtual teams" or employees linked electronically who may or may not ever have met in person.[32] Managers frequently face situations in which they must seek and combine judgments in group meetings. This is especially true for nonprogrammed decisions, which are novel, with much uncertainty regarding the outcome. In most organizations, it is unusual to find one individual making decisions on such problems on a regular basis. The increased complexity of many nonprogrammed decisions requires specialized knowledge in numerous fields, usually not possessed by one person. This requirement, coupled with the reality that the decisions made must eventually be accepted and implemented by many units throughout the organization, has increased the use of the collective approach to the decision-making process. The result for many managers has been an endless amount of time spent in meetings of committees and other groups.

7-4a Individual Versus Group Decision Making

There has been considerable debate over the relative effectiveness of individual versus group decision making. Groups usually take more time to reach a decision than individuals do, but bringing together individual specialists and experts has its benefits because the mutually reinforcing impact of their interaction results in better decisions.[33] In fact, a great deal of research has shown that consensus decisions with five or more participants are superior to individual decision making, majority vote, and leader decisions.[34] You can see this phenomenon at work in examples ranging from the trivial to the important. Finance professor Jack L. Treynor, for instance, devised an experiment in which he asked his students to guess how many jelly beans were in a jar and found that the *group's* average guess was off by just 2 percent even though few of the students were that close. Or consider the show "Who Wants to Be a Millionaire?" When a contestant on the show is stumped by a question, he has a couple of choices in asking for help: the audience or someone he's designated as an expert. The experts do a reasonable job: They get the answer right 65 percent of the time. But the audience is close to perfect: It gets the answer right 91 percent of the time.[35]

Further research has found that groups supported by an electronic group support system (GSS) exchanged far more information and reached more effective decisions than those groups not so supported.[36] Unfortunately, open discussion has been found to be negatively influenced by such behavioral factors as:

1. The pressure to conform.
2. The influence of a dominant personality type in the group.
3. *Status incongruity,* as a result of which lower-status participants are inhibited by higher-status participants and "go along" even though they believe that their own ideas are superior.
4. The attempt of certain participants to influence others because these participants are perceived to be expert in the problem area.[37]

Certain decisions appear to be better made by groups, while others appear better suited to individual decision making. Nonprogammed decisions appear to be better suited to group decision making. Such decisions usually call for pooled talent in arriving at a solution; the decisions are so important that they are usually made by top managers and to a somewhat lesser extent by middle managers.

In terms of the decision-making process itself, the following points concerning group processes for nonprogrammed decisions can be made:

1. Groups are probably superior to individuals because of the greater amount of knowledge available to groups.
2. In *identifying alternatives,* the individual efforts of group members are necessary to ensure a broad search in the various functional areas of the organization.
3. In *evaluating alternatives,* the collective judgment of the group, with its wider range of viewpoints, seems superior to that of the individual decision maker.
4. In *choosing an alternative,* it has been shown that group interaction and the achievement of consensus usually result in the acceptance of more risk than would be accepted by an individual decision maker. In any event, the group decision is more likely to be accepted as a result of the participation of those affected by its consequences.

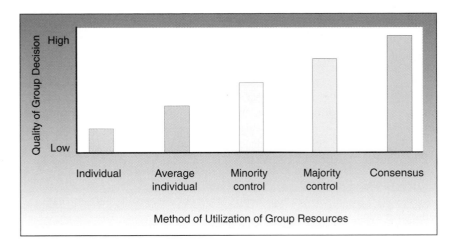

5. *Implementation* of a decision, whether or not it is made by a group, is usually accomplished by individual managers. Thus, since a group cannot be held responsible, the responsibility for implementation necessarily rests with the individual manager.

Figure 7-5 summarizes the research on group decision making. It presents the relationship between the probable quality of a decision and the method utilized to reach the decision. It indicates that as we move from "individual" to "consensus," the quality of the decision improves. Note also that each successive method involves a higher level of mutual influence by group members. Thus, for a complex problem requiring pooled knowledge, the quality of the decision is likely to be higher as the group moves toward achieving consensus.

7-4b Creativity in Group Decision Making

If groups are better suited to nonprogrammed decisions than individuals, then it is important that an atmosphere fostering group creativity be provided. In this respect, group decision making may be similar to brainstorming in that discussion must be free flowing and spontaneous. All group members must participate, and the evaluation of individual ideas must be suspended in the beginning to encourage participation.[38] However, a decision must be reached, and this is where group decision making differs from brainstorming.

7-4c Techniques for Stimulating Creativity

It seems safe to say that in many instances group decision making is preferable to individual decision making, but there are drawbacks. You may have heard the statement "A camel is a racehorse designed by a committee." This simply alludes to the fact that a committee may bring more issues to a problem than need to be considered. In a classic study of group decision making, Cohen and March identified what they called a **garbage can phenomenon**.[39] People will often use committee meetings to air their special grievances or bring up a preferred solution. For example, an information technology specialist may always bring up a technology-related solution to problems.

While the necessity and the benefits of group decision making are recognized, numerous problems are also associated with it, some of which have already been noted. Practicing managers need specific techniques that will enable them to increase the benefits from group decision making while reducing the problems associated with it.

Next we examine three techniques that, when properly utilized, have been found to be extremely useful in increasing the creative capability of a group in generating ideas, understanding problems, and reaching better decisions. Increasing the creative capability of a group is especially necessary when individuals from diverse sectors of the organization must pool their judgments to create a satisfactory course of action for the organization. The three techniques are:

▶**garbage can phenomenon**
A commonplace occurrence in group decision making where individuals bring their favorite problems or solutions to each group meeting.

1. brainstorming,
2. the Delphi Technique, and
3. the Nominal Group Technique.

Brainstorming   In many situations, groups are expected to produce creative or imaginative solutions to organizational problems. In such instances, **brainstorming** has often been found to enhance the group's creative output. The technique of brainstorming includes a rigorous set of rules. The purpose of the rules is to promote the generation of ideas while avoiding the inhibitions many people feel in group settings. The basic rules are as follows:

▶ **brainstorming** A technique for simulating creativity by using a rigorous set of rules that promote the generation of ideas while avoiding the inhibitions that many people feel in group settings.

- No idea is too ridiculous. Group members are encouraged to state any extreme or outlandish idea.
- Each idea presented belongs to the group, not to the person stating it. In this way, it is hoped that group members will utilize and build on the ideas of others.
- No idea can be criticized. The purpose of the session is to generate, not evaluate, ideas.

Brainstorming is widely used in advertising and some other fields, where it is apparently effective. In other situations, it has been less successful because there is no evaluation or ranking of the ideas generated. Thus, the group never really concludes the problem-solving process.

The Delphi Technique   The **Delphi Technique** involves the solicitation and comparison of anonymous judgments on the topic of interest through a set of sequential questionnaires that are interspersed with summarized information and feedback of opinions from earlier responses.[40]

▶ **Delphi Technique**
A technique for stimulating creativity that involves soliciting and comparing anonymous judgments on the topic of interest through a set of sequential questionnaires that are interspersed with summarized information and feedback of opinions from earlier responses.

The Delphi process retains the advantage of having several judges while removing the biasing effects that might occur during face-to-face interaction.[41] The basic approach has been to collect anonymous judgments from group members by mail questionnaire. The members independently generate their ideas to answer the first questionnaire and return it. A process administrator then summarizes the responses as the group consensus and feeds this summary back along with a second questionnaire for reassessment. Based on this feedback, the respondents independently evaluate their earlier responses. The underlying belief is that the consensus estimate will result in a better decision after several rounds of anonymous group judgment. While it is possible to continue the procedure for several rounds, essentially no significant change occurs after the second round of estimation.

The Nominal Group Technique (NGT)   The **Nominal Group Technique** (NGT) has gained increasing recognition in health, social service, education, industry, and government organizations.[42] The term *Nominal Group Technique* was adopted by earlier researchers to refer to processes that bring people together but do not allow them to communicate verbally. Thus, the collection of people is a group "nominally," or "in name only."

▶ **Nominal Group Technique (NGT)** A technique for generating ideas that involves the anonymous contribution of ideas in a group setting.

Basically, NGT is a structured group meeting that proceeds as follows: A group of seven to ten individuals sit around a table but do not speak to one another. Rather, each person writes ideas on a pad of paper. After five minutes, a structured sharing of ideas takes place. Each person presents one idea. A person designated as recorder writes the ideas on a flip chart in full view of the entire group. This continues until all of the participants indicate that they have no further ideas to share. There is still no discussion.

The output of this phase is a list of ideas (usually between eighteen and twenty-five). The next phase involves structured discussion in which each idea receives attention before a vote is taken. This is achieved by asking for clarification or stating the degree of support for each idea listed on the flip chart. The next stage involves independent voting in which each participant, in private, selects priorities by ranking or voting. The group decision is the mathematically pooled outcome of the individual votes.

The Delphi Technique and NGT are similar in many ways. Basic differences between them are:

Management Focus on Innovation

Using "Groupware" to Improve Decision Quality

Communications technology is all about being in two places at one time and is a great tool if used properly. Bob Carman, a program manager at Rocketdyne, created a virtual work group of experts outside of those in the company. With the virtual team, Rocketdyne was able to create a new engine for Boeing, test it in computer simulations, and bring it in under budget. Companies considering this new model of work groups should be aware of the need to manage them successfully. There are three rules that need to be obeyed for success.

Rule 1: Exploit diversity in those who will be working on the project. Get the best people to be found to fill the gaps in the company's expertise.

Rule 2: Use technology to simulate reality. Find a system for communication that suits the group; e-mail is not suggested as the best solution to intergroup communication.

Rule 3: Hold the team together through skills that keep the work group happy and productive. The authors suggest that the reasons these small groups are not used more often is due to organizational inertia rather than opposition to the method.

Source: Adapted from Ann Majchrzak, Arvind Malhotra, Jeffrey Stamps, and Jessica Lipnack, "Can Absence Make a Team Grow Stronger?" *Harvard Business Review,* May 2004, pp. 131–136.

1. Delphi participants are typically anonymous to one another, while NGT participants become acquainted.
2. NGT participants meet face-to-face around a table, while Delphi participants are physically distant and never meet face-to-face.
3. In the Delphi process, all communication between participants is by way of written questionnaires and feedback from the monitoring staff. In NGT, communication is direct between participants.[43]

Practical considerations, of course, often influence which technique is used.[44] For example, such factors as the number of working hours available, costs, and the physical proximity of participants will influence which technique is selected.

The discussion here has not been designed to make you an expert in the Delphi process or NGT. The purpose has been to indicate the frequency and importance of group decision making in every type of organization. The three techniques discussed are practical devices whose purpose is to improve the effectiveness of group decisions.

Decision making is a common responsibility shared by all executives, regardless of functional area or management level. Every day, managers are required to make decisions that shape the future of their organization as well as their own futures. The quality of these decisions is the yardstick of their managers' effectiveness. Some of these decisions may have a strong impact on the organization's success, while others will be important but less crucial. However, all of the decisions will have some effect (positive or negative, large or small) on the organization. The Management Focus on Innovation box highlights new software that is assisting companies in group decision making and collaboration.

7-5 Information Technology and Decision Making

Organizations today have access to more information than ever before. The abundance of newspapers, journals, magazines, TV and radio programs, seminars, and the explosive growth of the Internet has led many commentators to label this the **Information Age**.[45] The sheer volume of information available to the modern manager presents a challenge and raises important questions about the impact of information management tools on the functioning of organizations. Understanding this impact becomes even more crucial as organizations strive to increase competitiveness and productivity in the face of global pressures.

In decision-making situations, managers can't possibly use "all available information." That may have been possible at one time in history, but it simply isn't possible today. It would take anyone more than a lifetime to gather and process "all available information." The challenge for managers is to collect, process, and warehouse the most relevant information to make effective decisions in the present and future.

▶**Information Age** The period characterized by the abundance of newspapers, journals, magazines, television and radio programs, seminars, and the explosive increase in the use of computers and especially the Internet.

TABLE 7-3	Attribute	Description
Attributes of Useful Information	Accessible	Information can be obtained easily and quickly.
	Timely	Information is available when needed.
	Relevant	Managers need the information to make a particular decision.
	Accurate	Information is error free.
	Verifiable	Information is confirmed.
	Complete	All details needed are available.
	Clear	Information is stated in such a way that no facts are misunderstood.

▶**data warehousing** The storage of pieces of knowledge, often in the form of stories, for easy access for those who have future need of it.

▶**data mining** The use of software to search through the warehouse of stored information for relevant bits.

▶**data mart** A subset of a data warehouse that is easier for people to search for the data and information they need.

▶**search engines** Internet services that locate information on the World Wide Web using key words or phrases.

▶**software agents** Software tools that will perform services for an individual on the World Wide Web. For example, a person may request than an agent find the lowest price for a new computer.

▶**decision support systems (DSS)** Interactive information systems that enable managers to gain instant access to information in a less-structured format than a traditional management information system of database.

Many organizations today have developed tools for warehousing and retrieving information for use throughout their firms. **Data warehousing** is the process of collecting pieces of knowledge, often in the form of stories, that might be useful to someone in similar situations in the future. These data are then stored in a database with easy access for those who have a need for it.[46] **Data mining** is the use of software to dig through the warehouse of stored information to search for the relevant bits. It is touted by software manufacturers as having the ability to discover information that will contribute to resolving business problems or creating business opportunities.[47] **Data marts** is a term being used to describe a subset of a data warehouse that is easier for people to search for the data and information they need.[48] **Search engines** and **software agents** help managers find the bits of information that are relevant to their current situation.[49]

Managers today must be able to make decisions quickly to keep pace with competition. Yet, if an organization isn't prepared to handle a large volume of information or if the information doesn't reach key decision makers, the volume of information and its speed of travel are of no value. Two important points for managers to remember are that not all information is useful, and useful information is better if it's widely shared.

7-5a Attributes of Useful Information

Not all information is appropriate for making a decision. For information to be truly useful it must be accessible, timely, relevant, accurate, verifiable, complete, and clear.[50] Table 7-3 summarizes these attributes. As the table shows, the requirements for useful information are fairly rigorous and may be difficult to meet. For instance, when information is needed quickly, accuracy may be sacrificed for speed; information obtained quickly may not be error free.

7-5b Information Sharing

A major challenge facing organizations is the manner in which information is shared among employees. Because of the abundance of information, much relevant information never reaches the people who can benefit from it the most.

In today's economy, information—more than capital assets and natural resources—is the key to growth and competitiveness. Some managers withhold information from workers because they're afraid employees will use the information against them or somehow share it with competitors. Unfortunately, workers can't respond to the need for continued improvement without information. Organizations that train people in the value of information and how to use it and share it gain competitive advantage over those who don't.

7-6 Decision Support Systems

A **decision support system (DSS)** is an interactive information system that enables managers to gain instant access to information in a less-structured format than a traditional management information system (MIS) or database. DSS software combines corporate information on past performance with what's currently taking place; it allows managers to

Management Information System	Decision-Support System	TABLE **7-4**
1. The main effect is on structured tasks where standard operating procedures, decision rules, and information flows can be reliably predefined.	1. The impact is on decisions in which there is sufficient structure for computer and analytic aids to be of value but where managers' judgment is essential.	**Differences Between an MIS and a DSS**
2. The main payoff is an improving efficiency by reducing costs, turnaround time, and so on, and by replacing clerical personnel.	2. The payoff is in extending the range and capability of managers' decision procedures to help them improve their effectiveness.	
3. The relevance for managers is the creation of a supportive tool, under their own control, that doesn't attempt to automate the decision process, predefine objectives, or impose solutions.	3. The relevance for manager's decision making is mainly indirect; for example, by providing reports and access to data.	
	4. A DSS tends to be aimed at the less well structured, underspecified problems that upper managers typically see.	
	5. It attempts to combine the use of models or analytic techniques with traditional data access and retrieval functions.	
	6. It focuses on features that make it easy to use by noncomputer people in an interactive mode.	
	7. It emphasizes flexibility and adaptability to accommodate changes in the environment and the decision-making approach to the user.	

Source: Adapted from V. Thomas Dock and James C. Wetherbe, *Computer Information Systems for Business,* West Publishing, 1988, p. 106.

work with large amounts of data not otherwise available to them. Through a DSS managers can obtain information about the firm, competitors, and the business environment. A modern DSS may include links to the World Wide Web and have built-in artificial intelligence that adjusts to group behaviors and needs.[51]

Decision support systems are inherently user-friendly. They use graphical user interfaces to help managers get to the information they need quickly and easily.[52] The main differences between a DSS and a traditional MIS are summarized in Table 7-4. A DSS supports managerial skills at all levels of decision making by providing instant response to managers' information needs. Thus, a DSS is a specialized MIS designed to improve the effectiveness of decisions.

An **executive information system (EIS)** is a user-friendly DSS designed specifically for executives. An EIS will be exceedingly easy to use, requiring that executives have no prior knowledge of computers or databases. A good EIS will consolidate the analysis provided by a DSS, interpret it in light of the organization's strategic goals, and present the results to executives in an easily understandable format. By moving a mouse or touching the screen the user directs the EIS to present relevant information.

Artificial intelligence allows computers to solve problems involving imagination, abstract reasoning, and common sense. Computer scientists are trying to empower computers to behave as though they could think by perceiving and absorbing data, reasoning, and communicating in ways similar to human behavior. The term **expert systems** refers to computer systems that can make decisions without human interaction. Such systems imitate human thinking and offer advice or solutions to complex problems in much the same way as a human expert would. Expert systems are used today to plan shipping schedules, provide financial advice to investors, and help managers respond to competition. Most of the leading financial institutions use expert systems in such areas as lending, financial planning, trading, fraud detection, auditing, and production selection.[53]

▶ **executive information system (EIS)** A user-friendly DSS designed specifically for executives; doesn't require prior knowledge of computers or databases but provides analysis by interpreting it in terms of the organization's strategic goals and presenting the results in an easily understandable format.

▶ **artificial intelligence** A computer program that allows computers to solve problems using imagination, abstract reasoning, and common sense.

▶ **expert systems** Computer systems that can make decisions without human interaction.

Since decision support systems can provide information to managers covering a wide range of factors, expert systems generally cover much smaller fields of knowledge. Expert systems are usually built from decision rules used by experts in a specific field. The user interacts with the system, each asking questions of the other. An expert system provides recommendations and explains the logic used to arrive at those recommendations. While experts systems are yet to make the logical decisions humans can make, the quality of expert system decisions continues to improve as the technology improves.

Management Summary

- Planning and decision making are two managerial activities that cannot be separated. Every stage of planning involves decision making.

- The quality of management decisions determines to a large extent the effectiveness of plans.

- Managers are evaluated and rewarded on the basis of the importance, number, and results of their decisions.

- Decisions may be classified as programmed or nonprogrammed, depending on the type of problem. Each type requires different kinds of procedures and applies to very different types of situations.

- Decision making is a many-phased process. The actual choice is only one phase.

- Different managers may select different alternatives in the same situation. This is because of differences in values and in attitudes toward risk.

- Managers spend a great deal of time in group decision making. This is especially true for nonprogrammed decisions. Much evidence exists that, in certain situations, group decisions are superior to individual decisions. However, there are exceptions, and group decision making itself can create problems.

- Much evidence exists to support the claim that in most instances group decisions are superior to individual decisions. Three relatively new techniques (brainstorming, the Delphi Technique, and the Nominal Group Technique) have the purpose of improving the effectiveness of group decisions.

- Information technology is increasingly being applied to assist managerial decision making.

- Information has unique characteristics that make it different from other organizational resources. Managers must understand these differences to use information effectively.

Key Terms

artificial intelligence (p. 165)
benchmarking (p. 154)
brainstorming (p. 162)
data mart (p. 164)
data mining (p. 164)
data warehousing (p. 164)
decision (p. 148)
decision support systems (DSS) (p. 164)
delegation (p. 155)
Delphi Technique (p. 162)

executive information system (EIS) (p. 165)
expert systems (p. 165)
formative feedback (p. 156)
garbage can phenomenon (p. 161)
Information Age (p. 163)
intuitive decision making (p. 151)
Nominal Group Technique (NGT) (p. 162)
nonprogrammed decision (p. 150)
policy (p. 150)
proactive decision (p. 151)

problem (p. 152)
programmed decision (p. 150)
reactive decision (p. 151)
satisficer (p. 155)
search engines (p. 164)
software agents (p. 164)
summative feedback (p. 156)
systematic decision making (p. 151)
values-based decision making (p. 157)

Review and Discussion Questions

1. What is a decision?

2. We make decisions daily. Describe in detail a programmed decision you make each day. Why do you consider it to be programmed? Was it ever a nonprogrammed decision? If so, discuss why.

3. Describe what you believe is a nonprogrammed decision that you recently made. Describe the circumstances surrounding the decision and state why you believe it was nonprogrammed. Did this belief influence your decision-making approach? In what ways?

4. Reexamine the decision you described in question 3 and discuss it in terms of the decision-making process outlined in the chapter.

5. Select a major political or business decision with which you are familiar. Evaluate the decision in terms of how good you think it was. Be specific, and state how you determined the quality of the decision.

6. What type of risk taker do you believe you are? Indicate how the characteristic has influenced some decisions that you have made recently.

7. Describe a group decision-making situation in which you were involved. Did any problems develop? Describe them in detail. Was the decision reached by the group different from the one you would have made as an individual? Do you think that the group decision was better? Why?

8. Have you ever used a computer or the Internet to help you make a decision? How can these tools help the average manager in making better decisions?

9. Think of a decision that you or someone you know has made recently. Do you believe that any of the various influences on the decision-making process discussed in the chapter could have affected the outcome? Discuss each influence and indicate how it may have affected the decision.

10. In your opinion, what are the advantages and shortcomings of group decision making?

Practice Quiz

Note: You can find the correct answers to these questions by taking the quiz and then submitting your answers in the Online Edition. The program will automatically score your submission. If you miss a question, the program will provide the correct answer, a rationale for the answer, and the section number in the chapter where the topic is discussed.

Indicate whether the sentence or statement is true or false.

_____ 1. A manager's reactive, intuitive decision will be better if it's based on training and experience with similar situations.

_____ 2. Without goals and objectives, there would be <u>no</u> way to make decisions because there would be no way to evaluate their effectiveness.

_____ 3. For a complex problem requiring pooled knowledge, the quality of the decision is likely to be **higher** as the group moves toward achieving consensus.

_____ 4. Because decision support systems can provide information covering a wide range of factors, expert systems generally cover much smaller fields of knowledge and are built from decision rules used by experts in a specific field.

Identify the letter of the choice that best completes the statement or answers the question.

_____ 5. Decision making often reflects the manager's effort to do all of the following EXCEPT _____.
a. make sense of a complicated environment.
b. attain some control.
c. achieve some sense of order.
d. reduce his or her responsibility.

_____ 6. Given that decision making is ultimately a _____ process, it is fraught with complexities and ambiguities.
a. mechanical
b. intuitive
c. human
d. methodical

_____ 7. Formative feedback should be used _____ the implementation process.
a. before
b. during
c. after

_____ 8. Risk is everywhere and it is unavoidable. The issue for managers is not whether to take risks, but how to take _____ risks.
a. expected
b. maximum
c. minimum
d. reasonable

_____ 9. Which of the following is NOT one of the three techniques that are useful in increasing the creative capability of a group in generating ideas, understanding problems, and reaching better decisions?
a. brainstorming
b. the Nomad Trek Technique
c. the Delphi Technique
d. the Nominal Group Technique

_____ 10. The Nominal Group Technique refers to a decision-making process that brings people together but does not allow them to _____.
a. look at each other.
b. touch each other.
c. communicate verbally.
d. do prior research.

_____ 11. The final step in the decision making process is to _____.
a. implement the decision.
b. seek approval for the decision.
c. monitor the results of the decision.
d. seek more information about the problem.

____ **12.** The technique of examining the practices of other firms that are regarded as leaders in that practice is called _____.

    a. feedback.

    b. monitoring.

    c. quality control.

    d. benchmarking.

____ **13.** _____ is the condition that occurs when lower-level individuals feel inhibited in group decision making when higher level individuals are part of the group.

    a. nominal group.

    b. groupthink.

    c. status incongruity.

    d. benchmarking.

____ **14.** Groups are better suited to _____ decisions than are individuals.

    a. non-programmed.

    b. systematic.

    c. programmed.

    d. intuitive.

____ **15.** Using a committee meeting to air specific grievances is a common decision making phenomenon known as _____.

    a. groupthink.

    b. brainstorming.

    c. garbage can.

    d. data mining.

Case Study

General Motors Changes Its Culture Based on GoFast Approach

Driven by changes in human resources, automotive giant General Motors is cutting bureaucracy and cultivating a get-it-done culture. The result is innovation, action, and millions of dollars in savings.

Two words run together tell the story of GM: GoFast. Hoping to halt sluggish *decision making* and inject *speed* and a sense of urgency into its global workforce of nearly 350,000, GM came up with the slogan in 2000. At the time, the company was in a downward spiral and steadily losing market share to highly competitive Japanese, German, and Korean auto manufacturers. Top leadership at GM knew that something had to be done to shake things up. GoFast, with human resources managers in the vanguard, would be the name of the program that would lead the charge. Today, 7,000 GoFast workshops later, the term is part of GM's culture, shorthand for ending cumbersome bureaucratic process by dealing with a problem immediately. "Just say 'GoFast' and everyone knows what you mean," says Kathleen Barclay, vice president of global human resources.

GM won the Workforce Management's Optimas Award for general excellence for turning its workforce managers into strategic partners. The company allowed workforce management to go beyond its traditional supporting role to help reshape corporate behavior with innovative ideas and technology. In addition to the GoFast workshops, salaried GM workers are given individual responsibility to contribute to corporate business results in an initiative called the Performance Management Process. The PMP program establishes individual business objectives for salaried employees that must be linked to the worker's unit and, in turn, to the company's overall goal. Today, 80 percent of GM's executives strongly agree that they are personally being held accountable for business results, compared to only 50 percent a few years ago, according to an in-house survey.

Some of the dollar payoffs have been equally dramatic. GoFast workshops produced documented savings of more than $500 million. Technology innovations are also part of the cost-cutting. Company executives found that if they trained local dealers by using satellite feeds to monitors set up in service bays, rather than using classrooms, they could reduce training costs from $89 per student hour to $38. That change so far has saved GM $50 million.

Now that the old decentralized structure has been replaced by a more centralized system of management, talent is rising to the top in previously unknown ways. There has been an 80 percent increase in the number of women executives at GM, with a 180 percent increase in the number of women in the top 450 positions in the company.

The reorganization that produced those results continues, with human resources managers operating as chief agents of the corporate overhaul. GM management concedes that its *decision making* was slow, lumbering and bureaucratic. Among the chief problems feeding the poor business results were highly decentralized, competitive business units. Barriers had been set up between the corporate units. Communication was poor. GM's chairman and CEO, Rick Wagoner, wanted to see the internal barriers torn down and the company moving forward with one mind toward common goals. And he wanted the entire corporation to be infused with what he called "a sense of urgency."

"In my mind, HR is paramount to our reorganization effort," Wagoner said. Barclay and her team began by taking a look at the way human resources itself was performing. "HR had traditionally been positioned in such a way that it was spending a lot of time on transactional and administrative activities," Barclay said. "We really needed to have a fundamental transformation of what human resources meant to the company as a whole." Barclay and her team surveyed top GM executives in manufacturing, engineering, vehicle sales, and other areas of the company, asking how human resources could add value and help drive change. The effort resulted in a strategic framework developed in 2001 that is still used today. It involves retraining human resources managers to think globally, learn to manage change, develop business acumen, and forge relationships with other GM workers. Then came programs like GoFast and PMP.

Simplified, GoFast works this way: once a problem has been identified, then executives and other salaried employees responsible are brought together for a one-day session. The process might involve 6 to 20 key players. A *decision* to fix the problem is made on the spot.

Efforts to change the GM culture are ongoing. "Human resources has a big role to play in *making* the company behave differently, and leveraging the strengths of the company and helping the company change its *speed* to go faster in *decision making*," Barclay said. "We have company-wide objectives around the world. We have everyone driving toward the same objectives."

Questions for Discussion

1. Do you think it is helpful to have a slogan like "GoFast" when a company is attempting to make a change throughout its entire operation? Explain.

2. Speed and urgency are the two dominant themes of GM's GoFast decision-making philosophy. How do these two concepts differ? How do they reinforce one another?

3. Why was it necessary to involve human resources in the GoFast transformation? Do you think it was necessary to have training sessions? Explain.

Source: Adapted from Douglas P. Shuit, "GM Goes Fast," *Workforce Management,* March 2004, pp. 36–38.

Internet Exercise

Thinking About Expert Systems

One of the more challenging problems in the Information Age is to imbue computers and computer networks with genuine intelligence. One way of doing so is to create so-called expert systems. Computer scientists and information technologists have for many years been searching for the holy grail of an electronic brain that can literally perform as well as or better than a human in certain specialized areas. In 1997, IBM used its supercomputer named "Deep Blue" to beat Gary Kasparov, the reigning world chess champion. This shocking achievement led many to reconsider the power of computing and its ability to mimic human thought. Students can learn more about this famous match at the following website:

http://www.research.ibm.com/deepblue/home/html/b.html

The challenge to create expert systems is that much of what an expert "knows" cannot be put into words. For example, to make this point, students should be asked to explain to another classmate how they ride a bike. The art of bike riding is largely ineffable—literally, unable to be articulated. The following website will help students understand better the nature of expert systems and how they currently are developed:

http://www.aaai.org/AITopics/html/expert.html

Students should visit this website outside of class, and think about the following questions:

1. What is meant by the term "knowledge engineer"? What role do knowledge engineers play in developing an expert system?

2. What is meant by the term "production rule"? Do you think knowledge is composed primarily of "production rules"? Explain.

3. What are the limitations of using expert systems in the workplace? What are some of the benefits of an expert system as compared with a human expert?

Experiential Exercise

Lost-at-Sea Decision Making

Purpose: The purpose of this exercise is to offer you the opportunity to compare individual versus group decision making.

Setting Up the Exercise: You are adrift on a private yacht in the South Pacific. As a consequence of a fire of unknown origin, much of the yacht and its contents have been destroyed. The yacht is now slowly sinking. Your location is unclear because of the destruction of critical navigational equipment and because you and the crew were distracted trying to bring the fire under control. Your best estimate is that you are approximately 1,000 miles south-southwest of the nearest land.

Exhibit 7-1 contains a list of fifteen items that are intact and undamaged after the fire. In addition to these articles, you have a serviceable rubber life raft with oars, large enough to carry yourself, the crew, and all the items listed here. The total contents of all survivors' pockets are a package of cigarettes, several books of matches, and five $1 bills.

1. Working independently and without discussing the problem or the merits of any of the items, your task is to rank the fifteen items in terms of their importance to your survival. Under column 1, place the number 1 by the most important item, the number 2 by the second most important, and so on through number 15, the least important. When you are through, *do not discuss* the problem or your rankings of items with anyone.

2. Your instructor will establish teams of four to six students. The task for your team is to rank the fifteen items, according to the group's consensus, in the order of importance to your survival. Do not vote or average team members' rankings; try to reach agreement on each item. Base your decision on knowledge, logic, or the experiences of group members. Try to avoid basing the decision on personal preference. Enter the group's ranking in column 2. This process should take between twenty and thirty minutes, or as the instructor designates.

3. When everyone is through, your instructor will read the correct ranking, provided by officers of the U.S. Merchant Marine. Enter the correct rankings in column 3.

4. Compute the accuracy of your individual ranking. For each item, use the absolute value (ignore plus and minus signs) of the difference between column 1 and column 3. Add up these absolute values to get your *individual accuracy index.* Enter it on the worksheet that follows.

5. Perform the same operation as in Step 4, but use columns 2 and 3 for your group ranking. Adding up the absolute values yields your *group accuracy index.* Enter it on the worksheet.

6. Compute the *average* of your group's individual accuracy indexes. Do this by adding up each member's individual accuracy index and dividing the result by the number of group members. Enter it on the worksheet.

7. Identify the *lowest* individual accuracy index in your group. This is the most correct ranking in your group. Enter it on the worksheet.

A Learning Note: This exercise is designed to let you experience group decision making. Think about how discussion, reflection, and the exchange of opinions influenced your final decision.

EXHIBIT 7-1 **Worksheet**

Items	(1) Individual Ranking	(2) Group Ranking	(3) Expert's Ranking
1-gal. plastic 2% milk container (one-fourth filled)	_____	_____	_____
Net bag containing 12 oranges	_____	_____	_____
50 ft. of 1/4-in. nylon rope	_____	_____	_____
30-gal. black plastic garbage bag containing 4 empty 3-liter soda bottles and assorted paper trash	_____	_____	_____
Round white fabric plastic tablecloth (8 ft. in diameter)	_____	_____	_____
1-gal. plastic water bottle (one-half filled)	_____	_____	_____
Waterproof floating flashlight	_____	_____	_____
Small first aid kit (containing 10-yd. roll of 2-in. cotton gauze bandage, 1-oz. tube of antibiotic cream, 8-oz. tube of Preparation-H®)	_____	_____	_____
11-in. floating fishing knife in sheath with stainless steel blade	_____	_____	_____
Inflated rubberized fabric float (6 ft. × 3 ft.) with corner grommets	_____	_____	_____
Nautical chart of the Caribbean	_____	_____	_____
Plastic folding chaise lounge with yellow canvas seat and back	_____	_____	_____
Styrofoam cooler with lid (24 in. × 16 in. × 12 in.)	_____	_____	_____
Sea survival kit (containing shark repellant, hooks, and fishing line)	_____	_____	_____
34 large (30 gal.) black self-tying plastic bags (found in Styrofoam cooler)			

Part

3

Job Design

Organizational Structure and Design

Organizing

Managing Human Resources

Managers must create order out of chaos. Left to itself, any system will tend toward disorder. That is consistent with the laws of thermodynamics. Management is needed to organize the resources of the organization to pursue goals. Not only must resources be organized but also they must be organized in a way that maximizes their efficient use.

A significant part of organizing resources involves organizing human resources. People need to know what is expected of them in any organization. Managers can help people understand their roles through efficient job or work design. Chapter 8 examines work design and its role in effective organizational design.

In Chapter 9, you'll learn the different ways that managers have structured organizations. You'll also learn effective techniques for organizing in the modern economy. Tall organization hierarchies are no longer the most typical way to organize. Modern workers require more autonomy and authority. This means that flatter and fewer organizational levels have become more widely used.

Organizational design is the creation of departments, divisions, or other organizational units. Managers establish organizational units to develop efficiencies. Often, such units become dysfunctional and need to be reexamined. Thus, organizational design doesn't occur only with new organizations; it occurs regularly with existing organizations. You'll learn in Chapter 10 that human resources must be managed and led in any type of organization.

Job Design

CHAPTER OBJECTIVES

1 Define what is meant by the terms job design and job description.

2 State how jobs differ in range, depth, and relationships.

3 Explain why perceived job content is important.

4 Discuss ways managers can change both the range and the depth of jobs to increase performance.

5 Explain how jobs can be enriched.

6 Describe teleworking, flextime, and job sharing.

CHAPTER OUTLINE

Managing Today

"Offshoring" Creates Jobs and Can Teach a Lesson

Global giants aren't the only firms cutting costs and shifting jobs overseas. Increasingly, small businesses are finding that "offshoring" jobs is contributing to the firm's performance. An example is the story of Rajeev Thadani, who wanted to expand Claimpower, Inc., his medical billing service in Fairlawn, NJ. He decided to outsource some of the jobs to India. He flew to his native Bombay and hired four locals to help file insurance claims on behalf of New Jersey doctors. They use software that Mr. Thadani, a programmer, developed for the job.

From a five person New Jersey business, Claimpower now has 35 employees in India. His client list has increased to 41 doctors from 10. All of this has occurred in three years. He is planning to add a sales team and over twelve more employees in the U.S. and another 30 in India. His goal is to handle claims of 500 doctors across the United States. Mr. Thadani has created jobs in India and in the United States.

The typical operating job at Claimpower involves workers imputting figures on a computer, printing forms, proof-

ing the forms, stuffing envelopes, and phoning insurance companies. The jobs in India pay between $133 to $633 per month, which is good by local standards. The costs of conducting the operational work in New Jersey were too high. As he plans to expand both the New Jersey and Bombay workforce he knows that the creation of more jobs was not possible without "offshoring" the early work to India.

Mr. Thadani's son, who was working for Claimpower part time, learned his lesson about "offshoring" firsthand. Mr. Thadani informed him that the job he was doing was being sent to India. The son learned skills to perform different tasks. The lesson learned is that it is important to keep skills ahead of the curve in the job market.

Source: Adapted from Craig Karmin, "Offshoring Can Generate Jobs in the U.S.'" *Wall Street Journal,* March 16, 2004, pp. B1 and B7.

▶**job design** The result of job analysis that specifies job range, depth, and relationships.

Jobs are the building blocks of organizational structures. **Job design** refers to the process by which managers determine individual job tasks and authority. Apart from the very practical issues associated with job design, that is, issues that relate to effectiveness in economic, political, and monetary terms, job designs have social and psychological implications. Jobs can be sources of psychological stress and even mental and physical impairment. On a more positive note, jobs can provide income, meaningful life experiences, self-esteem, esteem from others, regulation and patterns of workflow, and association with others. The performance of organizations and people depends largely on how well jobs are designed. The opening Managing Today vignette, "Offshoring Creates Jobs and Can Teach a Lesson," emphasizes how designing work can result in the creation of jobs.

▶**quality of work life** A formal program that attempts to integrate employee needs and well-being to improve productivity, increase work involvement, and provide higher levels of job satisfaction.

The issue of designing jobs has gone beyond the determination of the most efficient way to perform tasks. The concept of **quality of work life** is now widely used to refer to the satisfaction of workers' personal needs. The emphasis on satisfaction of personal needs does not imply less emphasis on organizational needs. Instead, contemporary managers are finding that when employees' personal needs are satisfied, the performance of the organization itself is enhanced.[1] Job design and redesign techniques attempt (1) to identify the most important needs of employees and the organization and (2) to remove obstacles in the workplace that frustrate those needs. Managers hope that the results are jobs that (a) fulfill important needs and (b) contribute to individual and organizational performance. The remainder of this chapter reviews selected job design techniques that facilitate the achievement of personal and organizational performance.

8-1 Job Analysis

▶**job analysis** A process of determining what tasks make up the job and what skills, abilities, and responsibilities are required of an individual to successfully accomplish the job.

Job analysis is the process of determining the tasks that make up the job and the skills, abilities, and responsibilities that are required of an individual to successfully accomplish the job. Job analysis achieves two vital purposes in the organization: (1) it specifies the tasks that must be accomplished to complete a job; and (2) it determines the skills and knowledge necessary to perform the tasks.[2] The information about a job is contained in what are called a *job description* and a *job specification.* The relationship between job analysis, job description, and job specification is presented in Figure 8-1.

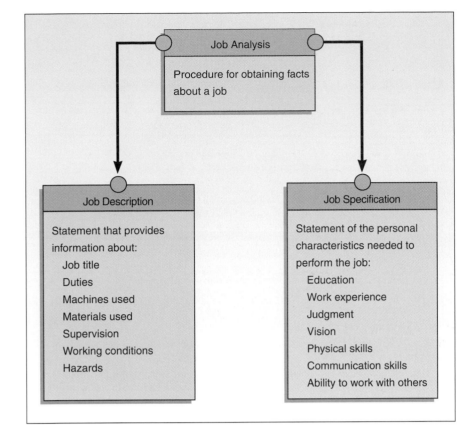

Figure 8-1
Job Analysis Components

Job analysis provides information that can be used by every manager within the organization. For example, to recruit and select effectively, qualified personnel must be matched with job requirements. The relevant set of job information is provided by the job description and the job specification. Another use of job information is to establish proper rates of pay. To have an equitable pay system, it is necessary to have a complete job description. An example of a job description and a job specification for a project general manager is provided in Figure 8-2.

Performing an informative and accurate analysis of most jobs is no easy task. Considerable evidence suggests that the types of subjective elements often involved in job analysis are subject to systematic sources of inaccuracy.[3] The duties of managers, such as those presented in the job description for the project general manager in Figure 8-2, are difficult to spell out. However, because of the range and types of managerial behaviors and duties, there must be a careful analysis of each managerial job.

Some human resources professionals have referred to job analysis as the basic activity of human resources management. It is the starting point for nearly all personnel functions.[4] A typical job analysis involves five steps (see Figure 8-3):

1. Examine how each job fits into the overall organization. This step involves creating or reviewing the organization chart, focusing on the formal relationships among departments, jobs, and individuals.

2. Select the jobs to be analyzed. Managers must zero in on the specific jobs to be analyzed and determine that job's unique function within the overall organization.

3. Collect data on the jobs to be analyzed. Data must be collected on the characteristics of the job, the behaviors and activities it requires, and the necessary employee skills and knowledge.

4. Prepare a job description. The job description is a written summary of the job: its activities, equipment required to perform the activities, and the working conditions of the job. A good job description can also help the organization with planning, recruiting, and training. It also helps workers understand what a specific job entails and what jobs fit their skills and interests.

Figure 8-2
**Job Description and
Job Specification**

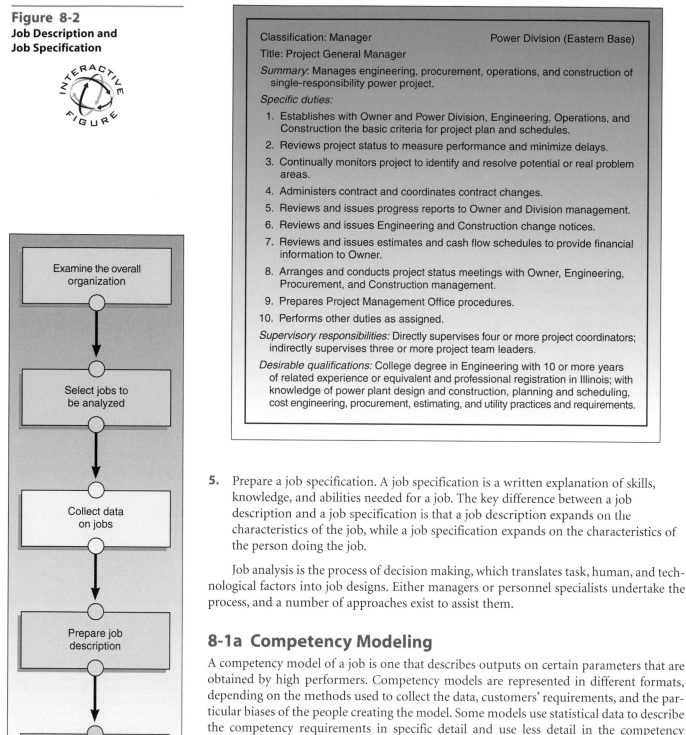

Classification: Manager   Power Division (Eastern Base)
Title: Project General Manager

Summary: Manages engineering, procurement, operations, and construction of single-responsibility power project.

Specific duties:

1. Establishes with Owner and Power Division, Engineering, Operations, and Construction the basic criteria for project plan and schedules.
2. Reviews project status to measure performance and minimize delays.
3. Continually monitors project to identify and resolve potential or real problem areas.
4. Administers contract and coordinates contract changes.
5. Reviews and issues progress reports to Owner and Division management.
6. Reviews and issues Engineering and Construction change notices.
7. Reviews and issues estimates and cash flow schedules to provide financial information to Owner.
8. Arranges and conducts project status meetings with Owner, Engineering, Procurement, and Construction management.
9. Prepares Project Management Office procedures.
10. Performs other duties as assigned.

Supervisory responsibilities: Directly supervises four or more project coordinators; indirectly supervises three or more project team leaders.

Desirable qualifications: College degree in Engineering with 10 or more years of related experience or equivalent and professional registration in Illinois; with knowledge of power plant design and construction, planning and scheduling, cost engineering, procurement, estimating, and utility practices and requirements.

Figure 8-3
Steps in a Typical Job Analysis

Examine the overall organization

↓

Select jobs to be analyzed

↓

Collect data on jobs

↓

Prepare job description

↓

Prepare job specification

5. Prepare a job specification. A job specification is a written explanation of skills, knowledge, and abilities needed for a job. The key difference between a job description and a job specification is that a job description expands on the characteristics of the job, while a job specification expands on the characteristics of the person doing the job.

Job analysis is the process of decision making, which translates task, human, and technological factors into job designs. Either managers or personnel specialists undertake the process, and a number of approaches exist to assist them.

8-1a Competency Modeling

A competency model of a job is one that describes outputs on certain parameters that are obtained by high performers. Competency models are represented in different formats, depending on the methods used to collect the data, customers' requirements, and the particular biases of the people creating the model. Some models use statistical data to describe the competency requirements in specific detail and use less detail in the competency descriptions. Others reverse this balance.

In the competency model for a district sales manager, for example, the approach might be to identify success factors (competencies), provide a behavioral description of each one, rank-order the factors by criticality, and establish a proficiency level for each factor. Success factors might include "leadership," "integrity," "self-motivation," and "tenacity."

Another type of competency model is one in which a specific competency is given a basic definition and behavioral anchors describe specific levels of expected performance behavior. The levels become more complex as the behaviors go up the scale. For example, the specific competency might be "organizational influence." The basic definition might include "the ability to influence others effectively . . . providing information and giving others ownership of their ideas." The behavioral anchors might include "relies on facts"

and "persuades." This type of model is useful for identifying and managing definitive performance expectations, and for identifying specific training and development needs.

In competency models, the job analysis is used to collect competency information—information that describes in detail the criteria for successful job performance. This detail typically includes information about tasks, responsibilities, duties, accountabilities, knowledge and skill requirements, and any other criteria for successful job performance.[5]

8-2 Job Design

Job design is the result of job analysis. A good job design will enable employees to exercise discretion in decision making in their work roles.[6] Successful managers involve employees in the job design process.[7] The manner in which jobs are designed has an important bearing on what they ultimately deliver to the organization. People can be kept under tight control and undertake tasks only as instructed, they can be made personally accountable for what is assigned to them, or they can share accountability with others.[8] An effective job design specifies three characteristics of jobs: range, depth, and relationships.

8-2a Range and Depth

Job range refers to the number of tasks a jobholder performs. The individual who performs eight tasks to complete a job has a wider job range than a person performing four tasks. In most instances, the greater the number of tasks performed, the longer it takes to complete the job.

A second job characteristic is **job depth,** the amount of discretion an individual has to decide job activities and job outcomes. In many instances, job depth relates to personal influence as well as delegated authority. Thus, an employee with the same job title and at the same organizational level as another employee may possess more, less, or the same amount of job depth because of personal influence.

Job range and depth distinguish one job from another not only within the same organization, but also among different organizations. To illustrate how jobs differ in range and depth, Figure 8-4 depicts the differences for selected jobs of business firms, hospitals, and universities. For example, business research scientists, hospital chiefs of surgery, and university presidents generally have high job range and significant depth. Research scientists perform a large number of tasks and are usually not closely supervised. Chiefs of surgery have significant job range in that they oversee and counsel on many diverse surgical matters. In addition, they are not supervised closely, and they have the authority to influence hospital surgery policies and procedures.

University presidents have a large number of tasks to perform. They speak to alumni groups, politicians, community representatives, and students. They develop, with the consultation of others, policies on admissions, fund-raising, and adult education. They can alter the faculty recruitment philosophy and thus alter the course of the entire institution. For example, a university president may want to build an institution that is noted for high-quality classroom instruction and for providing excellent services to the community. This

> ▶**job range** The number of tasks assigned to a particular job.

> ▶**job depth** The relative freedom that a jobholder has in the performance of assigned duties.

Figure 8-4
Job Depth and Range

	High Depth						
Low Range	BUSINESS automobile mechanics	HOSPITAL anesthesiologists	UNIVERSITY professors	BUSINESS research scientists	HOSPITAL chiefs of surgery	UNIVERSITY presidents	**High Range**
	BUSINESS assembly-line workers	HOSPITAL bookkeepers	UNIVERSITY graduate student	BUSINESS maintenance repairpersons	HOSPITAL nurses	UNIVERSITY department chairpersons	
	Low Depth						

thrust may lead to recruiting and selecting professors who want to concentrate on these two specific goals.

Examples of jobs that have high depth and low range are packaging machine mechanics, anesthesiologists, and faculty members. Mechanics, for example, perform the limited tasks that pertain to repairing and maintaining packaging machines. But they can decide how breakdowns on the package machine are to be repaired. The discretion means that the mechanics have relatively high job depth.

Highly specialized jobs are those that have few tasks to accomplish by prescribed means. Such jobs are quite routine; they also tend to be controlled by specified rules and procedures (low depth). A highly despecialized job (high range) has many tasks to accomplish within the framework of discretion over means and ends (high depth). Within an organization there typically are great differences among jobs in both range and depth. Although managers have no precise equations to use to decide job range and depth, they can follow this guideline: Given the economic and technical requirements of the organization's mission, goals, and objectives, what is the optimal point along the continuum of range and depth for each job?

8-2b Job Relationships

Job relationships are determined by managers' decisions regarding departmentalization bases and spans of control. The resulting groups become the responsibility of a manager to coordinate toward organization purposes. These decisions also determine the nature and extent of jobholders' interpersonal relationships, individually and within groups. Group performance is affected in part by group cohesiveness. And the degree of group cohesiveness depends upon the quality and kind of interpersonal relationships of jobholders assigned to a group.

The wider the span of control, the larger the group, and consequently the more difficult it is to establish friendship and interest relationships. Simply, people in larger groups are less likely to communicate (and interact sufficiently to form interpersonal ties) than people in smaller groups. Without the opportunity to communicate, people will be unable to establish cohesive work groups. Thus, an important source of satisfaction may be lost for individuals who seek to fulfill social and esteem needs through relationships with coworkers.

The basis for departmentalization that management selects also has important implications for job relationships. The functional basis places jobs with similar depth and range in the same groups, while product, territory, and customer bases place jobs with dissimilar depth and range in the same group. Thus in functional departments, people will be doing much the same specialty. Product, territory, and customer departments, however, are comprised of jobs that are quite different and heterogeneous. Individuals who work in heterogeneous departments experience feelings of dissatisfaction, stress, and involvement more intensely than those in homogeneous, functional departments. People with homogeneous backgrounds, skills, and training have more common interests than those with heterogeneous ones. Thus it is easier for them to establish social relationships, which are satisfying with less stress, but also less involvement in the department's activities.

8-3 Perceived Job Content

Perceived job content refers to aspects of a job that define its general nature as perceived by the jobholder as influenced by the social setting. It is important to distinguish between the objective properties and the subjective properties of a job as reflected in the perceptions of people who perform them. Managers cannot understand the causes of job performance without consideration of individual differences such as personality, needs, and span of attention. Thus if managers desire to increase job performance by changing job content, they can change job design, individual perceptions, or social settings. These factors are the causes of job content.

Individuals perceive and describe their jobs using many different adjectives. These adjectives describe aspects of the job's range, depth, and relationship and are termed *job characteristics.*

The job characteristics model (JCM) suggests that jobs should be designed to include five important core dimensions that increase motivation, performance, and satisfaction, reducing employee turnover and absenteeism. These five characteristics of perceived job content are discussed in more detail in the following:

> *Skill variety:* The degree to which the job requires a variety of different activities in carrying out the work.
>
> *Task identity:* The degree to which the job requires completion of an identifiable task or output.
>
> *Task significance:* The degree to which the job has an impact on other jobs within the organization or related organizations.
>
> *Autonomy:* The degree to which the job provides the worker with the freedom and discretion in setting work schedules, and in determining the appropriate means of doing the job.
>
> *Feedback:* The degree to which individuals are able to obtain data concerning the fulfillment of the job requirements.

The relative presence of these five key job characteristics creates different levels of three critical psychological states: experienced meaningfulness, experienced responsibility, and knowledge of results. These three states are necessary for job satisfaction and motivation. As Figure 8-5 shows, skill variety, task identity, and task significance contribute to a sense of meaningfulness. Autonomy is related to feelings of responsibility, and feedback is related to knowledge of results.

Managers must be aware that different employees have different capabilities and needs. These differences affect how the job characteristics approach to job design should be deployed. In Figure 8-5, a box labeled "Strength of employees' need for growth" is presented. This is designed to highlight the fact that people with a strong internal need to grow and expand their potential are expected to respond more strongly to attempts to alter these five core dimensions of jobs than those with a weak internal need to grow. As we will explore later, managers can use several strategies to ensure that employees grow at the pace they're comfortable with.

Differences in social settings of work also affect perceptions of job content. Examples of social setting differences include leadership style[9] and what other people say about the job.[10] As suggested, how one perceives a job is greatly affected by what other people say about it. Thus, if work colleagues state that their jobs are boring, one is likely to state that his or her job is also boring. If the individual perceives the job as boring, job performance will no doubt suffer. Job content, then, results from the interaction of many factors in the work situation.

8-4 Job Performance

The purpose of job design is to encourage job performance. Job performance includes a number of outcomes. In this section we discuss performance outcomes that have value to the organization and to the individual.

perceived job content The aspects of a job that define its general nature as perceived by the jobholder as influenced by the social setting.

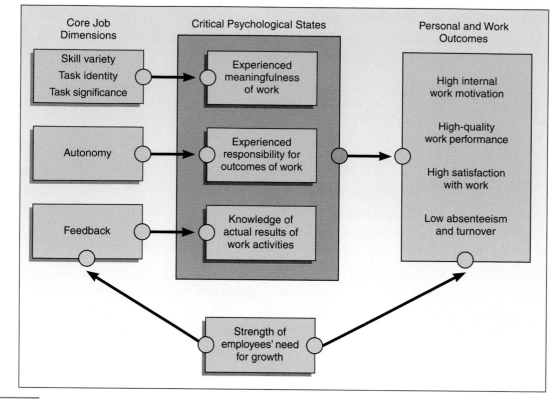

Figure 8-5
The Job Characteristic Approach

Source: Adapted from "Motivation Through
the Design of Work: Testing of a Theory,"
by J. Richard and R. G. Oldham from
*Organizational Behavior and Human
Performance,* August 1976, p. 256.
Reprinted by permission of Elsevier.

The Management Focus on Innovation box, "The Five-Alarm Job Design," illustrates how a company can create a highly desired great job.

8-4a Objective Outcomes

Quantity and quality of output, absenteeism, tardiness, and turnover are objective outcomes that can be measured in quantitative terms. For most jobs, implicit or explicit standards exist for these objective outcomes. Industrial engineering studies establish standards for daily quantity, and quality control specialists establish tolerance limits for acceptable quality. These aspects of job performance account for characteristics of the product, client, or service for which the jobholder is responsible. But job performance includes other outcomes.

8-4b Personal Behavior Outcomes

The jobholder reacts to the work itself and also reacts by either attending regularly or by being absent, by staying with the job or by quitting. Moreover, physiological and health-related problems can ensue as a consequence of job performance. Stress related to job performance can contribute to physical and mental impairment; accidents and occupationally related disease can also ensue.

8-4c Intrinsic and Extrinsic Outcomes

Job outcomes include intrinsic and extrinsic work outcomes. The distinction between intrinsic and extrinsic outcomes is important for understanding the reactions of people to their jobs. In a general sense, intrinsic outcomes are objects or events that follow from the worker's own efforts, not requiring the involvement of any other person. More simply, it is an outcome clearly related to action on the worker's part. Such outcomes typically are thought to be solely in the province of professional and technical jobs; yet all jobs potentially have opportunities for intrinsic outcomes. Such outcomes involve feelings of respon-

Management Focus on Innovation

The Five-Alarm Job Design

Gayle is convinced that she has a dream job. And she's not going to let anyone tell her differently. While others moan and complain about long hours and bad bosses, the paralegal at Alston & Bird, a prominent Atlanta law firm, is eager to show up for work and doesn't mind putting in a few extra hours, if necessary. "I've got a tremendous amount of responsibility, and the lawyers respect me," she says. "I feel stimulated and challenged, and there are terrific opportunities to grow professionally. I can't imagine a more interesting job or a better place to work."

At a time when job satisfaction is declining and loyalty is diminishing, Gayle might seem like a throwback to another era. Yet the 17-year veteran of Alston & Bird offers clear proof that an outstanding job and an excellent employer can redefine the physics of the labor universe. While pay and benefits play a key role in drawing talent, organizations that offer attractive and rewarding jobs are far more likely to slash turnover, pump up productivity and bolster the bottom line.

Some jobs, such as those in the entertainment industry or in political circles, might appear glamorous or offer plenty of cachet, but long hours, tough working conditions and a lack of advancement opportunities can shred employees and send them fleeing to other companies or industries. A hot job, more than anything else, offers opportunity and meshes with the current values, attitudes and desires of the workforce.

For employers, it's no trivial matter. Although it's possible to earn a profit with lackluster benefits and mediocre working conditions, there's a huge difference between "pay to play" and "play to win." Those who monitor the pulse of the market and understand what categorizes a job as hot, as well as how to develop effective recruiting strategies and how to create a compelling work environment, will emerge as the winners in today's high-stakes business derby. Companies that hit the mark in creating great jobs, such as Alston & Bird, reap huge rewards. The firm offers job sharing, flexible working hours, and ongoing training and learning and has designed jobs to provide maximum responsibility and autonomy. The 1,500-employee firm, rated number two on *Fortune* magazine's "100 Best Companies to Work For" list for 2004, has a low 7 percent turnover among its attorneys, compared to an industry average near 20 percent. Overall, it receives approximately 15,000 applications a year for about 200 openings.

Source: Adapted from Samuel Greengard, "The Five-Alarm Job," *Workforce Management,* February 2004, pp. 43–46.

sibility, challenge, and recognition; the outcomes result from such job characteristics as variety, autonomy, identity, and significance.[11]

Extrinsic outcomes, however, are objects or events that follow from the workers' own efforts in conjunction with other factors or persons not directly involved in the job itself. Pay, working conditions, co-workers, and even supervision are objects in the workplace that are potentially job outcomes but are not a fundamental part of the work. Dealing with others and friendship interactions are sources of extrinsic outcomes.

8-4d Job Satisfaction Outcome

Job satisfaction depends on the levels of intrinsic and extrinsic outcomes and how the jobholder views those outcomes. These outcomes have different values for different people. For some people, responsible and challenging work may have neutral or even negative values. For other people, such work outcomes may have high positive values. People differ in the importance they attach to job outcomes. Those differences alone would account for different levels of job satisfaction for essentially the same job tasks.

> **job satisfaction** A jobholder's satisfaction based on levels of intrinsic and extrinsic outcomes and the way the jobholder views those outcomes.

Another important individual difference is job involvement.[12] People differ in the extent that (1) work is a central life interest, (2) they actively participate in work, (3) they perceive work as central to self-esteem, and (4) they perceive work as consistent with self-concept. Persons who are not involved in their work cannot be expected to realize the same satisfaction as those who are. This variable accounts for the fact that two workers could report different levels of satisfaction for the same performance levels.

A final individual difference is the perceived equity of the outcome in terms of what the jobholder considers a fair reward. If the outcomes are perceived to be unfair in relation to those of others in similar jobs requiring similar effort, the jobholder will experience dissatisfaction and seek means to restore the equity, either by seeking greater rewards (primarily extrinsic) or by reducing effort.

8-5　Redesigning Job Range: Job Rotation and Job Enlargement

The earliest attempts to redesign jobs date to the scientific management era. The efforts at that time emphasized efficiency criteria. In so doing, the individual tasks that compose a job are limited, uniform, and repetitive. This practice leads to narrow job range and, consequently, reported high levels of job discontent, turnover, absenteeism, and dissatisfaction. Accordingly, strategies were devised that resulted in wider job range through increasing the required activities of jobs. Two of these approaches are job rotation and job enlargement.

8-5a　Job Rotation

▶**job rotation**　Rotating an individual from one job to another to enable the individual to complete more job activities because each job includes different tasks.

Managers of many organizations have utilized different forms of the **job rotation** strategy. This practice involves rotating an individual from one job to another. In so doing, the individual is expected to complete more job activities since each job includes different tasks. Job rotation involves increasing the range of jobs and the perception of variety in the job content. Increasing task variety should increase the intrinsic value associated with job satisfaction. However, the practice of job rotation does not change the basic characteristics of the assigned jobs. Critics state that this approach involves nothing more than having people perform several boring and monotonous jobs rather than one. However, large, innovative corporations such as Sony and Canon use job rotation among engineers as one strategy to encourage production innovations.[13] Small companies also use job rotation extensively. Research from the American Society of Training and Development showed that small companies use job rotation more extensively than large companies.[14] An alternative strategy is job enlargement.

8-5b　Job Enlargement

▶**job enlargement**　A job strategy that focuses on despecialization, or increasing the number of tasks that an employee performs.

The pioneering Walker and Guest study[15] was concerned with the social and psychological problems associated with mass-production jobs in automobile assembly plants. The researchers found that many workers were dissatisfied with their highly specialized jobs. In particular, they disliked mechanical pacing, repetitiveness of operations, and a lack of a sense of accomplishment. Walker and Guest also found a positive relationship between job range and job satisfaction. The findings of this research gave early support for motivation theories that predict increases in job range will increase job satisfaction and other, objective, job outcomes. **Job enlargement** strategies focus on the opposite of dividing work—they are a form of despecialization or increasing the number of tasks that an employee performs. For example, a job is designed such that the individual performs six tasks instead of three.

Although in many instances an enlarged job requires a longer training period, job satisfaction usually increases because boredom is reduced. The implication, of course, is that the job enlargement will lead to improvement in other performance outcomes.

The concept and practice of job enlargement has become considerably more sophisticated. In recent years effective job enlargement involves more than simply increasing task variety. In addition, it is necessary to redesign certain other aspects of job range, including providing worker-paced (rather than machine-paced) control.[16] Each of these changes involves balancing the gains and losses of varying degrees of division of labor.

Some employees cannot cope with enlarged jobs because they cannot comprehend complexity; moreover, they may not have an attention span sufficiently long to stay with and complete an enlarged set of tasks. However, if employees are known to be amenable to job enlargement and if they have the required ability, then job enlargement should increase satisfaction and product quality and decrease absenteeism and turnover. These gains are not without costs, including the likelihood that employees will demand larger salaries in exchange for their performance of enlarged jobs. Yet these costs must be borne if management desires to implement the redesign strategy that enlarges job depth and job enrichment. Job enlargement is a necessary precondition for job enrichment.

8-6 Redesigning Job Depth: Job Enrichment

The impetus for redesigning job depth was provided by Herzberg's two-factor theory of motivation.[17] The basis of his theory is that factors which meet individuals' need for psychological growth, especially responsibility, job challenge, and achievement, must be characteristic of their jobs. The application of his theory is termed **job enrichment.** The implementation of job enrichment is realized through direct changes in job depth. Managers can provide employees with greater opportunities to exercise discretion by making the following changes (see Figure 8-6):

▶ **job enrichment** A strategy that seeks to improve performance and satisfaction by building more responsibility, more challenge, and a greater sense of achievement into jobs.

1. *Direct feedback:* The evaluation of performance should be timely and direct.
2. *New learning:* A good job enables people to feel that they are growing. All jobs should provide opportunities to learn.
3. *Scheduling:* People should be able to schedule some part of their own work.
4. *Uniqueness:* Each job should have some unique qualities or features.
5. *Control over resources:* Individuals should have some control over their job tasks.
6. *Personal accountability:* People should be provided with an opportunity to be accountable for the job.

As the theory and practice of job enrichment have evolved, managers have become aware that successful applications require numerous changes in the way work is done. Some of the more important changes include delegating greater authority to workers to participate in decisions, to set their own goals, and to evaluate their (and their work groups') performance. Job enrichment also involves changing the nature and style of managers' behavior. Managers must be willing and able to delegate authority. Given the ability of employees to carry out enriched jobs and the willingness of managers to delegate authority, gains in performance can be expected. In fact, job enrichment can be a key outcome of reengineering projects. Performance support technology that makes people smarter (such as computers, decision support systems) can add job satisfaction through improved expertise and performance levels.[18] These positive outcomes are the result of increasing employees' beliefs that efforts lead to performance, that performance leads to intrinsic and extrinsic rewards, and that these rewards have power to satisfy needs. These significant changes in managerial jobs when coupled with changes in nonmanagerial jobs suggest the importance of a supportive work environment as a prerequisite for successful job enrichment efforts.[19]

Job enrichment and job enlargement are not competing strategies. Job enlargement but not job enrichment may be compatible with the needs, values, and abilities of some individuals. Yet job enrichment, when appropriate, necessarily involves job enlargement. (See the Learning Moment box, "Job Enrichment Reminder.")

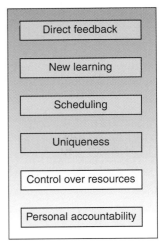

Figure 8-6
Redesigning Job Depth

LearningMoment _Job Enrichment Reminder_

Managers can use a number of job redesign approaches to improve performance. What works best is uncertain, but through observation and experience, managers can gauge what would be the most effective method or combination of designing a job. Job enlargement is the combination of tasks into a broader job. This is a redesign response to oversimplified jobs.

Job enrichment incorporates high-level motivators, including more job responsibility, greater recognition, more opportunities for personal growth, and greater job discretion or autonomy.

8-7 Other Job Redesign Approaches

In addition to or in conjunction with job rotation, job enlargement, job enrichment, and use of the job characteristics model, several other options are available. Organizations are continually searching for ways to add flexibility to jobs and work roles. A number of these approaches will be presented.

8-7a Job Sharing

▶**job sharing** A job arrangement in which two part-time employees perform the job duties and tasks that otherwise would be completed by one full-time employee.

Research has determined employees are very concerned about having greater control of balancing their work, family, and recreational lives. One approach that is directed at providing a better balance is called **job sharing.** This approach allows two or more part-time employees to jointly work a complete job. For example, one employee may work Monday and Friday, while a job sharing partner works Tuesday through Thursday.

The use of job sharing allows the work colleagues to care for children, attend school, care for elderly parents, or to better balance work and nonwork needs and choices.

8-7b Flextime

▶**flextime** A job arrangement that permits employees the option of selecting their starting and quitting times, provided that they work a certain number of hours per week.

Another approach to redesigning jobs lets employees have input in establishing their work schedules. **Flextime** is a schedule that allows workers to select starting and quitting times within limits set by management.[20] Rather than working the traditional eight-hour day, workers are given greater flexibility in deciding exactly when they will work. A person may work ten hours one day, and six the next, for example. Jobs designed using flextime include bank tellers, data entry clerks, lab technicians, nursing, and others.

Flextime programs have been successful for a number of firms. Over half the firms using flextime have reported improvements in areas such as productivity, labor costs, and morale.[21] One study found that flextime reduces paid absence, idle time, and overtime pay.[22] Another study reported that satisfaction with the work schedules and with interpersonal interactions improved significantly for both managers and nonmanagers.[23]

At the University of California–Irvine employees are able to establish their starting and ending times of work as well as deciding whether to work four or five days per week. One department requires the employees to be present at a core time, 9:00 a.m. until 2:00 p.m. These employees can then adjust their start and end hours around the core time.[24]

8-7c Teleworking

Teleworking (also referred to as telecommuting) involves workers who work from home full-time or some portion of their workweek and use the Internet, dial-up lines, or other forms of telecommunications.[25]

In 2003, the U.S. Labor Department estimated that over 23 million workers worked on-line from their home or some other location outside the home.[26] Teleworking was originally proposed as a creative way to save energy or increase productivity.[27] However, a 2001 survey of 150 executives in large U.S. companies found that 36 percent say there is no difference in productivity levels between teleworkers and on-site employees.

Two crucial issues have occurred in teleworking: how workers can be managed and how the work can be managed. Workers must learn how to work from an alternative work location. They must also acquire the discipline necessary to work untethered. There is also the challenge of determining how to do the work while being physically separated from colleagues and managers. A greater reliance on trust, commitment, and meeting deadlines is created by the teleworking approach. Managers and employees have to learn how to perform work using a remote work base.

John Chen, CEO of Sybase, states, "Creativity shouldn't get restricted by time and space. Telecommuting is almost a requirement."[28] The Families and Work Institute reports that 70 percent of employees surveyed were willing to change employers and 81 percent were willing to sacrifice advancement to obtain flexible work arrangements.[29]

Verifone, a division of Hewlett-Packard with more than 3,000 employees worldwide, has used telecommuting and virtual teams since 1981.[30] If a person lives in Colorado and can do the job in virtual space Verifone is not reluctant to hire him or her. Verifone requires

Management Focus on Innovation

Myths about Telework

Managers and nonmanagers hold a number of firm but false beliefs about such arrangements as teleworking.

Myth 1: *Teleworking is for everyone.* No, it is not. Being computer literate is one requirement, and today not everyone is comfortable with technology. In general, younger workers are more comfortable than older, more experienced, more knowledgeable workers are.

Myth 2: *The office is the most productive place to work.* No, there are a lot of distractions and time wasters in offices. However, there are distractions at home and in remote offices. Managing the distractions is a must for teleworkers. Once a system is in place, the wasted time is reduced and productivity improves.

Myth 3: *There is no teamwork in teleworking.* Traditional face-to-face meetings and time is reduced. However, technology empowers everyone to communicate, problem-solve, and learn. Contributions of team members is reflected more on the quality of the content and information than on the schmoozing that occurs in face-to-face teams.

Myth 4: *Teleworkers can take care of themselves.* Not exactly. Most people need support, coaching, and guidance on some issues. Also, people need access to the firm's systems, gadgets, and technical support.

their top-level executives to meet face-to-face with staff at remote offices as often as possible. Managers, scattered around the world, rotate meeting sites. Managers also have training courses available that address how to supervise and lead remote employees. The Verifone commitment to teleworking arrangements is accepted by managers and nonmanagers as a sound alternative to on-site, single-location job and work design.

The Management Focus on Innovation box "Myths About Telework" addresses a number of myths that have been associated with alternative work arrangements such as teleworking.

Astute managers carefully evaluate the pros and cons of teleworking options for their employees. In reviewing the process and procedures of a number of organizations there is a template or set of considerations that are worth considering when evaluating teleworking's value add for an organization. The Learning Moment box offers a few guidelines for managers and teleworkers to consider.

The positive benefits of any redesign effort are moderated by individual differences in the strength of employees' growth needs. That is, employees with strong needs for accomplishment, learning, and challenge will respond more positively than those with relatively weak growth needs. Employees forced to participate in job redesign programs but who lack either the skills or the ability to perform redesigned jobs may experience stress, anxiety, adjustment problems, erratic performance, turnover, and absenteeism.

The available research on the interrelationships between perceived job content and performance are meager. One recent survey of 30 actual applications of job redesign strategies confirms that failures are as frequent as successes.[31] It is apparent, however, that managers must cope with significant problems in matching employee needs, differences, and organizational needs.[32] The problems associated with job redesign are several, including the following:

1. The program is time consuming and costly.

2. Unless lower-level needs are satisfied, people will not respond to opportunities to satisfy upper-level needs. And even though our society has been rather successful in providing food and shelter, these needs regain importance when the economy moves through periods of recession and inflation.

3. Job redesign programs are intended to satisfy needs typically not satisfied in the workplace. As workers are told to expect higher-order need satisfaction, they may raise their expectations beyond that which is possible. Dissatisfaction with the program's unachievable aims may displace dissatisfaction with the jobs.

4. Finally, job redesign may be resisted by labor unions that see the effort as an attempt to get more work with the same pay.

LearningMoment _A General Guideline Template_

Managerial Behaviors

- Communicate clearly and frequently
- Provide all data, memos, and information provided to onsite workers
- Discuss issues, performance, and needs at least once weekly
- Ask for brief reports on work and goals accomplished (bi-monthly)
- Attempt to interact in person at least quarterly
- Provide formal feedback on performance

Teleworkers

- Provide comfortable work space
- Provide all necessary and updated equipment
- Maintain privacy
- Minimize interruptions
- Check regularly (daily) with supervisor and team

Privacy and Confidentiality

- Keep all materials and interactions confidential
- Back up systems
- Use passwords
- Protect against viruses and hackers

Practical efforts to improve productivity and satisfaction through implementation of job redesign strategy have emphasized autonomy and feedback. Relatively less emphasis has been placed on identity, significance, and variety.[33] Apparently it is easier to provide individuals with greater responsibility for the total task and increased feedback than to change the essential nature of the task itself. To provide identity, significance, and variety often requires enlarging the task to the point of losing the benefits of work simplification and standardization. But within the economic constraints imposed by the logic of specialization, it is possible to design work so as to give individuals complete responsibility for its completion to the end and at the same time to provide supportive managerial monitoring.

These and other problems account for many failed efforts to achieve satisfactory results with job redesign efforts. Despite the instances of failure, organizations continue to search for ways to improve job designs. The use of free agents on virtual teams is an example of an approach some firms use that is briefly discussed in the Management Focus on Leadership box, "Virtual Teams and Free Agents."

In general, the conclusion that one reaches when considering the experience of job redesign approaches is that they are relatively successful in increasing quality of output, but not quantity. This conclusion pertains, however, only if the reward system already satisfies lower-level needs. If it currently does not satisfy lower-level needs, employees cannot be expected to experience upper-level need satisfaction (intrinsic rewards) through enriched jobs. Since a primary source of organizational effectiveness is job performance, managers should design jobs according to the best available knowledge. At present, the strategies for designing and redesigning jobs have evolved from scientific management approaches to work design with emphasis on quality of work-life issues in the context of rapidly changing technology.

▶ *Management Focus* on **Leadership**

Virtual Teams and Free Agents

Virtual teams come together in cyberspace from across the country or world to work on a project or task. Some of these arrangements last a few days, while others last for a year or more. Some of the arrangements use global virtual teams (GVTs). A GVT is a temporary, culturally diverse, geographically dispersed, electronically communicating work group of members who think and act in concert.

The virtual team arrangement can be found in any industry. Motorola, Borg-Warner, Toyota, Novartis, and West Bend are examples of enthusiastic advocates of multidisciplinary virtual teams. These companies and a growing number of others use free agents on the virtual teams.

A free agent, or freelancer, is an independent contractor whose skills, interpersonal abilities, and creative talents are marketable. The free agent can work on many different projects with different colleagues. Perhaps as many as 30 million U.S. free agents work in virtual teams.

The use of free agents and virtual teams is not for every firm. Managing these kinds of units and people is challenging. Managers must adapt their on-site (in office, factory) style to the realities of working with individuals making inputs and contributions from different locations. This means giving up some degree of traditional control and working very hard to maintain trust and communication. Virtual teams and free agents, more than traditional job arrangements, need excellent managers who can communicate and lead from a distance.

Sources: Adapted from Michael Harvey, Milorad M. Novicevic, and Gary Garrison, "Challenges to Staffing Global Virtual Teams," *Human Resource Management Review,* September 2004, pp. 275–294; Cristina B. Givson and Susan G. Cohen (eds.), *Virtual Teams That Work: Creating Conditions for Virtual Team Effectiveness,* (San Francisco: Josey-Bass, 2003); Jon L. Pierce, Tatiana Kostova, and Kurt T. Dirks, "Toward a Theory of Psychological Ownership in Organizations," *Academy of Management Review,* April 2001, pp. 298–310; and Jane Lommel, "Virtual Companies Meet Needs of Constantly Changing Market," *Human Resource Management News,* September 1, 2000, p. 5.

8-8 The Future of the Job

Since the beginning of the Industrial Revolution people have predicted that machines would take over the jobs done by people. In the nineteenth century, Luddites reacted to this belief by destroying looms and spinning jennies that threatened their jobs. Karl Marx predicted a vast army of unemployed people created by capitalists who invested in automated factories. In the late 1940s, Norbert Weiner, a computing pioneer, predicted that computers would take over so many jobs that the Great Depression would look like a picnic in comparison. In the late 1950s and 1960s, movies and television picked up on the threat of "automation" and the potential loss of jobs.

Fear of what technology will do to people's jobs waxes and wanes. In the last few years, the fear has grown stronger again, especially after waves of corporate "downsizing" eliminated huge chunks of middle-management jobs. Are the fears of job loss from technology justified? In a way, yes. Technology has destroyed millions of jobs. A decade ago, the words on this page would have been set by a typesetter. That role is no longer needed as computers and word processing software have taken it over.[34]

In the past 200 years, millions of jobs have been destroyed due to the development of technology and machines. Over the same period, however, the number of jobs available in the economy has grown almost continuously, as have the real incomes of most people in the industrial world. Further, this growth has come about not in spite of technology, but largely because of it.

In short, it's without question that many people's lives have been disrupted as technology charges ahead and makes their role in organizations obsolete. Nonetheless, as John Kennedy put it, "If men have the talent to invent new machines that put men out of work, they have the talent to put those men back to work."[35]

That phrase is the key to jobs in the future. Managers and workers of all types will have less security in their jobs than people had in the past. The changed model of a career follows from the changed nature of work. The "job," a more-or-less set task that one does every day, is disappearing as routine office and factory work is automated. Today, people spend their days on projects, designing a new jetliner, launching a product, preparing a

Management Focus on Leadership

Rewarding Employees for Teamwork

Organizations will go to great lengths to make teams work. Unfortunately, evidence shows that a lot of this effort will be wasted if these organizations don't succeed in aligning the team concept with their business strategies and human resource management systems. The rationale behind teams is well defined. For many organizations, a wide gap exists between their initial expectations for teams and the results the teams achieve. One of the chief hurdles appears to be how to design a reward program that will both sustain team progress and reinforce the team structure. The success of teams lies in a partnership between HR strategists, line managers, and team members. Inattention to the key design factors in forging this partnership is likely to lead to the failure of the teams.

The effort to move jobs into team roles raises a series of difficult questions about how to design a teamwork structure. An integrated management model categorizes seven interrelated areas that every team champion will have to confront: leadership; values and cultures; work processes and business systems; organization, team, and job design; individual and team competencies; management processes and systems; and reward and recognition. It would be ideal to tackle the chal-lenges on all fronts, but in reality organizations will usually dive in at one spot and expand from there.

A division of Unisys, the information technology company, entered the process with "organization, team, and job design" as its primary focus. Relocating its back-office accounting function to the prairies, the company took advantage of the new site to make dramatic changes in the way people work. Today, more than 140 people are organized into ten teams at the Bismarck, North Dakota, office. These teams handle various accounting functions, such as the company's accounts payable and employees' business travel reimbursements. Each team takes care of an entire process, from opening mail to issuing checks, and seeks solutions internally to any problems it encounters. And while everybody gets an individual base wage, people also get paid for the performance of the team.

Sources: Adapted from Leigh J. Thompson, *Making the Team: A Guide for Managers,* (Upper Saddle River, NJ: Prentice Hall, 2004); Carl R. Weinberg, "Reward Strategies for Compensation Lessons from the Front," *Compensation and Benefits Review,* February 2001, pp. 6–14; and Steven E. Gross, "When Jobs Become Team Roles, What Do You Pay?" *Compensation & Benefits Review,* January/February 1997, pp. 48–51.

lawsuit, or reengineering the billing process. Projects are conceived, staffed up, completed, and shut down. Familiar signs of career progress—promotions from junior engineer to manager, and so on—have gone the way of the Taylorist division of labor. Today, the goal is growth in one's profession, not climbing the corporate ladder. The Management Focus on Leadership box "Rewarding Employees for Teamwork" takes a look at one profession that has created a legion of nomadic workers.

Regardless of where you work each day—whether at a large corporation, a small business, or the end of your dining room table—the message is the same: You are on your own. The paternalistic model of long-term employment is dead and buried. People must be prepared for a wide range of different types of work: consulting, temporary, running their own business, working from home, returning to college, shifting careers. Nearly 45 million Americans, about one-third of the workforce, are self-employed or working as temps, part-timers, or consultants. Table 8-1 provides six tips for staying ahead in this new age where the notion of the "job" is rapidly changing.[36]

TABLE 8-1 **Six Tips for Staying Ahead**	
1.	Continually evaluate your skills, competencies, and knowledge. Where are you currently? Where do you want to be in the future?
2.	Read, study, and update your knowledge and information. Keep informed by reading as much as possible.
3.	Study and observe how successful people talk, present themselves, make decisions, and handle crises. You can learn from others if you take the time.
4.	Work at being proficient with technology. Take courses, study how to use it effectively, and update yourself. The Information Age is here to stay. To be a part of it you must be computer literate.
5.	Keep alert for opportunities and projects that stretch your skills. Do not become comfortable with one set routine.
6.	The more experience you have the more attractive you are when vacancies or new projects emerge.

Management Summary

- Job design involves managerial decisions and actions that specify job depth, range, and relationships to satisfy organizational requirements as well as the social and personal requirements of the jobholders.

- Contemporary managers must consider the issue of quality of work life when designing jobs. The issue reflects society's concern for work experiences that contribute to the personal growth and development of employees.

- Strategies for increasing the potential of jobs to satisfy the social and personal requirements of jobholders have gone through an evolutionary process. Initial efforts were directed toward job enlargement. This strategy produced some gains in job satisfaction but did not change primary motivators such as responsibility, achievement, and autonomy.

- During the 1960s, job enrichment became a widely recognized strategy for improving quality of work-life factors. This strategy is based on Herzberg's motivation theory and involves increasing the depth of jobs through greater delegation of authority to jobholders. Despite some major successes, job enrichment is not universally applicable because it does not consider individual differences.

- Individual differences are now recognized as crucial variables to consider when designing jobs. Experience, needs, values, and perceptions of equity are some of the individual differences that influence the reactions of jobholders to their jobs. When individual differences are combined with environmental, situational, and managerial differences, job design decisions become increasingly complex.

- The most recently developed strategy of job design emphasizes the importance of core job characteristics as perceived by jobholders. Although measurements of individual differences remain a problem, managers should be encouraged to examine ways to increase positive perceptions of skill variety, task identity, task significance, autonomy, and feedback. By doing so, the potential for high-quality work performance and high job satisfaction is increased.

- Many organizations have attempted job redesign with varying degrees of success. The current state of research knowledge is inadequate for making broad generalizations regarding the exact causes of success and failure in determining the applicability of job redesign in their organizations.

Key Terms

flextime (p. 184)
job analysis (p. 174)
job depth (p. 177)
job design (p. 174)

job enlargement (p. 182)
job enrichment (p. 183)
job range (p. 177)
job rotation (p. 182)

job satisfaction (p. 181)
job sharing (p. 184)
perceived job content (p. 179)
quality of work life (p. 174)

Review and Discussion Questions

1. Explain the difficulties that management would encounter in attempting to redesign existing jobs as compared with designing new jobs.

2. What cost savings can an organization realize by using telecommuters? Offshore employees?

3. What are the characteristics of individuals who would respond favorably to job enlargement, but not to job enrichment?

4. To what extreme can an individual firm redesign jobs to include motivational factors? Are there economic, social, and legal limits?

5. Explain the relationships between feedback as a job content factor and personal goal setting. Is personal goal setting possible without feedback? Explain.

6. How could a manager determine that the job of a software programmer should be redesigned?

7. Which of the job core dimensions do you now value most highly? Explain and list them in rank order of importance to you.

8. In your own work experience have managers been concerned with developing challenging jobs? How do your experiences compare to the practice of devising challenging objectives?

9. What are some of the advantages and disadvantages for two individuals who are sharing a job?

10. Why is it important for managers to fully understand the advantages and disadvantages of teleworking?

Practice Quiz

Note: You can find the correct answers to these questions by taking the quiz and then submitting your answers in the Online Edition. The program will automatically score your submission. If you miss a question, the program will provide the correct answer, a rationale for the answer, and the section number in the chapter where the topic is discussed.

Indicate whether the sentence or statement is true or false.

_____ 1. Job analysis has been referred to by some human resources professionals as the basic activity of human resources management.

_____ 2. Successful managers involve employees in the job design process.

_____ 3. Group performance is affected in part by group cohesiveness.

_____ 4. People with a strong internal need to grow and expand their potential respond more strongly to attempts to alter the five core dimensions of jobs than those with a weak internal need to grow.

_____ 5. Job enrichment can be a key outcome of job reengineering projects.

_____ 6. Over half the firms using overtime pay have reported improvements in productivity, labor costs, and morale.

_____ 7. Job enlargement is the combination of tasks into a broader job. This is a redesign response to overly complicated jobs.

Identify the letter of the choice that best completes the statement or answers the question.

_____ 8. Managers cannot understand the causes of job performance without consideration of individual differences such as personality, needs, and _____ .
  a. education levels.
  b. monetary needs.
  c. span of attention.
  d. interpersonal skills.

_____ 9. Another factor in job satisfaction is the perceived equity of the outcome in terms of what the jobholder considers a fair _____ .
  a. workday.
  b. reward.
  c. quota.
  d. workload.

_____ 10. Nearly _____ of the American workforce is self-employed or working as temps, part-timers, or consultants.
  a. one-fourth
  b. one-third
  c. one-half
  d. all

_____ 11. A crucial issue associated with teleworking is how _____ .
  a. workers should be paid.
  b. work should be managed.
  c. work should be assigned.
  d. bonuses should be allocated.

_____ 12. _____ is a schedule that allows workers some control over when they start and finish the formal workday.
  a. Job rotation
  b. Performance management
  c. Flextime
  d. Offshoring

_____ 13. The characteristics of a job (e.g., engineer, teachers, judge) that have an impact on other jobs within or outside the organization (e.g., company, school, court) is called _____ .
  a. feedback cycle.
  b. task unit.
  c. task enlargement.
  d. task significance.

_____ 14. The discretion an individual exercises over a job/work/task is called the _____ .
  a. job specialty.
  b. job range.
  c. job depth.
  d. job relationship.

_____ 15. The application of Herzberg's two-factor motivation theory is referred to as _____ .
  a. job rotation.
  b. cycle time.
  c. job sharing.
  d. job enrichment.

Case Study

Generational Differences and Job Satisfaction

Workforce data from Randstad North America and Roper Starch Worldwide give employers new insights into what they should consider to attract and retain the most talented workers, thereby reducing operational costs associated with recruiting and hiring new employees.

One *Randstad North American Employee Review* explored generational mind-sets about satisfaction, motivation, and success in today's workforce. It identified the three key elements that drive employee satisfaction, and it also uncovered some myths about the way Mature Workers, Baby Boomers, GenXers, and GenYers view work, which may help employers better understand and manage employees of different generations.

Generational Differences

The Randstad Review unveils information regarding some generational myths and stereotypes. For instance, rather than being stagnant in a job while waiting for retirement, 81 percent of Mature Workers (ages 55 to 69) are interested in trying new things. GenXers' work styles do not mirror the myth of being job-hopping slackers; 77 percent of GenXers (ages 21 to 35) say that success is finding a company where you want to work for a long time, and 73 percent find satisfaction in knowing their work helps clients or customers.

Baby Boomers may be known as the selfish "Me" generation, but in reality Baby Boomers (ages 36 to 54) truly want to make a contribution to their clients and employers.

GenYers are often viewed as having a sense of entitlements and wanting opportunities handed to them; however, the truth is, GenYers (born after 1980) have an entrepreneurial spirit that makes them very self-reliant, the survey found.

Success in the workplace is not judged just by the size of a paycheck. *The Randstad Review* found three key elements that drive employee satisfaction: trust, flexibility, and a career mind-set. Nine out of ten employees (91 percent) define true success as being trusted to get a job done, surpassing fulfillment from money or a title. Flexibility is still important to the 2001 workforce—employees are not willing to give up the flexible work schedules that have emerged over the last ten years—and 67 percent of people ranked flexibility as part of their definition of workplace success. Employees who have some flexibility in when, where, or how they do their work are satisfied with their jobs.

A survey by the Society for Human Resource Management (SHRM) and CNNf showed significant generational differences. Mature workers indicated that compensation contributed significantly more to their overall job satisfaction than did GenXers. The GenX and GenY respondents reported that they base more of their satisfaction on work/life issues, career advancement opportunities, and communication between them and management than on compensation.

Questions for Discussions

1. Since there apparently are differences across generations regarding work design and flexibility preferences, what should managers do to help employees satisfy these different needs?

2. What value is provided to managers by having available survey results like the *Randstad North America Employment Review* studies and the SHRM and CNNF survey?

3. Do the results from *Randstad North American Employee Review*, SHRM, and CNNf surveys apply to employees operating from remote work sites? Explain.

Sources: Adapted from Dolly Penland, "Marking Time," *Jacksonville Business Journal,* October 22, 2004; www.kennedyinfo.com "Recruiting Trends," May 17, 2001; and Claire Raines and Jim Hunt, *The Xers and Boomers: From Adversaries to Allies,* (New York: Crisp, 2000).

Internet Exercise

Government Oversight

The government has developed a number of rules, regulations, and guidelines for various alternative work arrangements. Some of the rules are federal and others are local or state. By searching and analyzing information on the Internet, what should managers be aware of in terms of government oversight and requirements regarding the following?

- Telecommuting
- Job Sharing
- Free Agents
- Offshoring
- Temporary Workers

A few sites to start your search are the Occupational Safety and Health Administration Department of Labor (OSHA) www.osha.gov, www.opm.gov/ocp/aws/, and www.vtpi.org/tdm/tdm15.

Experiential Exercise

Your Job Preferences Compared with Others

Purpose: This exercise identifies what makes a job attractive or unattractive to you. Managers could use preferences of employees, if known, as information to develop and restructure jobs that are more attractive, rewarding, and generally more fulfilling. This type of information would permit a manager to create a positive motivational atmosphere for subordinates.

Setting Up the Exercise:

1. Think about your present job (if you have one) or the type of job you would like. Decide which of the following job factors is most important to you. Place a *1* in front of it. Then decide which is the second most important to you and place a *2* in front of it. Keep ranking the items in order of importance until the least important job factor is ranked *14.* Individuals differ in the order in which these job factors are ranked. What is your present preference?

    ____ Advancement

    ____ Pay (income received for working)

    ____ Fringe benefits (vacation period, insurance, recreation facilities)

    ____ Schedule (hours worked, starting time)

    ____ Location (geographic area: Midwest, South, West, East, Southwest)

    ____ Supervisor (a fair, influential boss)

    ____ Feedback (receiving prompt, meaningful, and accurate feedback on job performance)

    ____ Security (steady work, assurance of a future)

    ____ Challenge (interesting and stimulating work)

    ____ Working conditions (comfortable and clean work area)

    ____ Co-workers (colleagues who are friendly, interesting)

    ____ The organization (working for a company you are proud of)

    ____ Responsibility (having responsibility to complete an important job)

    ____ Training and development opportunities (the ability to receive training and development in the organization or through external sources)

2. Now rank the job factors as you think other members of your class would rank them. Look around and think how the average person in your class would rank the job factors.

    ____ Advancement

    ____ Pay

    ____ Fringe benefits

    ____ Schedule

    ____ Location

    ____ Supervisor

    ____ Feedback

    ____ Security

    ____ Challenge

    ____ Working conditions

    ____ Co-workers

    ____ The organization

    ____ Responsibility

    ____ Training and development opportunities

3. The instructor will form four-to-six-person groups to discuss the *individual* and *other* rankings. Each group should calculate averages for both rankings. What does this show? The members of the group should discuss these average scores.

4. The average individual and average other rankings should be placed on the board or flip chart and discussed by the entire class.

A Learning Note: Individuals consider different factors important. Can a manager realistically respond to a wide range of different preferences among subordinates?

Organizational Structure and Design

9

Managing Today

Mail-Well Restructures and Streamlines Its Operations

In 2002, executives at Mail-Well, Inc., a $1.8 billion printing company, decided that the firm was due for a structural overhaul. The plan they conceived reshaped the company into two business segments instead of three, remapped its geographic organization, unified its sales offering, and streamlined its management structure.

After selling most of its non-core assets, the company consolidated its commercial printing and envelope business into a single group for direct sales to national and local accounts. The unit, called the "Commercial Segment," consists of 36 printing plants and 29 envelope plants, which account for about $1.4 billion of the company's revenues. Once dispersed across seven territories, the Commercial Segment now has just five regions. Mail-Well's executives stated that the former operating structure didn't support the company's strategy for customer service and growth. "We want to function as a single entity and to present ourselves to customers and prospects as a unified company with a single point of entry," explained Gordon Griffiths, president of the Commercial Segment.

Keith Larson, Mail-Well's executive vice president of sales and marketing, explained that the company had been based on the traditional consolidator model. That is, "we bought 140 companies and then left them alone. But we learned that being a holding company wasn't enough." He described Mail-Well's new value proposition as a triangle, in which understanding the customer forms the base while connecting the parts of the organization and customizing products and services are the sides. "The message is that we understand our clients' visual communication needs and connect our resources to deliver those customized messages and solutions."

In addition, Larson noted, local service will remain crucial to the company's relationships with customers. "Our plants, which are located in close proximity to the customers they serve, are equipped to produce quick-turn, short-run work with the convenience and versatility of a local provider." Mail-Well's restructuring has an intense customer focus, and is expected to position the company for continued growth in the coming years.

Source: Adapted from "Mail-Well Executives Note Gains in Big Restructuring," *Graphic Arts Monthly,* April 2004, p. 22.

The concept of organizational structure will be introduced by describing the typical experience of an individual taking her first job. More than likely, you have worked for a company, or perhaps a church, governmental agency, or summer camp. Perhaps you are now employed. One of the first things your boss told you was what your job would involve—what equipment you should use, what you should produce, and who you work with. For example, if you were employed as a bank teller, you were told how to deal with each type of customer transaction such as deposits, withdrawals, check cashing, and even loan payments. Each type of transaction required a slightly different method, and you were taught those methods.

You also quickly learned which other people you had to work with to complete your job satisfactorily. For example, you were perhaps required to secure the approval of another person before you could cash a check for someone who was not a customer of the bank. In this instance, you were acting on orders or directives that defined how much authority you had to complete a transaction. In any setting, an individual's job is specified in terms of basic tasks and authority to complete those tasks.

You also quickly found out another piece of important information; that is, just what your boss expected of you. Your boss is the individual who supervises your work to see that you do it properly and within the bounds of your authority. But perhaps more importantly, your boss has authority over you. She has the right to tell you what to do, and to evaluate your work. If the boss is pleased with your performance, then you know that you have a good chance to continue working and even to get pay raises and promotions.

Another important piece of information is the names of others under your supervisor. These other people are the members of your department, or unit, or group. Chances are, all of your coworkers' jobs are more or less similar. If you are a teller, your boss is the head teller. Some of your coworkers may have more tasks than others and more freedom (autonomy) to do those tasks. You also may find out (or suspect) that those coworkers make more money than you do.

If you continue to work in the bank, you will discover that people in your department come and go. Some will get fired; some will be promoted to other jobs. But as quickly as

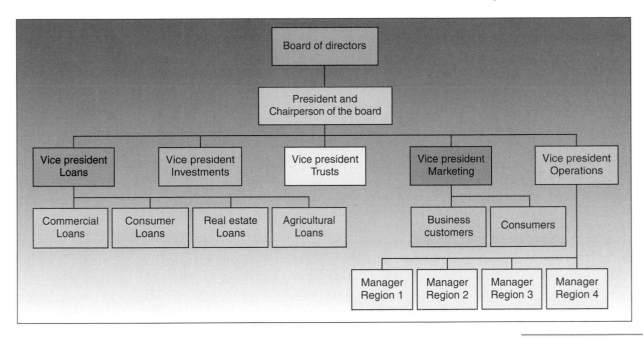

Figure 9-1
Security Bank
Organization Chart

one person leaves a job, another person usually will be hired to fill it. Thus, you begin to realize that the work goes on despite the comings and goings of different people. It may even be that your boss—the head teller—changes. Your original boss may be promoted, or may retire, or may quit to take another job. But soon, another person will take the job; perhaps a teller in your department has been promoted. These experiences should cause you to understand that the bank has created ways to avoid dependence on individuals. It has devised, in effect, a system of jobs, departments, and authority that enables the work to be done irrespective of the particular individuals who are employed at the time. That system and its parts are the bank's organizational structure.

As you gain experience in your job, and as you become more familiar with what goes on in the bank, you begin to see that banks consists of numerous jobs and departments. You also discover that your boss has a boss who in turn has a boss. You may even be curious enough to ask someone about how the bank is run. When you first began your job you may have been given some company literature, such as an annual report or employee handbook. There, you likely would see an organization chart. Figure 9-1 is an example of a bank's organization chart.

An organizational chart shows jobs and departments and is the most tangible depiction of an organizational structure. Reporting relationships and channels of communication are indicated by the solid lines connecting the positions. Now you see the whole complicated picture. What does the chart really show? What concepts enable you to understand it? Why is the bank organized in the way it is and not in some other way? Why were you hired? How could the organization be changed? This chapter and those that follow will present ideas that will enable you to answer questions such as these.

9-1 Organizational Structure

Organizational structure is the framework of jobs and departments or divisions that directs the behavior of individuals and groups toward achieving the organization's goals and objectives. A good organizational structure is aligned with an organization's strategy. "Alignment" means that the organization's structure is such that it facilitates realization of the organization's goals and objectives. **Organizational strategy** specifies *what* will be accomplished. Organizational structure specifies *who* will accomplish what and *how* it will be accomplished.

Over the last 125 years, organizations have experimented with a variety of structures designed to facilitate the achievement of goals. This chapter explores some of these structures. In the last chapter you explored the elements of job design and analysis. Using a

organizational structure The formally defined framework of task and authority relationships. The organization structure is analogous to the biological concept of the skeleton.

organizational strategy The general approaches the organization uses to achieve its organizational objectives. These approaches include market penetration, market development, product development, and diversification strategies.

physics metaphor, the job can be seen as the "atom" or "basic building block" of organizational design. The next task for managers after having defined the basic building blocks is to combine them logically, physically, and socially to pursue organizational goals. This is the fundamental challenge of organizational design: grouping jobs for the most effective, efficient use of resources to achieve organizational goals.

An effective organizational structure doesn't often occur by chance or luck. Managers must design effective structures. The Managing Today vignette describes how Mail-Well senior executives restructured the $1.8 billion company to be more responsive to customers. Many organizations find themselves, after years of growth, to have developed layers of bureaucracy between decision makers and customers. When that happens, the organization can become less responsive to customer needs and make itself vulnerable to more agile competitors. Mail-Well recognized its need to regain contact with customers before a crisis arose. Smart managers are constantly reviewing their organizational structure to ensure that it is optimally suited for achieving the organization's goals. In creating an organizational structure managers are faced with myriad decisions and alternative courses of action. Should the organization be centralized or decentralized? Should it allow managers a wide or narrow span of control? Should it be a flat or tall hierarchy? We explore these questions next.

9-2 Determining Organizational Structure

Most of you have probably already worked in some type of organization, but you may not have given much thought to the way things were organized. For example, if you worked in a fast-food restaurant, did you take note of how the manager organized the staff? Some people were cooks. Some were cashiers. And still others had odd jobs like washing the dishes or cleaning up in the dining area. These different tasks were staffed by individuals working within the organizational structure. Effective organizations have unobtrusive structures that seem natural and unforced to the workers. But achieving such a natural-seeming structure isn't easy. Managers are faced with at least four choices about organizational design:

▶ **authority** The legitimate right to use assigned resources to accomplish a delegated task or objective; the right to give orders and to exact obedience.

1. *Degree of Specialization*   This refers to the extent to which individual jobs are specialized. Most organizations consist of specialized jobs, with workers performing different tasks. By dividing tasks into narrow specialties, managers gain the benefits derived from *division of labor*. These benefits include minimal training required for the jobs, and economic gains from employees who find ways of doing their jobs very efficiently. In our technology age, division of labor also refers to deciding when to use humans and when to use technology for many tasks. For example, it is very common today to have incoming customer calls screened by sophisticated answering systems prior to a human coming on the line. While many callers find this frustrating, the division of labor between man and machine is an effective way for companies to control costs and manage rapid growth.[1]

▶ **employee empowerment** The management practice of pushing decision-making authority down the chain of command to the individuals or groups responsible for carrying out tasks.

2. *Delegation of Authority*   When designing an organizational structure, managers must consider the extent to which authority will be distributed throughout the organization. **Authority** is defined as *the organizationally sanctioned right to make a final decision.* Managers delegate certain tasks to others to help them achieve more than they possibly could on their own. Authority in organizations can be centralized or decentralized. Today, many companies practice a form of delegation known as **employee empowerment.** This technique combines delegation with training to ensure that the individuals to whom tasks are delegated have the skills required to make sound decisions.[2]

▶ **departmentalization** The process of grouping jobs together on the basis of some common characteristic, such as product, client, location, or function.

3. *Type of Departmentalization*   **Departmentalization** is the process of grouping jobs according to three key factors: logic, physical location, and social harmony. Departmentalization is key to the flow of work in an organization and has become especially challenging for modern managers with far-flung, global operations and employees who "telecommute" to work and rarely set foot in the office.

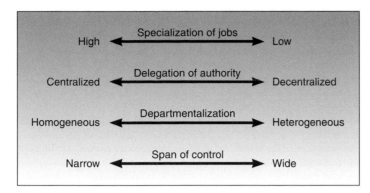

Figure 9-2
Designing Organization
Structure

4. *Span of Control* **Span of control** refers to the number of people who report to one manager or supervisor. The objective in establishing span of control is to determine the optimal design: wide or narrow? A wide span of control (flat organizational structure) results in a large number of workers reporting to one supervisor. A narrow span of control (tall organizational structure) results in a small number of people reporting to a single manager.

▶ **span of control** The number of subordinates who report to a superior. The span of control is a factor that affects the shape and height of an organization structure.

Figure 9-2 shows that these organizational design decisions managers face are not discrete, either-or decisions. Each of them is best represented as a continuum. The challenge for managers is finding the location on these continua that, when combined, produce the most effective results for the organization.

The four organizational design decisions that managers must make are important and complex. To help you understand these decisions a little better, we'll explore each in more detail.

9-2a Degree of Specialization

Job specialization is typically used to refer to the extent of variety in a given job. Ordinarily, we think of those jobs with low variety as higher in specialization and, thus, requiring less training and education. This is not always the case, however. Consider the cardiovascular surgeon. Such a person is considered a "specialist." The very nature of a surgeon's work is to focus on a single area of medical expertise and develop a very high level of competence and reliability. Think about it. If you required heart surgery, would you rather have it done by someone who has done hundreds of them, or by someone who "dabbles" in a wide variety of types of surgery?

Today, job specialization is not associated with scientific management, where management determined workers' jobs and the worker specialized in that job alone. The concept of specialization has changed from that perspective, but it still carries with it the efficiencies that Frederick Taylor and his scientific management disciples sought. Today's workers specialize in jobs or tasks, and they are encouraged to design their own work and enhance their specialized skills. The modern specialist, be it the cardiovascular surgeon or the assembly line worker, has far more autonomy to study his or her work, experiment with better ways of doing tasks, and extend the proficiencies gained into related areas than the worker of the scientific management era.

Effective managers seek to develop specialists in this modern sense of the term. This can be done by encouraging workers to regard whatever they do as a "profession." We don't question the fact that major league sports players typically play the same position and same sport for an entire career. We often watch them as they struggle through good times and bad. The best ones never cease in their efforts to be the best they can be. Managers must create jobs that are deep enough to encourage a commitment to the pursuit of excellence.[3] This is done through job design, job enlargement, and job enrichment, concepts you studied in the previous chapter. In addition, managers should find ways for people in disparate parts of the organization to share knowledge and insights with one another.

Management Focus on Innovation

Non-Technology Factors Linked to Overall Increases in Worker Productivity

A study by the Federal Reserve Bank of San Francisco sought to identify the causes of worker productivity increases over the past decade. In the wake of rapid technological advances in the 1990s, many have attributed the productivity gains of the decade primarily to innovations in software and hardware. While these factors are important, the authors of the Federal Reserve study found that non-technology workplace innovations are also important factors in the productivity gains. The most significant such factors were: pro-

duction ideas drawn from non-managerial employees, job rotation and job sharing, and tying compensation to performance. In fact, the researchers noted that these non-technology factors account for as much as 89 percent of the observed productivity gains.

Source: James Mehring, "What's Lifting Productivity?" *Business Week,* May 24, 2004, p. 32.

Knowledge is gained through the use of cross-functional teams, task forces, and job rotation or job sharing. These facilitate formal and informal interactions between employees. This is sometimes known as the "bumblebee" effect—when professionals work in different parts of the firm, moving between the country, lines of service, and industry axes. Ideas thus cross-pollinate as professionals develop networks that access the firm's dispersed experiences. These emergent communities, created by the complex division of labor, are at the core of knowledge generation. The Management Focus on Innovation box describes a study of workplace practices that have contributed to productivity gains over the past decade. As noted, workplace innovations such as job rotation are important factors in these gains.

9-2b Delegation of Authority

In practical terms, delegation of authority concerns the relative benefits of decentralization, that is, delegation of authority to the lowest possible level in the managerial hierarchy. The concept of **decentralization** does not refer to geographic dispersion of the organization's operating units; rather, it refers to the delegated right of managers to make decisions without approval by higher management. Of course, managers must be clear that they can delegate authority, but they cannot delegate accountability. Ultimately, the manager is accountable for the organization's effectiveness.[4]

> **decentralization** The process of pushing downward the appropriate amount of decision-making authority. All organizations practice a certain degree of decentralization.

Today's workplace is characterized by managers who are comfortable delegating authority to workers.[5] Empowering employees to make decisions and to devise their jobs according to what they think is best is difficult for many managers. They fear a loss of control and worry that employees may misuse their new powers. Usually, these fears are unfounded. Modern workers are typically more highly educated than the laborers of Frederick Taylor's day. They have the intellectual skills and knowledge to make good decisions, or to know when they need help in making good decisions. Table 9-1 provides tips for effective delegating.

Delegation of decision making is the center of a decentralized organizational structure. Command-and-control, hierarchical organizations have highly centralized structures. As already mentioned, the trend today is toward more delegation and less centralized organizational structures. Let's examine the advantages and disadvantages of decentralized authority.

Advantages of Decentralized Authority   Some experts believe that decentralization encourages the development of professional managers. As decision-making authority is pushed down in the organization, managers must adapt and prove themselves if they are to advance. That is, they must become generalists who know something about the numerous job-related factors that they must cope with in the decentralized arrangement.

Managers in a decentralized structure often have to adapt and to deal with difficult decisions, so they gain experience necessary for promotion into positions of greater authority and responsibility. In a decentralized structure, managers can be readily com-

TABLE 9-1

The Art of Delegating

- *Determine what to delegate.*   Identify and list responsibilities that need to be assigned to others. Try to be as specific as possible.

- *Match projects to staff members.*   Determine which assignments would be best suited to each employee. Also try to offer individuals projects you know they will enjoy. They'll jump into the work more enthusiastically.

- *Communicate your expectations.*   Don't simply provide a laundry list of tasks. Instead, explain the ultimate objectives of the project and how it helps your department or the company achieve certain goals.

- *Follow up.*   Occasionally check on the individual's progress to find out if he or she needs additional assistance or guidance. Your role is to help remove any obstacles, but you still need to trust the person to complete the task.

- *Show appreciation.*   A heartfelt "thank you" can go a long way toward motivating someone. You might also recognize the person in a team meeting.

Source: Adapted from "The Art of Delegation," by Liz Hubler, *Office Pro,* April, 2001, p. 7. Copyright © 2001. Reprinted by permission of IAAP via Copyright Clearance Center.

pared with their peers on the basis of actual decision-making performance, not personality. In effect, the decentralized arrangement can lead to a more equitable performance appraisal program and to a more satisfied group of managers.

The decentralized arrangement also can lead to a competitive climate within the organization. In such a structure, managers are motivated to excel since they are compared with their peers on various performance measures. Their relative performance in this context can affect their career path (promotions, pay increases, travel opportunities, etc.).

In the decentralized pattern, managers likewise can exercise more autonomy and satisfy their desires to participate in problem solving. This freedom can lead to managerial creativity and ingenuity, which contribute to the flexibility and profitability of the organization. E. F. Schumacher is a management thinker who wrote a book in 1973 called *Small Is Beautiful.* Schumacher believed that large corporations created bureaucratic inefficiencies and caused an individual to feel like "a small cog in a vast machine." Despite this, Schumacher realized that large organizations are here to stay. Thus, he counseled managers to achieve "smallness" within their larger organizations through decentralization. Through greater decentralization, he said, large corporations could retain individual intuition and entrepreneurial zeal.[6] Today, Schumacher's language of "smallness" has been replaced by terms such as "lean" and "agile." Lean organizations are those that have eliminated unnecessary steps in key processes.[7] Agile organizations are those that are able to change rapidly as competitive conditions and/or customer needs change.[8]

Disadvantages of Decentralized Authority   Decentralization has disadvantages, and they must be weighed against the advantages. Most advocates of decentralization recognize that if an organization shifts from centralized to decentralized authority, certain costs may be incurred. These are some of the costs:

1. Managers must be trained to handle decision making, and this may require expensive formal training programs.

2. Since many managers have worked in centralized organizations, it is uncomfortable for them to delegate authority in a decentralized arrangement. Their attitudes are difficult to alter, and attempts often lead to resistance.

3. Accounting and performance appraisal systems must be made compatible with the decentralized arrangement, and this can be costly. Administrative costs are incurred because new or altered accounting and performance appraisal systems must be tested, implemented, and evaluated.

These are, of course, only some of the disadvantages of decentralizing. As with most issues, there is no definite, clear-cut answer to whether decentralization is better for an organization. But one prerequisite for successful decentralization is thorough consideration of each organization factor (e.g., work force requirements, size, and control mechanisms).

▶**chain of command** The formal channel that defines authority, responsibility, and communication relationships from top to bottom.

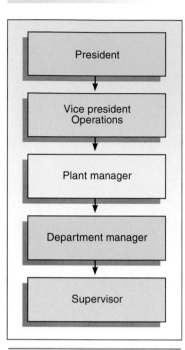

Figure 9-3
Chain of Command

▶**boundaryless organization** Where the formal structure characteristics such as spans of control, departmentalization, and a rigid chain of command is minimized or eliminated.

Figure 9-4
Communication Bridge

The Chain of Command and Authority One result of delegated authority is the creation of a chain of command. The **chain of command** is the formal channel that defines the authority, responsibility, and communication relationships from top to bottom in an organization. Figure 9-3 depicts the chain of command for a hypothetical managerial hierarchy. In theory, the chain should be followed whenever directives are passed downward or whenever communications are passed upward and downward.

At the same time, there must be means to bypass the formal chain when conditions warrant. Consequently, a subordinate often is empowered to communicate directly with a peer outside the chain. However, the appropriate superiors must indicate beforehand the circumstances under which the crossovers will be permitted. Figure 9-4 shows a bridge between F and G (the dashed line), which D and E have approved. In special circumstances, F and G may communicate directly without going through channels, yet both would be accountable only to their respective superiors—in this case, D and E.

Many modern scholars, and some practicing managers, suggest that organizations can function more effectively without a clear chain of command. They argue that the traditional organizational pyramid with its downward chain of command is becoming obsolete as new models for new kinds of organizations evolve. Some have argued for what is referred to as a **boundaryless organization.** Such organizations are characterized by semipermeable boundaries between organizational departments and divisions. Boundaryless organizations still have workgroups and teams, but they are fluid and invite participation from individuals from diverse parts of the organization.[9]

The Line-Staff Distinction In examining organizational structure, you must be careful to distinguish between line and staff. Line positions are defined as those involved in operational activities in a direct sense, that is, creating, financing, and distributing a good or service. Staff positions, meanwhile, are advisory and facilitative functions supporting the line activities. The line function contributes directly to the accomplishment of the major objectives of the organization, and the staff function contributes to their accomplishment indirectly.

Figure 9-5 illustrates a line and staff organization design of a hypothetical firm. If you assume that the organization depicted in Figure 9-5 is a manufacturing firm, you should be able to differentiate between line and staff positions. Using the criterion that the line functions contribute directly to the firm's objectives should lead you to the conclusion that the marketing and production departments perform activities directly related to the attainment of a most important organizational objective—placing an acceptable product on the market. You also can see that the activities of the managers of environmental control and human resources are advisory in nature. Their activities are helpful in enabling the firm to produce and market its product, but they do not directly contribute to the process. Thus environmental control and human resources are considered to be staff departments in this particular firm.

9-2c Types of Departmentalization

The *logic of departmentalization* is based on how best to group jobs according to the task at hand and the required individuals and jobs to complete it. Of course, the manager

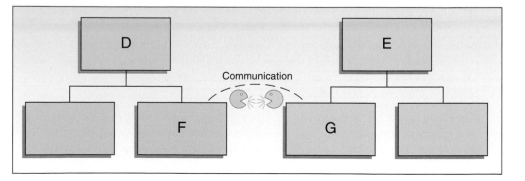

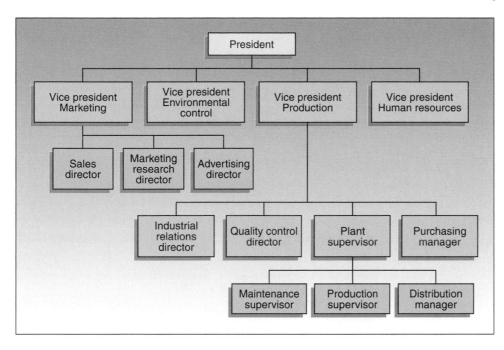

Figure 9-5
**Line and Staff Design
(Partial Organization Chart)**

decides on the "task at hand." A product doesn't dictate the order of assembly; logic and the demands of efficiency do. Research has suggested that product quality is affected by interdepartmental conflict and connectedness.[10] Thus, it's important for managers to group tasks in a way that minimizes conflicts.

Another factor in departmentalization is *physical location.* In a plant, jobs are organized into departments based in part on the layout of the organization's physical space. For example, a company with copious physical space may decide to separate sales from marketing. A company with limited space may group the two to save on that particular limited resource.

The final factor in departmentalization is **social harmony.** Managers must be attuned to the social relationships in an organization and be careful not to create a departmental structure that creates disharmonies. For example, in software companies, application developers may dislike administrators. Creating a single department that placed the two different groups in close proximity may be counterproductive. Good managers don't fancy themselves as social workers who wish to create harmony where it doesn't exist. Good managers accept current reality and design the organizational structure that works best with things as they are. This is not to say that managers shouldn't attempt to change attitudes in the long run—clearly, they should if those attitudes block progress. But, in the short run the work must get done. And good managers balance long-range change efforts with the immediate demands of meeting day-to-day organizational objectives.

social harmony A factor in departmentalization. Managers must be attuned to the social relationships in an organization and be careful not to create a departmental structure that creates disharmonies.

Functional Departmentalization
Jobs can be grouped according to the functions of the organization. A business firm includes such functions as production, marketing, finance, accounting, and human resources. A hospital consists of such functions as surgery, psychiatry, housekeeping, pharmacy, personnel, and nursing.[11] The functions of a fictitious entity we'll call Security Bank are the basis for the departments at the very top of its organizational chart, as shown in Figure 9-6. Within each of the five departments, individuals perform specialized jobs in the areas of loans, investments, trusts, marketing, and operations. A partial organization chart for a manufacturing firm is shown in Figure 9-7. It reflects the basic functions required to manufacture and sell a product.

An important advantage of functional departmentalization is that it makes use of the benefits of specialization. That is, you may logically set up departments that consist of experts in particular fields such as production or accounting. By having departments of specialists, a manager creates, at least theoretically, the most efficient unit possible.

Figure 9-6
Security Bank: Partial Organization Chart, Functional Departmentalization

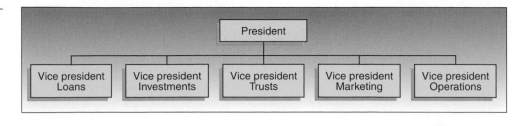

Figure 9-7
Business Firm: Partial Organization Chart, Functional Departmentalization

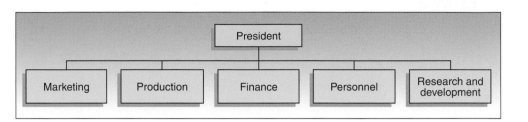

A major disadvantage of the functional arrangement, however, appears when specialists, working with and encouraging one another in their respective areas of expertise and interest, let the organizational objectives take a back seat to departmental objectives. Accountants may see only accounting problems, and not those of production or marketing or those of the overall organization. In other words, identification with the department and its objectives is often stronger than identification with the organization and its objectives.[12] This can be a problem if departmental goals are not adequately aligned with organizational goals.

Geographic Departmentalization   Another commonly used departmental basis is built around geography. All activities in a geographic area are assigned to a particular manager. This individual is in charge of all operations in that geographic area. The operations department of the Security Bank is subdivided into four geographic regions, each served by a branch bank. Figure 9-8 depicts that part of Security Bank that is organized according to territorial bases. If you were a teller in a branch bank in Region 1, your boss likely would report to the manager of that geographical area.

A business firm that is widely dispersed geographically often will use a geographic departmentalization basis. Firms whose operations are similar from region to region frequently use the territorial basis. Chain stores, railroads, airlines, and large consulting firms all establish departments along territorial lines.

An advantage often associated with geographic departmentalization is that it provides a training ground for new managers. The company can place managers out in territories and then assess their progress. The experience managers gain away from headquarters can provide invaluable insights into how the organization's products or services are accepted in the field. The geographic basis also enables the firm to develop local market areas and adjust more quickly to local customers' needs.

Figure 9-8
Security Bank: Partial Organization Chart, Territorial Departmentalization

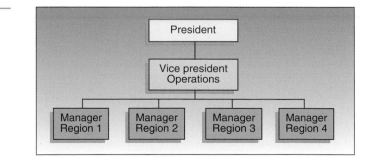

Management Focus on Diversity

Advertising Firm Develops Structure Based on Diversity

Media Planning, the media buying and planning operation of Havas Advertising, plans to sort out America's great melting pot for its clients with the launch of a multicultural unit. "Media Planning Diversity," a unit that specializes in working on media placement directed at Hispanic, African-American, and other ethnic groups, will group together clients already at Havas or Media Planning, including MCI WorldCom, the second largest Hispanic advertiser in the United States; Reckitt Benckiser's Lysol; and Volkswagen.

The unit will have about nine planners and buyers, who will come from both within the agency and from new hires. Currently, Hispanic marketing will be the largest piece of the spending at Media Planning Diversity. Media Planning has a natural affinity for the market because its worldwide CEO, Fernando Rodes Vilas, is Spanish.

Source: Adapted from Richard Linnett, "Media Shop Gets Diversity Unit," *Advertising Age,* May 7, 2001, p. 8.

The disadvantages of territorial departmentalization include difficulties in maintaining consistent adherence to company policy and practices, duplication of effort, and the necessity of having a relatively large number of managers. Companies that use territory as a primary basis for departmentalization often need a large headquarters staff to control the dispersed operations.

Product Departmentalization In many large, diversified companies, activities and personnel are grouped on the basis of product. As a firm grows, coordinating its various functional departments becomes more difficult, and product departmentalization can ease coordination problems. This form of organization allows personnel to develop total expertise in researching, manufacturing, and distributing one product line. See the Management Focus on Diversity Box: "Advertising Firm Develops Structure Based on Diversity" for a discussion of one company's method of departmentalizing its clients based on their ethnic diversity. Concentrating authority, responsibility, and accountability in a specific product department allows top management to better coordinate its activities. The need for coordinating production, engineering, sales, and service cannot be overestimated. Figure 9-9 is a partial organizational chart that represents a large electrical products company.

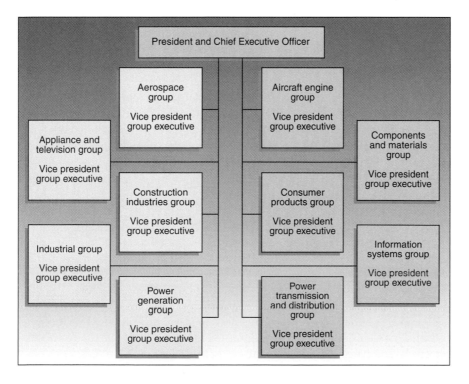

Figure 9-9
Business Firm: Partial Organization Chart, Product Departmentalization

Figure 9-10
Security Bank: Partial Organization Chart, Product Departmentalization

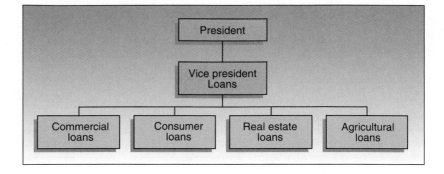

Within each of these product groups, you find production and marketing personnel. Since group executives coordinate the sale, manufacture, and distribution of a product, they become overseers of a profit center. This is how profit responsibility is exacted from product organizational arrangements. Managers establish profit goals at the beginning of a time period and then compare the actual profit with the planned profit. This approach is used in the Buick, Cadillac, Chevrolet, Pontiac, and Saturn divisions of General Motors. Product-based organizations can also be found in health care as well as in business.[13] The disadvantages of product-based organizations stem from the need to create relatively independent divisions. Each division must have all the resources and types of jobs necessary to be in business. Each division also must have accountants, lawyers, engineers, market researchers, and scientists assigned to it. Therefore, the product-based organization runs the danger of duplication of effort among its divisions. Research into organizational design best practices has shown that the most effective way to use product departmentalization is to ensure flexible boundaries between business units. Flexible boundaries allow organizations to reduce overall costs and to be more adaptive in response to market pressures.[14]

Product-based departmentalization is used in the Security Bank example. The vice president of the loan department is responsible for four units—commercial loans, consumer loans, real estate loans, and agricultural loans. The partial organizational chart is shown in Figure 9-10.

Customer Departmentalization   Customer-oriented departments are found frequently in educational institutions. Some educational institutions have regular (day and night) courses and extension courses. In some instances, a professor will be affiliated solely with the regular students or the extension students. In fact, the titles of some faculty positions often specifically mention the extension division. Some department stores also are departmentalized on a customer basis. They have such groupings as women's wear, men's wear, and teens.

The advantages and disadvantages of customer- or client-based organizations are identical to those of product organizations. Figure 9-11 depicts how Security Bank uses customers as the basis for organizing its marketing function. The bank's management believes that marketing and promotional efforts differ enough for business and nonbusiness customers so that specialization along those two lines is justified. The emergence of the service sector as a major source of business activity has encouraged managers to consider customer contact as a basis for organizing.[15]

Multiple Bases for Departmentalization   The methods just cited for dividing work are not exhaustive; there are many other ways to combine jobs into departments. Furthermore, most large organizations are comprised of departments using different methods. For example, at the upper levels of management, the vice presidents reporting to the president may represent different product groups. At the level directly below the vice presidents, the managers may be part of a particular function. The next level in the organization may include a number of different technical classifications. This multiple division of work in organizational design is illustrated in Figure 9-12. The figure's business example can be compared with the banking example in Figure 9-1.

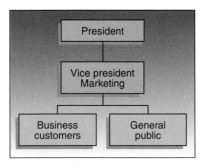

Figure 9-11
Security Bank: Partial Organization Chart, Customer Departmentalization

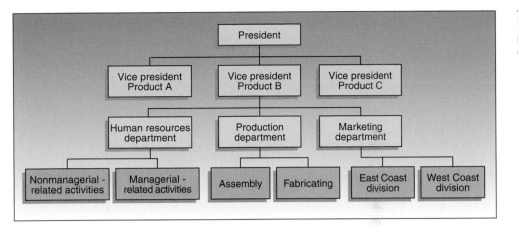

Figure 9-12
Business Firm:
Organization Chart

The principle of departmentalization specifies the general purpose to be followed when grouping activities. But the basis actually chosen is a matter of balancing advantages against disadvantages. For example, the advantage of departmentalizing on the basis of customers or products is that it can bring together under the control of a single manager all the resources necessary to make the product for the customers. In addition, specifying objectives is made considerably easier when the emphasis is on the final product. At the same time, this ease of objective identification and measurement can encourage individual departments to pursue their own goals at the expense of company objectives. A second disadvantage of product and customer departmentalization is that the task of coordinating the activities tends to be more complex. Reporting to the unit manager are the managers of the various functions (production, marketing, and personnel, for example) whose diverse but interdependent activities must be coordinated.

Departmentalization based on functional operations has certain advantages and disadvantages. The primary advantage is that such departmentalization centers on specific skills and training, and activities assigned to the departments emphasize the skills that individual members bring to the job. Because of the similarity of the subordinates' jobs, coordinating the activities of functional departments is considerably less complex than coordinating the activities of product departments. But functional departments have disadvantages as well. The principal disadvantage is that they cannot provide managers sufficient job depth to make their jobs challenging. Since creating functional departments involves breaking up a natural work flow and assigning parts of that flow to each department, every department manager must work very hard to coordinate the work of his or her section with the work of all the other departments.

9-2d Span of Control

The determination of appropriate bases for departmentalization establishes the kinds of jobs that will be grouped together—but not the *number* of jobs to be included in a specific group. That involves the issue of *span of control*. Generally, a span of control comes down to the decision of *how many people a manager can effectively oversee;* that is, will the organization be more effective if the manager's span of control is relatively large or small?[16]

Consider, for instance, the impact of different spans of control. In Figure 9-13 you see a graphic comparison of two structures, each with twenty-four nonmanagerial employees. In the first case, the maximum span of control is twelve, and there are two levels of management and three managers (a president and two supervisors). In the second case, the maximum span of control is four, and there are three levels of management and nine managers (a president, two department heads, and six supervisors).

The exact number of jobs (and people) reporting to a manager cannot be stated in specific terms for all managers in all organizations. Rather, the only feasible approach to determining optimal span of control is to weigh the relative importance of a number of factors.[17] Those factors include the following:

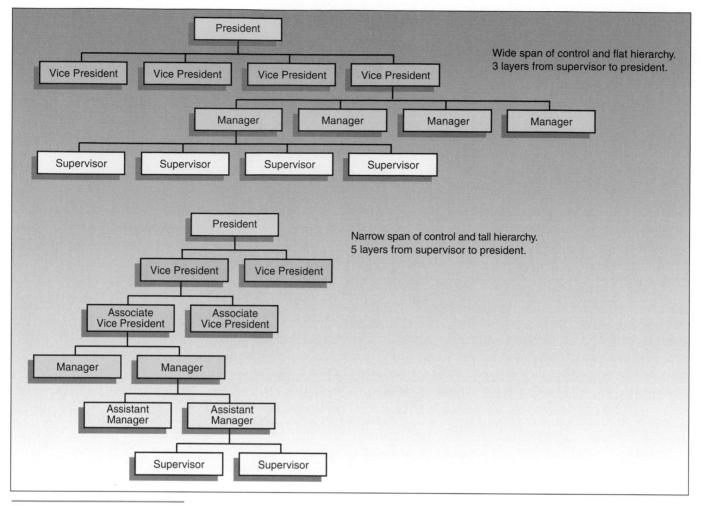

Figure 9-13

Wide and Narrow Spans of Control

1. *The competence of both the manager and the subordinates* The more competent they are, the wider the span of control can be.

2. *The degree of interaction that is required among the units to be supervised* The more the required interaction, the narrower the span of control must be.

3. *The extent to which the manager must carry out nonmanagerial tasks* The more technical and job-related work the manager has to do, the less time is available to supervise others, and thus the narrower the span of control must be.

4. *The relative similarity or dissimilarity of the jobs being supervised* The more similar the jobs, the wider the span of control can be; the less similar the jobs, the narrower it must be.

5. *The extent of standardized procedures* The more routine the jobs of subordinates are, and the greater the degree to which each job is performed by standardized methods, the wider the span of control can be.

6. *The degree of physical dispersion* If all the people to be assigned to a manager are located in one area, and within eyesight, the manager can supervise relatively more people than one whose people are dispersed throughout the plant or countryside at different locations.

Many studies have attempted to determine the exact relationships between these factors and the span of control. One review of these studies notes that they are, by and large, inconclusive. The actual spans of control in organizations result from the interplay of events and personalities unique to the particular organization.[18] Luther Gulick, an influential management scholar who is closely associated with the concept of "span of control," advocated that managers should oversee only a relatively small number of subordinates.[19]

9-3 Globalization and Implications for Organizational Design

The modern global economy has burst on the scene rather suddenly with the demise of worldwide communism and the opening of vast new markets. Many large and small organizations are taking advantage of the global economy in two primary ways: selling products and services around the world and outsourcing non-mission critical operations to strategic partners around the world. Each of these challenges to modern organizational design is explored next.

9-3a Selling Products and Services Around the World

Selling products to international markets poses new challenges for organizations that are structured primarily for domestic sales. As many firms have discovered through a trial-and-error process, simply exporting organizational structure to foreign locations is often not an effective strategy. To compete successfully in global markets, companies have discovered that paying attention to local customs and culture is important. In addition, global sales and service functions require integration of company knowledge and information on a global scale. Virtual work teams and telecommunication links have enabled firms to maintain tight control of costs and provide a high level of services to customers.

9-3b Outsourcing Operations Around the World

Many companies, primarily manufacturing but also retailing firms, are taking advantage of production operations all over the world to achieve cost savings and reliable supply lines.[20] Companies such as Nike, the "Big Three" automakers in the United States, Cummins Engine Company, Boeing, Wal-Mart, and others have used global outsourcing as part of their overall strategies.[21]

Outsourcing allows companies to focus on core competencies, and take advantage of strategic partnerships with other firms whose competencies are complementary or synergistic. In this way, for example, Nike is able to focus on design and marketing, leaving manufacturing to other companies that specialize in that part of the business. For example, Nike sources more than 30 percent of its manufacturing to China.[22] The challenge for Nike is managing the entire process from raw material acquisition to end user. In modern terms, this is known as **supply chain management (SCM)**.

Supply chain management refers to a company's efforts to organize and control its global sourcing. Modern firms with global suppliers can be viewed as being in the center of a constellation of firms, each of which adds value to the product.[23] Managing this constellation can be very difficult for firms because, despite advances in information technology, unexpected events and complexities are the rule rather than the exception in international business.

Today, companies are increasingly outsourcing non-core business processes to foreign labor markets where costs are lower.

> **supply chain management (SCM)** A company's efforts to organize and control its global sourcing.

Business Process Outsourcing (BPO)   With the increasing education levels around the world, BPO is no longer confined to routine manufacturing jobs or boiler-room telemarketing centers.[24] Today's outsourcing involves complex work that requires extensive preparation and training. For example, Indian radiologists now analyze computed tomography (CT) scans and chest X-rays for American patients out of an office park in Bangalore. In the United States, radiologists are among the highest-paid medical specialists, often earning more than $300,000 per year to evaluate magnetic resonance imaging (MRI), CT scans, and X-rays. In Bangalore, radiologists work for less than half that. Not far from the radiology lab in Bangalore, Ernst & Young has 200 accountants processing U.S. tax returns. Starting pay for an American accountant ranges from $40,000 to $50,000; in Bangalore accountants are paid less than half that.[25] In the next 15 years, Forrester Research predicts that 3.3 million service jobs will move to countries such as India, Russia, China, and the Philippines. That is the equivalent of 7.5 percent of all jobs in the United States right now.[26]

Management Focus on Ethics

In the Real World Does BPO Increase the U.S. Unemployment Rate?

The Labor Department, in its numerous surveys of employers and employees, has never tried to calculate the number of jobs that are shifted overseas as a result of BPO. But the offshoring of work has become so noticeable that experts in the private sector are trying to quantify it. Initial estimates are that at least 15 percent of the 2.81 million jobs lost in America since the recession began have reappeared overseas. Productivity improvements at home account for the great bulk of the job loss. But the estimates suggest that work sent offshore has raised the U.S. unemployment rate by four tenths of a percentage point or more.

Among economists and researchers, one high-end job-loss estimate comes from Mark Zandi, chief economist at Economy.com, who calculates that 995,000 jobs have been lost overseas since the recession began in March 2001. That is 35 percent of the total decline in employment since then. Most of the loss is in manufacturing, but about 15 percent is among college-trained professionals.

Source: Adapted from Louis Uchitelle, "A Missing Statistic: U.S. Jobs that Went Overseas," *The New York Times,* October 5, 2003.

The outsourcing revolution has led to job losses and job shifts for many people. Some groups and analysts assert that outsourcing is an unethical business practice because it moves jobs from the U.S. to offshore locations. But, as the Management Focus on Ethics box observes, outsourcing has not affected the number of jobs in the U.S.

9-4 Dimensions of Structure

The four design decisions (division of labor, departmentalization, span of control, and delegation of authority) result in a structure of organizations. Researchers and practitioners of management have attempted to develop their understanding of relationships between structures and performance, attitudes, satisfaction, and other variables thought to be important. The development of understanding has been hampered not only by the complexity of the relationships themselves, but also by the difficulty of defining and measuring the concept of organizational structure.

Although universal agreement on a common set of dimensions that measure differences in structure is neither possible nor desirable, some suggestions can be made. Currently, three dimensions are often used in research and practice to describe structure: formalization, centralization, and complexity.[27]

9-4a Formalization

formalization The degree to which an organization's expectations as to the means and ends of work are specified and written.

The dimension of **formalization** refers to the extent to which expectations regarding the means and ends of work are specified and written. An organization structure that is described as highly formalized would be one in which rules and procedures are available to prescribe what each individual should be doing. Such organizations would have written standard operating procedures, specified directives, and explicit policies. In terms of the four design decisions, formalization is the result of high specialization of labor, high delegation of authority, the use of functional departments, and wide spans of control.[28]

1. High specialization of labor, such as in the auto industry, is amenable to the development of written work rules and procedures. The jobs are so specialized as to leave little to the discretion of the job holder.

2. Functional departments are made up of jobs which have great similarities. This basis brings together jobs which make up an occupation such as accountants, engineers, machinists, and the like. Because of the similarity of the jobs and the rather straightforward nature of the department's activities, management can develop written documents to govern the department's activities.

3. Wide spans of control discourage one-on-one supervision. There are simply too many subordinates for managers to keep up with on a one-to-one basis. Consequently, managers will require written reports to inform them.

4. High delegation of authority creates the need to have checks on its use. Consequently, the organization will write guidelines for decision making and will insist upon reports that describe the use of authority.

Although formalization is defined in terms of the existence of written rules and procedures, it is important to understand how they are viewed by the employees. Some organizations may have all the appearances of formalization, complete with thick manuals of rules, procedures, and policies, but employees do not perceive them as affecting their behavior. Thus, even though rules and procedures exist, they must be enforced if they are to affect behavior.[29] This is made all the more complex in the modern, flexible workplace as managers strive to implement managerial rules while needing to ensure a degree of operational flexibility that relies on informality.[30]

9-4b Centralization

Centralization refers to the location of decision-making authority in the hierarchy of the organization. More specifically, the concept refers to the delegation of authority among the jobs in the organization. Typically, researchers and practitioners think of centralization in terms of (1) decision making and (2) control. But despite the apparent simplicity of the concept, it can be complex.

> **centralization** Describes the location of decision-making authority in the organization's hierarchy; refers to the delegation of authority among the organization's jobs.

The complexity of the concept derives from three sources: First, people at the same level can have quite different decision-making authority. Second, not all decisions are of equal importance in organizations. For example, a typical management practice is to delegate authority to make routine operating decisions (i.e., decentralization), but to retain authority to make strategic decisions (i.e., centralization). Third, individuals may not perceive that they really have authority even though their job descriptions include it. Thus, objectively they have authority, but subjectively they do not.[31]

The relationships between centralization and the four design decisions are generally as follows:

1. The higher the specialization of labor, the greater the centralization. This relationship holds because highly specialized jobs do not require the discretion that authority provides.
2. The greater the use of functional departments, the greater the centralization. The use of functional departments requires that the activities of the several interrelated departments be coordinated. Consequently, authority to coordinate them will be retained in top management.
3. The wider the spans of control, the greater the centralization. Wide spans of control are associated with relatively specialized jobs, which as we have seen have little need for authority.
4. The less authority is delegated, the greater the centralization. By definition of the terms, centralization involves retaining authority in the top-management jobs, rather than delegating it to lower levels in the organization.

9-4c Complexity

Complexity is the direct outgrowth of dividing work and creating departments. Specifically the concept refers to the number of distinctly different job titles, or occupational groupings, and the number of distinctly different units, or departments. The fundamental idea is that organizations with a great many different kinds and types of jobs and units create more complicated managerial and organizational problems than those with fewer jobs and departments.

> **complexity** Difference among jobs as the direct outgrowth of dividing work and creating departments.

Complexity, then, relates to differences among jobs and units. It, therefore, is not surprising that differentiation is often used synonymously with complexity. Moreover, it has become standard practice to use the term *horizontal differentiation* to refer to the number of different units at the same level;[32] *vertical differentiation* refers to the number of levels in the organization. The relationships between complexity (horizontal and vertical differentiation) and the four design decisions are generally as follows:

1. The greater the specialization of labor, the greater the complexity. Specialization is the process of creating different jobs and thus more complexity. Specialization of labor contributes primarily to horizontal differentiation.

2. The greater the use of territorial, customer, and product bases, the greater the complexity. These bases involve the creation of self-sustaining units that operate much like freestanding organizations. Consequently there must be considerable delegation of authority and consequently considerable complexity.[33]

3. Narrow spans of control are associated with high complexity. This relationship holds because narrow spans are necessary when the jobs to be supervised are quite different from one another. A supervisor can manage more people in a simple organization than in a complex organization. The apparently simple matter of span of control can have profound effects on organizational and individual behavior. Hence, we should expect the controversy that surrounds it.

4. The greater the delegation of authority, the greater the complexity of the organization. Delegation of authority is typically associated with a lengthy chain of command, that is, with a relatively large number of managerial levels. Thus delegation of authority contributes to vertical differentiation.

The discussion of the relationships between dimensions of organizational structure and the four design decisions are summarized in Table 9-2. The table notes only the causes of high formalization, centralization, and complexity. However, the relationships are symmetrical: the causes of low formalization, centralization, and complexity are the opposite of those shown in Table 9-2.

Organizations differ in their degree of formalization, centralization, and complexity. The important managerial issue is the relationship between these dimensions and individual, group, and organizational performance.[34]

9-5 Organizational Design

In this chapter we have seen that organizational structure is the framework of jobs and departments that directs the behavior of individuals and groups toward achieving an organization's objectives. Structure provides the foundation within which the organization functions, and managers must design an organizational structure that enhances the organization's overall strategy. Managers have many alternatives in developing an organizational structure. **Organizational design** is the process by which they develop an organizational structure. Since organizational structure is determined by specialization of jobs, delegation of authority, departmentalization, and span of control, organizational design includes coordinating these dimensions of organizational structure and deciding the extent to which the organization will be specialized, centralized, and so on. Modern researchers have developed sophisticated modeling and simulation tools for managers to use to determine optimal organizational designs under different scenarios. These new models are too complex to elaborate in this introductory text. It is enough for our purposes here to make you aware that such new tools exist. Most managers hire consultants or university professors to assist them in applying these new tools to their particular situations.[35]

▶ **organizational design** The process by which managers develop an organization's structure.

TABLE 9-2 **Relationship Between Organizing Decisions and Organization Dimensions**	High formalization is the result of:	1. High specialization. 2. Functional departments. 3. Wide spans of control. 4. Delegated authority.
	High centralization is the result of:	1. High specialization. 2. Functional departments. 3. Wide spans of control. 4. Centralized authority.
	High complexity is the result of:	1. High specialization. 2. Territorial, customer, and product departments. 3. Narrow spans of control. 4. Delegated authority.

Two extreme models of organizational design—the mechanistic model and the organic model—have provided much of the framework for understanding organizational design.[36]

9-5a The Mechanistic Model

In the early part of the twentieth century, many organizations and managers were guided by the principles of scientific management. They designed organizational structures that reduced jobs to basic, repetitive tasks. The focus was on maximizing efficiency. Workers were regarded as parts of the organizational machine. This view of the workplace and its guiding principles has come to be known as the **mechanistic model.** The term describes a rigid organization that attempts to achieve peak production and maximum efficiency through rules, standard operating procedures, centralized authority, and unambiguous chain of command.

Two types of organizational structures that you've already studied can be considered mechanistic models: Taylor's scientific management, and Weber's bureaucracy. Each of these organizational designs tried to reduce work into simple, discrete tasks. Taylor focused his attention on the worker and how to make the worker more efficient by applying scientific method to his or her job. Weber focused on communication and authority relationships within the organization, and how to make them more efficient by logically arranging them in a centralized bureaucracy.

Before we go too far in criticism of the mechanistic model of the organization, it should be pointed out that it also offers tremendous strengths. The mechanistic model introduced the application of analysis and division of labor to the workplace. Each of these tools is still used today in almost every work setting. Fast-food restaurants, health clubs, churches and synagogues, and nonprofit organizations will all have some division of labor. Each will probably also have managers who analyze work flow to determine if improvements can be made. These contributions of the mechanistic model must be recognized and understood.

At the same time, there is much to criticize in the mechanistic model. You've already learned that scientific management, if used too intensively, can lead to worker malaise or rebellion. Overly rigid work rules, repetitive tasks, and loss of autonomy can lead workers to be *less* productive. Modern managers have learned that most jobs don't have a "one best way" of being done. They've learned that different workers have different work styles. They've also learned that *empowering* workers to make decisions about how best to fulfill their responsibilities leads to high performance and high productivity.

The mechanistic model, while still influential in modern organizations, has given way to other designs. One prominent model that takes off from the more fluid design of biological organisms is called the organic model.

9-5b The Organic Model

The organic model of organizational design is in sharp contrast to the mechanistic model. The **organic organization** seeks to maximize flexibility and adaptability. The organic model encourages greater empowerment of employees to take advantage of the potential that each person brings to the office. The organic model de-emphasizes specialization of jobs, status, and rank. Horizontal and lateral relationships are as important as vertical relationships.[37]

The organic organization provides individuals with a supportive work environment and builds a sense of personal worth and importance.[38] Thus, managers in organic organizations encourage and motivate employees to reach their potential. This type of organization tends to be decentralized, and communication flows throughout the organization rather than through the chain of command. Typically, organic organizations base departmentalization on product and customer rather than on function.

Intuitively, you may believe that the organic organization is superior to the mechanistic model. The organic model with its encouragement of human potential and focus on employee empowerment certainly does offer some employees a better work environment. But don't forget, the goal of any organization must be to create the most efficient and productive means of delivering products and services. Organizations that don't strive for high

> **mechanistic model**
> An organization design in which there is differentiation of job task, rigid rules, and a reliance on top-management objectives.

> **organic organization** An organization with a behavioral orientation, participation from all employees, and communication flowing in all directions.

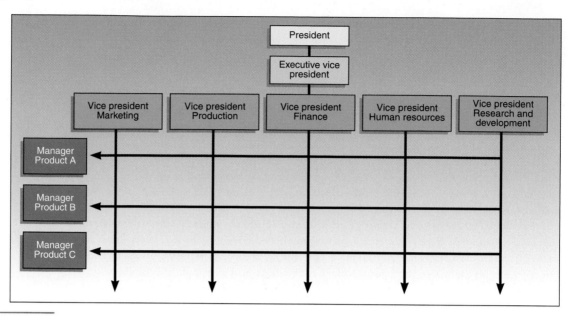

Figure 9-14
Matrix Organizational Structure

performance will be outperformed by others. Employee empowerment and development can be carried too far if a manager begins to regard that as the focus of his or her work. Effective managers don't lose sight of organizational goals. They develop and empower employees to the extent that those are effective techniques for achieving organizational outcomes.

9-5c Other Forms of Organizational Design

Many other forms of organizational design have been developed or are emerging in response to the rapidly changing environment. Increased global competitiveness, decentralization of authority, mergers and acquisitions, information technology, and consolidation of industries are just a few of the factors causing organizations to search for new designs. This section looks at several additional forms of organizational design.

▶**matrix organization**
A design in which a project-type structure is imposed on a functional structure.

The Matrix Organization   An emerging organization design, termed **matrix organization,** combines functional and product departmental bases.[39] Companies such as American Cyanamid, Caterpillar Tractor, Hughes Aircraft, ITT, Monsanto Chemical, National Cash Register, Prudential Insurance, TRW, and Texas Instruments are only a few that have experimented with a matrix design. Public sector users include public health and social service agencies.[40] Although the exact meaning of matrix organization is not well established, the most typical meaning sees it as a balanced compromise between functional and product organization, between departmentalization by process and by purpose.[41]

The matrix organizational design achieves the desired balance by superimposing, or overlaying, a horizontal structure of authority, influence, and communication on the vertical structure. The arrangement can be described as in Figure 9-14, where personnel assigned in each cell belong not only to the functional department, but also to a particular product or project. For example, manufacturing, marketing, engineering, and finance specialists will be assigned to work on one or more projects or products A, B, C, D, and E. As a consequence, personnel will report to two managers, one in their functional department and one in the project or product unit. The existence of a dual authority system is a distinguishing characteristic of matrix organization.

Matrix structures are found in organizations that require responses to rapid change in two or more environments, such as technology and markets, which face uncertainties that generate high information-processing requirements, and which must deal with financial and human resources constraints.[42] Managers confronting these circumstances must obtain certain advantages, which are most likely to be realized with matrix organization.[43]

Advantages of Matrix Organization   A number of advantages can be associated with the matrix design. Some of the more important ones are as follows:

Efficient use of resources Matrix organization facilitates the utilization of highly specialized staff and equipment. Each project, or product unit can share the specialized resource with other units, rather than duplicating it to provide independent coverage for each.

Flexibility in conditions of change and uncertainty Timely response to change requires information and communication channels that efficiently get the information to the right people at the right time. The result is a quicker response to competitive conditions, technological breakthroughs, and other environmental conditions.

Technical excellence Technical specialists interact with other specialists while assigned to a project. These interactions encourage cross-fertilization of ideas. Each specialist must be able to listen, understand, and respond to the views of the other. At the same time, specialists maintain ongoing contact with members of their own discipline because they are also members of a functional department.

Freeing top management for long-range planning An initial stimulus for the development of matrix organizations is that top management increasingly becomes involved with day-to-day operations. Environmental changes tend to create problems with cross-functional and product departments that cannot be resolved by the lower-level managers.

Improving motivation and commitment Project and product groups are composed of individuals with specialized knowledge. Management assigns to them, on the basis of their expertise, responsibility for specific aspects of the work. Consequently, decision making within the group tends to be more participative and democratic than in hierarchical settings.

Providing opportunities for personal development Members of matrix organizations are provided considerable opportunity to develop their skills and knowledge. They are placed in groups consisting of individuals representing diverse parts of the organization. The experience broadens each specialist's knowledge not only of the organization but also of other scientific and technical disciplines.

The Virtual Organization We are rapidly moving toward a distributed workforce that uses electronic technology to link workers and functions at scattered sites. This change is altering the nature of work, from the sales representative whose company database allows her to give customers immediate information on new product features, to the shipping employee who can monitor goods in real time. The growth of the virtual organization will be fueled by three factors:

- The rapid evolution of electronic technologies, which are facilitating the digital, wireless transfer of video, audio, and text information.

- The rapid spread of computer networks, in which the United States now maintains a strong global advantage over many other countries, including Japan.

- The growth of telecommuting, which will enable companies to provide faster response to customers, reduce facility expenses, and help workers meet their child- and eldercare responsibilities.

One implication of this trend is that people will need to develop specialized communication and planning skills to succeed in the virtual work environment. Traditionally, managers who lacked communication and planning skills often compensated through iterative face-to-face discussions, requiring team members to come back to them again and again to clarify performance goals or decision-making authority. To capitalize on the flexibility and speed that are possible through distributed, networked teams, managers and team members will have to form clear, up-front agreements regarding:

1. Performance expectations.
2. The team's priorities.
3. How communications are to be carried out among members.
4. The degree of resource support for virtual employees.

Electronic networking can redistribute power in organizations. Computer networks make it technically feasible for employees to skip levels in the chain of command, providing senior managers with direct feedback on performance problems and questions regarding organizational issues. Electronic bulletin boards let workers anonymously raise organizational issues, and they provide an effective rumor-control mechanism. But networks can also make employees at remote sites feel as if they are part of the team.

One impact of these trends is that, over the next few years, managerial performance will be based less on the ability to direct and coordinate work functions and more on improving key work processes. To ensure high performance, virtual managers will need to instill trust and cooperation between members of off-site work teams. It is not enough for these teams simply to be linked together by e-mail. Team members need to interact on a regular basis. Three problems in particular will require virtual managers' prompt attention:

1. *Nonresponsiveness* Virtual managers will need to ensure that remote teams of workers respond to one another at least as well as they would in a traditional work environment, and probably better.

2. *Location-Centric Words and Actions* Managers must ensure that remote teams don't use colloquialisms or local terms that are inscrutable to others. Virtual teaming requires constant attention to the communication process.

3. *Loss of "Water-Cooler" Time* Employees need informal or "leisure" time to freely share information. Virtual managers must ensure that such informal communication opportunities are available to virtual teams.[44]

Within stable-state organizations, a good manager is viewed as someone who consistently maintains solid performance within a team, while company loyalty is synonymous with defending the value of the organization's policies, procedures, and processes. In contrast, the dynamic organization recognizes the need for continuous improvement to meet changing customer requirements and competitor actions. In such organizations, managers will be increasingly judged on their ability to identify and implement improvements and to encourage innovative thinking from team members, while professionals will be judged on their ability to adapt quickly to widely different work environments.

Finally, the dynamic organization will require workers to be able to jump quickly into new ventures and manage temporary, project-focused teams, as more and more of their work responsibilities will lie outside of the traditional "work niche" consisting of a rigid job description and functional organizational "home."

The Multidivisional Organization

The **multidivisional,** or **"M-form,"** organization has emerged in a high-performance organizational form that allows highly interdependent operating units or divisions.[45] Each division's product or value added is different from other divisions, but they all share common resources, such as technology, skill, and information. The M-form design tries to strike a balance between autonomy and interdependence. With this design, each unit is expected to act independently to maximize profits. But success depends on sharing limited resources among the divisions. The key to this type of design is ensuring that this form of cooperation doesn't stifle creativity and independence. Figure 9-15 shows an M-form organizational design.

The Network Organization

A **network organization** is a flexible, usually temporary set of alliances among disparate companies that have come together for a specific, single purpose.[46] This is a dynamic organizational design, meaning that the parts that have been brought together for a specific purpose are not likely to hold together beyond that. A major advantage of the network design is that it allows organizations to focus on that which they do best—their "core competence." In this way, organizations can discontinue those activities that are not part of its core and that may be handled better by another company. This practice has come to be known as **outsourcing.** Outsourcing is simply the practice of one company contracting with another to provide products or services that are not part of the first company's core activities.

This design is gaining popularity around the world as the global economy continues to mature. Strategic partners can be added to a network of relationships as needed. For

▶**multidivisional (M-form) organization** A high-performance organization form that allows highly interdependent operating units or divisions.

▶**network organization** A flexible, usually temporary set of alliances among disparate companies that have come together for a specific, single purpose.

▶**outsourcing** The practice of one company contracting with another to provide products or services that are not part of the first company's core activities.

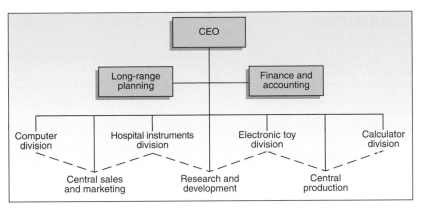

Figure 9-15
The Multidivisional (M-Form) Organization

example, a company expanding into a foreign market may add a broker or trading company to its network.

In addition, the network organization allows companies to shift away from underperforming units. If a network member isn't performing at the levels expected, it is jettisoned in favor of a new partner.

Management Summary

- The organizing function includes action steps that managers take to determine which jobs and which authority relationships are necessary to implement plans and policies.

- The four primary decisions that managers make when performing the organizing function are: job design, departmentalization bases, spans of control, and delegated authority. Conceptually, these decisions are different, but in practice they are highly interrelated.

- Job design involves deciding the appropriate tasks and authority to be assigned to each job and jobholder.

- Departmentalization involves deciding the bases to use in grouping jobs that are to be directed by a manager. The bases typically used are function, territory, customer, and product.

- The number of individuals who report to a manager determines her span of control. Deciding the appropriate

span is a key organizing decision, and although there are no precise rules, managers can follow guidelines to determine optimal spans.

- The delegation of authority involves providing jobholders with the right, or the freedom, to make decisions without approval by higher management. The relative advantages of centralization versus decentralization must be weighed, however.

- All organization structures can be described in terms of three dimensions: formalization, centralization, and complexity. The decisions that managers make regarding job design, departmentalization, spans of control, and delegation of authority determine the dimensions for a particular organization.

Key Terms

authority (p. 196)
boundaryless organization (p. 200)
centralization (p. 209)
chain of command (p. 200)
complexity (p. 209)
decentralization (p. 198)
departmentalization (p. 196)
employee empowerment (p. 196)

formalization (p. 208)
matrix organization (p. 212)
mechanistic model (p. 211)
multidivisional (M-form) organization (p. 214)
network organization (p. 214)
organic organization (p. 211)
organizational design (p. 210)

organizational strategy (p. 195)
organizational structure (p. 195)
outsourcing (p. 214)
social harmony (p. 201)
span of control (p. 197)
supply chain management (SCM) (p. 207)

Review and Discussion Questions

1. What are primary purposes of organizational structure?

2. Assume that the management of a large company has completed its review of progress toward annual profit objectives. The review indicates that the company is significantly below its target profit. Explain how the causes of the poor performance might be traced to the organizational structure.

3. From your own work experience, what important information is not shown in the Security Bank organizational chart (Figure 9-1)?

4. Use the four elements of organizational structure to describe your college or university.

5. Why is it necessary to create staff positions in organizations? Do these positions reduce the authority of line managers? Explain.

6. Summarize the advantages and disadvantages of decentralization. Describe a situation where decentralization is highly effective.

7. Use the three dimensions of organization structure to compare and contrast two organizations that you know about.

8. How is a functional-base organization most effective in obtaining the advantages of specialization of labor?

9. What factors other than structure contribute to organization performance? Explain.

10. Evaluate Motorola's solution to the problem associated with excessive numbers of managers and managerial layers.

Practice Quiz

Note: You can find the correct answers to these questions by taking the quiz and then submitting your answers in the Online Edition. The program will automatically score your submission. If you miss a question, the program will provide the correct answer, a rationale for the answer, and the section number in the chapter where the topic is discussed.

Indicate whether the sentence or statement is true or false.

1. A wide span of control (flat organizational structure) results in a small number of workers reporting to one supervisor.

2. Delegation of decision making is the center of a centralized organizational structure.

3. One result of delegated authority is the creation of a chain of command.

4. The more authority that is delegated, the greater the centralization of the organization.

5. Electronic networking can redistribute power in organizations.

Identify the letter of the choice that best completes the statement or answers the question.

6. An important advantage of functional departmentalization is that it makes use of the benefits of _____ .
   a. generalization.
   b. specialization.
   c. human resources.
   d. globalization.

7. _____ allows personnel to develop total expertise in researching, manufacturing, and distributing one product line.
   a. Product departmentalization
   b. Geographic departmentalization
   c. Functional departmentalization
   d. All of the above

8. At the present time, three dimensions are often used in research and practice to describe structure. Which of the following is NOT one of those dimensions?
   a. formalization
   b. internalization
   c. centralization
   d. complexity

9. The rapid evolution of electronic technologies, the rapid spread of computer networks, and the growth of telecommuting has fueled the growth of the _____ organization.
   a. matrix
   b. organic
   c. multidivisional
   d. virtual

10. The _____ can be seen as the "atom" or basic building block of the organization.
    a. organization chart
    b. strategy
    c. job
    d. department

11. The organizationally sanctioned right to make a final decision is known as _____ within the organizational structure.
    a. specialization
    b. authority
    c. departmentalization
    d. span of control

12. A narrow span of control indicates a _____ organizational hierarchy.
    a. tall
    b. horizontal
    c. formal
    d. informal

13. Organizational _____ refers to the dispersion of decision authority throughout the organization.
    a. departmentalization
    b. formalization
    c. devolution
    d. decentralization

14. _____ refers to the degree to which an organization specifies the means to achieve organizational goals and objectives.
    a. Departmentalization
    b. Specialization
    c. Formalization
    d. Decentralization

Indicate whether you agree with the sentence or statement.

15. It is possible for large organizations to use multiple organizational methods.

Case Study

Life Time Design Onshore/Offshore Organizational Structure

Wesley Bertch and his team learned a few lessons about offshore outsourcing through the hard knocks academy. Bertch leads the software development group at Life Time Fitness, a high-growth, national health and fitness chain. Life Time offers its customers health clubs; spas and salons; member services, such as personal training and swimming lessons; a nationally distributed magazine; and energy bars, powders, and other consumer goods. Life Time also has a corporate wellness unit that sells products and services to thousands of companies. In addition to supplying these various divisions with information technology systems, Life Time provides services to its internal real-estate group. Keeping pace with the growing software needs of so many diverse business units is a huge challenge.

Unfortunately, Bertch's internal staff of 15 programmers was able to produce only about one-third of the output he needed. With a limited budget and demand for greater output, he reasoned that offshore software development was the ideal solution. Bertch needed to augment his internal team in a cost-effective way, without sacrificing quality.

From an organizational perspective, Life Time met the key criteria for offshoring: centralized IT, process maturity, and years of experience working with Indian companies and technical workers, both in the United States and offshore. Life Time had executive sponsorship and commitment. It even had the perfect project to test the outsourcing waters: a small, low-risk web application for its real-estate division. The application's purpose was to provide screens for entering new location information.

The vendor Life Time invited to implement the project was an Indian firm that had been successfully supporting the company's sales-force-automation implementation. With this prior history of working together, both sides thought the web application project would be relatively easy. The vendor agreed to take on the project for a fixed fee of $20,000, with a nine-week time line.

Both parties agreed that the vendor should perform all phases of the project, from gathering business requirements through quality assurance. Life Time's internal staff was to monitor and participate as necessary. If the project proved successful, Life Time promised the offshore vendor that there would be much more project work in the future. The two organizations established a project team to manage the project. The following list shows the roles that were established on the project management team.

Life Time's Offshore Development Team

On-Site Liaison: Supplied by the vendor, acted as a bridge between the Life Time team and the offshore project manager. This person was on a senior level technically and had strong communication skills.

On-Site Business Analyst: Supplied by the vendor, completed the application's functional requirements, then returned to India to act as offshore project manager.

Offshore Project Manager: Tracked tasks and schedules for three offshore team members: a Java developer, a JSP developer, and a tester.

Offshore Technical Manager: Supervised the Life Time project, as well as three others.

Life Time Software Manager: Coordinated Life Time team with the on-site liaison to provide code reviews, database design, and general advice.

Life Time Project Manager: An individual in Life Time's real-estate division served as the internal business champion.

The project got off to a good start. The vendor's business analyst met frequently with the real-estate division's users and, with the on-site liaison, worked to document all the functional and user interface requirements within four weeks.

By week three, however, Life Time's software manager noticed problems in the software. His review of the functional specifications revealed problems in the requirements, particularly in the interface specifications. For example, the user interface as laid out forced the users to reenter data they had previously entered, and the screen flow was confusing. The on-site liaison countered that although the interface had problems, it complied with the documented business requirements.

To ensure that Life Time would get what it needed, Bertch extended the project time line, agreed to a cost increase of $7,000 to allow for additional analysis and better interface design, and dedicated internal Life Time analysis and user interface experts to guide the final version of the documentation.

After the vendor's business analyst finalized the documentation, he returned to India and, in an effort to exploit his knowledge of the project requirements, was reassigned as the offshore project manager. By this point, the offshore technical manager had lined up the offshore project team, so the coding design began in earnest.

Once offshore, however, the project started to unravel. Upon receiving the offshore vendor's database design, Life Time's lead data architect declared it to be the worst he'd ever seen. There were so many critical database flaws—more than 100—that Life Time's architects were unable to log them all within the scheduled one-week review period.

The database was not the only problem. Determined to impress Life Time with their programming prowess, the offshore developers insisted on completing the entire code design before allowing Life Time to review it. Confident in their original code design, the offshore team had launched immediately into writing Java code before Life Time's review. Unfortunately, the eventual review determined that the offshore team's design patterns weren't in accordance with the standards Life Time follows, invalidating all the offshore team's Java code.

In two weeks, the offshore team had gone from proud and eager to embarrassed and dejected. Once the stark reality of the logged defects sank in, the team knew there was no way it could straighten out the code design and then code and test the applications within the set time frame. Frustration levels were high on the offshore team, and the on-site liaison became increasingly defensive. The internal Life Time team was disappointed and annoyed as well, but accepted the fact that mistakes were bound to happen on the first end-to-end offshore project. The Life Time team valued a quality final product much more than time line precision. Nevertheless, as Life Time learned later, the offshore team began working extra-long hours to avoid asking for a time extension.

Given all the problems up to that point, Bertch sensed the project was at risk so he flew to India to meet with the offshore team. The visit was informational and warm feelings prevailed, but by this time the application was in the testing phase and nearly complete. Not long after the India trip, the offshore team delivered the tested and "finished" application. According to the on-site liaison, all Life

Time needed to do was perform a user-acceptance review and sign off on the project's successful delivery.

Instead, Bertch decided to perform some quality assurance with his internal team. In less than a day, one Life Time tester and one developer found more than 35 defects, many of them fatal. The offshore team categorized the hundreds of newly found defects as "in scope" (these they fixed) or "out of scope" (these were deemed Life Time's problem). Even after the vendor fixed the "in scope" defects, the application was unusable. And fixing it meant it would be late and even more over budget. At this point, Bertch decided the best course was to take delivery of the application and overhaul the code internally.

Reflecting on his offshoring experience, Bertch said, "You might assume that, given our dismal experience with offshore development, we have written off this model completely. Not so. Offshore may still hold promise as a way to cost-effectively extend our current team. What would we do differently? Instead of relying on the ven-dor to institute the offshore processes and team, we would set that up ourselves. Ideally, we would have a developer from our internal team relocate to India to build and manage a competent offshore team, perhaps within leased space at an existing development facility."

Questions for Discussion

1. Did Life Time have enough structure to manage this project effectively? What might you have done differently?

2. What unique challenges do you think are present when two companies attempt to work together to structure a project? What unique challenges are present when these two companies are separated by an ocean? By cultures?

3. Why did this project fail?

Source: Wesley Bertch, "Why Offshore Outsourcing Failed Us," *Network Computing,* October 16, 2003, pp. 65–68; Rick L. Click and Thomas N. Duening, *Business Process Outsourcing: The Competitive Advantage* (Hoboken, NJ: John Wiley & Sons, October 2004), pp. 39–42.

Internet Exercise

Understanding the Virtual Organization

The Virtual Enterprise Forum is a website dedicated to researching and understanding virtual organizations, virtual teams, and the distributed workforce. Students should be instructed to visit the following website and complete the exercises.

> http://www.ve-forum.org

One of the features of this website is the *Online Journal of Organizational Virtualness.* Students should visit the site outside of class and be instructed to complete the following exercises:

1. Select an article from the *Online Journal of Organizational Virtualness.*

2. Read the article and prepare a one-page abstract to distribute and discuss in class.

3. Come up with at least two questions about the article that you would like to explore further. Contact the author of the article via e-mail and ask him or her to provide you with answers to your questions. Ask whether there is anything about the article the author would like to change or update.

It's possible that several students will select the same article, and that they will all be contacting the same author for answers to questions. Instructors should inform students about proper e-mail etiquette and how to politely inform authors of the purpose of their inquiry and how to clearly state their questions.

Experiential Exercise

Designing a New Venture

Purpose: The purpose of this exercise is to provide students with first-hand experience in organizing a new business venture.

Setting Up the Exercise: In the early 1970s, George Ballas got so frustrated trying to keep his lawn neatly trimmed around the roots of oak trees that he developed what is now called the Weed Eater. The original Weed Eater was made from a popcorn can that had holes in it and was threaded with nylon fishing line. Weed Eater sales in 1972 totaled $568,000; but by 1978, sales were in excess of $100 million. There are now twenty or so similar devices on the market.

Two brothers from Pittsburgh, George and Jim Gammons, are starting a new venture called Lawn Trimmers, Inc. They are attempting to develop an organization that makes a profit by selling lawn trimmers that do not wear out for over 2,000 trimming applications. The Weed Eater and similar products often have breaks in the nylon lines that require the user to turn off the trimmer and readjust the line. The Gammons brothers have developed a new type of cutting fabric that is not physically harmful and cuts for over 2,000 applications.

To sell the lawn trimmers, the Gammons brothers will have to market their products through retail establishments. They will make the products in their shop in Pittsburgh and ship them to the retail establishments. The profits will come entirely from the sales of the lawn trimmers to retail establishments. The price of the product is already set, and it appears that there will be sufficient market demand to sell at least 6,000 lawn trimmers annually.

1. The instructor will set up teams of five to eight students to serve as organizational design experts who will provide the Gammons brothers with the best structure for their new venture. The groups should meet and establish a design that would be feasible for the Gammons at this stage in their venture.

2. Each group should select a spokesperson to make a short presentation of the group's organizational design for the Gammons.

3. The class should compare the various designs and discuss why there are similarities and differences in what is presented.

A Learning Note: This exercise will show that organizational design necessitates making assumptions about the market, competition, labor resources, scheduling, and profit margins, to name just a few areas. There is no one best design that should be regarded as a final answer.

Source: Adapted from Royston Greenwood, "How Investment in Organizational Design Impacts the Effectiveness of KM," *Knowledge Management Review,* September/October 2000, pp. 10–11.

Managing Human Resources

10

Managing Today

Employee Fitness: A Word of Caution

Suppose you are evaluating the credentials of applicants for a high-energy position in your new start-up company. Applicant No. 1 lists as hobbies triathlons, mountain biking, and weight lifting. This applicant looks like he could lift a building.

Applicant No. 2 is shaped like a Bartlett pear and lists his hobbies as grilling steak and watching golf. A pack of cigarettes shows through his shirt pocket.

Who should be selected? Did you select the fit, muscle-toned, and energetic No. 1? If a candidate is rejected because of the way he looks, like a pear, you may be in for some legal problems. Managers now are being challenged on these kinds of decisions.

In the District of Columbia a manager who engages in personal appearance discrimination (a protected class under the D.C. Human Rights Act—www.glaa.org/archive/1997/schwbect.shtml) can find himself or herself facing a plaintiff's lawyer.

The Americans with Disabilities Act (ADA) can be used by individuals who believe that because they are over their ideal body weight they failed to be hired for a job.

The Health Insurance Portability and Accountability Act (HIPAA) prevents employers from restricting entry into group health plans or charging a higher premium to certain participants on the basis of health status (i.e., existing or prior medical condition, disability, or health claims history).

What is happening is that managers now must be knowledgeable about laws, restrictions, and requirements when hiring employees. Applicant No. 1 may be better than Applicant No. 2 but the hiring decision better not be made on the basis of the way the person looks and seems to project health and energy. Maybe Applicant No. 2 has a non-life-threatening condition that is an ADA-recognized disability. Because of the disability the individual is restricted from physically working out. Being careful in selecting employees is obviously important to organizations to avoid lawsuits.

Sources: Adapted from Craig Hall's "Employees: Wellness—and Beyond," *Occupational Health & Safety,* September 2004, pp. 46–49; Peter Petesch, "Workplace Fitness or Workplace Fits?" *Human Resource Magazine,* July 2001, pp. 137–140; and Kathy Schwappach, "More Leeway for Workers, More Work for HR," *HR Magazine,* March 2001, pp. 60–68.

A manager's greatest responsibility is to select, direct, develop, and evaluate the people of the organization. As the Managing Today opening vignette illustrates, managers now must be knowledgeable about laws and regulations. The failure to properly select, develop, or evaluate people can result in lawsuits and unnecessary costs. The manager who understands human resource management issues is able to optimally attract, retain, and motivate people. People are the sources of all productive effort in organizations. Organizational performance depends on individual and team performance.

In this chapter we apply the elements of the organizing function to human resources. You should develop greater understanding of how managers define standards, acquire information, and take corrective action in the process of managing human resources.

This chapter addresses human resource principles and practices. It suggests that high-performing organizations build their competitiveness by developing their people. In large, formal organizations such as Lufthansa, Daimler-Chrysler, or Honda, human resources are usually managed through a distinct department or division. In small organizations it's often up to the company founders to handle all of the human resource issues. This is no small feat as, even for the small business, human resource management is becoming increasingly complex. In the next section, we'll look at human resource management and some of the leading issues confronting managers today. Some of the most significant issues identified by human resource managers are presented in the following Management Focus on Leadership box, "Human Resource Challenges Are Important."

10-1 Human Resource Management

The Human Resource Management (HRM) at Sun Microsystems serves the needs of that organization and facilitates the accomplishment of its objectives. But without modifications, its program would probably not be well suited for Burger King or Caterpillar. Each company develops its own HRM program after considering such factors as size, type of skills needed, number of employees required, unionization, clients and customers, financial posture, and geographic location.

> # *Management Focus* on **Leadership**
>
> ## Human Resource Challenges Are Important
>
> Human resource management offers a number of challenges to managers. The American Society of Training Directors (ASTD, www.astd.org) and the Society for Human Resource Management (SHRM, www.shrm.org) collected information from human resource (HR) professionals on the biggest challenges. The top six issues cited by the professionals were:
>
> 1. Staffing/Attracting New Talent/Retention
> 2. Training/Learning
> 3. Fast Growth/Change Management/Culture
> 4. Attitude/Morale/Motivation/Productivity
> 5. Management/Supervisor Issues and Development Needs
> 6. Aligning Human Resources with Business Strategy
>
> Whether other professionals consider these six issues as the most pressing challenge is not certain. Financial managers perceive challenges in financial terms, while lawyers view the world in legalistic terms. Unless, however, managers attend to these HR issues, the likelihood that firms can accomplish objectives will be low.
>
> *Source:* Adapted from "ASTD/SHRM Research Results," www.personneldecisions.com, July 2001.

A successful HRM program requires participation by managers because it is they who must interpret and implement policies and procedures. Line managers must translate into action what an HRM department provides.[1] Without managerial support at the top, middle, and lower levels, HRM programs cannot succeed. Therefore, it is important that managers clearly understand how to mesh their responsibilities with those of the HRM department.

For many years the HRM function wasn't thought to be directly related to a company's profit margins. A company's HRM approach usually wasn't included in a company's overall strategic plan, and HRM managers often occupied staff rather than line positions. In other words, HRM was often seen as a "supporting" function, rather than a function related to productivity and competitiveness.

Those days are long gone, however. Firms today are pitted against one another in a bitter struggle for the best talent. Technical talent, managerial talent, and the plain-old ability to think critically are hot skills that corporate recruiters seek today. In the modern organization, mind skills are usually favored over hand skills, and companies are competing feverishly with one another to attract the best and brightest. They're also competing with one another to develop that talent as quickly as possible, and then retain it to their advantage. This battle to attract, develop, and retain talent has elevated the HRM department and HRM manager to a more lofty plane in many organizations.[2]

Human resource management can be defined as the process of accomplishing organizational objectives by acquiring, retaining, developing, and properly using the human resources in an organization. The notion of accomplishing objectives is a major part of any form of management. Unless objectives are regularly accomplished, the organization ceases to exist.

The *acquisition* of skilled, talented, and motivated employees is an important part of HRM. The **acquisition phase** involves recruiting, screening, selecting, and properly placing personnel.

The **retention** of competent individuals is important to any organization.[3] If qualified individuals regularly leave a company, it becomes continually necessary to seek new personnel. This costs money and is time consuming. In stark contrast to the downsizing wave that hit U.S. companies in the last decade, many companies now are taking proactive steps to retain key employees over the long term.[4]

The opposite of retention is, of course, **termination,** which is an unpleasant part of any manager's job. Employees occasionally must be terminated for breaking rules, failing to perform adequately, or job cutbacks. Before managers fire employees they should be aware of a changing legal environment that makes the procedure more hazardous than ever.[5] The procedures for such terminations usually are specified by an HRM staff expert or are covered in a labor-management contract.

▶**human resource management** The process of accomplishing an organization's objectives by acquiring, retaining, developing, and properly using its human resources.

▶**acquisition phase** A step in human resources management that involves recruiting, screening, selecting, and properly placing personnel.

▶**retention** An employer's ability to hold employees.

▶**termination** Ending an employee's employment.

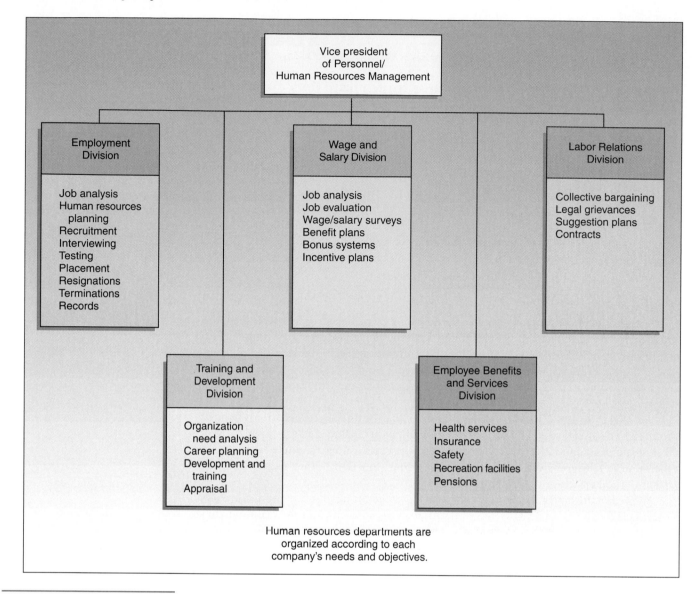

Human resources departments are organized according to each company's needs and objectives.

Figure 10-1

Example of a Personnel/ Human Resources Management Department

▶**proper use of people**
An understanding of both individual and organizational needs so that the full potential of human resources can be employed.

Developing personnel involves training, educating, appraising, and generally preparing personnel for present or future jobs. These activities are important for the economic and psychological growth of employees. Self-realization needs cannot be satisfied in an organization that does not have an efficient set of development activities. Developing employees is also essential to a firm's productivity and performance. Robert T. Robertson, CEO of Con-Way Transportation Services, for example, cites employee development as essential to his firm's highly effective customer services. He says developing employees is central to helping them make contributions to the company's services to customers, a key competitive arena in the shipping industry.[6]

The **proper use of people** involves understanding both individual and organizational needs so that the full potential of human resources can be employed. This part of human resources management suggests that it is important to match individuals over time to shifts in organizational and human needs.

HRM in larger organizations such as NYNEX, Bausch & Lamb, Polaroid, and Marriott is performed in a staff department like the one shown in Figure 10-1. Remember, however, that each company organizes its department according to its own set of needs and objectives. Each department activity utilizes some form of control. A few of the HRM activities and their control mechanisms will be discussed.

10-2 Human Resource Planning

Human resource planning is a process that involves two steps: forecasting future human resource needs, and planning how to fulfill and then manage those needs. Forecasting future needs is a difficult process. Some organizations rely on mathematical projections to determine their future human resource needs. They collect data on such factors as the available supply of human resources, labor-market composition, the demand for products, new research breakthroughs, and competitive wage and salary programs. From these data and previous records, managers then can use statistical procedures to make forecasts. Of course, unpredictable events can alter trends. But when such surprises seldom occur, fairly reliable forecasts are possible.

Anticipating future business and environmental demands requires a planning system. The activities that a manager could follow in such a system include the following:

1. *Human resource inventory*–assessing the personnel skills, abilities, and potential present in the organization.
2. *Forecasting*—predicting future personnel requirements.
3. *Human resource plans*—developing a strategy for recruiting, selecting, placing, transferring, and promoting personnel.
4. *Development plans*—ensuring that properly trained managers are ready to take over vacant or new jobs.

Estimating based on experience is a more informal forecasting procedure. Department managers and supervisors may be asked for opinions about future human resource needs. Some managers are confident in human resource planning; others are reluctant to offer an opinion or are not reliable forecasters.

> **human resource planning**
> Estimating the size and makeup of the future workforce.

10-2a Recruiting Activities

If human resource needs cannot be met within the company, outside sources must be tapped. An attractive organization such as Microsoft keeps a file on applicants who sought employment with it over the past year. Even though these applicants were not hired, the applicant frequently maintains an interest in working for a company with a good reputation and image. By carefully screening these files, some good applicants can be added to the pool of candidates.

Advertisements in newspapers, trade journals, and magazines notify potential applicants of openings. Responses to advertisements will come from both qualified and unqualified individuals. Occasionally, a company will list a post-office box number and not provide the company name. This form of advertisement is called a *blind ad*. Such advertisements eliminate the necessity of contacting every applicant. However, they do not permit a company to use its name or logo as a form of promotion. Some organizations are effectively using their own employees in newspaper and magazine ads.

The following Management Focus on Diversity box, "Valuing Diversity," illustrates how firms are advertising to attract minority job applicants.

The college campus is one of the most important sources for recruiting lower-level managers. Many colleges and universities have placement centers that work with organizational recruiters. The applicants read advertisements and information provided by the companies, and then they sign up for interviews. The most promising applicants are invited to visit the companies for more interviews.

To find experienced employees in the external market, organizations use private employment agencies, executive search firms, or state employment agencies. Some private employment agencies and executive search firms are called *no-fee agencies,* which means that the employer pays the fee instead of the applicant. An organization is not obligated to hire any person referred by the agency, but the agency usually is informed when the right person is found.

For many midsized firms, networking is an effective recruiting strategy. For ASAP Software Express, Inc., for example, networking draws in at least one-third of new hires. Anastasi Carr, human resource manager of the Buffalo Grove, Illinois, firm, said, "The

Management Focus on **Diversity**

Valuing Diversity

Spurred by the recognition that a diverse workforce adds value and is important to a firm's success, diversity-oriented ads are being used. Microsoft has developed a series of "Valuing Diversity" advetorials—short essays in the opinion-editorial pages of major newspapers around the country. The ads tell a story, stating that 800,000 skilled technology jobs are going unfulfilled in the United States, and this shortage is "expected to worsen" in the next five years.

Pitney Bowes advertises in major magazines and states, "We're interested in genius . . . not genes . . . genius is diverse." Bristol-Myers Squibb, in magazine and newspaper ads, states, "We believe that diversity is the cornerstone of a high performance organization."

A manager explains Prudential's (www.prudential.com) diversity ads by stating, "Our corporate culture is diverse, so we want recruiting to be diverse, because that brings a variety of new ideas and perspectives into the company. We also want to sell to a diverse audience, and someone who sees a recruitment ad that focuses on diversity may also become a customer."

Research studies have shown that minority job seekers look for firms with a proven diversity record. A Wetfeet.com study found that 16 percent of respondents looked at a diverse workforce as a key indicator of a firm's commitment to diversity. In the study one-third of respondents eliminated a company from employment consideration because of a lack of gender or ethnic diversity.

Source: Adapted from Ruth E. Thaler–Carter, "Diversify Your Recruitment Advertising," *HR Magazine,* June 2001, pp. 57–59; Taylor Cox, Sr., Paul H. O'Neill, and Robert E. Quinn, Sr., *Creating the Multicultural Organization: A Strategy for Capturing the Power of Diversity,* (New York: John Wiley, 2001).

---

bottom line is we don't have hundreds of resumes coming in each week without going out to get them."[7]

A number of firms are using software programs to improve their recruiting effectiveness. The following Management Focus on Technology box, "Software Doesn't Replace Hard Work," explains a number of myths that need to be revealed.

10-3 Equal Employment Opportunity

Managers today of organizations both large and small must be aware of their obligations to hire and retain individuals in a nonbiased manner. This point was illustrated in the Managing Today opening vignette. The Civil Rights Act of 1964 and the Equal Employment Opportunity (EEO) Act of 1972 have had far-reaching effects on employment practices in the United States. No organization is immune from these important changes in U.S. law. Basically, EEO means that employers cannot discriminate against employees or prospective employees on the basis of their race, color, religion, sex, or national origin.

EEO laws and regulations are enforced by the Equal Employment Opportunity Commission (EEOC). The federal government attempts to provide equal opportunities for employment without regard to race, religion, age, creed, sex, national origin, or disability through Title VII of the Civil Rights Act of 1964 and the Equal Employment Opportunity Act of 1972.[8] These laws have broad coverage and apply to any activity, business, or industry in which a labor dispute would hinder commerce. The laws also cover state and local governments, governmental agencies, and agencies of the District of Columbia.

Some of the specific provisions of the Equal Employment Opportunity Act of 1972 are shown in Figure 10-2.

Title VII provides that an employer may lawfully hire a person based on his or her religion, sex, or national origin if such is a **bona fide occupational qualification (BFOQ)** for the job. A BFOQ is a qualification that is reasonably necessary for the normal operation of the particular business. For example, it would be unreasonable to expect an employer to have to consider male candidates for an attendant position in a female washroom, or vice versa. In such situations, a person's sex is a BFOQ that would allow an employer to "discriminate" on the basis of sex.

The legal procedures regarding equal employment opportunities and recruitment are important to employers. Organizations have to adjust to and work with these laws. Although adjustments are sometimes difficult, they seem to be a better alternative than becoming involved in long and costly court battles. Providing equal opportunities to all

bona fide occupational qualification (BFOQ) A qualification that is reasonably necessary for the normal operation of the particular business.

Management Focus on **Technology**

Software Doesn't Replace Hard Work

Applicant-tracking systems and recruiting software can cost anywhere from a few thousand dollars to several million dollars, depending on the size of the organization, the scope of the project, and the particular application

With that investment, time to hire may plunge by two-thirds and cost per hire by 40 percent or more. Many organizations also reduce turnover by 10 percent or more by hiring more effectively up front. In many cases, however, the technology proves to be a disappointment.

Here are some of the fallacies that some companies have uncovered:

You can handle all recruiting online. There's no question that the Web has made it a lot simpler to reach hot prospects—and for them to reach you. It can also slash recruiting costs dramatically. However, it's not the only game in town. Recruiters with solid industry connections are essential for finding candidates for senior- and executive-level positions, and valuable for combing through piles of resumes for many other positions. What's more, paper-based resumes can yield impressive results.

The software will find the best candidates. It's tempting to think that an applicant-tracking system will mine all the resumes that stream in, monitor job boards, and land all the A-players your organizations desires. Unfortunately, switching on a totally automated system is a recipe for disaster.

Companies are advised to attract desirable candidates through a well-designed corporate website, job boards, professional journals, job fairs, and highly targeted advertising. And use recruiters—internally or externally—who understand the needs of the organization.

Today's applicant-tracking software doesn't require training. One of the biggest mistakes of using software systems is that too often the human resources staff and recruiters are given approval on a system without adequate training. That can lead to bad searches and interviews with unqualified applicants. Simply typing in keywords is no guarantee of success.

Source: Adapted from "Myths About Recruiting Technology," *Workforce Management,* October 2004, p. 70.

---

qualified job applicants makes sense both legally and morally. The vast majority of managers in organizations believe that all citizens have a right to any job they can perform reasonably well after a sufficient amount of training.

The legal procedures that must be followed are now becoming more complicated as globalization continues. The Management Focus on Globalization box, "Implications of Laws," examines a few examples of this complexity.

Figure 10-2
Key EEO Provisions

Some of the specific provisions of the Equal Employment Opportunity Act of 1972 are:

It is unlawful for an employer to fail or refuse to hire or to discharge any individual, or otherwise to discriminate against any individual with respect to compensation, conditions, or privileges of employment because of race, color, religion, sex, age, or national origin. This applies to applicants for employment as well as current employees.

Employers may not limit, segregate, or classify employees in any way that would deprive them of employment opportunities because of race, color, age, religion, sex, or national origin.

The EEOC has the power to file action in a federal district court if it is unable to eliminate alleged unlawful employment practices by the informal methods of conference, conciliation, and persuasion.

Employment tests may be used if it can be proven that they are related to the job or promotion sought by the individual. Tests should be validated within each company.

No discriminatory statements may be included in any advertisements for job opportunities.

Management Focus on Globalization

Implications of Laws

Managers must now consider the implications of laws in other countries when making decisions or conducting business. The European Union Data Privacy Directive (www.dss.state.ct.us/digital/eupriv.html) imposes stringent requirements on organizations before personal data can be collected or used. It also prohibits business transactions with countries that do not have similar privacy policies in place. The directive covers all persons living within the European Union, citizen or not, U.S. organizations employing Europeans, or U.S. expatriates in Europe.

U.S. laws also have a long reach. A new European equal rights directive prohibits discrimination based on age, an issue first addressed through U.S. laws. Sexual harassment laws also are impacting other countries. The member states of the European Union (all twenty-five) each have laws that define sexual harassment and make it unlawful to subject anyone to a hostile work environment or to quid pro quo harassment in the workplace.

Countries across the world are examining and adopting each other's best practices at an accelerating rate. As borders become more porous in the global economy the laws of one country increasingly affect people and organizations in other countries.

Sources: Adapted from "Europa," www.europa.eu.int, November 23, 2004; and "Going Global," *Workplace Visions,* July 11, 2001, Society for Human Resource Management.

10-3a Selection Activities

selection of personnel The hiring process that depends largely on an organization's needs and compliance with legal requirements.

The **selection of personnel** depends largely on organizational needs and on compliance with legal requirements. Discriminatory practices in recruiting, testing, and offering a job are illegal, as defined in the Civil Rights Act of 1964 and the Equal Employment Opportunity Act of 1972. A few of the important legal guidelines affecting the staffing selection step are described in Table 10-1.

The actual selection process is a series of steps. It starts with initial screening and ends with the orientation of newly hired employees. Figure 10-3 presents each step in the process. Recognizing human resource needs through the planning phase of staffing is the point at which selection begins. Preliminary interviews are used to screen out unqualified applicants. This *screening* often is the first personal contact a person has with an organization. If the applicant passes the preliminary screening, he or she then usually completes an application.

Interviews   Interviews are used throughout the selection process. Interviewers usually first acquaint themselves with the job analysis information. Second, they review the application blank information. Third, they typically ask questions designed to give better insight into the applicants, and they add this information to that on the application blank.

T A B L E 10-1 **Some Legal Guidelines for the Selection Step in Staffing**	Selection Screening Steps	Legal Activities	Illegal Activities
	Tests	Can be used if they have been validated	Can't be used when there is no relationship between test results and performing the job
	Interview information	1. To ask if a person is a U.S. citizen	1. To require citizenship or ask proof of citizenship
		2. To ask about convictions for crime	2. To ask if person has ever been arrested
	Age	To require proof of age after hiring	To require birth certificate
	Racial identity	To keep records on racial and ethnic identity for purposes of reporting	To ask for race, creed, or national origin in application or interview

Figure 10-3
Selection Steps

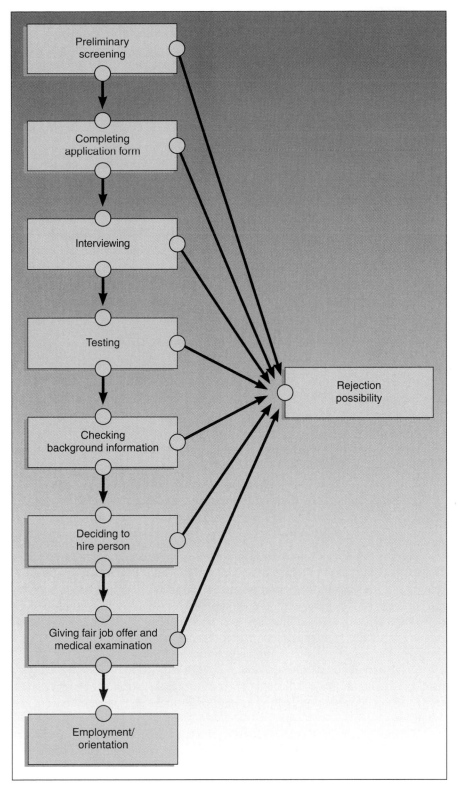

Three general types of interviews are used: structured, semistructured, and unstructured. In the **structured interview,** the interviewer asks specific questions of all interviewees. In the **semistructured interview,** only some questions are prepared in advance. This approach is less rigid than the structured interview and allows the interviewer more flexibility. The **unstructured interview,** meanwhile, allows the interviewer the freedom to discuss what even he thinks is important. Comparing answers across interviewees is rather difficult, however.

▶ **structured interview**
An interview for which the interviewer prepares questions in advance and asks these specific questions of all interviewees.

▶ **semistructured interview**
An interview for which the interviewer prepares some questions in advance but has flexibility in the questions to ask.

▶ **unstructured interview**
An interview for which the interviewer has the freedom to discuss whatever information is considered important.

Another type of interview that has been gaining some adherents is the group or panel interview. In this type of interview, a job candidate meets with an entire work group to discuss job requirements, qualifications, and general personality issues. Such an interview helps the work group determine whether the candidate will "fit in" to the prevailing culture. Research has indicated that group or panel interviews better predict job success than interviews conducted by only a single individual.[9]

▶**selection tests** Common tests used to screen applicants.

Testing   **Selection tests** have become a common method of screening applicants.[10] Selection tests are costly, time consuming, and have legal implications.[11] But they do have several advantages:

1. *Improved accuracy in selecting employees.* Individuals differ in skills, intelligence, motivation, interests, needs, and goals. If these differences can be measured, and if they are related to job success, then performance can be predicted to some extent by test scores.

2. *Objective means for judging.* Applicants answer the same questions, under test conditions, and their responses are scored. One applicant's score then can be compared with the scores of other applicants.

3. *Information on the needs of present employees.* Tests given to present employees provide training, development, or counseling information.

Despite these advantages, tests have been—and probably will remain—controversial. Key legal rulings and fair-employment codes have helped create strict procedures for developing tests. The following criticisms have been directed at testing programs:

1. Tests are not infallible. Tests reveal what persons *did* do in a testing situation, not what they could do on the job. Some of the best test performers may be the poorest job performers.

2. Tests are given too much weight. Tests cannot measure everything about a person. They can never substitute for good judgment.

3. Tests discriminate against minorities. Ethnic minorities, such as blacks and Mexican-Americans, may score lower on certain paper-and-pencil tests because of cultural bias. The Civil Rights Act of 1964 prohibits employment practices that artificially discriminate against individuals on the basis of test scores.

The U.S. Supreme Court made a landmark ruling related to tests in the *Griggs v. Duke Power Company* case in 1971.[12] Six years earlier, Duke Power had established a policy requiring job applicants to satisfactorily pass a number of tests and have a high school education to qualify for placement and promotion. A group of black employees challenged these requirements, arguing that they were denied promotions because of the testing policy. The Supreme Court ruled that neither the high school requirement nor the test scores showed a relationship to successful job performance.

Organizations using any test now must carefully examine how the scores are used. And test results must be validated. There must be statistical proof that test scores are related to job performance. Testing, however, still can be an important part of the recruiting process.[13]

The steady growth in employee testing has led to a broad range of psychometric tests. To select and use tests effectively, managers must establish the qualities or characteristics to be assessed, and they must check the validity of the tests that claim to produce such data. Test selection should start by addressing the following criteria:

1. What qualities or characteristics have been shown to correlate with high or low performance standards in the relevant job?

2. Are there any valid tests that will help to identify and assess these qualities?

Because no test reaches 100 percent validity, they should rarely be the sole basis of a job appointment. Normally, tests need to be considered alongside an interview, previous employment history, and references.[14]

The Hiring Decision Once the preliminary screening steps are completed—evaluating the application blanks, interviewing, and testing—and the organization considers making an offer, a *background check* usually is made. The background check consists of verifying various facts and collecting additional data from references and previous employers. The organization also attempts to gather facts about the applicant's previous record of job performance. If reference checks yield favorable information, the line manager and an employment division representative usually meet to decide the type of compensation and benefit offer that will be made.

Many firms don't have even the most basic controls in place to ensure a sound employment selection process. However, mistakes and oversights that lead to poor employee development often begin with the hiring decision. Some steps managers can take to ensure sound employment decisions are:

1. Inform candidates up front of the recruiting procedures. If candidates believe that the prospective employer will contact former supervisors, verify education, and check criminal records, they are more likely to be honest and straightforward.

2. Require candidates to complete an application form that includes a signed statement from the applicant confirming the accuracy of the information provided and consenting to a background check.

3. Follow up reviews of the application with a telephone interview. An initial telephone interview can help qualify the candidates. "Red flags" identified in the review process could be confirmed or refuted at this stage through direct questions.

4. Ask the right questions. Direct questions should be asked during interviews to determine resume fact from fiction.

5. Conduct mandatory background checks, including criminal records and verification of employment and education histories.[15]

10-3b Orientation and Training

If new employees are properly oriented, several objectives can be accomplished. First, start-up costs can be minimized. A new employee can make costly mistakes unless tasks, expectations, procedures, and other matters are properly explained. Anxieties can be reduced and realistic job expectations can be created by a good **orientation.**[16] Caterpillar, Inc., for example, launched an employee-orientation program that orients new employees not only to Caterpillar but also to its location in Peoria, Illinois. The orientation consists of a week-long program followed by Monday-morning sessions for two and a half months. While the initial program focuses on Caterpillar, the Monday morning sessions cover both the culture of the community and of Caterpillar.[17]

> **orientation** A process of providing new employees specific information about their organization.

Training of human resources involves change: change in skills, attitudes, knowledge, and behaviors. Many organizations today employ large staffs of people whose primary function in the organization is to train other employees. Many companies are successfully empowering employees in this way to enhance productivity and corporate performance.

Many companies have developed their own "universities" to enhance employee training and expand the curriculum offered. Corporate universities can be found at McDonald's (Hamburger U), Men's Wearhouse (Suits U), General Motors (GMU), and many others. In fact, there were more than 1,600 corporate universities in 2000, up from about 400 in 1988.[18] Each of these firms, and many others, is involved in training to enhance their competitive position. The premise behind their efforts is that the more employees know about their business, the economy, themselves, and their fellow employees, the better they will perform. This premise has been supported by research that shows the benefits, in general, of training.

Despite this research, however, nothing can be said about the benefits of particular training programs or approaches. In one humorous example, Dilbert cartoon creator Scott Adams posed as a consultant to Logitech International, the world's largest producer of computer "mice." With the approval of Logitech cofounder and vice chairman Peirluigi

Zappacosta, Adams trained a group of executives on how to establish a mission statement. The group went from their former statement, "to provide Logitech with profitable growth and related new business areas," to the verbose and inscrutable, "The New Ventures Mission is to scout profitable growth opportunities in relationships, both internally and externally, in emerging, mission inclusive markets, and explore new paradigms and then filter and communicate and evangelize the findings." Adams revealed his prank after the group had approved the new mission, proving that it's often difficult for managers to discriminate between valuable knowledge and worthless claptrap.[19]

10-3c Performance Evaluation

performance evaluation
A postcontrol technique that focuses on the extent to which employees have achieved expected levels of work during a specified time period.

Performance evaluation processes and procedures accomplish two broad and several specific purposes. For most managers, performance appraisal is the most distasteful part of their job. In fact, an increasing number of managers have abolished the use of traditional performance appraisals. But the process can be made far less painful if managers think of it as a three-step process: (1) collect the necessary data; (2) evaluate the employee's performance; (3) write the performance review.[20] The two broad purposes are termed (1) *judgmental* and (2) *developmental*.[21]

judgmental purposes The use of performance evaluation results as bases for salary, promotion, and transfer decisions.

Judgmental Purposes   When performance evaluation results are the basis for salary, promotion, and transfer decisions, **judgmental purposes** are being served. The immediate objective is to improve performance by rewarding high performers. Managers who use performance evaluation for judgmental purposes must evaluate performance accurately and precisely and distribute rewards on the basis of performance. Failure to do so undermines the judgmental purposes and causes employees to be cynical about the process.

Managers become judges when judgmental purposes are sought. Subordinates being evaluated, meanwhile, recognize that their financial and career interests are at stake. So they tend to play passive, reactive roles and are frequently defensive. The atmosphere in which performance evaluations are undertaken is often colored by suspicion and distrust. Managers and subordinates alike are uncomfortable about the process, particularly when the information about performance is potentially inaccurate and when the performance standards are invalid.

developmental purpose
A performance evaluation policy of informing employees of their strengths and weaknesses and ways to improve their skills and abilities in an effort to improve performance through self-learning and personal growth.

Developmental Purposes   The second broad purpose of performance evaluation is to improve performance through self-learning and personal growth. The **developmental purpose** is accomplished when employees are made aware of their strengths and weaknesses and of ways to improve their skills and abilities.

The focus of attention is less on the appraisal of past performance and more on the improvement of future performance. The manager's role in the process is to counsel, guide, and generally be helpful as subordinates seek, through active involvement, a better understanding of their potential for improved performance. Managers should avoid judgmental terms such as *good–bad, positive–negative,* and *right–wrong*. Instead, they should help employees identify areas in need of improvement.

The two general purposes of performance evaluation are not mutually exclusive. Managers must, however, identify the purposes of performance evaluation and provide for those purposes by adopting appropriate procedures.

performance standards
Standards that form the basis for appraising an individual employee's effectiveness during the performance evaluation.

10-3d Performance Standards

The performance evaluation program at any level within the organizational hierarchy must, at some point, focus on **performance standards.** In performance evaluation, the standard is the basis for appraising the effectiveness of an individual employee.

relevant requirement
A measure used as a performance standard must be determined to have a significant and determinable necessity (relevance) to the individual and the organization.

Requirements of a Performance Standard   At least four requirements must be met before a measure can qualify as a performance standard. First is the **relevant requirement**—the measure must be relevant to the individual and the organization. Determining what is relevant is itself controversial. Some person or group must make a judgment about what constitutes relevance.

Second is the **stable requirement**—the standard must be reliable. This involves agreement of different evaluations at different points in time. If the results from two different evaluations diverge greatly, the standard is probably unreliable. Third is the **discriminatory requirement**—the performance standard must distinguish between good, average, and poor performers. The fourth requirement is the **practical requirement**. The standard must mean something to the evaluator and the person evaluated.

Another element of a performance standard that is increasingly recognized as integral to enhancing employee productivity is feedback. Humans, by nature, are self-regulating. When we receive feedback from our actions, we change automatically. For example, when a driver feels the bumps of the lane markers he or she makes a steering adjustment. The feedback of the bumps, not a remedial Steering 101 course, changes the behavior. Research has shown that relevant feedback is the most important element of behavior change.[22]

Single or Multiple Standards   Ample evidence supports arguments for either single or multiple standards. In some situations, especially at the policymaking level, a single standard is needed to reach a managerial decision. In cases involving promotion, salary and wage decisions, and transfer and counseling, multiple standards can be useful in illustrating why a particular decision is made or why a specific development program is recommended. It is extremely difficult to make a promotion decision on the basis of a single criterion.[23]

10-3e Administering Performance Evaluation

Although developing a systematic program for performance evaluation is extremely important, other managerial practices regarding performance evaluation are just as significant. Managers must decide (1) who will do the rating, (2) who will be rated, (3) when the rating should take place, and (4) how to perform in the evaluation interview.

Who Should Evaluate?   Five possible parties can serve as evaluators: (1) the supervisor or supervisors, (2) organizational peers, (3) the person being evaluated, (4) subordinates, and (5) individuals outside the work environment. In most situations, the evaluator is the immediate supervisor of the person evaluated. Because of frequent contact, he or she is assumed to be most familiar with the employee's performance. In addition, many organizations regard performance evaluation as an integral part of the immediate supervisor's job. The supervisor's evaluations often are reviewed by higher management, thereby maintaining managerial control over the evaluation program.

The major claims in support of self-evaluation are that this approach improves the employee's understanding of job performance, increases the personal commitment of employees because of their participation in the process, and reduces the hostility between superiors and subordinates over ratings. Some employers fear, however, that self-ratings will be unusually high.

In organizations that enjoy a high level of trust, subordinates sometimes can rate their managers. Organizations with a history of antipathy between managers and nonmanagers, however, should not expect to obtain valid information by such means.

Support has emerged for increased use of multiple evaluators. The major advantage of using a combination of superior, peer, and self-ratings is that a great deal of information is gained about the employee.[24] In making decisions about promotion, training and development, and career planning, a manager needs as much information as possible to suggest the best course for the employee. One innovation that uses multisource evaluation is known as **360-degree feedback.** This form of evaluation involves gathering information about a person's behavior from a boss or bosses, direct reports, colleagues, team members, internal and external customers, and suppliers. Several companies that have used 360-degree feedback successfully include Canadian Imperial Bank of Commerce, Northwestern Mutual Life Insurance Company, and NALCO (a specialty chemical company based in Naperville, Illinois).[25]

When to Evaluate   There is no specific schedule for evaluating employees. In general, however, one formal evaluation a year is provided for older or tenured employees. Recently

> **stable requirement** The requirement that a performance evaluation standard must be reliable; that is, different evaluations performed at different times should be in agreement.

> **discriminatory requirement** The requirement that a performance evaluation standard must recognize the difference between good, average, and poor performers.

> **practical requirement** An evaluation standard that must have meaning to the evaluator and the person evaluated.

> **360-degree feedback** A form of performance evaluation that involves gathering information about a person's behavior from a boss or bosses, direct reports, colleagues, team members, internal and external customers, and suppliers.

hired employees usually are evaluated more frequently than others. The time to evaluate will depend on the situation and on the intent of the evaluation. If performance evaluations are too far apart or occur too frequently, the ratee may not be able to use the feedback to make improvements.

An evaluation program conducted solely to rate employees soon will lose any potential value or motivational impact unless it is integrated with the main emphases of the organization. The judgmental and developmental purposes best show through when both the person being evaluated and the evaluator understand each other's role in the process. The evaluator must clarify, coach, counsel, and provide feedback. On the other hand, the person being evaluated must understand evaluator expectations, his or her own strengths and weaknesses, and the goals to be accomplished. These various roles can become clear if the performance evaluation program is considered a continual process that focuses both on task accomplishments and on personal development.

The Evaluation Interview   Regardless of how individual job performance information is collected, the evaluator must provide formal feedback to the person being evaluated. Without formal feedback, the employee will have difficulty making the modifications necessary to improve performance, difficulty matching his or her individual job performance expectations with those of the evaluator, and difficulty assessing the progress being made toward accomplishment of career goals.[26]

The feedback interview should be part of any performance evaluation program from the beginning.[27] The interview should focus on the job performance of the employee. Generally, evaluators feel uncomfortable about discussing the problems of those they rate.

On the other hand, employees often become defensive when evaluators point out weaknesses or failures. As criticism increases, the defensiveness of subordinates increases. Furthermore, praise in the feedback sessions is often ineffective, since most evaluators first praise, then criticize, and finally praise to end the session. Employees become conditioned to this sequence.[28]

Too often, performance evaluation interviews focus on the past year or on plans for the short run. Rarely do a manager and subordinate discuss careers.[29] But managers should understand the requirements for the various career tracks within the organization. The manager should be able to help create challenging but not unattainable job tasks for subordinates. This will help prepare subordinates for future jobs requiring more skills and abilities. Managers should discuss the lifelong sequence of job experiences of subordinates as part of the performance evaluation feedback interview. Only when career goals are considered can the evaluation process become a developmental experience as well as a judgmental analysis of job performance.

Although the particular needs of each organization, manager, and individual must be considered, some general guidelines can be suggested. In Figure 10-4, suggestions for preparing and conducting the appraisal interview are stated.

10-3f Traditional Performance Evaluation Methods

Managers usually attempt to select a performance evaluation procedure that will minimize conflict, provide ratees with relevant feedback, and contribute to the achievement of organizational objectives. Basically, managers must try to develop and implement a performance evaluation program that also can benefit other managers, the work group, and the organization.

As with most managerial procedures, there are no universally accepted methods of performance evaluation to fit every purpose, person, or organization. What is effective in Dell Computer will not necessarily work in IBM. In fact, what is effective within one department or one group in a particular organization will not necessarily be right for another unit or group within the same company.

Graphic Rating Scales   The oldest and most widely used performance evaluation procedure, the graphic scaling technique, has many forms. Generally, however, the rater is

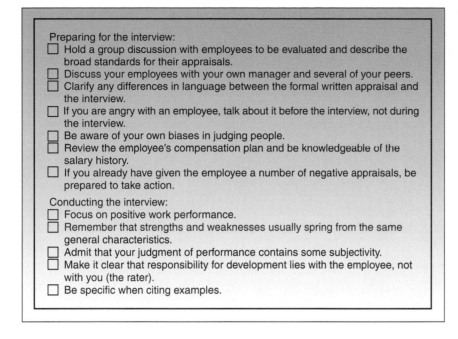

Figure 10-4
Guidelines for Preparing and Conducting an Appraisal Interview

Inside the figure:

Preparing for the interview:
- ☐ Hold a group discussion with employees to be evaluated and describe the broad standards for their appraisals.
- ☐ Discuss your employees with your own manager and several of your peers.
- ☐ Clarify any differences in language between the formal written appraisal and the interview.
- ☐ If you are angry with an employee, talk about it before the interview, not during the interview.
- ☐ Be aware of your own biases in judging people.
- ☐ Review the employee's compensation plan and be knowledgeable of the salary history.
- ☐ If you already have given the employee a number of negative appraisals, be prepared to take action.

Conducting the interview:
- ☐ Focus on positive work performance.
- ☐ Remember that strengths and weaknesses usually spring from the same general characteristics.
- ☐ Admit that your judgment of performance contains some subjectivity.
- ☐ Make it clear that responsibility for development lies with the employee, not with you (the rater).
- ☐ Be specific when citing examples.

supplied with a printed form, one for each subordinate to be rated. The form lists a number of job performance qualities and characteristics to be considered. The rating scales are distinguished by (1) how exactly the categories are defined, (2) the degree to which the person interpreting the ratings (e.g., the superior) can tell what response was intended by the rater, and (3) how carefully the performance dimension is defined for the rater.

Each organization devises rating scales and formats that suit its needs. Figure 10-5 is an example of a rating form used in some organizations. The general form displayed in Figure 10-6 is used by a state university to evaluate technical and staff personnel. Each form attempts to clarify the meanings of each of the rating factors.

Ranking Methods Some managers use a rank order procedure to evaluate all subordinates. The subordinates are ranked according to their relative value to the company or unit on one or more performance dimensions. The procedure followed usually involves identifying the best performer and the worst performer. These are placed in the first and last positions on the ranking list. The next best and next poorest performers then are filled in. This continues until all subordinates are on the list. The rater is forced to discriminate by the rank-ordering performance evaluation method.

Some problems are associated with the ranking method. One is that ratees in the central portion of the list likely will not be much different from one another on the performance rankings. Another problem involves the size of the group of subordinates being evaluated. Large groups are more difficult to rank than small groups.

LearningMoment *The Law*

The laws regulating equal employment opportunity (EEO) are intended to eliminate discrimination in any aspect of employment and the managing of human resources. The laws are intended to ensure that any job applicant or employee is fairly judged on characteristics related to the performance of work tasks they are being hired to perform.

The Equal Employment Opportunity Commission (EEOC, www.eeoc.gov) has the responsibility and authority to enforce and oversee the rules and regulations.

Figure 10-5
Typical Graphic Rating Scale

	Outstanding	Good	Satisfactory	Fair	Unsatisfactory
Name _____ Dept. _____ Date _____					
Quantity of work Volume of acceptable work under normal conditions Comments:	☐	☐	☐	☐	☐
Quality of work Thoroughness, neatness, and accuracy of work Comments:	☐	☐	☐	☐	☐
Knowledge of job Clear understanding of the facts or factors pertinent to the job Comments:	☐	☐	☐	☐	☐
Personal qualities Personality, appearance, sociability, leadership, integrity Comments:	☐	☐	☐	☐	☐
Cooperation Ability and willingness to work with associates, supervisors, and subordinates toward common goals Comments:	☐	☐	☐	☐	☐
Dependability Conscientious, thorough, accurate, reliable with respect to attendance, lunch periods, reliefs, etc. Comments:	☐	☐	☐	☐	☐
Initiative Earnest in seeking increased responsibilities; self-starting, unafraid to proceed alone Comments:	☐	☐	☐	☐	☐

Ford Motor Company has used a rank order system of appraisal in which it is mandated that 5 percent of senior managers must be given the lowest of three rating grades. Those who didn't improve after two years could be demoted or fired. This system has resulted in six age-discrimination lawsuits.[30] In their lawsuits employees and former employees charged that the ranking system and mandate resulted in weeding out older, white, male workers.

In a memo to Ford employees, CEO Jacques Nasser said that the 5 percent mandate was being eliminated. He claimed the ranking approach was never intended to single out employees by age or race. The system, which was used to evaluate 18,000 managers and supervisors, also required coaching of employees throughout the year.

weighted checklist A rating system consisting of statements that describe various types and levels of behavior for a particular job. Each of the statements is weighted according to its importance.

Weighted Checklists A **weighted checklist** consists of a number of statements describing various types and levels of behavior for a particular job or group of jobs. Each statement has a weight or value attached to it. The rater evaluates each subordinate by checking the statements that best describe the behavior of the individual. The check marks and the corresponding weights then are summated. Figure 10-5 illustrates a form of the weighted checklist.

The weighted checklist makes the rater think in terms of specific job behavior. However, this procedure is difficult and very costly to develop. Separate checklists usually are established for each job or group of jobs.

```
Name _____        Social Security No. _____
Job Title _____
Bureau/center _____

                                                              Rating x Weight = Score

1. Demonstrated personal characteristics                      _____    20%    _____
      Consideration should be given to job knowledge,
      judgment, communication skills, attitude, ability to
      deal with people (superiors, subordinates, clients,
      and other university personnel), initiative, and so on.

2. Performance of assigned duties                             _____    60%    _____
      Consideration should be given to the degree of
      program goal accomplishment, quality of service
      provided, quality of program activities (workload
      and clients generated), degree of supervision
      and/or guidance required, quality of reports,
      contribution to public relations, improvements
      generated in program to which assigned,
      clients'/students' reactions, and so on.

3. Contribution outside area of assigned duties              _____    20%    _____
      Consideration should be given to suggestions for
      furthering the Office for Research, contribution to
      new program development, public relations
      activities, contribution to improving relations with
      the college and university, and state agencies.

                                                  Total score          _____

Comments: _____
_____
_____
_____
      Date                                                        Signature
```

Figure 10-6
Personnel Evaluation

Descriptive Essays The essay method of performance evaluation requires that the evaluator describe each employee's strong and weak points. Some organizations require every evaluator to discuss specific points, while others allow them to discuss whatever they believe is appropriate. One problem with the unstructured essay evaluation is that it provides little opportunity to compare employees on specific performance dimensions. Another limitation involves the variations in the writing skills of evaluators. Some simply are not very good at writing descriptive analyses of subordinates' strengths and weaknesses.

Rating Errors The numerous traditional performance evaluation methods each have problems and potential *rating errors.* The major problems and errors can be *technical* in the form of poor reliability, poor validity, little practicality, or evaluator misuse. In some situations, evaluators are either extremely harsh or easy in their evaluations. These are called *strictness* or *leniency* rater errors. The harsh evaluator tends to give lower-than-average ratings to subordinates. The lenient evaluator tends to give ratings that are higher than average. These kinds of rating errors typically result because the evaluator applies his or her own personal standards to the particular performance evaluation system being used. For example, the words *outstanding* or *average* may mean different things to various evaluators.

Rating errors can be minimized if evaluators consider the following:

1. Each dimension addresses a single job activity rather than a group of activities.

2. The evaluator can observe the behavior of the employee on a regular basis.

3. Terms such as *average* are not used on rating scales, since different evaluators react differently to such words.

4. The evaluator does not have to evaluate large groups of subordinates. Fatigue and difficulty in discriminating among ratees become major problems when large groups of subordinates are evaluated.

5. Evaluators are trained to avoid leniency, strictness, and other rating errors.

6. The dimensions being evaluated are meaningful, clearly stated, and important.

Another possibility is to use more elegant forms of performance evaluation that attempt to minimize rating errors.[31] Two of the more elegant approaches are **behaviorally anchored rating scales (BARS)** and **management by objectives (MBO)**.

10-3g Progressive Performance Evaluation Methods

In an effort to improve traditional performance evaluations, some organizations have used various behaviorally based and goal-setting programs. The behaviorally based programs attempt to examine what the employee does in performing the job. The objective, or goal-setting, programs typically examine the results of accomplishments of the employee.

> **behaviorally anchored rating scales (BARS)** Rating scales developed by raters and/or ratees that use critical behavioral incidents as interval anchors on each scale; uses about six to ten scales with behavioral incidents to derive the evaluation.

> **management by objectives (MBO)** A planning and controlling method that comprises two meetings between the superior and the subordinate: (1) first to discus goals and to jointly establish attainable goals for the subordinate and (2) later to evaluate the subordinate's performance in terms of the goals that have been set.

Behaviorally Anchored Rating Scales   Behaviorally anchored rating scales (BARS) are constructed through the use of "critical incidents."[32] *Critical incidents are examples of specific job behaviors that determine various levels of performance.* Once the important areas of performance are identified and defined by employees who know the job, critical incident statements are used to discriminate among levels of performance. The form for a BARS usually covers six to ten specifically defined performance dimensions, each with various descriptive behaviors. Each dimension is based on observable behaviors and is meaningful to the employees being evaluated.

An example of BARS for a competence performance dimension for engineers is presented in Figure 10-7. The dimension is defined for the evaluator; the behaviors define the particular response categories for the evaluator, and the response made by the evaluator is precise and easy to interpret. The feedback provided by the BARS is clear and meaningful. For example, if the employee is given a 1.5 on this dimension, he or she is provided with the specific behavior that the evaluator evaluated.

A number of advantages are associated with the use of BARS. Since job-knowledgeable employees participate in the actual development steps, the final evaluation form should be acceptable as a measure of actual performance.

The use of BARS also provides valuable insight into developing training programs. The skills to be developed are specified in terms of actual behavioral incidents rather than abstract or general skills. Trainees in a BARS-based program could learn expected behaviors and how job performance is evaluated.

A behaviorally anchored evaluation system may minimize rating errors. However, some critics of BARS have presented results indicating that the approach is not always the most relevant, stable, and practical. These critics also suggest that more research comparing BARS with traditional evaluation methods is needed.

Despite the time, the cost, and the procedural problems of developing and implementing BARS, this system seems to have some advantages. Specifically, a BARS program could minimize subordinates' defensive attitudes toward evaluation. By being involved in the development of BARS, subordinates can make their input known. This input can be incorporated into the final BARS. The BARS development steps could include both superiors and subordinates. In a sense, then, all parties involved can contribute to the creation of the evaluation criteria (dimensions) and the behavioral incidents that are used to define each level of performance.

Another advantage of using BARS is that the evaluation program concentrates on job-specific and job-relevant behaviors. Many performance evaluation programs are abstract and meaningless to either the employees or the evaluators. Thus, when giving feedback to employees, the evaluators must convert the ratings to examples of actual job behavior. There are, in many cases, variances in the evaluators' ability to make these conversions from the rating scale to meaningful job behaviors. The BARS already contain behaviors that the superior can use in developing the evaluation counseling interview.

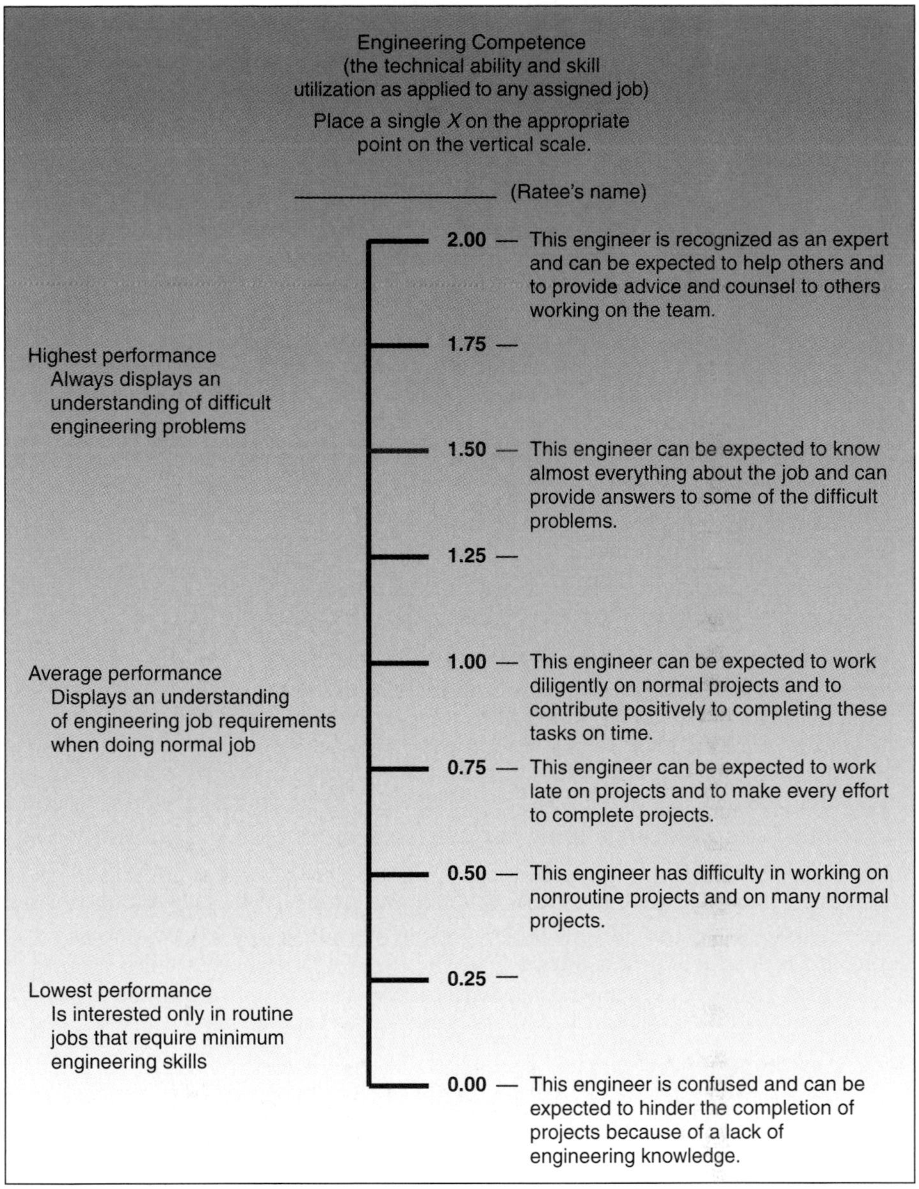

Engineering Competence
(the technical ability and skill
utilization as applied to any assigned job)

Place a single *X* on the appropriate
point on the vertical scale.

_____ (Ratee's name)

2.00 — This engineer is recognized as an expert
and can be expected to help others and
to provide advice and counsel to others
working on the team.

1.75 —

Highest performance
Always displays an
understanding of difficult
engineering problems

1.50 — This engineer can be expected to know
almost everything about the job and can
provide answers to some of the difficult
problems.

1.25 —

Average performance
Displays an understanding
of engineering job requirements
when doing normal job

1.00 — This engineer can be expected to work
diligently on normal projects and to
contribute positively to completing these
tasks on time.

0.75 — This engineer can be expected to work
late on projects and to make every effort
to complete projects.

0.50 — This engineer has difficulty in working on
nonroutine projects and on many normal
projects.

0.25 —

Lowest performance
Is interested only in routine
jobs that require minimum
engineering skills

0.00 — This engineer is confused and can be
expected to hinder the completion of
projects because of a lack of
engineering knowledge.

Figure 10-7
A BARS Performance Dimension

Management by Objectives (MBO) In most traditional and BARS evaluation programs, the evaluator is making judgments about the performance of *activities*. Many managers believe that a *results-based* program is more informative. As discussed in Chapter 5, a results-based program is called *management by objectives* (MBO). This program typically involves the establishment of planning objectives by the manager alone or jointly by the manager and the subordinate.

MBO is far more than just an evaluation approach. It usually is a part of an overall motivational program, planning technique, or organizational change and development program. Here, we only explore the idea of MBO as an alternative to traditional performance evaluation methods.

An MBO performance evaluation program focuses on the employee's achievements. The key features of a typical MBO program include the following:

1. The superior and the subordinate meet to discuss and set objectives for the subordinate for a specified period of time (e.g., six months or one year).

2. Both the superior and the subordinate attempt to establish objectives that are realistic, challenging, clear, and comprehensive. The objectives should be related to the needs of both the organization and the subordinate.

LearningMoment *No One "Best Way"*

Why, when, and how to conduct performance appraisals is not a set-in-concrete approach. Appraising a person's previous performance and then predicting what his or her performance will be in the future is tricky at best. Who should do the appraisal, when it should be conducted, and how to conduct it are all opinion and preference issues. There is no one "best way" or time to conduct performance appraisals. Regardless, however, of how and when performance appraisal data and information are assembled, the evaluation must provide sound formal feedback. Forgetting or not providing feedback defeats the purpose of helping employees make the changes needed to improve performance.

3. The standards for measuring and evaluating the objectives are agreed upon.
4. The superior and the subordinate establish some intermediate review dates when the objectives will be reexamined.
5. The superior plays more of a coaching, counseling, and supportive role and less of a judgmental role.
6. The entire process focuses on results and on the counseling of the subordinate, and not on activities, mistakes, and organizational requirements.

MBO-type programs have been used in organizations throughout the world.[33] As with the performance evaluation programs already discussed, there are both advantages and potential disadvantages associated with the use of MBO. The fact that MBO stresses results is a benefit that can also be a problem. Focusing only on results may take attention away from the process of accomplishing the objectives. A subordinate receiving feedback about what has been achieved still may not be certain about how to make performance corrections. A manager may tell a subordinate that the quality control goal was missed by 3.5 percent, but this type of feedback is incomplete. The subordinate who has failed to meet the quality control goal needs guidance and advice on how to accomplish it in the future.[34]

10-4 Compensation

Compensation is the HRM activity that deals with every type of reward that individuals receive for performing organizational tasks. It is basically an exchange relationship. Employees exchange their labor for financial and nonfinancial rewards. Financial compensation is both direct and indirect. **Direct financial compensation** consists of the pay an employee receives in the form of wages, salary, bonuses, and commissions. **Indirect financial compensation** (also called "benefits") consists of all the rewards that are not included in direct compensation, such as vacation time and insurance coverage.

From the employees' perspective, pay is a necessity in life. The compensation received from work is one of the chief reasons people seek employment. Pay is the means by which they provide for their own and their families' needs. For some people, compensation may be the only (or certainly a major) reason why they work. Others find compensation a contributing factor to their efforts. But pay can do more than provide for employees' psychological needs. It can also indicate their value to the organization.

Payroll often exceeds 50 percent of an organization's overall expenses. The objective of the traditional compensation function is to create a system of rewards that is equitable to employer and employee alike. The desired outcome is employees who are attracted to the work and motivated to do a good job for the employer. Research has indicated seven criteria for compensation system effectiveness:

- *Adequate:* Minimum government, union, and managerial pay levels should be met.
- *Equitable:* Everyone should be paid fairly, in line with their effort, abilities, and training.

> **direct financial compensation** Consists of pay an employee receives in the form of wages, salary, bonuses, and commissions.

> **indirect financial compensation** Consists of all the rewards, such as vacation time and insurance coverage, not included in direct compensation.

- *Balanced:* Pay, benefits, and other rewards should provide a reasonable total reward package.
- *Cost-effective:* Pay should not be excessive, considering what the organization can afford to pay.
- *Secure:* Pay should be enough to help employees feel secure and aid them in satisfying basic needs.
- *Incentive providing:* Pay should motivate effective, productive work.
- *Acceptable to the employee:* Employees should understand the pay system and feel that it is reasonable for the enterprise and themselves.

These seven criteria can be combined in a number of ways, comprising what is known as the **compensation system.** Most organizations have compensation systems that specify pay levels, benefits packages, and other rights, privileges, and perks that go along with jobs and job classes. Some organizations, such as government offices, have rigorous job classes, payment schedules, and benefit plans. Others, such as new ventures and "virtual" organizations, have little or no specified compensation systems.

10-4a Compensation Systems

Employees can be paid for the time they work (flat rates), the output they produce (individual incentives), or a combination of these two factors. In the following sections, we explore some of the strategies that are being used in organizations to compensate people for their contributions.

Flat Rate Compensation   In the unionized firm where wages are established by collective bargaining, single **flat rates** are usually paid. These are often set rates for various job classifications. For example, a company may have a policy that clerk typists are paid $9.00 per hour, while assembly line employees are paid $17.50 per hour. Often, these rates are paid regardless of experience or seniority. Unions have historically insisted on ignoring performance differentials in compensation for a variety of reasons. They contend that performance measures are inequitable. Jobs need cooperative effort that could be destroyed by wage differentials. Sales organizations, for example, pay a flat rate for a job and add a bonus or incentive to recognize individual differences.

Choosing to pay a flat rate versus different rates for the same job depends on the objectives the compensation analyst establishes. Recognizing individual differences makes the assumption that employees are not interchangeable or equally productive. By using pay differentials to recognize these differences, managers try to encourage an experienced, efficient, and satisfied workforce.

Individual Incentives   Perhaps the oldest form of compensation is the **individual incentive plan** in which the employee is paid for units produced. Individual incentive plans take several forms: piecework, production bonuses, and commissions. These methods seek to achieve the incentive goal of compensation.

Straight **piecework** usually works as follows: An employee is guaranteed an hourly rate (often the minimum wage) for performing an expected minimum output (the standard). For production over the standard, the employer pays so much per additional pieces produced. This is probably the most frequently used incentive pay plan. The standard is set through work measurement studies as modified by collective bargaining. The base rate and piece rate may emerge from data collected by pay surveys.

A variation of the straight piece rate is the **differential piece rate.** In this plan, the employer pays a smaller piece rate up to the standard and then a higher piece rate above the standard. Research indicates that the differential piece rate is more effective than the straight piece rate, although it is much less frequently used.[35]

Production bonus systems pay an employee an hourly rate. Then a bonus is paid when the employee exceeds the standard, typically 50 percent of labor savings. This system is not widely used today.

---

compensation system
An organization's established procedure that specifies pay levels, benefits packages, and other rights, privileges, and perks according to job classification.

flat rates   A pay scale established by collective bargaining.

individual incentive plan
A compensation plan that pays the employee for units produced; includes piecework, production bonuses, and commissions.

piecework   A compensation plan that bases pay rate on the number of pieces produced; a type of individual incentive plan.

differential piece rate
A compensation plan in which an employer pays one rate per piece up to a certain standard number and then a higher rate per piece.

production bonus systems
A system that pays an employee an hourly rate. Then a bonus is paid when the employee exceeds the standard, typically 50 percent of labor savings.

▶ **commission** A compensation plan that is the equivalent of straight piecework and typically a percentage of the item's price.

Commissions are paid to sales employees. Straight commission is the equivalent of straight piecework and is typically a percentage of the item's price. A variation of the production bonus system for sales is to pay salespeople a small salary (usually called a "draw") and commission or bonus when they exceed standards.

Individual incentives are used more frequently in some industries (clothing, steel, textiles) than others (lumber, bakery, beverage) and more often in some jobs (sales, production) than others (maintenance, clerical). Individual incentives are possible only in a situation where performance can be well specified in terms of output. In addition, employees must work independently of each other so that individual incentives can be applied equitably.

The research results on the effectiveness of individual incentives are mixed. Most studies indicate they do increase output, although other performance criteria may suffer. For example, in sales, straight commissions can lead to less attention being paid to servicing accounts. Working on hard-to-sell customers may be neglected because the salesperson will elect to sell to easy customers. There is also evidence of individual differences in the effect of incentives on performance.[36] Some employees are more inclined to perform better than others. This should not be a surprise since we know that people have varying motivations at work.

Gainsharing Incentive Plans

▶ **gainsharing plan** A group incentive compensation plan whose purpose is, through a financial formula, distributing organizationwide gains.

Gainsharing plans are companywide group incentive plans designed to unite diverse organizational elements behind the common pursuit of organizational goals by allowing employees to share in the profits.[37] Perhaps this type of system is best described as "a system of management in which an organization seeks higher levels of performance through the involvement of its people."[38] The system has proven to be exceptionally effective in enhancing organizationwide teamwork. Gainsharing plans that use cash awards and have been in place for at least five years have shown productivity ratio improvements resulting in labor cost reductions of 29 percent.[39]

Since the early 1980s an increasing number of companies have been implementing gainsharing plans using a formula that establishes a bonus based on improved productivity. Gainsharing rewards are normally distributed on a monthly or quarterly basis.[40] The factors that dictate a gainsharing plan's success include: (1) company size, (2) age of the plan, (3) the company's financial stability, (4) unionization, (5) the company's technology, and (6) employees' and managers' attitudes. A gainsharing plan is expensive to administer; projected benefits must be weighed against costs.

Linking pay to group performance and the creation of team spirit are two reasons cited for gainsharing's rising popularity.[41] For gainsharing to succeed, it must be supported by management. Management must also understand what gainsharing can and can't accomplish in order to optimize their type of group-based incentive program.

Employee Stock Option Plans

▶ **employee stock option plans (ESOP)** A program that awards company stock to employees as a form of compensation; usually employees are allowed to purchase shares of company stock at a discount from the market prices after a specified performance standard has been surpassed.

Employee stock option plans (ESOP) are increasingly used by firms to attract and retain top-notch talent. Five to 10 percent of U.S. companies offer stock option plans to all employees, typically granting from 100 to 200 option shares annually, or an amount based on a percentage of salary. The use of stock options helps to create a companywide "ownership" culture by focusing employees' attention on the employers' financial performance. Broad-based stock option plans are most commonly found in high-technology, telecommunications, and pharmaceutical companies.[42]

10-4b The Equal Pay Act

Today U.S. women working full-time earn only about 70 to 75 percent of what men earn.[43] Historically it was felt that women worked sporadically to bring in money for luxuries. The Virginia Slims opinion poll of 1990 found that women and men work for the same primary reason.[44]

The Equal Pay Act (1963) amending the Fair Labor Standards Act is the first antidiscrimination law relating directly to women. The act applies to all employers and employees covered by the Fair Labor Standards Act, including executives, managers, and professionals. The Equal Pay Act requires equal pay for equal work for men and women. It defines equal work as employment requiring equal skills, effort, and responsibility under similar working conditions.[45]

Under the Equal Pay Act, an employer can establish different wage rates on the basis of (1) seniority, (2) merit, (3) performance differences (quantity and quality of work), and (4) any factor other than sex. Shift work differentials are also permissible. But all these exceptions must apply equally to men and women. Since passage of the act the female–male earnings gap has narrowed slightly. In an effort to close the remaining earnings gap, there has been a growing movement in the past few years to have the widely accepted concept of equal pay for equal jobs expanded to include equal pay for comparable jobs.[46] Thus, for young people entering the workforce today, there is practically no difference between wages for men and women within a single job; the male–female wage discrepancy is heavily generational.

10-4c Comparable Worth

The doctrine of comparable worth (sometimes called pay equity) is not a position that provides that women and men be paid equally for performing equal work. **Comparable worth** is a concept that attempts to prove and remedy the allegation that employers systematically discriminate by paying women employees less than their work is intrinsically worth, relative to what they pay men who work in comparable professions. The term *comparable worth* means different things to different people. Comparable worth relates jobs that are dissimilar in their content (for example, nurse and plumber) and contends that individuals who perform jobs that require similar skills, efforts, and responsibilities under similar work conditions should be compensated equally.[47]

Advocates of comparable worth depend primarily on two sets of statistics to demonstrate that employers discriminate against women employees. First, they point to statistics that show that women earn from 59 to 88 percent less than men overall. Second, women have tended to be concentrated in lower-paying, predominately female jobs.[48] In spite of the fact that more women are entering the workforce, about one-fourth of all women employed in 1988 worked in three job categories: secretarial/clerical, retail sales, and food preparation and service.[49]

> **comparable worth** A compensation concept that attempts to prove and remedy the allegation that employers systematically discriminate by paying women employees less than their work is intrinsically worth, relative to what they pay men who work in comparable professions; sometimes called *pay equity.*

10-5 Benefits and Services

Indirect financial compensation, called **fringe benefits,** consists of all financial rewards that are not included in direct financial compensation. Unlike pay for performance programs and incentive plans, benefits and services are made available to employees as long as they are employed by the organization. Annual surveys suggest that about 75 percent of all U.S. workers say that benefits are crucial to job choice. If limited to only one benefit (beyond cash), 64 percent say that health care is most important.[50]

Employee benefits and services are part of the rewards of employment that reinforce loyal service to the employer. Major benefits and services programs include pay for time not worked, insurance, pensions, and services like tuition reimbursement.

This definition of benefits and services can be applied to hundreds of programs. There is a lack of agreement on what is or is not to be included, the purposes to be served, responsibility for programs, the costs and values of the various elements, the units in which the costs and values are measured, and the criteria for decision making. Compensation decisions with respect to indirect compensation are more complex than decisions concerned with wages and salaries.

> **fringe benefits** Indirect financial compensation consisting of all financial rewards not included in direct financial compensation.

10-5a Benefits Required by Law

The programs offered in work organizations today are the product of efforts in this area for the past sixty years. Before World War II, employers offered a few pensions and services because they had the welfare of employees at heart or they wanted to keep out a union. But most benefit programs began in earnest during the war, when wages were strictly regulated.

The unions pushed for nonwage compensation increases, and they got them. Court cases in the late 1940s confirmed the right of unions to bargain for benefits: *Inland Steel v. National Labor Relations Board* (1948) over pensions, and *W.W. Cross v. National Labor Relations Board* over insurance. The growth of benefit programs indicates how much unions have used this right. In 1929 benefits cost employers 3 percent of total wages and salaries; by 1949 the cost was up to 16 percent, and in the 1970s it was nearly 30 percent. By 1990 costs of benefits and services totaled about 50 percent.[51]

10-5b Additional Benefits and Retirement Plans

In addition to benefits required by the law (such as unemployment insurance, social security, and workers' compensation), many employers also provide other kinds of benefits: compensation for time not worked, insurance protection, and retirement plans. There are many differences in employers' practices regarding these benefits. The most widely used benefits include paid vacations, holidays, sick leave, life insurance, medical insurance, and pension plans.

10-5c Child Care

Two important parts of benefits packages are child care and elder care. Nearly 50 percent of today's workers are women and as many as 70 percent of these women have children under age six at home. The Bureau of the Census reports that working mothers pay about $15.1 billion per year for child care while they work. The U.S. Department of Labor predicts that in the first decade of the twenty-first century more than 80 percent of women between the ages of twenty-five and forty-four will be working outside the home at least part-time. This suggests that child care programs will become a necessity.

10-5d Elder Care

People age sixty-five or older will comprise 23 percent of the U.S. population by 2050.[52] Recent research shows that at least 20 percent of all employees already provide assistance to one or more elderly relatives or friends. On average, these employees spend between six and thirty-five hours per week providing this care. At least 50 percent of these employees also have children at home. The burden falls most heavily on the working woman who traditionally took care of elderly relatives and did not work outside the home. Employees who are also caregivers to seniors experience the following problems: missed work (58 percent), loss of pay (47 percent), and less energy to do their work well (15 percent).

10-6 Special Issues in Human Resources

A number of special issues such as sexual harassment and substance abuse have become significant in the workplace.

10-6a Sexual Harassment

According to public opinion polls, the majority of American women believe they have experienced sexual harassment on the job. As the law has evolved, two types of conduct have been found to constitute sexual harassment in violation of Title VII of the Civil Rights Act. The first type, originally identified in 1977, is the designated *tangible job benefit*, also known as *quid pro quo harassment*. This form of harassment occurs when an employee's career path is directly impacted by a supervisor's unwelcome requests for sexual favors or other sexual advances (www.hr-guide.com).

A second type of sexual harassment is a *hostile work environment*. The elements necessary for proving a hostile work-environment-related sexual harassment claim are stated by a New York State case:

> A person would have to show that (1) he or she belongs to a protected group (i.e., female or minority group); (2) he or she was subject to unwelcome sexual harassment as defined

above; (3) the harassment complained of was based upon his or her membership in the protected class; and (4) the harassment complained of affected the terms, conditions, or privileges of his or her employment.

The creation of a work environment in violation of Title VII can occur in many ways depending on the size of the workforce, managers' sensitivity to sexual harassment, and the dynamics of the workplace.

As Clarence Thomas's 1991 Senate confirmation hearings regarding his nomination to the U.S. Supreme Court illustrate, sexual harassment cases are difficult to unravel. Often they involve one person's word against another's. The nation watched as Anita Hill described a series of incidents she found offensive. Clarence Thomas denied that the incidents occurred. Thomas was eventually confirmed to the Supreme Court seat, but the hearings were a catalyst in sexual harassment becoming a major concern across the United States.

Sexual harassment can cause lasting emotional damage, depression, and reduced productivity. Each of these consequences is costly to individuals and organizations. One study estimated that the cost to the federal government resulting from sexual harassment over a two-year period was about $267 million.

The seriousness of sexual harassment and why it must be dealt with through policies, increased awareness, and training are captured by a statement of the U.S. Merit Protection Board:

> Victims pay all the intangible emotional costs inflicted by anger, humiliation, frustration, withdrawal, dysfunctional family, and other damages that can be sexual harassment's aftermath. Victims of the most severe forms of harassment, including rape, can face not only severe emotional consequences, but also the possibility of a life-threatening disease. Some victims may leave jobs for one with a lower career path in order to escape the sexual harassment.[53]

Due to its trauma and potential impact, sexual harassment demands prompt managerial action. It is impossible for a worker to pay attention to the quality of production or service when harassment is occurring. Corrective action is required because of the need to protect the rights of every worker. It is also required because the law (although it's gray in some areas) indicates that employers are liable for sexual harassment. In fact, employers may also be responsible for the acts of their employees. For example, where an employer (or an employer's agents) knows or should know of the harassment and fails to take immediate and corrective action, the employer may be held liable. Sending a clear message that sexual harassment of any form will not be tolerated is a recommended course of action.[54]

The following Management Focus on the Law box, "Jury Verdict Against the Hospital," illustrates how costly a lawsuit and jury award involving sexual harassment can be to an organization.

10-6b Substance Abuse

Substance abuse (www.4intercept.com) is a major problem that may impact the safety, productivity, and image of organizations.[55] An American Management Association survey indicates that about 75 percent of major U.S. companies now engage in drug testing.[56] Most major corporations also conduct preemployment substance abuse testing. Like many forms of testing, substance abuse screening has passionate opponents. Claims that it is inaccurate, an invasion of privacy, and demeaning are well articulated. But so long as there are estimates that any firm with more than six employees has a substance abuser, testing is likely to continue. It is also estimated that substance abuse costs U.S. industry over $100 billion annually because of lost productivity. Substance abusers are absent two and a half times more days than nonabusers, file five times the number of medical claims and workers' compensation claims, and have four times as many on-the-job accidents. Clearly programs and policies are needed to reduce the burden of substance abuse.

Management Focus on the Law

Jury Verdict Against the Hospital

The U.S. Equal Employment Opportunity Commission (EEOC) announced that a federal jury awarded $4,050,000 to Stephanie Denninghoff following a four-day trial conducted on her behalf by the U.S. Equal Employment Opportunity Commission (EEOC) against bon Secours DePaul Medical Center, Inc. for unlawful retaliation. The jury awarded $1,050,000 in compensatory damages and $3 million in punitive damages to Ms. Denninghoff after she was forced to resign from her position as Director of Operative Services following her attempts to prevent sexual harassment in the hospital's operating rooms and facility. "I feel vindicated," said Stephanie Denninghoff, following the jury's verdict.

The EEOC's lawsuit filed in U.S. District Court of the Eastern District of Virginia involved the unlawful termination of Stephanie Denninghoff from her position at DePaul, in retaliation for Ms. Denninghoff's role in addressing complaints by employees about sexually harassing behavior in the operating room environs by a nurse. Complaints were made to Ms. Denninghoff about a nurse's hugging, kissing, embracing, and rubbing doctors and other staff members. Ms. Denninghoff, in her capacity as the nurse's supervisor, with the involvement of Human Resources, verbally warned the nurse about this behavior being inappropriate.

Following the nurse's counseling, the evidence showed that the nurse complained to doctors and staff members about being treated unfairly, threatened to quit, and ultimately did so. Several doctors complained to management about Ms. Denninghoff's role in addressing this behavior and one prominent doctor threatened to remove his business from DePaul Hospital unless Ms. Denninghoff was terminated and the nurse brought back to the hospital. Subsequently, Ms. Denninghoff was asked to resign her position or be terminated, allegedly for a "breach of confidentiality." Having no choice, Ms. Denninghoff resigned and filed a complaint with the EEOC. The evidence at trial demonstrated, and the jury determined, that the real reason Ms. Denninghoff was forced to resign was because of her involvement in the situation with the nurse. The nurse whose inappropriate behavior had been complained about returned to work at the hospital six days after Ms. Denninghoff was forced to leave.

Source: Adapted from "Workplace Answers," www.workplaceanswers.com/news/41.asp, November 3, 2003.

Management's most powerful tool to combat substance abuse is an informed, educated workforce. Detecting substance abuse or a related problem requires careful observation and proper training. Signs of possible substance abuse include the following:

* Difficulty in recalling instructions
* Frequent tardiness and absence
* Numerous restroom breaks
* Extended work and lunch breaks
* Difficulty in getting along with coworkers
* Increased off- and on-the-job accidents
* Dramatic change in personality [57]

Can managers be good observers and diagnosticians? Sometimes. But patterns of behavior suggesting substance abuse could also be caused by family problems, workplace stress, or physical health problems. Taking drugs on the job is illegal, while having family problems isn't.

The controversy about substance abuse detection and testing is likely to continue unabated. The need is for a policy and program that (1) explains the company's philosophy on substance abuse, (2) describes the firm's policy on testing, (3) implements a discipline and rehabilitation program, (4) communicates the program to all employees, and (5) educates managers on how to enforce a fair substance abuse policy and program.[58] The foundation of an effective approach to preventing substance abuse is a clear, coherent program. Certainly substance abuse is unacceptable in the workplace. Therefore employers must reserve the right to test even though they'll probably exercise the right sparingly. Dealing fairly with substance abuse problems sends a positive message to employees and customers.

Management Summary

- Evaluating the performance of human resources is a key managerial responsibility. Effective performance evaluation can help accomplish such goals as increased motivation and improved knowledge.

- To be effective as a management control activity, performance evaluation must be based on specific standards. These performance standards must be relevant, stable, practical, and capable of distinguishing different levels of performance.

- To administer a performance evaluation program, managers must make several key decisions, including who should do the rating, when to rate, and how the evaluation interview will be performed.

- Traditional performance evaluation methods use some form of rating scale that requires managers to rate their subordinates on a number of dimensions.

- In reaction to some of the problems inherent in traditional performance evaluation methods, two recently developed methods, behaviorally anchored rating scales and management by objectives, have been widely adopted.

- Behaviorally anchored rating scales use critical incidents or specific job behaviors that determine different levels of performance.

- Sexual harassment and substance abuse are significant problems in the workplace that managers must deal with so that the well-being of the workforce and job performance can be optimized.

Key Terms

360-degree feedback (p. 231)
acquisition phase (p. 221)
behaviorally anchored rating scales (BARS) (p. 236)
bona fide occupational qualification (BFOQ) (p. 224)
commission (p. 240)
comparable worth (p. 241)
compensation system (p. 239)
developmental purpose (p. 230)
differential piece rate (p. 239)
direct financial compensation (p. 238)
discriminatory requirement (p. 231)
employee stock option plans (ESOP) (p. 240)

flat rates (p. 239)
fringe benefits (p. 241)
gainsharing plan (p. 240)
human resource management (p. 221)
human resource planning (p. 223)
indirect financial compensation (p. 238)
individual incentive plan (p. 239)
judgmental purposes (p. 230)
management by objectives (MBO) (p. 236)
orientation (p. 229)
performance evaluation (p. 230)
performance standards (p. 230)
piecework (p. 239)
practical requirement (p. 231)

production bonus systems (p. 239)
proper use of people (p. 230)
relevant requirement (p. 231)
retention (p. 221)
selection of personnel (p. 226)
selection tests (p. 228)
semistructured interview (p. 227)
stable requirement (p. 231)
structured interview (p. 226)
termination (p. 221)
unstructured interview (p. 227)
weighted checklist (p. 234)

Review and Discussion Questions

1. Explain why both developmental and judgmental purposes are difficult to achieve in performance evaluation.

2. Can you pay a person a different rate because of gender? Explain.

3. Explain why diversity advertising for job applicants has become an important part of recruitment.

4. What would be the major reasons why a firm such as General Dynamics in San Diego would use its current employees' pictures in its recruitment ads?

5. What role does the government play in human resource management activities and programs? Should its role be larger or smaller? Discuss.

6. Describe and distinguish between the various traditional performance evaluation methods.

7. Explain the differences between behaviorally anchored rating scales and traditional rating scales.

8. What type of compensation package do you prefer at this point in your career? Do you believe your preferences will change over time? Why?

9. What type of questions could be more easily asked by using a computer system than by using a traditional one-on-one interviewing format?

10. Explain the basic features of a management by objectives performance evaluation program.

Practice Quiz

Note: You can find the correct answers to these questions by taking the quiz and then submitting your answers in the Online Edition. The program will automatically score your submission. If you miss a question, the program will provide the correct answer, a rationale for the answer, and the section number in the chapter where the topic is discussed.

Indicate whether the sentence or statement is true or false.

1. The EEOC now has the power to file action in a federal court if it is unable to eliminate alleged unlawful employment practices by the informal methods of conference, conciliation, and persuasion.

2. An MBO performance evaluation program focuses on the employee's achievements.

3. The **preliminary interview process** is the HRM activity that deals with every type of reward that individuals receive for performing organizational tasks.

4. Today, U.S. women working full time earn about 85 percent of what men earn.

5. Court cases in the late 1940s confirmed the right of unions to bargain for benefits.

6. People age 65 or older will comprise 23 percent of the U.S. population by 2050.

7. Sexual harassment can cause lasting emotional damage, depression, and reduced productivity.

Identify the letter of the choice that best completes the statement or answers the question.

8. Research has shown that _____ is the most important element of behavior change.
a. a role model
b. a pay raise
c. relevant feedback
d. a good manager

9. Critical incidents are examples of specific job behaviors that determine various levels of _____ .
a. injury.
b. reward.
c. competence.
d. performance.

10. An American Management Association survey indicates that approximately _____ of major U.S. companies now engage in drug testing.
a. 25 percent
b. 50 percent
c. 75 percent
d. 90 percent

11. The acquisition phase of human resource management includes _____
a. placement.
b. screening.
c. recruiting.
d. all of the above.

12. Selection testing of human resources is _____ .
a. outdated.
b. based on meta-analysis.
c. involved with legal issues.
d. preferred to interviewing.

13. The most widely used performance evaluation procedure is the _____ .
a. BARS.
b. essay.
c. weighted checklist.
d. graphic rating scale.

14. Indirect financial compensation is also referred to as _____ .
a. salary.
b. stock system.
c. benefits.
d. red line method.

15. Under the Equal Pay Act, an employer can establish different wage rates on the basis of _____ .
a. religious preference.
b. merit.
c. gender.
d. school grade point average.

Case Study

Performance Appraisals Getting the Boot

Performance appraisals have come under fire and criticism for many years. W. Edwards Deming, the world-renowned quality management guru, despised the use of appraisal systems. He believed they are built of negative factors, missing goals, and command-and-control oversight.

In many organizations there is an emphasis on shared leadership, empowerment, teamwork, and retaining top employees. Using a nit-picking appraisal approach is not in line with employee needs to personally develop and grow. A survey performed by the Society for Human Resource Management (SHRM, www.shrm.org) and Personnel Decisions International (PDI, www.pdi.com) found that 32 percent of the professional human resource professionals surveyed indicated that they were "unsatisfied" or "very unsatisfied" with their firms' appraisal systems.

If there is no appraisal system, what will take its place? Coens, Jenkins, and Block, in their book *Abolishing Performance Appraisals: Why They Backfire and What to Do Instead* (San Francisco: Berrett-Koehler, 2000), have plenty of suggestions for managers. They suggest that performance management replace performance appraisal. Performance management rests on the following principles:

- Goals should be set and agreed upon by both the manager and the employee.
- Metrics for measuring the employee's success in meeting these goals should be clearly articulated.
- Employees should be able to think of their managers as coaches who are there not to pass judgment but to help them achieve success.

These principles emphasize that instead of pinpointing where employees fall short, a new way of results-oriented and coaching-based thinking is advocated. Formal performance appraisal is considered outdated, adversarial, and too negative.

The debate is whether goal setting, employee involvement, and coaching can effectively replace the type of systems that are still widely used: graphic rating scales, ranking methods, weighted checklists, descriptive essays, and behaviorally anchored rating scales.

Questions for Analysis

1. Why is it too general to claim that performance appraisals are negative and not worthy of being used?
2. What are some positive and negative features of the recommendations of Coen, Jenkins, and Block?
3. Do you believe that performance appraisals will be abolished in the next decade? Why?

Source: Adapted from Marc J. Epstein and Jean-Francois Manzoni, *Performance Measurement and Management Control: A Compendium of Research* (San Deigo: Elsevier 2004); Brian E. Becker, Mark A. Huselid, and David Ulrich, *The HR Scorecard: Linking People, Strategy and Performance* (Cambridge, MA: Harvard Business School Press, 2001); Tom Coens, Mary Jenkins, and Peter Block, *Abolishing Performance Appraisals: Why They Backfire and What to Do Instead* (San Francisco: Berrett-Koehler, 2000); and Dayton Fandray, "The New Thinking In Performance Appraisals," www.zigonperf.com/freeresources.asp.

Internet Exercise

Company Sexual Harassment Policies

Sexual harassment in the workplace is a costly and prevalent problem in organizations. It is not only a problem in the United States but also around the world. Use the Internet to find and review the sexual harassment policies of *two* American and *two* non-American companies.

1. Are there similarities and differences that really stand out in the policies?
2. Do you believe that sexual harassment policies can make a difference in reducing the prevalence of this behavior? Why?

Experiential Exercise

A Control Procedure: Your Personal Performance Appraisal

Purpose: The purpose of this exercise is to apply performance appraisal guidelines to your own activities and objectives.

Setting Up the Exercise:

1. Write a paragraph (150 words or less) describing a successful you. What would make you successful? Select school, your job, your family, or personal life as a reference point. In your paragraph, list the outcomes (results) that would mean you were successful (e.g., *school*—grade point average, 3.3, graduated with honors, receiving highest grade on final; *job*—promoted to next level in two years, receiving recognition, receiving large merit increase).

2. Using the chart that follows, for the reference point (choose one), select five areas of major concern and the measures of success you would use. Determine whether the measures of success are subjective or objective. Do they have a time frame?

3. Develop the major areas of concern into specific personal objectives—one for each major area of concern. The objectives should be one *single* sentence, clearly stated, with a time period specified. Rank the objectives from the most important to the least important.

4. The instructor will form groups of three students to share their success stories, measures of success, and objective statements. Are there differences in what are considered success measures, objectives, and priorities?

A Learning Note: Even self-performance appraisal is a control procedure. It serves to direct individual behavior toward objectives that are meaningful, clear, comprehensive, and challenging. Explicit objectives that are well stated must be carefully worked on. Skill in developing objectives can be improved with practice. Good objectives can be helpful in planning, organizing, and controlling behavior and attitudes.

Major Area of Concern	How Is Success Measured?	Subjective/Objective	Time Frame Yes/No
1. _____	_____	_____	_____
_____	_____		
2. _____	_____	_____	_____
_____	_____		
3. _____	_____	_____	_____
_____	_____		
4. _____	_____	_____	_____
_____	_____		
5. _____	_____	_____	_____
_____	_____		

Ranked Objectives

1. _____

2. _____

3. _____

4. _____

5. _____

Leading

Leadership is perhaps the most important role in a manager's portfolio. At the same time, it's perhaps the most difficult role. Leadership requires resolve and commitment. It requires a sense of urgency and the ability to motivate. Above all, it requires vision.

This part of the text examines leadership from a variety of perspectives. Chapter 11 explores the various theories that have been applied to understanding the phenomenon of leadership. Who has it? How does one become a leader? You'll learn the difference between leadership and management. You'll also learn how to develop the skills necessary to be a leader today.

Chapter 12 explores the various techniques managers use to motivate others to pursue organizational goals. Leadership requires followers. Recruiting followers to a cause requires communication skills, enthusiasm, and commitment. Leaders must walk the walk and talk the talk. They must understand how to motivate individuals as well as groups.

Motivating others requires interpersonal communication skills. Chapter 13 explores communications and how to improve your ability to work with others. Communication is a complex process involving verbal and nonverbal messages. In addition, communication is a two-way process that requires strong listening skills. The complex communication environment and the skills necessary to navigate successfully within it are explored in Chapter 13.

The modern workplace makes extensive use of teams and work groups. Communication with and within these groups requires skill. Chapter 14 explores the skills needed to communicate with individuals and teams in the modern workplace. It also examines the different types of groups and management strategies to implement to deal with conflicts between groups.

Elements of Leadership

CHAPTER OBJECTIVES

1 Define what is meant by the term *leadership.*

2 Explain why leadership is a necessary management function.

3 Describe the two primary functions of leadership.

4 Distinguish management from leadership.

5 State the three general approaches to the study of leadership.

6 Describe the basic conclusions of contingency theory.

7 Discuss why the maturity level of followers would be expected to change over time.

8 Define what is meant by the term *transformational leadership.*

CHAPTER OUTLINE

Managing Today

The Essential Ingredient: Good Leaders Are Good Listeners

What distinguishes great leaders, whether in business or sports, from the rest? The ability to listen. Those who are wrapped up in themselves and unaware of the reality surrounding them will never produce success.

Basketball legend Bill Russell drives home the point of listening. In his book, *Russell Rules,* he wrote that "80% of people hear while only 20% really listen." Absorbing the right information, discerning the difference between what people say and what they mean, working well with others—all these benefits of really listening are present in successful chief executives. Here are some business all-stars whose acute ears help make their companies rewarding investments:

> Max DePree won renown for his office furniture maker, Herman Miller, with its benevolent employment practices and state-of-the-art products. DePree insisted that management lavish attention on its employees and its customers—a practice that many companies make only a pretense of doing. The result is that employees at every level of the Herman Miller organization feel they are part of the team. Small wonder the company comes up with furniture designs that people like to use and look at.

> J.M. Smucker has been dominated by one family for four generations. Nevertheless, the descendants of Jerome Smucker aren't stuck in their ways. They're ever alert for what kids and adults want to eat. Maybe nobody has the time anymore to spread jam on toast. The Smuckers have figured out how to shift into portable snacks. Witness two very successful product launches: Smucker's Uncrustables, a line of thaw-and-serve crustless peanut butter and jelly sandwiches, and Smucker's Snackers, which combines peanut butter and jelly with crackers.

Listening, like leadership, is a skill that can be learned. Leadership coach Terry Pearce says that good leaders learn how to empathize, build consensus, lead without dominating, and, most critically, they listen to understand. Pearce teaches listening in three quick steps: (1) Pause ten seconds before answering—try it, it's painful! (2) Ask a question to clarify intent. (3) Respond with feelings as well as facts. In today's business environment, where people are rushed to do more with less and have to prioritize on a day-to-day basis, they have a tendency to simply not take the time to talk with one another and, more important, to listen to one another.

Not only do leaders have to make the effort to hear more than they want to, but they also have to make an effort to really understand what is being said. Breaking through their own personal "listening" barriers is a true challenge, but it will lead to a true understanding of what's being communicated.

Sources: Adapted from John W. Rogers, Jr., "Listen Up," *Forbes,* August 20, 2001, p. 172; Patricia Sellers, Ahmad Diba, and Ellen Florian, "Get Over Yourself," *Fortune,* April 30, 2001, pp. 76–81; and Jack Clark, "Let's Talk," *Business Credit,* November/December 2000, pp. 10–13.

Leadership is an important and necessary skill for achieving individual, group, and organizational performance. Managers, whether they are chief executive officers or first-level supervisors, influence attitudes and expectations that encourage or discourage performance, secure or alienate employee commitment, and reward or penalize achievement. Despite the growth of large, impersonal organizations, people still relate to leaders. We see this in our everyday lives, and we make judgments about the leaders of our business, governmental, and educational organizations. Leadership does make a difference.

This chapter reviews some influential theories and ideas about leadership. Efforts to analyze effective leadership have focused on three general areas: (1) *the personal characteristics of leaders,* (2) *the behavior of leaders,* and (3) *the situations in which leaders are found.* Despite the extensive research into leadership, it is impossible to state that there is one best way to lead. Rather, the prevailing view of leadership is that the best way to lead varies with each situation. That is, a good leadership style in one situation may, when practiced in another situation, result in chaos, nonperformance, and unfulfilled goals.

Leadership involves other people. Therefore, where there are leaders, there must be followers.[1] Leadership can arise in any situation where people have combined their efforts to accomplish a task. Thus, leaders may or may not be managers. Within the organization, informal groups develop, and within those groups are people who influence the behavior of other group members. Such people are the **informal leaders.** Individuals who influence the behavior of their assigned groups are the **formal leaders** of organizations. The emphasis in this chapter is on formal leadership, that is, managers who must exhibit leadership behavior.

Leading and being a manager are not necessarily the same. Managers are people formally recognized in the organization's hierarchy. They are expected to plan, organize, con-

▶**informal leaders** People who lead their groups, divisions, or departments based on their leadership skills, and not on formal authority or titles.

▶**formal leaders** Individuals who lead their assigned groups, divisions, or departments by virtue of their position and title.

trol, and make effective decisions. It is correct to state that a good manager is always a good leader, but a good leader is not necessarily a good manager. The key difference between leadership and management has been described as follows:

> Leadership is a part of management but not all of it. . . . Leadership is the ability to persuade others to seek defined objectives enthusiastically. It is the human factor which binds a group together and motivates it toward goals. Management activities such as planning, organizing, and decision making are dormant cocoons until the leader triggers the power of motivation in people and guides them toward goals.[2]

According to a study conducted by *BT.Novations*, a management consulting firm in Provo, Utah, the definitions and perceptions of what people consider true leadership within their organizations doesn't necessarily include management jobs. The study asked more than 2,500 white-collar employees to identify a leader within their organization. Nearly 85 percent of the individuals identified by the respondents did not hold a management position. The study results reflect the trend of creating and operating flatter organizations by reducing the number of midlevel managers, according to Kurt Sandholtz, vice president for *BT.Novations* and the survey's project leader. "Companies are more team-based and free-flowing than they were 25 years ago," says Sandholtz. "Managers today have a broader span of control, and this means key contributors are stepping up and making things happen within their companies."[3]

11-1 Defining "Leadership"

Leadership is not an easy term to define precisely. We define **leadership** as "the ability to influence through communication the activities of others, individually or as a group, toward the accomplishment of worthwhile, meaningful, and challenging goals." First, this definition indicates that one cannot be a leader unless there are people (e.g., coworkers, followers) to be led.[4] Second, leadership involves the application of influence skills. The use of these skills has a purpose, to accomplish goals. Finally, an objective of leadership is to bring about influence so that important goals are achieved. This influence is brought about not only directly through authority or motivation, but also indirectly through role-modeling. Research has shown that employees generally have higher expectations of leaders as models or exemplars of the organization.[5]

> **leadership** In the context of management theory, a person's ability to influence the activities of followers in an organizational setting. Management theory emphasizes that the leader must interact with his or her followers to be influential.

11-2 The Core of Leadership: Influence

The exercise of influence is the essence of leadership behavior. The use of influence as a *primary* method of affecting the organization is perhaps the major difference between leaders and managers. Leaders use influence as their primary tool to move the organization toward its goals. Of course, managers too must use influence and show leadership. However, a manager also uses such tools as compensation, employee feedback and evaluation, and organizational structure to move an organization.

Seven influence strategies have been proposed as vital for practicing leadership roles:[6]

* Reason—Using facts and data to develop a logically sound argument
* Friendliness—Using supportiveness, praise, and the creation of goodwill
* Coalition—Mobilizing others in the organization
* Bargaining—Negotiating through the use of benefits or favors
* Assertiveness—Using a direct and forceful approach
* Higher Authority—Gaining the support of higher levels in the hierarchy to add weight to the request
* Sanctions—Using rewards and punishment

A study of 360 first- and second-level managers in the United States, Great Britain, and Australia assessed their personal influence strategies.[7] The most popular methods used with subordinates were reason and assertiveness, while the least-used methods were higher authority and sanctions. The study also determined that managers with the power to control resources use a greater variety of influence strategies. This study suggests that using influence is a fundamental activity in organizations.

Leaders need to learn a variety of influence strategies; they cannot rely solely on the traditional strategy of exercising the power they possess by virtue of their position in the formal hierarchy or informal group. In addition, in modern organizations it's recognized that employees should be allowed to influence the way the organization works. Organizational psychologist Noel M. Tichy said, "The ultimate test for a leader is not whether he or she makes smart decisions and takes decisive action, but whether he or she teaches others to be leaders and builds an organization that can sustain success even when he or she is not around."[8] Others, such as Boston Philharmonic (www.bostonphil.com) founder and conductor Benjamin Zander, define leadership in terms of the ability to think creatively. Zander says that a leader's role is to help people realize and understand "distinctions." He demonstrates his point through music, highlighting nuances that untrained listeners would not detect to help them think "out of the box" and realize the possibilities that lie hidden beneath the surface.[9] Most analysts of leadership would agree that it involves engaging employees, getting them involved in creating results at all levels of the organization.[10]

11-3 Distinguishing Management from Leadership

The distinction between management and leadership is controversial. No clear line separates the two. It goes without saying that managers must often be leaders, and that leaders must often be managers. Nonetheless, there does seem to be some truth to the idea that management is different from leadership.

Harvard Business School's Abraham Zaleznick supports this notion. He thinks that the distinction between leadership and management lies in the focus of the role. Managers must focus on moment-to-moment organizational performance. Leaders, on the other hand, focus on the long-term goals of an organization. In Zaleznick's terminology, managers are primarily concerned with *process* and leaders are primarily concerned with *substance*.[11]

Perhaps an example would help to make this distinction clearer. Michael Dell is the CEO of Dell Computers (www.dell.com). He started the company from his dorm room at the University of Texas, selling made-to-order computers over the telephone. Realizing that the demand for his computers far outstripped his ability to supply them, he quit school and launched his company. As his company grew, Dell became immersed in endless details about work flow, product quality, and supply chain management. It wasn't long before he realized that he was in trouble. Dell Computer experienced difficult times due to production problems, questionable product quality, and uncertain market focus. Michael Dell realized that he was better as a leader than as a manager. He had the vision that created the company, but he wasn't very good at managing the day-to-day details involved in operating the growing company.[12]

This is a common problem many entrepreneurs like Michael Dell face. They are good visionaries and are very influential, but they often aren't very good managers. Fortunately for Michael Dell, he realized his limitations before the company got into too much trouble. He went out and hired the best operations, financial, and other executive officers he could find to handle the day-to-day management of his company. Today, Dell Computers is a major international competitor and one of the most respected companies in America.[13]

The process versus substance distinction is useful in understanding the contrast between management and leadership. However, don't begin to think that the roles are distinct in organizations. Most managers must also be leaders and most leaders must also be managers. The distinction is really based on a continuum. Managers primarily are concerned with process, and leaders primarily are concerned with substance. Figure 11-1 displays this continuum.

Typically, good leaders sacrifice micromanagement of the bottom line in favor of a macroscopic understanding of the enterprise, its associates, and its strategic direction. Although it has never been conclusively proven that leaders produce lower profits than managers, they do tend to create more inspired, more empowered associates—willing to serve to the ends of the earth—and leaders are significantly less likely to be deemed a "workaholic," "ogre," or "taskmaster" by their associates or colleagues.[14] In his popular

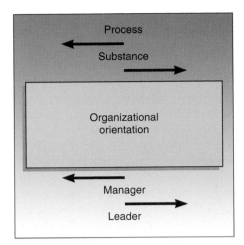

Figure 11-1
The Management-Leadership Continuum

book *Good to Great,* author and business researcher Jim Collins identified what he referred to as **Level Five Leadership.** Level Five leaders are individuals who usually have risen up within a particular industry and who lead primarily by example. They are not concerned with being "the CEO" or with being a "celebrity"; they are focused on results and do whatever is necessary to achieve them.[15]

11-4 Approaches to Understanding Leadership

Leadership has been one of the most studied topics in management, yet the conclusions reached have been contradictory, exaggerated, and controversial. Part of the problem lies in the definitions, measurements, and theories used to study leadership. The three main approaches at the center of the debate surrounding leadership are as follows:

* **Trait Theory of Leadership**   Attributes performance differences among employees to the individual characteristics (traits) of leaders.
* **Behavioral Theory of Leadership**   Attributes performance differences to the behaviors and style of leaders.
* **Contingency Theory of Leadership**   The leader's behavior and style in combination with situational factors are the key reason for performance differences.

Over the years each of these main approaches has been refined and various dimensions have been added, but they still remain the primary basis for leadership theory, research, and application discussions.

11-5 Trait Theory of Leadership

We observe good leaders such as Carly Fiorina of *Hewlett-Packard,* Debbi Fields of *Mrs. Fields' Cookies,* and Steve Jobs of *Apple Computer.* So it's natural to ask whether the secret

▶ **Level Five Leadership**   Level Five leaders are individuals who usually have risen up within a particular industry and who lead primarily by example.

▶ **trait theory of leadership** A theory that attempts to specify which personal characteristics (physical, personality, mental) are associated with leadership effectiveness. Trait theory relies on research that relates various traits to effectiveness criteria.

▶ **behavioral theory of leadership** A theory that attributes performance differences to the behaviors and style of leaders.

▶ **contingency theory of leadership** A theory that attributes performance differences to the leader's behavior and style in combination with situational factors.

LearningMoment   *Leaders Versus Managers*

Leadership is an elusive characteristic that is often easy to spot but very difficult to define. What makes someone a good leader? Think about three strong leaders that you know. What makes them good leaders? Do they possess common characteristics? Now think about three strong managers that you know. What makes them good managers? How are they different from leaders?

A good analogy to keep in mind when comparing management to leadership is: Managers climb the corporate ladder, leaders make sure the ladder is leaning against the right wall.

of leadership is to be found in the individual characteristics of leaders. Are there differences between leaders and nonleaders in terms of personality traits, physical characteristics, motives, needs? Many people believe that effective leadership has roots in a particular personality trait. Some even assume that unless one possesses that trait, he or she is doomed to failure as a leader.

The trait theory of leadership constitutes an important but somewhat controversial approach to understanding leadership. Boiling leadership down to specific human traits or characteristics seems simplistic. What trait or combination of traits could be consistently linked with leadership? None have been found. For example, not all effective leaders are tall or exceptionally smart. Not all effective leaders are charismatic or glib. In addition, there are cultural differences in the traits that are necessary for effective leadership. A good leader in an American company may not have the traits needed to be successful in, say, a Chinese corporation.

Although the trait theory has its problems, it can't be denied that leaders exhibit traits that followers admire. The systematic study of the personal characteristics and traits of leaders began as a consequence of the need for military officers during World War I. Many business and governmental organizations also began researching the characteristics that distinguished their most effective managers from the less effective managers. The studies that attempt to identify these traits have produced a lengthy list. They are grouped into six categories:

1. *Physical traits*—age, height, weight.
2. *Background characteristics*—education, social class or status, mobility, experience.
3. *Intelligence*—ability, judgment, knowledge.
4. *Personality*—aggressiveness, alertness, dominance, decisiveness, enthusiasm, extroversion, independence, self-confidence, authoritarianism.
5. *Task-related characteristics*—achievement need, responsibility, initiative, persistence.
6. *Social characteristics*—supervisory ability, cooperativeness, popularity, prestige, tact, diplomacy.

Even today, some executives involved in the recruitment and selection of managers believe that the trait theory is valid. However, the comparison of leaders by various physical, personality, and intelligence traits has resulted in little agreement.[16] Similarly, many scholars used to think that entrepreneurs had certain traits in common. As with leadership, it has been exceedingly difficult to pin down any so-called traits that all entrepreneurs share.[17]

11-5a Physical Traits

Some advocates of the trait theory contend that the physical characteristics of a person affect ability to influence followers. For example, an extensive review of twelve leadership investigations showed that nine of the studies found leaders to be taller than followers; two found them to be shorter; and one concluded that height was not the most important factor.[18] Other physical traits that have been studied with no conclusive results include weight, physique, and personal appearance. One physical characteristic that consistently has been associated with leadership is "energy level." Sustained high achievement requires physical stamina, and research has shown that good leaders typically have high energy levels and an ability to tolerate stress.[19]

11-5b Personality

A number of studies have found several personality factors to be related in some, but not all, cases of effective leadership.[20] These studies have found that leaders with the drive to act independently and with self-assurance (e.g., with confidence in their leadership skills) are successful in achieving task and group performance. Research suggests that leadership in the modern workplace requires intelligence, common sense, high energy levels, a willingness to work hard, and good timing.[21] Further, leadership scholar Max DePree lists twelve attributes of successful leadership:[22]

Management Focus on Ethics

Why Should Leaders Be Ethical?

Where the general manager/chief executive officer is clearly supportive and models ethical behavior, a positive culture will permeate the whole organization. General managers, CEOs, and other senior managers must give strong messages about ethical behavior. Positive and effective messages provide the foundation on which to build a culture of proper, ethical behavior.

How do leaders establish ethical behavior? First, they have to establish some things that they believe in—based on their knowledge, education, experience, and background. To be consistent and strong, leaders have to be guided by their basic beliefs. Then they take their beliefs and mold them into a way of being effective, a style of leading, a way of showing that "here's what I believe in" and "here's why" and "here's how we can make progress by living this way." Then, leaders need to work closely with the people around them, persuade them, lead them. That's what leaders are for—to have ideas and to sell those ideas, to listen, and to get people to move with them. So, first leaders have to believe, then they have to find a way to be effective, and then they have to work with people to cause them to join with the leader in doing what they're doing.

Sources: Craig Thomas, "The Ethical Leader," *Executive Excellence,* May 2001, p. 15; and Robert Ball, "Practical Difficulties with Ethics," *Public Management,* April 2001, pp. 3–4.

1. Integrity
2. Vulnerability
3. Discernment
4. Awareness of the human spirit
5. Courage in relationships
6. Sense of humor
7. Intellectual energy and curiosity
8. Respect for the future, regard for the present, understanding of the past
9. Predictability
10. Breadth
11. Comfort with ambiguity
12. Presence

In fact, there may be as many personality attributes of leaders as there are scholars of the topic. Nonetheless, you can probably find some similarity across the different lists. Common themes that seem to emerge include: intelligence, curiosity, empathy, and high energy.[23] Another leadership factor that has been the subject of much study over the recent past is ethics. The Management Focus on Ethics box, "Why Should Leaders Be Ethical?," discusses how the ethics of leaders influences the culture of the organization.

11-5c Intelligence

After surveying the literature, one scholar concluded that leadership ability is associated with the judgment and verbal facility of the person.[24] Another researcher concluded that within a certain range, one's intelligence is an accurate predictor of managerial success.[25] Above and below this range, the chances of successful leadership decrease significantly. However, the leader's intelligence should be close to that of the followers. The leader who is too smart or not smart enough may lose the followers' respect.

Warren Bennis, a scholar of leadership, has argued that leaders of the future will need very high IQs to deal with increasingly complex organizations. He said, "The basis for effective leadership in the future will be the cognitive capacity to deal with complex issues. I think that by 2020 we will see chairs of neuroscience in business schools to deal with these issues." Bennis still believes that leaders are made rather than born. However, "We must make people brainier and we really need to rethink how we educate people to go into business."[26]

11-5d Emotional Intelligence

Daniel Goleman and his colleagues have done extensive research into the effects of emotions on leadership behavior.[27] In particular, these researchers have examined the extent to which a person's knowledge of their own and others' emotions enables then to be more effective managers and leaders. Their claims are emphatic: "A leader's premier task—we could even say his primal task—is emotional leadership." The researchers are emphatic in asserting that when they talk about emotional intelligence they are not just talking about "touchy-feely" stuff. They state: "Managing for financial results begins with the leader managing his inner life so that the right emotional and behavioral chain reaction occurs."[28] The authors suggest that a person's emotional intelligence may be at least partially genetically determined. They state that a person's emotional skills are not "genetically hardwired" like eye color or skin tone, but they do have a "genetic component." They present a five-step program for people—of all ages—to improve their emotional skills:

1. Decide who you want to be.
2. Determine who you are now.
3. Develop a path from where you are to where you want to be.
4. Determine how to make changes permanent.
5. Find out who can help you get where you want to go.

11-5e Ghiselli's Leadership Trait Studies

Edwin E. Ghiselli, an important scholar of leadership, has studied eight personality traits and five motivational traits.[29] Ghiselli's research findings suggest the relative importance of the traits as noted in Figure 11-2.

Figure 11-2
The Relative Importance of Leader Characteristics and Effective Leadership

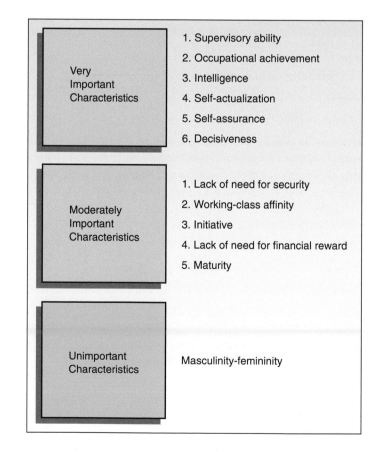

11-5f Charismatic Leadership

Another trait that is often associated with leadership is "charisma." Warren Buffett at *Berkshire Hathaway*, Steve Ballmer of *Microsoft*, and Donald Trump are examples of leaders with charisma. A charismatic leader is a person who by force of personal abilities and style is capable of having a profound and extraordinary effect on followers.[30] The **charismatic leadership** view combines both traits and behaviors to describe this type of leader.

What Buffett, Ballmer, and Trump are able to do because of their energy, self-confidence, and dominating personalities is to project a conviction in the moral rightness of their beliefs.[31] Charismatic leaders generate excitement and increase the expectations of followers through their visions of the future. Research suggests that charismatic leadership is a function of what followers perceive. Some fortunate individuals are born with this gift, but most charismatic leaders apparently learn it and use it with great success.[32]

Some theorists propose that charisma is distributed throughout the organization. We usually only read about world-class leaders.[33] However, there are executives, middle-level managers, salespersons, and truck drivers who possess charisma. In management it is difficult to be a successor to a charismatic leader. Through interviews with ninety reputedly charismatic leaders, researchers identified a set of behavior strategies used by these individuals as follows:

1. *Focusing attention* on specific issues of concern, concentrating on analysis, problem solving, and action.
2. *Communicating* with empathy and sensitivity.
3. *Demonstrating consistency* and trustworthiness by one's behavior, being honest, sticking with a decision, and following through on decisions.
4. *Expressing active concern for people* including one's self, thus modeling self-regard, and reinforcing feelings of self-worth in others.[34]

Notice that the first two behaviors are task oriented and the latter two are people oriented. Others have developed a matrix of five characteristics of charismatic leaders:

1. Strategic vision and articulation
2. Sensitivity to the environment
3. Unconventional behavior
4. Personal risk
5. Sensitivity to other's needs

These five factors are good predictors of whether people consider a leader charismatic or noncharismatic. Their presence in a leader is significantly associated with the perception that that leader is charismatic.[35] One leader who had all of the five characteristics was Robert Wood Johnson, founder and longtime chairman of *Johnson & Johnson.* Johnson knew that the core advantage of his company was the creativity and innovation of his people. The Management Focus on Innovation box, "Johnson & Johnson Leadership Emphasizes Innovation," highlights the Johnson & Johnson culture of innovation.

Much more theoretical work and research is needed to explore a more complete picture of charismatic leadership behaviors and traits, but the initial set of findings is interesting.[36] The initial findings also indicate that charismatic leaders are not all born, which suggests that individuals may be trained or developed in management programs to use charismatic leadership behaviors.

11-6 Behavioral Theory of Leadership

The disappointing results of the search for leadership traits have led to a somewhat different line of thought. Rather than focusing on the *characteristics* of effective leaders, an alternative is to focus on their **behavior.** The question of behavioral leadership theories then becomes: What do effective leaders *do* that ineffective ones *do not do?* For example, are effective leaders democratic rather than autocratic, permissive rather than directive, person-oriented rather than task-oriented? Or are effective leaders characterized by some

▶ **charismatic leadership**
Charismatic leaders generate excitement and increase the expectations of followers through their visions of the future.

▶ **behavior** Any observable response given by a person.

Management Focus on Innovation

Johnson & Johnson Leadership Emphasizes Innovation

To say the least, Johnson & Johnson company chairman Robert Wood Johnson was ahead of his time when he wrote the Company Credo in the 1940s. The Credo took the unusual step of declaring that the organization's primary responsibility was to "the doctors, nurses, and patients . . . mother and fathers and all others who use our products and services." This customer-driven focus had been the basis of J&J's success to that point, and it continues to pervade the company today, serving as common ground for the organization's 170 operating companies. J&J's business today is driven by three basic commitments:

1. Commitment to the Credo
2. Commitment to decentralized management
3. Commitment to the long term

Within the Credo's framework—and in some ways because of it—J&J constantly emphasizes innovation, often measuring its success by the percentage of sales from products introduced in the last five years. In the 1980s, this percentage was around 30 percent. Today, it is close to 35 percent. As a result of this high level of innovation, the organization has increased its sales by more than $3 billion and added over 8,000 new employees since 1995.

Sources: Robert M. Fulmer, "Frameworks for Leadership," *Organizational Dynamics,* March 2001, pp. 211–220; and Robert M. Fulmer, Philip A. Gibbs, and Marshall Goldsmith, "Developing Leaders: How Winning Companies Keep on Winning," *Sloan Management Review,* Fall 2000, pp. 49–59.

---

balance of these behaviors? This line of questioning is based on the reasoning shown in Figure 11-3.

Terms such as *permissive-directive, democratic-autocratic,* and *person-oriented-task-oriented* are nearly synonymous. Generally, these terms refer to whether the leader's behavior reflects *primary* concern for the work or for the people who are doing the work. We noted earlier that the essence of leadership is getting work done through others. One point of view holds that the best way to lead is to be task-oriented.

11-6a Task-Oriented Leadership

Scientific management techniques such as time and motion study, work simplification, and piece-rate incentive pay plans emphasize the need for leaders to plan each worker's job tasks and job outcomes. The leader is assumed to be the most competent individual in planning and organizing the work of subordinates. According to a major proponent of scientific management:

> The work for every workman is fully planned out by the management at least one day in advance, and each man receives . . . complete written instructions, describing in detail the task which he is to accomplish, as well as the means to be used in doing the work.[37]

To ensure that each task is performed according to the plan, the worker is paid on an incentive basis. The performance standards are stated in terms of quantity and quality of output, and the worker is paid for each unit of acceptable quality.

The terms used to refer to leader behaviors that are concerned primarily with task-oriented leadership include directive, production-oriented, autocratic, and initiating structure. Each of these terms is used in contemporary management and leadership liter-

Figure 11-3
Behavior of Effective Leaders

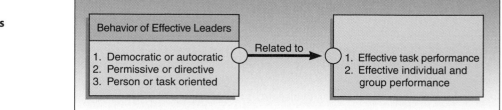

ature. Although the origins of task-oriented leadership can be found in literature first published some seventy years ago, some modern leaders still believe that task-oriented behavior is the most effective for obtaining performance. At the same time, an emerging perspective that has gained wide influence is person-oriented leadership.

11-6b Person-Oriented Leadership

Rensis Likert is a pioneer in the development of the idea that the behaviors of the most effective leaders are person-oriented. Likert and his associates at the *University of Michigan* have conducted studies in various organizational settings such as industrial, governmental, educational, and health care. These studies have led Likert to conclude that the most effective leaders focus on the human aspects of their groups. They attempt to build effective teamwork through supportive, considerate, and nonpunitive *employee-centered* behavior. Such leaders were found to be more effective than those who emphasized *task-centered* behavior; that is, leaders who specifically detailed the work of subordinates, closely supervised them, and rewarded them only with financial incentives.[38]

The concept that people seek a wide array of satisfactions through work is at the core of many management practices. It is not surprising that it should also be the underpinning of a popular point of view regarding leadership.

Thus, it would seem that we are left with the choice that the effective leader is *either* task-oriented *or* person-oriented, *but not both*. And if this is the case, then aspiring leaders need only a narrow range of skills. If the most effective leaders are task-oriented, then leaders need only be skilled in the technical aspects of planning and organizing the work of others. But if the most effective leaders are person-oriented, then human relations and interpersonal skills are required. But what if both points of view are correct? Some believe that effective leaders are equally task- and person-oriented in their behavior toward subordinates.

11-6c Combining Task- and Person-Oriented Leadership

The idea that the one best way to lead effectively requires a balance between task- and person-oriented behavior has considerable appeal. Two approaches to studying this idea have become well known in the theory and practice of leadership:

1. Two-Dimensional Theory
2. Managerial Grid Theory

Two-Dimensional Theory   One of the most significant investigations of leadership began immediately after World War II at Ohio State University. The researchers associated with this program have produced many studies of leadership effectiveness. The two key concepts in the two-dimensional theory are **initiating structure** and **consideration.** Initiating structure refers to task-oriented behavior in which the leader organizes and defines the relationships in the group, establishes patterns and channels of communications, and directs the work methods. Consideration refers to person-oriented behavior in which the leader exhibits friendship, trust, respect, and warmth toward subordinates.

Generally, the behaviors of leaders who emphasize initiating structure fall into a consistent pattern. They tend to insist that subordinates follow rigid structures in work methods; they insist on being informed; they push their subordinates for greater effort; they decide in detail what shall be done and how it shall be done. Considerate leaders express appreciation for jobs well done, stress the importance of high morale, treat everyone as equals, and are friendly and approachable. The difference between managers high on initiating structure and high on consideration is displayed in Figure 11-4.

One study of the relationship between initiating structure and consideration and leadership effectiveness focused on first-level management—supervisors in a manufacturing facility. The measures of leadership effectiveness included proficiency ratings made by top management, absenteeism, accident rates, grievances, and turnover. The study found that supervisors of line departments (production) scored high on proficiency ratings if they

▶ **initiating structure**
Leadership acts that develop job tasks and responsibilities for followers.

▶ **consideration** Behaviors by a leader that imply supportive concern for the followers in a group.

Figure 11-4
Two-Dimensional Leadership Theory

Initiating Structure	Consideration
• Insist on rigid work methods.	• Express appreciation for job well done.
• Insist on being informed.	• Stress importance of high morale.
• Push subordinates for increased effort.	• Treat all employees as equals.
• Decide in detail on what to do and how to do it.	• Be friendly and approachable.

also scored high on initiating structure and low on consideration. However, supervisors of staff departments were most proficient when they scored low on initiating structure and high on consideration. Subsequent studies tended to conclude that supervisors who score high on both dimensions generally are more effective than those who score low.[39]

Managerial Grid Theory   One highly publicized leadership behavior model, developed by Robert Blake and Jane Mouton, is called the **managerial grid.** According to the proponents of this theory, leaders are most effective when they achieve a high and balanced concern for both people *and* task.[40] This idea is shown in Figure 11-5. Each leader, according to the model, can be rated somewhere along each of the axes from 1 to 9 depending on his or her orientation.

Although there are eighty-one possible positions in the grid, attention is drawn to five of them:

managerial grid A highly publicized leadership behavior model developed by Blank and Mouton that considers leaders as most effective when they achieve a high and balanced concern for both people and task.

1. *The 9, 1 leader* is primarily concerned for production and only minimally concerned for people. This type of leader, categorized under the term *task management,* believes that the primary leadership responsibility is to see that the work is completed.

2. *The 1, 9 leader* is primarily concerned for people and only incidentally concerned for production. This leader, who practices *country club management,* believes that a supervisor's major responsibility is to establish harmonious relationships among subordinates and to provide a secure and pleasant work atmosphere.

3. *The 1, 1 leader,* under the classification of *impoverished management,* is concerned neither for production nor people. This leader would attempt to stay out of the way and not become involved in the conflict between the necessity for production and the attainment of good working relationships.

4. *The 5, 5 leader* reflects a middle-ground position and thus practices *middle-of-the-road management.* A leader so described would seek to compromise between high production and employee satisfaction.

5. *The 9, 9 leader's* behavior is the most effective—it is the one best way. This style, termed *team management,* is practiced by leaders who achieve high production through the effective use of participation and involvement of people and their ideas.

The managerial grid is used to assess the actual leadership styles of men and women prior to training. An important assumption of this approach is that people can be trained to become 9, 9 leaders. Thus a 1, 9 or a 9, 1 leader can change and become more effective by learning the behaviors associated with 9, 9 leadership.

The significant contribution of the two-dimensional and managerial grid theories is that they force us to seek more complete answers to the question "What is effective leadership?"

The study of leadership behavior is a step in the direction of determining what leaders actually do in their leadership roles. However, most behavior-based explanations of leadership fail to specify how a follower's behavior affects a leader.[41] For example, a hard-

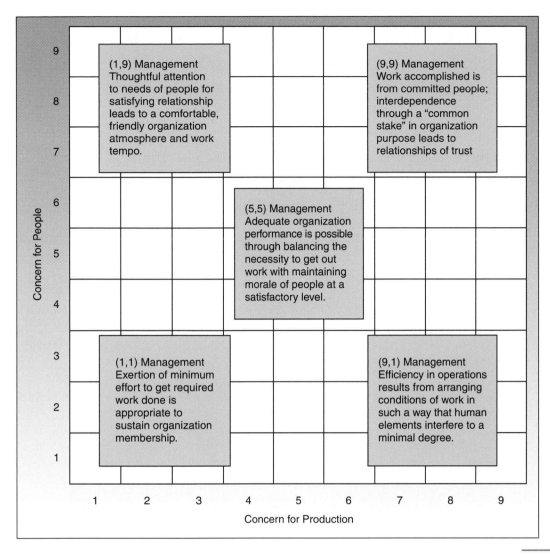

Figure 11-5
The Managerial Grid

Source: From *The Managerial Grid*
by Robert R. Blake and Jane S. Mouton.

working, productive computer programmer may cause her supervisor to be supportive or people-oriented, rather than the other way around. Perhaps the interaction between leaders and followers is more important than influence attempts initiated by the leader.

Another weakness in the behavior-based explanations is the failure to include an analysis of the situation in which the leader must perform. Like the trait explanation, the behavior models neglect the type of situation—routine, crisis, novel. What is good leadership behavior in a hostile merger situation may be far from ideal in a situation that requires teamwork to beat back a main competitor in the marketplace.

11-7 Contingency Theory of Leadership

An increasing number of researchers are prone to believe that the practice of leadership is too complex to be represented by unique traits or behaviors. Rather, a current idea is that effective leadership behavior is contingent upon the situation. But even this idea is not now fully settled. One variation of the idea assumes that leaders must change behaviors to meet situational needs. A second variation assumes that leaders' behaviors are difficult to alter and that the situation itself must be changed to make it compatible with the leaders' behavior.

The contingency theory of leadership is considerably more complex than either the trait or the behavioral approach. As indicated in Figure 11-6, effective leadership depends on the interaction of the leader's personal characteristics, the leader's behavior, and factors in the leadership situation. In a sense, the situational approach is based on the idea that effective leadership cannot be defined by any one factor. This approach does not deny the

Figure 11-6
The Situational Approach to Effective Leadership

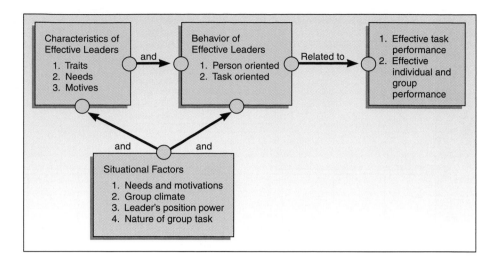

importance of the leader's characteristics or behavior. Rather, it states that *both* must be considered in the context of the situation.

11-7a Leadership Flexibility: Fit the Style to the Situation

A recurring theme in leadership theory and practice is the concept of *participation* by subordinates in decision making. This theme originated in the writings of the behavioral approach to management, and it has held a prominent place in the thinking of managers for the last forty years. The fundamental idea is shown in Figure 11-7.[42]

At the extremes of this continuum are boss-centered leadership and subordinate-centered leadership. Between these extremes are five points representing various combinations of managerial authority and subordinate freedom. One of the extreme positions, boss-centered leadership, represents a manager who simply makes a decision and announces it. The subordinate-centered leader permits subordinates to participate fully in decision making. Within prescribed limits, the subordinates act as partners with the leader.

The proponents of participative management believe that the difficulty is not so much in convincing people that they must change their behavior as the situation changes, but in teaching leaders how to recognize the need for the change. A number of guidelines have been proposed to help leaders identify situations that lend themselves to participative decision making.

Whether a leader should make the decision and announce it (boss-centered) or share the problem with subordinates and seek group consensus (subordinate-centered) depends on the interaction of factors related to the problem and to the subordinates. Factors related to the *problem* are:[43]

1. The likelihood that one solution to the problem is more effective than another.
2. The extent to which the leader has sufficient information to make a high-quality decision.
3. The extent to which alternative solutions are known with some certainty.

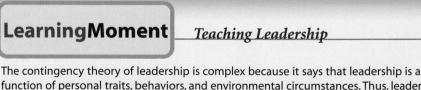

LearningMoment   *Teaching Leadership*

The contingency theory of leadership is complex because it says that leadership is a function of personal traits, behaviors, and environmental circumstances. Thus, leadership is something that may emerge in anyone under the appropriate circumstances. What implications does this theory have on the teaching of leadership? Can people be taught to be leaders even though much of the environment in which they find themselves is beyond their control?

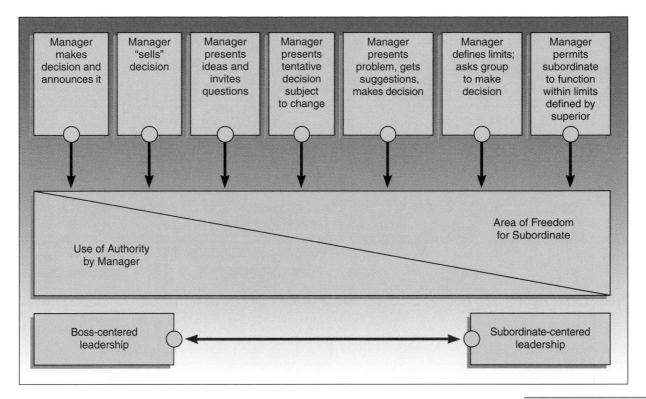

Figure 11-7
Continuum of Leadership Behavior

Factors related to *subordinates* are:

1. The likelihood that effective implementation of the solution depends on subordinates accepting it as appropriate.

2. The likelihood that if the leader makes the decision, the subordinates will accept it.

3. The extent to which subordinates recognize and accept the organizational objectives to be attained by the solution.

4. The likelihood that conflict among subordinates will result if the preferred solution is adopted.

In a practical sense, combining these seven factors creates different situations. At one extreme are situations for which a number of solutions exist, none of which require acceptance by subordinates for effective implementation. The manager should make the decision and announce it. On the other hand, participation is warranted to the extent that only one solution is likely and its consequences are not known with certainty *and* subordinates have relevant information *and* their acceptance is necessary for implementation. The effective leader changes style whenever the situation demands it. That is, the leader is flexible enough to be relatively task-centered or employee-centered as situations change.

Contingency theory also suggests that leadership style should be matched to the strategic choices available in the firm's competitive environment. Research has indicated that senior executives who align their strategic choices to the competitive environment are more successful than those who cling to a single strategic direction.[44]

11-7b Leadership Flexibility: Fit the Style to the Maturity Level of Followers

Paul Hersey and Kenneth H. Blanchard have developed a situational theory of leadership. They call it the **life cycle theory**.[45] This explanation is based on the belief that the most effective leadership style varies with the maturity of followers. *Maturity* is viewed as consisting of two components—job-related maturity and psychological maturity. Job-related maturity refers to the ability to perform a task. Psychological maturity refers to a person's willingness to perform a job. Four distinct levels of maturity exist:

▶ **life cycle theory** A theory of leadership that suggests that leaders must adjust their leadership style based on the maturity of those being led. In this case, "maturity" refers to the followers' ability to perform the assigned tasks.

M1: Person is unwilling and unable to perform the job

M2: Person is unable but willing to perform the job

M3: Person is able but unwilling to perform the job

M4: Person is able and willing to perform the job

The life cycle theory suggests that as the individual matures from M1 to M4, the leadership style must change to fit that changing maturity level. Hersey and Blanchard identified four leadership styles:

S1: Telling—the leader has to tell the employee what to do in great detail

S2: Selling—the leader has to sell the employee on the value of the task

S3: Participating—the leader participates in the task with the employee

S4: Delegating—the leader fully delegates the task to the employee

Figure 11-8 shows how these maturity levels and leadership styles interact. As you can see, the leader shifts his or her style to match the maturity level of the employee in a seamless fashion.

There are some exceptions to the life cycle theory. For example, when faced with a crisis situation involving filling an important order, a leader may find it necessary to be very

Figure 11-8
Situational Leadership

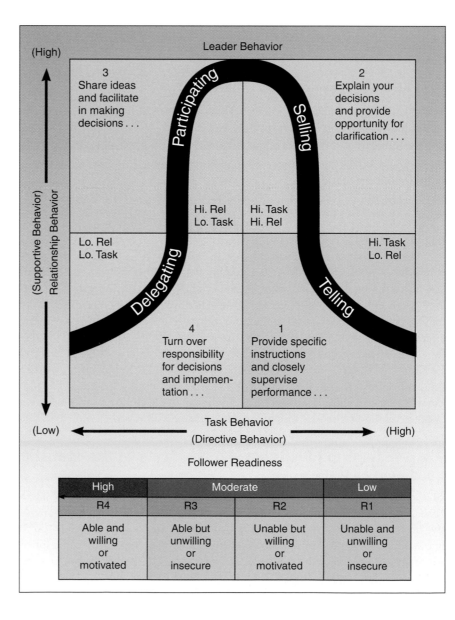

task-oriented (e.g., use telling style [S1] even when the followers are very mature [M4]). However, using the high task-low relationship leadership style over an extended period of time will likely result in a backlash from the followers. A mature follower wants to be treated in a particular way.

The life cycle theory has intuitive appeal. However, the theory assumes that leaders are perceptive enough to accurately pinpoint maturity levels. The theory also assumes that followers will agree with a leader's assessment of their maturity level. Using the parent-child example, we know how much disagreement can occur in determining maturity levels.

Also, the life cycle theory assumes that a leader is flexible enough to move through four phases or back and forth. Is this amount of flexibility possible? Hersey and Blanchard think so, but research evidence to support their views is quite limited. In fact, the validity of measurement instruments and the relationship of the model to performance has not been carefully investigated by independent researchers.

Despite some shortcomings, the life cycle theory has generated interest among practicing managers. It calls attention to the need to be flexible. Leadership is, after all, a dynamic process that requires flexibility. Also, the life cycle theory illustrates the interactive nature of leadership. That is, a leader can influence followers, but followers, because of their maturity level, can also influence leadership behavior.

11-7c Leadership Inflexibility: Fit the Situation to the Leader's Style

Using a considerable body of research evidence, Fred E. Fiedler has developed an important contribution to the situational theory of leadership.[46] He identifies three important situational factors or dimensions that he believes influence the leader's effectiveness. The dimensions are the following:

1. **Leader-member relations** This refers to the degree of confidence the subordinates have in the leader. It also includes the loyalty shown to the leader and the leader's attractiveness.

2. **Task structure** This refers to the degree to which the subordinates' jobs are routine rather than nonroutine.

3. **Position power** This refers to the power inherent in the leadership position. It includes the rewards and punishments typically associated with the position, the leader's official authority (based on ranking in the managerial hierarchy), and the support that the leader receives from superiors and the overall organization.

Fiedler has obtained data that relate leadership style to the three-dimensional measures of different situations. Fiedler's measure of leadership style distinguishes between leaders who tend to be permissive and considerate and foster good interpersonal relations among group members and leaders who tend to be directive, controlling, and more oriented toward task than people. Fiedler suggests that leaders who are directive and leaders who are permissive can function best in certain types of situations. Instead of stating that a leader must adopt this or that style, Fiedler identifies the type of leader who functions best in a given situation. According to Fiedler, we should not talk simply about good leaders or poor leaders. A leader who achieves effectiveness in one situation may not be effective in another. The implication of this logic is that managers should think about the situation in which a particular leader (subordinate manager) performs well or badly. Fiedler assumes that managers can enhance subordinates' effectiveness if they carefully choose situations that are favorable to the subordinates' styles.[47]

Fiedler's "fit of the leader to the situation" approach is known as **Fiedler's LPC theory.** This nomenclature is due to the fact that Fiedler measured a leader's style using an instrument that identified the leader's least preferred coworker (LPC). The LPC measures the leader's behavioral style in terms of task orientation and people orientation. With this measure, a leader who identified his LPC in terms critical of the worker's task initiative and accomplishment was described as task-oriented. If the leader identified the LPC in relatively positive terms (that is, the leader preferred not to work with this person but found little to criticize), the leader was described as people-oriented.

leader-member relations A factor in the Fiedler situational model of leadership that refers to the degree of confidence, trust, and respect that followers have in the leader.

task structure Refers to the degree of routineness found in a job; a highly routine job is said to have high task structure.

position power A factor in the Fiedler situational model of leadership that refers to the power inherent in the leadership position.

Fiedler's LPC theory A leadership theory that fits the leader to the situation; uses an instrument to identify the leader's least preferred coworker (LPC).

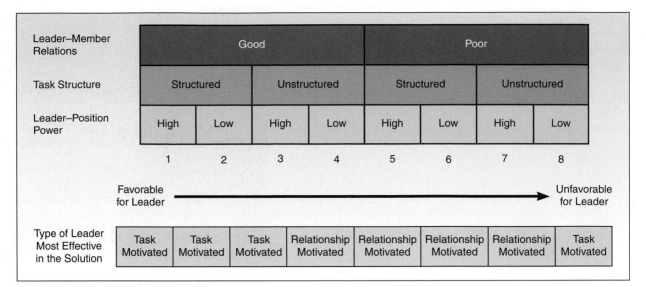

Leader–Member Relations	Good				Poor			
Task Structure	Structured		Unstructured		Structured		Unstructured	
Leader–Position Power	High	Low	High	Low	High	Low	High	Low
	1	2	3	4	5	6	7	8

Favorable for Leader →————————————————————————→ Unfavorable for Leader

Type of Leader Most Effective in the Solution	Task Motivated	Task Motivated	Task Motivated	Relationship Motivated	Relationship Motivated	Relationship Motivated	Relationship Motivated	Task Motivated

Figure 11-9
Fiedler's Analysis of Situations in Which the Task- or Relationship-Motivated Leader Is More Effective

Fiedler found that, for particularly difficult work conditions (poor relationships with workers, little power over workers, and an unstructured task) or relatively undemanding work situations (good relationships with workers, high power over workers, and a clearly structured task), the effective leader needed to be task-oriented. In mixed (not easy, not difficult) situations, a people-oriented style worked best. These relationships are illustrated in Figure 11-9.

Although Fiedler and associates cite extensive research to support the theory, critics suggest that the theory has measurement problems and that a limited number of situational variables are incorporated. The measures Fiedler uses to assess a person's preferred leadership style are claimed to be unreliable and unstable. There is also the criticism that the theory fails to specify what an effective leader actually does in various situations.[48]

11-7d Path-Goal Theory of Leadership

House and Mitchell's path-goal leadership theory is based on the expectancy theory of motivation.[49] The role of the leader in this theory is twofold:

1. Clarify for the follower the path by which an individual can achieve personal goal and organizational outcomes; and
2. Increase rewards that are valued by the follower.

In a sense, the leader facilitates organizational learning by helping followers better understand how their actions are linked to organizational rewards. Effective leaders help workers engage in behaviors that lead to rewards they value. Path-goal theory identifies four types of leader behaviors:

1. *Directive Behaviors* The leader makes task expectations clear by setting goals, structuring work flow, and providing feedback through regular performance appraisals. This is similar to the "initiating structure" behavior examined earlier.
2. *Supportive Behaviors* The leader demonstrates concern for the worker and, when problems occur, is ready to offer advice. These behaviors are similar to the "consideration" behaviors examined earlier.
3. *Participative Behaviors* The participative leader actively seeks ideas and information from workers. Participative behavior implies that workers participate in decisions that affect them and their work.
4. *Achievement Behaviors* Achievement leadership translates into setting expectations and task goals at a high level. This involves making the job challenging but not impossible to accomplish.

These four behaviors form a repertoire of actions a leader might exhibit under different work situations. The theory also suggests that the leader has the ability to increase rewards valued by workers.

Path-goal theory prescribes which leader behaviors are likely to be effective under different situational constraints. Leaders are expected to change their behavior as the situation warrants. This theory views leadership as the vital link between the organization and the individual worker. Leaders need to motivate workers to understand how their work efforts are tied to valued salary increases, promotions, praise, recognition, and respect.

Some pragmatic procedures for improving a leader's relations, task structure, and position power are as follows:

- Leader-member relations could be improved by restructuring the leader's group of subordinates so that the group is more compatible in terms of background, educational level, technical expertise, or ethnic origin.

- The task structure can be modified either in the structured or the nonstructured direction. A task can be made more structured by spelling out the jobs in greater detail. A task can be made less structured by providing only general directions for the work that is to be accomplished.

- Leader position power can be modified in a number of ways. A leader can be given a higher rank in the organization or more authority to do the job. In addition, a leader's reward power can be increased if the organization delegates authority to evaluate the performance of subordinates.

11-8 Modern Views of Leadership

The study of leadership will probably never end. The topic is important enough that managers and executives—and others—will seek out new insights and understandings of this elusive human quality. Today, thinkers with a wide variety of intellectual backgrounds are offering their perspectives on leadership. Stephen R. Covey is best known for his book *The 7 Habits of Highly Effective People.*[50] In that book, Covey identified seven habits that his research indicated are critical to being an effective person at work, at home, and in other walks of life. The seven habits he defined are:

1. *Be Proactive:* Being proactive means more than taking initiative—it means begin responsible for your own life.
2. *Begin with the End in Mind:* Begin each day with the image of the end of your life as your frame of reference or criterion by which everything else is examined.
3. *Put First Things First:* This is the day-to-day enactment of the first two habits; it is the day-to-day and moment-to-moment task of effective self-management.
4. *Think Win/Win:* Win/win is a frame of mind that constantly seeks mutual benefit in all human interactions.
5. *Seek First to Understand, Then to Be Understood:* In order to effectively interact with other people, you must first listen to and understand them.
6. *Synergize:* This term refers to the concept of "creative cooperation"—the effort to make more out of social relationships than appears to be available.
7. *Sharpen the Saw:* This habit refers to the need to rejuvenate and revitalize on a regular basis.

Covey has now recently extended his list of habits with a new book called *The Eighth Habit: From Effectiveness to Greatness.*[51] In this book, Covey says the eighth habit has been necessitated by the onset of the knowledge revolution, the Internet, and the rise of the so-called knowledge worker. According to Covey, the eighth habit is "Find Your Voice and Inspire Others to Find Theirs." This is based on the belief that today's knowledge workers seek more from their work than previous generations. They not only seek meaningful employment—they want that meaning to express their own talents and value systems.

In contrast to Covey, Warren Bennis of the *University of Southern California* centers his work on leadership in the characteristics and behaviors of actual living leaders. One of his more popular books, *On Becoming a Leader,*[52] focused on individuals such as *A&M Record Company* owner Herb Alpert; Betty Friedan, cofounder of the *National Organization of Women;* Norman Lear, television producer; Sydney Pollack, Oscar-winning motion-picture director; and Larry Wilson, founder of *Wilson Learning Corporation.* Bennis writes in a more down-to-earth style than Covey. He doesn't purport to uncover any natural or universal laws but focuses on what leaders actually do.

Bennis and Covey are similar, however, in creating popular books about leadership that are not based on rigorous research. One of the more thoroughly researched works on leadership in the last forty years is by Michael D. Cohen and James G. March. Their work resulted in a book titled *Leadership and Ambiguity.*[53] The book is not as popular as Covey's or Bennis's, largely because it is full of inscrutable mathematics and graphs. Nonetheless, Cohen and March's work has been widely hailed for its rigor and comprehensiveness. They developed a set of new metaphors that describe organizations as "organized anarchy" and decision situations as "garbage cans." In essence, they state, a leader navigates the organized anarchy by applying a light touch.

Leaders recognize that most decision situations are like garbage cans in that they allow people who have a favorite theory or idea to bring them out in decision situations. Thus, don't be surprised to find the IT manager suggesting an IT solution to every problem, or the HRM managers suggesting an HR solution to every problem. The effective leader allows individuals to bring their ideas to decision situations, but then is unafraid to choose an alternative that seems best given the organization's goals.

Several theorists use the term *transformational leadership* to describe an inspirational form of leader behavior based on modifying followers' beliefs, values, and ultimately their behavior. In contrast, transactional leadership is more closely related to both behavioral and situational leader behaviors. Transactional leaders appeal to workers' rational exchange motives. Workers exchange labor for wages. Leaders help clarify the path from effort to reward. For the worker, this is a form of self-interested exchange—do this and you get rewarded. For the leader, it is a process of keeping workers loyal to organizational goals.

Another currently popular view of leadership is that organizations can make the most effective use of leadership when it's developed throughout the organization. This view is especially important in the post-downsizing era when many layers of middle management have been slashed from the organizational chart. Those who remain must accept new leadership responsibilities as the global economy continues to put new competitive pressures on organizations. The Management Focus on Globalization box, "Wal-Mart Focuses on Developing International Leaders," examines how Wal-Mart empowers individual managers for overseas assignments.

Whatever view of leadership you think is best, there is no shortage of texts on the topic. As in all things, no view is probably completely "correct." Your best bet as you search through some of this literature on your own is to use what works from each thinker. In time, you may have enough leadership experience of your own to pen a book on the topic yourself.

LearningMoment *The Organized Anarchy*

Cohen and March describe organizations as "organized anarchies." This term is used to remind managers and leaders that perfect or complete control of the organization is not possible. Discuss how this idea fits with modern concepts of "employee empowerment" and "boundaryless organizations."

Management Focus on Globalization

Wal-Mart Focuses on Developing International Leaders

Wal-Mart's strong financial position and the availability of acquisition candidates assure its ability to expand globally. But that's only one part of the equation. The other key element for expansion—and one that has been seen as a limiting factor in the past—is the preparedness of Wal-Mart's people to take on the challenge of entering new countries. When Wal-Mart enters a new country, it has an individual ready for the top leadership position as a result of a program called Accelerated International Management. Wal-Mart identifies people that have the potential and desire to be country presidents.

CEO John Menzer, along with COO Craig Herkert and other top international executives, have made people development a top priority for good reason. Attracting, retaining, and developing quality people is one of the greatest challenges any rapidly expanding organization faces, and it is especially true for

Wal-Mart given its international growth plans. The company's track record has been to enter a new market every year or every other year, so entry into another new market is inevitable because it has been about two years since Wal-Mart entered the United Kingdom by acquiring ASDA.

Another key initiative is the International Leadership Development program. It involves people from various countries working in other countries to expose them to new ideas, while they provide the host country with their skills. There are twenty-five Wal-Mart de Mexico associates, for example, working in U.S. stores, while there are seventeen U.S. associates working at ASDA.

Source: Adapted from "People Power Bridges Operations from Bentonville to Beijing," *DSN Retailing Today,* June 5, 2001, p. 9.

Management Summary

- Leadership is the ability to influence followers toward the accomplishment of worthwhile, meaningful, and challenging goals.

- The trait approach to leadership relates personal characteristics and effective leadership. Despite much study and effort, no conclusive results are available to guide managers in selecting future leaders.

- The idea that effective leaders behave differently from ineffective leaders has led to inconclusive results. An important issue is whether an individual can shift between person-oriented behavior and task-oriented behavior.

- More attention is being paid to the charismatic leader or those individuals who, because of their energy, self-confidence, and dominating personality, project a conviction in the moral rightness of their beliefs.

- The situational approaches to leadership are more complex than the trait and behavior approaches. The complexity arises from the necessity to consider the interactions of the leader, behavior, and situation.

- The situational approaches are based on two different assumptions about leadership flexibility. One approach assumes that leaders can and must change their behavior to fit the situation. The other assumes that leaders cannot change their behavior but must change the situation.

- The most important conclusion to be made from leadership theory is that managers must understand their own abilities and their impact on others.

Key Terms

behavior (p. 259)
behavioral theory of leadership (p. 255)
charismatic leadership (p. 259)
consideration (p. 261)
contingency theory of leadership (p. 255)
Fiedler's LPC theory (p. 267)

formal leaders (p. 252)
informal leaders (p. 252)
initiating structure (p. 261)
leader-member relations (p. 267)
leadership (p. 253)
Level Five Leadership (p. 255)

life cycle theory (p. 265)
managerial grid (p. 262)
position power (p. 267)
task structure (p. 267)
trait theory of leadership (p. 255)

Review and Discussion Questions

1. Do you believe that a manager can be effective if she is not considered by subordinates to be a leader? Explain.

2. Can leadership concepts be applied in the classroom setting? That is, can the teaching styles of your professors be described as person-oriented and task-oriented? Are these distinctions useful for analyzing why some professors are more effective than others? Explain.

3. Leadership obviously is one factor that contributes to the performance of a group or an organization. What other factors can you think of, and how important are they in comparison to leadership?

4. It is often said that leaders are born, not trained. In light of what you have studied about the trait theory of leadership, how would you respond to that statement?

5. "Person-oriented leadership is OK if you are only interested in employee satisfaction, but if you want to get the job done, then task-oriented leadership is the only way." Evaluate this quotation.

6. What is your reaction to the idea that an effective leader must be able to shift from person orientation to task orientation as the situation dictates? Do you believe that you can be flexible in your behavior? Explain.

7. Describe in practical terms the ways in which a manager's job can be altered to fit his or her leadership style.

8. In how many of the eight situations described in Fiedler's theory have you had work experience? Describe in detail one of those experiences and determine whether the manager was using the "appropriate" style.

9. What does maturing mean in job and in psychological terms?

10. Evaluate the strengths and shortcomings of the managerial grid theory of leadership. Can you think of situations where a 9, 1 leader or a 1, 9 leader may be more effective than a 9, 9 leader? Explain.

Practice Quiz

Note: You can find the correct answers to these questions by taking the quiz and then submitting your answers in the Online Edition. The program will automatically score your submission. If you miss a question, the program will provide the correct answer, a rationale for the answer, and the section number in the chapter where the topic is discussed.

Indicate whether the sentence or statement is true or false.

1. The most popular methods used to influence subordinates are reason and assertiveness, while the least-used methods are higher authority and sanctions.

2. Leaders must focus on moment-to-moment organizational performance; managers must focus on the long-term goals of an organization.

3. In Abraham Zaleznick's terminology, managers are primarily concerned with process; leaders are primarily concerned with substance.

4. Process-focused managers are seldom leaders, and substance-focused leaders seldom manage processes.

5. The trait approach to leadership attempts to relate personal characteristics to effective leadership.

6. The situational approach to leadership is less complex than the trait and behavior approaches.

Identify the letter of the choice that best completes the statement or answers the question.

7. Which of the following is NOT one of the three primary theories at the center of the debate surrounding leadership?
   a. trait theory of leadership
   b. behavioral theory of leadership
   c. cultural theory of leadership
   d. contingency theory of leadership

8. Which of the following is NOT one of the behavior strategies identified through interviews with ninety charismatic leaders?
   a. focusing attention on specific issues of concern, concentrating on analysis, problem solving, and action
   b. communicating with empathy and sensitivity
   c. demonstrating consistency and trustworthiness
   d. expressing active concern for people
   e. remaining calm under pressure

9. The two key concepts in the two-dimensional theory are **initiating structure** and _____.
   a. consideration.
   b. interpersonal skills.
   c. effectiveness.
   d. driving product development.

10. The life cycle theory of leadership states that leadership is a dynamic process that requires _____.
   a. advanced age.
   b. experience.
   c. flexibility.
   d. opportunity.

11. The situational theory of leadership is based on the manner in which two primary factors interact. One factor is leadership behavior, the other is _____.
   a. leadership attitude.
   b. follower readiness.
   c. leadership traits.
   d. follower attitudes.

12. In his book "Good to Great" Jim Collins asserted that the _____ leader is one who usually rises up through the ranks and is not caught up with the "celebrity" aspect of being a CEO.
   a. great
   b. good
   c. level V
   d. situational

D **13.** Daniel Goleman and his colleagues suggest that it is a leader's _____ that is most important in determining their success within the organization.
   a. charisma
   b. intelligence
   c. people skills
   d. emotional intelligence

C **14.** Steven Covey has written a very successful book called "The 7 Habits of Highly Effective People". He has recently written a new book that asserts that there is an eighth habit that effective people practice. This eighth habit is best expressed as _____.
   a. the "garbage can" theory of leadership.
   b. treat the organization as an anarchy.
   c. find your voice and help others find theirs.
   d. the manager climbs the ladder, the leader makes sure it is leaning against the right wall.

B **15.** The definition of leadership used in this book emphasizes the importance of _____ skills.
   a. power
   b. influence
   c. writing
   d. social

Case Study

The Story of the H.M.S. *Endurance*

Dogged by failure and bad luck, Sir Ernest Shackleton was nevertheless called "the greatest leader that ever came on God's earth, bar none." He failed three times in polar exploration. In 1902, he was part of Captain Robert Falcon Scott's expedition to the South Pole on the *Discovery* when they were forced to turn back. In 1908, commanding his own similar expedition, he had to turn back only 97 miles from the Pole after realizing it would be certain death by starvation to go on. Nonetheless, he was knighted for his efforts. The 1914–1916 expedition aboard the H.M.S. *Endurance* was his greatest failure: he lost his ship even before touching Antarctica. But he reached a new pinnacle in leadership when he successfully led all the members of his crew to safety after a harrowing two-year fight for their lives.

By 1914, despite the tragic death of Captain Scott's party, beaten to the South Pole by the Norwegian *Amundsen,* Shackleton had rekindled public enthusiasm for polar exploration with his idea of crossing Antarctica on foot with dogs and sledges—something not in fact achieved until Vivian Fuchs did it in the 1950s with motor vehicles.

Nearly 5,000 applications poured in, from which Shackleton hired about 30 men. Polar expeditions were typically composed of two sections, a shore party of explorers and scientists and the ship's crew. Shackleton always remembered what a London theatrical manager once told him about the challenge of forming a repertory company: "Character and temperament matter quite as much as acting ability." He said he had to balance science or seamanship "against the kind of chaps they were." Shackleton built his crew around a core of experienced workers—what he called "old dogs." He chose a reliable deputy, Frank Wild, who shared his views of leadership and was, above all, loyal. Reginald James, the physicist, was asked if he could sing—Shackleton saw this as a touchstone for team spirit. He looked always for a temperamentally happy person, telling the meteorologist Leonard Hussey: "Loyalty comes easier to a cheerful person." He knew that candidates hungry for the job usually proved their mettle.

He also rotated work assignments so that everyone over time worked alongside everyone else in the group, breaking down hierarchies and cliques. He lent a hand with menial tasks and was a consistent presence in the work area. His participation allowed him to show by example how he expected things to be done; it gave him a better understanding of the effort involved; it helped him evaluate the strengths and weaknesses of each individual; it gave a certain dignity to all the jobs and it enhanced his standing with the crew. Most of all, it allowed him to bond with his men.

Shackleton used mealtimes to chat and joke with the men, to hear their ideas and relax as comrades. It was a rule to hold a concert every Saturday night, and when, on finally abandoning the sinking *Endurance,* the men had to leave behind treasured possessions, Shackleton insisted that one man save his banjo because it would help keep up everyone's spirits in the stranded months ahead. Happiness and comfort, he knew, were not expendable.

Once the *Endurance* became stuck in the ice, in view of its base but unable to reach it, Shackleton had to find a way of tackling the crushing disappointment. He maintained the established routine so that the men felt secure. He focused on making sure every man had the strength for the ordeal ahead, encouraging healthy eating, vigorous sport, and some means of relaxation for everyone. He used the new science of psychology: although the men had to eat fresh meat—seals and penguins—in order to avoid scurvy, they rebelled while the ship still had stocks of canned food. Shackleton waited until the first kill of seal and penguin was brought aboard, then announced there was only enough for the officers and scientists: the mess deck would have to wait for the next kill. The seamen promptly dispatched a representative to demand their contracted right to a quarter of all provisions: they never rejected fresh meat again. Another technique he used for defusing any resentment over food sharing was to get a man to stand with his back to the food as each portion was doled out and call a colleague's name: that way, no one was able to pick their own share.

Shackleton believed in hands-on training but only when necessary; he expected the men to do well and intervened only when they did not. By conveying trust in their abilities, Shackleton got the best from each man. He also developed a personal relationship with each: on the *Endurance* his method was to keep the ship's library in his cabin, so that he could chat with the men as they came to borrow books. With the *Endurance* stuck fast, the expedition was stranded on a vast, unstable layer of ice on the surface of the Weddell Sea in a temperature of –16 degrees Fahrenheit. The boss gathered the whole group around him and spoke simply from the heart. He gave a realistic appraisal of the situation, explained the options and offered his plan of action, asking for their support. He appeared calm, confident, and strong. Years later, one of the men recalled: "He spoke to us in a group, telling us that he intended to march the party across the ice to the west . . . that he thought we ought to manage five miles a day and that if we all worked together it could be done."

The men were more than 1,000 miles from any other human being, and hundreds of miles from land. For three days they struggled, not managing more than a mile a day. Shackleton halted the march and announced plans for survival on the ice floe. He balanced the personalities in each tent, established as normal a routine as possible, and planned for the worst if the ice gave way under a tent. On November 21, 1915, the *Endurance* finally broke apart and sank. Without emotion or melodrama, he told the men: "Ship and stores have gone, so now we'll go home."

His plan was for the lifeboats to be hauled over the ice to the open sea and then rowed to the nearest whaling station. After a forced stop of three months, the boats were finally launched, but more trouble lay in wait. They had to abandon the voyage on uninhabited Elephant Island, 60 miles away: one boat with Shackleton and five men would make a bid for South Georgia, 800 miles away. It sounded impossible, and this time Shackleton could not take his trusted deputy Wild, who was needed to manage the stranded party. They could easily have given up hope once "the Boss" had left. Typically, Shackleton took the expedition's two malcontents with him so that they would not damage morale among those left behind.

The impossible was done. The boat landed on South Georgia in seventeen days—a feat that is still regarded as one of the greatest boat journeys ever made. After a further ten days of struggling across the inhospitable and mountainous island, the party reached the whaling station. Their colleagues were rescued from Elephant Island with not a life lost. Wild had followed Shackleton's example, keeping the routine going, with entertainments and little celebrations, staving off depression by keeping everyone busy.

Shackleton once summed up how he viewed life and leadership. "Some people say it is wrong to regard life as a game. I don't think so. Life to me means the greatest of all games. The danger lies in treating it as a trivial game, a game to be taken lightly, and a game in which the rules don't matter much. The rules matter a great deal. The game has to be played fairly . . . and even to win the game is not the chief end. The chief end is to win it honorably and splendidly."

His supreme legacy was his example of how to persevere against seemingly insurmountable odds. When he was asked by the headmaster of a boys' school what advice he might like to pass on, Shackleton told him: "The only message I can think of for your boys is: in trouble, danger, and disappointment, never give up hope. The worst can always be got over."

Questions for Discussion

1. What general lessons about leadership can be learned from Shackleton's example? What lessons can be carried over to managing business organizations?

2. What do you think were the distinguishing leadership behaviors that Shackleton displayed? What were his distinguishing leadership traits? Do you think he displayed emotional intelligence? Explain.

3. Do you think that Shackleton's example is in line with Covey's seven habits of highly effective people? Explain.

Source: Adapted from Margaret Kelly, "Leading in a Crisis," *Executive Excellence,* October 2004, p. 4; "The Importance of Being Ernest," *Director,* March 2001, pp. 76–79; *Shackleton's Way,* by Margot Morrell and Stephanie Capparell, published by Nicholas Brealey on March 8, 2001; and Alfred Lansing, *Endurance: Shackleton's Incredible Voyage* (Carroll & Graf Publishers: March 1, 1999).

Internet Exercise

How Good a Leader Are You?

One of the truly valuable qualities of the Internet is the ability to easily collect normative information from a lot of people that enables individuals to compare themselves anonymously on a wide range of characteristics. On-line personality tests, IQ tests, and other quizzes and questionnaires can be fun and informative. One area in which on-line testing has been developed is leadership.

The following website provides a short on-line test for students to determine their leadership abilities.

http://health.discovery.com/tools/assessments.html

Students should be instructed to visit this website outside of class, take the short on-line leadership test, and print their test feedback. They should bring the results to class and be prepared to discuss the results with others. To protect the anonymity of students, instructors should request a copy of each student's feedback form and then list the various categories on the board or on an overhead projector. Discussion should center on the validity of the testing, the accuracy of the feedback, and the nature of the questions that were asked. Students should be challenged to take additional on-line leadership tests to see if there is consistency in their scores.

Experiential Exercise

Task and People Orientations

Are you task- or people-oriented? Or do you have a balanced style of leading? The following items describe the people- or task-oriented aspects of leadership. Use any past or present experience in leading a group of people as you complete the thirty-four-item scale. Circle whether you would most likely behave in the described way: always (A), frequently (F), occasionally (O), seldom (S), or never (N).

Source: The T/P Leadership Questionnaire was adapted from *Organizations and People* 4th Edition, by J. B. Ritchie and P. Thompson. Copyright © 1988. Reprinted with permission of South-Western, a division of Thomson Learning.

A F O S N **1.**   I would most likely act as the spokesperson of the group.

A F O S N **2.**   I would encourage overtime work.

A F O S N **3.**   I would allow employees complete freedom in their work.

A F O S N **4.**   I would encourage the use of uniform procedures.

A F O S N **5.**   I would permit employees to use their own judgment in solving problems.

A F O S N **6.**   I would stress being ahead of competing groups.

A F O S N **7.**   I would speak as a representative of the group.

A F O S N **8.**   I would encourage members for greater effort.

A F O S N **9.**   I would try out my ideas in the group.

A F O S N **10.** I would let members do their work the way they think best.

A F O S N **11.** I would be working hard for a promotion.

A F O S N **12.** I would tolerate postponement and uncertainty.

A F O S N **13.** I would speak for the group if there were visitors present.

A F O S N **14.** I would keep the work moving at a rapid pace.

A F O S N **15.** I would turn the members loose on a job and let them go to it.

A F O S N **16.** I would settle conflicts when they occur in the group.

A F O S N **17.** I would get swamped by details.

A F O S N **18.** I would represent the group at outside meetings.

A F O S N **19.** I would be reluctant to allow the members any freedom of action.

A F O S N **20.** I would decide what should be done and how it should be done.

A F O S N **21.** I would give some members some of my authority.

A F O S N **22.** Things would usually turn out as I had predicted.

A F O S N **23.** I would allow the group a high degree of initiative.

A F O S N **24.** I would assign group members to particular tasks.

A F O S N **25.** I would be willing to make changes.

A F O S N **26.** I would ask the members to work harder.

A F O S N **27.** I would trust the group members to exercise good judgment.

A F O S N **28.** I would schedule the work to be done.

A F O S N **29.** I would refuse to explain my actions.

A F O S N **30.** I would persuade others that my ideas are to their advantage.

A F O S N **31.** I would permit the group to set its own pace.

A F O S N **32.** I would urge the group to beat its previous record.

A F O S N **33.** I would act without consulting the group.

A F O S N **34.** I would ask that group members follow standard rules and regulations.

T _____ P _____

The T/P Leadership Questionnaire is scored as follows:

a. Circle the item numbers for statements 8, 12, 17, 18, 19, 29, 33, and 34.

b. Write the number 1 in front of item number if you responded S (seldom) or N (never) to that statement.

c. Also write a number 1 in from of item numbers not circled if you responded A (always) or F (frequently).

d. Circle the numbers that you have written in front of the following statements: 3, 5, 8, 10, 15, 18, 19, 21, 23, 25, 27, 29, 31, 33, and 34.

e. Count the circled number 1s. This is your score for concern for people. Record the score in the blank following the letter P.

f. Count the uncircled number 1s. This is your score for concern for task. Record this number in the blank following the letter T.

Motivation

CHAPTER OBJECTIVES

1 Define the meaning of *motivation*.

2 Explain the difference between content and process theories of motivation.

3 Discuss how incentives can be used to motivate some, but not every individual.

4 State why individuals react differently to being frustrated or blocked in satisfying their needs.

5 Discuss how reinforcement theory principles can be applied by a manager to influence behavior.

6 Describe why money is not always a motivator of employee behavior in organizations.

7 Explain the different kinds of quality of work life programs that managers are now using in organizations.

CHAPTER OUTLINE

Managing Today

Executive Compensation

In the wake of publicized scandals and perceived abuses, federal taxing authorities are going into action in the area of executive compensation. The Internal Revenue Service (IRS) has established a compliance initiative focusing on the tax treatment of virtually every area of executive compensation.

Can executives justify their high pay and benefits packages?

This is a difficult question for the IRS, general public, or stockholders to answer. Table A below provides the total compensation for six investment bank CEOs in 2003 and 2002.

Many advocates of attractive compensation packages for executives claim that the high pay is driven by perform-

ance. However, a pay-for-performance link has not been displayed for most executive-level managers. The impact of not fully supporting a pay-for-performance link for executives on those employees below the executive level (e-level) is something to seriously consider when motivation is the topic.

Source: Adapted from Paul Hodgson, "The Wall Street Example: Bringing Excessive Executive Compensation into Line," *Ivey Business Journal,* May/June 2004, pp. 1–6; Douglas Faucette, "Heightened Director Responsibilities in Setting Executive Compensation," *Executive Compensation Issues,* October 2004, pp. 100–103; and Mark Hamilton, "Executive Compensation Issues: New IRS Focus," *Executive Compensation Issues,* October 2004, pp. 22–25.

TABLE A			Total Compensation on Wall Street 2003/2002		
Company Name	**Ticker**	**CEO**	**2003 Total Compensation $**	**2002 Total Compensation $**	**Increase/ (decrease) %**
Bear Stearns Companies Inc. (The)	BSC	James E. Cayne	33,925,412	28,367,933	19.59
Citigroup Inc.	C	Sandord I. Weill (former CEO)	54,063,222	13,366,676	304.46
Goldman Sachs Group, Inc. (The)	GS	Henry M. Paulson	21,400,579	9,511,884	124.99
Lehman Brothers Holdings Inc.	LEH	Richard S. Fuld	52,954,039	28,709,101	84.45
Merrill Lynch & Co., Inc.	MER	E. Stanley O'Neal	25,344,265	12,404,473	104.32
Morgan Stanley	MWD	Philip J. Purcell	23,324,053	23,680,325	1.50
S&P 500 (matched sample)			4,630,349	3,656,536	22.84

Motivation is a general term used to describe the process of starting, directing, and maintaining physical and psychological activities. It is a broad concept that embraces such internal mechanisms as (1) preferences for one activity over another, (2) enthusiasm and vigor of a person's responses, and (3) persistence of organized action toward relevant goals.[1] The word *motivation* comes from the Latin *movere* "to move."

No manager has ever "seen" motivation, just as no manager has ever "seen" thinking, perceiving, or learning. All that a manager sees is behavior and changes in behavior. To explain or justify these observed behaviors, managers make inferences about underlying psychological processes—inferences that are formalized in the concept of motivation. Thus, in a formal sense **motivation** is defined as "all those inner striving conditions described as needs, drives, desires, motives, and so forth. It is an inner state that activates or moves."

Instead of using a formal interpretation of motivation to accomplish the job of managing other employees, a manager observes behavior and makes inferences about motiva-

▶ **motivation** The inner strivings that initiate a person's actions.

tion. If an employee displays the following type of behavior, he or she is considered to be motivated:

* Is regularly present on the job
* Puts forth her best effort
* Is always working at performing the job
* Is directing her efforts toward the accomplishment of meaningful goals

In essence, managers observe presence on the job, effort, persistence, and goal-orientation, and make inferences about whether or not an employee is motivated. As the Managing Today opening vignette suggests, executive compensation is so high for a select few it may result in a backlash at lower levels in an organization. For example, are employees going to be motivated to accomplish challenging goals if a few top-level executives are receiving such seemingly lucrative compensation packages?

12-1 Motivation and Behavior

All behavior is in some way motivated. People have reasons for doing what they do—for behaving in the manner that they do. All human behavior is directed toward certain goals and objectives. Such goal-directed behavior revolves around the desire for *need satisfaction*. A *need* is a physiological, psychological, or sociological want or desire. A need is "satisfied" when it is fulfilled. In general, people are moved to seek happiness in everything they do. Business consultant Tom Morris, in his book *If Aristotle Ran General Motors: The New Soul of Business*, contends that engaging workers' hearts, not just their minds, is the next catalyst for success in business.[2] Managers can use knowledge of the triggers of human motivation and performance and the incentives that stimulate it to improve worker productivity. The following Management Focus on Leadership box, "A Number of Triggers in Motivation," explores a number of possible triggers for motivation and peak performance.

12-1a Motivation

An unsatisfied need initiates motivation as shown in Figure 12-1. An unsatisfied need causes tension (physical, psychological, or sociological) within the individual or group, leading to some kind of behavior (to seek a means) to satisfy the need and thereby reduce the tension. Note that this activity is directed toward a goal; arrival at the goal satisfies the need. For example, a thirsty person needs water, is driven by thirst, and is motivated by a desire for water in order to satisfy the need.

Depending on how well the goal is accomplished, the inner state is modified as shown by the feedback loop in Figure 12-1. Thus, motivation begins with an unsatisfied condition and ends with movement to release that unsatisfied condition, with goal-directed behavior as a part of the process.

12-1b Motivation and Performance

In reviewing the general motivation model shown in Figure 12-1, it is important to point out that motivation and performance are distinct concepts. Managers are concerned about

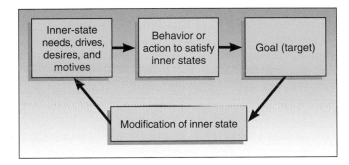

Figure 12-1
Model of the Motivation Process

Management Focus on Leadership

A Number of Triggers in Motivation

Sustaining a high level of motivation and performance requires high energy, physical and emotional strength, and sharp intellect. Managing an outstanding performer is often more difficult than managing a poor performer. The manager has the responsibility to maintain excellence.

Loehr and Swartz offer managers and organizations a performance hierarchy as a starting point in helping employees achieve and sustain high performance. They have worked with professional athletes such as tennis player Monica Seles and golfer Mark O'Meara. The hierarchy is used to highlight the Ideal Performance State (IPS). Put simply, the best and more

highly motivated performers tap into positive energy at all levels of the performance pyramid (www.corporateathlete.com/pages/legal.html).

The motivation level of managers and nonmanagers is increased when all levels of the performance pyramid (see figure below) are in sync.

The word *spiritual* prompts the most conflicting debate. By spiritual the authors mean the pyramid develops the energy that is unleashed by tapping into one's deepest values and defining a strong sense of purpose. A spiritual capacity serves as a powerful motivator.

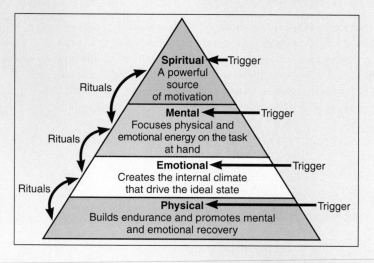

Source: Adapted from Steven Farmer and Anson Seers, "Time Enough to Work: Employee Motivation and Entertainment in the Workplace," *Time & Society,* September 2004, pp. 265–284. *Source for figure:* Adapted from Jim Loehr and

Tony Schwartz, "The Making of a Corporate Athlete," *Harvard Business Review,* January 2001, pp. 120–128. Copyright © 2001 by the Harvard Business School Publishing Corporation; all rights reserved.

employees accomplishing significant work goals. The successful accomplishment of work goals is the result of a number of factors such as the effort, time, and commitment of the employee. There is also the employee ability factor, as well as the type of support and guidance provided by the manager.[3] It is important for a manager to note that some of the factors that result in accomplished goals are internal, a part of the employee's makeup or characteristics.

Since both internal and external factors interact in accomplishment of goals, it is important for the manager to not reach incorrect or incomplete conclusions about motivation. A manager, for example, may notice a drop in performance and react by increasing the incentive pay for producing each unit. The manager's reaction is an attempt to increase the employee's motivation level and to show the employee how interested the manager is in performance. However, the drop in performance may be due to illness, to personal problems, or to dissatisfaction with the job.

Managerial mistakes in diagnosing what are thought to be motivational (inner-state) problems are common in work settings. Other factors interact with motivation to determine if job performance goals will be accomplished. The employees' abilities, outside work activities, available resources, working conditions, and the style of management are important factors to consider when diagnosing what is thought to be a motivation problem.

Managers should be aware of two types of rewards: *intrinsic* and *extrinsic.*[4] Intrinsic rewards are the natural rewards a person receives by performing a task or activity. The

Management Focus on Leadership

Making Intrinsic Motivation Better

There are times that a person feels energized by the work or tasks he or she is performing. The sense of energy, pride, and awareness of performing work that is valuable is powerful. It is intrinsically or personally (from within the person) generated.

On other occasions, work is depressing, energy sapping, and mechanical. You feel like you are working to earn the paycheck. This is the extrinsic or outside-rewarded motivation side of the coin.

One explanation that is based on research work proposes four building blocks for sustaining intrinsic motivation. Managers and workers together can build intrinsic motivation. The building blocks are shown in the chart below.

The manager must play a role in each of these four areas. In diagnosing work and activities, addressing the choice, competence, meaningfulness, and progress building blocks of intrinsic motivation is important for employees to accomplish performance goals. Managers can become leaders by helping employees in these four intrinsic motivation areas.

Choice	Competence	Meaningfulness	Progress
• Delegate activity • Trust in workers • Security (no punishment for honest errors • Communication	• Knowledge • Positive feedback • Challenge • Skill recognition	• An exciting vision • Whole task to complete • Relevant tasks	• Milestones • Celebrations • Measurement of improvement

Source: Adapted from Rob L. Martens, Judith Gulikers, and Theo Bastiaens, "The Impact of Intrinsic Motivation on E-learning in Authentic Computer Tasks," *The Journal of Computer Assisted Learning,* October 2004, pp. 369–377; Stephen Reiss, "Multifaceted Nature of Intrinsic Motivation: The Theory of 16 Basic Desires," *Review of General Psychology,* September 2004, pp. 179–193; Kenneth W. Thomas, "Intrinsic Motivation and How It Works," *Training,* October 2000, pp. 130–135; and Kenneth Carlton Cooper and Ken Cooper, *Effective Competency Modeling and Reporting* (New York: AMAOM, 2000).

completion of a project or the solving of a problem may yield a sense of accomplishment and personal fulfillment. Learning how to complete a difficult task is another intrinsic type of reward.

Extrinsic rewards are provided or given by another person for completing a task or activity. They are tangible and can be visible to others. When a department earns, divides, and issues an annual bonus to employees an extrinsic reward has been given. If you were given a promotion for excellent performance, you would be given something tangible and observable. The Management Focus on Leadership box, "Making Intrinsic Motivation Better," provides some building blocks that can be used to increase the strength of intrinsic motivation.

Managers use rewards to motivate employees to perform their jobs, work well with others, attend work, and remain with the organization.[5] Managers can provide directly extrinsic rewards. However, they can only hope to provide work, tasks, and activities that can yield intrinsic (nonobservable) rewards to employees. As experienced managers know, people want extrinsic and intrinsic rewards.[6]

Incentives are an important part of human motivation. Unfortunately, many managers miss the productivity advantages of providing incentives to employees because they mistakenly believe that it will lead to a sense of entitlement. That is, many managers refuse to provide incentives because they believe it will raise an employee's expectations. The key is to link incentives to performance, so that employees are clearly aware of their control of the rewards they attain.[7]

12-2 Need-Based Theories of Motivation

Over the years psychologists have studied a number of concepts that have represented the energetic force that constitutes human motivation. The most commonly used concept in theories of work motivation is *needs*. These theories are referred to as being based on a

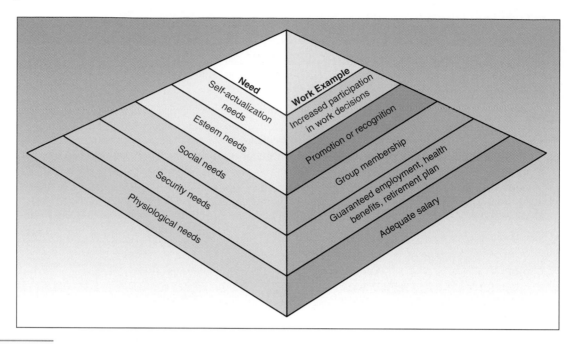

Figure 12-2
Maslow's Hierarchy of Needs

content explanation of needs. It is important to note again that *needs* are internal and they cannot be observed directly.

Needs may be classified in different ways. Many of the early management theorists regarded monetary incentives as the prime motivating means. These writers were influenced by the classical economists of the eighteenth and nineteenth centuries, who emphasized the rational pursuit of economic objectives and believed that economic behavior was characterized by rational economic calculations. Today, some behavioral scientists and managers hold that though money obviously is an important motivator, people seek to satisfy needs that are other than purely economic.

12-2a Maslow's Hierarchy of Needs

Most behavioral scientists now agree that human beings are motivated by the desire to satisfy many needs. But there is a wide difference of opinion as to what those needs and their relative importance are. Abraham Maslow, a clinical psychologist, developed a widely publicized theory of motivation called the **hierarchy of needs** (www.maslow.com).

▶**hierarchy of needs** Maslow's framework of five core needs to explain human's motivation.

Maslow's hierarchy of needs is widely accepted today in management theory and practice, because it seems to make sense and is easy to understand.[8] This theory of motivation is based on two important assumptions:

1. Each person's needs depend on what he already has. Only needs not yet satisfied can influence behavior. A satisfied need cannot influence behavior.
2. Needs are arranged in a hierarchy of importance. Once one need is satisfied, another emerges and demands satisfaction.

Maslow believed five levels of needs exist. These levels are (1) physiological, (2) safety, (3) social, (4) esteem, and (5) self-actualization.[9] He placed them in a framework he called the *hierarchy of needs*. This is presented in Figure 12-2.

Maslow stated that if all of a person's needs are unsatisfied at a particular time, the most basic needs will be more pressing than the others. Needs at a lower level must be satisfied before higher-level needs come into play, and only when they are sufficiently satisfied do the next needs in line become significant. Let us briefly examine each need level.

▶**physiological (basic) needs** Needs of the human body, such as food, water, and air.

Physiological needs   This category consists of the basic needs of the human body, such as food, water, and sex. Physiological needs will dominate when all needs are unsatisfied. In such a case, no other needs will serve as a basis for motivation. As Maslow states, "A person who is lacking food, safety, love and esteem would probably hunger for food more strongly than for anything else."[10] Organizational factors that might satisfy physiological needs include enough pay to permit an employee to survive and working conditions that permit a healthy environment.

Safety needs   Safety needs include protection from physical harm, ill health, economic disaster, and the unexpected. From a managerial standpoint, safety needs manifest themselves in attempts to ensure job security and to move toward greater financial support.

Social needs   Social needs are related to the social nature of people and to their need for companionship. This level in the hierarchy is the point of departure from the physical or quasi-physical needs of the two previous levels. Nonsatisfaction in this level of needs may affect the individual's mental health. Organizational conditions that help to satisfy these needs include encouraging team building, providing supportive supervision practices, and permitting coworkers the opportunity to interact socially on the job.

Esteem needs   Esteem needs comprise both the awareness of one's importance to others (self-esteem) and the actual esteem of others. The satisfaction of esteem needs leads to self-confidence and prestige. Organizations can support the satisfaction of these needs by recognizing good performance and permitting employees to work autonomously to complete challenging and meaningful job tasks.

Self-actualization needs   Maslow defines these needs as the "desire to become more and more what one is, to become everything one is capable of becoming."[11] The satisfaction of self-actualization needs enables individuals to realize fully the potentialities of their talents and capabilities. Maslow assumes that the satisfaction of self-actualization needs is possible only after the satisfaction of all other needs. Moreover, he proposes that the satisfaction of self-actualization needs will tend to *increase* the strength of those needs. Thus, when people are able to attain a state of self-actualization, they will tend to be motivated by increased opportunities to satisfy that level of needs. Organizations can help employees satisfy self-actualization needs by encouraging creativity, allowing risk-taking decision making, and supporting workers in their efforts to develop their skills.

> **safety needs** Needs include protection from physical harm, ill health, economic disaster, and the unexpected.

> **social needs** Needs for social interaction and companionship.

> **esteem needs** The awareness of the importance of others and of the regard accorded by others.

> **self-actualization needs** The human need to fully realize one's potential.

Maslow's ideas are easy to recall and continue to play an influential role among practicing managers and human resource professionals.[12] However, there are significant problems with this perspective. First, Maslow himself recognized that the hierarchy is not a stair-step approach. Human needs are multiple and they often occur simultaneously. Second, we have to consider the relative level of the need that is present at a given time. Being thirsty is a relative concept. If you're in a desert and have no water, the need will probably influence 100 percent of your behavior. On the other hand, if you're mildly thirsty all morning but you're writing the weekly report, your behavior may be more determined by a deadline than your thirst. Third, Maslow's theory describes needs as internal; it says nothing about the environment's effect on behavior. How are needs determined? For example, the need for new clothes may be determined by comparing our clothes with those worn by friends, models, or prestigious people. Functionally our clothes may be fine but by comparison to our friends' clothing, they might look old or out of style. So what might be considered a lower-order need for clothing becomes translated into a higher-order need for self-esteem.

To a large degree, Maslow's ideas help us understand that everyone has basic needs that must be satisfied. One way to satisfy these needs is through work. But the complexity of the need satisfaction process makes simple prescription problematic. Maslow's need hierarchy describes a model of basic human needs but offers little practical guidance for motivating workers.

For example, the Management Focus on Information Technology box, "Technology Workers Require New Form of Motivation," discusses how managers can motivate the new breed of technology workers. Many of them have already achieved riches beyond their wildest dreams. They also have titles and most of their needs fulfilled. However, some managers have found that glory, or recognition for their achievements, can be an effective motivating factor for today's technology workers.

Management Focus on Technology

Technology Workers Require New Form of Motivation

Technology management must creatively address the motivational needs of technology workers (TWs). That's because TWs control more technology than management does. Since technology is so crucial to the daily functioning of the firm, managerial attention and creativity are needed.

Money has long been used to reward system developers, consultants, and administrators. Fortunately, TWs are distracted by being able to afford luxury items beyond their wildest dreams. But good times have limits. How many TVs can a person watch? How many parking places can one find? How many heirs can one provide for?

Companies are turning to glory as the prime motivator. Glory is more subjective and plentiful than money and power. Examples of glory and what must be done to obtain it include: participation in the stock purchase plan for just being an employee; Analyst of the Quarter recognition for creating a needed spreadsheet; a dinner for two for creating software; training certificates for attending team-building seminars; quality circle membership for participating in TQM; an afternoon off with pay for helping orient three new hires.

The possibilities for bestowing glory are endless. All that's needed is documentation that the employee is deserving. The ensuing admiration of colleagues generates warm feelings that can't be had any other way.

Glory allows TWs to be motivated through recognition. Being recognized among your peers is motivational. It is a sign of performing well and accomplishing an important task or activity. The sense of fulfillment from recognition must be balanced with other motivators such as fairly disturbed compensation, vacation time, and some degree of autonomy. Recognition even for TWs can only be one of a number of extrinsic and intrinsic motivational rewards.

Sources: Adapted from John M. Ivancevich and Thomas N. Duening, *Managing Einsteins: Leading High Tech Workers in the Digital Age* (New York: McGraw-Hill, 2002); Vincent Alonzo, "Revenge of the Nerds," *Incentive,* April 1997, pp. 50–52; and Dennis Coleman, "To Motivate Nerds, Spread the Glory," *Upside,* September 1996, p. 28.

12-2b McClelland's Achievement-Motivation Theory

David McClelland, a psychologist, studied the conditions under which people develop a motive to achieve, and its impact on behavior.[13] The term *achievement* is used to mean both a need and a motive (www.accel-team.com/human_relations/hrels_06_mcclelland.html). McClelland and his colleagues devised a way to measure the strength of a need and then looked for relationships between strength of needs in different societies, conditions that had fostered the needs, and the results of needs in work organizations.

Participants were shown pictures and asked to make up stories about them, that is, to describe what was happening in the picture and what the probable outcome would be. McClelland assumed that what a person perceived and reported in the pictures (called the *Thematic Apperception Test* [TAT]) reflected the person's values, interests, and motives. McClelland stated, "If you want to find out what's on a person's mind, don't ask him, because he can't always tell you. Study his fantasies and dreams. If you do this over a period of time, you will discover the themes to which his mind returns again and again. And these themes can be used to explain his actions."[14]

From individuals' responses to a series of pictures, McClelland calculated scores for three human needs—need for achievement, need for affiliation, and need for power. The need for achievement was designated as n Ach. For example, one picture was of a boy holding a violin. Table 12-1 provides hypothetical stories prepared by a person who scored high on need for achievement and one who scored low on need for achievement.

Self-motivated need achievers like to set their own goals. Goals that they set are moderately difficult but are not impossible to achieve. Also, those with high needs for achievement like to receive feedback on their performance.[15] Successful salespeople usually have a high level of achievement motivation, for example.[16] These people set moderately difficult but achievable goals for themselves.[17]

The need for affiliation (n Aff) is the desire to work and to be with other people. There is a high need to socially interact, to support others, and to be concerned with the development and growth of others. The n Aff is similar to Maslow's social need.

The need for power (n Pow) refers to the desire to have impact, to be influential, and to have control over others. McClelland proposes that there are two "faces of power"—one

High n Ach Story	Low n Ach Story	**T A B L E 12-1**
The boy just completed a long, daily violin lesson. He is happy with his improvement and thinks that his daily practice is well worth the hard work. He knows that to become a top concert violinist by age nineteen, he will have to practice when his friends are partying, playing baseball, dating, and attending musical concerts. He wants to be the best and is willing to pay the price.	Jim is simply holding his dad's violin. He likes the music it makes, but feels that his dad spends too many hours playing the instrument. If only he could play without having to practice like his dad. It seemed that practicing was boring and would take away valuable time from his friends and his girlfriend. Maybe there were other instruments that are easier to learn to play. Then again, maybe he should be a good listener of music performed by others.	**Examples of n Ach Stories**

positive and one negative. The positive face emphasizes a concern for helping others achieve goals. The negative face is aimed at personal gain; it is designed to create a dominance over others.

McClelland's research suggests that these three needs have implications for job selection, placement, motivation, and training. For example, individuals can increase their achievement motivation when they are taught how to set goals that stretch their skills. Also, a person who has a high n Aff and a low n Pow and is given an assignment where power must be used will have a difficult time succeeding.[18]

A problem with McClelland's theory rests in measuring the needs. The TAT is a projective device that is prone to error and subjective bias by raters who interpret the stories written (www.learner.org/exhibits/). There is also the problem of the writing ability of individuals. One person may have a flair for writing, while another may write in a stilted and ponderous manner. The person's writing skills will influence how the stories are rated.

12-2c Herzberg's Two-Factor Theory

Frederick Herzberg advanced a theory of motivation based on a study of need satisfactions and on the reported motivational effects of those satisfactions on 200 engineers and accountants. His approach is termed the **two-factor theory of motivation.**[19]

Herzberg asked the participants in his study to think of times when they felt especially good and especially bad about their jobs (www.skymark.com/resources/leaders/herzberg.asp). Each person was then asked to describe the conditions that caused those feelings. Significantly, the individuals *identified different work conditions for each of the feelings.* For example, if managerial recognition for doing an excellent job led to good feelings about the job, the lack of managerial recognition was seldom indicated as a cause of bad feelings.

Based on this research, Herzberg reached the following two conclusions:

1. Although employees are dissatisfied by the absence of some job conditions, the presence of those conditions does not cause strong motivation. Herzberg called such conditions *maintenance factors* or *hygiene factors*, since they are necessary to maintain a minimum level of need satisfaction. He also noted that these have often been perceived by managers as factors which can motivate subordinates, but that they are, in fact, more potent as dissatisfiers when they are absent. He concluded that there were ten maintenance factors, namely:

   • Company policy and administration
   • Technical supervision
   • Interpersonal relations with supervisor
   • Interpersonal relations with peers
   • Interpersonal relations with subordinates

▶**two-factor theory of motivation** The theory, popularized by the work of Frederick Herzberg, that the absence of some job conditions dissatisfies employees but that the presence of those conditions doesn't build employee motivation, and that the absence of other job conditions doesn't dissatisfy employees but that their presence builds employee motivation.

Figure 12-3
Contrasting Views of Satisfaction-Dissatisfaction

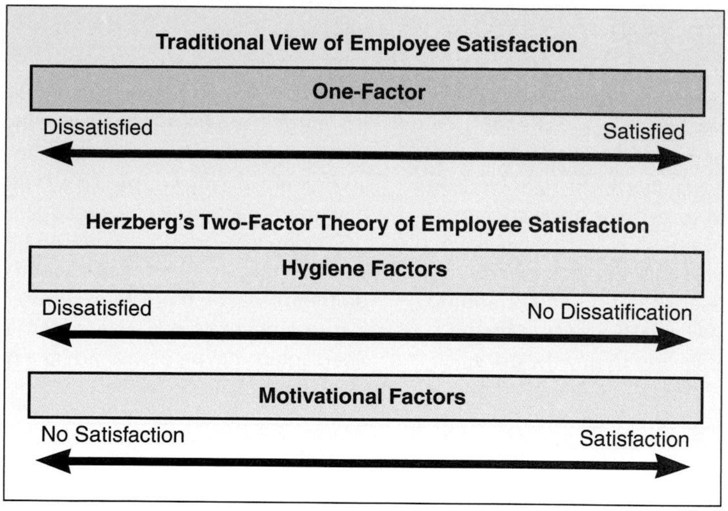

- Salary
- Job security
- Personal life
- Work conditions
- Status

2. Some job factors, which Herzberg calls *motivators,* cause high levels of motivation and job satisfaction when present. However, the absence of these factors does not prove highly dissatisfying. Herzberg described six of these motivational factors:

- Achievement
- Recognition
- Advancement
- The work itself
- The possibility of personal growth
- Responsibility

Prior to Herzberg's research, managers viewed job satisfaction and dissatisfaction as opposite ends of the same continuum, as shown in Figure 12-3. Herzberg's research findings introduced the notion of two continuums. If employees are not satisfied, they indicate no satisfaction, and not dissatisfaction.

The motivational factors are job centered. They relate directly to the job itself, that is, the individual's job performance, the job responsibilities, and the growth and recognition obtained from the job. The maintenance factors are peripheral to the job and are more related to the external environment of work. The distinction between motivational and maintenance factors is similar to the distinction between *intrinsic* and *extrinsic* rewards. Intrinsic rewards are part of the job and occur when the employee performs the work; the work itself is rewarding. Extrinsic rewards are external rewards (e.g., receiving a paycheck) that have meaning or value after the work has been performed or away from the workplace. They provide little, if any, satisfaction when the work is being performed.

Since conducting the original study Herzberg has cited numerous replications supporting his position.[20] These studies were conducted with professional women, hospital maintenance personnel, agricultural administrators, nurses, food handlers, manufacturing supervisors, engineers, scientists, military officers, managers ready for retirement, teachers, technicians, and assemblers. Some of the studies were conducted in cultural settings beyond the United States, in Finland, Hungary, the Soviet Union, and Yugoslavia.

Herzberg reports that American, Japanese, and Italian employees are motivated by similar job motivations. About 80 percent of the factors that are intrinsic to the job result in satisfying job experiences for workers across these different cultures.[21] He has concluded that there are more commonalities among workers throughout the world than were originally assumed in studying motivation. Employees in Italy, like those in the United States, are motivated by their own inherent need to succeed at a challenging task. The manager in Rome or Chicago needs to provide opportunities for employees to achieve so they will become motivated.

Herzberg's theory of motivation has generated quite a bit of controversy. Three main criticisms have been directed at it and its accompanying research. Doubts have been raised about the Herzberg methodology (his use of the structured interview to collect information). Other researchers have used other methods and have failed to replicate his findings.[22] Thus, there is a possibility that his results may have been influenced by the method used to collect the information.

Some claim that the two sets of job factors uncovered by Herzberg are not independent.[23] Some individuals are motivated by salary, while other individuals are not at all motivated by advancement opportunities. In fact, some individuals perceive advancement as something to avoid. Sex differences also have been found. Some female workers report that interpersonal relations are important motivators.

A third criticism is that Herzberg proposed a theory of motivation based on the responses of engineers and accountants.[24] Can such a theory be generalized to nonprofessionals and less-educated employees? Any theory based on such a limited sample, such as only engineers and accountants, should be considered cautiously.

Despite some criticisms, Herzberg's theory of motivation has stimulated discussion and further research into motivation. Herzberg has looked at and discussed motivation in terms that managers understand. He has done so without loading his discussion with the psychological terminology that managers typically gloss over and ignore.

12-2d Maslow and Herzberg: Comparisons

There is much similarity between Herzberg's and Maslow's models. A close examination of Herzberg's ideas indicates that what he actually was saying is that some employees may have achieved a level of social and economic progress in our society such that the higher-level needs of Maslow (esteem and self-actualization) are the primary motivators. However, these employees still must satisfy their lower-level needs to maintain their present state. Thus, money might still be a motivator for nonmanagement workers (particularly those at a minimum-wage level) and for some managerial employees. Herzberg's model adds to the need hierarchy model because it distinguishes between the two groups of motivational and maintenance factors and points out that the motivational factors often are derived from the job itself. Figure 12-4 compares the two models.

LearningMoment *Content Theories*

Content theories of motivation use individual needs to help explain the behaviors and attitudes of people at work. Each content explanation discusses a slightly different set of needs. However, all are in agreement that unfulfilled needs create tension and energy that initiate behaviors and attitudes. Managers can create work cultures and contexts in which needs can be fulfilled through excellent performance of the work or tasks.

Figure 12-4
Comparison of the Maslow and Herzberg Models

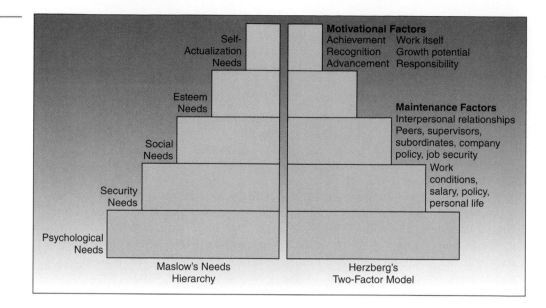

Maslow's Needs Hierarchy: Psychological Needs, Security Needs, Social Needs, Esteem Needs, Self-Actualization Needs

Herzberg's Two-Factor Model:

Motivational Factors
Achievement   Work itself
Recognition   Growth potential
Advancement   Responsibility

Maintenance Factors
Interpersonal relationships
Peers, supervisors, subordinates, company policy, job security
Work conditions, salary, policy, personal life

12-3 Process Theories of Motivation: Expectancy Theory

There are three popular cognitive process explanations of motivation. These approaches explain the internal processes taken by individuals in achieving positive motivation. One process theory of motivation was developed by Victor H. Vroom, and it expands on the work of Maslow and Herzberg.[25] Vroom's **expectancy theory of motivation** views motivation as a process governing choices. Thus, an individual who has a particular goal must practice a certain behavior to achieve it. He or she weighs the likelihood that various behaviors will achieve the desired goal, and if a certain behavior seems to be more successful than others, that behavior likely will be the one the goal-seeker selects.

In the *expectancy motivation model*, motivation, or the force to perform, is defined as expectancy times instrumentality times valence, or $M = E \times I \times V$. The theory proposes three determinants of motivation:

1. *The expectancy that individual effort will result in performance.* Employees generally are motivated to exert effort if they believe their effort will result in high performance.

2. *The belief that performance will result in reward.* Employees are motivated if they believe performance will lead to desired rewards. The employee considers whether performance is *instrumental* in achieving rewards.

3. *The valence of rewards.* Valence refers to an employee's preference for rewards he believes will result from performing well. A manager who provides rewards that have low valence (are not highly preferred) is not likely to see that rewards bring much improvement in performance.

Expectancies are probabilities calculated by a person's thought processes. If a person decides that if she works hard, she will be a high performer, expectancy is likely to be close to 1.00, or certainty. On the other hand, if a person decides that no matter how hard she works; there is little likelihood that she will be a high performer, expectancy will be close to 0.

Whether or not high performance is associated with desired outcomes is determined by examining what is called *instrumentality* in the expectancy theory. Instrumentalities are correlations or indicators of association, which range from −1.00 to +1.00. If a person sees no association between high performance and an outcome such as a merit pay increase, the instrumentality is 0. On the other hand, if a person believes high performance is always

expectancy theory of motivation A theory that defines motivation, or the force to perform, as defined as expectancy times instrumentality time valence, $M = E \times I \times V$.

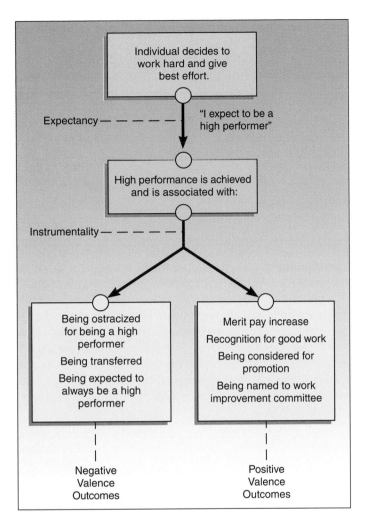

Figure 12-5
Expectancy Theory from
a Manager's Perspective

associated with a merit pay increase, the instrumentality is +1.00. Since instrumentality is an indicator of association or correlation, it can range from −1.00 to +1.00.

Valences are the values an individual attaches to work outcomes, such as a merit pay increase, a promotion, a transfer to a new group, more job responsibility, or having a longer workday. If one desires an outcome, it has a positive valence; if one does not prefer an outcome, it has a negative valence; if one is indifferent to a particular outcome, it is considered to have a zero valence.

Expectancy theory predicts that motivation to work will be high in the following instances:

1. *Expectancy is high*—The employee feels that high performance can be attained.
2. *Instrumentality is high*—The employee associates high performance with a desired (positive valence) outcome such as a merit pay increase.
3. *Valence is high*—The employee has a high preference for a merit pay increase.

Since $M = E \times I \times V$, all three components in the equation must be high to achieve optimal motivation. A zero for expectancy, instrumentality, or valence means that there is no motivation. Figure 12-5 illustrates a general and a work-related example of the expectancy theory.

An important contribution of the expectancy theory is that it explains how the *goals* of individuals influence their *effort* and that the behavior individuals select depends on their assessment of whether it will successfully lead to the goal. For example, members of an organization may not all place the same value on efforts to increase employee involvement. Research has shown that employees who volunteer for such programs evaluate their outcomes more favorably than those who don't volunteer. In fact, individual commitment to employee involvement programs is directly related to their appraisal of potential program outcomes.[26]

Vroom believes that what is important is the perception and value that the individual places on certain goals. Suppose that one individual places a high value on a bonus and perceives high performance as instrumental in reaching that goal. Accordingly, this individual will strive toward superior performance to achieve the bonus. However, another individual may value relationships with co-workers. The individual, therefore, is not likely to emphasize superior performance to achieve the goal. Think of expectancy theory in terms of two workers, where one worker has the goal of monthly sales of e-learning courseware of $50,000 and another the goal of monthly sales of e-learning courseware of $28,000. How might their respective efforts and behaviors in selling the on-line courseware for a company such as SmartForce vary?

Research studies of expectancy theory usually involve asking employees to estimate the expectancy they have of being an outstanding, good, or average performer.[27] In addition, the employees are asked to estimate the association (instrumentality) of performance and outcomes (pay, promotion). They also are asked to rate or rank the valence of outcomes. Their responses then are combined to determine the degree of effort (motivation) expended.

For the most part, empirical studies provide some support for the expectancy theory.[28] However, many factors besides expectancy, instrumentality, and valence may influence the amount of effort expended on the job, and accurately measuring the factors in the expectancy theory is difficult. Is it really possible to have people report on their expectancies, instrumentalities, and valences? How can their answers be measured? Researchers who have tested various portions of the expectancy model have not yet completely resolved these questions.[29]

The expectancy theory does have several important practical implications managers should consider, however. They can:

1. *Determine what outcomes employees prefer.* Communicating with employees to determine their preferences is important for developing reward packages that can stimulate motivation.
2. *Define, communicate, and clarify the level of performance that is desired.* An employee needs realistic and meaningful performance goals before he can exert proper effort.
3. *Establish attainable performance goals.* Setting impossible goals will create frustration and confusion and lower motivation.
4. *Link desired outcomes to performance goal achievement.* A manager should spell out how and when performance will be rewarded. Every effort should be made to link performance and rewards.

12-4 Process Theories of Motivation: Equity Theory

J. Stacy Adams's equity theory concerns workers' perceptions of (cognitive process) how they are being treated. In particular, equity theory is based on the assessment process workers use to evaluate the fairness or justice of organizational outcomes and the *adjustment process* used to maintain perceptions of fairness.[30] The concepts of fairness and equilibrium (internal balance) are central to equity theory. The basic idea in equity theory is that an employee first considers her input (effort) and then her outcomes (rewards). Next the employee compares her personal ratio of effort to reward to the ratio of a referent. The referent is usually another employee doing basically the same work, some standard ratio based on a fair day's work, or another employee at approximately the same level in an organization.

▶**reference ratio** The ratio comparing a person's input to outcome.

This ratio of comparing a person's input to outcome is called a **reference ratio.** If the employee believes that his input-to-outcome ratio is lower than the reference ratio, he can (1) reduce his effort or (2) seek higher rewards to bring his input-to-outcome ratio in line with the reference ratio. Conversely, if the employee's ratio is higher than the reference ratio, she can increase her effort or reduce her rewards. If Georgia feels that she's overrewarded for her work, she might feel guilty. To reduce this tension, she could work harder or find more work to do. Her actions would reflect the need to adjust her internal state of fairness. Likewise, John (an underrewarded worker) is off-balance in the opposite direction. He too would seek an equity adjustment. If no pay increase appeared to be forthcoming, theory suggests that he'd decrease his effort to again create an equitable outcome.

Note that a worker's inputs and outcomes need not be in exact balance to one another as long as the reference ratio imbalance matches the worker's ratio. That is, a worker may feel that she is working very hard, but she may not feel unfairly treated as long as her comparison workers are also working very hard. Many workers are willing to work hard as long as the burden is shared. Equity theory helps to account for workers' feelings of mistreatment by highly paid managers.

Managers should also be wary that workers from different cultures have different equity sensitivities. Research has shown that in addition to varying equity sensitivities across cultures, diverse individuals also have different approaches to organizational citizenship.[31] Managers should also be aware that equity sensitivity will vary to some extent between individuals from similar cultural backgrounds.[32]

There has been some criticism from practicing managers about the value of equity theory. There is not clear evidence that employees change their behavior as they are overcompensated or receive more than they deserve. Second, equity theory explanations of motivation focus on the person's perception of the fairness of the amount and allocation of rewards among individuals. This notion of fairness is referred to as **distributive justice**.[33]

There is also the notion of **procedural justice**. That is, the perceptions of the person about the process (e.g., reward allocation based on performance review ratings) used to determine how to distribute rewards. Procedural justice affects trust, commitment, and loyalty.[34] A procedural justice assumption is that people are going to be more motivated to perform at a high level when they perceive the programs used to make decisions about the distribution of outcomes as fair. Employees will be more motivated if they believe that their performance is being accurately assessed. Conversely, if employees perceive that the performance appraisal program is biased or inaccurate, they will be less motivated to perform well.

▶ **distributive justice** The concept that different rewards to individuals should not be based on arbitrary criteria.

▶ **procedural justice** The concept that a reward should be clearly stated and impartially provided.

12-5 Reinforcement Theory of Motivation

Reinforcement theory is another widely practiced theory of motivation. Reinforcement theory considers the use of positive or negative reinforcers to motivate or to create an environment of motivation. This theory of motivation is not concerned with needs or why people make choices. Instead, it is concerned with the environment and its consequences for the person; that is, behavior is considered to be environmentally caused.

The explanation of why people continue to work hard, according to reinforcement theory, centers on Thorndike's law of effect, which states that behavior that results in a pleasing outcome will likely be repeated; however, behavior that results in an unpleasant outcome is not likely to be repeated.[35]

Operant conditioning is a powerful tool used for changing employee behavior. The term *operant conditioning* in the management literature applies to controlling work behavior by manipulating the consequences. It is based on the research work of psychologist B. F. Skinner and is built on two principles: (1) Thorndike's law of effect and (2) properly

▶ **reinforcement theory** Theory of motivation that considers the use of positive or negative reinforcers to motivate or create an environment of motivation.

 **LearningMoment** *Process Theories*

Process theories address the cognitive approach taken by individuals. The expectancy theory describes internal processes of choice. Equity theory explains how people react when they feel unfairly rewarded for work performance. Process theories offer more dynamic explanations of motivation since they focus on cognitive process and behavior.

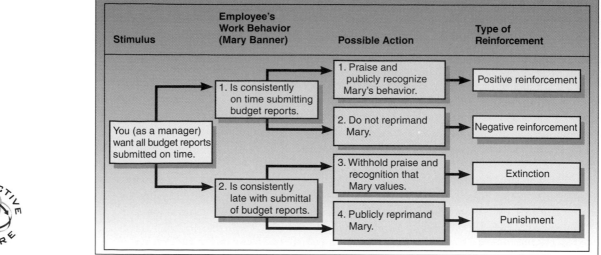

Stimulus	Employee's Work Behavior (Mary Banner)	Possible Action	Type of Reinforcement
You (as a manager) want all budget reports submitted on time.	1. Is consistently on time submitting budget reports.	1. Praise and publicly recognize Mary's behavior.	Positive reinforcement
		2. Do not reprimand Mary.	Negative reinforcement
	2. Is consistently late with submittal of budget reports.	3. Withhold praise and recognition that Mary values.	Extinction
		4. Publicly reprimand Mary.	Punishment

Figure 12-6
Four Types of Reinforcement Available to Managers
Source: Adapted from Abraham Maslow, "A Theory of Human Motivation," *Psychology Review*, 50, pp. 370–96.

▶**behavior modification**
An approach to motivation that uses principles of operant conditioning. Operant behavior is learned on the basis of consequences. If a behavior causes a desired outcome (for managers) it is reinforced (positively rewarded), and because of its consequences it is likely to be repeated. Thus, behavior is conditioned by adjusting its consequences.

▶**positive reinforcement**
An increase in the frequency of a response that results when the response is followed by a positive reinforcer.

▶**negative reinforcement**
An increase in the frequency of a response that is brought about by removing a disliked event immediately after the response occurs.

▶**punishment** The introduction of something disliked or the removal of something liked following a particular response in order to decrease the frequency of that response.

scheduled rewards influence individual behaviors.[36] **Behavior modification** is the term used to describe techniques for applying the principles of operant conditioning to the control of individual behavior.

Suppose you are a manager and your employee Mary Banner is always late with required budget reports. There are four types of reinforcement that you could use. First, you could focus on reinforcing the desired behavior (which, in this example, is preparing budget reports on time). You could use positive or negative reinforcement. **Positive reinforcement** would include rewards such as praise, recognition, or a pay bonus. **Negative reinforcement** also focuses on reinforcing the desired behavior. However, instead of providing a positive reward, the reward is that the employee avoids some negative consequence. Thus, Mary would complete the report on time to avoid the negative consequence of being reprimanded by her manager.

Alternatively, the manager might focus on reducing the tardiness of submitting the budget report by use of two other reinforcements: extinction or punishment. Through the use of extinction (withholding positive reinforcement), Mary might unlearn her bad habit of submitting late reports. Another method that reduces the frequency of undesired behavior is called **punishment.** In this case, punishment could involve the manager's public reprimand of Mary for submitting a late report. These four types of reinforcement that a manager can apply are presented in Figure 12-6.

12-6 Managerial Approaches for Improving Motivation

Managers can use several approaches to motivate workers to perform more effectively. Two approaches, however, have been especially effective: linking pay to job performance, and quality of work life programs.

12-6a Pay and Job Performance

Pay often can be used to motivate employee performance.[37] But a pay plan also must (1) create the belief that good performance leads to high levels of pay, (2) minimize the negative consequences of good performance (in which the better you do, the more they give you to do), and (3) create conditions in which rewards other than pay are seen to be related to good performance. These three conditions follow from the expectancy theory of motivation, which states that individuals will be motivated to seek goals they value and can attain.

Pay for performance plans are not new. The most common types are individual (e.g., merit pay), team (e.g., gainsharing), and organizational (e.g., profitsharing). For example, increasing a person's pay based on performance appraisal results is a technique used in some firms. The assumption is that the performance appraisal results are valued and reliable. Unfortunately, this assumption is often seriously questioned because of poorly designed and administered appraisal programs.[38]

Pay for performance programs based on weak or controversial performance measures are not always trusted. Quibbling over whether to award a 3 percent or 4 percent raise based on performance measures can take a lot of time and energy to resolve. Equity, expectancy, and reinforcement issues are important in attempting to resolve any debate about the accuracy and fairness of the pay for performance decision.

12-6b Quality of Work Life Programs

Quality of work life (QWL) is defined as an attempt through a formal program to integrate employee needs and well-being with the intention of improved productivity, greater worker involvement, and higher levels of job satisfaction. It strives to better personalize the workplace by improving the quality of a person's daily existence on the job. A combination of factors has led to this increased interest in improving QWL. Managerial concern about productivity, government regulations such as Title VII of the Civil Rights Act, the Occupational Safety and Health Act (1970), the Fair Labor Standards Act of 1963, and increased competition for personnel have encouraged companies to pay more attention to QWL.

Programs for QWL improvements range from those requiring minor changes in the organization to those requiring extensive modifications in structure, personnel, and the utilization of resources. Three types of QWL programs are quality circles, employee stock ownership plans, and the use of alternative work schedules.

Quality Circles   Faced with sluggish productivity, an increasingly competitive work market, and inflation, some managers have discovered and experimented with **quality circles** (QCs). Quality circles are small groups of workers (seven to twelve) who meet regularly (weekly in most cases) with their supervisor as the circle leader to solve work-related problems (e.g., quality, quantity, cost).

quality circles Small groups of workers who meet regularly with their supervisor as their leader to solve work-related problems.

QCs give the employee opportunity for involvement, social-need satisfaction, participation in work improvement, challenge, and opportunity for growth. They are, in essence, vehicles for providing employees with opportunities to satisfy lower- and upper-level needs, as stated by Maslow, through the motivators described in Herzberg's theory. Participation in QCs provides the vital Herzberg-type motivators to even the lowest-level employee. Members assume responsibility to identify and analyze problems in their work areas.

Although in most cases QCs meet for only about an hour a week, this meeting carries over into the rest of the week. Circle activities are carried to breaks and lunchtimes. Also, members continue to think about the points raised in the meetings. Frequently, circle members meet on their own time to complete QC assignments such as comparing their own circle's progress with that of other QCs.

The QC provides employees with an opportunity to be a part of a team seeking common goals. Matching the worker's needs to company goals can be accomplished in a QC. Organizational goals can be reached while personal needs keep the process moving forward. However, like any managerial program with motivational overtones, QCs have some risks. QCs are *not* the answer to all motivational problems.

American companies began experimenting with QCs in the late 1970s. While these early efforts were hailed as revolutionary efforts at participative management, many of the efforts ended up in failure. There were some successes. Federal organizations such as the Norfolk, Virginia, Naval Shipyard, NASA's Lewis Space Center, and the U.S. Customs Service reported varying degrees of success. At the same time, model Japanese companies had as many as 75 percent of their employees involved in QCs.[39]

Research has shown that managers must be aware of two important factors when implementing use of QCs:

1. Employees must be trained in the process of quality circles.
2. The quality circle process will differ from industry to industry.[40]

Managers should also be aware that another potential problem with QCs is managerial resistance. QCs encourage people to voice opinions, make suggestions, and display their ideas about work. This practice theoretically reduces the "administrative distance" between workers and manager. The result is that some managers feel threatened by what they perceive as a loss of power, status, prestige, and authority. They may consciously or subconsciously hinder the work and processes of the QC.

Employees may resist QCs as well. They may not want to accept the additional responsibilities that come with QCs. They may feel that management support is not strong enough, or that they don't have the skills that are needed to be effective in a QC environment.[41]

Still another potential area of difficulty is the role of the QC leader. In organizations, managers and supervisors take leadership roles. However, in the QC, the leader is not in an authority position. She is instead a facilitator, a discussion leader who helps the group reach solutions. The leader who attempts to autocratically enforce his viewpoints quickly loses the respect, cooperation, and attention of the QC members. Many managers have a difficult time making the transition from a legitimate authority position in the formal hierarchy to the role of a facilitator in a QC.

Employee Stock Ownership Plans (ESOPs)

Ever since 1974, when Congress enacted the first of a series of tax measures designed to encourage ESOPs, the number of employee-owned (or partially owned) companies has grown (www.nceo.org/library/eo100.html). Employee owners publish the *Milwaukee Journal,* sell home improvement products at Lowe's Companies, provide physical therapy at Ewing and Thomas in New Port Richey, Florida, and fly airplanes for United Airlines.

Worker ownership is a democratic ideal that was created in the 1950s by a lawyer, Louis Kelso. He was able to convince Senator Russell Long to provide the idea with appropriate statutory legitimation plus a number of special tax incentives.[42] The 1986 Tax Reform Act has made ESOPs even more agreeable in terms of tax deduction incentives.

Rosen and Quarrey studied forty-five ESOP companies, looking at data for each during the five years before it instituted the plan and then five years after. Five comparison companies for every ESOP were selected from *Dun & Bradstreet* in terms of business type, size, and location. Sales and employment growth were closely monitored. The data were clear in showing that some companies did better after setting up ESOPs.

Further analysis of attitude data indicated that workers enjoyed participating in decision making, were enthusiastic about owning a part of the company, and had better morale after the ESOP was established.

Clearly not all organizations can or should establish ESOPs. There must be further research on what ESOPs can and cannot do in terms of productivity, morale, and QWL.[43] In some cases employees in ESOPs who feel that they can share ideas, opinions, and creativity with their organizations apparently are self-motivated to work hard and long hours.

Flexible Work Schedules

Each year an increasing number of organizations are adopting alternative work schedules; that is, a work schedule that is not a traditional 8:00 A.M. to 5:00 P.M. schedule. Employee preferences, management flexibility, the growing number of single-parent families, and the anxiety of traveling to and from work during peak traffic times are reasons why alternative work schedules are growing in popularity.

At the turn of the twentieth century, the average workweek was about sixty hours long. Today the workweek average is around thirty-eight to forty hours weekly. About 20 percent of the workforce uses shift schedules; that is, one week a worker works from 7:00 A.M. to 3:00 P.M.; the next week from 3:00 P.M. to 11:00 P.M.; and the next week from 11:00 P.M. to 7:00 A.M. This type of shift schedule is difficult for employees in terms of sleeping patterns, eating habits, and family relations and interactions. A popular alternative to the standard schedule or a shift schedule is the flextime arrangement. Flextime is a schedule that gives an employee some choices as to when he will work. There is a *core* time when the employee must be at work and a *flexible* time when the employee chooses the remaining work time. The core time may be from 10:00 A.M. to 2:00 P.M. For this four-hour period the worker must be present. The worker then must schedule another five hours of work around the core. One person may elect to work from 8:00 A.M. to 5:00 P.M.; another may decide to work from 10:00 A.M. to 7:00 P.M.; and still another may decide to work from 5:00 A.M. to 2:00 P.M. Each of the employees works nine hours and each is present during the *core* time.

Another alternative is to work a "compressed" workweek.[44] Instead of working a five-day schedule, the employee may elect to extend the workday and work only four days, eleven hours a day.

Some banks and related establishments use *permanent part-time* employees; that is, part-time help is used on a regular basis for, say, four hours a day, five days a week (1:00 P.M. to 5:00 P.M.).[45] Another form of part-time employment is called *job sharing*. In such a schedule two employees divide a full-time job. Each person may work half the job or one person may work 60 percent of the hours and the other works the remaining 40 percent of the time.

Some firms permit telecommuting. By using computer terminals linked to mainframes in the main office or plant, work information can be exchanged. According to the Olsten Forum on Managing Workplace Technology, 51 percent of the 300 North American firms surveyed allow some form of telecommuting. Of those responding, 74 percent expect the practice to increase, and 45 percent said it enhances productivity.[46] In 1997, 11 million employees were classified as telecommuters, triple the number that were so classified in 1990.[47] The practice is likely to continue to increase as, by and large, telecommuters report satisfaction with this work arrangement.[48]

Each of these alternative work arrangements has some potential motivational value. Workers are given more freedom of choice to make decisions about their work schedule. This permits employees electing one of these alternative options the opportunity to decide when to conduct personal business and how to spend their workday.

12-6c A Critique of Performance-Based Rewards

The use of rewards has come to be very natural in work, school, and child rearing at home. Researcher Alfie Kohn (www.alfiekohn.org) offers a compelling set of criticisms of performance-based rewards. He contends that rewards and punishments are just two sides of the same coin, and the coin doesn't buy very much.[49] He suggests that managers must move beyond the use of rewards or punishments. Kohn raises some interesting arguments based on his review and interpretation of the research literature. His arguments are interesting and provocative enough that managers should at least be aware of the points he raises.

A few of Kohn's criticisms are these:

Rewards injure relationships. Individual rewards for performance create jealousies, envy, competition, and shame. The person not rewarded feels badly. There are always comparisons of what each person received. The result is less interpersonal goodwill and less working together.

Rewards are really punishment. An individual who is extrinsically rewarded is reminded each time he or she receives something that the "boss" is in control. Pleasing the boss, being politically correct, and staying in a subservient role are forms of punishment.

Rewards have a Skinner bias. B. F. Skinner is a behaviorist who conducted most of his experiments on rodents and pigeons and wrote most of his books about people. Basing reinforcement applications at work on pigeon- and rodent-dominated research is absurd. Emotions in employees are powerful, yet they are ignored by Skinner.

Rewards ignore reasons. What makes incentive pay plans and other forms of extrinsic rewards so appealing is that they are quick fixes. Issuing these kinds of rewards does not require managers to pay any attention to why a particular behavior occurred. Why was John's bonus larger than Mark's bonus? What were the behavioral differences between John and Mark?

Rewards discourage risk taking. When people are driven by rewards, their focus becomes more narrow, their creativity wanes, and they are not inclined to take risks. Taking risks may distract them from receiving a reward. Keeping a narrow, less risky orientation becomes preferred.

Kohn's critique is worthy enough to ask managers to think about the points he raises. It is unlikely in the foreseeable future to expect performance-based rewards to vanish in work organizations.[50] One of Kohn's limitations is that he provides no organizational suggestions or prescriptions for replacing rewards. His emphasis on child rearing and raising good children without "goodies" (rewards) is not applicable to work organizations without much more compelling translation and research work on his part or on the part of other researchers.

Management Summary

- Motivation is not something that can be seen. All that a manager can observe are changes in behavior. From these changes a manager makes inferences about motivation or what we define as all those inner-striving conditions described as needs, drives, desires, and motives that direct and maintain behavior.

- Rewards are of two types: *intrinsic* when a person derives satisfaction from performing the work or task itself and *extrinsic* when a person derives satisfaction from receiving something from an external party.

- Maslow proposed that each person has a hierarchy of five needs—physiological, safety, social, esteem, and self-actualization. Needs at the lower level must be adequately satisfied before high-level needs emerge and play a role in shaping behavior.

- McClelland studied the conditions under which people develop a motive to achieve and its impact on behavior. He identified three important needs—achievement, affiliation, and power.

- When a person is blocked from satisfying needs, a variety of constructive or defensive behaviors can occur—the choice in dealing with need satisfaction.

- Herzberg proposes a two-factor theory of motivation. One set of job conditions called the maintenance factors is needed to maintain a minimum level of satisfaction. On the other hand, motivational factors result in higher levels of motivation and job satisfaction.

- Vroom suggested an expectancy theory of motivation; that is, an individual engages in deciding what type of behavior is likely to result in his being able to achieve desired goals.

- The reinforcement theory of motivation uses positive or negative reinforcers to help motivate individuals. B. F. Skinner's application of behavior modification utilizes reinforcement theory to influence individual behavior.

- A provocative critique of reward systems is provided by Alfie Kohn. He offers reasons why reward systems are not very effective. His view comes up short on presenting what organizations should be doing, the costs, and the complexity of doing away with extrinsic rewards.

Key Terms

behavior modification (p. 292)
distributive justice (p. 291)
esteem needs (p. 283)
expectancy theory of motivation (p. 288)
hierarchy of needs (p. 282)
motivation (p. 278)

negative reinforcement (p. 292)
physiological (basic) needs (p. 282)
positive reinforcement (p. 292)
procedural justice (p. 291)
punishment (p. 292)
quality circles (p. 293)

reference ratio (p. 290)
reinforcement theory (p. 291)
safety needs (p. 283)
self-actualization needs (p. 283)
social needs (p. 283)
two-factor theory of motivation (p. 285)

Review and Discussion Questions

1. Quality of work life (QWL) programs sound interesting and attractive. They are used in a handful of organizations. Why, however, are QWL programs not used in a majority of organizations?

2. What is the problem with a manager concluding that motivation and performance are the same or are similar concepts?

3. The manager of a fast-food restaurant was overheard saying, "I believe that money is the best of all possible motivators. You can say what you please about all the other nonsense, but when it comes right down to it, if you give a guy a raise, you'll motivate him. That's all there is to it." In light of what we have discussed in this chapter, advise this restaurant manager.

4. Think of a situation from your personal experience in which two individuals reacted differently to frustration. Discuss each situation and the reactions of the two individuals. Can you give a possible explanation of why they reacted differently?

5. Some critics of behavior modification programs state that most of the declared successes are based on short-term results. These critics contend that a proper evaluation over a longer period of time would show negative results for these programs. Comment.

6. Since motivation can't be seen, is it difficult to measure? What kind of problems would exist if a person attempted to use the *Thematic Apperception Test* (TAT) to assess the motivation levels of a group of subordinates?

7. This chapter emphasizes that managers must be familiar with the fundamental needs of people in order to motivate employees successfully. Select two individuals with whom you are well acquainted. Do they differ, in your opinion, with respect to the strength of various needs? Discuss these differences and indicate how they could affect behavior. If you were attempting to motivate those persons, would you use different approaches for each? Why?

8. Alfie Kohn's critique of reward programs is compelling. What is the value of knowing about his concerns and attempting to solve the issues he raises?

9. Assume that you have just read that the *goals* of individuals influence their *effort* and that the behavior they select depends on their assessment of the probability that the behavior will lead to the goal. What is your goal in this management course? Is it influencing your effort? Do you suppose that another person in your class might have a different goal? Is his effort (behavior) different from yours? Could this information be of any value to your professor?

10. What is the difference between intrinsic and extrinsic rewards? What types of rewards fit each category? What role can a manager play in making sure that both of these types of rewards are available to employees?

Practice Quiz

Note: You can find the correct answers to these questions by taking the quiz and then submitting your answers in the Online Edition. The program will automatically score your submission. If you miss a question, the program will provide the correct answer, a rationale for the answer, and the section number in the chapter where the topic is discussed.

Indicate whether the sentence or statement is true or false.

1. An unsatisfied need causes tension within the individual or group, which leads to some kind of behavior to satisfy the need and thereby reduce the tension.

2. Maslow stated that if all of a person's needs are unsatisfied at a particular time, the most basic needs will be more pressing than the others.

3. Self-motivated need achievers like to set their own goals.

4. Herzberg reports that American, Japanese, and Italian employees are seldom motivated by similar job motivations.

5. Worker ownership of a company is an idea that was created in the 1950s by a lawyer.

Identify the letter of the choice that best completes the statement or answers the question.

6. The key to avoiding a sense of entitlement is to link incentives to _____ so that employees are clearly aware of their control of the rewards they attain.
   a. attendance
   b. seniority
   c. pay scale
   d. performance

7. The most commonly used concept in theories of work motivation is _____.
   a. wants.
   b. constraints.
   c. rewards.
   d. needs.

8. Since $M = E \times I \times V$, all three components in the equation must be _____ to achieve optimal motivation.
   a. high
   b. low

9. The ratio of a comparison person's input to outcome (reward) is called a _____ ratio.
   a. reference
   b. preference
   c. equity
   d. justice

10. According to the 1997 Olsten Forum on Managing Workplace Technology, 51 percent of the 300 North American firms surveyed allow some form of _____.
    a. flextime.
    b. profit sharing.
    c. telecommuting.
    d. job sharing.

11. One of the most common pay for performance plans is_____.
    a. off work pay.
    b. seniority pay.
    c. merit pay.
    d. team developmentary.

12. The concept of procedural justice has an impact on_____.
    a. loyalty.
    b. commitment.
    c. trust.
    d. all of the above.

13. Although David McClelland's theory of achievement motivation is interesting and elegant there is a problem with measurement. He uses the _____, which is subject to error and rater bias.
    a. need audit
    b. Thematic Apperception Test
    c. Nominal Group Test
    d. WonderlicTest

14. The most accurate comment to make about intrinsic motivators is that they are _____.
    a. personal and job related.
    b. based on external rewards.
    c. personality traits.
    d. observable and objective.

15. In the expectancy theory of motivation when instrumentality is nonexistent or of zero value then the motivation strength or power would be _____.
    a. moderately high.
    b. at least as strong as valence strengths.
    c. zero.
    d. 1.0000 + 1.00.

Case Study

Proposing to Work Flextime

Some believe that flextime is a crucial part of creating a workforce in which both companies and workers can adapt to changing technology and shifting family duties. A few examples illustrate that individuals can prepare their own proposal so that their bosses consider a number of work options for them to continue working.

All this may seem like a lot of homework, but it can pay off. Kristin's vice president was against her part-time telecommuting plan when her immediate boss first mentioned it to him. "He was kind of shoving her out the door, saying, 'That's not going to work,'" recalls Kristen, a program manager who live is Missouri. But after her boss handed him her well-documented written proposal, based on a template she found on-line, "He came back and said it was the most impressive proposal he'd seen, and that given the time I'd put into it, we ought to give it a try," Kristen says.

The best all-round website is www.workoptions.com. This site covers four options—part-time hours, a compressed workweek, job-sharing, and telecommuting. The site lays out some excellent homework for wannabes, with checklists of things to do before approaching the boss. This includes boning up on workplace policies and precedents, such as finding out whether others have been granted schedule changes and how they worked out.

Shannon long dreamed of working from home. Stuck in traffic commuting for more than an hour a day, wishing for more personal time, she hated "feeling like I was in the rat race," says Shannon, a health care consultant. But she hadn't a clue how to ask her boss for a change.

She found help in an unexpected place, the Internet. On a friend's advice, she searched websites on job flexibility and found a template for a telecommuting proposal to hand to her boss. After some homework and preparation, she presented the proposal and won approval. She's now seven weeks into her new work-at-home setup, and it's going well.

More than half the workforce wishes for some kind of change in their hours on the job, according to research by the Families and Work Institute, New York. But from the perspective of many individuals, as the old saying goes, you can't get there from here. Unless you employer is among a minority that has adopted and truly embraces clear, fair alternative-work policies, surmounting obstacles to changing your work setup can be a mystifying challenge.

The Internet has the potential to change all that. If you know where to look online, you can find some of the best strategies that have come out of more than a decade of flexibility research and practice. Templates for a detailed written proposal, background on the business reasons for offering flexibility, Q&As by experts, and even a screening test to help you figure out whether you're suited to work independently can all be found on the Web.

There are plenty of other things you'll need that you can't find on-line. You'll need goodwill with your bosses, earned through hard work, and a good track record on the job to lend your proposal credibility. You'll also need a fundamental understanding of the objectives of your business, to show how your proposed new setup will serve its needs.

You may need lots of patience. One customer-service manager I've corresponded with labored for two years to get her employer's approval for job-sharing, as her boss's bosses dithered over such steps as adjusting health benefits. By practicing perseverance, she eventually got approval.

You also need courage. If you work in a rigid culture, you risk being written off as uncommitted, or consigned to somebody's lay-off list if you ask for an oddball work setup—not matter how skillfully you ask. Though Shannon knew she had the work ethic to be a successful telecommuter, she didn't muster the courage to propose it until she and her husband decided to move to another state for his work, forcing her to either quit or work from home.

Questions for Discussion

1. What benefits are provided by using a template to prepare a personal telecommuting proposal for a manager to consider?

2. Why would a manager resist an employee's proposal to telecommute?

3. What work ethic must a person have to be a good candidate for telecommuting?

Source: Adapted from Sue Shellenbarger, "If You'd Rather Work in Pajamas, Here Are Ways to Talk the Boss into Flex-time," *Wall Street Journal,* New York: February 13, 2003, p. D1. Copyright © 2003 Dow Jones & Co. via Copyright Clearance Center.

Internet Exercise

Purpose: The purpose of this exercise is to compare the importance of various individual motivational factors among several people so that an awareness of differences and similarities is brought into focus.

Setting Up the Exercise:

1. Individually complete the ranking priority form shown below, using Herzberg's twelve factors which develop his two-factor theory of motivation. Those factors are:

Pay	Policies
Benefits	Achievement
Supervision	Challenge
Working conditions	Responsibility
Rules	Recognition
Procedures	Autonomy

2. After the ranking has been individually completed, the instructor will form groups of four to six students to discuss their rankings.

3. Each group will appoint a spokesperson to report to the entire class on how individual rankings differed in his group.

A Learning Note: This exercise will illustrate that there are major individual differences in motivational preferences. The difficulties managers face in addressing such individual differences should become clear.

Priority of Motivation Factors
(most influential first)

1. _____
2. _____
3. _____
4. _____
5. _____
6. _____
7. _____
8. _____
9. _____
10. _____
11. _____
12. _____

Experiential Exercise

Creating a Motivational Climate

The chapter discusses a variety of approaches for motivating employees. Some firms use a combination of approaches. There are also a host of what are called motivational speakers, consultants, and trainers. Tony Robbins, Zig Zigler, and Tom Peters are three of these motivational gurus. Find three other motivational gurus whom organizations use to pump up the work environment. Find out the background of these individuals, whom they work for, and with what line of thinking they are associated. Do not use Robbins, Zigler, or Peters as your three gurus. However, looking them up may help you with your exercise.

Communications
Skills test   88%

What motivates you
At work

150-200 words

Interpersonal and Organizational Communications

13

Managing Today

Lessons on Communicating and Leadership

When former treasury secretary Robert Rubin left his post as CEO of Goldman Sachs in 1992 to join the Clinton administration, he admitted he "didn't have the foggiest notion" of the inner workings of the White House and Capitol Hill. But Rubin had developed a habit earlier in his career that he quickly put to good use: after filling a legal pad with questions, he began making the rounds, interviewing Washington insiders—including members of other political camps—to gather information and advice.

"I arrived in Washington knowing a good bit about how Wall Street worked and some of what I knew was very useful. But I also had a strong appreciation for how much I didn't know about the ways of Washington," Rubin noted. "My chief asset in navigating this unknown terrain was a recognition and a readiness to learn."

By actively soliciting advice and a wide range of opinions, Rubin did what successful leaders have done for centuries, says leadership expert Saj-Nicole Joni: assemble a team of advisors who ensure that the leader can undertake the right kind of exploratory thinking and be challenged by multiple perspectives outside his office walls. Joni researched successful leaders and their teams for three years, talking to hundreds of top executives around the globe. Successful leaders, she concludes, are the ones who understand that they need different kinds of conversations with advisors outside the executive suite and beyond the daily work of running a complex organization. "Leaders need external thinking partners on the team so that they can explore sensitive issues with high trust and external perspective," says Joni. "Your ability to get results in increasingly boundaryless organizations depends on how well you can orchestrate your network of important relationships. You can't realize your full potential alone. And you cannot sustain full potential alone."

Conversations with these advisory teams are broad-ranging, and fall into one or more of four basic categories. But leaders who are not making time regularly for all four kinds of conversations as part of leadership work today run the risk of being blindsided by the competition, a new market entry, or unforeseen events such as the creation of new governmental regulations.

- **The visionary conversation.** The primary purpose of this kind of dialogue is to imagine the different, possible futures that you might create, and use that insight in the present. In this kind of conversation, you and your advisors consider world trends— micro- and macroeconomics, global and political realities, scientific and technological developments—sometimes as much as seven to ten years into the future.

- **The sounding-board conversation.** This conversation takes place when you want to work with someone who has the right expertise to take a "third opinion" look at a new strategy, marketing idea, or potential product. You and your advisors look together at the implicit assumptions involved in the course of action, check them against external reality, and vet the decision in multiple ways, considering, for instance, its legal, political, and environmental implications

- **The big-picture conversation.** In this conversation, you and your advisor step back and look at all the things that are going on, making sure that where you intend to go is consistent with your mechanisms for getting there. The purpose is to make sure that nothing has been left out, that your thinking hasn't become blinkered by a too-narrow corporate focus.

- **The "expertise in inquiry" conversation.** In these dialogues, you are looking for more than an expert problem-solving conversation. You are looking not only to develop your knowledge but also fundamental models and new ways of thinking about the terrain. Joni says, "The leadership terrain is complex, and the thinking required to master that terrain is demanding. Thus, learning what you are not a master of is just as important as developing your thinking skills."

Sources: Adapted from Nick Morgan, "The Third Opinion: How Leaders Can Get the Advice They Really Need," *Harvard Management Communication Letter,* Summer 2004, pp. 3–5; Robert Rubin, *In An Uncertain World: Tough Choices from Wall Street to Washington* (New York: Random House, 2003); and Saj-Nicole Joni, *The Third Opinion: How Successful Leaders Use Outside Insight to Create Superior Results* (New York: Portfolio/Penguin, 2004).

Communicating and communication are vital aspects of the managerial function of leading. Without communications, managers cannot *influence* individuals and groups to attain performance objectives. Effective communication is at the very heart of managerial performance.

Keeping people informed about company strategies is critically important in organizations of all sizes. Research conducted by the MCG Consulting Group on leadership found that communication skills is one of the five most important characteristics of leadership, along with vision, initiative, judgment, and motivation.[1] Not communicating with employees—or not allowing them access to important information—can exact a heavy price. A communications gap doesn't only undermine morale and performance, it can ultimately impact the bottom line:

- Over a five-year period, companies with higher scores on information-sharing had higher return on investment and higher return on sales than companies with low scores, according to a University of Michigan survey.

- An analysis of data from employee attitude surveys at Hewlett-Packard and GE found strong correlation between improved two-way employee/supervisor communication and increased productivity and employee retention.

- At Sears, analysts found that a five-point improvement in employee attitudes—a factor often tied to information-sharing—will drive a 1.3 percent increase in customer satisfaction and a 0.5 percent improvement in revenue growth.[2]

Opening information channels and making sure that communication flows in the right directions can be critical to performance. In addition, holding back information may prove destructive, giving employees and even customers the wrong signals.

In Chapter 2, we explored Henry Mintzberg's assumptions and research, which views the manager's job in terms of three primary managerial roles.[3] Communication is at the core of each of these roles. For example:

1. The manager's *interpersonal* roles require constant communication between managers and subordinates, customers, suppliers, peers, and superiors. The Mintzberg research indicates that managers spend about 45 percent of their contact time with peers, about 45 percent with people outside their work unit, and about 10 percent with superiors.

2. In the *informational* roles, managers seek information from all their contacts that may affect their job performance and goal accomplishment. Managers also send information to others inside and outside their unit and the organization.

3. The manager's *decisional* roles involve using information, contacts, and relationships to allocate limited resources, solve conflict-laden situations, and initiate problem-solving solutions. Once a decision is made by a manager, it must be communicated clearly to others.

The roles introduced and discussed by Mintzberg indicate that managers rarely get to do their thinking and contemplating alone. Interacting and orally communicating with others are major activities of managers. Studies indicate that managers spend from 60 to 80 percent of their time at work involved with oral communications.[4] Even with the myriad new communications tools now available in the workplace, traditional forms of communication continue to predominate. Research has shown that the new forms of communication do not replace more traditional forms, they simply supplement them.[5]

This chapter considers organizational communications. We begin by developing a framework for understanding communications. Then, organizational communication and the various formal and informal channels are explored. Next, we examine interpersonal communication styles, followed by consideration of some of the problems associated with interpersonal communications. The chapter concludes with a discussion of the causes and cures of communication breakdowns and discusses techniques managers can use to improve organizational communications.

13-1 A Framework for Understanding Communications

Communication is defined as the transmission of mutual understanding through the use of symbols. If mutual understanding does *not* result from the transmission of symbols, there is no communication. Figure 13-1 reflects the definition and identifies the important elements of communication.

As shown in Figure 13-1, the process of communication can be broken down into basic elements: the *source, encoding,* the *message,* the *medium, decoding,* the *receiver, noise,* and *feedback.* In simple terms, an individual or a group of individuals (the communicator) has an idea, message, or understanding to transmit to another individual or group of individuals (the receiver). To transmit the idea, the communicator first must translate it into a

▶**communication** The transmission of mutual understanding through the use of symbols.

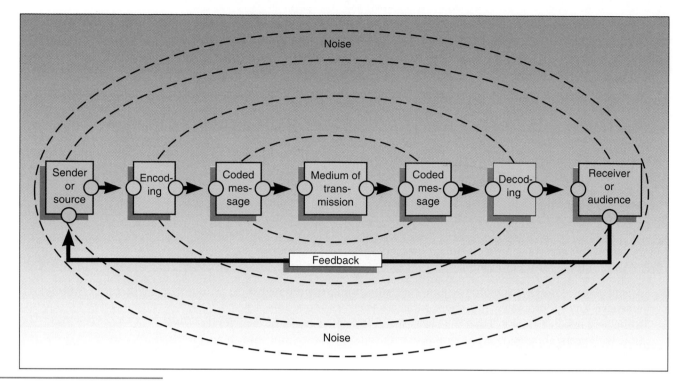

Figure 13-1
The Communication Process

language (encoding) and send the message by verbal, nonverbal, or written means (the medium). The message is received through the senses of the receiver and translated (decoded) into a message received. Occasionally, noise enters the communication picture. That is, some form of interference occurs at some point in the process. Communication interference must be reduced or eliminated so that an understanding between the sender and receiver can result. By a nod of the head, a facial expression, or action, the receiver acknowledges whether understanding has been achieved (feedback). Let us examine each element more closely.

13-1a The Communicator

Communicators in an organization can be managers, nonmanagers, departments, or the organization itself. Managers communicate with other managers, subordinates, supervisors, clients, customers, and parties outside the organization. Nonmanagers likewise communicate with managers and nonmanagers, clients, customers, and external parties. People in sales departments communicate with people in production departments, and engineering personnel communicate with product design teams. Communications between individuals within the organization are important means for coordinating the work of separate departments.

13-1b Encoding

The communicator's message must be translated into a language that reflects the idea; that is, the message must be encoded. The reader of spy novels is familiar with the scene in which the enemy (or friendly) agent has a message to send to headquarters. To prevent opposing agents from obtaining the message and understanding it, the agent transmits the message in *code*, a language presumably known only by the agent and headquarters. In situations less dramatic and intriguing, encoding usually is the selection of language specific to the purpose of the communicator's message. The encoding action produces the communicable message.

A manager usually relies on languages, words, symbols, or gestures that portray his thoughts and feelings. The purpose of **encoding** is to translate thoughts and feelings into a code that others are able to understand. In some cases, this may involve using jargon.

▶**encoding** The translating of a communication into an understandable message by a communicator.

LearningMoment *Translating Technical Jargon*

It's very important that managers learn to communicate with others who are both less technically trained and more technically trained. Managers who talk down to subordinates less technical than themselves lose their respect. Likewise, managers who attempt to "fake" their technical competence with those more highly trained lose their respect. Managers must learn to translate their technical code into a language that others can understand, and they must not be afraid to ask for appropriate translations when they lack technical knowledge.

People trained in nearly any profession will have a "technical" language they use to talk among themselves about the problems and issues within that profession. However, professionals in organizations must often deal with others who do not have their level of training and experience. They must take extra care to encode their messages in a language the nonprofessionals can understand in order for communication to occur.

13-1c The Message

The output of the encoding process is the *message*. The purpose of the communicator is expressed in the form of the message—either verbal or nonverbal. Managers have numerous purposes for communicating, such as to have others understand their ideas, to understand the ideas of others, to gain acceptance of themselves or their ideas, and to produce action. The message, then, is what the individual hopes to communicate, and the exact form that the message takes depends to a great extent on the medium used to carry it. Decisions relating to the two—message and medium—are inseparable.

The most famous discussion of the message component of communications was raised by Marshall McLuhan. His observation that "the medium is the message" conveys the idea that form overwhelms content. This controversial thesis lies behind much of the modern distrust of major media—and the belief that most of them operate with a "hidden agenda."[6]

13-1d The Medium

The *medium* is the carrier of the intended message. Organizations provide information to their members by a variety of means, including face-to-face communication, telephone, group meetings, computers, memos, policy statements, reward systems, bulletin boards, production schedules, company publications, and sales forecasts.

Unintended messages can be sent by silence or inaction on a particular issue as well as by decisions on which goals and objectives are *not* to be pursued and which methods are *not* to be utilized. Finally, such nonverbal media as facial expressions, tone of voice, and body movements also can communicate an unintended or intended message.

LearningMoment *Hidden Agendas in Communication*

McLuhan's belief that "the medium is the message" suggests that people use communication forms to deliver important parts of a message. For example, a face-to-face meeting is often considered more appropriate for serious communication than brief e-mails. What "message" do you think people send when they use interoffice memoranda? The telephone? An employee newsletter?

Management Focus on Innovation

Tele-Immersion Offers New Promise for Remote Communications

Tele-immersion, a new medium for human interaction enabled by digital technologies, approximates the illusion that a user is in the same physical space as other people, even though the other participants might in fact be hundreds or thousands of miles away. It combines the display and interaction techniques of virtual reality with new vision technologies that transcend the traditional limitations of a camera. Rather than merely observing people and their immediate environ- ment from one vantage point, tele-immersion stations convey them as "moving sculptures," without favoring a single point of view. The result is that all the participants, however distant, can share and explore a life-size space.

Source: Adapted from Jaron Lanier, "Virtually There," *Scientific American,* April 2001, pp. 66–75.

---

media richness The capacity of a medium to convey data.

bandwidth The amount of data that can be squeezed through an electronic medium.

information richness The ability of information to change understanding within a time interval.

Another factor that is important in choosing a medium is **media richness,** the capacity for a medium to convey data.[7] One medium may be richer than another; that is, one medium may have a greater capacity to carry data than another. Data-carrying capacity refers to the degree to which a medium can effectively and efficiently convey data. Several criteria are used to evaluate a medium's richness: its capacity for timely feedback; its capacity for multiple uses, such as audio and video; the extent to which the message can be personalized; and the variety of symbolic messages that can be encoded (for example, emotional expressions as well as natural language). In modern terms, media richness is similar to **bandwidth.** Bandwidth refers to the amount of data that can be squeezed through an electronic medium.

Another important concept is **information richness.** Information richness is the ability of information to change understanding within a time interval. Communication transactions that can overcome different frames of reference or clarify ambiguous issues to change understanding are considered rich. Communications that require a long time to enable understanding or that cannot overcome different perspectives are lower in richness. In a sense, richness pertains to the learning capacity of a communication.[8]

The Management Focus on Innovation box, "Tele-Immersion Offers New Promise for Remote Communications," discusses advances in video conferencing that may enable greater communication richness in our increasingly global and virtual business world.

13-1e Decoding

decoding The process by which receivers translate a message into terms meaningful to them.

Decoding refers to the process by which receivers *translate* the message into terms meaningful to them. For example, in the spy business, if headquarters uses the same code book that the secret agent used in preparing the coded message, then the message it receives will be the same as what was sent. But if the code is known only to the agent, then no common understanding can be reached. In a business organization, if the message that the chief executive receives from the accounting department includes many technical terms that are known only to accountants, no communication occurs. An often-cited complaint in organizations with departmental structures is that the various units cannot communicate. Each department has a language and symbols that persons outside the group have difficulty decoding. This lack of a common language leads to inefficiencies, high costs, and decreasing competitiveness.

13-1f The Receiver

Communication requires a *receiver* who must be taken into account when a communicator attempts to transmit information. "Telling isn't teaching" if the teacher uses language that the student cannot understand (cannot decode). Engineers cannot expect to communicate to nonengineers if the symbols they use are beyond the receivers' training and ability to comprehend. Effective communication requires that the communicator anticipate the receiver's decoding ability. *Effective communication is receiver oriented, not sender oriented.*

Today's multicultural workplaces pose another problem for receiving messages as they were intended. Managers today must be certain that their messages are tailored to the language or cultural backgrounds of receivers.[9] Unintended insults or confusions can escalate rapidly into widespread organizational problems.

13-1g Noise

Noise is any element or condition that disturbs or interferes with the effective sending and receiving of communication. Disturbances or interferences can occur at any point in the communication process. A manager may not be able to express himself well; a subordinate may be bored and not pay attention to what a manager says; memos may be poorly reproduced and thus hard to read; or an electrical power surge may shut down the organization's computer. These are all examples of noise. They disturb and interfere with the regular flow of information. Managers must take action whenever possible to reduce noise.

▶**noise** Any element or condition that disturbs or interferes with sending and receiving effective communication.

13-1h Feedback

Feedback enables the communicator to determine if the message has been received and if it has produced the intended response. *One-way* communication processes do not allow receiver-to-communicator feedback. *Two-way* communication processes, however, do. For the manager, communication feedback may present itself in many ways. In face-to-face situations, *direct* feedback is possible through verbal exchanges as well as through subtle means such as facial expressions that indicate discontent or misunderstanding. In addition, communication breakdowns may be indicated by *indirect* means, such as declines in productivity, poor quality of production, increased absenteeism or turnover, and conflict or a lack of coordination between units.

▶**feedback** An element that enables the communicator to determine whether a message has been received and whether it has produced the intended message.

13-2 Organizational Communication: Formal Channels

Managers must provide for organizational communication in three distinct directions, downward, upward, and horizontal. These three formal channels of communication and a few examples for each direction flow are provided in Figure 13-2. Since these three directions summarize the paths that official communications travel in an organization, let's briefly examine each of them. The manager who understands and examines the formal flow of communication is better able to appreciate the barriers to effective organizational communication, as well as the means for overcoming them.

13-2a Downward Communication

Downward communication flows from individuals in higher levels of the organization to those at lower levels. The most common forms of downward communication are job instructions, official memos, policy statements, procedures, posters, manuals, and company publications. In many organizations, downward communication often is both inadequate and inaccurate, and employees typically receive such tremendous amounts of downward communication that they selectively decide which messages to fully receive, which to partially receive, and which to disregard.

The key aspect of downward communication is that subordinates tend to react most effectively to those matters they judge to be of the greatest personal interest to the boss. Among the range of policies, recommendations, guidelines, and directives that come from above, subordinates tend to select those most in keeping with their perception of their boss's character, personal motivation, and style. Those downward communications that match subordinates' impressions of their boss's preferences are given priority for follow-up action.[10] Managers must be aware of this selective screening of downward communication. Having clear principles and clear organizational goals will ensure that employees pay attention to those messages that affect organizational performance.

▶**downward communication** Communication that flows from individuals at higher levels. The most common type of downward communication is job instructions that are transmitted from the superior to the subordinate.

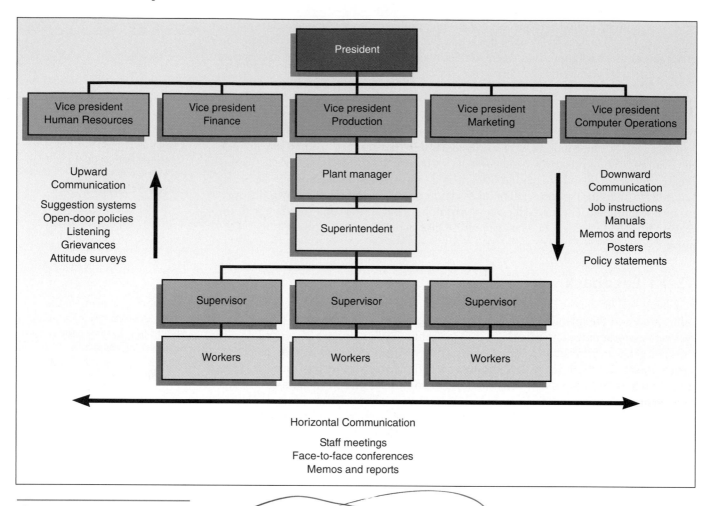

Figure 13-2
Formal Organizational Channels of Communication

▶ **upward communication**
Communication that flows from individuals at lower levels of an organization structure to those at higher levels.

13-2b Upward Communication

A high-performing organization needs effective **upward communication** as much as it needs effective downward communication. Effective upward communication—getting messages from employees to management—is difficult to achieve, especially in larger organizations. Some studies suggest that of the three formal communication channels, upward communication is the most ineffective. Upper-level managers often don't respond to messages sent from lower-level employees, and lower-level employees often are reluctant to communicate upward, especially when the message contains bad news.[11] However, upward communication is often necessary for sound decision making.

Widely used upward communication devices include *suggestion boxes, group meetings, participative decision making,* and *appeal or grievance procedures.* In the absence of these flows, employees find ways to adapt to nonexistent or inadequate upward communication channels. In the absence of sanctioned upward communication channels, employees may resort to inventing their own channels, including such unwanted techniques as "underground" employee publications. To prevent this, managers should make sure they have well-known methods for employees to be able to communicate upward.

Effective upward communications are important because they provide employees with opportunities to be *heard.* However, research has shown that workers generally will not speak their minds if they know their comments will reach management with their names attached.[12] Besides traditional methods of communicating with employees, managers must also develop ways for employees to express themselves anonymously. This can be done with suggestion boxes, exit interviews by a third party, or anonymous focus groups conducted by a third party. It may be difficult for some managers to relinquish control over the upward communication channel, but the alternative—not getting valuable information from employees—could be far worse.

13-2c Horizontal Communication

Often overlooked in the design of most organizations is provision for the formal *horizontal* flow of communication. When the supervisor of the accounting department communicates with the director of marketing concerning advertising budget expenditures, the flow of communication is horizontal. Although vertical (upward and downward) communication flows are the primary considerations in organizational design, effective organizations also need **horizontal communication.** Horizontal communication—for example, between production and sales departments in a business organization and between different departments within a hospital—is necessary for the coordination of diverse organizational functions.

Managers who recognize the need for horizontal communication can appoint committees of representatives from various departments. The use of routinely scheduled interdepartmental staff meetings can facilitate horizontal communication. The more interdependent the work of the departments, the greater is the need to formalize horizontal communication. Of the three formal communication channels, horizontal communication tends to be the most effective. Messages are often sent and accurately received, and feedback is frequently obtained.[13]

The Internet and corporate intranets have introduced new opportunities for horizontal or lateral communications in companies. Many companies are using the technology to share best practices information across departments and divisions.[14] For example, problems often occur during the handoffs from one link to another in the product-creation process or service-delivery chain. Often, one group doesn't realize it is creating problems. A survey of a retail company found that more than 25 percent of store employees identified a significant communication barrier with a particular department in the distribution centers. Yet the employees didn't see any barriers at all and would have continued creating the same problems endlessly if they hadn't been compelled to address the underlying issues.

An organization's formal structure (see Figure 13-2) can have impacts on its flow of communication. The three basic patterns of formal communication—upward, downward, and horizontal—are spelled out by the relationships depicted in an organization chart. However, communication involves people as well as structure. Managers and employees tend to adapt and modify the formal channels to suit their needs, goals, and time. In some cases, *informal* channels emerge to supplant the formal channels.

13-3 Organizational Communication: Informal Channels

Research suggests that communications do not flow randomly within organizations, nor do they necessarily follow the formal pathways published in an organizational chart.[15] Many organizations have extensive networks of informal communications. Employees of large organizations readily acknowledge the existence of so-called water cooler gossip, rumors, and stories. The study of informal pathways has been helped by a method known as sociometry. In sociometry, members of a group or unit are asked about the other members with whom they communicate.[16] Then a diagram of these patterns, known as a **sociogram,** is drawn showing the pathways used for communication.

An example of a sociogram is shown in Figure 13-3. It was developed after asking members of a department to list whom they communicate with on technical job-related problems, issues, or concerns. Some of the connections shown in Figure 13-3 have arrowheads on one end, indicating that that person passes information on to another person, while others have arrowheads at both ends, suggesting that that person gives and receives information. By constructing sociograms such as the one in Figure 13-3, the patterns of informal communications can be graphically represented. This can provide a manager with insights into the informal patterns as well as the formal patterns that control the flow of communications within a department.

The sociogram shows that three close-knit **cliques** tend to communicate on a regular basis. These cliques have formed because of common interests, physical proximity, or sim-

> **horizontal communication**
> Communication that occurs when the communicator and the receiver are at the same level in the organization.

> **sociogram** A graphical presentation of pathways used for communication; shows who is communicating with whom.

> **cliques** Groups within an organization that tend to communicate internally on a regular basis.

Figure 13-3
Sociogram: Informal Communication Patterns on Technical Aspects of the Job

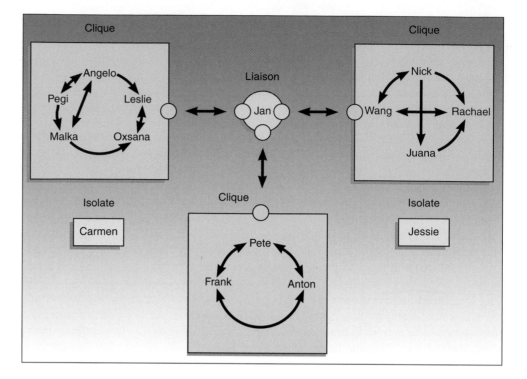

isolates Individuals or small groups within an organization that tend not to communicate with other individuals and/or groups.

liaison The role played by individuals or small groups in an organization to facilitate communication among isolates and cliques.

ilar jobs. On the other hand, Carmen and Jessie are revealed as **isolates** who communicate with no one on technical matters. Being an isolate may indicate such things as having different goals from others in the unit or being disaffected from the job.

The sociogram also singles out a **liaison** person, Don, who is not a member of a clique but is at the center of information flow. Don has contact with the three cliques and serves as a liaison who ties the unit together on technical matters. Liaisons have been referred to as "the 'cement' that holds the structural 'bricks' of an organization together; when the liaisons are removed, a system tends to fall apart into isolated cliques."[17]

The informal organization in corporate life is widely underappreciated among practicing managers. As a result, many managers don't have a mastery of the workings of the informal organization and often downplay its comparative importance. Because the informal organization allows and encourages open relationships and interaction between people as individuals more than as post-holders, it tends to work with much shallower status hierarchies, which can be completely level or even inverted in some circumstances. The informal communication channel brings benefits to the overall organization through the provision of essential communication services.[18] It can also bring some negative elements to the organization as the informal communication channel is the primary vehicle for back stabbing and other nonproductive forms of conversation.[19] A few elements of the informal channels of organizational communication are explored next.

13-3a The Grapevine

An informal communication pathway that is recognized as a part of organizational life is called the **grapevine.** The use of the term *grapevine* is said to have originated during the Civil War, when telegraph lines were strung loosely between trees, and soldiers said the wires resembled a grapevine. Messages that were difficult to decipher were said to have come through "the grapevine."

Today's grapevine cuts across formal channels of communication. Through it passes an assortment of facts, opinions, suspicions, and rumors that typically do not move through the formal channels. Research suggests the following:

grapevine An informal communication network in organizations that short-circuits the formal channels.

1. Organizations have several grapevine systems.
2. Information traveling in a grapevine does not follow an orderly path.
3. Organizationally related grapevine information is about 75 percent accurate.[20]

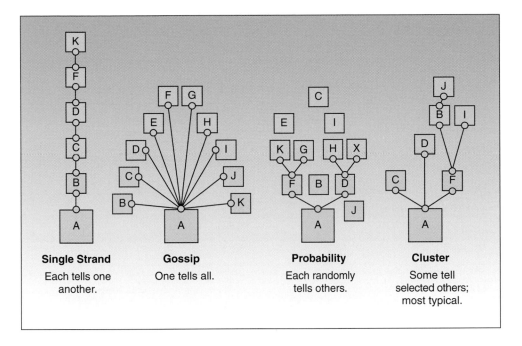

Figure 13-4
Grapevine Patterns

Source: Keith Davis, *Human Behavior at Work: Organizational Behavior,* 6th ed. (New York: McGraw-Hill, 1981), p. 339. Reprinted by permission of The McGraw-Hill Companies.

A survey conducted by *Coleman Consulting Group* of more than 22,000 employees operating on shift work schedules found that 55 percent said the majority of information they receive comes via the grapevine.[21] The patterns of grapevine communication are shown in Figure 13-4. The cluster pattern, in which only select individuals repeat what they hear, is the pattern most commonly found in organizations.

13-3b The Rumor

The grapevine is so much a part of organizational life that it is futile for management to attempt to eliminate it as an informal channel. However, a manager must recognize that a grapevine can be troublesome if it serves as a constant source of **rumors.** Rumors are an everyday part of business and management; it is estimated that over 33 million rumors are generated in U.S. businesses every day.[22]

A rumor can be defined as an unverified belief that is in general circulation inside the organization (an internal rumor) or in the organization's external environment (an external rumor).[23] A rumor has three components. The *target* is the object of the rumor. The *allegation* is the rumor's point about the target. And the rumor has a *source*, the communicator of the rumor. Often, individuals will attribute a rumor to a prestigious or authoritative source to give the rumor more credibility.[24]

Some rumors that travel through the company grapevine or outside the organization are true; however, sometimes they are not. Regardless of their validity, rumors tend to flourish if their content is entertaining, important, and ambiguous. Entertaining rumors have staying power because people find them interesting to think about and pass on to others.

Important rumors have staying power because their information concerns people. For example, rumors often run rampant in a company shortly after it has been acquired by another firm. Many rumors are believed because the information is important to the acquired workforce. Employees seek information to reduce their uncertainty and anxiety about their jobs and the company's future. Ambiguous rumors have staying power because their lack of clarity makes it difficult to quickly refute and dismiss the rumor.[25]

Managers and employees in the global workplace endorse rumor as an important information source, according to research conducted by *International Survey Research.* The company polled more than 2 million employees, primarily managers, all over the world. All industries were represented. Respondents were asked to indicate total agreement with the following statement: "We usually hear about important matters first through rumors." Table 13-1 shows the percentage of workers from a variety of countries who agreed that rumors are important sources of information in an organization.[26]

> **rumors** Unverified beliefs that circulate in an organization or into its external environment; comprises the *target* (the rumor's object), the *source* (the rumor's communicator), and the *allegation* (the rumor's point about the target).

TABLE 13-1 **Percentage of Workers Who Believe Rumors Are Important**		
United Kingdom		73%
United States		69%
Hong Kong		68%
Thailand		66%
Canada		63%
South Africa and France		62%
Taiwan		61%
Brazil and Australia		59%
Netherlands and Singapore		58%
Mexico and Germany		57%
India		54%
Malaysia		52%
The Philippines		51%
China		51%
Switzerland		47%
Japan		42%

Grapevines, rumors, and gossip are deeply ingrained in organizational life, so managers must be tuned in and listening to what is being said. Falsified facts traveling through the rumor mill can be corrected by feeding accurate information to primary communicators or liaison individuals. Also, managers can use informal communication systems such as the grapevine to benefit programs, policies, or plans. The grapevine can provide yet another, albeit weak, communication vehicle to keep the workforce informed about job-related matters.

13-4 Interpersonal Communication

One type of communication travels from individual to individual in face-to-face and group settings. Such flows are termed **interpersonal communications,** and the forms vary from direct verbal orders to casual, nonverbal expression. Interpersonal communication is the primary means of managerial communication; on a typical day, over 75 percent of a manager's communications occur via face-to-face interactions.[27]

The problems that can arise when managers attempt to communicate with other people can be traced to *perceptual* and *interpersonal style* differences. Each manager perceives the world in terms of his or her background, experiences, personality, frame of reference, and attitude. The primary manner in which managers relate to and learn from the environment (including people in that environment) is through information received and transmitted. The way managers receive and transmit information partly depends on how they relate to themselves and others. The way a manager commonly relates to others is known as "interpersonal style." We'll explore this concept next. In addition to interpersonal style, interpersonal communications are affected by the amount of **information** the various parties to a communication have. Differences in access to or possession of information can create communication challenges.

13-4a Interpersonal Styles

Interpersonal styles differ among individuals, and understanding these differences is important for managerial and organizational performance. **Interpersonal style** refers to the way in which an individual prefers to relate to others. The fact that much of the interactions among people involve communication indicates the importance of interpersonal style.[28]

▶**interpersonal communications** Communications that comprise the full range of direct verbal and nonverbal signals that pass between and among individuals in the workplace.

▶**information** Derived from data; essentially, data that are organized for a specific purpose.

▶**interpersonal style** The way in which an individual prefers to relate to others.

Figure 13-5
Identify the Group
Where You Belong

INTERACTIVE FIGURE

Select the six traits that best describe you.

☐ Direct	☐ Bold	☐ Daring
☐ Self-starter	☐ Challenge-oriented	☐ Competitive
☐ Enthusiastic	☐ Persuasive	☐ Sociable
☐ Inspiring	☐ Talkative	☐ Optimistic
☐ Amiable	☐ Relaxed	☐ Patient
☐ Good listener	☐ Steady	☐ Logical
☐ Perfectionist	☐ Analytical	☐ Precise
☐ Diplomatic	☐ Accurate	☐ Restrained

Based on your answers above, you belong in group:

Group 1: direct, bold, daring, self-starter, challenge-oriented, competitive

Group 2: enthusiastic, persuasive, sociable, inspiring, talkative, optimistic

Group 3: amiable, relaxed, patient, good listener, steady, logical

Group 4: perfectionist, analytical, precise, diplomatic, accurate, restrained

Some communication style differences among people are unintentional or unconscious. For example, research into differences between male and female voice tones has indicated that they differ acoustically, and sex-stereotyped attributions are formed based on gender of voice. This research reported that men's voices are less nasal than women's voices, and that nasality of voice is inversely related to perceptions of persuasiveness. In other words, the less nasal the voice, the more persuasive it was perceived to be by listeners.[29]

Good communicators learn to recognize their interpersonal style and the styles of others. They also learn to modify their style to enhance the likelihood of effective communications. For example, look at the following groups of words, and identify which group you are most like, and which you are least like (see Figure 13-5):

- Group 1: direct, bold, daring, self-starter, challenge-oriented, competitive
- Group 2: enthusiastic, persuasive, sociable, inspiring, talkative, optimistic
- Group 3: amiable, relaxed, patient, good listener, steady, logical
- Group 4: perfectionist, analytical, precise, diplomatic, accurate, restrained

Let's say that you are most like Group 2, and least like Group 4. You work with a colleague who is quiet, cautious, analytical, and somewhat pessimistic, a behavioral style clearly quite different from yours. If you communicate with your usual enthusiastic, optimistic verve, it is likely to be less effective when dealing with this person. Learning to adapt your style, however, diminishes communication tension. In this situation, by simply moderating some of your enthusiasm and slowing down your pace of speech you will inevitably establish better rapport.[30]

13-4b Communication and Information

Information is held by you and by others. Interpersonal communications is largely focused on transmitting information from one person to another person or persons. But you or they may not have all the necessary facts.

Figure 13-6
Interpersonal Styles and Communication

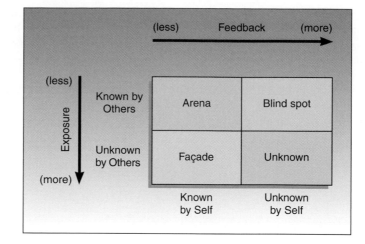

The Johari Window is a popular and easily understood model of communication developed by psychologists Joseph Luft and Harry Ingham. The Johari Window is essentially an information processing model. The model uses a two-by-two matrix to reflect the interacton of two sources of information: the self and others. The four quadrants representing the "interpersonal space" identify how the particular information-processing elements affect the quality of relationships.

The different combinations of knowing and not knowing information are shown in Figure 13-6. The figure identifies four regions, or combinations, of information known and unknown by self and others.

The Arena

The region most conducive to effective interpersonal relationships and communications is termed the **arena.** In this setting, all the information necessary to carry on effective communication is known to both the sender (self) and the receivers (others). As expressed in the current cliché, each party to the communication knows where the other comes from. In practical terms, if a communication attempt is in the arena region, the parties to the communication share identical feelings, data, assumptions, and skills that bear on the attempt.

The Blind Spot

When relevant information is known to others but not to you, a **blind spot** results. In this context, a person (self) is at a disadvantage when communicating with others because he cannot know the others' feelings, sentiments, and perceptions. Consequently, interpersonal relationships and communications suffer.

When one party is unable to know her true feelings or sentiments about an issue, she may be unable to perceive accurately the information received from others. The idea of *selective perception* is related to blind-spot problems, since an individual experiencing a blind spot likely will be unable to receive and decode information properly. The greater the blind spot, the smaller the arena, and vice versa.

The Façade

When information is known to the self but unknown to others, the person (self) may resort to superficial communications; that is, he may present a **façade.** A façade is a false front. The façade area is particularly damaging when a subordinate "knows" and an immediate supervisor "does not know." The façade, like the blind spot, diminishes the arena and reduces the possibility of effective communication.

The Unknown

If neither party in a communication pattern knows the relevant feelings, sentiments, and information, each party is functioning in **the unknown** region. Such a situation often is stated as "I can't understand them, and they don't understand me." In this predicament, interpersonal communications are sure to suffer. The unknown factor often occurs in organizations when individuals in differing technical areas must coordinate their activities through communications.

arena The theoretical "best place" for communication where each party knows each other's positions and motivations well. This is the most effective domain for interpersonal communications.

blind spot When relevant information is known to others but not to a particular individual. In this context, the individual is at a disadvantage when communicating with others because he or she cannot know the others' feelings, sentiments, and perceptions.

façade When information is known to an individual but unknown to others, the individual may resort to superficial communications; that is, he or she may present a false front.

the unknown If neither party in a communication pattern knows the relevant feelings, sentiments, and information, each party is functioning in the unknown region.

Thus, we see that the larger the areas affected by blind spots, façades, and unknowns, the smaller the arena. But how can we reduce those areas and enlarge the arena? Interpersonal communication problems are the results of unsound relationships. An individual can improve unsound relationships by adopting two strategies—exposure and feedback.

Exposure   Increasing the arena area by reducing the façade area requires that one be open and honest in sharing information with others. The unwillingness of companies to discuss salary matters is an example of inadequate exposure. The process that the self uses to increase the information known to others is termed **exposure** because it leaves one in a vulnerable position. Exposing one's true feelings and sentiments is a ploy that involves some risk.

> **exposure** The process that the self uses to increase information known to others.

Feedback   When the self does not know or understand, more effective communications can be developed through feedback from those who do know. Thus, the blind spot can be reduced with a corresponding increase in the arena. Whether feedback is possible depends on the individual's willingness to hear it or the willingness of others to give it. Thus, the individual is less able to control the provision of feedback than the provision of exposure. Obtaining feedback is dependent on the active cooperation of others, while exposure requires the active behavior of the individual and passive listening by others.

13-5 Types of Interpersonal Communication

Interpersonal communication is of two types: verbal and nonverbal. Verbal communication is *talking* or *writing* to someone. Most managers are good at verbal communications and have learned how to speak and write clearly and succinctly. Often, managers are less well informed about the power of nonverbal communication. The subtle facial expressions or body language managers use, deliberately or not, can have a profound effect on the morale of a workforce. For example, if a manager shows stress in a time of crisis, the employees will probably be more concerned about their situation than if the manager displays confidence and resolve. In such a situation, the nonverbal cues a manager sends to employees can have a more dramatic effect on performance than any verbal message. We examine each type of communication in more detail in the following sections.

13-5a Verbal Communication

There are essentially two types of **verbal communication**: oral and written. However, these forms have many permutations that make them incredibly complex. Oral communication, for example, can be face-to-face or mediated by technology, such as a telephone. Most of you reading this will probably agree that communicating by telephone is quite different than face-to-face communication. This difference is magnified in emotional or complicated interactions.

> **verbal communication** Communication by talking or writing.

Oral Communication   **Oral communication** takes place when the spoken word is used to transmit a message. Conversations can take place in person, via telephone, or through some other mechanism that allows individuals to speak to one another. Oral communication enables prompt, two-way interactions between parties. Many meetings and conferences that involve people from different locations, even different parts of the world, are conducted using videoconferencing so that participants can interact personally. Perhaps the major benefit of this type of communication is that ideas can be interchanged and prompt feedback can be provided. Questions can be addressed, positions and issues debated, and a plan for action or resolution established. Oral communication that takes place in person also allows the use of gestures, facial expressions, and other emotions such as tone of voice. As the Management Focus on Technology box, "IM Is Catching on in Organizational Communications," indicates, instant messaging technology is becoming as ubiquitous as e-mail and voice mail in the workplace.

> **oral communication** The transmission and receipt of messages that occurs when the spoken word is used to transmit a message.

Oral communication, because of its immediacy, can occasionally result in poor communication. If, for instance, a person becomes angry, noise enters the communication process. Messages that are not clearly encoded may also fail to communicate the intended

Management Focus on Technology

IM Is Catching on in Organizational Communications

Instant messaging (IM), formerly a technology reserved for teens who were not allowed to use the telephone after 9:00 P.M. has found broad acceptance within the enterprise. Some startling new statistics reveal just how important this mode of communicating has become to worldwide commercial activity:

• 85 percent of all enterprises in North America use some form of IM.

• 20 percent of all enterprises worldwide now use IM, and that number is expected to rise to 80 percent by 2008.
• 11.4 billion instant messages are sent daily. That number is expected to hit 45.8 billion by 2008.
• Over 830 million active IM accounts were recorded by the end of 2004.

Source: Adapted from "Hooked on IM" *CRN,* September 13, 2004, p. 37.

idea. A hurried manager may give an oral instruction or initiative without thinking about the outcome. While feedback is immediate, it may also be without thought, reducing the quality of the communication. Individuals often feel the need to respond immediately in a face-to-face meeting, when in fact they should take some time to prepare a well-thought-out response.

Research has indicated that 67 percent of new employees recruited from full-time education start their careers without essential interpersonal skills. Human resource professionals believe that "soft" skills should be an essential part of academic training. Oral communication was cited as the number one soft skill but was perceived to be sorely lacking among recruits coming straight from higher education.[31] At the same time, students in business communication programs rate oral communication less positively than either written or e-mail communication.[32]

written communication The transmission and receipt of messages through the written word.

Written Communication Transmitting a message through the written word is called **written communication.** This type of communication can help eliminate the problem we just discussed. Written messages allow a manager to think about the message, reread it several times, and perhaps get others to review the message before it's transmitted. The receiver can take time to read the message carefully and accurately. Written messages are also more permanent than oral, providing a record of the communication. Whether it's a long report or a short memo, written communication can be referred to in the future as needed. Managers often find it necessary to document their decisions for legal reasons.

Despite the advantages of written communication, managers generally prefer to communicate orally. Written communication takes more time to prepare and does not allow interaction or immediate feedback. Managers rely on two-way communication to resolve problems quickly. It takes much longer to get ideas on paper, to distribute them to others, and to receive written responses; a telephone call or a meeting is quicker. Written communication, by its formal nature, may also discourage open communication. E-mail, a form of written communication, is more timely and allows quick response, perhaps explaining its popularity.

13-5b Nonverbal Communication

nonverbal communication The transmission and receipt of messages by some medium other than verbal or written.

Communication that is nonverbal can occur in any interaction between individuals. A manager's nonverbal behavior may communicate a stronger message than information presented in a memo, policy statement, or conversation.[33] **Nonverbal communication** is present in the vocal cues, facial expressions, posture, or spatial orientation of a sender. For example, did you know that covering the mouth with the hands, rubbing the side of the nose, or jerking the head quickly could be signs that a person is attempting to be deceptive?[34]

Communicating nonverbally involves the sending and receiving of messages by some medium other than verbal or written. One researcher has found that only 7 percent of a message's impact comes from its verbal content. The rest of the impact is nonverbal—38 percent from vocal inflection and content, and 55 percent from facial content.[35] When a sender's communication is contradictory (the nonverbal message contradicts the verbal message), the receiver places more weight on the nonverbal content of the overall communication.[36]

The vocal part of a message pertains to how it is transmitted. A message can be transmitted loudly or softly, quickly or slowly, with controlled or uncontrolled inflection, or with a high or low pitch. The method of transmission adds meaning to the receiver who assesses these cues. For example, suppose a manager who is usually calm and collected delivers a high-pitched, uncontrolled message to his subordinates. The subordinates are likely to infer from the message that the manager is under heavy pressure. This interpretation may cause them to listen more attentively, since it is not normal for the manager to seem so troubled.

Body expressions are another important source of nonverbal communication. Eckman and Friesen have classified body language into five types of expression.[37] **Emblems** are gestures that are much like sign language (the hitchhiker's thumb, the OK sign with thumb and forefinger, the "V" sign for victory). These movements quickly convey an understood word or phrase. **Illustrators** are gestures that illustrate what is being said (a raised forefinger to indicate the first point of a sender's position, extended hands to illustrate the size of an object). **Regulators** are movements that regulate a conversation. For example, an upraised palm from the receiver tells a sender to slow down, an arched eyebrow can convey a request for the sender to clarify what has been said, and a nod of the head indicates understanding. Emblems, illustrators, and regulators are consciously used by individuals in communication.

Two other types of body expressions, *adapters* and *affect displays,* are often subconsciously communicated and can reveal much about a sender's and a receiver's feelings and attitudes. **Adapters** are expressions used to adjust psychologically to the interpersonal climate of a particular situation.[38] Usually learned early in life, adapters are frequently used to deal with stress in an interpersonal situation. Drumming fingers on a table, tugging a strand of hair, or jiggling a leg or foot are all ways of releasing some degree of stress.

Affect displays are usually subconscious expressions that directly communicate an individual's emotions. Most affect displays are facial expressions, which are a particularly important communicator of a person's feelings. There is a long-held assumption that a person's emotions are mirrored in her face and that these emotions can be "read" with a great deal of accuracy. For example, many communications experts agree that a smile communicates friendship, affection, and a desire to be helpful. Infrequent eye contact conveys dislike and an ill-at-ease feeling about the subject being discussed.

Affect displays are also expressed in body positions. For example, a "closed posture" (arms folded across the chest, legs crossed) communicates defensiveness and often dislike. Interestingly, body positions can visibly convey a high degree of rapport between the sender and receiver. Communications researchers have found that when rapport exists, the two individuals mirror each other's movements—shifting body position, dropping a hand or making some other movement at the same time. If a rapport is abruptly ended in a conversation, the "mirror" is quickly broken.[39]

The image that a person projects through body language and overall appearance is a concern of many employees in organizations. Dress is particularly important in business. Many organizations implement dress codes to communicate a particular employee and company image to customers and other constituents. It's imperative that managers be aware of their body signals and tone to ensure that they correspond with the intended message. For example, if a manager shifts his eyes and looks away while speaking, other people won't trust his message. If a manager raises her voice in a questioning tone while giving out quotas, she'll sound as though she doesn't believe they're attainable. If a manager wants to be seen as a leader, he'll need to stand up straight, make eye contact, and smile. Those signals project confidence and energy. On the other hand, if he walks with his shoulders slumped and head down, speaks in a flat tone, and fidgets often, he'll likely be seen as indecisive, negative, or inexperienced.[40]

One other important but often overlooked element of nonverbal communication is **proxemics,** which is defined as an individual's use of space when interpersonally commu-

▶**emblems** Nonverbal communication that resembles sign language; examples include a "thumbs up" gesture indicating approval.

▶**illustrators** Physical gestures that illustrate what is being said (e.g., extended hands to indicate the size of an object); a form of body language.

▶**regulators** Physical movements that regulate a conversation (e.g., nodding the head to indicate understanding); a form of body language.

▶**adapters** Physical expressions used to adjust psychologically to the interpersonal climate of a particular situation; frequently used to deal with stress (e.g., drumming fingers on a table); a form of body language.

▶**affect displays** Usually subconscious expressions that directly communicate an individual's emotions (e.g., a "closed posture" that communicates defensiveness); a form of body language.

▶**proxemics** An individual's use of space when communicating with others.

nicating with others. According to Edward Hall, a prominent researcher of proxemics, people have four zones of informal space, which are spatial distances they maintain when interacting with others: the intimate zone (from physical contact to eighteen inches); the personal zone (from one and a half to four feet); the social zone (from over four to twelve feet); and the public zone (more than twelve feet).[41] For Americans, supervisor-subordinate relationships begin in the social zone and progress to the personal zone after mutual trust has been developed.[42] An individual's personal and intimate zones comprise a "private bubble" of space and are considered to be private territory not to be entered by others unless invited.

Proxemics affects interpersonal communication when the proxemic behavior of the sender and receiver differs. For example, assume that you communicate, like most Americans, standing in the social zone while interacting at a social gathering such as a cocktail party. However, in the South American culture, a personal-zone distance is considered more natural in such situations. You are talking with a South American businessperson at a cocktail party who is assuming a personal-zone distance. How would you feel? Typically in such a situation, an individual feels so uncomfortable with the person standing "too close" that any verbal communication is not heard. Conflicts in proxemic behavior often create a substantial barrier to effective communication. Such conflicts can also influence each individual's perceptions of the other (you may view the South American as pushy and aggressive; he may see you as cold and impolite).

13-6 Why Communications Break Down

A manager has no greater responsibility than to develop effective communications. However, communications often break down for various reasons. Problems occur both in formal **organizational communications,** such as public relations press releases, and in interpersonal communications. In general, managers should recognize that a breakdown can occur whenever any one of the elements of communication—sender, encoding, medium, decoding, receiver, or feedback—is defective.

13-6a Conflicting Frames of Reference

Individuals can interpret the same communication differently, depending on their previous experiences. This type of communication breakdown is related to the *encoding* and *decoding* elements. When the receiver and sender use the same encoding and decoding language, they can achieve common understanding. But each of us is unique in background and experience. Words can take on different meanings for different people. In terms of interpersonal communication, the arena area is relatively small when compared to blind spots, façades, and unknown area. To the extent that individuals have distinctly different *frames of reference*, communications among these individuals will be difficult to achieve.

Science historian Thomas Kuhn famously wrote that science progresses via a never ending series of "paradigms."[43] A **paradigm** is a frame of reference that scientists use to understand the natural world. Scientists are trained within a particular paradigm, learn which problems are important, and develop solutions to those problems all within the same frame of reference. Kuhn demonstrated that scientific progress is most profound not when a problem within a particular paradigm is solved, but rather when a new paradigm is invented and new problems are created. For example, Isaac Newton's view of the universe led to certain scientific procedures and approaches. However, this view was inadequate to account for phenomena at light speed. Only Albert Einstein's insight known as general relativity enabled scientists to understand how the world behaves in these unique conditions.

Managers too are constrained to some extent by the frame of reference—the paradigm—they've adopted as part of their experience and training. For this reason, it's often difficult for managers to solve problems when economic or competitive conditions change. To be effective, managers must recognize the constraints of their frame of reference and be proactive in seeking to change it when it is no longer effective.

One consequence of different frames of reference among individuals is that communications become distorted. For example, managers have different perceptions than do

organizational communications Information that flows outward from the organization to the various components of its external operating environment. Whatever the type of organization, the content of this information flow is controlled by the organization (e.g., advertising in business organizations).

paradigm A frame of reference used to understand the world.

their subordinates; district sales managers have different perceptions than do salespersons. In an organization, the *jobs* that people perform will create different, potentially conflicting, frames of reference. For example, a pricing problem will be viewed differently by the marketing manager than by the plant manager. An efficiency problem in a hospital will be viewed by the nursing staff from its frame of reference and its experiences, and this may result in interpretations that differ from those of the staff physicians.

Different *levels* in the organization will also have different frames of reference. First-line supervisors have frames of reference that differ in many respects from those of vice presidents. As a result, the needs, values, attitudes, and expectations of these two groups will differ, and this often will result in unintentional distortions of the communications between them. Neither group is wrong or right. In any situation, individuals will choose that part of their own past experiences that relates to their current experiences and helps them form conclusions and judgments. Unfortunately, such incongruities in encoding and decoding can result in barriers to effective communication.

13-6b Selective Perception

Selective perception occurs when people block out new information, especially if it conflicts with what they believe. Thus, when people receive information, they are apt to hear only those words that affirm their beliefs. Information that conflicts with preconceived notions either is not noted or is distorted to confirm their preconceptions.

For example, a notice may be sent to all operating departments that costs must be reduced if the organization is to earn a profit. Such a communication may not achieve its desired effect if it conflicts with the "reality" of the receivers. Operating employees, for instance, may ignore or be amused by the notice in light of the large salaries, travel allowances, and expense accounts of some managers. Whether these expenditures are justified is irrelevant; what is important is that such preconceptions result in breakdowns in communication. In other words, if people hear only what they want to hear, they cannot be disappointed.

> **selective perception** The process of blocking out new information, especially if it conflicts with what the receiver believes.

13-6c Value Judgments

In every communication situation, receivers make **value judgments** by assigning an overall worth to a message prior to receiving the entire communication. Such value judgments may be based on the receiver's evaluation of the communicator, the receiver's previous experiences with the communicator, or the message's anticipated meaning. Thus, a hospital administrator may pay little attention to a memorandum from a nursing team leader because "she's always complaining about something." An employee may consider a merit evaluation meeting with the supervisor as going through the motions because she perceives the supervisor as being more concerned about administrative matters than performance.

> **value judgments** The assignment by a receiver of an overall worth to a message before the receiver receives the entire communication.

13-6d Status Differences

Every employee has a particular status in an organization that is determined by such factors as position, title, pay, office size, and other factors. Communication is often hindered when **status differences** exist between communicators. For example, subordinates are usually reluctant to be open and honest in their communications with supervisors who have higher status and more power. Few are willing to provide their bosses with frank feedback concerning their decisions or actions because of concern about their supervisors' reactions.[44] As a result, many managers don't receive needed accurate feedback; what little feedback they receive is *filtered*. That is, the sender manipulates the information so it is perceived as positive by the receiver. Filtering occurs at all levels of the organization.

> **status differences** The differences between communicators that often hinder the communication.

13-6e Security

The security of the information channel is an increasingly important consideration for employees. The Internet and other electronic communication technologies have increased

Management Focus on Ethics

Communication Privacy in the Age of the Internet

A survey by the American Management Association shows that about 78 percent of companies in the United States monitor their employees in some way. Sixty-three percent monitor employee Internet use, 47 percent store and review employee e-mail messages, 15 percent view employees by video, 12 percent review and record phone messages, and 8 percent review voice-mail messages.

Of course, there are valid reasons for some monitoring. More than 75 percent of companies say that it helps them combat personal use of the Internet during business hours. Employers also have an incentive to ensure that employees don't unwittingly or intentionally divulge company trade secrets and intellectual property by way of their communications. Furthermore, employers want to prevent or remedy any

defamatory statements made by employees in electronic and other communications.

Still, workers have legitimate concerns that their privacy rights might be invaded. The primary federal statute in this area is the Electronic Communications Privacy Act (ECPA). The ECPA bars the intentional interception of any wire, oral, or electronic communication, or the unauthorized access of stored communications. The ECPA does have three exceptions. The exceptions generally allow employers to monitor business-related phone calls, to monitor communications when there has been employee consent, and to retrieve and access stored e-mail messages.

Source: Adapted from Eric J. Sinrod, "Who's Watching You?" *Computerworld,* June 11, 2001, p. 34.

---

opportunities for people to exchange information with one another. On-line discussion forums, chat rooms, and virtual meetings have been enabled by network technologies. Paradoxically, the potential for communications to be monitored through these channels has led some employees to *reduce* their amount of communication. Organizations large and small are struggling with issues of employee privacy that have arisen in computer-mediated communications. The Management Focus on Ethics box, "Communication Privacy in the Age of the Internet," examines this issue more closely.

13-6f Source Credibility

> **source credibility** The trust, confidence, and faith that the receiver has in the words and actions of the communicator.

Source credibility refers to the trust, confidence, and faith that the receiver has in the communicator's words and actions. The level of credibility that the receiver assigns to the communicator, in turn, directly affects how the receiver views and reacts to the words, ideas, and actions of the communicator. Thus, how subordinates view a communication from their manager is affected by their evaluations of the manager. The degree of credibility they attach to the communication is heavily influenced by their previous experiences with the manager. Hospital medical staff members who view the hospital administrator as less than honest, manipulative, and not to be trusted are apt to assign inaccurate motives to any communication from the administrator. Union leaders who view managers as exploiters and managers who view union leaders as inherent enemies are unlikely to engage in much real communication.

13-6g Time Pressures

> **time pressures** Communication problems caused by inadequate time.

The pressure of time is an important barrier to communication. An obvious problem is that managers do not have the time to communicate frequently with every subordinate. **Time pressures** often can lead to serious problems. **Short-circuiting** is a failure of the formally prescribed communication system often resulting from time pressures. It means simply that someone who normally would be included has been left out of the formal channel of communication.

> **short-circuiting** The failure of the formally prescribed communication system, often as the result of time pressures.

13-6h Information Overload

In decision making, one of the necessary conditions for effective decisions is the presence of *information*. In fact, because of advances in communication technology, difficulties may arise not from the absence of information but from *excessive* information. Managers often are deluged by information and data. They cannot absorb or adequately respond to all of the messages directed to them. They screen out the majority of messages, which in effect means that these messages are never decoded. Thus, the area of organizational communication is one in which "more" is not always "better."

13-6i Semantic Problems

Communication is the transmission of *information* and *understanding* through the use of *common symbols*. Actually, we cannot transmit understanding. Usually we can only transmit information in the form of words, which are the common symbols. Unfortunately, the same words may mean entirely different things to different people. The understanding is in the receiver, not in the words.

When a plant manager announces that a budget increase is necessary for the growth of the plant, the manager may have in mind the necessity for new equipment, and expanded parts inventory, and more personnel. To the existing personnel, however, growth may be perceived as excess funds that can be used for wage and salary increases.

Again, because different groups use words differently, communication often can be impeded. This is especially true with abstract or technical terms or phrases. A **cost-benefit analysis** would have meaning to persons involved in the administration of the hospital but probably would mean very little to the staff physicians. In fact, it might even be scorned by the latter. Such concepts as *trusts, profits,* and *Treasury bills* may have concrete meanings to bank executives but little or no meaning to bank tellers. Thus, because words mean different things to different people, it is possible for a communicator to speak the same language as a receiver but still not transmit *understanding*.

Occupational, professional, and social groups often develop words and phrases that have meaning only to group members. Such special language can serve many useful purposes. It can provide group members with feelings of belonging, cohesiveness, and, in many cases, self-esteem. Special languages also can facilitate effective communication *within* the group. The use of in-group language can, however, result in severe *semantic problems* and communication breakdowns when outsiders or other groups are involved. Technical and staff groups often use such language in an organization, not for the purpose of transmitting information and understanding, but to communicate a mystique about the group or its function.

> ▶ **cost-benefit analysis**
> A technique for evaluating individual projects and deciding among alternatives.

13-6j Poor Listening Skills

Effective interpersonal communication requires that each participant not only hear the words that are said but also understand their meaning. This task requires the ability to listen—to focus on the speaker, block out distractions, and carefully comprehend the communicator's message. Although listening is a key requirement for effective communication, most individuals listen at only a 25 percent level of efficiency.[45]

Several factors hinder effective listening. Perhaps the primary obstacle is in an individual's free time while listening. On average, an individual speaks about 125 words a minute but listens at a rate that is more than three times as fast (from 400 to 600 words a minute). As a result, 75 percent of listening time is free time—that is, time to become mentally sidetracked by any number of distractions.[46] The physical surroundings, the speaker's appearance, his mention of a controversial concept or idea, or a problem nagging at the listener—can all compete for a listener's attention.[47]

13-7 How Communications Can Be Improved

Managers striving to become better communicators must accomplish two separate tasks. First, they must improve their messages—the information they wish to transmit. Second, they must improve their own *understanding* of what other people are trying to communicate to them; they must become better encoders and decoders. *They must strive not only to be understood but also to understand.* The techniques discussed here will help managers to accomplish these two important tasks.

Figure 13-7
10 Commandments for Effective Listening

Source: Kent Davis, *Human Behavior at Work: Organizational Behavior,* 6th Edition, p. 396. Reprinted by permission of The McGraw-Hill Companies.

Ten Commandments for Effective Listening

1. **Stop talking!** You cannot listen if you are talking.
   Polonius (*Hamlet*): "Give every man thine ear, but few thy voice."

2. **Put the talker at ease.** Help him feel that he is free to talk. This is often called a permissive environment.

3. **Show her that you want to listen.** Look and act interested. Do not read your mail while she talks. Listen to understand rather than to oppose.

4. **Remove distractions.** Don't doodle, tap, or shuffle papers. Will it be quieter if you shut the door?

5. **Empathize with him.** Try to put yourself in his place so that you can see his point of view.

6. **Be patient.** Allow plenty of time. Do not interrupt her. Don't start for the door or walk away.

7. **Hold your temper.** An angry person gets the wrong meaning from words.

8. **Go easy on argument and criticism.** This puts him on the defensive. He may "clam up" or get angry. Do not argue; even if you win, you lose.

9. **Ask questions.** This encourages her and shows you are listening. It helps to develop points further.

10. **Stop talking!** This is first and last because all other commandments depend on it. You just can't do a good listening job while you are talking.

Nature gave people two ears but only one tongue, which is a gentle hint that they should listen more than they talk.

13-7a Effective Listening

To *understand,* managers first must *listen.* One way to encourage someone to express true feelings, desires, and emotions is to listen. Just listening is not enough, of course. You must listen with understanding. Figure 13-7 provides a list of the "Ten Commandments for Effective Listening."

No communications occur until managers make the *decision to listen.* The guidelines in Figure 13-7 are useless unless one realizes that effective communication involves understanding as well as being understood.

13-7b Following Up

Following up involves assuming that you are misunderstood. Whenever possible, managers should attempt to determine whether their intended meaning was actually received. As we have seen, meaning often is in the mind of the receiver. An accounting unit leader in a government office communicates notices of openings in other agencies to the accounting staff members. Although this action may be understood among longtime employees as a friendly gesture, a new employee might interpret it as an evaluation of poor performance and a suggestion to leave. The manager can circumvent problems caused by miscommunication by following up to ensure people have received the intended message.

13-7c Regulating Information Flow

Regulating the flow of communications ensures an optimum flow of information to managers and reduces the likelihood of **communication overload.** Both the quality and quantity of communications should be regulated. The idea is based on the **exception principle of management,** which states that only significant deviations from policies and procedures should be brought to the attention of managers.

13-7d Utilizing Feedback

Feedback is an important element in effective two-way communication. It provides a channel for receiver response. Through feedback, the communicator can determine whether the message has been received and if it has produced the intended response.

In face-to-face communication, direct feedback is possible. In downward communication, however, inaccuracies often occur because there is insufficient opportunity for

▶**communication overload** The inability to absorb or adequately respond to messages directed to a person because of the excessive amount of information and data they must absorb.

▶**exception principle of management** Theory that states that only significant deviations from policies and procedures should be brought to the attention of managers.

feedback from receivers. Thus, distributing a memorandum on an important policy statement to all employees does not guarantee that communication has occurred. An organization needs effective upward communication if its downward communication is to have any chance of being effective. The point is that developing and supporting feedback involves far more than following up on communications.

13-7e Empathy

Empathy is the ability to put oneself in the other person's role and to assume the viewpoints and emotions of that person. This involves being a listener rather than a talker. Empathy requires communicators to place themselves in the receivers' positions and anticipate how the message is likely to be decoded.

> **empathy** The ability to put oneself in another person's role and to assume that person's role and to assume that person's viewpoints and emotions.

It is vital that a manager understand and appreciate the process of decoding. Decoding involves perceptions, and the message will be filtered through the perceptions of the receiver. For vice presidents to communicate effectively with supervisors, for faculty to communicate effectively with students, and for government administrators to communicate effectively with minority groups, empathy is often an important ingredient. Empathy can reduce many of the barriers to effective communication that we have discussed. The greater the gap between the experiences and background of the communicator and the receiver, the greater is the effort that must be made to find a common ground of understanding—ground on which there are overlapping fields of experience.

13-7f Simplifying Language

Complex language has been identified as a major barrier to effective communication. Students often suffer when their instructors use technical jargon that transforms simple concepts into complex puzzles.

Schools are not the only places, however, where complex language is used. Government agencies are known for their often incomprehensible communications. We have noted instances in which professional people attempt to use their in-group language to communicate with individuals outside their group. Managers must remember that effective communication involves transmitting *understanding* as well as information. If the receiver does not understand, then there has been no communication. In fact, many of the techniques discussed in this section work solely to promote understanding. Managers must encode messages in words, appeals, and symbols that are meaningful to the receiver.

13-7g Organizational Stories

Many scholars have asserted that narrative as a rhetorical method be afforded greater recognition in professional management education. Narrative—which is defined as a depiction of a sequence of events, real or fictional, to illustrate a truth or to create shared meaning—operates at a high level of rhetorical power in every context because stories are the way we make sense of our lives. Stories anchor the chaos of events in our experiences, beliefs, and values. Recently, narrative has been given much attention as a means of understanding organizations as well as analyzing and interpreting organizational culture. Managers who understand the view that human communication can be seen as stories, who understand that narrative influences what constitutes good reasons for an audience, and who understand and reflect on their own narratives will have greater success in communication at work.

Managerial careers put managers in communities of stakeholders (clients, patients, investors) for whom professionals must interpret bodies of knowledge to lead, to serve, and, above all, to meet their professional goals. In organizations, as old patterns of managerial control disappear, professionals communicate with colleagues from a wide variety of job knowledge and experiences. Narrative allows the communicator to forge relationships with diverse audiences well beyond those afforded by a technical argument. Narrative—storytelling—is a widely adaptable, audience-based means by which professionals can exercise leadership or simply collaborate on discrete goals by communicating to persuade diverse audiences.[48]

13-7h Final Comments

In conclusion, it would be hard to find an aspect of a manager's job that does not involve communication. If all members of the organization had a common point of view, communicating would be easy. Unfortunately, each member comes to the organization with a distinct personality, background, experience, and frame of reference. The structure of the organization itself influences status relationships and the distance (levels) between individuals, and these in turn influence the ability of individuals to communicate.

In this chapter, you have been introduced to the basic elements in the process of communication and what it takes to communicate effectively. These elements are necessary whether the communication is face-to-face or written and whether it occurs vertically or horizontally within an organization. Several common communication barriers exist, and there are several ways to remove them. Often, however, there is insufficient time to utilize many of the techniques for improving communications, and such skills as empathy and effective listening are not easy to develop. Communicating is a matter of transmitting and receiving, and managers must be effective at both. They must understand as well as be understood.

Management Summary

- Communication is the process of achieving common understanding. For managerial purposes, it is undertaken to achieve an effect.

- Organizational communication flows downward, upward, and horizontally.

- There are both formal and informal communication channels in most organizations.

- The elements of communication are the sender, encoding, the message, the medium, decoding, the receiver, noise, and feedback. All of these elements must be in harmony if communication is to achieve understanding and be effective.

- A crucial factor in determining the effectiveness of formal communications in an organization is the way in which the organization is structured.

- Interpersonal communication styles must be adapted to ensure effective communications.

- Verbal communication includes both speaking and writing.

- Rumors are an everyday part of organizational life. Regardless of their validity, rumors tend to flourish when they are viewed by the receiver as important, entertaining, and ambiguous.

- Such psychological factors as perception, personality, and interpersonal style are critical in determining the effectiveness of interpersonal communications.

- Nonverbal communication is an important source of information about people's thoughts and feelings. Voice, body expressions, style of dress, and proxemics are all important mechanisms of nonverbal communication.

- The extent to which individuals share understanding depends on their use of feedback and exposure. Balanced use of both is the most effective approach.

- Communication barriers can be identified in organizations and in people. Effective managers can remove or at least minimize these barriers by developing effective listening skills and empathy, by following up on their communications, regulating information flow, using feedback, and simplifying their language.

- Conflicting frames of reference is a common source of communication barriers in organizations.

Key Terms

adapters (p. 317)
affect displays (p. 317)
arena (p. 314)
bandwidth (p. 306)
blind spot (p. 314)
cliques (p. 309)
communication (p. 303)
communication overload (p. 322)
cost-benefit analysis (p. 321)

decoding (p. 306)
downward communication (p. 307)
emblems (p. 317)
empathy (p. 323)
encoding (p. 304)
exception principle of management (p. 322)
exposure (p. 315)
façade (p. 314)
feedback (p. 307)

grapevine (p. 310)
horizontal communication (p. 309)
illustrators (p. 317)
information (p. 312)
information richness (p. 306)
interpersonal communications (p. 312)
interpersonal style (p. 312)
isolates (p. 310)
liaison (p. 310)

media richness (p. 306)
noise (p. 307)
nonverbal communication (p. 316)
oral communication (p. 315)
organizational communications (p. 318)
paradigm (p. 318)
proxemics (p. 317)

regulators (p. 317)
rumors (p. 311)
selective perception (p. 319)
short-circuiting (p. 320)
sociogram (p. 309)
source credibility (p. 320)
status differences (p. 319)

the unknown (p. 314)
time pressures (p. 320)
upward communication (p. 308)
value judgments (p. 319)
verbal communication (p. 315)
written communication (p. 316)

Review and Discussion Questions

1. Several studies indicate that managers are poor listeners. As one subordinate commented, "The boss doesn't listen; she argues." What factors in the workplace hinder a manager's ability to listen?

2. Explain the relationship between organizational structure and communication flows within the organization.

3. As a chief communications officer within an organization, what strategies would you implement to stop damaging rumors you've identified in the organization?

4. Which barriers to communication are most controllable by managers? Explain.

5. What, if anything, can managers do to remove barriers to communication that are beyond their control?

6. Of the "Ten Commandments for Effective Listening," which commandment do you believe is the most difficult to successfully obey? Explain.

7. How would you apply the concept of proxemics in designing an office that facilitates open, effective communication?

8. In your experience, which communication element has often been the cause of your failures to communicate? What can you do to improve your ability to communicate?

9. Many managers today use e-mail for their written communications. What are some drawbacks of relying on e-mail? What are some benefits?

10. How should managers deal with the problem of conflicting frames of reference among different organizational departments? Explain.

Practice Quiz

Note: You can find the correct answers to these questions by taking the quiz and then submitting your answers in the Online Edition. The program will automatically score your submission. If you miss a question, the program will provide the correct answer, a rationale for the answer, and the section number in the chapter where the topic is discussed.

Indicate whether the sentence or statement is true or false.

_____ 1. People trained in nearly any profession use "jargon" to talk among themselves about the problems and issues within that profession.

_____ 2. Research has shown that workers generally will not speak their minds if they know their comments will reach management with their names attached.

_____ 3. Falsified facts traveling through the rumor mill can be corrected by feeding accurate information to primary communicators of liaison individuals.

_____ 4. Research indicates that nasality of voice is inversely related to perceptions of persuasiveness. In other words, the less nasal the voice, the more persuasive it is perceived by listeners.

_____ 5. Conflicts in proxemic behavior often create a substantial barrier to effective communication.

Identify the letter of the choice that best completes the statement or answers the question.

_____ 6. _____ between individuals within an organization is important for coordinating the work of separate departments.
   a. Competition
   b. Cooperation
   c. Communication
   d. Friendship

_____ 7. Which of the following is NOT used to evaluate a medium's richness?
   a. its capacity for timely feedback
   b. its capacity for multiple uses, such as audio and video
   c. the extent to which the message can be personalized
   d. the variety of symbolic messages that can be encoded
   e. the ability of the receiver to understand the message

_____ 8. In face-to-face situations, _____ is possible through subtle means, such as facial expressions that indicate discontent or misunderstanding.
   a. direct feedback
   b. indirect feedback

_____ 9. Routinely scheduled interdepartmental staff meetings can facilitate _____ communication.
   a. upward
   b. downward
   c. horizontal

_____ 10. To understand, managers must first _____.
   a. speak.
   b. think.
   c. listen.
   d. filter.

_____ 11. Most individuals listen at only a _____ percent level of efficiency.
   a. 10
   b. 25
   c. 40
   d. 65

____ **12.** Managers should attempt to determine whether their intended meaning was actually received. In the context of effective communication, this is known as

_____.

    a. regulating information flow.

    b. utilizing feedback.

    c. following up.

    d. empathy.

____ **13.** The ability of information to change understanding within a time interval is known as _____.

    a. information richness.

    b. information economy.

    c. information specialization.

    d. media richness.

____ **14.** Which of the following is a form of upward communication in the workplace?

    a. policies

    b. mission statements

    c. strategies

    d. grievance

____ **15.** _____ is an example of an informal channel of communication in an organization.

    a. The grapevine

    b. A policy

    c. The employee handbook

    d. The organizational mission

Case Study

The Horse Whisperer

A Lesson in Communication

Monty Roberts, the horse whisperer who was the inspiration for the book and movie of the same name, has identified and explained an effective nonverbal language that he's practiced for more than fifty years with astonishing results. Roberts, sixty-five, has proved more than 1,000 times that he can take a wild horse and, in roughly thirty minutes, become the chairman of every encounter.

Roberts learned his craft the hard way. He watched his father "break" horses by tying them up with ropes and whipping them to break their spirit. The sights and sounds of horses being tortured were unbearable to young Monty. So he found another way. At age six, he showed his father that by "whispering"—using body language—he could partner with a horse in three days, as opposed to the three weeks or longer required for his father's brutal methods.

Wild Horses at Work

"If people do their work because they're frightened not to do it," says Roberts, "would they do it as well if they weren't frightened? We go to work and hide. We join a team to get cover, to get the light off of us. Or we hide from ourselves. That's not what we want in the people who work for us. It's not what we want to be."

"Let's look at it from the power of the creature," Roberts says. "Think like the flight animal, which is essentially what a horse is. Now, make me believe that hitting or scaring the flight animal can convince it that together, we can do great work. Words can hurt as much as whips can. Some people say, 'I'd almost rather someone hit me than demean and cut me with words.' If we recognize that violence can take the form of words, we'll recognize that there is a lot of violence in corporate America."

Many of the horses that enter the ring with Roberts fear being killed by him. "Those big flight animals are always ready to run," Roberts says. "It's the same with humans. The bosses who act aggressively are the ones with the smallest hearts. They're the cowards. They've learned to act out in a violent fashion. They have used that cowardice to tell themselves, 'If I don't do this, I'll lose my grip.' Way down the ladder, you have to realize that and get those people to see that violence is hurting them.

"Some of the biggest bullies in corporate America have come to my ranch to watch me work with wild horses. One morning, one CEO decided to have a cigarette before setting out. He wanted oth-ers to have to wait for him so that he could prove his power. I said to his people, 'Come on, let's get started.' His assistant said, 'We have to wait for the boss.' 'No we don't,' I said. Off we go, and I watch that CEO throw the cigarette away and hear him grumble, and I immediately launch into a diatribe about what it is about CEOs that causes them to do that kind of thing. In less than three hours, he comes up to me and says, 'I'm starting to see that some things I do hold the company back.'

"When you reduce it to a fight or a battle of wills, a horse, a child, or an adult develops a mentality that he won't be ruled by anybody. You bully people with words or taunts, and you can't lead them—no matter how much you pay them.

"The other night, I worked with a crippled horse that couldn't trot anymore. The owners put it in a field and were practically starving it. Its hair was white where it had been whipped. A woman had just bought the horse, and it refused to load into her trailer. It couldn't stand the sound of metal, because it reminded it of the buggy in the back. It would go into a complete panic when the woman tried to load it. I worked with the horse. I wanted it to trust me and to be with me. I established that I was not going to harm the animal. I showed it that I was the strong one. Horses and people want to follow someone they can trust. Leaders who can quiet that fight-or-flight instinct in others are the ones who take charge. I was able to gain the horse's trust by repeatedly coming up to it and patting its blind side, where it was unprotected; by showing it that I was not going to get angry or violent, rewarding it instead with a rub between the eyes for even small wins; and by showing it that I wasn't going to go away or give up. Eventually, I walked into the trailer, and the horse followed me of its own volition."

Roberts suggests that managers look at themselves as a horse whisperer, and they will relate to people more generously. They will begin to treat others with instinctive respect. Whispering is a great metaphor because there is anger in people that shows up in countless acts. The most common act of anger is not listening.

"I can't come to grips with how much violence there is among people," Roberts laments. "No one of us was born with the right to say to any other creature, 'I'll hurt you.' Anger is never the answer. It's an act of frustration. It's okay to kick a computer, or to throw a chair across the room. But you never do that to another living being."

So what would work in a human whisperer? The answer is that listening fosters whispering. The asked question is an opportunity for adult human whispering. When you ask the horse-in-the-human a question—and even invite him to ask one back—he invariably enters a childlike innocence and freshness. Fight, flight: Both become irrelevant.

Questions for Discussion

1. How can we use the lessons of the horse whisperer to improve interpersonal communications at work?

2. Do you think that most people are good listeners? Why? Are you a good listener?

3. What does Roberts mean when he says that there is too much "violence" in the way people communicate at work? Do you agree with him? Explain.

Source: From, "Whisper, Don't Shout," by Harriet Rubin from *Fast Company,* April 2001. Copyright © 2005 Gruner & Jahr USA Publishing. Reprinted with permission.

Internet Exercise

Assess Your Interpersonal Communication Skills

A good way to constantly improve as a manager and as a person is to receive feedback on your personal skills, knowledge, and ability. Many managers today hire personal "coaches" who help them understand their strengths and weaknesses. Another technique that is less "public" is to take standardized tests that will provide feedback that is private.

Queendom is an Internet magazine with a difference: It provides an interactive avenue for self-exploration with a healthy dose of fun . . . and thus its motto is serious entertainment. Queendom develops its own professional-quality interactive tests, giving readers the opportunity to look into their personality, relationships, intelligence, and health.

Students should be encouraged to test their interpersonal communication skills by clicking on the link shown below. The on-line test should take about twenty minutes. Students should be encouraged to share their findings with the class during the next class period.

http://www.queendom.com/tests/relationships/communication_skills_r_access.html

Experiential Exercise

Perceptual Differences

Purpose: To illustrate how people perceive the same situation differently through the process of selective perception.

Setting Up the Exercise: The instructor will divide the class into groups of four students each. Then, complete the following activities:

1. As individuals, complete the following quiz. Do not talk to your group members until everyone in the class has finished.

2. Your instructor will provide the answers to the fifteen questions. Score your responses.

3. As a group, discuss your members' responses. Focus your discussion on the following questions:

   a. Why did perceptions differ across members? What factors could account for these differences?

   b. Most people don't perform very well with this quiz. Why? What other factors beyond selective perception can adversely affect performance?

A Learning Note: This exercise aptly demonstrates the wide variety of perceptual differences among people when considering a situation where little factual information is provided. The exercise should also indicate that most people selectively perceive the information they are comfortable with in analyzing the situation. Many will also subconsciously fill in gaps of information with assumptions they suppose are facts.

Quiz: The Robbery

The lights in a store had just been turned off by a businessman when a man appeared and demanded money. The owner opened a cash register. The contents of the cash register were scooped up, and the man sped away. A member of the police force was notified promptly.

Answer the following questions about the story by circling T for true, F for false, or ? for unknown.

1. A man appeared after the owner turned off his store lights.	T	F	?
2. The robber was a man.	T	F	?
3. The man who appeared did not demand money.	T	F	?
4. The man who opened the cash register was the owner.	T	F	?
5. The store owner scooped up the contents of the cash register and ran away.	T	F	?
6. Someone opened a cash register.	T	F	?
7. After the man who demanded money scooped up the contents of the cash register, he ran away.	T	F	?
8. While the cash register contained money, the story does not state how much.	T	F	?
9. The robber demanded money of the owner.	T	F	?
10. A businessman had just turned off the lights when a man appeared in the store.	T	F	?
11. It was broad daylight when the man appeared.	T	F	?
12. The man who appeared opened the cash register.	T	F	?
13. No one demanded money.	T	F	?
14. The story concerns a series of events in which only three persons are referred to: the owner of the store, a man who demanded money, and a member of the police force.	T	F	?
15. The following events occurred: someone demanded money, a cash register was opened, its contents were scooped up, and a man dashed out of the store.	T	F	?

Source: William V. Haney, *Communication and Interpersonal Relations: Text and Cases* (Homewood, IL: Richard D. Irwin, 1979), pp. 250–51.

Work Groups and Teams

CHAPTER OBJECTIVES

1. State the reasons why groups are formed within organizations.

2. Describe the difference between formal and informal groups

3. Define the work group from a manager's perspective.

4. Explain how work groups can apply pressure to an individual member and cause the member to conform to norms.

5. Discuss management strategies that can be implemented to deal with intergroup conflict.

6. Describe the advantages and disadvantages of virtual teams.

Managing Today

Teamwork Brings Success to Investment Firm

Teamwork is an important element in the success of Malvern, PA, based Stoneridge Investment Partners. John Stocke, CIO for Stoneridge, can boast about the firm's sophisticated information technology and quantitative research tools, but the foundation of the company's success is its ability to utilize its human talent. Stocke contends that his group's partnership with the investment team has been critical in the firm's drive to preserve capital. "The main advantage is the cohesiveness of the team and that fact that we work well together. Between us, we have a great deal of knowledge in certain areas and are able to have our knowledge converge. I also consider each one a friend as well as a partner," Stocke noted.

Stocke explained that the team uses a quantitative research tool, which screens data via investment sector. Once the screening is complete, the team then does its buying and selling. This process of collaboration is carried out daily. The interaction between the information technology people, who strive to provide more and better data, and the investment analysts, who must sift through the data to make stock picks for clients, is critical to the firm's long-term success rate.

Source: Adapted from "Teamwork Is Key for Success for Boutique Firm," *Investment Management Weekly,* October 18, 2004, p. 7.

---

work group A collection of interacting employees (managerial or nonmanagerial) who share certain norms and are striving toward member need satisfaction through the attainment of group goals.

This chapter is concerned with the issues of managing work groups and group processes in organizations. Managers and researchers have paid special attention to the group processes that affect individuals and organizations. Thus, any presentation of management would be incomplete if it did not include a framework for understanding the nature and characteristics of work groups. A **work group** is defined as a collection of interacting employees (managerial or nonmanagerial) who share certain norms and are striving toward member need satisfaction through the attainment of group goals. The work group is the smallest formal organization of people within a firm. As such, a work group represents the most basic level of collective work activity.

The term **work team** describes a special type of organizational work group. The primary difference between a work team and a work group is the way in which they are governed. Generally, teams are self-managing and have a great deal more decision autonomy than work groups.

work team A special type of organizational work group; teams are self-managing and have a great deal more decision autonomy than work groups.

This chapter will give you (1) a classification of the different types of groups, (2) some knowledge about the reasons for the formation and development of groups and teams, (3) an understanding of some characteristics of groups, and (4) some insights into the outcomes of group membership.

14-1 A Managerial Model of Group Factors

Figure 14-1 depicts a general model of group factors a manager can use to gain some understanding of group dynamics and outcomes. The model indicates that two types of groups, formal and informal, exist in organizations. These groups either are formed by management or naturally evolve. Teamwork is important in nearly every type of business today. The Managing Today story highlights how an investment firm blends high-tech research tools into its stock-picking processes using a team-based approach. It is vital for managers to recognize that all workplace innovation, whether high tech or low tech, will have a ripple effect throughout the organization. Using teams to integrate various work units during the organizational change process can help ensure a successful transition.[1]

A group, once it evolves or is formed, begins a specific pattern of development. Like individuals, over time groups become more efficient and more productive.[2] As a group develops, it begins to exhibit various typical characteristics such as norms, cohesiveness, and political maneuvering. The characteristics and their intensity, clarity, and frequency all culminate in a unique group personality.

outcomes The tangible consequences of a group's existence.

A group's existence also has tangible consequences, called **outcomes.** They include performance, the number of units produced or services provided, and for individual members, satisfaction arising from group affiliation.

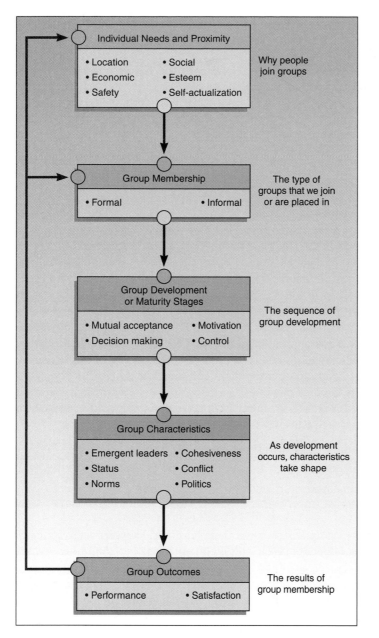

Figure 14-1
Model of Organizational Groups: Reasons for, Types of, Development, Characteristics, and Outcome

According to the model in Figure 14-1, group outcomes are influenced by individual needs and proximity, the type of group, the stage of group development, and the personality of the group, which is built up by its characteristics. These outcomes provide standards by which management can assess group effectiveness.

14-2 Categories of Groups

Managers and nonmanagers belong to a number of different groups within organizations, and individual memberships in groups often overlap. In some instances, individuals are members of a group because of their position in the organization. But through contacts they make in the group, they may also see some members informally.

14-2a Formal Work Groups

All employees are members of at least one group based on their positions in the organization. These **formal groups** are the departments, units, project teams, and so on, that the organization forms to do the work. The demands and processes of the organization lead

▶ **formal groups** The departments, units, and project teams that an organization forms to do the work.

to the formation of these groups. Two specific types of formal groups are *command* and *task* groups.

The Command Group   The **command group** is specified by the organizational hierarchy, usually outlined on the organization chart. The subordinates who report directly to a supervisor make up a command group. The relationship between a department manager and his three supervisors in a machine shop, for instance, is indicated in the organization chart. As the span of control of the department manager increases, the size of the command group also increases.

> **command group** The group shown on an organization chart that reports to a single manager.

The Task Group   A number of employees who work together to complete a specific project or job are considered a **task group.** A manufacturing, office work, or development process that requires a great deal of interdependence is an example of a task group. For example, suppose that three office clerks are required to: (1) secure the file of an automobile accident claim; (2) check the accuracy of the claim by contacting the persons involved; and (3) type the claim, obtain the signatures of those involved, and refile the claim. The activation of the file and the things that must be done before the claim is refiled constitute required tasks. The process creates a situation in which three clerks must communicate and coordinate with each other if the file is to be handled properly. Their interactions facilitate the formation of a task group. Or consider a team of software engineers working together to ensure that a new application performs as expected in the organization. To achieve that end, the development process requires individuals who can observe and record the work process, those who can draft the high-level design features of the application, and those who can write the code that underlies the various features of the application.[3]

> **task group** A formal group put together temporarily to complete a specific job or project.

Committees are very common in organizations. Committees actually are task groups established for such purposes as:

- Exchanging views and information
- Recommending actions
- Generating ideas
- Making decisions

Committees can achieve all of these purposes. However, a group may have difficulty coming to decisions. Managers typically attempt to keep a committee's size relatively small, since size affects the quality of a group's decisions. Increasing a committee's size tends to limit the extent to which its members want to or can communicate, and members tend to feel threatened and less willing to actively participate. The perceived threat can lead to increased stress and conflict. Stress and conflicts are outcomes that do not facilitate the generation of good committee decisions.

The *committee chairperson* is expected to provide proper direction. Ordinarily, successful committees have chairpersons who understand group processes. Such chairpersons see that the committee's objectives and purposes remain clear. They encourage committee members to participate and know how to move the committee toward its objectives.

The following guidelines can aid committee chairpersons:

1. Be a careful listener, and keep an open mind.
2. Allow each member to voice opinions; do not place your opinion above those of others.
3. Get everyone involved in the committee's activities.
4. Display an active interest in the purpose of the committee and in the ideas of its members.
5. Help the committee focus on the task at hand and on the progress being made.

Committee members also must be responsible for creating an atmosphere of cooperation within the group. Research indicates that in cooperative groups, as distinguished from competitive groups, one finds:

1. Stronger motivation to accomplish the task.
2. More effective communication.
3. More ideas generated.
4. More membership satisfaction.
5. More group performance.

Thus, when cooperation prevails, the results are generally positive. Communication, satisfaction, and productivity all tend to be more positive in a cooperative committee. Both the committee's chairperson and its members are important determinants of cooperative committee efforts.

14-2b Informal Work Groups

Whenever employees associate on a fairly regular basis, groups tend to form, and their activities may differ from those required by the organization. The **informal groups** are natural groupings of people in the workplace. They do not arise as a result of deliberate design but evolve naturally. The evolution of informal groups follows a path in response to the common interests, needs, or attractions of members. Informal groups often develop within formal groups because of certain values or needs that members find that they have in common. The informal group is not sanctioned by management, and its membership usually cuts across a number of formal groups. Two types of informal work groups are *interest* and *friendship* groups.

The Interest Group   Groups often form because their members share a common interest in some particular job-related event or possible outcome. This type of group can be viewed as an **interest group,** since the members have joined together to achieve some objective, such as an equitable pension payment. The members of the group may or may not be members of the same command or task group.

The Friendship Group   In the workplace, drawn together by common characteristics such as age, ethnic background, political sentiment, or family structure, employees often form **friendship groups.** These groups frequently extend their interaction and communication to off-the-job activities. For example, the members become friends in the workplace, then bowl together, or attend sporting events together, or take their families on picnics together.

The formation of informal groups in an organization does not signal anything especially good or bad about management practices. The informal groups evolve naturally in response to the needs, interests, or characteristics of the members. Few, if any, organizations have no informal groups. Therefore, if you look only at the formal groupings in an organization chart, you are likely to have only a partial view of the important group memberships of employees.

Figure 14-2 classifies groups on the basis of formality, informality, and type. Many individuals are members of several or all of these groups at the same time. Not all groups can be neatly placed on a formal-informal continuum, however.

14-3 The Formation of Work Groups

By going to work for an organization, you are actually joining a group. Once individuals become members of the organization, they are placed in, or volunteer for, various group memberships. They also join or create informal groups, because of common interests and characteristics. These and other reasons for group formation suggest that common *location, economic background,* and *attitudes* strongly influence people to join formal groups and join or establish informal groups.

▶**informal group** Natural grouping of people based on common interests or needs.

▶**interest group** An informal group formed to achieve some job-related, but personal, objective.

▶**friendship group** An informal group that evolves because of some common characteristic, such as age, political sentiment, or background.

Figure 14-2
Informal-Formal Group Types

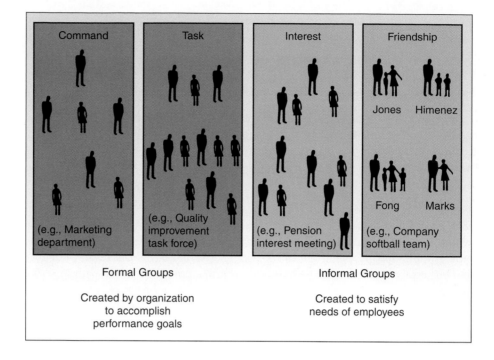

14-3a Location

When people are in close proximity, they tend to interact and communicate. Some degree of interaction and communication is necessary for group formation, particularly informal groups.

In organizations, a typical practice is to position workers with similar occupations together. For example, in the construction of a home, the bricklayers perform their jobs side by side. The same situation exists in offices, where clerks or secretaries are located next to one another.

14-3b Economic Background

In some cases, work groups form because individuals believe that they can gain economic benefits on their jobs if they band together. For example, individuals working at different stations on an assembly line may be paid on a group-incentive basis. Whatever the particular group produces determines the wages of each member. Since the workers all want to increase their wages, they will interact and communicate with one another. By working as a group instead of as individuals, they may actually obtain higher economic benefits.

Another example of how the economic motive affects the formation of informal work groups is a nonunion organization formed by workers to bring pressure on management for more economic benefits. The group members have a common interest—increased economic benefits—which leads to group affiliation.[4]

14-3c Attitude

Workers in organizations also are motivated to form work groups so that needs other than economic can be more satisfied. Workers who join together informally to improve productivity, quality, and customer satisfaction are acting only indirectly in their economic interests. They may have little or no clear understanding of the impact of their efforts on their economic benefits. Managers must learn to appeal to the attitudinal needs and/or emotional needs of employees to reap additional productivity gains.[5] The following Management Focus on Teamwork box, "Teams and Emotional Intelligence," describes group emotional intelligence and the role it can play in individual and group behavior.

Management Focus on Teamwork

Teams and Emotional Intelligence

Study after study show that teams are more creative and productive when they can achieve high levels of participation, cooperation, and collaboration among members. These are not behaviors that a manager can demand. Drisket and Wolff's research found that three basic conditions need to be present before such behaviors can occur: mutual trust among members, a sense of group identity (a feeling among members that they belong to a unique and worthwhile group), and a sense of group efficacy (the belief that the team can perform well and that group members are more effective working together than apart).

At the core of these three conditions are emotions. Trust, a sense of identity, and a feeling of efficacy occur in work cultures where emotion is well handled, so groups benefit by building their emotional intelligence.

Yes, teams have emotional intelligence. In most cases emotional intelligence has been discussed as an individual compe-tency. However, since a large amount of work in organizations is done in teams, understanding the emotional intelligence of teams is becoming an important managerial competency.

Emotionally competent teams face difficult situations without pointing fingers or ignoring feedback. IDEO, an industrial design firm, is a good model for exploring how group emotional intelligence works. The IDEO teams respect individual members' emotions. IDEO team members also confront one another when they break norms. There is also a continual seeking out of feedback. The result of IDEO's approach is teams that are cohesive, productive, and popular.

Sources: Adapted from Vanessa Urch Drisket and Steven B. Wolff, "Building the Emotional Intelligence of Groups," *Harvard Business Review,* March 2001, pp. 80–90; and Daniel Goleman, *Working with Emotional Intelligence* (New York: Bantam Doubleday Dell, 2000).

14-4 The Development of Work Groups

While informal groups develop in a nonstructured way, formal groups usually go through various stages of group and team development. Research has identified four distinct stages that most groups and teams go through as they develop: forming, storming, norming, and performing (Figure 14-3).

Group development describes the progression from a collection of people brought together for a common purpose to a well-functioning unit whose individual members cooperate to pursue a common goal.

14-4a Stage 1: Forming

Forming is the beginning stage of group development where individuals are brought together for a specific purpose. In this stage, the group members come together as a functioning unit. They agree to rules of conduct and the goals of the team. Group hierarchy and roles begin to develop, and a formal group leader is typically appointed to facilitate further group development. Research suggests that after groups have become operational they return briefly to the "forming" stage at the beginning of each meeting.[6]

14-4b Stage 2: Storming

This is the most turbulent stage of group development. *Storming* refers to the fact that, after initial niceties, the group falls into a process of confronting conflicts and discovering ways to keep the group focused. During this stage, group members learn to accept individual differences, and the beginnings of a collective "group personality" emerge. This personality is a result of shared values and purposes. There is also an informal vying for power within the group that occurs in this stage. Group members negotiate roles that are needed for effective group functioning and members tend to adopt and maintain those roles for the duration of the group.

14-4c Stage 3: Norming

During the *norming* stage the group establishes its long-term vision and how it will function over time. The agreement among members on a long-term vision is referred to as

> **group development** The phases or sequences through which a group passes, such as mutual acceptance, decision making, motivation, and control.

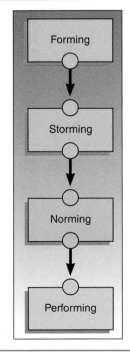

Figure 14-3
Stages of Group Development

shared values. The group's norms are the unwritten rules of correct behavior and decorum. For example, most groups develop seating patterns that are very stable. You may have noticed this yourself, as students in management courses will typically choose the same seat in a classroom for each meeting even though seats have not been assigned. This informal seating pattern is a group norm. Although group norms are rarely formalized, deviation from them may subject a group member to punishment, humiliation, or ostracism.

14-4d Stage 4: Performing

The final stage of group development is reached when a group is able to begin *performing* the task it was designed to address. During this stage, a group that has held together begins to fine-tune its work patterns. Group members may carefully redefine roles as needed. The group will help develop skills of individual members, as they are needed. The group may also recruit new members as it determines gaps in skill sets among existing members.

At each stage in the group development process, the group is confronted with increasingly difficult decisions. One of the greatest challenges is how best to reward individual contributions and still maintain the group's integrity. In mature groups, individual efforts are integrated into group functions.

14-5 Characteristics of Work Groups

Creating an organizational structure can result in such characteristics as specified relationships among subordinates, superiors, and peers; leaders assigned to positions; standards of performance; a status rank order according to the positions that individuals are filling; and group politics. Work groups also have characteristics similar to those of other organizations, including leaders, standards of conduct, reward and sanction mechanisms, and political maneuvering. An effective group is one that fully utilizes the skills and abilities of each of its members. Groups continue to be effective as long as they are able to engage the enthusiasm, skills, and intelligence of members.

A good way of thinking about the relationship between a member and the group is as a type of exchange. The group member gives time, energy, knowledge, and emotion while the group provides the member with need satisfaction. Group membership has the potential to satisfy several common human needs, including the need for achievement, the need for power, and the need for affiliation.[7] Many group members derive satisfaction from knowing that their contributions to a group were essential in helping it reach its goals. Group membership is also a primary mode of social interaction for many people in organizations. Organizational citizenship behaviors play a big role in work group effectiveness. Research has indicated that helping behavior and sportsmanship had significant effects on performance quantity and performance quality among work groups.[8]

Table 14-1 lists ten characteristics of effective groups.

14-5a Role Making in Groups

All work groups are defined by roles that members in the group perform and by the hierarchy or status of these roles. As discussed in Chapter 1, a *role* is a set of shared expectations regarding a member's attitude and task behavior within the group. At the most basic level, a group will have two roles: leader and member.

The greater the group's task complexity, the more roles will emerge. Group member agreement about the role to be performed is referred to as the sent role. The **sent role** is in essence the formal requirements of the role within the group. The **received role** is the role recipient's understanding of what the sent role means. In other words, the sent role may be received differently by different people. The **enacted role** is how the received role is expressed or redefined by the individual assuming the role.[9] This is how formal group expectations are transmitted, filtered, and processed for action by the role occupant. We all have different backgrounds, values, education, and beliefs about how the job should be done. All of these factors are brought to the forefront during role creation and enactment processes.

sent role Group member agreement about the role to be performed.

received role The role recipient's understanding of what the sent role means.

enacted role The manner in which the received role is expressed or redefined by the individual assuming the role.

TABLE 14-1

Characteristics of Effective Groups

1. All group members understand group roles and expectations.

2. Group members have developed a good working relationship.

3. Group members are attracted to the group and are loyal to the leader.

4. Group members have a high degree of trust and confidence in one another.

5. Group activities such as decision making and problem solving occur in a supportive atmosphere.

6. The group leader's role is to create a supportive atmosphere in which group work occurs. The leader should (1) seek information from group members about decisions that will affect them and (2) provide information that they need to do their jobs better.

7. The group should attempt to develop each member's full potential.

8. An atmosphere that encourages members to influence each other should be maintained. Influence ensures that new ideas enter the group and that dominant personalities work to the group's betterment.

9. The process for selecting a group leader should be based on the qualities that the individual brings to the group that encourage a supportive and open atmosphere.

10. Communication among members and the leader should be encouraged. If problems exist, free and open communication will bring problems to the surface.

Source: Adapted from Rensis Likert, *New Patterns of Management* (New York: McGraw-Hill, 1961), pp. 162–71. Used with permission of The McGraw-Hill Companies.

14-5b Problems in Role Making

Role creation with groups is not without its share of problems. Common problems include role conflict, role ambiguity, and role overload.[10]

Role conflict represents the incompatibility between the role's requirements and the individual's own beliefs or expectations. Remember, we all assume multiple roles in many different aspects of our lives. For example, a worker could simultaneously hold the roles of mother, wife, devoted church leader, manager, and engineer. It is easy to see that many of these different roles have required behaviors that may conflict with one another.

Such internal conflict can come from a variety of sources. One source, *interrole conflict,* occurs when two different types of roles collide. A manager may have to fire an employee who is also a friend. The friend part of him doesn't want to fire the employee, but his job requires him to do so. *Intrarole conflict* occurs when two similar roles come in conflict—for example, when your boss tells you to increase productivity and your workers are pushing for better working conditions. In this example, you are simultaneously a subordinate and a superior. Further, you believe that the organization needs greater productivity and also that the work rules make for dissatisfied and unmotivated workers. *Intersender conflict* occurs when contradictory messages come from the same source. Your boss preaches that quality is the most important aspect of your work. However, he insists on hiring low-skilled workers who can't fully utilize the robotics that are a major determinant of quality in the company. *Person-role conflict* occurs when an individual's beliefs are in direct conflict with the requirements of his or her role. For example, you know that a product batch is defective and shipping the products could possibly cause consumer injury and increase liability for the firm. You've also received a memo from your boss insisting your job is to help build sales volume by expediting the shipment of as many products as possible. You know shipping the product is wrong but you feel compelled to make your volume quota. Such role conflicts have a direct effect on organizational citizenship behaviors.[11]

In **role ambiguity,** role requirements are not clear. In general, role ambiguity results when the role occupant is not sure how to fulfill role requirements. Simple routine roles rarely generate ambiguity. In a routine role, such as an assembly line job, role requirements are specific or decision criteria are simple. Professional roles present a greater chance of

role conflict The incompatibility between the role's requirements and the individual's own beliefs or expectations.

role ambiguity The situation existing when role requirements are unclear.

role ambiguity. Managers often face a technical situation that they are not trained to fully understand, and they must decide to rely on a subordinate's judgment. The ambiguity for the manager is whether to consult a staff specialist (which might waste time) or go with the subordinate's judgment. The manager knows full well that he'll be held responsible regardless of a positive or a negative outcome. Managers should understand that role ambiguity is a stressor in the workplace. It can be mitigated to some extent by a worker's commitment to the firm.[12]

▶ **role overload** A condition that occurs when a task's demands overwhelm the role occupant's ability to perform the task.

Role overload is a condition in which a task's demands overwhelm the role occupant's ability to perform the task. Too much, too little, or conflicting information may surpass the role occupant's ability to perform the task at a satisfactory level. With the emphasis on "lean organizations" and the corresponding reduction of America's white-collar workforce, it's very likely that role overload will be a common contributory symptom of role stress reported by those who remain.

Role conflict, role ambiguity, and role overload are all potential problems that can decrease a group's effectiveness. Managers must recognize the potential problems that can undermine a group's overall performance.

14-5c The Group Leader

One of the most important group roles is that of the group leader. The leader emerges from within an informal group and is accepted by the group members. In the formal group, however, the leader is appointed.

Leaders in many formal groups are followed and obeyed because employees perceive them as possessing the power and influence to reward them or punish them if they do not comply with requests. This is not always an accurate perception, however. As organizations have continued to move toward self-managed teams, group leaders are often not in hire-fire or reward-punish positions.

The informal leader emerges from within the group and serves a number of functions. First, any group of individuals without a plan or some coordination becomes an ineffective unit. Its members are not directed toward the accomplishment of goals, and this can lead to a breakdown in group effectiveness. The leader initiates action and provides direction. If there are differences of opinion on a group-related matter, the leader attempts to settle the differences and to move the group toward accomplishing its goals.

Second, some individual must communicate the group's beliefs about policies, the job, the organization, the supervision, and other related matters to nonmembers.[13] The nonmembers could include members of other groups, supervisory personnel, and the union. In effect, the group leader communicates the values of the group.

The characteristics of informal group leaders can be summarized as follows:

1. The leadership role is filled by the individual who possesses the attributes that members perceive as being critical for satisfying their needs.

2. The leader embodies the values of the group and is able to perceive those values, organize them into an intelligible philosophy, and verbalize them to nonmembers.

3. The leader is able to receive and interpret communication relevant to the group and to effectively communicate important information to group members.

In most groups, leaders perform two specific roles. A leader who performs the *task role* typically concentrates on accomplishing the desired goals, such as providing a number of units within quality and cost standards or delivering a product to a customer. The task role requires the leader to accomplish something specific of importance to the membership.

Leaders of groups also perform a *supportive,* or *maintenance, role,* which involves personally helping members, listening to their problems, and encouraging group cohesiveness. While the task role is job oriented, the supportive role is people oriented. Both orientations are important for accomplishing group performance and satisfaction.[14] In some groups, one person performs both roles. In other groups, two individuals perform the roles.

14-5d Group Status

Status is the rank, respect, or social position that an individual has in a group. Managers have relative status that depends on their positions in the hierarchy; that is, the top managers of the firm have more status than middle managers, and the middle managers have more status than lower-level managers. The top-level positions have more authority, responsibility, power, and influence—and thus are accorded more status.

A similar status system develops in groups. For many different reasons, members are accorded status by their groups. Individuals in leadership roles possess status because of their roles. Consequently, they are ranked highly in the group-status hierarchy.

Other factors influence the status systems of groups. Many groups consider the seniority of a member to be important. A worker having more seniority is often thought of as being "organizationally intelligent," which means that she knows how to adapt to the demands of supervisors, subordinates, or peers. This ability to adjust is an important status factor with group members.

The individual's skill in performing a job is another factor related to status. An individual with expertise in the technical aspects of the job is given a high-status ranking in some groups. This type of status does not mean that the individual actually utilizes the skill to perform more effectively, but simply that the group members admire this skill.

14-5e Group Norms and Compliance

A **group norm** is an implicit or explicit agreement among the group members as to how they should behave. The more a person complies with norms, the more the person accepts the group's standards of behavior.

Work groups can utilize norms to bring about acceptable job performance. Three specific social processes bring about compliance with group norms: *group pressure, group review and enforcement,* and *personalization of the norms.*

> **group norm** Explicit or implicit agreement among a group's members about how they should behave.

Group Pressure   The pressure to adhere to a specific group norm can bring conformity to the behavior of the group's membership. Conformity occurs when a person complies with a group's wishes because of the pressure it applies or fear of future group pressure. Complying with group pressure does not mean the person agrees with the group's wishes.

Group Review and Enforcement   If group members, either veterans or newcomers, are not complying with generally accepted norms, a number of different approaches may be employed. One soft approach is a discussion between respected leaders and the nonconformists. If discussion does not prove effective, more rigorous corrective action is used, such as private and public scolding by the members. The ultimate enforcement is to drop the deviating members from the group. A vital role for managers is to allow groups enough space to develop their own interpersonal commitments without waiting too long for performance to commence. This balancing act can be very difficult for managers accustomed to intervening at the slightest hint of trouble. However, sometimes the best action for a manager is thoughtful nonaction—especially in the early stages of group formation when groups are establishing their own norms.[15]

Personalization of Norms   Behavioral patterns are influenced significantly by values. Values, in turn, are influenced by the events occurring around individuals; values are learned and become personalized. For example, the norm of a work group may be to treat college graduates *and* persons who did not go to college equally. This norm may be accepted by a group member as morally and ethically correct. Prior to group affiliation, the member may have displayed little interest in whether an individual attended college. However, based on a feeling of fairness, the member personalizes this group-learned norm, and it becomes a standard of her behavior.

Figure 14-4
Positive and Negative Group Norms

Condition Performance	Positive Group Norm +	Negative Group Norm −
Output	Members work hard to produce at optimal skill levels.	Members work just hard enough to get by.
Quality	Members take pride in producing quality products.	Members pay enough attention to quality to keep management minimally happy.
Absenteeism	Members pride themselves on being present.	Members are not interested in good attendance.
Supervisor relations	Members respect supervisors and are honest in their interactions.	Members distrust management and hold back vital information.
Honesty	Members are against stealing and slowdowns.	Members encourage some pilferage and slow down the line when everyone seems tired.
Wages/salaries	Members expect a fair day's pay for a good day's work.	Members expect to be taken care of despite a lack of effort—the "organization owes me" attitude.

The group norms can either be positive or negative as far as a manager is concerned. However, both types of norms typically are encountered when compliance is the issue of concern. Figure 14-4 illustrates some examples of work conditions for which groups often establish norms. Positive and negative norms are presented to portray what managers often must face.

14-5f Group Cohesiveness

group cohesiveness The attraction of individual members to a group in terms of the strength of the forces that impel them to remain active in the group and to resist leaving it.

The flip side of group pressure is a phenomenon known as **group cohesiveness.** In a cohesive group, the various members of the group have aligned their interests by choice rather than pressure. Cohesive groups are aligned on the long-term goals of the group, but may not agree on each detail about how to achieve these goals. Aligning groups on the long-term goals via persuasion rather than pressure can lead to high morale and high performance.[16]

Cohesiveness refers to the extent that group members are attracted to each other and to the group values. It is the pressure on the individual member to remain active in the group and to resist leaving it.[17]

All characteristics of groups are influenced in some degree by group cohesiveness. For example, the greater the attraction within the group, the more likely its members will adhere closely to a group norm such as a production level.[18] Group cohesiveness influences a variety of outcomes, including organizational commitment, job satisfaction, motivation, and role conflict.[19]

Some of the conditions that can enhance or reduce cohesiveness are presented in Figure 14-5.

The Size of the Work Group It is important that group members interact and communicate. If a group is so large that members do not know one another, it is unlikely that the group will be cohesive. Managers have learned than an inverse relationship exists

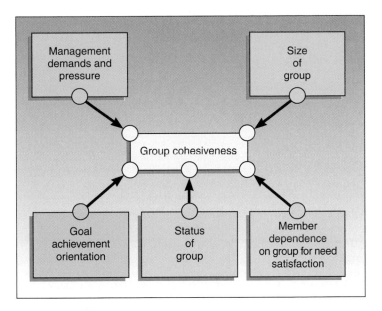

Figure 14-5
Factors Contributin
to Group Cohesiven

between group size and group cohesiveness.[20] As the size of a group increases, its cohesiveness decreases. Project *teams* are most effective with four to seven members. Once a *team* grows beyond seven persons, its internal maintenance consumes a disproportionate share of *team* energy. The number of relationships increases as the *team* grows, factions form, responsibility wanes, and accountability erodes.[21]

The Spacing of the Work Group   This is a rather new phenomenon related to the use of information technology. Work groups no longer need to be physically present to complete their tasks. Telecommuting has emerged in an era where large numbers of employees work from their homes or remote telecenters. In either case, these workers often work with people whom they rarely meet in person. Tasks and responsibilities are conducted through electronic media. Managers must learn to work with such "virtual teams" to ensure the same level of productivity—or higher—as would occur in a more traditional work team situation.

Virtual Teams   Virtual teams are composed of individuals who operate across space and time and who communicate mainly through electronic technologies. E-mail, video-conferencing, electronic chat rooms, intranets, and networked computers let members in virtual teams work together in a coordinated manner. Decisions can be made from a distance and communicated to virtual team members.[22]

Technology, information, and knowledge databases make it possible to operate across space, time, and boundaries. Virtual team members can review, use, and implement resources that everyone can share. The issue of distance between team members is insignificant because of a reliance on electronic technologies. Team members from any geographical location can be in contact with all or some of the virtual team with the click of a mouse.[23]

Organizations have been able to assemble cross-functional virtual teams to solve problems, service customers, form alliances, and negotiate business transactions. Companies such as IBM, Procter & Gamble, AT&T, and Hewlett Packard have partially or completely eliminated traditional offices for field sales and customer service. The old-fashioned office has been replaced with individuals and teams with portable computers, cellular phones, videoconferencing, and fax machines that permit remote or mobile work flexibility.[24]

The freedom and autonomy of being on a virtual team is appealing to some individuals. Executives like the concept especially when it results in significant reductions in real estate cost. The virtual arrangements also make it possible for increased interaction between sales personnel and customers.

Management Focus on **Information Technology**

Virtual Workers Still Crave Interpersonal Interaction

A future of teleworking *virtual teams*—all sharing ideas, developing products, and coordinating projects without ever meeting their teammates in person—has yet to arrive, much like the vaunted paperless office.

Even in the world's most technologically interconnected societies, telecommuting is not as widespread among twenty-first-century infotech workers as pundits have been predicting for some three decades. A recent study reports that only 4 percent of Finnish workers said they were performing telework (defined as work done at home under an employment contract); another 4 percent had tried telework. But more than 90 percent said they had never even experimented with it.

The need for a live, physical connection with collaborators may be why working "virtually" is so unpopular, suggest researchers conducting the study at the University of Tampere Department of Sociology and Social Psychology. They also fault old-fashioned management attitudes that prevent organizations from instituting changes that could save on office overhead and workers' commuting time.

But workers may have another fear: loss of identity and distinction. One price of working in a team is the need to surrender your unique ideas into a group's intellectual identity, according to a study by scholars at Stanford Graduate School of Business and elsewhere. In a *virtual* team, your contributions may be deposited into a database, becoming the property of the organization. If your hard-earned experience, knowledge, and wisdom can no longer be traced directly to you, what future do you have in the Knowledge Economy?

"It's a real fear," says Margaret Neale, one of the study's authors. "Technology has the potential to destabilize the relationship between organizations and employees."

Similarly, because *virtual* workers and teleworkers are isolated from their colleagues, they lose opportunities to benefit from other people's ideas and experience and hence to replenish their own intellectual reservoirs, says Neale. Thus, while technology enables them to disseminate information to each other and the organization quickly, virtual *teams* are less able to transfer implicit knowledge.

Source: Adapted from Cynthia G. Wagner, "Fear and Loathing in the Virtual Workplace," *The Futurist,* March/April 2004, pp. 6–7.

Despite the potential benefits of having virtual teams, there are occasions when face-to-face interaction is needed to solve a personal or emotional issue. The Management Focus on Information Technology box indicates that there are some problems associated with being a virtual worker. While it sounds appealing to imagine working from a home office with virtual collaborators around the world, many such workers have found there are disadvantages associated with the isolation.

The advantages of flexibility with virtual teams are likely to be a major consideration when weighing the benefits and costs of such an arrangement.[25] As an example of this major benefit the development of the Boeing 777 aircraft is often cited. This aircraft was developed primarily through the work of virtual teams. About 238 teams used a network of 1,700 individual computer systems to link everyone together. Teams in Seattle; Japan; Wichita, Kansas; Philadelphia, and many other locations worked and communicated electronically. The efficiency was superb, and the results included a well-designed aircraft, team cohesiveness, and met deadlines.

The growing popularity of virtual teams has resulted in software technology for sharing documents, organizing calendars, and identifying areas of responsibility in specific teams.[26] Eroom.net (www.eroom.net) is a tool designed to help virtual team members feel like a part of the team. Members can share documents, compare schedules, and conduct threaded discussions. The tool allows a member to see which teammates are on-line and also provides a means to summon members to a virtual chat room. Other tools such as Skype (www.skype.com) enable live voice communications from PC to PC anywhere in the world for free. These innovations have made it easier for people to collaborate at a distance. Research has determined that regular communication among collaborators is more important in virtual teams than in organization-centered teams.[27]

The Dependence of the Members on the Work Group The greater the individual's dependency on the group, the stronger will be his or her attraction for it. Individuals join groups because the groups can help them satisfy economic and sociopsychological needs. A group that is able to satisfy a significant portion of an indi-

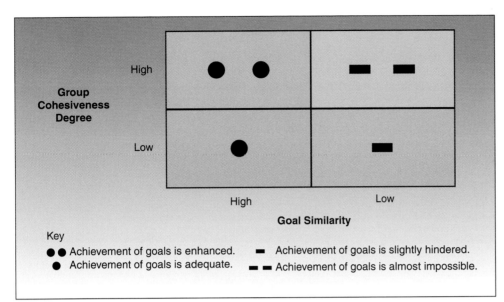

Figure 14-6
Cohesiveness and Goal Similarities: Similarity Between Group and Organization Performance Goals

vidual's needs will be attractive to that individual. Group processes such as interaction with coworkers and overall friendship may make the group a key factor in the individual's life. Thus, what the group stands for, its norms, and its membership are bonds that tie the individual to the group.

The Achievement of Goals   The attainment of some set of group-established goals (e.g., better production than another group) influences the group's members. For example, if a work group attains a highly desired rating for completing a task, then a value of belonging to that group is enhanced. Its members feel pride in being part of a group that has achieved a superior performance.

Work groups that have successfully attained goals are likely to be highly cohesive units. The members tend to be more attracted toward one another because they have worked together in the past and their efforts have resulted in achieving goals. Thus, success and cohesiveness are interrelated: Success in goal achievement encourages cohesiveness, and cohesive work groups are more likely to attain goals. Managers know, however, that although group cohesiveness can lead to the achievement of goals, cohesiveness can prove detrimental when group and organization goals are incompatible.

Managers clearly must recognize that they will have a difficult job if a group is highly cohesive but has performance goals that differ from those of the organization. On the other hand, a cohesive group whose goals are similar to those of management can be a very enjoyable unit to manage. The possible relationships between cohesiveness and goal similarities are illustrated in Figure 14-6. The ideal situation occurs when the highly cohesive group's goals are similar to those of the organization, which is shown as the ●● cell in Figure 14-6.

The Status of the Group   In an organizational setting, groups typically are ranked in a status hierarchy. A status hierarchy may develop among groups for many different reasons, including the following:

1. The group is rated higher than another group in overall performance; this rating measures success in an organization.

2. To become a member of the group, individuals must display a high level of skill.

3. The work being done by the group is dangerous, or financially more rewarding, or more challenging, than other work.

4. The group is less closely supervised than other groups.

5. In the past, members of the group have been considered for promotion more often than members of other groups.

Figure 14-7
Symptoms of Groupthink

Source: Irving L Janis, *Victims of Groupthink.* Copyright © 1972 by Houghton Mifflin Company. Adapted with permission.

> ### Symptoms of Groupthink
>
> • **Having illusions of group invulnerability.** Members of the group believe it is basically beyond criticism or attack.
>
> • **Rationalizing unpleasant and disconfirming data.** Members of the group refuse to accept contradictory data or to consider alternatives thoroughly.
>
> • **Believing in inherent group morality.** Members of the group believe it is "right" and above any reproach by outsiders.
>
> • **Stereotyping competitors as weak, evil, and stupid.** Members of the group refuse to look realistically at other groups.
>
> • **Applying direct pressure to deviants to conform to group wishes.** Members of the group refuse to tolerate a member who suggests the group may be wrong.
>
> • **Using self-censorship by members.** Members of the group refuse to communicate personal concerns to the group as a whole.
>
> • **Having illusions of unanimity.** Members of the group accept consensus prematurely without testing its completeness.
>
> • **Guarding minds.** Members of the group protect the group from hearing disturbing ideas or viewpoints from outsiders.

These are only some of the criteria that affect the status hierarchy of groups. Generally, the higher a group ranks in the intergroup status hierarchy, the greater its cohesiveness. However, the higher-status groups appear attractive only to some nonmembers. Individuals outside the group may not want to become members of a high-status group because membership entails close adherence to group norms.

Management Demands and Pressure   Another agent for group cohesiveness is management demands and pressure. In many organizations, management has a significant impact on group cohesiveness. The members of groups tend to stick together when superiors pressure them to conform to some organizational norm.

The group cohesiveness attributed to managerial demands may be either a short-run or long-run phenomenon. In some cases, a loosely knit group (low in cohesiveness) may interpret a company policy statement as a threat to the job security of its members. Consequently, the group may become a more cohesive and unified whole to withstand the perceived management threat. After the danger is past (e.g., the policy statement is rescinded), the group may drift back toward low cohesiveness. In other cases, the cohesiveness may be a longer-lasting phenomenon.

When groups are characterized by high conformity and cohesiveness, a phenomenon called **groupthink** might occur.[28] Groupthink exists when a group believes that it is invincible, rationalizes away criticisms, believes that everyone should comply with a group norm, and is characterized by unanimity among its members. When left unchecked, groupthink can lead to decisions that run counter to the organization's long-term strategies and goals.[29] Figure 14-7 identifies a number of symptoms of groupthink, which must be overcome if group effectiveness is to be restored.

Several managerial actions can minimize the groupthink phenomenon. Preventive actions include the following:

• Assigning the role of critical evaluator to all members of the group. Critical thinking should be encouraged, supported, and rewarded.

• Encouraging members to be impartial and to engage in open interaction instead of sticking with predetermined preferences.

• Establishing subgroups to work on problem issues and to then share with the total group the proposed solutions.

• Including outside experts in group discussions and permitting them to challenge the views expressed by members.

groupthink A phenomenon that occurs when a group believes that it is invincible, ignores criticism, attempts to bring noncomplying members into line, and feels that everyone is in agreement.

- Having at least one group member play the devil's advocate and challenge the majority position.

- Developing an analysis of how the group's decision will affect other groups. Discuss the consequences of the group's proposal so that changes can be made before action is taken.

- Holding a "second chance" meeting at which every group member expresses any doubts about the decision.

These preventive actions do have disadvantages.[30] For instance, the open dialogue, debate, and exchange of ideas is likely to lead to prolonged delays in decision making. Can a manager afford the time in a crisis situation? A crisis may require quick communications, quick discussions, and group meetings with time deadlines.[31] Bringing in outside experts also can create problems. Although experts have much to offer, their use increases the risk of security leakage. One of the most effective techniques for eliminating groupthink is to ensure that someone always plays **devil's advocate,** asking the hard questions about a decision and group tendencies.[32]

14-5g Group Politics

Political maneuvering to obtain limited resources is a common group characteristic. Since organizations typically work with scarce resources, **group politics** is a problem that managers become involved with on a regular basis.

Group politics exists when the behavior of the group is specifically self-serving. When a group acts to enhance its own position, regardless of the costs of the action, it acts politically. Often, self-serving group behavior creates such strained group relationships that both organizational and group performances suffer. When a situation becomes an "us" versus "them" or a "my group" versus "your group" controversy, there are self-serving overtones. Through their actions and their dealings with groups, managers set the tone for the political maneuvering that emerges.[33]

Two types of managerial behaviors can create the atmosphere for group politics— offensive and defensive. *Offensive political behavior* by a group manager includes power building, exploiting or calling attention to the weaknesses of others, and sabotaging the work of others.

Defensive political behavior by a group manager can mean maneuvering in response to others. Placing the blame on another group, covering up mistakes, or even working hard to direct attention away from weaknesses are examples of defensive political behavior.

By example, managers often can create the environment for the degree and kind of politics in organizations. Subordinates look to managers for direction. When managers use political maneuvers, subordinates tend to imitate this action. Managers can modify such behavior by examining their political tendencies:

- Is this action only self-serving?

- Will this action hurt another group or person?

- Will organizational performance be improved by this action?

Confronting these questions can help managers become more aware of the political impact of their behavior. When the behavior initiated by a manager involves working together with other groups, organizational performance can be enhanced.

14-5h Cultural Diversity

Members in most organizational groups today will differ from each other in important ways, such as age, gender, ethnic background, disabilities, religious affiliation, and lifestyle. In fact, research has shown that cultural diversity in the workplace is good for business. However, research has also shown that firms that pursue diversity for its own sake do not gain the advantages of firms that pursue diversity for performance reasons.[34]

▶ **devil's advocate** A person playing devil's advocate will intentionally attempt to argue against the prevailing wishes of the group.

▶ **group politics** The use of self-serving tactics to improve a group's position relative to that of other groups.

Cultural diversity has many implications for group performance.[35] Different rules and traditions across the diverse backgrounds of individual group members serve to complicate interpersonal interactions. Research has generally shown that groups with a substantial degree of cultural diversity are not able to solve complex problems as effectively as homogeneous groups.[36] Managers often overlook the relationship between high performance and the ability for group members to work effectively with diverse individuals. To interact productively in a diverse group it's necessary to respect other cultures and create new ways of integrating diverse viewpoints, expanding the range of acceptable means for achieving organizational goals.[37]

Managing diverse groups has become a critical challenge in organizations. In fact, firms that don't include diversity as part of their business plan might be at a competitive disadvantage.[38]

The characteristics of groups described in this section provide an overview of how managers can think about and understand group behavior and performance. Despite being able to understand groups and their characteristics, managers won't be able to eliminate intergroup conflict. Conflict is a natural part of any system that has scarce resources. Managers must understand conflict as a natural occurrence. In the next section, we explore the nature of intergroup conflict and several ways to manage it.

14-6 Intergroup Conflict

Conflict occurs when one party perceives that another party has frustrated, or is about to frustrate, the accomplishment of a goal. Conflict is not limited to interacting groups; it also occurs within groups, between individuals, and between organizations.[39] We will focus here on **intergroup conflict** within organizations.

> **intergroup conflict**
> The disagreements, hostile emotions, and problems that exist among groups as a result of limited resources, communication problems, differences in perceptions and attitudes, and lack of clarity.

One way to view conflict is to consider it as a sequence of episodes.[40] The sequence is as follows:

- *Latent conflict*—conditions for conflict exist: two groups competing for scarce resources, for example.
- *Perceived conflict*—group members realize that there is conflict between groups.
- *Felt conflict*—the members involved feel tense or anxious.
- *Manifest conflict*—behaviors clearly demonstrate that one group is attempting to frustrate another group.
- *Conflict aftermath*—the situation after the conflict is minimized or eliminated.

Since conflict can progress to the manifest stage, it can have dysfunctional consequences for organizations and individuals. Conflict can arouse emotions and anxiety, lower satisfaction, and decrease performance. Research has shown that the greater the perceived threat, the greater decrement in problem-solving effectiveness.[41] Managers must solve the conflict and get groups once again working cooperatively toward the accomplishment of organizational and individual goals. Yet cooperation is not always the most desirable result of group interaction. For example, two groups may cooperate because they both oppose the introduction of new equipment being installed to improve cost control. In this instance, the cooperation of the groups can make the trial period of testing the new equipment a bad experience for management.

There are many reasons for conflict among groups. Some of the more important ones relate to limited resources, communication problems, differences in interests and goals, different perceptions and attitudes, and lack of clarity about responsibilities.

14-6a Limited Resources

Groups that possess an abundance of materials, money, and time usually are effective. However, when a number of groups are competing for limited resources, conflict often results. The competition for equipment dollars or merit increase money or new positions can become fierce.

14-6b Communication Problems

Groups often become very involved with their own areas of responsibility. They tend to develop their own unique vocabulary. Paying attention to an area of responsibility is a worthy endeavor, but it can result in communication problems. The receiver of information should be considered when a group communicates an idea, a proposal, or a decision. Misinformed receivers often become irritated and then hostile.

14-6c Different Interests and Goals

A group of young workers may want management to do something about an inadequate promotion system. However, older workers may accuse management of ignoring improvements in the company pension plan. Management recognizes the two different goals but believes the pension issue is the more pressing and addresses it first. The groups want management to solve both problems, but this may not be currently possible. Thus, one group, that of the young workers, may become hostile because it feels it has been ignored.

14-6d Different Perceptions and Attitudes

Individuals perceive things differently. The groups to which they belong also can have different perceptions. Groups tend to evaluate in terms of their backgrounds, norms, and experiences. Since each of these can differ, there is likely to be conflict among groups. Most groups tend to overvalue their own worth and position and to undervalue the worth and position of other groups.

14-6e Lack of Clarity

Job clarity involves knowing what others expect in terms of task accomplishment. Yet in many cases, it is difficult to specify who is responsible for a certain task. For example: Who is responsible for the loss of a talented management trainee—the personnel department or the training department? Who is responsible for the increased sales revenue—marketing or research and development? The inability to pinpoint positive and negative contributions causes groups to compete for control over the activities that are more easily associated with specific effort.

14-7 Managing Intergroup Conflict

The management of intergroup conflict involves determining strategies to minimize such causes. Management reaction to disruptive intergroup conflict can take many different forms.[42] But management usually will first try to minimize the conflict indirectly, and if this fails, become directly involved.

The *indirect approach* refers to techniques managers might use that don't require their direct intervention. The *direct approach* refers to managers becoming personally involved in resolving intergroup conflicts. Each approach is examined in more detail in the following sections.

14-7a The Indirect Approach

Initially, managers often avoid direct approaches to solving conflict among groups. Unfortunately, *avoidance* does not always minimize the problem. Matters get worse because nothing is being done, and the groups become more antagonistic and hostile.

Another indirect strategy is to encourage the groups to meet and discuss their differences and to work out a solution without management involvement. This strategy can take the form of bargaining, persuasion, or working on a problem together.

Bargaining involves having the groups agree about what each will get and give to the other. For example, one group may agree to give another group quick turnaround time on the repairs of needed equipment if the second group agrees to bring complaints about the quality of repairs to it before going to management. Bargaining between two groups is successful if both groups are better off (or at least no worse off) after an agreement has been reached.

Persuasion involves having the groups find areas of common interest. The groups attempt to find points of agreement and to show how these are important to each of the groups in attaining organizational goals. Persuasion is possible if clashes between group leaders do not exist.

A problem can be an obstacle to a goal. For groups to minimize their conflicts through *problem solving*, they must agree at least generally on the goal. If there is agreement, then the groups can propose alternative solutions that satisfy all parties involved. For example, one group may want the company to relocate the plant to a suburban area and the other group may want better working conditions. If both parties agree that a common goal is to maintain their jobs, then building a new facility in an area that does not have a high tax rate may be a good solution.

14-7b The Direct Approach

To improve intergroup relations, greater integration or collaboration among groups must occur. Various strategies can be used effectively to increase integration. Management can use *domination* to minimize conflict by exercising its authority and requiring that a problem be solved by a specific date. If management uses authority, the groups may join together to resist domination. Management thus becomes a common enemy, and the groups forget their differences in order to deal with their opponent.

Another direct approach is to *remove the key figures* in the conflict. If a conflict arises because of personality differences between two individuals, removing them is a possible solution. This approach has three problems. First, the key figures who are to be removed may be leaders of the groups. Removing them could make the groups more antagonistic and lead to greater conflict. Second, it is difficult to pinpoint accurately whether the individuals in conflict are at odds because of personal animosities or because they represent their groups. Third, removal may create martyrs. The causes of the removed leaders may be remembered and fought for, even though the leaders themselves are gone.

Management also can establish a task force with representatives from groups in conflict to work on problems. The task force will develop ideas and procedures for improving group interaction to be presented to their groups.[43]

A final direct strategy to minimize conflict is to find *superordinate goals*. These are goals desired by two or more groups that can only be accomplished through the cooperation of the groups. When conflicting groups have to cooperate to accomplish a goal, conflict can be minimized. For example, a companywide profit-sharing plan may encourage groups to work together. If company profits are distributed among employees at the end of the year, conflict among groups can reduce the amount of profits that each employee receives. Thus, the superordinate goal, generating profit, may take precedence over group conflict.

14-8 Group Outcomes: Performance and Satisfaction

The purpose of group membership is to achieve group performance. Too little emphasis has been placed on group performance.

In recent years, social psychologists have increased their efforts to understand group performance. Some contributors to group performance are (1) *perceived freedom to participate,* (2) *perceived goal attainment,* and (3) *status consensus.*

14-8a Perceived Freedom to Participate

A group member's perception of freedom to participate influences his need satisfaction and performance. Work group members who perceive themselves as active participants report that they are more satisfied, whereas those who perceive their freedom to participate as insignificant are typically the least-satisfied members in a work group.

The freedom-to-participate phenomenon is related to the entire spectrum of economic and sociopsychological needs. For example, individuals' perceived ability to participate may lead them to believe that they are valued members of the group. This assumption can lead to the satisfaction of social, esteem, and self-actualization needs, which in turn leads to high levels of performance.

14-8b Perceived Goal Attainment

Perceiving that you are progressing toward the attainment of desired goals is an important factor in the performance of group members. Members of groups that have clearly progressed toward results indicate higher levels of satisfaction than members of groups that have not progressed adequately. Goal attainment is effective performance.

14-8c Status Consensus

Status consensus is defined as agreement about the relative status of all group members. Suppose a person has a high rank or worth because he has a valued characteristic such as education but is not experienced to perform a group role. In that case, a lack of status consensus or **status incongruence** would exist. A recent college graduate might face status incongruence if she is placed in a position to lead a group of experienced technicians. This lack of consensus between education and experience for the position would create an uncomfortable work atmosphere. According to formal organization procedures, the leader has the authority and the responsibility to direct the group. However, the experienced workers likely would not trust the untested opinions and ideas of the new, inexperienced leader. The result might be covertly slowing down performance or even sabotaging the young leader's directives. In any event, a lack of status consensus within a group can cause decreased performance and less satisfaction.

Managers must work with groups and know how they function and perform. Managers who understand groups are better able to turn inevitable group characteristics into positive forces to accomplish desirable performance objectives. Without a solid understanding of group structure, processes, development, and consequences, the manager is placed at an uncomfortable disadvantage. Figure 14-8 presents guidelines that managers can use to learn more about their groups.

▶ **status consensus** Agreement as to the relative status of all group members.

▶ **status incongruence** A behavioral factor in group decision making where lower-status individuals are inhibited by higher-status individuals in the group.

14-8d Developing Teams

Organizing, managing, and evaluating workplace teams is a difficult process. In the several decades since teams have become a more vital component of many organizations, several lessons have been learned on how managers can more effectively utilize the team

Area of Concern	Questions to Answer
1. Activities	Who does what job in the group?
2. Interactions	Who initiates contact? How frequently? On what issues?
3. Norms	What are the task and the behavioral norms? How clear are the norms to the members?
4. Leaders	Who are the informal leaders?
5. Status	What is the status order?
6. Cohesiveness	How cohesive is the group? On what issues is its cohesiveness greatest?
7. Group politics	How much political maneuvering goes on in the group?
8. Performance	How does the group's performance compare to that of other groups? Has its performance fluctuated? When?

Figure 14-8
Checklist for Learning About Groups

approach. Research by McKinsey & Company, for example, has uncovered the following ten principles of "team-driven companies."[44]

1. *Organize around processes rather than task.* Performance objectives should be based on customer needs such as service. The processes that meet those needs should be the major components of the company.

2. *Flatten the hierarchy by grouping subprocesses.* Teams should be arranged in parallel, with each doing many steps in a process, not a series of teams with each doing a few steps.

3. *Give leaders responsibility for processes and process performance.* Self-managed teams are responsible for multiple tasks. Team members possess a set of skills relevant to the groups' tasks and have discretion over the methods of work, task schedules, assignment of members to different tasks, compensation, and feedback about performance for the group as a whole.[45]

4. *Link performance objectives and evaluation of all activities to customer satisfaction.* Everything should be driven by the customer; successful performance also means customers have been satisfied.

5. *Assign performance objectives to teams, not individuals.* This makes teams the focus of organizational performance and design. Individuals cannot continuously improve quality and work flows.

6. *Assign managerial tasks to teams as much as possible.* Workers' teams should be responsible for activities such as hiring, evaluating, and scheduling.

7. *Emphasize the need for workers to develop several competencies.* In a team-driven company, only a few specialists are needed. Productivity can be increased by asking the team to take on more difficult tasks and asking team members to serve as consultants to other teams.[46]

8. *Train team members on a just-in-time, need-to-perform basis.* Information should go directly to those who can use it in their jobs. Trained and empowered workers know how to use information.

9. *Put team members in touch with customers.* Field trips and spots on problem-solving teams can bring team members closer to customers. Knowledge of customer needs is then reflected in teamwork.

10. *Reward skill development and team performance.* Performance evaluation should focus on team achievements rather than individual achievements. It is counterproductive to talk about teamwork while evaluating and rewarding individuals.

Management Summary

- Managers must deal with formal and informal groups. Even in the most efficiently managed organizations informal groups will emerge.

- Groups are formed to satisfy needs—organizational, economic, and sociopsychological.

- Groups develop over a period of time and because of interaction. This suggests that if a mature group is what a manager wants, then the group will have to be kept together.

- The different types of groups that managers are involved with as members or leaders include task, command, friendship, and interest groups. Each of these types satisfies some set of needs of the group members.

- Group characteristics include group leaders, status, norms, cohesiveness, politics, and diversity. These are areas that managers must learn about through careful observation.

- Group cohesiveness and conformity may result in groupthink—everyone goes along with the group because it is all-powerful.

- Group politics can have a negative impact on performance. Providing a good model that minimizes political maneuvering is one procedure a manager can adopt to minimize the dysfunctions of group politics.

- To improve the ability to work effectively with groups, it is important for the manager to study, observe, and to ask the right questions.

Key Terms

command group (p. 332)
devil's advocate (p. 345)
enacted role (p. 336)
formal groups (p. 331)
friendship groups (p. 333)
group cohesiveness (p. 340)
group development (p. 335)
group norm (p. 339)

group politics (p. 345)
groupthink (p. 344)
informal groups (p. 333)
interest group (p. 333)
intergroup conflict (p. 346)
outcomes (p. 330)
received role (p. 336)
role ambiguity (p. 337)

role conflict (p. 337)
role overload (p. 338)
sent role (p. 336)
status consensus (p. 349)
status incongruence (p. 349)
task group (p. 332)
work group (p. 330)
work team (p. 330)

Review and Discussion Questions

1. Explain how a group can exercise control over its members.

2. A manager stated that if he were doing a good job of managing, no informal groups would be formed by subordinates. Do you agree? Explain.

3. Why is it better for managers to try indirect methods of resolving intergroup conflict before becoming directly involved?

4. Why has the concept of a virtual team become a more widely used approach in the past few years?

5. Why would it be difficult for a group leader to blend the talents of a group of creative individuals?

6. What happens within a group during the "storming" stage of group development?

7. What role does diversity play in work groups? Should managers be concerned to eliminate or promote diversity on work teams? Explain.

8. Should a manager be excited about having a highly cohesive group of subordinates?

9. Why is self-serving group behavior usually viewed as group politics?

10. Why is being a good listener an important requirement for serving as the chairperson of a committee?

...d the correct answers to these questions by taking the
...ubmitting your answers in the Online Edition. The program
...tically score your submission. If you miss a question, the pro-
... provide the correct answer, a rationale for the answer, and the
sec...n number in the chapter where the topic is discussed.

Indicate whether the sentence or statement is true or false.

1. In some cases, work groups form because individuals believe that they can gain economic benefits on their jobs if they band together.

2. At each stage in the group development process, the group is confronted with increasingly difficult decisions.

3. The diverse backgrounds of individual group members tend to simplify interpersonal interactions.

4. Firms that don't include diversity as part of their business plan are at a competitive advantage.

5. Conflict is a natural part of any system that has abundant resources.

6. Common location, common attitudes, and common economic background strongly influence people to join both formal and informal groups.

Identify the letter of the choice that best completes the statement or answers the question.

7. Which of the following does NOT happen during the storming stage of group development?
 a. Members learn to accept individual differences.
 b. Informal vying for power occurs.
 c. Members negotiate roles.
 d. The group establishes its long-term vision.

8. Groups continue to be _____ as long as they are able to engage the enthusiasm, skills, and intelligence of members.
 a. viable
 b. creative
 c. effective
 d. fresh

9. Three specific social processes bring about compliance with group norms. Which of the following is NOT one of those processes?
 a. group pressure
 b. group review and enforcement
 c. personalization of the norms
 d. role overload

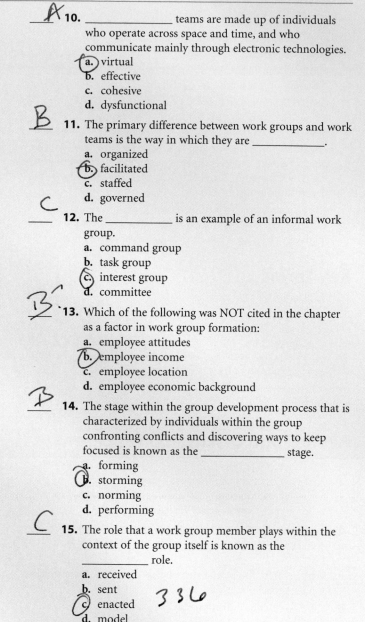

10. _____ teams are made up of individuals who operate across space and time, and who communicate mainly through electronic technologies.
 a. virtual
 b. effective
 c. cohesive
 d. dysfunctional

11. The primary difference between work groups and work teams is the way in which they are _____.
 a. organized
 b. facilitated
 c. staffed
 d. governed

12. The _____ is an example of an informal work group.
 a. command group
 b. task group
 c. interest group
 d. committee

13. Which of the following was NOT cited in the chapter as a factor in work group formation:
 a. employee attitudes
 b. employee income
 c. employee location
 d. employee economic background

14. The stage within the group development process that is characterized by individuals within the group confronting conflicts and discovering ways to keep focused is known as the _____ stage.
 a. forming
 b. storming
 c. norming
 d. performing

15. The role that a work group member plays within the context of the group itself is known as the _____ role.
 a. received
 b. sent
 c. enacted
 d. model

Case Study

Radius: A Restaurant Built on Teamwork

When visiting a great restaurant, one notices the special ambience, superb cuisine, and the superior service. Radius in Boston has these three ingredients. However, it also has another crucial factor that is less obvious to customers: a commitment to teamwork.

The teamwork starts in the kitchen. The Radius kitchen is made up of stations: meat, fish, garde, and pastry. Two people work at each station, and they have full responsibility for their part of the meal. The pastry team plans, cooks, and prepares the pastries.

The career ladder inside the kitchen is different from that in most restaurants. In most places, cooks start out as garde managers and work their way up to preparing fish and meat. At Radius, cooks work at stations for six weeks and then rotate to another. Job rotation is used for everyone on the kitchen team.

Weekly meetings are held to discuss the business, customer complaints, and special compliments received. The sous chefs and the pastry chefs meet with the back waiters and the waiters' support staff to go over issues, dishes, and procedures. Because servers at Radius announce each course, they need to know what is on each plate, how to present it to a guest, and how to pronounce it.

A daily meeting focuses on the behind-the-scene operations. About thirty staffers meet with the chef and co-owner Michael Sedlow to discuss the evening plans. Every detail about the specials, the fine wines, and the sauces is reviewed and discussed.

Then there is the daily service meeting. All the wait staff, floor managers, hosts, and hostesses go over the floor plan, assignments, the night's reservations, who the customers are, how to pronounce customers' names, and similar details. The special dishes are explored. For example, a server is asked to describe the dish: What are the red beads around the plate? "Spicy tomato oil."

The unusual attention to detail, pride in being a part of Radius, and the customer compliments make all of the commitment to teams a special experience. Radius believes that with the team approach it will soon be ranked among the top twenty-five restaurants in the country.

Questions for Discussion

1. How can meetings to go over details encourage and generate team cohesiveness?

2. What are the benefits of establishing a station-based kitchen that uses teams to start and finish the work?

3. Do you believe that the Radius approach to teamwork would totally eliminate any type of conflict? Why?

Sources: Gina Imperato, "Their Specialty? Teamwork," *Fast Company,* January/February 2000, p. 54; and Chris Komisarjevsky and Reiva Komisarjevsky, *Peanut Butter and Jelly Management: Talks from Parenthetical Lessons for Managers* (New York: AMACOM, 2000).

Internet Exercise

Examining Virtual Work Tools

For this exercise, students will examine a variety of tools that are available on the Internet to enable and empower virtual workers. This exercise can be done in class—especially classrooms with wireless Internet connectivity—or outside of class.

Students should visit the following websites and evaluate the underlying technologies and their potential use by workers in virtual work groups and teams.

1. www.skype.com

2. www.salesforce.com

3. www.teamspace.com

4. www.microsoft.com/windows/netmeeting/

5. www.communityzero.com

6. www.ipswitch.com/Products/collaboration/workgroup. html?google

7. www.smoothprojects.com

Evaluate each of the listed products and services in light of the following questions:

1. What does each product do?

2. How does the product enable virtual teamwork?

3. What is the price of the service? How economical is the product/service?

Experiential Exercise

Group Brainstorming in Action

Purpose: The purpose of this exercise is to provide experience in group brainstorming—to learn to use and pool the ideas, good and bad, of group members.

Setting Up the Exercise: The rules for the group brainstorming session are:

- Each group member is to contribute at least two ideas. The ideas must be written on a sheet of paper.
- The instructor (or group leader) will write each idea on a chalkboard or flip chart.
- Every idea will be recorded, no matter how unrealistic.
- While ideas are being recorded, there must be no evaluation by other group members. This is an important part of brainstorming, the freedom to simply "say it like it is" and have no fear of being evaluated.

1. The instructor will form groups of six to eight persons. A group leader will be elected. The leader serves mainly as a recorder of ideas. He or she should also contribute ideas.

2. The groups will brainstorm and develop solutions to the following problem:

   The Midwest region of the United States is becoming known as the "rust bowl" of America. Steelworkers and autoworkers have been losing their jobs. Today, there are only 260,000 steelworkers in the United States, while in 1977 there were 460,000. Most of the job loss has occurred in the "rust bowl" states—Illinois, Michigan, Ohio, Indiana, and Pennsylvania. The dire prediction is that those who have lost their jobs will never again work in steel mills or auto plants. The jobs are lost forever. Assume that this prediction is basically correct. Using a brainstorming method, develop some solutions that labor, management, and government can take to ease the social, emotional, and psychological pain of job-loss victims. What should and can be done?

3. Each group member independently is to develop two solutions for the job-loss problem. After about twenty minutes, begin recording the solutions.

4. Discuss the brainstorming procedure in the group. What would be the next step to take once brainstorming is completed, if it were being done in an organization?

A Learning Note:

This exercise will indicate that it is rather difficult to brainstorm. The technique sounds easy, but it is difficult to accomplish. Group members will find that during the brainstorming, it is difficult to refrain from evaluating the quality of each idea.

5

Controlling

Organizational control is fundamental to effectiveness. As organizations pursue goals, they must be aware of how they stand with respect to those goals. Is progress being made? If not, what factors are standing in the way? These are the types of questions that managers address as part of the controlling function.

Chapter 15 examines some of the basic elements of controlling, including setting standards of performance, using information technology, and factors affecting quality and productivity.

Chapter 16 examines the types of control measures that managers have traditionally used. These include financial controls and key ratios, process flow diagrams, and cost analysis. This chapter also examines some of the control measures that have evolved out of the quality management approach.

Elements of Controlling

15

357

Managing Today

Customer Input Used to Develop Hotel Standards

A lot of hotel operations experience goes into setting a brand's quality standards, but that process is never far removed from the adage that the customer is always right. Although hotel guests don't take part in management meetings that set, enforce, refine, and amend quality standards, their feedback—formal and informal—is one of the major concerns driving development of quality standards.

David O'Shaughnessy, group executive vice president at Accor Lodging North America, said development of quality standards for the company's Motel 6 and Red Roof Inn brands started with internal discussion about what was important to guests. Those conclusions were validated through focus groups conducted with customers across the country. "We prioritized what the customers told us, we took what we had, and then the standards were developed," O'Shaughnessy said. "It's constantly evolving, but everything we do is for the customer."

Customer feedback is only part of what goes into developing quality standards. Most hotel companies rely on comments from front-line employees in addition to decisions made by those in the company who have expertise in the subject. But in the end, everything is done with an eye toward pleasing guests. The most important reason for development of quality standards is a desire for consistency, and that also has its basis in guest satisfaction and pleasure.

As much as customers and employees are involved, the initial development of standards and the implementation of new standards rests with the leaders of the franchisor, management company, or owner. The natural role of those entities is to come up with a quality plan that will drive business to properties and have customers loyally returning.

O'Shaughnessy said Accor also has evolving standards, but that some standards will never be changed. "What we measure today does not always include the obvious because those things are so embedded in our product that it is only natural to do things a certain way," he said.

He said employees from different properties are encouraged to share success stories relating to standards and problems with current standards with each other. "Employees really respond well when you tailor programs to their needs and let them know they are part of setting the standards. There are many who are part of the process, but the goal is always to please the guest with a high-quality, consistent brand."

Sources: Adapted from Robert A. Nozar, "Guests' Input Helps Develop Standards," *Hotel & Motel Management,* May 7, 2001, p. 36; and Jeff Higley, "Accor Officials See Red," *Hotel & Motel Management,* April 30, 2001, pp. 3–4.

▶**controlling function** The actions and decisions that managers undertake to ensure that actual results are consistent with desired results.

Today, it is more critical than ever to improve an organization's performance.[1] The **controlling function** consists of *actions and decisions managers undertake to ensure that actual results are consistent with desired results.* The key to effective *controlling* is to plan for specific performance results. Unless managers decide in advance what level of performance they want, they will have no basis for judging actual performance. As described in earlier chapters, when managers plan, they establish the ways and means to achieve objectives. These objectives are the targets, the desired results, that management expects the organization to achieve.

After planning, managers must deploy their organizations' resources to achieve results. And although resources can be allocated and activities can be planned, managers must recognize that unforeseen events such as fuel shortages, strikes, machine breakdowns, competitive actions, and governmental influence can sidetrack the organization from its initial plans. Thus, managers must be prepared and able to redirect their organization's activities toward accomplishing the original objectives. To do this, managers must understand the concept of *necessary conditions for control.*

▶**perceived value** The value customers place on a good or service as opposed to its cost or price.

The Managing Today opening vignette highlights quality control efforts undertaken by Accor North America for its Red Roof Inn and Motel 6 franchises. Accor's leaders took the critical step of inviting customer input into the standard-setting process. Since quality is largely a function of customer **perceived value,** including customer feedback in the standard-setting stage of the control process is very important.

15-1 Necessary Conditions for Control

Effective control requires three basic conditions:

1. *Standards* that reflect the ideal outcomes.
2. *Information and measurement* that indicate deviations between actual and standard results.
3. *Corrective action* for any deviations between actual and standard results.

The logic is evident: Without standards, there can be no way of knowing the situation, and without provision for action to correct deviations, the entire control process becomes a pointless exercise.

15-1a Standards

Standards are derived from objectives and have many of the same characteristics. Like objectives, standards are targets; to be effective, they must be stated clearly and be related logically to objectives. Standards are the criteria that enable managers to evaluate future, current, or past actions. They are measured in a variety of ways, including physical, monetary, quantitative, and qualitative terms.[2] For example, Raybestos Brakes has worked hard on establishing performance standards for replacement brake parts. "The first reason for this is to establish a benchmark for safety," said Larry Pavey, president. "Without some type of standards, performance and safety are left for each manufacturer to define. This means that the highway becomes the research and development lab, where accidents reflect product failure."[3]

> **standards** Conditions for control derived from objectives.

The various forms standards take depend on *what* is being measured and on *the managerial level responsible* for taking corrective action. As a manager moves up in an organization, the standards for which he is accountable become more abstract, and the causes for deviations become more difficult to identify. Chief executive officers gauge the success of their organizations against standards such as "service to the public," "quality health care," and "customer satisfaction." These abstract criteria have no obvious method of measurement. But managers at the top of an organization are not the only ones who must deal with difficult-to-measure standards. For example, managers of staff units that provide service to line units also have problems determining standards to guide their units' actions.

Performance standards should be aligned not only with overall organizational goals but also with the firm's reward and compensation plan. Research has determined that employees are more willing to accept and live up to performance standards if they are reasonable given the compensation and other rewards they receive. Standards that are overly rigorous compared with the compensation are likely to be ignored or violated. In setting performance standards, managers must be aware both of organizational goals and of how they intend to reward people for achieving them.[4]

15-1b Information and Measurement

Information that reports actual performance and permits appraisal of that performance against standards is necessary. This usually involves some type of objective measurement but also could include subjective or qualitative reports about performance.[5] Objective information is most easily acquired for activities that produce specific results. For example, production and sales activities have easily identifiable end products for which information is readily obtainable. The performance of legal departments, research and development units, or personnel departments is more difficult to evaluate, however, because the outputs of these units are difficult to measure.

> **information** Derived from data; essentially, data that are organized for a specific purpose.

While objective measurement of performance is necessary to manage an organization, too much measurement of performance can actually be detrimental to organizational performance. Some organizations compile information in too much detail, needlessly driving

Management Focus on Technology

Effective Technology Buying Requires Clear Standards

Regular reporting of information technology (IT) buyers' performance—in terms of clear measures like contributions to earnings per share—is an important best practice, according to members of the Society for Information Management's IT Procurement Working Group.

Well documented, valid metrics demonstrate the value that dedicated IT purchasing expertise and management can create for a company. This demonstrated value then inspires technology end users to support the buying group's initiatives for cutting costs and improving service levels. It also inspires them to involve the IT buying group very early in their technology acquisition processes. Such support and involvement,

say the experts, leads to increasingly innovative programs for cutting IT costs, improving service, and creating value for the business through better management of the information technology buy.

"I think metrics are extremely important," says Gary Beaudreau, vice president, technology acquisition, State Street Corp., Quincy, MA, and a co-chair of the IT Procurement Group. "I find that companies most successful at making improvements are those that have good measurement systems that are very visible and well communicated."

Source: Adapted from Susan Avery, "Measuring Purchasing's Value," *Purchasing*, July 19, 2001, pp. 45–47.

up reporting expenses. Managers must learn to balance their need to know with the operating results of the company.[6] The Management Focus on Technology box, "Effective Technology Buying Requires Clear Standards," discusses how clear metrics help IT buyers justify their purchases and track their effectiveness.

15-1c Corrective Action

▶**corrective action** The actions a manager takes to bring a system back into conformance with performance standards.

Corrective action depends on the discovery of deviations and the ability to take necessary action. The people responsible for taking the corrective action must know that (1) they are indeed responsible and (2) they have the assigned authority to take those steps. The jobs and position descriptions must include specific statements clearly delineating these two requirements. Otherwise, the control function likely will fall short of its potential contribution to organizational performance. Responsibilities that fall between the jobs of two individuals are undesirable, but sometimes unavoidable. Managers who work in organizations facing uncertain and unpredictable environments often confront unanticipated situations—the kinds not stated in job descriptions.

The essential elements of management control are diagrammed in Figure 15-1. The control function involves implementing *methods* that will provide answers to three basic questions:

1. What are the planned and expected results?
2. By what means can the actual results be compared with the planned results?
3. What corrective action is appropriate from which authorized person?

Often, the corrective action that is required involves disciplining an employee or employees. If someone is not performing according to expectations, managers are obligated to step in and take corrective action. It's important for managers to remember that performance-based corrective action should not be construed as punishment.[7] Rather, corrective action should be delivered and received in a constructive manner. Yet managers should leave no doubt about the performance expectations of a job. Consequences of nonperformance should be clear but not bellowed or broadcast to employees. Managers should focus on the rewards of high performance (the carrot) more than the consequences of nonperformance (the stick). Employees generally respond more favorably to promises of reward than threats of punishment.

▶**service level agreements (SLAs)** The fine-grained details about performance expectations and potential remedies if performance falls short of those expectations.

Corrective action today also involves managing the performance of other companies who are serving as vendors or strategic partners. The primary instrument of controlling the performance of other companies—particularly information technology service providers—is the contract and related **service level agreements (SLAs).** Service level agreements are the fine-grained details about performance expectations and potential

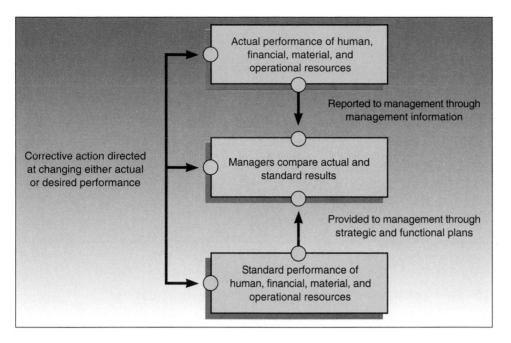

remedies if performance falls short of those expectations. Managers today increasingly work with business-to-business vendors for a wide range of services, allowing the buying company to focus on its core competencies. Because of this, managers should be aware of the pitfalls of managing the performance of another firm, and the role of SLAs in setting standards and providing cause for corrective action if needed.[8]

15-2 Three Types of Control Methods

Control methods can be classified according to their focus. Three different types of control methods are identified in Figure 15-2.

15-3 Preliminary Control

Preliminary control (also called "feedforward control") methods increase the possibility that future results will compare favorably with planned results. Policies are important

▶ **preliminary control** The methods that focus on the acquisition of resources.

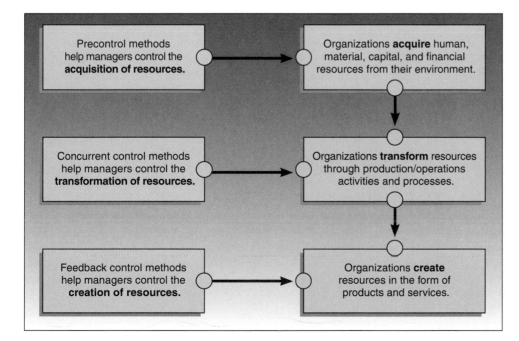

precontrol methods because they define appropriate future action. Other precontrol methods involve human, capital, and financial resources.

15-3a Preliminary Control of Human Resources

Preliminary control of human resources depends on job requirements. Job requirements predetermine the skills needed by the jobholders. Knowing the kind of person a job candidate is will not do any good without first knowing what kind of person the company is looking for. A variety of tools are available to managers today to assess the organization's culture and the skill requirements of a job. These data are then used to develop a questionnaire for job applicants. These screening tools are a form of precontrol—they ensure to a high degree of accuracy that the person being hired matches the needs and culture of the organization.

Appropriate attention to preliminary control of human resources ensures that the organization will meet its needs through the skills, abilities, and attitudes of its employees. With the increasing focus on knowledge as an important organizational asset, the search, screening, selection, and training of new employees has become a vital function. Where human resources managers had been considered to have staff rather than line responsibilities, many firms today place human resources managers in the direct chain of command. These firms realize that it's no longer appropriate to consider human resources management as a supporting function. It has direct impact on the firm's productivity through its recruiting, selection, hiring, and employee retention practices. HR has come to be regarded as a strategic asset to many organizations.[9]

15-3b Preliminary Control of Materials

Preliminary control of materials involves ensuring that the raw materials a firm purchases meet quality standards. At the same time, a sufficient inventory or just-in-time delivery system must be in place to ensure that a firm can meet customer demand. Imagine a fast-food restaurant that ran out of hamburgers just as the local football game ended and hungry fans came streaming in. The lost food sales and lost goodwill could be very costly to the firm. Or imagine the restaurant had plenty of burgers, but the meat was low quality and many people got sick. Again, the best production processes in the world can't make up for poor preliminary control of materials.

15-3c Preliminary Control of Capital

Preliminary control of capital reflects the need to replace existing equipment or to expand the firm's productive capacity. Capital acquisitions can be precontrolled by establishing criteria of potential profitability that must be met before the acquisitions are authorized. Decisions involving the commitment of present funds in exchange for future funds are termed **investment decisions.** Control methods that screen investment proposals are derived from financial analysis. There are several methods that managers use to control capital, three of these are the _payback method, rate of return on investment,_ and _discounted rate of return._

▶**investment decisions**
Commitments of present funds in exchange for potential future funds; controlled through a capital budget.

Additional cash inflow before taxes (labor cost savings)	$20,000
Less: Additional taxes	
Additional income	$20,000
Depreciation ($40,000/4)	$10,000
Additional taxable income	$10,000
Tax rate	0.36
Additional tax payment	$3,600
Additional cash inflow after taxes	$16,400
The payback period can be calculated as follows: $40,000/$16,400 = 2.44 years	

TABLE 15-1

Payback Method

The Payback Method   This is the simplest method of capital control. The **payback method** calculates the number of years needed for the proposed capital acquisition to repay (pay back) its original cost out of future cash earnings. For example, a manager is considering implementing new information technology that would reduce labor costs by $20,000 per year for each of the four years of the new equipment's expected life. The cost of the technology is $40,000. If we use a 34 percent marginal corporate tax rate, the additional after-tax inflow from which the equipment's cost must be paid is calculated as illustrated in Table 15-1.

The proposed new information technology would repay its original cost in about two and a half years; if the predetermined standard requires a payback of three years or less, the information technology would be an appropriate investment for the firm.

The payback method suffers from many limitations as a standard for evaluating capital resources. It doesn't produce a measurement of profitability. More important, it doesn't take into account the *time value of money;* that is, it doesn't recognize that a dollar today is worth more than a dollar at a future time. Other capital control methods do include these important considerations. The primary reason for using the payback method is that in situations where the technology changes rapidly and new products become obsolete quickly, corporations should look for investment opportunities that pay back within a short period of time.

Rate of Return on Investment   One alternative measure of profitability, consistent with methods routinely used in accounting, is the simple **rate of return on investment,** often called the return on investment or "ROI." Using the preceding example, the calculation would be as illustrated in Table 15-2.

The calculated rate of return would then be compared with some standard of minimum acceptability, and the decision to accept or reject would depend on that comparison. In this case, if the standard rate of return were 10 percent, the purchase of the information technology would be a good investment. The measurement of the simple rate of return has the advantage of being easily understood. It has the disadvantage of not including the time value of money. The discounted rate of return method overcomes this deficiency.

Discounted Rate of Return   The **discounted rate of return** is a measurement of profitability that takes into account the time value of money. It is similar to the payback

▶**payback method** The payback method calculates the number of years needed for the proposed capital acquisition to repay (payback) its original cost out of future cash earnings.

▶**rate of return on investment** The ratio of the annual returns to the initial cost of the investment.

▶**discounted rate of return** The rate of return that equates future cash proceeds with the initial cost of an investment.

Additional gross income	$20,000
Less: Depreciation ($40,000/4)	$10,000
Taxes	$3,600
Total additional expenses	$13,600
Additional net income after taxes	$6,400
The rate of return is the ratio of additional net income to the original cost: $16,400/$40,000 = 16%	

TABLE 15-2

Rate of ROI

method; only cash inflows and outflows are considered. The method is widely used because it is considered the correct method for calculating the rate of return. Based on the preceding example, the discounted rate of return is calculated as:

$$\$40,000 = \$16,400/(1+r)^n$$

In this equation, r is equal to the discount rate and n is the number of periods to be discounted. The discount rate can be determined in a number of ways. It can be a preestablished **hurdle rate** the company wants to achieve in all its investments. This is a rate established by policy and is deemed to be the minimally acceptable level of return for an investment to be eligible for further consideration. Another way is to determine the **opportunity cost** of the investment. This would be the rate of return that a firm could earn if it invested the capital in something else. This would be a rate established by the market. The number of periods to be discounted (n) is the expected useful life of the equipment.

Students familiar with finance will recognize this analysis as the standard *present value* analysis usually taught in introductory finance courses. The rationale of this method can be understood by thinking of the $16,400 inflows as cash payments received by the firm. In exchange, for each of these four payments of $16,400, the firm must invest $40,000 at the beginning of the period.

15-3d Preliminary Control of Financial Resources

Preliminary control of financial resources must be available to ensure the payment of obligations arising from current operations. Materials must be purchased, wages paid, and interest charges and due dates met. **Budgets**—particularly cash and working capital budgets—are the principal means for precontrolling the availability and cost of financial resources. These budgets anticipate the ebb and flow of business activity when materials are purchased, finished goods are produced, goods are sold, and cash is received. This cycle of activity, the **operating cycle,** results in a problem of *timing* the availability of cash to meet the obligations. As inventories of finished goods increase, material, labor, and other expenses are incurred and paid, and the supply of cash decreases. As inventory is sold, the supply of cash increases. Precontrol of cash requires that funds be available during the period of inventory buildup, and that cash be used wisely during periods of abundance.

15-4 Concurrent Control

Concurrent control consists primarily of actions by supervisors who direct the work of their subordinates. **Direction** refers to the acts managers undertake (1) to instruct subordinates in the proper methods and procedures, and (2) to oversee the work of subordinates to ensure that it is done properly. Direction follows the formal chain of command, since the responsibility of each manager is to interpret for subordinates the orders received from higher echelons. The relative importance of direction depends almost entirely on the nature of the tasks subordinates perform. The manager of an assembly line that produces a component part requiring relatively simple manual operations may seldom engage in direction. On the other hand, the manager of a research and development unit must devote considerable time to direction. Research work is inherently more complex and varied than manual work and requires more interpretation and instruction.

Directing is the primary activity of the first-line supervisor, but every manager in an organization engages at some time in directing employees.[10] As a manager moves up the hierarchy, however, the relative importance of directing diminishes and other responsibilities become more important.

Other factors also determine differences in the form of direction. For example, direction is basically a process of *interpersonal communication,* so the *amount* and *clarity* of information are important factors. Subordinates must receive sufficient information to carry out the task, and they must understand that information. On the other hand, too much information and too much detail can be damaging. The manager's mode and tone of voice used in delivering the information also can greatly influence the effectiveness of direction.

---

hurdle rate The standard established by a company for financial performance of an investment or capital expenditure.

opportunity cost The cost of using cash or other resources for a particular purpose to the exclusion of other potential uses (opportunities).

budget A predetermined amount of resources linked to an activity.

operating cycle The set of activities, including their costs, that are involved in the conversion of raw materials into finished goods ready for sale.

concurrent control The techniques and methods that focus on the actual, ongoing activity of the organization.

direction A method of concurrent control that refers to the manager's act of interpreting orders to a subordinate.

LearningMoment   *Empowerment and Concurrent Control*

Employee empowerment has become a leading mantra among management scholars and practitioners alike. Empowerment of employees drives decision making and authority to the level of the worker carrying out workplace tasks. This movement has received acclaim for promoting more rapid and better decision making. Concurrent control suggests that managers are watching employees. To what extent does this interfere with the practice of "empowerment"? Is it possible that managers can employ concurrent control systems in a culture of employee empowerment?

Effective direction depends on effective communication. A directive must be reasonable, intelligible, appropriately worded, and consistent with the overall objectives of the organization. The subordinate rather than the manager will decide whether these criteria have been met. Many managers have assumed that their directives were straightforward and to the point and then discovered that their subordinates had failed to understand them or had refused to accept them as legitimate.[11]

The process of direction involves not only the *manner* in which directives are communicated but also the *manner* of the person who directs.[12] A supervisor may be autocratic or democratic, permissive or directive, considerate or inconsiderate. Each of these could have different impacts on the effectiveness of direction as a concurrent control technique. Direction involves day-to-day overseeing of the work of subordinates. As deviations from standards are identified, managers must take immediate corrective action by coaching their subordinates and showing them how to perform their assigned tasks appropriately.

Using the authority of position to achieve concurrent control has become increasingly difficult. Rapidly changing markets and technology often force managers to use decision-making approaches outside the formal chain of command. These approaches bring together employees with the expertise to solve the problem or to make the decision. In such settings, influence, not authority, is the appropriate way to manage.

15-5 Feedback Control

Feedback control employs *historical* outcomes as bases for correcting *future* actions. For example, a firm's financial statements can be used to evaluate the acceptability of historical results and to determine if changes should be made in future resource acquisitions or operational activities. Four feedback control methods are widely used in business:

> **feedback control** The techniques and methods that analyze historical data to correct future events.

1. Financial statement analysis.
2. Standard cost analysis.
3. Employee performance evaluation.
4. Quality control.

The following discussion provides basic descriptions of these methods.

15-5a Financial Statement Analysis

A firm's accounting system is a principal source of information managers can use to evaluate historical results. Periodically, the manager receives a set of financial statements that usually includes a cash flow statement, income statement, and balance sheet. These financial statements summarize and classify the effects of transactions in assets, liabilities, equity, revenues, and expenses—the principal components of the firm's financial structure.

The **income statement** (also called the "profit and loss statement") tells a manager whether the firm is able to make a profit from operations. This statement is divided into three parts: revenues, cost of goods sold, and expenses. *Revenues* refers to the money taken in (cash or credit) for sale of goods. The *cost of goods sold* is the amount the firm had to

> **income statement** A statement (also called the "profit and loss statement") that tells a manager whether the firm is able to make a profit from operations. This statement is divided into three parts: revenues, cost of goods sold, and expenses.

pay to acquire the goods it sells. *Expenses* refers to the cost of "doing business." For example, salaries, rent, utilities, insurance, and many other items are expenses. If revenues exceed the cost of goods sold plus expenses, the firm has made a profit.

The **balance sheet** provides managers with a "snapshot" of the firm's financial condition at a specific point in time. The firm's assets are matched against its liabilities and owner's equity. At all times assets are equal to liabilities plus equity. This is expressed as:

Assets = Liabilities + Owner's Equity

The ratio of liabilities to equity is an important one for firms. It tells managers how much of a firm is owned by equity holders (typically, owners) and how much of the firm is leveraged (owned by lenders).

The **cash flow statement** provides managers with a view of the firm's cash position. Cash is the most liquid and fungible asset a firm has. It can be used to pay bills, invest in new equipment, invest in research and development, and keep a firm afloat during downturns in the business cycle. Because of the importance of cash, it is important to track its inflows and outflows. The cash flow statement provides managers with projections of a firm's cash position based on assumptions about standard income (cash inflows) and expenses (cash outflows) over time.

A detailed analysis of a firm's financial statements enables managers to determine the adequacy of the firm's earning power and its ability to meet current and long-term obligations. Managers must have measures of and standards for profitability, liquidity, and solvency. Whether a manager prefers the rate of return on sales, on owner's equity, on total assets, or a combination of all three is an individual choice. What's important is to establish a performance standard and to stick with it over time. Use of the same measure over time allows managers to determine trends.

The measures of liquidity reflect the firm's ability to meet current obligations as they become due.[13] The most often used measure is the **current ratio** (the ratio of a firm's current assets to current liabilities). The standard of acceptability depends on the particular firm's operating characteristics. Bases for comparison are available from trade associations that publish industry averages. A tougher test of liquidity is the **acid-test ratio,** which relates only cash and near-cash items to current liabilities.

The relationship between current assets and current liabilities is an important one. The composition of the current assets is an equally important measure. **Accounts receivable turnover** and **inventory turnover** are two measures of the composition of current assets. Accounts receivable turnover is the ratio of credit sales to average accounts receivable. This ratio indicates how rapidly credit sales are being turned into cash. A lower ratio would indicate a time lag in the collection of receivables. This could strain the resources of a firm that was short on cash for expenses. Appropriate corrective action might involve a tightening of credit standards or a more vigorous effort to collect outstanding accounts.

The **inventory turnover ratio** consists of comparing cost of goods sold with average inventory. A high ratio could indicate a low inventory balance in relation to sales. Conversely, a low ratio might indicate an overinvestment in inventory to the exclusion of other, more profitable assets. Whatever the case, the appropriate ratio must be established by the manager, based on the firm's experience within its industry and market.

Inventory Turnover Ratio = Cost of Goods Sold/Average Inventory

Another financial measure is **solvency.** Solvency refers to the firm's ability to meet its long-term obligations—its fixed commitments. An appropriate balance must be maintained—a balance that protects the interest of the owner yet doesn't ignore the advantages of long-term debt as a source of funds. A commonly used measure of solvency is the ratio of net income before interest and taxes (usually called EBIT or EBITDA) to interest expense. This indicates the margin of safety between profits and expenses related to repayment of loans. Naturally, most firms prefer a high ratio on this measure.

Solvency = EBIT/Interest Expense

balance sheet The balance sheet provides managers with an "snapshot" of the firm's financial condition at a specific point in time. The firm's assets are matched against its liabilities and owner's equity.

cash flow statement The cash flow statement provides managers with a view of the firm's cash position.

current ratio The ratio of a firm's current assets to its current liabilities.

acid-test ratio A test of liquidity that relates only cash and near-cash items to current liabilities.

accounts receivable turnover The ratio of credit sales to average accounts receivable that indicates how rapidly credit sales are being turned to cash.

inventory turnover A measure of the composition of current assets by comparing cost of goods sold to average inventory.

inventory turnover ratio A comparison of cost of goods sold to average inventory.

solvency A firm's ability to meet its long-term (fixed) obligations.

Firms also use **debt ratios** to assess the amount of financing being provided by creditors. Two popular debt ratios are the **debt to equity ratio** and the **debt to asset ratio.** The debt to equity ratio is a measure of the amount of assets financed by debt compared to that amount financed by profits retained by the firm and equity investments. The debt to asset ratio is an expression of the relationship of the firm's total debts to its total assets.

Debt to Equity Ratio = Assets Financed by Debt/Assets Financed by Equity

Debt to Asset Ratio = Total Debts/Total Assets

> **debt ratios** Measures of the amount of financing being provided by creditors.

> **debt to equity ratio** A measure of the amount of assets financed by debt compared to the amount financed by profits retained by the firm and equity investments.

15-5b Standard Cost Analysis

Standard cost accounting systems are considered a major contribution of scientific management to organizational control. A **standard cost system** provides information that allows managers to compare actual costs to budgeted, or predetermined, costs. This information allows managers to take corrective actions if the actual costs exceed budgeted amounts. The first use of standard costing was to control manufacturing costs. Today, standard costing is applied to selling, general, and administrative expenses.

To understand standard costing, consider how it is applied to manufacturing. The three elements of manufacturing costs are labor, direct materials, and overhead. For each of these, an estimate must be made of cost per unit of output. For example, the direct labor cost per unit of output consists of the standard usage of labor and the standard price of labor. The standard usage can be derived from time studies that determine the standard output per labor hour. The standard price of labor is fixed by the salary schedule as it applies to the type of work that is necessary to produce the output. A similar determination is made for direct materials. Thus, the standard labor and standard materials costs might be as follows:

> **debt to asset ratio** An expression of the relationship of the firm's total debts to its total assets.

> **standard cost system** A system that provides information that allows managers to compare actual costs to budgeted or predetermined costs.

* Standard labor usage per unit: 2 hours
* Standard wage rate/hour: $8.00
* Standard labor cost (2 × $8.00): $16.00
* Standard material usage/hour: 6 pounds
* Standard material price/pound: $.30
* Standard material cost (6 × $.30): $1.80

The accounting system enables the manager to compare incurred costs and standard costs. Today, cost accounting practices are undergoing significant changes to keep pace with the rapidly evolving business environment. **Activity-based costing (ABC),** a system of cost accounting based on actual processes (activities) rather than labor and materials, has been increasingly used in businesses of all types.[14] Its underlying principle is that activities consume resources and production is a sequence of activities. The labor costs of an activity can be traced by assessing the portion of each person's time spent on the activity. In this way, ABC can trace costs across departmental lines if a particular activity involves more than one organizational unit. The Management Focus on Ethics box, "The Ethics of Finance," highlights the key issue of ethical practices in accounting. Firms must ensure that their accounting practices are ethical to maintain shareholder, customer, and employee trust.

> **activity-based costing (ABC)** Activity-based costing is a system of cost accounting based on actual processes (activities) rather than labor and materials.

15-5c Employee Performance Evaluation

Employee performance evaluation is an important element of control, motivation, and reward. It is often the most neglected aspect of a manager's duties because many managers are uncomfortable in providing honest feedback to others about their performance. However, if handled correctly, employee performance evaluations do not have to make people uncomfortable. The most important thing for managers to remember when conducting

Management Focus on Ethics

The Ethics of Finance

In the securities business, the "market" is a synthesis of information that investors trust to be reliable in all material respects. Accountants supply an important element by faithfully translating economic events of organizations into a common language. Paradoxically, the image of accountants' honesty and ethics ranks just above average and well below the top as compared with other professions. The findings of a 2001 Gallup poll of 1,000 Americans show only 38 percent thought the honesty and ethics of accountants were either "high" or "very high." This resulted in a rank of twelfth out of thirty-two professions mentioned in the survey, placing accountants ahead of senators, business executives, and journalists. At the very lowest were lawyers, stockbrokers, and labor leaders. Car salesmen came in last. Considered most honest and ethical were nurses and other medical professionals.

Source: Adapted from Curtis C. Verschoor, "Strengthening the Ethics of Finance," *Strategic Finance,* March 2001, pp. 20–21.

---

evaluations is that they must be *objective*. Being objective means that the manager has established evaluation techniques ahead of time and has been collecting relevant data on employee performance to enable independent assessment of how well performance matches pre-established goals.

We have discussed employee performance evaluation techniques at length elsewhere in this text (see Chapter 10). Here, we simply want to emphasize the importance of employee evaluation in the control function of management. The **performance review** is the formal meeting between the manager and the subordinate that occurs once or twice per year. This is a form of feedback control that helps the employee understand how well they are performing with respect to their goals. Managers should not wait for these biannual meetings to provide employees with performance feedback, however. Problems that arise between meetings should be handled using other types of interventions. These between-meeting interventions would be a form of concurrent control. Of course, managers should also *praise and reward* outstanding performance between formal reviews as another form of concurrent control. Finally, all performance evaluation should be conducted against the backdrop of preexisting goals and objectives. This form of preliminary control sets the standards for employee performance and allows for objective evaluation over time.

> **performance review** The formal meeting between the manager and the subordinate that occurs once or twice per year.

15-5d Quality Control

Quality has a number of different definitions. Table 15-3 provides just a few that have been used over the years.

Despite these many perspectives on quality, the customer is the key perceiver of quality because his or her purchase decision determines the success of the organization's product or service, and often the fate of the organization itself. A consumer's perception of a product/service's "excellence" is generally based on the degree to which the product or service meets his or her specifications and requirements. Specifically, a consumer perceives "excellence" by evaluating one or more dimensions of quality, which are summarized in Table 15-4. In judging the quality of a Sony television set, for example, a prospective buyer may examine *performance*, how well the TV set performs its primary function. (Is the picture sharp, the color vivid, the sound clear?) The set's extra *features* such as automatic fine tuning may be evaluated. The rate of repair or *reliability* may be a factor as well as *serviceability*, the convenience and quality of repair should a breakdown occur. *Conformance*, for example, the set's compatibility with a VCR of another brand, may be assessed. *Durability*, the typical life span of the set, may also be examined as well as the visual appeal of its design *(aesthetics)*. Sony's reputation for product quality may also influence the consumer's evaluation of the set's overall quality *(perceived quality)*.[15]

Two points are noteworthy concerning a consumer's "perception of excellence" or quality. First, consumers emphasize different dimensions of quality when judging a prod-

TABLE **15-3**

Definitions of Quality

Definitions of quality are personal and idiosyncratic. These concise, clear, and meaningful definitions are arranged by category of focus.

1. Manufacturing based
   "Quality [means] conformance to requirements."—Philip B. Crosby
   "Quality is the degree to which a specific product conforms to a design or specification."—Harold L. Gilmore

2. Customer based
   "Quality is fitness for use."—J. M. Juran
   "Total Quality is performance leadership in meeting customer requirements by doing the right things right the first time."—Westinghouse
   "Quality is meeting customer expectations. The Quality Improvement Process is a set of principles, policies, support structures, and practices designed to continually improve the efficiency and effectiveness of our way of life."—AT&T
   "You achieve customer satisfaction when you sell merchandise that doesn't come back and a customer who does."—Stanley Marcus

3. Product based
   "Differences in quality amount to differences in the quantity of some desired ingredient or attribute."—Lawrence Abbott
   "Quality refers to the amount of the unpriced attribute contained in each unit of the priced attribute."—Keith B. Leffler

4. Value based
   "Quality is the degree of excellence at an acceptable price and the control of variability at an acceptable cost."—Robert A. Broh
   "Quality means best for certain customer conditions. These conditions are (a) the actual use and (b) the selling price of the product."—Armand V. Feigenbaum

5. Transcendent
   "Quality is neither mind nor matter, but a third entity independent of the other two ... even though Quality cannot be denied, you know what it is."—Robert Pirsig
   "A condition of excellence implying fine quality as distinct from poor quality.... Quality is achieving or reaching the highest standard as against being satisfied with the sloppy or fraudulent."—Barbara W. Tuchman

Sources: Adapted from *Fortune,* March 22, 1993, p. 21; and V. Daniel Hunt, *Quality in America* (Burr Ridge, Ill.: Irwin/McGraw-Hill, 1992), p. 21.

uct or service. Because of these differences in consumer preferences, a company may choose to emphasize one or a few dimensions of quality rather than compete on all eight dimensions.

Second, perceiving "excellence" can be highly subjective. Some dimensions such as *reliability* or *durability* can be quantified by simply reviewing the product's records. However, other dimensions such as *aesthetics* depend on personal likes and dislikes, which are

TABLE **15-4**

Dimensions of Quality

Dimension	Example
Performance:	The product/service's primary operating characteristics
Features:	Secondary, "extra" characteristics
Reliability:	Consistent performance within a specific period
Conformance:	Degree to which design and characteristics meet specific standards
Durability:	The length of a product/service's useful life
Serviceability:	The speed, courtesy, competence, and ease of repair
Aesthetics:	The looks, taste, feel, sound, smell of a product/service
Perceived quality:	Quality conveyed via marketing, brand name, reputation

Source: Adapted from David A. Garvin, "Competing on the Eight Dimensions of Quality," *Harvard Business Review,* November–December 1987, pp. 101–9.

Figure 15-3
The Price/Quality Relationship

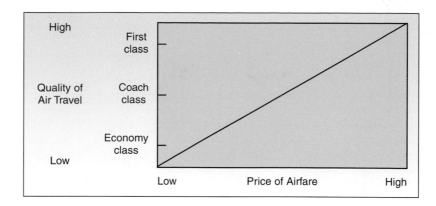

highly subjective. Differences in preferences and the subjectivity of perceptions underscore the need for organizations to obtain accurate market information concerning consumer perceptions and preferences.[16]

One other important element of the quality concept concerns the relationship between quality and price. In many cases, the relationship between a product's or service's quality and price is positive and linear, as shown in Figure 15-3.[17] If quality increases, so will the price (given that price reflects the cost of providing the product or service). This relationship is particularly strong when an organization produces a product or service that rates highly on all eight dimensions of quality. However, sometimes a higher level of quality does not result in a higher price when improving quality actually reduces the *cost of quality.*

Cost of Quality   To understand this relationship, it is first necessary to understand the concept of cost of quality and its component parts. An organization's *cost of quality* is the total expense involved in ensuring that a product or service meets established quality standards. The cost of quality is comprised of three types of costs.

▶ **prevention costs** The costs of preventing product or service defects.

1. **Prevention costs** are the costs of preventing product or service defects—the precontrol aspect of quality control. Examples of prevention costs are the expenses of effective employee training, reengineering the product's manufacturing process, or working with suppliers to ensure that materials are of high quality.

▶ **appraisal costs** All expenses involved in directly evaluating quality.

2. **Appraisal costs** are all expenses involved in directly evaluating quality, such as the costs of quality inspection and testing.

▶ **failure costs** The costs incurred by a defective product or service.

3. **Failure costs** occur once a defect is produced and identified. If the defect is found before the product leaves the plant, the failure costs are *internal* (e.g., the costs of scrapped material or of reworking the defective part or product). If the defect is found by the customer, *external* failure costs are incurred (the costs of recalled products, customer complaints, and a damaged product image).[18]

▶ **hidden costs** Costs of operating that don't appear on a firm's income statement but affect the profitability of the firm.

These three components' costs are often called **hidden costs,** because they are not directly measured as part of an organization's operations.[19] Individually, these hidden costs comprise a different proportion of the total cost of quality because they are incurred at different points of the production process. Figure 15-4 represents what is often referred to as the quality **funnel principle.** According to this principle, the nearer to the start of the production process the hidden costs are incurred, the lower the cost of quality. This is the case because, as the product or service progresses through the process, more resources are invested such as labor, time, and materials. The greater the amount of resources invested, the higher the cost of rejection (and quality).

▶ **funnel principle** This principle states that the earlier in the production process quality problems are detected, the less is their cost to the organization.

Applying this principle, prevention costs are incurred primarily at the beginning of the production process and are the least expensive component (5 to 10 percent of total quality costs). Failure costs are incurred mostly at the end of the process and thereafter and are the most expensive component (65 to 75 percent). Appraisal costs are incurred primarily during the production process and are larger than prevention but smaller than failure costs (20 to 25 percent of total quality costs).[20]

Importantly, many companies are shifting their quality control emphasis to prevention (precontrol). They are increasing prevention costs of quality by focusing more on

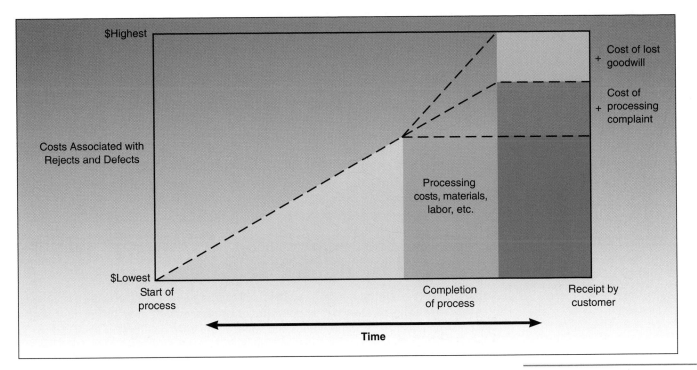

$Highest

Costs Associated with
Rejects and Defects

Processing
costs, materials,
labor, etc.

+ Cost of lost
  goodwill

+ Cost of
  processing
  complaint

$Lowest
Start of
process

Completion
of process

Receipt by
customer

Time

Figure 15-4
The Funnel Principle: Quality Costs as a Function of Time

such preventive mechanisms as employee training and the design of the manufacturing process. Over time, this increase in prevention quality costs produces larger returns. Quality is improved. Appraisal costs are reduced because improved prevention reduces the need for inspection and testing activities. Above all, failure costs—the most costly quality component—are reduced because the service or product is produced right the first time. Overall quality costs decline.

Factors Affecting Quality   Quality has been defined as a function of customer expectations. The greater the perceived value of a product or service, the higher are customer expectations for quality. A trip to Disney World inspires a higher perception of perceived value than a trip to a local amusement park, for example. This expectation translates to pricing, management of the customer experience, and control methods and measurements used. Effective management of quality depends on a number of factors:

* Policy
* Information
* Engineering and design
* Materials
* Equipment
* People
* Field support

An integrated quality control system must focus on these factors.

Policy   Management establishes policies concerning product quality. These policies specify the standards or levels of quality to be achieved in a product or service; they can be an important precontrol and concurrent control means for ensuring quality. For example, Paine's Recycling and Rubbish Removal, Simsbury, Connecticut, uses a simple "Three S" policy to enhance quality and customer satisfaction:

* Satisfaction—Doing the job right the first time;
* Safety—For all customers and employees; and
* Specifications—Use the proper equipment to do the job well.

Owner Russell Paine says, "Commitment to the Three S policy begins at the top and extends throughout the company. Everyone is aware that their paycheck is generated by the customer and that it originates with customer satisfaction."[21]

Managers generally consider three factors in determining policy for quality: the product or service's market, its competition, and image. An evaluation of the market provides an indication of customer expectations of quality and the price they are willing to pay for it. Quality expectations and price, for example, widely differ in the luxury car and economy car markets within the auto industry. Quality levels provided by the competition also affect policy because the company's products or services must be competitive quality wise to succeed in the marketplace.

Besides considering the market and competition, management must also consider the organization's image. Making a low quality product that is inconsistent with a firm's image may damage long-term interests. For example, marketing a low-priced Porsche or a new and low-priced Baskin-Robbins ice cream flavor might create a backlash from regular customers. Customer images of these products (and their loyalty) may be tarnished if they associate a lower-priced product or service with lower quality.

Information Information plays a vital role in setting policy and ensuring that quality standards are achieved. Concerning policy, accurate information must be obtained about customer preferences and expectations and about competitor quality standards and costs. *Competitive benchmarking* is an effective approach to obtaining valuable information about a competitor's quality standards and costs.[22] Also, new computer technology is enabling organizations to quickly obtain and evaluate information about the quality of products while they are being produced.

Engineering and Design Once management has formulated a policy concerning quality, it is the engineer or designer who must translate the policy into an actual product or service. The engineer/designer must create a product that will appeal to customers and that can be produced at a reasonable cost and provide competitive quality. This need to integrate cost, quality, and customer satisfaction has led to a process known as "concurrent engineering." This process replaces the traditional, sequential product design process with simultaneous design by integrated, multifunctional teams operating in cooperation with both customers and suppliers. The objective is to achieve "right the first time" production of new products in less time, with better quality and at lower cost.[23]

Materials A growing number of organizations are realizing that a finished product is only as good as materials used to produce it. In this regard, many manufacturing companies are implementing a new precontrol strategy with material suppliers. They are reducing their number of suppliers, for example, weeding out the lower-quality vendors and focusing on developing effective, long-term relationships with the better ones.

Equipment The ability of equipment, tools, and machinery to accurately and reliably produce desired outputs is important, especially in manufacturing industries. If the equipment can meet acceptable tolerances, at competitive costs and quality, an organization will have the opportunity to compete in the marketplace.

People While materials, design, and equipment are important ingredients to quality, the employee is the vital contributor to quality. Working individually, or as teams, employees take the ingredients and process them into a final product or service of quality. Management must train employees not only in the specialized knowledge of producing a quality product or service but in an *attitude* of quality.

Field Support Often, the field support provided by the supplier determines a product's quality image *(perceived quality)*. IBM, General Electric, and Sears Roebuck have reputations for providing strong field support for their products. This is not to say that the products of these firms are necessarily the best in their industries. Many customers select

IBM computers, General Electric refrigerators, and Sears Roebuck dishwashers because the field support of these firms is considered excellent.

15-6 Statistical Process Control (SPC)

The use of statistical process control has long played an important role in business and industry.[24] **Statistical process control (SPC)** is based on two assumptions: (1) nature is imperfect and (2) variability exists everywhere in systems. Therefore, probability and statistics play a major role in understanding and controlling complex systems.[25] Charts, diagrams, and graphs are conceptual tools managers can use to summarize statistical data, measure and understand variation, assess risk, and make decisions. **Statistics** is defined as "that branch of applied mathematics which describes and analyzes empirical observations for the purpose of predicting certain events as a basis for decision making in the face of uncertainty."[26] Statistics come in two varieties: descriptive and inferential.

15-6a Descriptive Statistics

Descriptive statistics are a computed measure of some property of a set of data, making possible a statement about its meaning. An example of a descriptive statistic is the average (mean) time it takes to answer the telephone in the customer service department. Other descriptive statistics include the mode (the most common data point) and the median (the point at which 50 percent of the other points lie above and 50 percent below). Mean, median, and mode are also often referred to as measures of central tendency.

15-6b Inferential Statistics

Inferential statistics are computations done on a set of data, or among several sets of data, that are designed to facilitate prediction of future events, or to guide decisions and actions. An example of an inferential statistic might be the correlation of the average time the customer service department takes to answer the telephone with customer attitudes about the organization. It might be found that faster average response time is correlated with increased customer satisfaction. In that case, this statistic would be a catalyst to action centered on reducing telephone response time.

15-6c Types of Process Variation

Variation exists in any process. Because of this, no two products or service encounters are exactly alike. *The control of quality is largely the control of variation.* The job of SPC is to limit this variation within an acceptable range. So does a manager determine what is acceptable variation?

There are two types of variation in any system: random and nonrandom. *Random variation* is often referred to as the "normal" variation of a system. Random variation potentially affects all components of a process. *Nonrandom variation* is not considered to be part of the normal causal processes of a system. This type of variation leads to unpredictable outcomes, something management wants to eliminate.

Random and nonrandom variation are explained in turn by two different types of causes: common and special. **Common cause variation** is just the random variation in a system and, typically, can't be completely eliminated. Managers should work to minimize the range of common cause variation as part of their continuous improvement process. *Range* refers to the extreme upper and lower measures of a variable.

Special cause variation, on the other hand, is due to some *external* influence upon a system. This could be anything from drug abuse by workers to earthquakes. Managers want to eliminate special cause variations to the extent possible. In our examples, this would be done by screening workers and offering drug abuse counseling, or by locating in areas not prone to earthquakes. A **stable system** is one that has eliminated special cause variation and is subject only to the unavoidable (yet reducible) common cause variation.

Without getting into the mathematics, SPC involves statistical sampling and the use of graphs to determine acceptable variation. Samples of an important variable within a

statistical process control (SPC) A control process based on two assumptions: nature is imperfect and variability exists everywhere in systems; uses probability and statistics to understand and control complex systems.

statistics "That branch of applied mathematics which describes and analyzes empirical observations for the purpose of predicting certain events as a basis for decision making in the face of uncertainty," according to Gabriel Pall.

descriptive statistics Computed measures of some property of a set of data, making possible a statement about its meaning.

inferential statistics Computations done on a set of data, or among several sets of data, designed to facilitate prediction of future events or to guide decisions and actions.

common cause variation The random variation in a system that typically can't be completely eliminated.

special cause variation A variation due to some external influence on a system.

stable system A system that has eliminated special cause variation and is subject only to the unavoidable (yet reducible) common cause variation.

Figure 15-5
Normal Curve

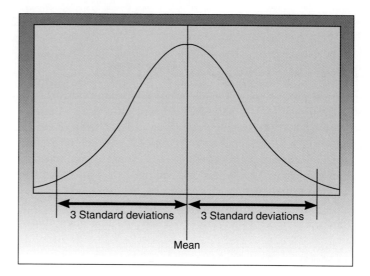

3 Standard deviations   3 Standard deviations

Mean

process are collected and its values are plotted on a graph, usually a control chart. Using *standard deviation* (a standard measure of variation around a mean), upper and lower control limits can be established. Typically, these limits are set at three standard deviations above and below the mean. Based on statistical theory, this should account for over 99 percent of all data points. In other words, assuming the data points are normally distributed, 99 percent will fall within three standard deviations above or below the mean. Figure 15-5 shows a **normal curve** (also called a *bell-shaped curve*) the mean, and three standard deviation units from the mean in each direction. As you can see, the area of the curve is a mathematical abstraction useful in describing a set of natural events. It isn't a law of nature, but it has proven to be useful in describing a wide range of phenomena. Managers who find a data point that's beyond the three standard deviation units above or below the mean can be confident that they have an unexpected event and that intervening action may be necessary.

> **normal curve** A statistical representation that applies to a wide range of phenomena that can be measured on a two-by-two scale. No matter the data being collected, the results tend to align according to the normal curve with most data tending toward the mean or average, and increasingly fewer data tending above and below the mean.

15-6d Using SPC

Using SPC, managers can determine whether variation in a system is within expected parameters or whether the variation is beyond expected parameters.[27] Any system, over a period of time, will experience some variation on a critical measure around an average (mean) value. Using statistical techniques managers can establish *upper and lower control limits* around the mean that define normal variation. System performance within these control limits is said to be subject to common cause variation. Managers shouldn't take action to correct common cause variation.

On the other hand, system performance that goes beyond either the upper or lower control limits is possibly due to special cause variation. Managers who detect special cause variation in their system should take corrective action.

LearningMoment   *Generate a Normal Curve*

A good way to understand the universal application of the normal curve is to prepare one using common data. For example, ask everyone in your class to tell you their height in inches. Plot the data and their frequency on a graph, using the x axis for frequency and the y axis for height in inches. If you have enough data points (twenty to thirty should be sufficient) a normal curve should emerge. You'll find some people on the low end of the scale, some on the high end, and most bunched in the middle around the mean. We don't have to know your city, your school, or your class to be confident that the normal curve relationship will apply to the height of your classmates.

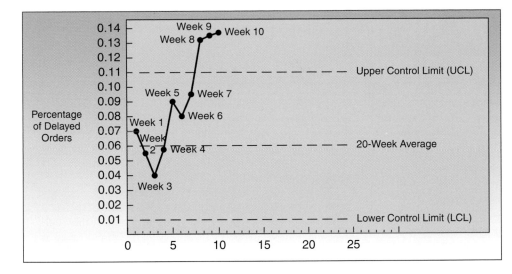

Figure 15-6
Control Chart of Delayed Orders
Note: Weeks 1 through 7 are within the control limits established during the 20-week baseline period. Weeks 8 through 10 show a consistent run beyond the upper control limit and suggest that a special cause variation may be at work.

As an example, consider a firm that wants to establish quality control over one of its key suppliers. One critical measure may be the percentage of orders that are delayed each week. To develop a baseline, the company may randomly sample 100 orders each week from this supplier for, say, twenty weeks to develop a mean percentage of orders that are delayed. With these data it's possible to establish upper and lower control limits. The range of values within these limits would be the range of expected variation due to common causes. If the mean percentage of delays during the twenty-week baseline period is .06 and the upper and lower control limits are .11 and .01, respectively, then any subsequent weeks where the percentage of delays is between these values is probably due to common cause variation (e.g., traffic conditions, worker absences, misplaced orders).

However, if for several weeks the manager notices that the percentage of delays is above .11 (or below .01), a special cause may be operating and action may need to be taken. Some possible causes are (1) the supplier was bought out and is under new management or (2) a trucker strike is delaying deliveries. Quality-based managers use statistical measures to know when key processes are affected by special cause variation and need immediate attention.

Figure 15-6 shows a control chart based on the preceding scenario. A **control chart** is a record of the targeted activity over time, with established upper and lower control limits. Control charts are an important tool in SPC, used to determine if a process is behaving as intended or if there is some unnatural variation.[28] The horizontal axis is divided into units of weeks, and the vertical axis into units of percentage of orders delayed. The upper and lower control limits, as well as the mean, are based on the twenty-week baseline period during which these measures were taken. As you can see from the plotted data points, weeks 1 through 7 are within the upper and lower control limits and their deviation from the mean can be attributed to common cause variation. However, weeks 8 through 10 are beyond the upper control limit. A prudent manager would watch closely for a continuation of this trend, which may indicate a special cause is operating.

The practice of quality management in any type of organization—whether it's service, manufacturing, retail, nonprofit, or something else—can benefit from applying statistical methods to organizational processes or customer expectations.[29] Although statistical techniques are common to most quality management environments, each manager must decide how best to apply these techniques to his or her own organization. What's common across organization types is the fundamental purpose of quality control—to minimize variation.

▶ **control chart** A record of an organization's targeted activity over time, with established upper and lower control limits.

> # *Management Focus* on Globalization

ISO 9000 Is a Global Quality Standard

The International Organization for Standards (ISO) introduced new quality management system standards known as ISO 9000. The Year 2000 revisions that were approved are as follows:

- ISO 9000: 2000, Quality Management Systems—Fundamentals and Vocabulary
- ISO 9001: 2000, Quality Management Systems—Requirements
- ISO 9004: 2000, Quality Management Systems—Guidelines for Performance

"The requirements of ISO 9001: 2000 maintain a greater focus on customer satisfaction, user needs, and continuous improvement of quality management systems than the 1994 version. The revised standard also shifts the requirements away from previously used manufacturing-oriented terminology and simplifies requirements for quality management system documentation. ISO 9001: 2000 is now the standard against which quality management systems are certified," said Jack West, chairman of the U.S. Technical Advisory Group to ISO Technical Committee 176.

ISO rules state that the standards be reviewed periodically because of technological and market developments. The 2000 revisions of the ISO 9000 series represent the most thorough overhaul of these standards since they were first published in 1987. The new versions take into account the developments in the field of quality and the considerable experience gained while implementing ISO 9000.

Source: Adapted from "ISO 9000: 2000 Quality Standards Approved," *Quality,* February 2001, pp. 14–17.

---

total quality control (TQC)
An approach to quality in organizations that seeks to achieve continual quality improvement in all aspects of the organization and to involve employees substantially in the improvement effort.

total quality management (TQM) The generic name given to the approach to quality-based management developed by W. Edwards Deming that is heavily oriented toward treating the *system* as the primary source of error or defects in manufacturing or service work.

International quality standards and quality system certification is provided through an organization called the International Organization for Standardization, or ISO. ISO has developed and promulgated quality standards since the 1940s. It is a nongovernmental body that is comprised of standards bodies from 140 countries. The common name for ISO standards is ISO 9000 (see the Management Focus on Globalization box, "ISO 9000 Is a Global Quality Standard"). These standards are developed through a rigorous process of consensus building across the participating standards bodies. Compliance with ISO standards is completely voluntary, although many firms are pressured by the market, by competitors, or by customers to obtain ISO certification.

SPC is the most narrowly focused of the approaches to quality control discussed in this section. It's concerned primarily with quantitative measures of performance, and doesn't address the issue of how to achieve performance improvements. **Total quality control (TQC)** and **total quality management (TQM)** focus on worker and manager behavior as well as techniques for controlling organizational performance through their activities.

Another approach to quality management that has many adherents around the world is referred to as "Six Sigma."[30] Six Sigma is the term used to refer to the six standard deviation distances between the points three standard deviations above and below a mean. Many training programs exist for managers who wish to become adept at the Six Sigma management approach, including several levels of certification that use the language of "belts"—similar to the certification levels in various martial arts. For example, the highest level of certification in Six Sigma is termed a "black belt."[31]

15-7 Total Quality Management (TQM)

Total quality management (TQM), the generic name given to the approach to quality-based management developed by W. Edwards Deming, is heavily oriented toward treating the *system* as the primary source of error or defects in manufacturing or service work (see Table 15-5).

Although quality management uses a myriad statistical techniques to control processes, there are also some fundamental lessons for control from a human psychology perspective. Deming stresses in his fourteen points such things as "pride of workmanship," "self-improvement," and "drive out fear." These are all elements of the "softer" side of management (the nonquantitative side) but equally important to master. Managers who only use SPC are likely to ignore the need for pride in workmanship that most workers share.

TABLE 15-5

Deming's Fourteen Points of Quality

1. *Create constancy of purpose for improvement of product and service.* Deming suggests a radical new definition of a company's role. Rather than to make money, it's to stay in business and provide jobs through innovation, research, constant improvement, and maintenance.

2. *Adopt the new philosophy.* Americans are too tolerant of poor workmanship and sullen service. We need a new religion in which mistakes and negativism are unacceptable.

3. *Cease dependence on mass inspection.* American firms typically inspect a product as it comes off the assembly line or at major stages along the way; defective products are either thrown out or reworked. Both practices are unnecessarily expensive. In effect, a company is paying workers to make defects and then to correct them. Quality comes not from inspection but from improvement of the process. With instruction, workers can be enlisted in this improvement.

4. *End the practice of awarding business on price tag alone.* Purchasing departments customarily operate on orders to see the lowest-priced vendor. Frequently, this leads to low-quality supplies. Instead, buyers should seek the best quality in a long-term relationship with a single supplier for any one item.

5. *Improve constantly the system of production and service.* Improvement isn't a one-time effort. Management is obligated to continually look for ways to reduce waste and improve quality.

6. *Institute training.* Too often, workers have learned their job from another worker who was never trained properly. They're forced to follow unintelligible instructions. They can't do their jobs well because no one tells them how to do so.

7. *Institute leadership.* The supervisor's job isn't to tell people what to do nor to punish them but to lead. Leading consists of (1) helping people do a better job and (2) learning by objective methods who needs individual help.

8. *Drive out fear.* Many employees are afraid to ask questions or to take a position, even when they don't understand what their job is or what's right or wrong. They will continue to do things the wrong way or not do them at all. Economic losses from fear are appalling. To ensure better quality and productivity, people must feel secure.

9. *Break down barriers between staff areas.* Often a company's departments or units are competing with each other or have goals that conflict. They don't work as a team so they can solve or foresee problems. Worse, one department's goals may cause trouble for another.

10. *Eliminate slogans, exhortations, and targets for the workforce.* These never helped anybody do a good job. Let workers formulate their own slogans.

11. *Eliminate numerical quotas.* Quotas take into account only numbers, not quality of methods. They're usually a guarantee of inefficiency and high cost. To hold their jobs, people meet quotas at any cost, without regard to damage to their company.

12. *Remove barriers to pride of workmanship.* People are eager to do a good job and get distressed when they can't. Too often, misguided supervisors, faulty equipment, and defective materials stand in the way of good performance. These barriers must be removed.

13. *Institute a vigorous program of education and retraining.* Both management and the workforce must be educated in the new methods, including teamwork and statistical techniques.

14. *Take action to accomplish the transformation.* A special top management team with a plan of action is needed to carry out the quality mission. Workers can't do it on their own, nor can managers. A critical mass of people in the company must understand the 14 points.

Sources: Adapted from W. Edwards Deming, *Out of the Crisis,* 2nd ed. (Cambridge, Mass.: MIT Center for Advanced Engineering Study, 1986). Reprinted by permission of The MIT Press.

Figure 15-7
Total Quality
Management Model

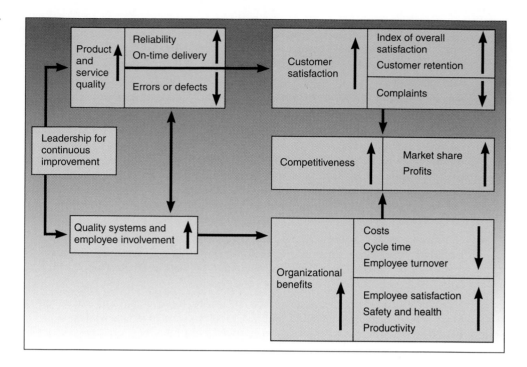

Thus, the *total* in total quality management requires managers to be familiar with a wide range of facts about the workplace, both those that can be described mathematically and those that can't. Figure 15-7 describes the benefits that accrue to an organization from paying attention to these nonquantitative aspects of a TQM approach.

Deming clearly outlined roles for workers and managers in a TQM-based workplace. In the following discussion, we briefly review the highlights of the worker's role and the manager's role in TQM.

15-7a The Worker's Role in TQM

In their book *In Search of Excellence,* consultants Tom Peters and Bob Waterman illustrate the importance of personal worker control in quality.[32] They describe an experiment designed to determine the effect of loud, disturbing noise on performing a mental task. The experimental group was provided a button it could press to eliminate the noise. The control group had no such button. In performing the mental task, the experimental group achieved five times the productivity rate and only 20 percent of the error rate of the control group. The significant point of this experiment is that, although the experimental group performed better, no one in the experimental group ever touched the button. Individuals who merely believed they had personal control over their working conditions achieved higher productivity and greatly reduced error rates compared with those who didn't believe they had control. A personal sense of control, not reduced noise, explained the difference between the two groups.

Deming provides an example of successful worker quality control in the production of stockings. Managers with the stocking company first recognized a problem in production costs when they faced a situation where costs were soon to exceed revenues. Management hired a statistician to help them diagnose their problem. The statistician recommended that the company send twenty supervisors to a ten-week training course to learn techniques for charting the number of defective stockings. When the supervisors returned, they were asked to apply some of the principles they had learned.

In all but two cases, defects fell within statistically established control limits with a mean defect rate of 4.8 percent per production worker (called "loopers" in the stocking business). Next, individual loopers were charted. Management found (1) an excellent looper whose skills were passed on to others by training them, (2) a looper who improved markedly with eyeglasses, and (3) a looper whose performance changed dramatically after charting. One of the loopers remarked, "This is the first time that anybody ever told me that care mattered." Within seven months, the mean number of defects dropped to 0.8 percent. Instead of 11,500 stockings rejected each week, only 2,000 were rejected.[33]

A quality-based system of control must be built on worker trust and pride of workmanship, which provides a basis for worker self-control.[34] In this quality-based view, control must be seen as an internal, individual process before it can result in an external process. Control becomes an internal quality guide practiced by all employees rather than an external set of rules applied by managers. Quality scholar Joseph Juran defines self-control as "A means of knowing what the goals are . . . a means of knowing what the actual performance is . . . a means for changing the performance in the event that performance does not conform to goals and standards."[35]

Using standards, workers have a quality-based strategy for determining those activities necessary and harmful to quality. Activities are built around the standards; irrelevant, redundant, or non-value-added activities are eliminated.

Although workers play an important role in implementing a TQM approach, management has the responsibility of leadership. In most organizations, workers below the managerial level are unlikely to lead a revolution in organizational philosophy. It's up to management to steer the ship. Managers must create the vision for the organization. This is no difference in a TQM environment or a scientific management environment.

15-7b The Manager's Role in TQM

Quality-based management believes control of work processes is effected first by the workforce, then by automation, then by managers, and finally by upper managers. Upper management is responsible for creating the system; workers are trained to maintain control. Thus, in a quality-based approach, control is located at the lowest levels of the firm—the workers on the line who provide the service.[36]

The traditional managerial control function has focused on supervision during the production process. Supervision has been widely practiced as a traditional method of keeping an eye on workers—looking for mistakes. Unfortunately, such extreme pressure to perform can lead to lower levels of quality and productivity.

Under the Deming approach, the responsibility for quality control ultimately rests with management. However, managers must also promote worker self-management or "quality-mindedness" practices, as Armand Feigenbaum refers to it.[37] To further employee self-management, managers must develop worker participation programs and policies. With knowledge of the company's costs and goals, workers have the knowledge, the tools, and the power to prevent problems from arising. Managers must also encourage employee suggestions and cost consciousness by recognizing and implementing worker quality improvement decisions. And, if there are problems, management should give workers the first opportunity to solve them.

Managers need patience to transform their organizations using the principles and tools of TQM. If a manager grows frustrated too soon with the lack of worker understanding or motivation to become involved in the new philosophy, he or she may not give it a chance to work.[38] Managers must realize this. Most workers want responsibility and control over their work. Most will understand and accept a new approach to their work if management demonstrates commitment to improving the system. That means workers need to be trained in the tools and techniques of TQM, SPC, and TQC. They need to be empowered to control their work processes. And they need to be encouraged constantly to develop pride in their work and their organization. These elements of quality are the least quantifiable, but no less important.

15-8 An Integrated Control System

Preliminary, concurrent, and feedback control methods are not mutually exclusive. Rather, they usually are combined into an integrated control system. Such a control system must provide for standards, information and measurement, and corrective action at every point, from input to process to output.

Managers desire manufacturing processes and customer service that produce output with zero defects and satisfied customers. But for many reasons, 100 percent, defect-free goods or perfect levels of service are nearly impossible to produce. The quality of raw materials varies, machines operate imperfectly, and employees have different levels of skills. Thus, managers know defects will be produced. The task for management is to minimize the defect rate. Today, quality has become an increasingly important control issue. Although quality perfection is unlikely, a growing number of companies are working to substantially improve the quality of the goods and services they produce.[39]

Quality has always been an important aspect of business management. High-quality products lead to customer goodwill and satisfaction. These, in turn, create repeat sales, loyal customers and clients, and testimonials to prospective customers or clients. Today, many organizations are elevating the importance of quality to a key element of their business strategy. The focus on meeting quality objectives is not limited to the production department. Top management considers quality improvement and high-quality standards to be vital corporate objectives. They—and in many cases employees companywide—are becoming actively involved in finding ways to improve quality.[40]

Management Summary

- Effective control depends on managerial decisions and actions to correct deviations between actual and planned results.

- The three necessary elements of control are predetermined standards, information, and corrective action.

- Precontrol methods and systems depend on information about characteristics and qualities of inputs—materials, capital, financial, and human resources. The foci of corrective action are the inputs themselves.

- Concurrent control methods and systems depend on information about ongoing activities and operations. The foci of corrective action can be activities and operations or the inputs, depending on the causes of the deviations between actual and desired performance.

- Postcontrol methods and systems use the information that measures the characteristics and qualities of actual results and performance. They involve taking corrective actions if those measures should be significantly out of line with expectations and or objectives.

- A growing number of companies are focusing on developing a superior quality control system because they are realizing customers want quality. Quality affects organizational performance, and high quality is the new standard for domestic and international competition.

- Consumers evaluate quality using eight dimensions: performance, features, reliability, conformance, durability, serviceability, aesthetics, and perceived quality.

- Developing an integrated quality control system requires defining quality characteristics and standards, developing a quality review program, building a commitment to quality among employees, and designing a quality measurement and reporting system.

- Advocates of a total quality control philosophy assert that companies should continually strive to improve quality in all operations of the organization, and that employees should be a key source of quality improvements.

Key Terms

accounts receivable turnover (p. 366)
acid-test ratio (p. 366)
activity-based costing (ABC) (p. 367)
appraisal costs (p. 370)
balance sheet (p. 366)
budget (p. 364)
cash flow statement (p. 366)
common cause variation (p. 373)
concurrent control (p. 364)
control chart (p. 375)
controlling function (p. 358)
corrective action (p. 360)
current ratio (p. 366)
debt ratios (p. 367)
debt to asset ratio (p. 367)
debt to equity ratio (p. 367)
descriptive statistics (p. 373)

direction (p. 364)
discounted rate of return (p. 363)
failure costs (p. 370)
feedback control (p. 365)
funnel principle (p. 370)
hidden costs (p. 370)
hurdle rate (p. 364)
income statement (p. 365)
inferential statistics (p. 373)
information (p. 359)
inventory turnover (p. 366)
inventory turnover ratio (p. 366)
investment decisions (p. 362)
normal curve (p. 374)
operating cycle (p. 364)
opportunity cost (p. 364)
payback method (p. 363)

perceived value (p. 358)
performance review (p. 368)
preliminary control (p. 361)
prevention costs (p. 370)
rate of return on investment (p. 363)
service level agreements (SLAs) (p. 360)
solvency (p. 366)
special cause variation (p. 373)
stable system (p. 373)
standard cost system (p. 367)
standards (p. 359)
statistical process control (SPC) (p. 373)
statistics (p. 373)
total quality control (TQC) (p. 376)
total quality management (TQM) (p. 376)

Review and Discussion Questions

1. Explain why predetermined standards are necessary for effective managerial control. Does the fact that management has set standards for crucial aspects of the organization guarantee that control will be effective? Why or why not?

2. Discuss how the college or university you attend controls the teaching performance of the faculty. Organize your answer in terms of the three types of control.

3. Discuss how managers should use and implement control policies in the organization. What is the role of employees in establishing and implementing policies?

4. Why are the standards that a CEO uses more ambiguous than the standards used by first-level managers?

5. What is the difference between descriptive statistics and inferential statistics?

6. Many managers assert that providing superior quality requires high manufacturing costs. However, some research

indicates that companies with the best quality earn the highest profits. Are these two statements contradictory? If so, resolve the contradiction.

7. What are the shortcomings of using statistical sampling in monitoring the quality of products or services?

8. In your opinion, what are the individual characteristics required to provide employees with effective direction? Explain.

9. Explain why the normal curve is a statistical abstraction with general application. Why does it describe such a wide range of phenomena?

10. Developing an integrated quality control system is a complex, challenging, and time-consuming task. What do you think are the challenges managers will face in introducing a quality control system to employees? What are the challenges of actually implementing such a system? Explain.

Practice Quiz

Note: You can find the correct answers to these questions by taking the quiz and then submitting your answers in the Online Edition. The program will automatically score your submission. If you miss a question, the program will provide the correct answer, a rationale for the answer, and the section number in the chapter where the topic is discussed.

Indicate whether the sentence or statement is true or false.

1. Capital acquisitions can be precontrolled by establishing profitability criteria that must be met before the acquisitions are authorized.

2. The **rate of return** is a measurement of profitability that takes into account the time value of money.

3. Research work is inherently more complex and varied than manual work and requires more interpretation and instruction.

4. A higher level of quality doesn't always result in a higher finished product price, as when improving quality reduces the cost of quality.

5. The greater the perceived value of a product or service, the higher are customer expectations for quality.

6. **Common cause variations** are just random variations in a system and, typically, can't be eliminated.

Identify the letter of the choice that best completes the statement or answers the question.

7. After planning, managers must_____their organization's resources to achieve results.
   a. inventory
   b. ration
   c. deploy
   d. estimate

8. The simplest method of capital control is the
   _____.
   a. payback method.
   b. rate of return on investment.
   c. discounted rate of return.

_C_ **9.** Which of the following is NOT one of the three elements of manufacturing costs?
   a. labor
   b. direct materials
   c. profit margins
   d. overhead

_A_ **10.** The most important thing for managers to remember when conducting employee evaluations is that they must be _____.
   a. objective.
   b. direct.
   c. precise.
   d. helpful.

_D_ **11.** Effective control of an organization requires three things: _____, measurement, and corrective action.
   a. authority
   b. leadership
   c. management
   d. standards

_B_ **12.** _____ control methods increase the possibility that future results will compare favorably with planned results.
   a. feedback
   b. preliminary
   c. concurrent
   d. financial

_B_ **13.** A simple method for the preliminary control of capital is the _____ method.
   a. solvency
   b. payback
   c. inventory turnover
   d. liquidity

_A_ **14.** Feedback control of human resources is usually done through a process known as a(n) _____.
   a. performance review.
   b. interview.
   c. performance exam.
   d. orientation.

_C_ **15** Managers should refrain from taking action on systems within the organization unless _____ variation has been detected through use of a control chart.
   a. common cause
   b. common type
   c. special cause
   d. special type

Case Study

BOSCH Uses Six Sigma to Improve Performance

A data-driven method for eliminating defects in any process from manufacturing to service, the Six Sigma methodology has been implemented by Bosch Security Systems worldwide. Bosch's goals for the program include changing its culture to be more proactive, driving fact-based decision making, and ensuring comprehensive and consistent approaches for all sites and parts of the organization.

Bosch is using the DMAIC (define, measure, analyze, improve, control) system, which is designed to enhance existing processes. It also is utilizing DESS (design for Six Sigma) to improve its development processes. DMAIC focuses on proactive problem-solving, while DESS centers on designing products and processes that perform at a Six Sigma level and enhance the customer experience.

"Six Sigma is consistent with the Robert Bosch quality improvement strategy, and it's been proven effective at many other successful companies, including other Bosch sites," noted Peter Ribinski, president/CEO for Bosch Security Systems in the U.S. "The program strongly supports our top three strategic objectives: improve the quality of products and processes; increase customer satisfaction and loyalty; and reduce costs."

Employees in several key areas are involved in the program including: engineering, purchasing, product management, quality/testing, manufacturing, and service/repair. The Six Sigma skills that they develop will apply to specific projects and their day-to-day responsibilities. Two types of "change agents" will be used: dedi-

cated product quality improvement managers and operational roles that will influence the majority of projects. "We anticipate that the significant cost savings will offset our investment in the program," Ribinski forecasted. "We have demonstrated our commitment to the Six Sigma program with our investment in time, solid leadership, full-time resources, training, win-win partnerships with suppliers, and infrastructure support."

Questions for Discussion

1. What do you think is meant by the term "fact-based decision making?" How should Bosch employees collect "facts" to enable decision making to proceed?

2. How will using Six Sigma and quality improvement techniques help Bosch reduce costs? What short-term costs may actually increase as the company transitions to the Six Sigma approach?

3. Why is it important to train employees in the Six Sigma philosophy? What did Deming say about employees in his TQM philosophy?

Source: Adapted from "Six Sigma Quality Implemented by Bosch," *Security Distributing & Marketing,* November 2004, p. 20.

Internet Exercise

On-line Customer Surveys Designed to Control Quality

Many organizations are using customer feedback surveys to enhance the level of the quality of their products and services. You may have seen these surveys in restaurants, at hotels, or in retail establishments. On-line services use the Web for administering their customer surveys. The following websites provide a few sources of on-line customer feedback surveys.

> http://www.usajobs.opm.gov/survey.htm
>
> http://www.dell.com/html/us/dellauction/survey.htm
>
> http://wedding.weddingchannel.com/help_guest/survey.asp

Questions for Discussion

1. Do you think the organizations that provide customer feedback surveys learn anything from the feedback they receive? Do you think they apply that knowledge to improve the quality of their services?

2. What flaws do you see in the surveys?

3. What benefits are there in on-line surveys over the traditional off-line versions?

Experiential Exercise

A Control System Profile

Purpose: This activity is designed to enhance students' understanding of the purpose, makeup, and operation of actual control systems in organizations.

Setting Up the Exercise: The instructor will divide the class into groups composed of four students each. Each group should complete the following project:

1. Select a control system that you would like to learn more about. The choices are numerous: budgeting, capital investment, performance appraisal, inventory control, quality control, and employee selection are all control systems that function in the typical organization. Identify an organization in your local community or in your college administration. Several control systems on campus are appropriate to study, such as student applicant selection.

2. Interview the individual who manages the respective control system. Your objective is to develop a written profile of the system. The interview should last approximately thirty minutes. Some suggested questions:

   a. What are the objectives of the control system?

   b. How are standards set and information collected to determine whether standards have been met?

   c. How has the control system changed over the years? What factors led to the changes?

   d. In what ways have you fine-tuned the system to meet your organization's particular needs and constraints?

   e. What are the challenges in implementing and managing the system?

3. Prepare a five-page written report on your findings. The paper should focus on presenting an overall profile of the objectives, makeup, and function of the system. You should also address how the system has evolved over the years and how the system is designed to meet the system's particular needs. Be sure to include any system problems you identified and suggest solutions.

A Learning Note: This exercise illustrates that control systems can widely differ across organizations because of each organization's particular needs and characteristics. Control systems are also quite fluid; they often are altered to accommodate particular circumstances and changes in the organization's processes.

Production, Operations, and Financial Controls

16

CHAPTER OBJECTIVES

1 Define the job of the production and operations manager.

2 State the methods managers can use to control the quality and quantity of production resources.

3 Define the necessary conditions for effective internal control of financial resources and assets.

4 Describe the principles of just-in-time inventory management and the challenges inherent in implementing the concept.

5 Discuss the advantages and disadvantages of enterprise resources planning (ERP) and supply chain management (SCM).

6 Discuss the uses and mechanics of the PERT and linear programming models for concurrent operations control.

CHAPTER OUTLINE

no quiz

Managing Today

Delphi Corporation Transforms Its Operations

Delphi Corporation, the world's largest maker of automotive and transportation electronics and systems, spent the last seven years successfully implementing lean manufacturing practices, achieving some incredible results. For the past two years, a major portion of this initiative has been directed at the transformation of the company's purchasing function into a lean, global supply management team. "To truly become a lean enterprise, we must partner with our suppliers to remove waste from our joint systems, allowing them to achieve similar results, and ultimately creating a lean, joint enterprise," J. T. Battenberg III, chairman, CEO and president, commented. "Our global supply management team is completely focused on optimizing the entire purchasing stream by engaging suppliers to reduce waste, eliminate unnecessary costs, improve quality and design, trim time-to-market, and elevate the financial performance of all the partners," he said. He cited the following points as critical to the company's transformation:

1. **Develop and manage to cost standards.** The intent is to establish new best-in-class levels of real cost that they can understand and that can be achieved by working jointly. "Cost management cannot be underestimated," Battenberg maintains. "Once you know what something really costs, the entire sourcing dynamic changes from an option mentality to a joint waste elimination focus."

2. **Develop commodity strategies and strategic suppliers.** Battenberg said that Delphi is focused on simplifying its message and aligning its management team on implementing common strategies globally. Concurrently, it is developing strategies, with the strategic sourcing teams determining the criteria that define all of Delphi's expectations for each and every key supplier. "We have to understand how we can work together to achieve mutual benefits," he said.

3. **Lean supplier development.** During 2004 Delphi placed fifty-two lean supplier development engineers into the global supply management team. "Together with supplier company personnel, our engineers are helping identify best practices leading to the best quality and lowest total cost for whatever we are buying," Battenberg said. "We map and we study the value stream, process by process by process." The process has been initiated with seventy-six of Delphi's largest suppliers in North America, Europe, and Asia- Pacific. In these companies the reduction in people costs has ranged from 20 percent to just under 50 percent. Productivity increases range from 30 percent to 60 percent, and first time quality has improved in a range from 10 percent to 45 percent.

Battenberg concludes: "We are trying to move to a lean enterprise and we're changing our sourcing model where we are now focused on relationship building so we can take our strategic suppliers with us on this most important journey."

Source: Adapted from "Lean Concept Drives Delphi's Global Supply Chain Management Initiative," *Supplier Selection & Management Report,* June 2004, pp. 1–3.

Managerial control of production and operations is critical to organizational performance no matter what type of company. Although modern organizations must undertake numerous activities, their ultimate fates depend in large part on how well managers control their productive resources. All other organizational activities, such as engineering, personnel, marketing, and research and development, support and depend on the primary activity of producing goods and services.

The Managing Today vignette focuses on Delphi Corporation, a manufacturer of parts for automobiles. Like many manufacturers, Delphi has a challenge when it comes to managing the many suppliers that furnish the company with raw materials and finished goods to be used in production. To remain competitive, Delphi must find ways to keep the costs of supplier management low. Nearly every business is concerned with managing its operating costs. This chapter will examine supply chain issues as a portion of the production/operations function. This chapter also examines several methods managers use to control productive resources. The presentation is organized around the three basic processes of production and operations: input, transformation, and output.

16-1 Production and Operations Control

▶**production** The total process by which a company produces finished goods and/or services.

People often confuse the terms *production, manufacturing,* and *operations.* They're related terms that have significantly different applications. **Production** refers to the total process by which a company produces finished goods and/or services. These processes involve

Organization	Inputs	Outputs or Production Processes	Products (Type)
Magazine publisher	Information in various forms (written, verbal, and photo or art pictorials), labor, energy, capital, ink, paper, tools, equipment, technology	Planning, budgeting, scheduling, design and layout, writing, editing, typesetting, art and photo preparation, management control, printing, folding, cutting, binding, shipping on time	Magazines (nondurable goods)
Hair-styling salon	Clients, hair knowledge, skills, information, hair care supplies, tools, technology, equipment, labor, energy, capital, water	Planning, budgeting, scheduling, ordering and handling materials, design, hair preparation, washing, conditioning, coloring, styling, meeting schedules, maintaining customer satisfaction (quality control)	Personal hair care (service)
Steel conduit manufacturer	Steel, chemicals, labor, energy, capital, tools, technology, equipment, water, location	Planning, budgeting, scheduling, ordering and handling materials, metal processing, labor organization, employee relations and safety, quality control, forming, cooling, storage and distribution, meeting schedules	Steel wire and pipe products (durable goods)

TABLE 16-1

Production Processes for Different Organizations

physical work, meetings and brainstorming, and planning. Table 16-1 provides examples of the production processes in different types of work environments.

Manufacturing refers only to the physical process of producing goods. The word *manufacturing* comes from the Latin words *mann* (hand) and *factor* (create or make)—in other words, handmade.

Operations are the functions needed to keep the company producing and delivering. They're literally any function or series of functions enacted to carry out a strategic plan. Operations for a manufacturer might include purchasing, materials management, production management, inventory, quality control, and other activities. Operations for a service business might include customer support, inventory (as in a retail operation), sales, after-sale support, marketing, and others. Managers must carefully structure and monitor operations to keep quality high and costs low. In addition, managers must be aware of the constant changes that are ongoing to create more effective and efficient operations.

▶ **manufacturing** The physical process of producing goods.

▶ **operations** The functions needed to keep a company producing and delivering.

16-2 The Role of the Production and Operations Manager

Production and operations (P&O) managers are responsible for producing the goods and services that businesses sell. There are many kinds of production and operations systems, just as there are many kinds of products demanded by the marketplace. Production and operations vary in size from a single person in a very small company to thousands of employees in a huge multinational enterprise. Production managers are needed not just for manufacturing, but for nearly any type of business that delivers a product or service to a customer. For example, Emma Rooney is the production manager for Birddog, a public relations and communications firm located in the U.K. Rooney manages the workflow, arranges production, and handles client invoicing and collections. Her title at Birddog is "Production Manager."[1]

The production goals of every business focus on producing output—goods and/or services—at the best quality possible within budget constraints. Thus, the P&O manager must organize and manage the production processes with efficiency and effectiveness. A P&O manager's job is to see that the operations necessary to achieve the company's production goals are carried out. To do this, these managers oversee a number of company operations. Typical functions include:

* Product planning
* Site location and layout
* Inventory control
* Purchasing and materials management
* Manufacturing and production
* Production control
* Quality control
* Plant management

In moderate-sized firms, the P&O manager is often a vice president who reports directly to top management; managers or supervisors representing the functions just mentioned report to the P&O manager.

P&O managers have product planning responsibilities such as preparing forecasts, schedules, and budgets in collaboration with top management, finance managers, and marketing managers. In start-up operations they might oversee site location and layout, hiring and training of employees, and selection and installation of an information technology infrastructure.

16-3 Organizing the Production Process

Just as a company can be organized in a variety of ways, titles can be applied to people within the company in a variety of ways. For example, the inventory control manager in one company may be called the purchasing and inventory control manager in another company. Knowing the exact titles and type of organization in place enables managers to have appropriate expectations and communicate effectively. Production and operations managers must fit into different types of organizations and be prepared to adapt to a variety of demands. The skills typically associated with production management include the abilities to plan, manage projects, map organizational processes, and juggle multiple competing demands on time and resources. Next we examine several different manufacturing organizational types.

16-3a Traditional Organizations

The organization chart in Figure 16-1 follows the traditional, or job-shop, form. It gives each manager a specific area of authority and responsibility; but it can also pit managers against each other. For example, if a purchasing manager has budgeted $50,000 for a quantity of a specific part and the inventory control manager must order them on a rush basis for $60,000, the purchasing manager's responsibility and authority are subordinated to the inventory manager's needs. Figure 16-1 shows typical departments in this type of organization and some common measures used in judging departmental performance. For example, the quality manager's performance would be appraised on the basis of costs, defect levels, and rework costs.

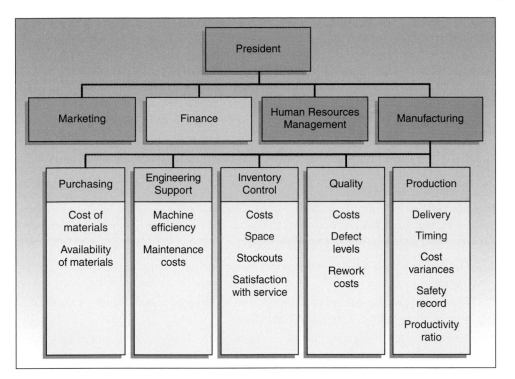

Figure 16-1
Traditional Manufacturing Organization

16-3b The Cellular Organization

In the past decade more and more companies have elected to use a **cellular organization** design for production. Here workers cooperate in teams (cells) to manufacture total products or subassemblies.[2] Each cell is responsible for the quality and quantity of its products. Each also has the authority to make adjustments to improve performance and product quality. Cell formation in cellular manufacturing deals with the identification of machines that can be grouped to create manufacturing cells and the identification of part families to be processed within each cell.[3] Figure 16-2 illustrates how, in the cellular arrangement, machines are arranged to handle all the operations needed to assemble the products. The parts follow a path through each cell to final assembly.

▶ **cellular organization**
An organization structured around units that complete entire assembly processes rather than a continuous line or linear production process.

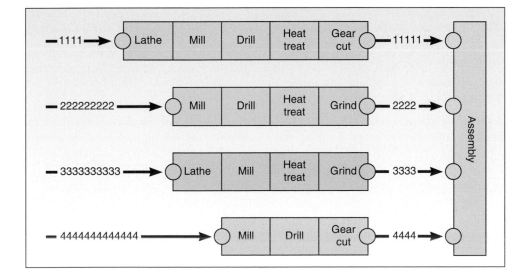

Figure 16-2
Cellular Manufacturing Layout

Source: From *Production and Inventory Management,* 1st edition, by Fogarty and Hoffman, copyright © 1983. Reprinted with permission of South-Western College Publishing, a division of Thomson Learning.

Interestingly, cellular manufacturing was pioneered in Russia, with early adoption among German and British manufacturers as well.[4] The basic difference between the cellular and the traditional organization is that workers in the cells are all responsible for their output. The linear competitiveness of the traditional structure is avoided. Instead, each individual is pressured to perform so that the group will succeed. Cells tend to be tightly self-monitoring and self-correcting. In a cellular organization companies tend to have much smaller staffs overall, with middle management positions reduced and lean management numbers at the top.

16-3c Process and Project Manufacturing

> **process manufacturing**
> A manufacturing approach that focuses on repetitive and mass production of goods.

How a company organizes may be related to the type of manufacturing carried on. **Process manufacturing,** for example, is carried on in various forms. This type of manufacturing applies various processes, or methods, to change materials into finished goods. Several processes that comprise this approach include:

- The *assembly process* puts parts together to form whole products, such as cars and trucks.
- The *continuous process* uses mass production techniques to make many items of one kind, such as roller bearings, nuts, or bolts.
- *Intermittent processing* uses one process for a batch of goods, and then changes processes to produce goods having some differences from the earlier batches (e.g., stainless steel restaurant kitchen drain-boards and fitted metal cabinets).
- The *analytic process* breaks down materials into components to extract the parts needed, as in oil refining and smelting.
- The *synthetic process* brings items together to create an entirely different product. For example, in the synthetic fabric industry and the rubber industry, chemical and heat processes change materials before being formed.
- The *extractive process* removes a product from raw material, as in coal mining.

> **project manufacturing**
> A manufacturing approach that focuses on major projects, such as bridges, dams, or buildings.

Project manufacturing usually involves very large projects for which materials and workers must be removed. There is no assembly line or workstation layout within a factory or shop; the product is built in place. Examples include the building of large ships, large printing presses, and high-rise office buildings.

16-4 Site Location and Layout

When a company starts up or opens a new branch, the P&O manager is heavily involved in planning the site location and layout. Company officers, engineers, and heads of departments add their ideas and lists of requirements.

16-4a Site Selection

A site may be bought or leased with or without a building already in place. If the site is to be leased, all managers involved should make their plans and submit their needs to a commercial or industrial real estate broker. The broker then submits a list of properties available in the area within the price range required. A site may come with a "build to suit" lease or may be a turnkey location whose building and interior facilities are already completed.

The type of business dictates the kind of facility. Service sector businesses often require small office facilities in heavy-traffic areas convenient to customers or to the electronic communications and other services the business itself requires. Heavy industry, on the other hand, requires vast space near interstate highways, rail spurs, or shipping ports to facilitate transportation to market. A production and operations manager's plan for site location considers most if not all of the following factors:

- Economies of cost or other economic advantages for land, buildings, or units

- Taxes, insurance, and other costs

- Proximity to related industries and suppliers, warehouses, and/or service operations

- Availability of an appropriate labor force, considering such factors as quality and cost

- Availability of economical transportation for materials and supplies as well as for finished goods

- Proximity to market for goods

- Air and water conditions

- Proximity to plentiful, economical energy services

- Climate and environment that's in line with the industry's needs and is amenable to employees' lifestyle

- Ample space for current and future needs of firm

- Proximity to such employee needs as housing, schools, mass transportation, religious facilities, day care, shopping, and recreational facilities

- Community receptiveness

Some site choices may be based on the overriding advantages of one factor, such as availability of labor or market, or low cost of land.[5] In recent years, for example, many American manufacturers have chosen to locate facilities in Mexico because of the low costs of land and labor. Clothing manufacturers have settled in China because of abundant cheap labor. Another increasingly popular production site is Eastern Europe. Major changes in the business climate and a large untapped market have made Russia, Poland, Hungary, and other central and eastern European countries intriguing options for joint ventures and new plants. In addition, many communities throughout the United States offer tax breaks and other incentives to companies to entice them.[6]

16-4b Site Layout

Just as it dictates the kind and location of facility, the type of business will determine the layout of the site selected. For each kind of business, P&O managers must meet different needs. Different kinds of production require varying space for assembly lines, workstations, or other specific arrangements for work layouts.

The manager must plan the layout in detail before the site is chosen. The plan must account for the needed square footage, work areas, office and conference areas, storage, and shipping and receiving needs. To draw up specific plans, managers use templates, models, drawings, and site layout software. In fact, site layout planning has become a focus of a great deal of innovation in software and computer simulations.[7] Leading software developers use fuzzy logic, optimization techniques, and other quantitative tools to create the most efficient layout for the business.[8]

LearningMoment | *The Importance of Site Layout*

Although it may seem a minor issue, site layout is an important consideration for a variety of reasons, including political, productivity, and communication concerns. People often regard the location of office space from a political perspective. For example, top executives usually get a "corner office" with multiple external views. People who have window offices usually outrank those with internal offices. Productivity is strongly affected by layout. Placing people who work together on projects in proximity to one another can greatly enhance productivity. In addition, such co-location can enhance communication.

16-5 Controlling Production and Operations

As noted in Chapter 15, control methods can be discussed in terms of the focus of their corrective action. Accordingly, production-operations control methods can be described as focusing on *inputs* (preliminary control), *transformation* (concurrent control), or *outputs* (feedback control).

16-5a Control of Inputs

Operations management involves acquiring resources (inputs) and allocating them among the resources' competing users. Preliminary control methods focus specifically on controlling the acquisition of resources. The resource acquired at the input end of the production process is usually designated as *raw material*. Control of inputs requires predetermining standards for the *quantity* and *quality* of raw materials. It also involves specifying standards for timely delivery.

Production managers make two key raw materials control decisions: (1) how *many* of each lot or batch of materials to order, and (2) how *often* to order each lot or batch. In resolving inventory problems, the manager initially must identify the cost factors that affect the choices being considered.

First are the **ordering costs,** incurred each time material is ordered from a supplier. These are the clerical and administrative costs per order, and they include the costs of placing the materials into inventory. Sophisticated mathematical models have been developed to help firms determine the costs and benefits of, for example, having multiple vendors as opposed to only a few or one. Companies such as Wal-Mart have excelled in managing multiple supplier relationships, enabling them to pass on cost savings to customers.[9]

Second, **carrying costs** are incurred whenever items are held in inventory. These include the interest on money invested in inventory and the cost of storage space, rent, obsolescence, taxes, protection, and insurance on losses due to theft, fire, and deterioration. Carrying costs usually are expressed as an annual figure and as a percentage of the average inventory. Some firms strive to minimize carrying costs by issuing a form of short-term financial security known as commercial paper. Commercial paper has a 270-day life cycle, enabling firms to obtain cash from investors who are secured by the firm's inventory carry.[10] Commercial paper is essentially a short term bond, and is available to investors through major stock exchanges such as the New York Stock Exchange.

To minimize *inventory costs,* a manager must minimize both ordering and carrying costs. These two costs are related to each other in opposing directions, as shown in Figure 16-3. That is, as ordering costs decrease, carrying costs increase. As the size of each order increases, the number of orders and the cost of ordering decrease. Yet, since larger quantities are being ordered and placed in inventory, the cost of carrying the inventory increases. For example, automobile retailers have reduced their inventory costs through aggressive use of the Internet. Major automobile dealers have set up direct order systems, allowing customers to order their vehicles directly from the factory. This helps the retailer reduce the inventory on the lot, reducing inventory costs by $150 to $700 per vehicle.[11]

The number of orders for a given time period is equal to usage for the period *(U)* divided by the size of each order *(Q),* or *U/Q.* The total ordering cost per period (week, month, or year) equals the cost of ordering each lot *(J) multiplied by the number of orders per period,* or

$$\frac{U}{Q}(J)$$

You can see that as the order size *(Q)* increases, fewer orders are required to meet the usage *(U)* for a period. Consequently, the ordering cost component will decrease. This is demonstrated by the downward sloping ordering cost curve in Figure 16-3.

The cost of carrying an item in inventory is calculated by multiplying the cost of the item *(V)* by a percentage figure (ordinarily the firm's cost of borrowing money) *(E),* or *VE.* This is management's estimate of carrying charges, taxes, insurance, and so on, per period,

ordering cost An element in inventory control models that comprises clerical, administrative, and labor costs.

carrying costs The costs incurred by carrying raw materials and finished goods in inventory.

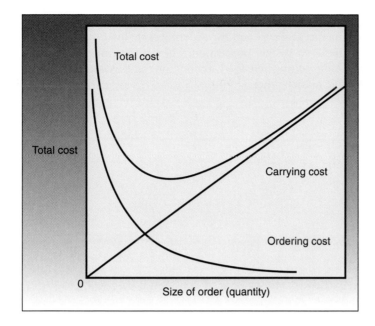

Figure 16-3
Relationship Between Ordering Costs and Carrying Costs

expressed as a percentage of the cost of inventory. The total carrying costs are equal to the cost of carrying one item *(VE)* multiplied by the average inventory Q/2. Note in Figure 16-3 that, unlike ordering costs, carrying costs increase as the size of the order increases. One particularly volatile component of carrying cost is the interest charge. Rising interest rates increase carrying cost and decrease the size of each order.

An example can show you why average inventory is Q/2. Assume that an organization orders and receives 500 items, and that it uses 100 each week. At the midpoint of the first week, it has 450. Figure 16-4 illustrates the number in inventory at the midpoint of each week, over a period of five weeks. Thus, an average of 250 (1,250 ÷ 5) parts is on hand over the five-week period. The average (250) also can be found by utilizing the formula Q/2, in this case, 500/2. Note, however, that the formula Q/2, as an approximation of average inventory, depends on how constant the rate of usage is.

Now assume that a production manager is attempting to solve an order quantity problem involving a component part. The yearly usage, which is constant for the part, is established as 1,000. The administrative and clerical costs of each order are $40. The manager estimates insurance and taxes to be 10 percent per year. The cost of a single part is $20. Thus, the following variables are involved: usage *(U)* = 1,000; order costs *(J)* = $40; insurance and taxes *(E)* = 10 percent; cost of the item *(V)* = $20.

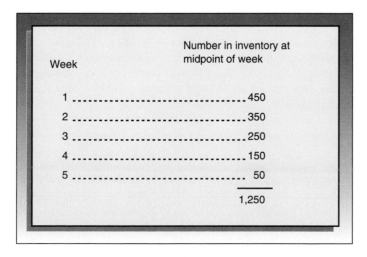

Figure 16-4
Average Inventory Analysis

Referring to Figure 16-3, you can see that the minimum total inventory cost is at the intersection of the carrying cost and the ordering cost. Total cost decreases as the size of the order increases—up to the intersection. Then it increases beyond the intersection. Thus, to solve for the point where the two lines intersect, we set the carrying cost and the ordering cost equal to each other:

$$\frac{Q}{2}(VE) = \frac{U}{Q}(J)$$

Solving for Q yields:

$$Q(VE) = \frac{2UJ}{Q}$$
$$Q^2(VE) = 2UJ$$
$$Q^2 = \frac{2UJ}{VE}$$
$$Q = \sqrt{\frac{2UJ}{VE}}$$

Economic Order Quantity (EOQ)

The final equation is commonly referred to as the *economic order quantity* (EOQ) formula and can be used to solve the inventory problem previously outlined. Using the data in the problem, you can determine the economic order quantity where $U = 1,000$, $J = \$40$, $E = 10$ percent, and $V = \$20$.

$$Q = \sqrt{\frac{2(1,000)(\$40)}{(\$20)(0.10)}}$$
$$Q = \sqrt{\frac{\$80,000}{\$2}}$$
$$Q = \sqrt{\$40,000}$$
$$Q = 200$$

The EOQ formula reveals that placing five lots of 200 each will be the least costly option.

The **EOQ model** here illustrates ordering an item in a job, lot, or batch manufacturing setting. A retail establishment, however, could also use the EOQ approach. In fact, the general approach of the model could be applied wherever an organization must purchase, or manufacture, a resource to hold in inventory.

However, in using the EOQ technique, it is important to understand the model's limitations. Perhaps the most serious shortcoming is the assumption of certainty in two of the formula's variables—unit demand (U) and cost (V). The demand for the unit is assumed to be known and constant, unchanging over a period of time. However, many factors can vary the demand for a unit, in particular the demand for the finished product of which the unit is a part. Changing economic conditions, changes in a competitor's product price, or many other circumstances can influence product demand, which can affect unit demand. The model also assumes that the price of a unit is constant. However, suppliers often provide price discounts when units are ordered in large quantities. This factor can influence inventory order decisions.

▶**EOQ model** The economic order quantity model, which is used to resolve problems regarding the size of orders. A manager concerned with minimizing inventory costs could utilize the model to study the relationships between carrying costs, ordering costs, and usage.

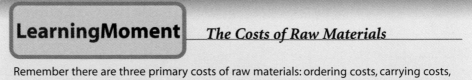

LearningMoment   *The Costs of Raw Materials*

Remember there are three primary costs of raw materials: ordering costs, carrying costs, and inventory costs. Ordering costs and carrying costs affect inventory costs in opposing ways. As carrying costs go down, ordering costs typically rise, and vice versa.

The model also assumes certainty concerning the time to order inventory. It assumes that the correct time is known. However, such problems as transportation delays and other requisition factors can vary the time required for the supplier to deliver the unit.

Just-In-Time (JIT) Manufacturing

Another approach to purchasing and inventory management that deals with the issue of timing is called **just-in-time (JIT) manufacturing.** The Toyota Motor Corporation is commonly cited as the originator of the JIT approach.[12] A JIT manufacturing approach requires that the exact quantity of raw materials, parts, and subassemblies are delivered to the part of the production process where they are needed at the precise time they are needed.[13] The JIT concept extends backward to suppliers and forward to customers. The goal is to match a firm's inputs with the production schedule that has, in turn, been timed to meet forecast market demand.

An efficient JIT system should result in low inventory and thus reduced costs due to reduced working capital. A JIT system can also save costs by reducing warehouse space that would be needed to hold inventory. Additionally, the space that would have been put to warehouse storage can be used for production, increasing the potential output for the firm.

> ▶ **just-in-time (JIT) manufacturing** An approach to inventory management designed to minimize inventory, boost plant productivity, and improve product quality.

Principles of JIT Manufacturing

When production and parts deliveries are organized on a JIT basis, quality is critical. Defective parts slow the process and defeat the purpose of the JIT system. Additionally, since JIT systems have little finished goods inventory, machine breakdowns are costly. Thus, careful attention to maintaining efficient equipment becomes a high priority. Machines must be in top working condition to fulfill the JIT demands. A top-quality repair team that can move into immediate action must be available if JIT is to work effectively. Just-in-time manufacturing is based on the following principles:[14]

Provide inventory (raw materials, work-in-process, finished goods) exactly when needed and no sooner.   Raw materials are received from suppliers just in time for use at machine A. No inventory stands waiting in materials storage. (In many plants using JIT, there is no materials storeroom; suppliers deliver materials directly to machine A.) Work-in-process inventory from machine A arrives exactly when needed at machine B, machine B's finished work is provided just in time for machine C, and so on. Finished goods inventory storage is eliminated. No inventory stands waiting anywhere for any purpose.

Eliminate safety stocks.   With this action, any problem in a machine shuts the production line down. All attention focuses on eliminating the problem. Consequently, production problems are solved more quickly.

Order materials and produce in small lots.   The precontrol of materials involves ordering in small quantities. Concurrent manufacturing control involves scheduling production in small lots. In small lot production, a unit proceeds more quickly through the production process. If machine A produces a defect in the unit, it is more quickly detected at machine B and solved before more units are wasted.

Maintain a stable production schedule.   Just-in-time manufacturing requires a continuous flowing, even, and stable production process. Concurrent production control must provide careful, advance scheduling to give suppliers sufficient notice concerning delivery times and to ensure a smooth, virtually nonstop production flow. Emergencies and expediting orders don't fit in the system.

Train employees to inspect quality while working on the product.   This action is not a core principle of JIT; however, many companies adopt the principle because this concurrent quality control is very compatible with the JIT concept.[15]

At first glance, JIT appears to pose two problems. The concept boosts setup costs because small lot production requires more setups. JIT also increases ordering costs because if materials are purchased in small quantities, more orders are required. The concept alleviates these problems with two additional principles:

Reduce setup times.   Given the greater number of setups, production downtime per setup must be reduced. Many companies have achieved reductions by finding faster ways to make machine adjustments, by altering the plant floor layout, and by making machine design changes. In the early 1970s, Toyota launched a companywide campaign to reduce setup times. One effort focused on cutting the time (one hour) required to ready 800-ton presses that form car fenders and hoods for a new lot of production. Over five years, Toyota reduced the setup time to twelve minutes. (A comparable U.S. competitor takes six hours to achieve the same setup.) Toyota is now working to achieve "single setups" (under ten minutes) and in some cases "one-touch setups" (under one minute).[16]

Reduce order costs.   This principle involves reducing the number of suppliers and focusing on developing long-term relationships with high-quality vendors. Suppliers should also be located close to the plant to reduce transport time (and thus lower order costs). Nearly 80 percent of Toyota's 220 suppliers are located within one hour of Toyota's plants.

Of course, JIT is not a perfect system. If something should go wrong in the manufacturer's supply chain, production could be slowed or even halted. A dramatic example of that occurred following the September 11, 2001, terrorist attacks in New York and Washington. Shortly after that event, Toyota came within fifteen hours of halting production of its Sequoia sport-utility vehicle in Princeton, Indiana. One of its suppliers was waiting for steering sensors normally imported from Germany, but no planes were allowed to enter the United States. Toyota, using a JIT system, had very few assemblies in the warehouse and was spared from shutting down only because the United States reopened its airways. Since then Toyota has worked with its suppliers to make sure they receive parts from *their* suppliers on time.[17]

16-5b Control of Transformation and Outputs

The transformation of raw material into finished output requires constant monitoring and control. Traditionally, organizations relied on multiple points of inspection to monitor production processes and initiate corrective measures when necessary. Note, however, that inspection locates problems only *after* they have already occurred. If a firm is producing a costly product, finding errors after they have occurred is too late.

To try to reduce errors and/or catch them before they have occurred, organizations of all types and sizes have put information technology to work to monitor production. Several systems that have evolved to help managers in the concurrent control of the production process include:

- Material Requirements Planning
- Enterprise Resource Planning
- Supply Chain Management
- Program Evaluation and Review Technique (PERT)

Each of these will be discussed briefly. For more in-depth treatment of each system, students can consult texts in operations management.

▶**materials requirements planning (MRP)** A computer-driven system for analyzing and projecting material needs and then scheduling their arrival at the right worksite at the right time in the right quantities.

Materials Requirements Planning (MRP)   **Materials requirements planning (MRP)** is a computer-driven system for analyzing and projecting materials needs and then scheduling their arrival at the right work site at the right time in the right quantities.[18] MRP works closely with the firm's master production schedule and considers such variables as lead time in ordering. MRP systems integrate a company's ordering, planning, and production scheduling to ensure optimization of resources. It also helps reduce overall IT costs by consolidating the various functions under a single application. Once available only to large firms, MRP software has been dramatically reduced in price and is now available to firms of nearly any size.[19]

MRP focuses on getting the right materials to the right place at the right time. In most cases, making "right" decisions requires a computer to handle all of the materials and components involved. The MRP computer application analyzes data from inventory, the master production schedule, and the bill of materials. The output includes inventory status, planned order timing, and changes in due dates because of rescheduling.

MRP is used in companies involved in assembly operations. Firms that produce large volumes of tools, generators, turbines, appliances, and motors are particularly attracted to MRP. It's also useful in companies that order a high number of units.

Enterprise Resource Planning (ERP)

Enterprise resource planning (ERP) software attempts to integrate all departments and functions across a company into a single computer system that can serve all those different departments' particular needs.

That integrated approach can have a tremendous payback if companies install the software correctly.[20] Take a customer order, for example. Typically, when a customer places an order, that order begins a mostly paper-based journey from in-basket to in-basket around the company, often being keyed and rekeyed into different departments' computer systems along the way. All that time spent in in-baskets causes delays and lost orders, and all the keying into different computer systems invites errors. Meanwhile, no one in the company truly knows what the status of the order is at any given point because there is no way for the finance department, for example, to get into the warehouse's computer system to see whether the item has been shipped.

ERP automates the tasks involved in performing a business process—such as order fulfillment, which involves taking an order from a customer, shipping it, and billing for it. With ERP, when a customer service representative takes an order from a customer, he or she has all the information necessary to complete the order (the customer's credit rating and order history, the company's inventory levels, and the shipping dock's trucking schedule). Everyone else in the company sees the same computer screen and has access to the single database that holds the customer's new order. When one department finishes with the order, it is automatically routed via the ERP system to the next department. To find out where the order is at any point, one need only log into the ERP system and track it down. With luck, the order process moves smoothly through the organization, and customers get their orders faster and with fewer errors than before. ERP can apply that same magic to the other major business processes, such as employee benefits or financial reporting.

Companies undertake ERP for three major reasons:

1. *To integrate financial data*—As managers try to understand the company's overall performance, they may find many different versions of the truth. Finance has its own set of revenue numbers, sales has another version, and the different business units may each have their own versions of how much they contributed to revenues. ERP creates a single version of the truth that cannot be questioned because everyone is using the same system.

2. *To standardize manufacturing processes*—Manufacturing companies, especially those with an appetite for mergers and acquisitions, often find that multiple business units across the company make the same widget using different methods and computer systems. Standardizing those processes and using a single, integrated computer system can save time, increase productivity, and reduce headcount.

3. *To standardize HR information*—Especially in companies with multiple business units, HR may not have a unified, simple method for tracking employee time and communicating with them about benefits and services. ERP can fix that.[21]

The Management Focus on Globalization box highlights Ansett Aircraft, a global supplier of parts to leading aircraft manufacturers, including Boeing and Airbus. Ansett was able to streamline its data processing and transaction tracking through implementation of a system-wide ERP software solution. Installing and implementing an ERP system is a complex and lengthy process. Even small firms can take twelve to fourteen months to fully install and debug an ERP system. Tales of troubled ERP installations are common. All the major ERP players, including *Baan, J.D. Edwards & Co., Oracle Corp., PeopleSoft,* and *SAP,* have at one time played the villain in the familiar story of troubled ERP installations. But the situation is looking up. In May 2001, Boston-based *AMR Research* predicted that total ERP company revenues will grow at a 14 percent compounded annual growth rate, improving to $36 billion in 2005 from $21 billion in 2001.[22]

> **enterprise resource planning (ERP)** Software that attempts to integrate all departments and functions across a company into a single computer system.

Management Focus on Globalization

Global Aircraft Parts Firms Integrates Disparate Systems Through ERP

Ansett Aircraft Spares and Services, an Australia-based product support company, services the commercial aviation community and has additional offices in the U.S. and the U.K. It generates revenue based on the number of quotes it can distribute for airplane parts each day. Ansett was losing a significant amount of money due to a wide range of parts indexing errors. The international company grew more rapidly than its current solution allowed. Ansett's IT systems consisted of one that managed inventory, sales, purchasing, and quoting, and another that managed invoicing. It needed a solution to bridge the gap.

The company elected to use a solution called Quantum Control *ERP* to bring everything in line. With more than eighteen modules, this *ERP* solution automated all aspects of the parts trading and repair process including inventory control, quoting, order processing, work orders, and accounting. Integrating the Quantum Control *ERP* system allowed Ansett to retain previous transaction histories, use current data maintained in the system, and launch new reporting features. The solution also brought into sync its *global* offices that were all running different solutions.

"The management is much easier," said Aren Gedikian, Ansett's systems support manager. "Other countries and other currencies can now use a single database, based in the United States, and connected using a mainframe." An *ERP* system will not only manage complex business processes to improve profitability, increase productivity, and allow a company to run more efficiently, but *ERP* will also bring together a company's *global* assets and ensure financials that span the time zones remain accurate and accessible.

Source: Adapted from Jennifer Jaroneczyk, "ERP Streamlines Global Finances," *Internet World,* September 2002, pp. 22–24.

Supply Chain Management (SCM)   All management theories and approaches evolve over time to meet changing competitive demands and to take advantage of emerging technologies. As more and more companies have been using computers, and as computers have become networked into vast communication systems, new capacities for managing production and operations have evolved. Today, organizations have linked their entire enterprise into a single information system. As a sale is made on the downstream side of the organization, information about that sale is transmitted upstream to pull new production through the system.

> **supply chain management (SCM)** A company's efforts to organize and control its acquisition and handling of raw materials and other supplies needed for operations.

Supply chain management (SCM) seeks to optimize the links between suppliers, manufacturing, distribution, and customers.[23] It's a technique that is especially important to build to order firms.[24] A *supply chain* is a network of facilities and distribution options that performs the functions of procurement of materials, transformation of these materials into intermediate and finished products, and the distribution of these finished products to customers. Supply chains exist in both service and manufacturing organizations, although the complexity of the chain may vary greatly from industry to industry and firm to firm. Most supply chains exhibit these basic characteristics:[25]

- The supply chain includes all activities and processes to supply a product or service to a final customer.
- Any number of companies can be linked in the supply chain.
- A customer can be a supplier to another customer so the total chain can have a number of supplier–customer relationships.
- While the distribution system can be direct from supplier to customer, depending on the products and markets, it can contain a number of distributors such as wholesalers, warehouses, and retailers.
- Products or services usually flow from supplier to customer. Likewise, design and demand information usually flows from customer to supplier. (Physical products move "downstream," while demand information flows "upstream.")

Traditionally, marketing, distribution, planning, manufacturing, and the purchasing organizations along the supply chain operated independently. These divisions within organizations have their own objectives, and these are often conflicting. Marketing's objectives of high customer service and maximum sales dollars conflict with manufacturing and

Management Focus on Technology

Caterpillar Links Suppliers to SCM System

Caterpillar launched a major supply chain management manufacturing collaboration initiative, with the realization that the project would require as much focus on new middleware as on the SCM business-to-business software. The multinational maker of construction and mining equipment, natural gas and diesel engines, and industrial gas turbines plans to use Dallas-based i2 Technologies' supply chain applications to share information with its suppliers as part of an effort to reduce inventories and shorten manufacturing times.

But Michael Hackerson, director of e-business at Caterpillar, said the most rigorous work will involve tying hundreds of suppliers into the new system. "You need a lot of middleware and hardware to link these companies together," Hackerson said. "Everyone's working on different systems, and you can't assume any of them can just plug into what we're building."

That's where IBM enters the equation. Its professional services division is being brought into the Caterpillar project to handle systems integration. In Caterpillar's case, middleware functions will be handled by IBM's WebSphere application server.

Caterpillar launched its SCM initiative in 2001, and executives at the company said they believe that the integration work was a necessary precursor to lowering its manufacturing costs. "We've already knocked down the prices we pay to our suppliers as much as possible," Hackerson said. "We've got to come up with a better way of doing business for both sides if we want to eliminate costs down the road."

Source: Adapted from Michael Meehan, "Caterpillar to Link Suppliers," *Computerworld,* September 17, 2001, pp. 2–6.

distribution goals. Many manufacturing operations are designed to maximize throughput and lower costs with little consideration for the impact on inventory levels and distribution capabilities. Purchasing contracts are often negotiated with very little information beyond historical buying patterns. The result of these factors is that there is not a single, integrated plan for the organization—there are as many plans as businesses. Clearly, a mechanism is needed through which these different functions can be integrated together. SCM is a strategy whereby such integration can be achieved.

SCM is typically viewed to lie between fully vertically integrated firms, where the entire material flow is owned by a single firm, and those where each channel member operates independently. Therefore, coordination between the various players in the chain is key in its effective management.

A wide variety of enterprise-wide software solutions have been developed to assist firms in their supply chain management. Supply chain management software solutions (such as *Manugistics, i2,* and *Logility*) coexist with, but are not the same as, ERP software solutions. ERP software generally encompasses all aspects of the business—order entry, distribution, procurement, production, logistics, inventory, and finance. The primary purpose of an ERP system is to control the flow and execution of transactional information across the supply chain. The Management Focus on Technology box, "Caterpillar Links Suppliers to SCM System," discusses the case of Caterpillar, a large industrial machinery manufacturer, attempting to control costs through an SCM application.

Supply chain management systems provide decision support for those decisions that must be made *prior* to execution. In essence, it performs the planning required to allow ERP systems to execute the plan. For superior competitive advantage, companies must implement a "closed-loop" SCM system that interacts with its ERP system. In a closed loop, the ERP system includes operational data (inventory movement, customer orders), tactical planning tools, and strategic planning tools brought together into a fully integrated environment. This environment must also be able to adapt to the ever-changing needs of the company. What is the bottom line? SCM is focused on planning and ERP is focused on execution.

There are problems with the new software tools. Research from the *Standish Group International,* for example, has shown that up to 90 percent of software projects take more time to implement than expected. Other critics say the complexity and rigidity of the software often causes project delays and failures. Problems also arise when a company has to adapt to the software's way of doing business, rather than the other way around.[26]

Program Evaluation and Review Technique (PERT)   Operations decisions based on concurrent control methods determine how much and when outputs will be produced. These decisions typically are termed *production scheduling*.

Managers can use network-scheduling models to combine and schedule resources or to control activities so plans are carried out as stated. Such models are especially suited for, but not restricted to, nonroutine projects, which are conducted a few times at most. In such projects, some type of coordination is needed to ensure that priority tasks are completed on time. Also needed is an approximation of how long the entire project will take. In summary, some method is needed to avoid unnecessary conflicts and delays. It should help keep track of all the events and activities on a specific project—and their interrelationships. Network models provide the means to achieve these goals. One widely used network model is the **Program Evaluation and Review Technique (PERT)**.

PERT (and its variations) probably is one of the most widely used production management methods. After the Special Projects Office of the U.S. Navy introduced it on the Polaris missile project in 1958, PERT was widely credited with helping to reduce by two years the time for the completion of the missile's engineering and development programs. By identifying the longest path through all of the necessary project tasks, PERT enabled the program managers to concentrate their efforts on these tasks, since they affected vitally the total project time. Today, almost every major government military agency involved in the space program utilizes PERT and other network models in planning and controlling their work on government contracts.

The aerospace business faces peculiar problems, but one-of-a-kind development work is an important element in many other kinds of organizations and industries as well. In addition to helping develop space vehicles and put astronauts on the moon, PERT also has been utilized successfully in:

- Constructing new plants, buildings, and hospitals
- Designing new automobiles
- Coordinating the numerous activities (production, marketing, etc.) involved in introducing new products
- Planning sales campaigns
- Planning logistic and distribution systems
- Coordinating the installation of large-scale computer systems
- Coordinating ship construction and aircraft repairs

Beyond its engineering applications, PERT also has been used successfully in coordinating the numerous activities necessary to complete mergers between large organizations. It has assisted economic planning in underdeveloped countries, and in small applications has helped coordinate and plan all the tasks necessary to organize large-scale conventions and meetings.

PERT networks are developed around two key concepts: activities and events. An **activity** is the work necessary to complete a particular event. An **event** is an accomplishment at a particular point in time. In PERT networks, an event is designated by a circle, and an activity is designated by an arrow connecting two circles. This is shown in Figure 16-5.

In Figure 16-5, two events are connected by one activity. The events are assigned numbers, and the activity is designated with an arrow. Each of the two events occurs at a specific point in time. Event 1 could represent "project begun," and Event 2 could represent

---

▶ Program Evaluation and Review Technique (PERT) A network management model that enables managers to focus on all necessary project tasks.

▶ activity The work necessary to complete a particular event in a PERT network that consumes time, which is the paramount variable in a PERT system. In PERT networks, three time estimates are used for each activity: an optimistic time, a pessimistic time, and a most likely time.

▶ event An accomplishment at a particular point in time in a PERT network; consumes no time.

Figure 16-5
The Basic Elements of a Simple PERT Network

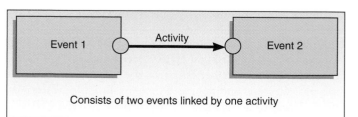

Event 1 — Activity → Event 2

Consists of two events linked by one activity

"project completed." The arrow connecting the two events, meanwhile, represents the activity—the actual work done—and the time necessary to complete it. Thus, the two events in Figure 16-5 designate the beginning and the end of the activity. The activity takes the time, not the event.

In constructing a PERT network, events and activities must be identified with enough precision that the manager can monitor accomplishments as the project proceeds. Four basic phases are needed when constructing a PERT network:

1. Define each activity to be done
2. Estimate how long each activity will take
3. Construct the network
4. Find the critical path—that is, the longest path in time—from the beginning event to the ending event

All events and activities must be sequenced in the network under a strict set of logical rules (e.g., no event can be considered complete until all preceding events have been completed). The rules should allow for the determination of the critical path.

The paramount variable in a PERT network is time—the basic measure of how long a project will take. Estimating the time each activity requires can be extremely difficult, however, since managers may not have similar experiences to compare.

Estimating activity time requirements is a technique for dealing specifically with uncertainty in making the job estimates. For example, assume you are trying to estimate how long it will take you to complete a term project for your management class. You know that one activity will be to collect certain information. If all goes well and you do not encounter any obstacles, you believe you can complete this activity in eight weeks. However, if you encounter obstacles (dates, parties, illness, materials not available in the library), the chances are greater that this activity will take much longer. Thus, you can estimate a variety of potential completion times for this part of your term project.

For projects using PERT, *three time estimates are required for each activity.* Each time estimate should be made by the individual or group most closely connected with, and responsible for, the particular activity. The following three estimates are needed:

1. *Optimistic Time (a).*   This is the time in which the project can be completed if everything goes exceptionally well and no obstacles or problems are encountered.
2. *Most Likely Time (m).*   This is the most realistic estimate of how long an activity might take. It is the average time you would expect to take if the activity were repeated often.
3. *Pessimistic Time (b).*   This is the time that would be required if everything went wrong and numerous obstacles and problems were encountered.

A PERT network of eight events is depicted in Figure 16-6. The three time estimates for each activity also are indicated.

Obviously, it would be extremely difficult to deal simultaneously with the optimistic time, the most likely time, and the pessimistic time. Fortunately, a method has been developed to arrive at one time estimate. An *expected time* (t_e), can be estimated satisfactorily for each activity by using the formula shown in Figure 16-7.

Figure 16-6
Expected Time (t_e)
for Each Activity

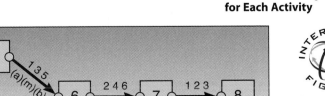

Figure 16-7
Expected Time Formula

$$t_e = \frac{a + 4m + b}{6}$$

a = Optimistic time

This is the time in which the project can be completed if everything goes exceptionally well and no obstacles or problems are encountered.

m = Most likely time

This is the most realistic estimate of how long an activity might take. It is the average time you would expect to take if the activity were repeated often.

b = Pessimistic time

This is the time that would be required if everything went wrong and numerous obstacles and problems were encountered. A PERT network of eight events is depicted in Figure 16-6. The three time estimates for each activity also are indicated.

Figure 16-8 depicts the network outlined in Figure 16-6 after the expected time (t_e) has been calculated for each activity. The sequence along the path 1, 2, 3, 5, 6, 7, 8 takes seventeen weeks, while the sequence along the path 1, 2, 4, 6, 7, 8 takes sixteen weeks. The critical path, then, is the one that takes the longest time (seventeen weeks).

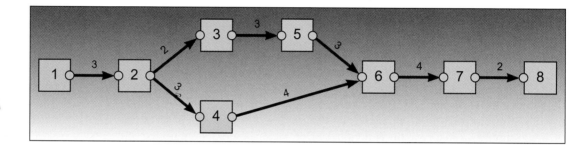

Figure 16-8
PERT Network

A major advantage of PERT is that the planning involved in constructing the network contributes significantly to the concurrent control of the project. The construction of the network is a very demanding but beneficial task that forces the manager to visualize the number and kinds of necessary activities and their sequences.

Final Thoughts on the Importance of Control   In this post-millennium economy, where corporate trust has eroded and people are unsure what to think about a firm's public comments about profits and losses, it's vital for managers to be informed about control. Not every manager needs to be an accounting or finance major, but they should know good numbers from bad and be prepared to stand behind them. Recently, the U.S. Securities and Exchange Commission has ordered corporate CEO's to "certify" the financial statements they release to the public. This is in response to the wave of accounting and corporate finance scandals that have affected firms such as Enron, WorldCom, and Tyco.

A working knowledge of control should also include understanding of technology innovations such as supply chain management (SCM) and enterprise resource planning (ERP). When well used, such innovations can greatly improve the operations and cost structure of a firm. However, when badly used and/or implemented, such innovations can lead to increased costs, headaches, and might even lead to a manager's dismissal.

As an aspiring manager you will need to develop working knowledge of each of these important areas of control. While you will not be able to do accounting or auditing as well as a CPA, you must be able to know a good CPA from a bad one. To be successful in your career as a manager, you will also need to stay in touch with developments in organizational control. New technologies, process improvements, and new managerial techniques are constantly arising and providing advantages to those who use them well.

Management Summary

- Effectively used, PERT can be a valuable control device. It provides time schedules for each activity and permits networks to be revised if unforeseen difficulties occur. Resources can be shifted, and activities can be rescheduled with a minimum of delay in the completion of the project.

- Effective control of production operations and financial resources requires an appropriate mix of precontrol, concurrent control, and postcontrol methods and policies.

- Production-operations control requires methods, procedures, and policies for the input, transformation, and output elements of production.

- Concurrent control in production-operations management is fundamentally a scheduling problem. Managers can use network and linear programming models to schedule the allocation of resources to different outputs.

- Just-in-time inventory management combines precontrol and concurrent control activities to minimize inventory and boost product quality, plant capacity, and productivity.

- Precontrol of financial resources is implemented through budgets, which specify standard levels for expense categories and organizational units.

- Concurrent control of financial resources depends on effective internal control procedures and policies.

Key Terms

activity (p. 400)

carrying costs (p. 392)

cellular organization (p. 389)

enterprise resource planning (ERP) (p. 397)

EOQ model (p. 394)

event (p. 400)

just-in-time (JIT) manufacturing (p. 395)

manufacturing (p. 387)

materials requirements planning (MRP) (p. 396)

operations (p. 387)

ordering cost (p. 392)

process manufacturing (p. 390)

production (p. 386)

Program Evaluation and Review Technique (PERT) (p. 400)

project manufacturing (p. 390)

supply chain management (SCM) (p. 398)

Review and Discussion Questions

1. Describe the financial and production-operations control system you would set up if you were the manager of a fast-food establishment. Be as specific as possible.

2. Discuss the differences between precontrol of capital equipment and precontrol of materials. Your answer should take into account the differences in setting standards, obtaining information, and taking corrective action.

3. Describe how you would determine whether a firm has an adequate internal control system for sales, cash, and accounts receivable.

4. The EOQ model is a useful technique for controlling the quantity of materials purchased. Explain how the model could be used to control the quantity of materials to be manufactured.

5. Given the limitations of the EOQ model, how should the model best be used in precontrolling an organization's materials?

6. Some observers assert that JIT inventory management simply won't work in some manufacturing organizations. Provide an example of an organization that would support their contention.

7. Are the principles of JIT applicable in service organizations? Explain.

8. Supply chain management has become an important consideration in the management of manufacturing operations. How do you think the principles and methods of SCM can be applied to a retail operation? A service business?

9. Enterprise resource planning (ERP) software such as SAP has had a tremendous impact on organizational control. What are the strengths and weaknesses of such systems? Discuss. Use the Internet to find articles on this issue.

10. Why is production scheduling fundamentally a problem of resource allocation?

Practice Quiz

Note: You can find the correct answers to these questions by taking the quiz and then submitting your answers in the Online Edition. The program will automatically score your submission. If you miss a question, the program will provide the correct answer, a rationale for the answer, and the section number in the chapter where the topic is discussed.

Indicate whether the sentence or statement is true or false.

_____ 1. Companies with a cellular organization tend to have much smaller staffs overall.

_____ 2. Some site choices may be based on the overriding advantages of a single factor, such as availability of labor or market, or the low cost of land.

_____ 3. Carry costs are incurred each time material is ordered from a supplier.

_____ 4. An efficient just-in-time system should result in low inventory.

_____ 5. Production managers may act as liaisons between executives and first-line supervisors.

_____ 6. Training employees to inspect quality while working on the product is a core principle of JIT.

Identify the letter of the choice that best completes the statement or answers the question.

_____ 7. Which of the following is NOT one of the three basic processes of production and operations?
   a. input
   b. output
   c. negotiation
   d. transformation

_____ 8. Just as it dictates the kind and location of facility, the type of business will determine the _____ of the selected site.
   a. layout
   b. price
   c. elevation
   d. neighbors

_____ 9. _____ parts slow the production process and defeat the purpose of the JIT system.
   a. Quality
   b. An oversupply of
   c. A shortage of
   d. Defective

_____ 10. When laying out a site plan, the manager should consider all of the following EXCEPT: _____ .
   a. square footage needs.
   b. storage needs.
   c. length of lease.
   d. shipping needs.

_____ 11. _____ refers to the physical process of producing goods.
   a. Production
   b. Operations
   c. Manufacturing
   d. Assembly

_____ 12. When workers are grouped together to complete the entire manufacture or assembly of a product the company is likely using a _____ form of organization.
   a. cellular
   b. intermittent
   c. continuous
   d. analytic

_____ 13. Which of the following is an example of an ordering cost?
   a. storage space
   b. inventory costs
   c. carrying costs
   d. placing materials into inventory

_____ 14. The software system that enables companies better to control processes from vendor management, to receiving, to outbound logistics is known as _____.
   a. enterprise resource planning.
   b. materials requirements planning.
   c. supply chain management.
   d. value chain management.

_____ 15. An approach for managing and controlling the time involved in the various operating activities of an organization is known as _____.
   a. value chain management.
   b. program evaluation and review technique.
   c. materials requirements planning.
   d. enterprise resource planning.

Case Study

Grocer Uses Supply Chain Management to Manage Inventory and Reduce Costs

For a closer look at the day-to-day challenges grocers face in operating their supply chains, all you need to do is examine the watercress. "Watercress has a shelf life of only one day," observed Diane Carter, director of supply chain operations of British grocer J. Sainsbury. "We have a number of items like that. Some have a shelf life that's measured in hours. As you can imagine, with a setting window as narrow as that, we can't afford to overstock. Our planning, forecasting, and logistics must be as efficient as possible," she said. Carter and company CIO Margaret Miller described Sainsbury's ongoing supply chain upgrade.

Sainsbury had several goals in its supply chain initiative. Improving inventory visibility was one of them. The origins of Sainsbury's supply chain initiative lie in a six-point transformation plan the grocer hatched in 2002. Among these points were the delivery of operational excellence, simplification of the business, and improvement of the customer-service offering.

Sainsbury quickly discovered that its existing IT systems would not support these goals. Many systems were antiquated or disparate. As an example of the grocer's IT inefficiency at the time, Miller cited the chain's point of sale (POS) system: "It was supported by 13 different platforms, including 'every flavor' of Unix, and some home-grown applications. Ninety-five percent of our IT budget was spent on just keeping the lights on," Miller said. "With that kind of a burden, we couldn't move aggressively, or improve cost efficiency."

The IT overhaul Sainsbury would undertake would be divided between three areas: Fifty percent of upgrade spending would go toward store systems. Another 30 percent would be spent on IT infrastructure, and the remaining 20 percent was earmarked for the supply chain. "Our strategy was to improve these areas with the aid of a small number of proven, strategic partners," Miller said.

Sainsbury brought Accenture on board to help, and addressed its POS woes with a new platform from Retalix. Over thirteen months, the grocer rolled the platform out to 14,000 units and trained 100,000 employees to use it. The POS deployment was spurred by more than a desire to cut costs. Miller explained that the upgrade also served to enhance Sainsbury's ability to collect transaction information, upon which all of its soon-to-be-upgraded forecasting engines would rely. Sainsbury also took pains to cleanse the transaction data it already had, added Carter. "It's the old computing proverb: Garbage in, garbage out," she said. "Gaps in sales history produce gaps in forecasting. We wanted our new forecasting engines to have the best fuel possible."

Much of that forecasting ability would come in the form of Retek's Advanced Inventory Planning (AIP) suite, which includes Retek Demand Forecasting (RDF) and Store Replenishment Planning (SRP). Those solutions went into place in 2003. Today, those solutions help Sainsbury manage nearly all 10 million of its stocking points. Furthermore, the grocer coupled those solutions with Retek Store Systems, which improves Sainsbury's visibility into its store-level item-level, in-stock positions.

"RDF is a robust product and a good fit for us," Carter said. "Within a week of going live with it, it was generating daily forecasts with custom alerts." The solution provides Sainsbury with a daily store/SKU-level order plan thirty-five days in advance, and weekly order plans forty weeks ahead. According to Carter, "The benefits were huge. We gave ourselves a clear visibility of demand, an ability to view and amend inventory data at multiple levels, even down to the SKU/store level."

Sainsbury also avails itself of the solution's promotional forecasting capabilities. Those are especially potent in Sainsbury's case, since so much rides on promotions. To illustrate, Carter noted that at Sainsbury, promotions drove up the sales of one particular brand of wine from its average of 500 cases per week to 128,000 cases per week.

Miller said that Sainsbury's implementation of the Retek solutions dramatically improved its on-shelf availability and produced annual cost savings upward of $100 million. To help Sainsbury act upon the forecasts produced, the grocer went live with the Retek Merchandising System in May 2003. The solution helps the grocer purchase more than 40,000 SKUs from its 2,400-plus suppliers, and manage Sainsbury's relationships with them. An integration with the British product data registry UDEX ensures that the solution works with accurate and up-to-date item information. The solution led to savings of $25 million, Miller said.

Sainsbury still isn't done upgrading. The grocer plans to implement Retek's Warehouse Inbound Planning (WIP) and Warehouse Replenishment Planning (WRP). Miller and Carter believe that those solutions will improve its control and visibility over its warehouse operations as the other solutions did for Sainsbury's store level. "Realistically, we can't implement those solutions until 2005 because they are still under development," Carter said.

Questions for Discussion

1. How does the shelf life of products affect a retailer's supply chain strategy? Explain.

2. Does a consumer electronics retailer have the same type of supply chain challenges as a grocer that features watercress? Explain the differences.

3. What role does information technology play in supply chain management for Sainsbury? Why does Sainsbury collect transactional information at the point of sale?

Sources: Adapted from Dan Scheraga, "Sainsbury's Supply Chain Gets Smarter," *Chain Store Age*, July 2004, pp. 30A–31A; Harry Yeates, "Cashing in on Electronic Labels," *Electronics Weekly*, November 10, 2004, p. 26; and Laura Rohde, "Sainsbury, Accenture to Redo Outsourcing Contract," *Computerworld*, October 25, 2004, p. 5.

Internet Exercise

Visit the ERP Research Center

Enterprise research planning (ERP) has become a major investment for firms of many sizes. The goal of ERP is to integrate a firm's entire supply chain to weed out inefficiencies and maximize productivity. While that is the purported goal of ERP, that ideal is not always realized.

Students of management don't have to be experts in ERP. Typically that role will be reserved for chief information officers (CIOs) or IT directors. Still, it's useful for managers at all levels to be aware of the strengths and limitations of ERP.

The following website is part of the *CIO Magazine's* list of online research centers.

http://www.cio.com/research/erp/edit/erpbasics.html

Students should visit the site outside of class with the following issues in mind. They should return to class and be prepared to discuss the issues.

1. What is ERP? What are its strengths? What are its limitations?

2. What types of companies can benefit from an ERP system?

3. What considerations must managers keep in mind when evaluating ERP systems from competing vendors?

4. What are the specific costs involved in implementing an ERP system? What types of "hidden costs" might also be part of implementing an ERP system?

5. What should managers do to make sure an ERP system is effective in their organization? How should managers introduce the system to employees?

6. How can managers "sell" the investment in an ERP system to top executives?

These questions will require the students to think beyond the material available at the website. Instructors should be sure to inform students that they will need to recall other things they've learned about effective planning, organizing, leading, and controlling to successfully answer the questions.

Experiential Exercise

A Strategic Control Decision Task

The plant manager of a major electronics manufacturer called a meeting with his immediate subordinates to discuss a major strategic control decision. The issue to be resolved concerned whether to go into the full-scale production and marketing of a new product, a miniature thermostat. The miniature thermostat, MT, had been under development for the past three years, and the manager believed that it was time to make a decision. The meeting was to be attended by the marketing manager, the production superintendent, the purchasing manager, and the plant cost accountant. The plant manager instructed each official to bring appropriate information and to be prepared to make a final decision regarding the MT.

Prior to the meeting, the plant manager noted the following facts concerning the MT:

1. Developmental efforts had been undertaken three years ago in response to the introduction of a similar product by a major competitor.

2. Initial manufacturing studies had indicated that much of the technology and know-how to produce the MT already existed in the plant and its workforce.

3. A prototype model had been approved by Underwriters' Laboratories.

4. A pilot production line had been designed and installed. Several thousand thermostats already had been produced and tested.

5. Market projections indicated that a trend toward miniaturization of such components as thermostats was likely to continue.

6. The competitor who had introduced the product was marketing it successfully at a price of $0.80 each.

7. The cost estimates derived by the cost accountant over the past two years consistently indicated that the firm could not meet the competitor's price and at the same time follow its standard markup of 14 percent of the selling price.

Because of his concern for the cost of the MT, the plant manager asked the cost accountant to brief the group at the outset of its meeting. The accountant's data are shown in the following table.

The accountant noted for the group that the firm would not be able to manufacture and sell the MT for less than $0.805 each, given

the present actual costs. In fact, meeting its markup objective would require a selling price of approximately $0.94 each, but that would be impossible, since the competitor was selling the same product for $0.80. She explained that if the MT could be manufactured at standard costs, it could compete successfully with the competitor's thermostat. She said that the company should abandon the MT if it could not be made at standard costs.

The marketing manager stated that the MT was an important product and that it was critical for the firm to have an entry in the market. He said that in a few years the MT would be used by all of the company's major customers and that the competition had already moved into the area with a strong sales program. He added that he did not place too much reliance on the cost estimates, because the plant had had so little experience with full-scale production of the MT and that, in any case, standard costs, though appropriate for cost containment, were inappropriate for decisions of this type.

The manufacturing superintendent stated that he was working with engineers to develop a new method for welding contacts and that if it proved successful, the direct labor cost would be reduced significantly. This would have a cumulative effect on costs, since overhead, spoilage, and selling and administrative expenses were based on direct labor. He also believed that with a little more experience, the workers could reach standard times on the assembly operations. He said that much progress in this direction had been made in the past four weeks.

The purchasing manager stated that material costs were high because the plant had not procured materials in sufficient quantities. She said that with full-scale production, material costs should decrease to standard.

Questions for Discussion

1. If you were the plant manager, what decision would you make regarding the MT?

2. If you decided to manufacture the MT, would your decision indicate that the standard of 14 percent markup was not valid?

3. Trace the relationships between precontrol, concurrent control, and postcontrol as revealed by the facts of the case.

	Actual Standard Costs	Costs
Direct labor	$0.059	$0.052
Direct material	0.340	0.194
Manufactured overhead (386% of standard direct labor)	0.228	0.228
Total manufacturing cost	$0.627	$0.474
Spoilage (10%)	0.063	0.047
Selling and administrative costs (40% of direct labor and overhead)	0.115	0.112
Total cost per MT	$0.805	$0.633
Required price to achieve 14% markup on selling price	$0.936	$0.736

Part **6**

**Managing
Change
and Innovation**

17 **Organizational Change
and Learning**

Nothing is more certain in modern organizations than that they will face change and need to change. The global economy has wrought extensive changes in competition, markets, and internal controls. Information technology is placing new demands on managers, workers, and executives. No one in the organization can be effective today without being familiar with networking technologies and the information and communication advantages they entail.

The final chapter (17) examines the need for organizational change and learning, common barriers to change and learning, and ways managers can break through those barriers. Change and learning are difficult for everyone. Managers have searched in vain for decades for the magic elixir that will ensure smooth and rapid implementation of their plans. The magic elixir doesn't exist. However, different tools and techniques for managing change will work in certain contexts. Modern managers must learn to diagnose the context and determine which tools may be most effective for managing change within that context.

Organizational Change and Learning

17

Managing Today

Successful Companies Adjust to Change

Managing change is one of the most difficult challenges that business organizations face today. Change is everywhere, it is inevitable, and dealing successfully with it is critical to an organization's success.

Change management is defined as the continuous process of aligning an organization with its marketplace—and doing it more responsively and effectively than competitors. For an organization to be aligned, the key management levers—strategy, operations, culture, and reward—must be synchronized continuously. Since change is an inevitable, ongoing process, these management levers must also be constantly altered.

Managing change includes identifying the destabilizing forces, determining your alignment in the market, electing the appropriate methods to use, creating the most effective change strategy, and applying them with the most accurate maneuvers. Managers, including managers of change, need to remember that they are changing and rearranging a variety of both human and nonhuman elements. Because change must be done thoughtfully and carefully, the preparation of a specific change management process can instruct an organization in the proper execution of change.

In the workplace, many significant changes are related to the implementation of new technologies: virtual teams, nonterritorial offices, mobile computing, EDI, e-mail; the noise about virtual this and virtual that gets louder every day, and more confusing as well. What are companies doing to get the kinks out of cyberspace? The following is a look at how a few companies are successfully "pushing the envelope" when it comes to cyberissues.

Buddy Up

It can get lonely in cyberspace. American Express, concerned that losing the "bullpen" atmosphere of the traditional sales office would affect sales, implemented a planned communications program using a "buddy system" as its centerpiece. In addition to regularly scheduled social/business cocktail parties, employees would buddy up with assigned personnel for electronic "schmooze sessions." Somewhat akin to the practice of gathering around the water cooler, these buddies talk openly via e-mail about business or personal matters, no matter which office or city they're working in.

Student Union

The ad agency Chiat/Day decided to design an in-house "student union" to bring together cyberemployees. A pioneer in nonterritorial workspace, Chiat/Day has team rooms in its New York office where people can work on long-term projects. It also has floating rooms for short-term projects. Workers can send e-mail from kiosklike computers scattered throughout the office or from unassigned office space, or from home. The student union is their water cooler; it allows electronically connected team players to stay socially connected not only to each other but to the company as well.

A Bulletproof System

Companies such as AT&T and Delta Consulting use what managers call "bulletproofing" to protect hardware and software operations. Bulletproofing can substantially minimize the amount of downtime or lost work from equipment or software failures, especially for remote workers who usually don't have access to alternate systems or machinery. To help these remote workers, companies are taking extra steps to scrutinize hardware and software for reliability and are using only well established, proven programs and hardware. Experts suggest that managers wait to upgrade to new versions until all the bugs have been worked out and reliability has been established.

Wireless Connections

Dallas-based Wyndham International Hotel provides wireless access to the hotel for frequent guests. The connection allows customers to book rooms, manage their accounts using wireless devices, and receive the latest on special services, discounts, and events.

Sources: Adapted from Stanley Slaughter, "Change Management," *Business Travel World,* November 2004, pp. 31–32; Robert Wasson, "Five Steps to Effective Change Management," *Engineering Management,* February/March 2004, pp. 14–15; "Quick Change Artists," *CIO* Magazine, August 2001; Dale G. Lake, "Making Change Happen One Person at a Time," *Human Resource Management,* Spring 2001, p. 89; Joanne Cole, "Pushing the Envelope in Cyberspace," *Getting Results... For the Hands-On Manager,* October 1997, p. 3; and Lisa M. Kudray and Brian H. Kleiner, "Global Trends in Managing Change," *Industrial Management,* May/June 1997, pp. 18–20.

▶**organizational change** The intentional attempt by management to improve the overall performance of individuals, groups, and the organization as a whole by altering the organization's structure, behavior, and technology.

This chapter explores the processes of **organizational change** and learning. The growing realization that organizations can become more effective through managerial applications of behavioral science has spawned a wealth of literature.[1] To provide a theme, the material is presented in terms of a model describing the important factors of the development process. For simplicity, the phrase the **management of change** is used to include the concept of organizational development in its broadest sense.

Change management is part science and part art.[2] The science part comes from knowing what techniques to apply to create effective, lasting, organizational change. The art part comes from knowing which technique to use in which situation. As the Managing Today opening vignette highlights, different organizations have used a variety of technologies to improve their effectiveness. They decided that changes in technology were worth the hard work.

> **management of change**
> (see p. 410) The concept of organizational development in its broadest sense.

Managers and organizations no longer have a choice. They must change and learn to compete, earn a profit, and survive. As will be revealed, managing and leading change is especially complex and difficult. Behavioral, emotional, organizational, time, resource, and historical factors can all be a part of the change process. Peter Senge, a recognized leader in introducing the concept of learning organizations, states:

> When I look at efforts to create change in big companies over the past 10 years, I have to say that change is possible—and enough evidence of failure to say that it isn't likely.[3]

Senge's comment reveals that change is a challenging job to say the least. How managers and leaders navigate this difficult endeavor can be improved if the concepts of change, resistance to change, strategies for change, and creating a learning organization are understood and appreciated.

17-1 A Model for Managing Change

The management of change is a systematic process that can be broken down into sub-processes, or steps. Figure 17-1 summarizes this process. It consists of seven steps linked in a logical sequence. A manager should consider each of these steps, either explicitly or implicitly, when undertaking a change program. The prospects for success are enhanced if each successive step is taken explicitly and formally.

In describing alternative change techniques and strategies, a number of strategies can be considered for adoption. No one change technique or change strategy can be thought of as superior and suitable for every situation.

Knowledgeable managers recognize the array of alternatives and are not committed to one particular approach to the exclusion of all others. At the same time, the effective manager avoids the pitfalls of stagnation. Thus, the management of change implies that the manager should adopt a flexible, forward-looking stance. Such a stance is essential in the change process outlined in Figure 17-1. Each step of the process is discussed in this chapter.

Note the change process in Figure 17-1 is a *continuous* process. It's a cycle that feeds back information; information that can be used for additional change and improvement. Once change is implemented it should be carefully monitored so that real time adaptations and improvements can be made. The failure to monitor change, unfortunately, is often bypassed in many organizations. As a result, little is known about the impact of the change on individual, team, and organizational performance variables.

17-2 Forces for Change

There are two types of forces for change: **external change forces** and **internal change forces.** The *external* forces are change in the marketplace, the technology, and the environment; these usually are beyond the control of the manager. *Internal* forces operate within the firm and to some extent can be controlled by managers.

> **external change forces**
> Forces for change outside the organization, such as the pricing strategies of competitors, the available supply of resources, and government regulations.

17-2a External Forces

Managers of business firms must respond to changes in the *marketplace,* the first external force for change. Competitors introduce new products, increase advertising, reduce prices, or improve customer service. In each case, a response is required, unless a manager is content to permit the erosion of profit and market share. Customer tastes and incomes also change. The firm's products may no longer have customer appeal. Or customers may become able to purchase more expensive, higher-quality forms of the same products. There is also an increasingly diverse customer population with many different tastes, needs, and preferences.

> **internal change forces**
> Forces for change that occur within the organization, such as communication problems, morale problems, and decision-making breakdowns.

Figure 17-1
Management of Change

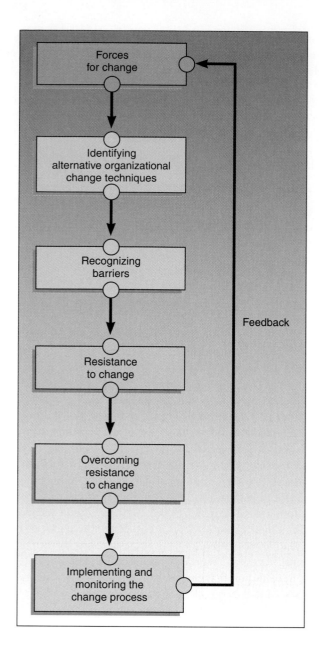

Changes in technology are constantly evolving and are considered a set of external forces. The knowledge explosion since World War II has brought new technology to nearly every management activity. Computers have made possible high-speed data processing and the solution of complex production problems. New machines and new processes have revolutionized manufacturing and distribution. Computer technology and automation have affected not only production techniques but also the social conditions of work.[4] New occupations have burst forth, and old occupations have faded away.[5] Sooner or later, delaying adoption of new technology that would reduce costs and improve quality will be reflected in the financial statement. Technological advance is a permanent fixture in contemporary society.[6]

Environmental changes are another external force for change. Managers must be tuned in to societal movements over which they have no control but which control the fates of their firms. The Management Focus on Diversity box illustrates changes in the makeup of the workforce that managers should be paying attention to every day. Albertsons is a company that is assertively responding to diversity issues.

Although business cycles are rather regular and periodic,[7] social changes are less cyclical and tend to catch business leaders unprepared.[8]

Management Focus on Diversity

Alberstons Becomes a Leader of Change

In a world of ever-increasing regulation, the term "diversity" is sometime misunderstood, lumped in with the mountain of dictates imposed upon business, many of which tend to restrain rather than enhance corporate performance. Even those CEOs who recognize the importance of diversity find themselves challenged to fully implement it in their companies.

This should be a major concern for boards and corporate leadership, because recognizing diversity's true meaning, and understanding its impact on a fundamental level, can pay huge dividends.

To really "get" diversity, it's important to understand the meaning of the word as applied to corporate culture. It's not only about eliminating prejudices, which have no place in our society. Organizations know they should hire qualified people regardless of color, gender, religion, sexual orientation, or any of the other many differences that distinguish a society. But diversity, in its purist sense, also means allowing people to be themselves—sharing ideas, taking risks, and adding value. Organizations constantly ask customers what they want to see in their local store and how they can make their lives easier by meeting those expectations. If you understand the diversity of the consumer base, if an organization can give these people what they want and make their lives easier and their shopping experience more enjoyable in the process, they'll keep those customers for life.

At Albertsons, there is a special emphasis on diversity. Early in 2004, Albertsons reached an important milestone by becoming the only company in the S&P 500 to have 50 percent female representation on the board of directors, which has since been exceeded. Women of all backgrounds are Albertsons primary shoppers, accounting for 85 percent of all purchasing decisions in our stores. So it makes strategic sense for women, arguably the people who can best relate to the needs and concerns of Albertson's company's principal retail audience, to sit on the highest levels of our company.

Those who don't understand the value of diversity often make the old argument challenging "diversity for its own sake."

But that criticism is losing steam, as the benefits of having a diverse workforce and management team make themselves known. Where it was once just a gut instinct, there is now research to prove that diversity works. For example, according to a study of the top 500 companies by the research firm Catalyst, companies with a higher representation of women in senior management outperform those with proportionately fewer women at the top. The trend held true across the broad spectrum of industries, and the numbers are significant—a difference of 35 percent return on equity and 34 percent on total return to shareholders.

Encouraging diversity fosters a culture in which people are encouraged to be themselves, to speak up, to take risks. Without risks, there will be no significant rewards. Each voice is an asset, and each idea another asset. As many of us have learned over time, even ideas that seem to lack merit at first glance should be listened to carefully, because one of them may be the jewel that will be incorporated into the business and improve results.

A few years ago, Albertsons, like every other retailer in the nation, focused increased attention on the Hispanic market. Hispanics were the fastest-growing ethnic group in the U.S., and one underserved in the consumer marketplace. Everybody added Latinos to their staffs, increased the number of products and services aimed at Hispanics, and did targeted advertising. This was fine. It was deserved. But with everybody doing about the same thing, no company gained a significant edge.

To keep diversity as a vibrant part of the corporate culture, it should be integrated from the point of hire, through orientation, and on every day on the job at every level of the organization. It's interesting how, by embracing diversity, stronger business results invariably occur and attendant career-advancement opportunities are developed.

Source: Adapted from Larry Johnston, "Making Diversity a Profitable Reality," *CEO Magazine*, December 2004, pp. 43–44.

17-2b Internal Forces

The forces for change within the organization can be traced to *processes* and *people.* Processes that facilitate change include decision making, communications, and interpersonal relations. Breakdowns or problems in any of these processes also can bring forces for change. Decisions may not be made, may be made too late, or may be of poor quality. Communications may be short-circuited, redundant, or simply inadequate. Tasks may or may not be completed or even started because the person responsible did not receive the instructions. Because of inadequate or absent communications, a customer's order is not filled, a grievance is not processed, an invoice is not filed, or a supplier is not paid. Conflicts between people and groups reflect breakdowns in the interaction among individuals.

Low levels of morale and high levels of absenteeism and turnover are symptoms of people problems. A strike or a walkout may be the most tangible sign of a problem. Such tactics usually are employed because they arouse the management to action. Most organizations inevitably maintain a certain level of employee discontent; yet it is dangerous to

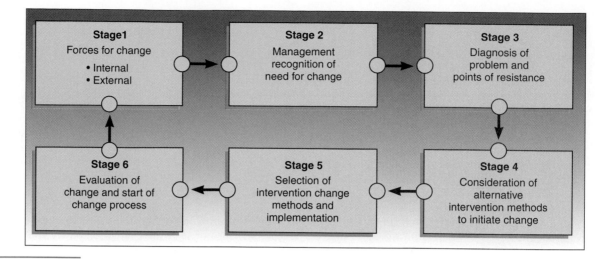

Figure 17-2
Framework for Managing Change

ignore employee complaints and suggestions.[9] But the process of change includes the *recognition* step, and this is the point at which management must decide to act or not to act.[10]

17-3 A Framework for Managing Change in Organizations

A framework can be useful for managing change and change processes. Figure 17-2 provides a process-oriented model for managing change that emphasizes six distinct stages in which managers must be knowledgeable and often make decisions. Stage 1, the forces for change, has already been discussed in terms of internal and external factors.

Distinguished psychologist Kurt Lewin introduced the notion of three stages in the change process: unfreezing, changing, and refreezing. The unfreezing phase is designated as Stage 2 in Figure 17-2. Managers must recognize that change is needed or that the present state is inadequate. Recognition is easy if the magnitude of the problems such as market share losses, a record increase in the number of equal employment opportunity discrimination suits, an ongoing loss of the most talented employees, or declining profit margins is significant. Unfortunately, the indicators that change is needed aren't always dramatic. A loss here and there, a complaining group of customers, a disgruntled software engineer, or a lost contract isn't always an indication that change is necessary.

Some companies have adopted a technique for helping managers recognize the need for change. The technique is known as the sense-and-respond (SR) model. The SR model involves sensing change earlier and responding to it faster. According to Steve Haeckel of the IBM Advanced Business Institute, the SR model requires managers to be very good at conceptual thinking.[11] That means managers must be able to think broadly and to entertain two or more (possibly contradictory) ideas about issues at the same time. The SR model requires that managers build an organizational context that delegates operational decision making and the design of adaptive systems to the people or teams accountable for producing results. The SR Corporation encourages all employees to be alert to changes in the environment and to act on those changes to improve the competitive position of the company.[12]

Stage 3 involves **diagnosis.** A sound diagnosis can provide invaluable information that helps unfreeze when problems are identified. Diagnosis can also clarify the problem and suggest what changes can solve it. Diagnosis can be conducted using a variety of techniques.

A diagnosis strategy developed by Lewin is known as **force field analysis.** This technique is a means of diagnosing situations and analyzing the various change strategies that can be used in a particular situation. According to the force field approach, an organization simultaneously faces driving forces for change (e.g., an aggressive competitor) and forces for maintaining the status quo (e.g., we have been beating competitors for years, there is no need to worry or change). In many situations considerable managerial skill is needed in order for driving forces to outweigh restraining forces.

▶**diagnosis** The use of data collected by interviews, surveys, observations, or records to learn about people or organizations.

▶**force field analysis** The process of identifying the forces that drive and the forces that resist a proposed behavioral, technological, or structural change.

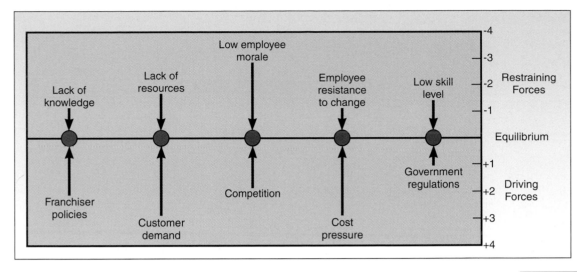

Figure 17-3
Driving and Restraining Forces in Fast-Food Restaurant Example

Once a manager determines that there's a gap between what's happening in the organization and what they'd prefer to be happening, then force field analysis becomes a useful tool. Before undertaking any change strategy, it's useful for managers to determine what they have working in their favor *(driving forces)* and what forces are working against them *(restraining forces)*. Since driving forces are pushing in a particular direction, they tend to initiate a change and keep it going. In terms of improving productivity in an organization, words of praise from a manager, effective reward systems, and a high level of employee involvement in decision making are examples of driving forces.

Restraining forces come in many shapes and forms. Low morale, anger, ingrained habits, group norms, fear of change, or inadequate work tools are examples of restraining forces. Equilibrium is the point at which the sum of the driving forces is equal to the sum of the restraining forces.

To understand Lewin's concepts better, imagine that you manage a fast-food restaurant. If you decide to initiate a change program in the restaurant, some of the driving forces might be customer demand, competition, cost pressures, government regulations, and franchise policies. Some of the restraining forces might be lack of resources, low employee morale, low employee skill level, employee resistance to change, or lack of knowledge about the change effort. Figure 17-3 illustrates the relationship between driving forces and restraining forces in this scenario.

In utilizing force field analysis for developing a change strategy, the following guidelines are useful:

1. If the driving forces far outweigh the restraining forces in power and frequency in a change situation, managers interested in driving for change can often push on and overpower the restraining forces.

2. If the reverse is true, and the restraining forces are much stronger than the driving forces, managers interested in driving for change have several choices. First, they can give up the change effort, realizing that it will be too difficult to implement. Second, they can pursue the change effort but concentrate on maintaining the driving forces in the situation while attempting, one by one, to change each of the restraining forces into driving forces or somehow to immobilize each of the restraining forces so that they are no longer factors in the situation. The second choice is possible, but very time consuming.

3. If the driving forces and restraining forces are fairly equal in a change situation, managers probably will have to begin pushing the driving forces while at the same time attempting to convert or immobilize some or all of the restraining forces.[13]

Stage 4 is the selection of a change intervention strategy. Several strategies, including survey feedback, team building, empowerment, and foresight-led change will be presented later.

> **LearningMoment**   _Lewin in Simple Terms_
>
> Lewin's force field theory explains how to initiate, manage, and stabilize the change process. What he is actually saying is that a person first has to unlearn old habits and attitudes. Once unlearning occurs, the individual must learn something new and also have the new learning reinforced.

After evaluating the pros and cons of various change techniques, one or some combination of alternatives should be selected and then implemented (Stage 5). Implementation should be given enough careful attention, time, and resources in order to bring about lasting change (refreezing).

Stage 6 in the change model points to evaluation and starting the process again. Managers want to learn whether changes have occurred and if so, what has been accomplished. Is the talent drain stopped or slowed? Has morale improved? Have customers returned? It's hard to measure change over time because there are often many uncontrollable changes that influence effects of the original change effort. In the middle of a structural change, a new government regulation may have been passed that directly affects employees in the units undergoing change. Suppose the regulation means that employees must now file additional government paperwork. But employees have continually complained about paperwork. Now, with the new regulation, there's even more paperwork. Did the structural change cause the lower morale that now exists or was it the new regulation? It would be hard to say what lies behind the lower morale.

Generally it's agreed that measuring skills, attitudes, and values before, during, and after change is difficult.[14] But there are attempts to measure reactions (Did you like the change program?), learning (What was learned?), and outcomes (Is quality of output higher, lower, or about the same?).

Based on years of research and attempts to measure changes in reaction, learning, behavior, and outcomes, some general guidelines are useful:

1. Measurements should be conducted over a period of time. Soon after change has occurred, participants may be generally excited and interested because they're being asked for responses. Conducting measurement over a period of time will identify lag effects, extinction effects, and long-term results.

2. When possible, compare groups that have undergone change and those that haven't faced change. Comparisons are a form of internal benchmarking—how does a unit that was changed compare on outcomes or behavior with a unit that wasn't changed?

3. Don't rely only on quantitative measures such as cost, profit, units produced, or defective units. What do participants say? How do participants look? What do participants do without being asked? These types of qualitative measures provide insight into effects of change.

These guidelines can be applied to both small or normal and major or radical changes. Unfortunately too many organizations bypass or weakly address Stage 6 because evaluation is difficult. But since change is a continual process, starting over requires feedback. The evaluation step can, if done properly, provide crucial and revealing feedback that influences Stage 1; that is, it becomes an internal-based force for change.

17-4 Identifying Alternative Change Techniques

The particular change technique chosen in Step 4 of the framework presented in Figure 17-2 depends on the nature of the problem. Management must determine which alternative is most likely to produce the desired outcomes.[15] In this section of the chapter, a number of change techniques are described. They are classified according to the major focus of the technique—namely, to change structure, behavior, or technology (see Figure 17-4).

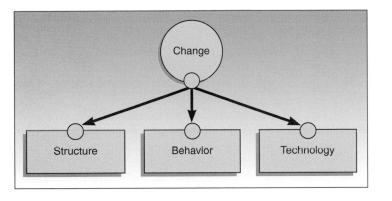

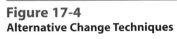

Figure 17-4
Alternative Change Techniques

17-4a Structural Change

Logically, organizing follows planning, since the structure is a means for achieving the objectives established through planning. **Structural change,** in the context of organizational change, refers to managerial attempts to improve performance by altering the formal structure of task and authority relationships.[16] But because structure creates human and social relationships that members of the organization may value highly, efforts to disrupt these relationships may be resisted.[17]

> **structural change** A planned change of the formally prescribed task and authority relationships in an organization's design.

Structural changes alter some aspects of the formal task and authority system. The design of an organization involves the specification of jobs, the grouping of jobs into departments, the creation of virtual teams and work to be done at remote sites (e.g., in the employee's home), the determination of the size of groups reporting to a single manager, and the distribution of authority—including the provision of staff assistance. Changes in the nature of jobs, bases for departmentation, the location of where work tasks are completed, and line-staff relationships are, therefore, structural changes.

Changes in the Nature of Jobs Changes in the nature of jobs originate with new methods and new machines. Work simplification and job enrichment are two examples of methods changes. Work simplification increases specialization, whereas job enrichment decreases it.

A job can be changed by altering (1) the job description, (2) the role expectations of a position, (3) the relationships among positions, and (4) work flow patterns. For example, a change in a job description means that the duties to be performed and the manager's expectations about the duties are changed.[18] A purchasing agent had his job description changed in an area involving his latitude for making purchasing decisions. After the change, he was able to make any purchasing decision without checking immediately with his manager. This change was structural. His increased authority also meant that he would have to work on Saturday evenings. This was a role expectation for purchasing agents with full purchasing decision authority.

Changes in the Basis for Departmentation Opinion is growing among managers and researchers that grouping jobs on the basis of function, territory, product, and customer does not occur in an orderly fashion.

Departmentation in some firms is based largely on a contingency perspective. The situation, people, resources, and external organizational forces appear to dictate largely what basis of departmentation will be used. The multiproducts and multi-industry organization require a significant amount of managerial coordination. Thus, experiments with different forms of departmentation and various managerial hierarchies are being conducted.[19]

An increasing number of firms are using teleworkers or individuals performing unit, department, or project jobs away from an office, factory floor, or cubicle. These workers may be a part of a formal department, unit, team, or project, but they receive, complete, and send work via fax, e-mail, and/or videoconferencing. There are over fifteen million teleworkers in the United States, and the trend is for an increase in the number of employees working remotely. Effectively coordinating, evaluating, and leading teleworkers is a task that a growing number of managers will have to learn.[20]

Changes in Line-Staff Relationships The changes normally include two techniques. The first and most common approach is to create staff assistance as a temporary or permanent solution. One response of manufacturing firms to the problem of market expansion is to create separate staff and service units. These units provide the technical expertise to deal with the production, financial, and marketing problems posed by expansion.

An illustrative case is a company that had grown quite rapidly after its entry into the fast-food industry. Its basic sources of field control were area directors who supervised the operations of the sales outlets of a particular region. During the growth period, the area directors had considerable autonomy in making the advertising decisions for their regions. Within general guidelines, they could select their own advertising media and formats and set their own advertising budgets. But as their markets became saturated and competitors appeared, corporate officials decided to centralize the advertising function in a staff unit located at corporate headquarters. Consequently, the area directors' authority was limited, and a significant aspect of their jobs was eliminated.

Elements of structural change often include plans, procedures, the span of control, and levels of organization. The point that should be taken, however, is not that any list of structural change approaches is incomplete, but that all structural parts are interrelated. Job changes do not take place in a vacuum; on the contrary, the change affects all surrounding jobs. The management of structural change must be guided by the point of view that all things are connected.

17-4b Behavioral Change

> **behavioral change techniques** Attempts to change employees' behavior to redirect and increase their motivation, skills, and knowledge bases.

Behavioral change techniques are efforts to redirect and increase employee motivation, skills, and knowledge bases. The major objective of such techniques is to coordinate performance of assigned tasks. The early efforts to change employee behavior date back to scientific management work-improvement and employee-training methods. These attempts primarily were directed at improving the skills and knowledge bases of employees. The employee counseling programs that grew out of the Hawthorne Studies were (and remain) primarily directed at increasing employee motivation.

Training and development programs for managers typically have emphasized interpersonal relationships and technical skills. These programs attempt to provide managers with basic technical and leadership skills. Since managers are concerned primarily with overseeing the work of others, these traditional programs emphasize techniques for dealing with people problems: how to handle the malcontent, the loafer, the troublemaker, the complainer. The programs also include conceptual material dealing with communications, leadership styles, and organizational relationships. The training methods often involve role-playing, discussion groups, lectures, and organized courses offered by the firm's training department or universities, consultants, and training corporations.

Training continues to be an important technique for introducing behavioral changes. In some applications, training has taken on a form quite different from that which developed under classical management theory. The vast majority of organizational development change techniques have been directed at changing the behavior of individuals and groups through problem solving, decision making, and communication. Team building and diversity training—the most commonly used change approaches—will be discussed in more detail.

At IBM a new form of compentency-based training is being used to change the leadership traits of managers. The accompanying Management Focus on Training box explains IBM's training program.

Team Building Team building enables work groups to do their work more effectively—to improve their performance.[21] The work groups may be established, or relatively new, command and task groups. The members of the work groups can be both internal and external to the organization.[22] The specific aims of the intervention include setting

> # *Management Focus* on Training

IBM's Program to Change Managerial Behaviors

It was at a client meeting in San Francisco in October 2002 that Sam Palmisano, IBM's new CEO, first unveiled the initiative he hoped would transform his company. The Internet really did change everything (the crash of the New Economy notwithstanding). In a hyperconnected world, IBM's clients needed to become "on-demand" companies, their every business process exquisitely calibrated to respond instantly to whatever got thrown at them. And to help them, IBM would have to do exactly the same thing.

When she heard about the new strategy, Donna Riley, IBM's vice president to global talent, remembers wondering whether the company had the right managers for its new direction. "If leadership is stuck in the past, and the business has changed, we have a problem," she says. By the spring of 2003, Palmisano and his leadership development team realized the strategy would indeed demand a new breed of boss—leaders who were sensitive to changes in their environment.

For help, Riley turned to the Hay Group, a consultancy firm that specialized in executive development. Hay had done work for IBM before, most notably in 1994 when, at former CEO Lou Gerstner's behest, the firm had interviewed a group of the company's top managers. As part of his turnaround strategy for the troubled company, Gerstner wanted to develop a new style of leader who could help transform his failed culture. Ultimately, Hay distilled eleven competencies from the interviews that would guide IBMers' performance as they pulled off one of the most remarkable corporate rebounds in history.

In the summer of 2003, Hay Group returned to conduct another set of interviews with thirty-three executives who had been identified as outstanding leaders in the new on-demand era—the folks who really got the new strategy and who were on the cutting edge in a high-performance culture. They were drawn from every division of the business, every part of the world, united by their extraordinary ability to get the job done. The plan was to put these top players under a microscope to attempt to determine how they thought about their jobs and the company; how they interacted with clients, peers, and subordinates; how they set goals and went about meeting them—in short, to extract the best practices from the best leaders to see if they could be duplicated.

In a series of three-and-a-half-hour interviews, the managers discussed circumstances in which they had been successful—or not. The interviews were supplemented by surveys of the people they worked with. Researchers then combed through the stories and accompanying data, looking for characteristics and qualities that distinguished these high performers.

Riley's team is now training IBM's executives in the new competencies. This year, only top management will be assessed against them. The next group—some 4,000 executives—will have a year to study the goals before being held accountable. But the new approach has already spurred some more flexible, collaborative efforts. Cross-functional teams from IBM's global services, software, and systems groups have helped Mobil Travel Guides transform itself from a travel content provider to a real-time, customized travel-planning service; a team of staffers from Big Blue's research, software, and consulting services helped Nextel dramatically improve its customer-care services.

In an interconnected world, such horizontal, collaborative networks of people clearly make more sense than rigid hierarchies. And leading in such a challenging environment is an acquired skill. "Leadership is a person journey for each person," says Riley, "But I think having a culture that says this stuff matters—particularly when it's linked to your business strategy—is a very powerful combination."

IBM's New Leadership Traits

If you were a leader at IBM, here's what you would be graded on.

Innovation that matters—for company and for the world

- **Thinking Horizontally:** Leverages IBM's enterprise capability to address client or market opportunities in new ways.
- **Informed judgment:** Synthesizes disparate sources of information to make an informed judgment regarding a strategic decision with both immediate and long-term implications.
- **Strategic risk-taking:** Innovates to create exponential growth, using multiple resources from around IBM.

Dedication to every client's success

- **Building client partnerships:** Builds ongoing, collegial relationships with key clients based on mutual strategic interests.
- **Collaborative influence:** Creates interdependence, building genuine commitment across organizational boundaries to a common purpose.
- **Embracing challenge:** Proactively builds in others the belief that they can innovate and grow the business.

Trust and personal responsibility in all relationships

- **Earning trust:** Does what is right for the long-term good of relationships inside and outside of IBM.
- **Enabling growth:** Changes systems or processes that impede growth and performance.
- **Passion for IBM's future:** Gets others energized to realize IBM's unique potential.
- **Developing IBM people and community:** Takes accountability for investing in the future leadership of IBM.

Source: Adapted from Linda Tischler, "IBM's Management Makeover," *FastCompany*, November 2004, pp. 112–113; Aaron Ricadela, "IBM Breaks Speed Record," *Information Week*, November 8, 2004, pp. 14–15.

goals and priorities, analyzing the group's work methods, examining the group's communication and decision-making processes, and examining the interpersonal relationships within the group.[23] As each of these aims is undertaken, the group is placed in the position of having to recognize explicitly the contributions, positive and negative, of each group member.[24]

The process by which these aims are achieved begins with *diagnostic* meetings. Often lasting an entire day, the meetings enable each group member to share with other members his or her perceptions of problems. If the group is large enough, subgroups engage in discussion and report their ideas to the total group. These sessions are designed for expression of the all members' views and to make these views public. That is, diagnosis, in this context, emphasizes the value of "open communication" of issues and problems that were previously discussed in secrecy.

Identifying problems and concurring on their priority are two important initial steps. However, a *plan of action* must be agreed on. The plan should call on each group member, individually or as part of a subgroup, to act specifically to alleviate one or more of the problems. If, for example, an executive committee agrees that one of the problems is lack of understanding of and commitment to a set of goals, a subgroup can be appointed to recommend goals to the total group at a subsequent meeting. Other group members can work on different problems. For example, if problems are found in the relationships among the members, a subgroup can initiate a process for examining the roles of each member.

Team-building interventions do not always require a complex process of diagnostic and action meetings. For example, the chief executive of a large manufacturing firm recognized that conflict within her executive group was breeding defensiveness among the functional departments. She also recognized that her practice of dealing on a one-to-one basis with executive group members, each of whom headed a functional department, contributed to the defensiveness and conflict. Rather than viewing themselves as team members with a stake in the organization, the department heads viewed one another as competitors. The chief executive's practice confirmed their belief that they managed relatively independent units.

To counteract the situation, the chief executive adopted the simple expedient of requiring the group to meet twice weekly. One meeting focused on operating problems, the other on personnel problems. The ground rule for these meetings was that the group must reach a consensus on each decision. After one year of such meetings, company-oriented decisions were being made, and the climate of interunit competition had been replaced by one of cooperation.

Team building also is effective when new groups are being formed. There are often problems when new organizational units, project teams, or task forces are created. Typically, such groups have certain characteristics that must be altered if the groups are to perform effectively. For example, the following combination of characteristics will lead to real problems:

1. Confusion exists as to roles and relationships.
2. Members have a fairly clear understanding of short-term goals.
3. Group members have technical competence that puts them on the team.
4. Members often pay more attention to the tasks of the team than to the relationships among the team members.

The result is that the new group will focus initially on task problems but ignore the relationship issues. By the time the relationship problems begin to surface, the group is unable to deal with them, and performance begins to deteriorate.

To combat these tendencies, a new group should schedule team-building meetings during the first weeks of its life. The meetings should take place away from the work site; one- or two-day sessions often are sufficient. The format of such meetings varies, but essentially their purpose is to provide time for the group to work through its timetable and the roles of members in reaching the group's objectives. An important outcome of such meetings is to establish an understanding of each member's contribution to the team and of the reward for that contribution. Although the reports of team building indicate mixed results, the evidence suggests that group processes improve through team-building efforts.[25] This record of success accounts for the increasing use of team building as an organizational development method.[26]

Diversity Training   **Diversity training** attempts to make the participants more aware of themselves and of their impact on diverse others.[27] "Sensitivity" in this context means sensitivity to self and to relationships with others. Diversity training stresses the *process* rather than the *content* of training and *emotional* rather than *conceptual* training. It is clear that this form of training is quite different from the traditional forms, which stress the acquisition of a predetermined body of concepts with immediate application to the workplace.

The process of diversity training includes a group of managers who, in most cases, meet away from their place of work. Under the direction of a trainer, the group usually engages in a dialogue that focuses on why some organizational acts and actors are seen as offensive while others are not.[28] The objective is to provide an environment that produces its own learning experiences. The unstructured dialogue encourages one to learn about the self in dealing with others. One's motives and feelings are revealed through behavior toward others in the group and through the behavior of others.

Managers should examine this technique critically to determine what kinds of behavioral changes are desirable and what kinds are possible. Certain conditions could limit the range of possible changes. In this light, managers must determine whether the changes induced by diversity training are instrumental for organizational purposes and whether the prospective participant could tolerate any anxiety generated by the training.

17-4c Technological Change

Technological change includes any application of new ways of transforming resources into products or services. In the usual sense of the word, technology means new machines—lathes, presses, computers, and the like. But the concept can be expanded to include all new techniques, whether or not they include new machines. From this perspective, the work improvement methods of scientific management can be considered technological breakthroughs. However, in this section, only those changes that can be linked to the introduction of a machine or a worker-machine process are discussed.

Technological change involving computers is being implemented by the majority of manufacturing and service organizations.[29] In service firms, computers now either perform or assist employees in performing a wide variety of tasks such as processing customer banking transactions, life insurance policies, and hospital admissions. Manufacturing processes continue to find new and effective ways to apply computer technology. In many plants, computers now control large parts of the manufacturing process such as materials handling, quality testing, and assembly. Some companies have created **flexible manufacturing systems.** These systems produce a part or product entirely by automation. From initial design to delivery, the unit is untouched by human hands.[30]

These technological changes have occurred largely because of the potential of high technology to lower production costs, to boost productivity, and to improve quality. However, although computer and robotics technologies have affected over half of America's jobs, the rate of high-tech implementation in U.S. organizations has fallen far short of projections. The reason: many high-tech changes haven't delivered expected results.

Many observers believe that the disappointing performance of such technological change is due to management's neglect of the structural and behavioral changes that must accompany technological change. Specifically, employees' jobs have not been redesigned in a way that both makes the best use of new technology and addresses the employees' social and psychological needs. A mismatch exists between technology and how workers perform their jobs, and how managers supervise the workers. Consequently, technology's potential isn't realized.[31]

This neglect is costly because computerizing the workplace requires major structural and behavioral changes for success to occur.[32] Changes are necessary in a number of areas, which are discussed in the following sections.

diversity training   A training technique that stresses the process rather than the content of training and emotional rather than conceptual training.

technological change A planned change in the machinery, equipment, or techniques used to accomplish organizational goals.

flexible manufacturing systems   Production systems that manufacture a part or product entirely by automation.

Employee Training Workers must be highly skilled to handle the substantial team responsibility for a major part of the manufacturing process. Team members must understand the technology to oversee machine functions and be skilled in diagnostic problem solving and communicating to quickly correct the glitches that sometimes occur. Thus, technological change essentially alters the amount and type of training that employees receive.

Compensation Many companies with a highly automated manufacturing process and employee teams have implemented a pay-for-knowledge compensation system. Individualized pay approaches, such as a piece rate system, don't work because the contributions of individual employees are difficult to measure. The pay-for-knowledge approach boosts team flexibility.

Management Style Because of the nature of their responsibilities, teams working with highly automated processes often have much more authority in performing their tasks than do individuals in more traditional, assembly-line-designed jobs. This increase in employee autonomy changes the nature of the manager's job. The emphasis shifts from supervision and control to coaching and consultation.[33] Technological change also requires that managers broaden their knowledge to include a thorough understanding of the new technology.

Technological innovations can change other aspects of the workplace. The changes can alter working conditions, the social relations among workers, career patterns, and promotion procedures, to name a few. The degree and extent of any changes in behavior and structure depend on the magnitude of the technological change. Essentially, the decision to adopt a technological change must involve consideration of the numerous behavioral and structural impacts that often occur. Those impacts must, in turn, be reconciled with the conditions that limit the scope and magnitude of the proposed change.

As the Management Focus on Ethics box, "Technology Change Creates Ethical Issues for Managers," discusses, technological changes in the workplace can often also lead to challenging ethical issues for managers.

The three major alternative approaches to change—structural, behavioral, and technological—attempt to improve performance by improving communication, decision making, attitudes, and skills. These approaches are based on the assumption that changes in structure, behavior, and technology can result in improvements for the organization, individuals, and groups. The three approaches are presented in Figure 17-5 as a system. That is, changes in one area are related to changes in other areas. The anticipated outcomes of this system of interrelated changes include the factors shown in Figure 17-5. Accomplishing all of the anticipated outcomes would be worthwhile for any manager. However, any successes may be limited because of implementation problems, resistance to change, and various other conditions.

17-5 Trends in Organizational Change

Forces primarily in the external environment during the start of the twenty-first century have encouraged two types of change in U.S. organizations: *downsizing* and *empowerment*. Each type of change usually brings about changes in the structural, behavioral, and technological aspects of the organization.

17-5a Downsizing

downsizing An organizational response to declining revenues and increasing costs that involves reducing the workforce and often closing and /or consolidating operations.

Declining revenues and increasing costs, mergers, and increasing international competition have intensified the need for organizations to be more efficient and productive. Many companies have responded to this need by **downsizing.** This major action involves reducing the size of the workforce and often closing some operations and consolidating others.[34]

The core task of the downsizing effort is determining what operations should be closed and which positions should be eliminated in the organization. Many companies

Management Focus on Ethics

Technology Change Creates Ethical Issues for Managers

Managers of public and private organizations have several responsibilities related to technology. They must develop and incorporate technological change into their organizations' daily operations. Managers must also make decisions concerning the potential effects of technological change on their workers, on their customers, and on society. The pace of technological change creates unique and ever-increasing burdens on managers' decision making. Consequently, managers may need help handling ethical issues raised by technology change.

Companies are not the only victims of unethical behavior. One study found that an overwhelming number of individuals reported uneasy feelings and concerns about technology-related problems. The survey found that 89 percent of the respondents felt that computers made it easier for someone to improperly obtain personal and confidential information; 76 percent suggested that because of computers, people have lost all control over how personal information is circulated; 69 percent noted that computers represent a threat to their personal privacy; and 66 percent indicated that there are not adequate safeguards to protect the privacy of personal information stored in computers.

Even these brief descriptions of technology-based ethical issues indicate that today's managers face a highly complex ethical arena. To effectively manage their organizations while coping with these ethical issues, managers should employ the following steps:

- Be aware of the issues.
- Develop an ethical framework.
- Be consistent.
- Communicate clearly.
- Stay alert.

Each of the five steps is very important. Yet the issue of staying alert stands out above all the others. The changing nature of technology and technology-based ethical issues requires managers to stay alert for emerging issues from current technologies and for emerging issues from new technologies. Effective management requires the ability to perceive and appreciate the implications of new circumstances and environments. Managers must successfully adapt to change. Ethical decision making is similar to many other management responsibilities: it requires that managers remain flexible and adaptable.

Sources: Adapted from Laura P. Hartman, *Perspectives in Business Ethics* (Burr Ridge, IL: McGraw-Hill, 2002); William P. Cordeiro, "Suggested Management Responses to Ethical Issues Raised by Technological Change," *Journal of Business Ethics,* September 1997, pp. 1393–1400; and Richard T. Herschel and Patricia Hayes Andrews, "Ethical Implications of Technological Advances on Business Communication," *Journal of Business Communication,* April 1997, pp. 160–170.

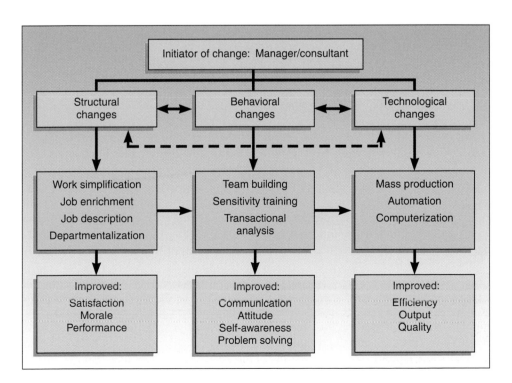

Figure 17-5
Three Change Approaches

identify units to be closed based on an analysis of each unit's financial performance and the company's projected future demand for its services. Market analysis of a product or service's future demand is conducted when a unit's operations are tied to output. Concerning positions, the content of jobs are analyzed to identify those that can be eliminated or consolidated with other positions.[35]

Once the downsizing decisions have been made, the most traumatic aspect of downsizing occurs—the actual shutdown of operations and employee layoffs. Some companies have attempted to help affected employees through this transition by providing advance notice, severance pay, extended health care benefits, and outplacement services.

However, despite organizational efforts, the period is exceptionally traumatic for employees who leave and for those who remain. Many management experts believe that downsizing is the primary contributor to a decline in employee loyalty in organizations.[36] Thus, once the actual downsizing decisions have been made, the organization is faced with rebuilding the company. Structural changes in job content, work flow, and organizational design must be implemented. Management also must focus on rebuilding commitment among retained employees, many of whom question the company's commitment to them. This task can be particularly challenging. Companies have responded in a number of ways.

In sum, downsizing is an often essential organizational change for companies striving to remain competitive in demanding external environments. However, the change is necessarily a painful one in many respects. Effective downsizing requires careful analysis of the companies' operations and a well-planned implementation that minimizes unnecessary human costs.

17-5b Empowerment

An increasingly competitive external environment demands that organizations produce better products and services and be more efficient in doing so. To meet this requirement, a rising number of companies are turning to employees, seeking their ideas and inputs and giving workers more autonomy in doing their jobs. The **empowerment** of individuals means granting them permission to utilize their talent, skills, resources, and experience to make decisions to complete their workloads.

> **empowerment** The practice of delegating authority and responsibility to employees.

In many cases, operating-level employees are making decisions in their work that previously were the domain of management. Examples of empowerment are found in making decisions about customer relationship management, investments, hiring people, just-in-time inventory management, total quality control, making computer purchases, and what alliances to form.

Instances of empowerment have occurred by redesigning jobs from an individual to team-based orientation. This structural change gives the responsibility for a major segment of work to a team of employees who often have the authority to schedule their own work, establish and monitor team performance measures, select and train their members, and solve production problems.

Empowerment has been credited with improving production and service quality and efficiency in a number of companies. However, this type of change often encounters several obstacles. A frequent problem is opposition to the change from managers who fear a loss of authority and power. Accustomed to a more authoritative style of management, some supervisors have difficulty in empowering subordinates and adopting a coaching rather than telling management style. Some employees also have difficulty in assuming the greater responsibility that empowerment requires. However, when these and other challenges are overcome, empowerment has produced some impressive results.[37]

17-6 Recognizing Limiting Conditions

> **leadership climate** The nature of the work environment that results from the leadership style and the administrative practices of managers.

The selection of a change technique is based on diagnosis of the problem, but it is also tempered by the conditions at the time. Three such conditions are the *leadership climate*, the *formal organization*, and the *organizational culture*.

Leadership climate refers to the nature of the work environment that results from the leadership style and the administrative practices of managers. Any change program not supported by management has only a minimal chance of success.[38] Management must be at least neutral toward the change. By not supporting the change, or by being unenthusiastic about it, a manager can undermine the efforts to change because she is in an authority position. The style of leadership itself may be the subject of change; for example, leadership training is a direct attempt to move managers toward a certain style—open, supportive, and group centered.

The **formal organization** must be compatible with the proposed change. This includes the effects on the organizational environment resulting from the philosophy and policies of top management, as well as legal precedent, organizational design, and the system of control. Of course, each of these sources of impact may be the focus of the change effort. The important point is that a change in one must be compatible with all of the others. For example, a change to technology that eliminates jobs contradicts a policy of guaranteed employment.

The impact of group norms and values and informal activities on **organizational culture** can influence the impact of a change program. The impact of traditional behavior, sanctioned by group norms but not formally acknowledged, was first documented in the Hawthorne Studies. A proposed change in work methods or the installation of an automated device can run counter to the expectations and attitudes of work groups. If such is the case, the manager implementing the change must anticipate resistance.

When managers evaluate the strength of limiting conditions, they are simultaneously considering the problem of objective setting. Many managers have been disappointed by change efforts that fell short of their expectations.[39] Particularly frustrated are those managers who cannot understand why the simple issue of a directive does not produce the intended response. Thoughtful managers will recognize that even as they attempt to make changes, other conditions enforce stability. The realities of limiting conditions are such that managers often must be content with modest change or even no change at all.

If a manager implements change without considering the constraints imposed by prevailing conditions within the present organization, the original problem may only get worse. Such change may actually result in further problems. Taken together, these constraints constitute the climate for change—positive or negative.

17-7 Resistance to Change

Most organizational change efforts eventually run into some form of employee resistance. Employee resistance to change is a behavioral and/or emotional response to actual, perceived, or imagined threats brought about by work change. Change triggers rational and irrational emotional reactions because of the uncertainty involved. Instead of assuming that employees will resist change or react in a particular manner, it is better to consider the general reasons why people resist change. Figure 17-6 illustrates a sample of some reasons for resisting change.

> **formal organization** The organization as it is drawn on the organization chart and as its titles and authority structure are designed.

> **organizational culture** The impact of group norms and values and informal activities on the organizational environment.

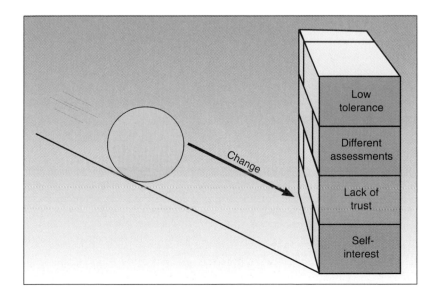

Figure 17-6
Common Reasons for Resisting Change

17-7a Why People Resist Change

Resistance to change in organizations is considered as being inevitable. It is a well-known phenomenon to any manager who has tried to bring about organizational change. A corollary to the view that people resist change is that the greater the magnitude of the change, the greater will be the resistance. The resistance to change can range from passive resignation to deliberate sabotage. Managers need to learn the various manifestations of how people resist change. Research has found there are four primary reasons people resist change as discussed in the following paragraphs.[40]

Parochial Self-Interest Some people resist organizational change out of fear of losing something they value. Individuals fear the loss of power, resources, freedom to make decisions, friendships, and prestige. In cases of fearing loss, individuals think of themselves and what they may have to give up. The fearful individual has only his parochial self-interest in mind when resisting change. The organization and the interests of coworkers are not given much priority.

Misunderstanding and Lack of Trust When individuals do not fully understand why the change is occurring, and what its implications are, they will resist it. Misunderstanding the intent and consequences of organizational change is more likely to occur when trust is lacking between the person initiating the change and the affected individual. In organizations characterized by high levels of mistrust, misunderstandings likely will be associated with any organizational change.

Different Assessments Since individuals view change differently—its intent, potential consequences, and personal impact—they often assess situations quite differently. Those initiating changes see more positive results because of the change, while those being affected and not initiating the changes see more costs involved with the change. Management might consider the change to a wireless computing approach a benefit, but others might consider the introduction of a wireless computing approach to be a signal of wanting employees to be connected to the firm 24/7.

Initiators of change often make two overly broad assumptions: (1) they have all the relevant data and information available to diagnose the situation; and (2) those to be affected by the change also have the same facts. Whatever the circumstances, the initiators and the affected employees often have different data and information. This leads to resistance to change. However, in some cases, the resistance is healthy for the firm, especially in the situation where the affected employees possess more valid data and information.

Low Tolerance for Change People resist change because they fear they will not be able to develop the new skills necessary to perform well. Individuals may understand clearly that change is necessary, but they are emotionally unable to make the transition. For example, this type of resistance is found in offices that introduce cubicles as the workstation, instead of private office spaces. Some individuals, and even their bosses, resist changes that can be interpreted as decreasing individual privacy.

LearningMoment *Creatures of Habit*

Most people are creatures of habit. Thus, there is a natural tendency to resist change, which can be frustrating to managers. However, by anticipating resistance and reasons for it, a manager can work to remove the problems and barriers. People will resist change, so managers must anticipate and work at reducing the resistance. After all, habit, fear, and uncertainty are powerful forces that people use to rationalize their resistance.

TABLE 17-1		Methods for Reducing Resistance to Change		
Approach	**Involves**	**Commonly Used When....**	**Advantages**	**Disadvantages**
1. Education and communication	Explaining the need for and logic of change to individuals, groups, and even entire organizations	There is a lack of information or inaccurate information and analysis	Once persuaded, people will often help implement the change	Can be very time consuming if many people are involved
2. Participation and involvement	Asking members of the organization to help design the change	The initiators do not have all the information they need to design the change, and others have considerable power to resist	People who participate will be committed to implementing the change and any relevant information they have will be integrated into the change plan	Can be very time consuming if participants design an inappropriate change
3. Facilitation and support	Offering retraining programs, time off, emotional support, and understanding to people affected by the change	People are resisting because of adjustment problems	No other approach works as well with adjustment problems	Can be very time consuming and expensive, and still fail
4. Negotiation and agreement	Negotiating with potential resisters; even soliciting written letters of understanding	Some person or group with considerable power to resist will clearly lose out in a change	Sometimes it is a relatively easy way to avoid major resistance	Can be too expensive if it alerts others to negotiate for compliance
5. Manipulation and co-optation	Giving key persons a desirable role in designing or implementing change process	Other tactics will not work or are too expensive	It can be a relatively quick and inexpensive solution to resistance problems	Can lead to future problems if people feel manipulated
6. Explicit and implicit coercion	Threatening job loss or transfer, lack of promotion, etc.	Speed is essential, and the change initiators possess considerable power	It is speedy and can overcome any kind of resistance	Can be risky if it leaves people angry with the initiators

Source: Reprinted by permission from "Choosing Strategies for Change," by John P. Kotter and Leonard A. Schlesinger (March–April 1979) *Harvard Business Review.* Copyright © 1979 by the Harvard Business School Publishing Corporation. All rights reserved.

A low tolerance for change also is found in individuals who resist change to save face. Making the necessary adjustments and changes would be, they assume, an open admission that some of their previous behavior, decisions, and attitudes were wrong.

17-7b Minimizing Resistance to Change

Resisting change is a human response, and management must take steps to minimize it. Reducing resistance can cut down on the time needed for a change to be accepted or tolerated. Also, the performance of employees can rebound more quickly if resistance is minimized.

A number of methods have been useful in decreasing employee resistance to change. Several important methods are listed here and are developed more fully in Table 17-1.

* Education and communication
* Participation and involvement
* Facilitation and support

- Negotiation and agreement
- Manipulation and co-optation
- Explicit and implicit coercion

17-8 Implementing and Monitoring the Change Process

The implementation of proposed change has two dimensions: *timing* and *scope*. *Timing* is knowing when to make the change. *Scope* is knowing how much of a change to make.

The matter of timing is strategic; it depends on a number of factors, particularly the organization's operating cycle and the groundwork that has preceded the change. A change of considerable magnitude should not compete with ordinary operations. For example, introducing a new electronic payment system in a retail store would not be a good idea during the Thanksgiving season. It might be easier to implement during a slack period. On the other hand, if the change is critical to the survival of the organization, then immediate implementation is in order.

The scope of the change depends on the change strategy. The change may be implemented throughout the organization and become established quickly. Or it may be phased into the organization level by level, department by department. The strategy of successful change utilizes a phased approach that limits the scope but provides feedback for each subsequent implementation.

The provision of feedback information is termed the *monitoring* phase. Figure 17-1 shows that information is fed back into the forces-of-change phase because the change itself establishes a new situation that might create problems.

The stimulus for change is a deterioration of performance objectives and standards that can be traced to structural, behavioral, or technological causes. The standards may be any number of indicators, including profit, sales volume, productivity, absenteeism, turnover, scrappage, and costs. The major source of feedback on those variables is the firm's management information system. But if the change includes the objective of improving employee attitudes and morale, the usual sources of information are limited, if not invalid.

To avoid the danger of overreliance on productivity data, the manager can generate ad hoc information to measure employee attitudes and morale. A benchmark for evaluation would be available if an attitude survey had been used in the diagnosis phase. The definition of acceptable improvement is difficult when attitudinal data are evaluated, since the matter involves "how much more" productive they should be. Nevertheless, if a complete analysis of results is to be undertaken, attitudinal measurements must be combined with productivity measurements.[41]

17-8a The Learning Organization

Since organizations are continuously changing they must learn from the past, competitors, and experts in order to remain competitive. Learning is a key ingredient in growing, becoming more effective, socially responsible, and sustaining the business model. Peter Senge, in his best-selling book *The Fifth Discipline*, described a **learning organization** as proactively creating, using, and transferring knowledge to change behavior.[42] Sharing knowledge, experiences, and ideas becomes a habit in a learning organization.

The Management Focus on Learning box, "Managerial Responsibilities for Learning," explains the role managers are playing in the development and growth of their employees.

Buckman Laboratories of Memphis, Tennessee, is held up as an example of a progressive learning organization.[43] The firm uses forums, training, electronic bulletin boards, virtual conference rooms, and presentations to share information and experiences (www.knowledge-nurture.com). By working together and sharing, the entire 1,200-member workforce is able to perform feats that previously were impossible. For example, a sales representative of Buckman was attempting to close a deal in Indonesia. The plant's

▶**learning organization**
An organization in which employees are engaged in problem solving, learning, and education so that continuous improvement in effectiveness is the result.

Management Focus on Learning

Managerial Responsibilities for Learning

Employees are developing new skills on the fly and in informal learning settings. IBM, Johnson & Johnson, the Men's Wearhouse, and EDS are among the companies who have moved a lot of learning from classrooms to informal settings. Now individuals share examples, stories, and ideas at lunch, in the hall, on the run. Gone are the days of managers having everyone trained exactly as needed in a classroom setting on a schedule.

George Zimmer, CEO of Men's Wearhouse, wants every employee to reach his or her potential. He has incorporated a concept called "cascading" in which everyone is responsible for the learning and development of their direct reports.

Siemens Power Transmission in Wendell, North Carolina, wanted to stop most of the "chit-chat" on the job until they found out that learning was rampant. Instead of what appeared to be idle chit-chat, employees were problem solving, sharing product and procedural information, and career counseling peers.

As more and more organizations are finding out, if employees are expected to learn continuously and managers are expected to accept accountability for learning, the company culture must effect those expectations. Only being a cheerleader for learning is not enough for managers. In learning organizations managers encourage, support, reward, and engage in learning.

Some predict that in the next decade the most critical competencies of managers, all types of industries, and also in non-profit organizations will become the ability to develop others, establish performance goals, and create fair and understandable metrics. Learning will play a prominent role in the attainment of the competencies. Manager-driven learning initiatives and support are becoming very common. The concept of the learning organization must include a discussion of the roles managers must play.

Sources: Adapted from French Caldwell, "The Future of Knowledge Management," *KM World,* October 2004, pp. 1–3; Donna Goldwasser "Me a Trainer? " *Training,* April 2001, pp. 60–66; and Charlotte Garvey, "The Whirlwind of a New Job," *HR Magazine,* June 2001, pp. 110–119.

decision-making team wanted a proposal within two weeks—an impossible task. The sales rep went to his on-line forum, explained his predicament, and within forty-eight hours had volumes of data, information, and facts to prepare the sales proposal. He made the two-week deadline with time to spare and closed the deal.

17-8b Learning Capabilities and Leadership

A number of factors that facilitate organizational learning have been identified. Table 17-2 presents ten different factors and briefly explains each of the factors. For example, an open climate (S) is displayed.[44] This depicts an openness to information, the encouragement of sharing, and debate. This factor is one of the trademarks of Buckman Laboratories previously presented.

Managers who also lead can create or contribute to the learning environment. The building and sustaining of a learning organization requires a commitment to learning, the generation of creative ideas that are implemented, and working to build cohesive teamwork, collaboration, and support. Table 17-3 presents a list of activities that can be performed to build learning.

A major result of an effective learning organization is that knowledge is managed more effectively.[45] **Knowledge management** is the sharing of information to achieve innovation, competitive advantage, and productive accomplishments. Although a learning organization leads to knowledge management, it is also true that, by managing knowledge, organizations will learn.

knowledge management
Refers to the many techniques managers can employ to capture and use the knowledge that is generated within the organization.

Learning and managing knowledge is not enough in a constantly changing work environment. Pfeffer and Sutton correctly suggest that many firms have fallen into a knowing-doing gap. What is learned and knowledge about change, strategies, and resistance must be converted into action and evaluation. It is easier and more comfortable to talk intellectually about empowerment, converting to more teleworking, or eliminating layers of management than to actually execute a change.[46] The challenge facing managers who understand change, learning organizations, and knowledge management is to become action-oriented and decisive.

T A B L E 17-2 **Factors That Facilitate Organizational Learning Capabilities**	**1.** Scanning imperative	Interest in external happenings and in the nature of one's environment. Valuing the processes of awareness and data generation. Curious about what is "out there" as opposed to "in here."
	2. Performance gap	Shared perception of a gap between actual and desired state of performance. Disconfirming feedback interrupts a string of successes. Performance shortfalls are seen as opportunities for learning.
	3. Concern for measurement	Spend considerable effort in defining and measuring key factors when venturing into new areas; strive for specific, quantifiable measures; discourse over metrics is seen as a learning activity.
	4. Experimental mind-set	Support for trying new things; curiosity about how things work; ability to "play" with things. Small failures are encouraged, not punished. See changes in work processes, policies, and structures as a continuous series of graded tryouts.
	5. Climate of openness	Accessibility of information, relatively open boundaries. Opportunities to observe others; problems/errors are shared, not hidden; debate and conflict are acceptable.
	6. Continuous education	Ongoing commitment to education at all levels; support for growth and development of members.
	7. Operational variety	Variety exists in response modes, procedures, systems; significant diversity in personnel. Pluralistic rather than monolithic definition of valued internal capabilities.
	8. Multiple advocates	Top-down and bottom-up initiatives are possible; multiple advocates and gatekeepers exist.
	9. Involved leadership	Leadership at significant levels articulates vision and is very actively engaged in its actualization; takes ongoing steps to implement visions; "hands-on" involvement in educational and other implementation steps.
	10. Systems perspective	Strong focus on how parts of the organization are interdependent; seek optimization of organizational goals at the highest levels; see problems and solutions in terms of systemic relationships.

Source: From B. Moingeon and A. Edmondson, in *Organizational Learning and Competitive Advantage* (Thousand Oaks, CA: Sage, 1996), p. 43. Reprinted by permission of Sage Publications Ltd.

TABLE 17-3	**Leadership Roles and Activities for Building a Learning Organization**		
Leadership Activities	**Role 1: Build a Commitment to Learning**	**Role 2: Work to Generate Ideas with Impact**	**Role 3: Work to Generalize Ideas with Impact**
Make learning a component of the vision and strategic objectives	X		
Invest in learning	X		
Publicly promote the value of learning	X		
Measure, benchmark, and track learning	X		
Create rewards and symbols of learning	X		
Implement continuous improvement programs		X	
Increase employee competence through training, or buy talent from outside the organization		X	
Experiment with new ideas, processes, and structural arrangements		X	
Go outside the organization to identify world-class ideas and processes		X	
Identify mental models of organizational processes		X	
Instill systems thinking throughout the organization		X	
Create an infrastructure that moves ideas across organizational boundaries		X	
Rotate employees across functional and divisional boundaries			X

Source: Based in part on D. Ulrich, T. Jick, and M. Von Gilnow, "High-Impact Learning: Building and Diffusing Learning Capability," *Organizational Dynamics,* Autumn 1993, pp. 52–66. Reprinted by permission of Elsevier.

Management Summary

- Organizational change is often inevitable. It also is necessary to improve the overall performance of the organization. Research has shown that planned change is more likely to bring about performance improvement than unplanned change.

- Employees resist the introduction of changes in structure, behavior, and technology. People resist change for economic reasons and for psychological reasons such as insecurity. Managers must be alert to any indication of resistance and they should also prepare subordinates for change.

- Before selecting change techniques, a manager must first recognize the need for change and conduct a thorough diagnosis so that problems can be uncovered.

- In recent years, many companies have introduced computers and robotics (technological change) into their production and service operations. However, often results have been unimpressive due to the neglect of needed structural and behavioral changes to maximize the effectiveness of high technology.

- The selection of a change technique should also consider limiting conditions in the organization such as the leadership climate, the formal organization, and the organizational culture.

- Successful organizational change requires that the scope (amount) of change is accurate and that the change is implemented at the right time.

- To monitor change, managers must collect data about whether objectives are being accomplished. Judging a major change a success even after one years' time is often premature.

- Organizations facing change must become efficient in how learning occurs and how knowledge is managed.

Key Terms

behavioral change techniques (p. 418)
diagnosis (p. 414)
diversity training (p. 421)
downsizing (p. 422)
empowerment (p. 424)
external change forces (p. 411)

flexible manufacturing systems (p. 421)
force field analysis (p. 414)
formal organization (p. 425)
internal change forces (p. 411)
knowledge management (p. 429)
leadership climate (p. 424)

learning organization (p. 428)
management of change (p. 411)
organizational change (p. 410)
organizational culture (p. 425)
structural change (p. 417)
technological change (p. 421)

Review and Discussion Questions

1. Some experts believe resistance to change is a natural human tendency based primarily on the fear of the unknown. Why do people resist structural, behavioral, and technological changes?

2. In your opinion, which force in the external environment exerts the most powerful influence on organizational change? Explain.

3. How can a manager apply Lewin's force field analysis in diagnosing a particular situation?

4. What value can be provided by an organization that is attuned to how and why learning must become a dominant part of its culture?

5. The following comment was overheard: "Structural, behavioral, and technological changes are all geared toward one major outcome, improved productivity. Thus, the best way to improve production output is to use the optimal mix

of change strategies, and this means everything available." Why is this statement incorrect?

6. Timing is the selection of the appropriate moment to initiate a change. Why is timing so important in implementing change?

7. Does implementing computerized technology in a plant's manufacturing operations exert more impact on structural or behavioral change? Explain.

8. What value can be added by an external consultant to a change program?

9. Why is there often more knowledge about a change program available than there is a desire on the part of managers to decisively initiate the program?

10. Attitude surveys are one approach to diagnosing organizational problems. What other tools or approaches could management use to perform the diagnostic task?

Practice Quiz

Note: You can find the correct answers to these questions by taking the quiz and then submitting your answers in the Online Edition. The program will automatically score your submission. If you miss a question, the program will provide the correct answer, a rationale for the answer, and the section number in the chapter where the topic is discussed.

Indicate whether the sentence or statement is true or false.

1. Although business cycles are rather regular and periodic, social changes are less cyclical and tend to catch business leaders unprepared.

2. The SR model requires that managers build an organization that delegates operational decision making and adaptive system design to the people or teams accountable for producing results.

3. Before undertaking any change strategy, it's useful for managers to determine what they have working in their favor (driving forces) and what forces are working against them (restraining forces).

4. Opinion is growing among managers and researchers that grouping jobs on the basis of function, territory, product, and customer does not occur in an orderly fashion.

5. A new group should schedule team-building meetings during the first weeks of its life.

6. Change triggers rational and irrational emotional reactions because of the uncertainty involved.

7. The greater the magnitude of the change, the greater will be the resistance.

8. Most people are creatures of habit.

Identify the letter of the choice that best completes the statement or answers the question.

9. _____ management is defined as the continuous process of aligning an organization with its marketplace.
   a. Strategic
   b. Organizational
   c. Product
   d. Change

10. Which of the following is the most important step that managers should take to effectively manage their organizations while coping with ethical issues?
   a. Be aware of the issues.
   b. Develop an ethical framework.
   c. Be consistent.
   d. Communicate clearly.
   e. Stay alert.

11. In the force field analysis, forces such as low employee morale and fear and anxiety about change are referred to as _____ .
   a. corporate realities.
   b. restraining forces.
   c. positive reverse factors.
   d. structural units.

12. One of the most important approaches for attempting to bring about behavioral changes is _____ .
  a. success planning.
  b. job redesign.
  c. compensation surveys.
  d. training.

13. When employees do not fully understand why a change program is being implemented and what the full range of implications will be, they will likely _____ .
  a. quit communicating with unit members.
  b. seek compensation.
  c. resist the change.
  d. reconsider their employment contract.

14. _____ is the sharing of information to achieve innovation, competitive advantage, and productive accomplishments.
  a. Performance gap fulfillment
  b. Multiple hourglass design
  c. Knowledge management
  d. Systems analysis

15. The final step (phase) in managing change is too often neglected. The emphasis of this final step is on _____ .
  a. force identification.
  b. evaluation.
  c. resistance to change.
  d. selecting the intervention method.

Case Study

Lighting the GE Way

Contrary to popular belief, Thomas Edison didn't invent the first lightbulb. It was Sir Joseph Wilson Swan, a British chemist, physicist, and inventor. Edison simply came up with one that could burn for 600 hours instead of 40, making it the first commercially viable "electric lamp" in history.

For scientists at General Electric's global research facility in Niskayuna, New York, that's more than trivia. It's a guiding principle for Anil, an amiable chemistry researcher who is trying to pull off an Edison-like feat. Anil and a cross-disciplinary team of scientists at the center want to develop a new kind of electric lamp using an emerging technology called organic light-emitting diodes (OLEDs), most easily thought of as light-up plastic.

Why? Call it creative destruction and dramatic change. Or, for the slightly more jaded perspective, call it trying for a miracle to salvage the iconic but struggling GE Lighting business (now part of GE's $14 billion consumer and industrial division). In 2002, it lost all of its Home Depot business to rival Philips. That single defeat wiped out a full 7 percent of the unit's annual sales. Business hasn't improved much since. And in a commodity line such as lighting, Anil's work also fits in nicely with CEO Jeffrey Immelt's push to foster innovations that let GE widen its margins with hard-to-copy products rather than competing on incremental improvements and price.

What's most striking about GE's renewed interest in innovation is not so much the technologies themselves, but how the company gets them from lab to market. "As a scientist, you have to figure out what makes this place tick. And it's not just technology," Anil says of GE's research center. "If you can't sell a project, then you're going to have a hard time here." So OLEDs may not be GE's most cutting-edge research project—that might be its nanotechnology or molecular-medicine efforts. But it is a technology that may one day save GE's flagging lighting business by, ironically, driving a stake through the lightbulb as we know it. So OLEDs provide an intriguing window onto how the company integrates long-range research into today's strategic planning and how new ideas get through the system without getting thwarted, blocked, or worse. How do you usher in a game-changing innovation and change that's years away from completion? Here's GE's shot at solving one of the oldest problems in business.

OLEDs are organic versions of LEDs—the stuff that makes our cell-phone buttons light up—with a couple of key differences. For starters, instead of emitting a single bright point of light like LEDs

do, OLEDs produce a patch of light over a wider area. Second, OLEDs consist of a thin, flexible, plastic-like material, unlike LEDs, which are fabricated as rigid semiconductor chips—a process that would be laughably expensive for general lighting. Anil hopes that the thin material will one day be printed using a cheap roll-to-roll process, as newspapers are. That flexibility opens up a range of imaginative possibilities, from lit ceiling tiles that would replace fluorescent overheads to illuminated curtains.

Anil began to take serious notice of OLEDs about five years ago. As a chemist in corporate R&D, he had a general interest in the technology as far back as 1989, when it was pioneered at Cambridge University. It wasn't until scientists showed that OLEDs could produce a white light, spelling opportunity for general lighting, that Anil's interest was fully piqued.

"Every year, OLED performance was getting exponentially better," he says. "One day I started plotting lines on a piece of paper showing this exponential growth, comparing it with conventional incandescent and fluorescent lighting technology. And you could see the lines start to intersect. So I'm thinking, "If we're a lighting company, there's both an opportunity and a threat here. This is a technology that could overtake us, and suddenly our own lighting business becomes meaningless.""

Inspired (and frightened) by his sketch, Anil began chasing some seed money within the company to see how OLEDs might fit in with GE's existing businesses. He was able to convince a handful of executive managers at the lab, and he got the money he needed to start. But to boost the project's initial funding and its staff from just Anil to a team of five, he enlisted the help of Greg. At the time, Greg was one of GE's business program managers—a liaison between the global research center and one of GE's business units. Together, they secured a grant from the U.S. Department of Energy to study OLEDs as an efficient lighting alternative.

When Jeffrey took the reins in 2001 from the legendary Jack Welch with a renewed focus on innovation, Anil knew that this leadership change was his opportunity. Under Welch, who considered investing in new technology to be a "wild swing," OLEDs would have likely remained a side project. Now they could be a full-time calling. It became a matter of Anil building support for the technology among scientists and engineers as well as the marketers and sales forces in the business units. "They said, 'Yes, we think it's important for GE to be in this,' " says Anil.

When it came time to present OLEDs as a candidate for advanced technology funding, Greg quips that he went in and told his bosses that "GE should invent a new lightbulb every hundred years or so."

OLEDs still face a long road. "You may start to see OLEDs showing up in niche architectural lighting in 8 to 10 years," says Kimberly, the director of technology and strategic research for iSuppli/Stanford Resources, a market research firm. "But you won't see something like flexible lighting for 15 or even 20 years." In fact, Kimberly says, the size of the OLED market for general lighting is impossible to forecast because so many technical questions remain unanswered.

This isn't news to GE. Proving commercial viability becomes more important as OLEDs develop. Scientists do their part through a process called "toll gating," in which they incrementally tackle risks that a promising technology will turn out to be a dud. Right now, Anil's team is at work on improving the brightness and duration of OLED lighting.

The other major hurdle is solving the production problems that would let you print OLEDs as you would a newspaper. OLEDs need to be hermetically sealed to work. Today that's accomplished by sandwiching the OLED material between two layers of glass. That's why it's premature to talk about roll-to-roll production. "In a way, those lines I plotted that showed the potential of OLEDs were deceptive, because there were things missing—like manufacturing," says Anil. "These are challenging problems. But we can either be scared by them or find a way to work around them."

While Anil's team works on those issues, a business unit's sales and marketing teams gather input about the technology from likely future customers. The net effect of this dance is that a technology must continually prove its market mettle if it hopes to continue along GE's path from lab to market. In theory, that means no new GE technology will hit the market unless there are customers already lined up.

How then does a technology like OLEDs not get lost in the strategic shuffle at a behemoth like GE, with $134 billion in annual sales? The answer lies in the company's yearly strategic planning process known as the S-1.

Contained within the consumer and industrial division's S-1 is a category labeled "innovation," under which projects fall into one of two subcategories: big bets and breakthroughs. OLEDs are listed as a breakthrough now, meaning they're still a corporate research project. Once technically viable, OLEDs would likely move to a big bet, where funding and technical development get handed over to the business unit.

GE's Rules for Innovation

Think like Edison. Thomas Edison was an inventor out to solve problems. Don't set out to invent new technology merely for technology's sake. Instead, define innovation in terms of a riddle you are seeking to solve.

Big ideas happen at the fringes. Recruit and retain talent from a broad spectrum of technical capabilities. When big brains look at problems in a different way—for example, physicists taking on chemistry problems—that's when breakthroughs can happen.

Make innovation pay its way. Business units should pony up for research they actually want rather than headquarters doling out all of R&D's budget, hoping for a breakthrough. Give early funding only to a handful of promising technologies.

Set intermediate goals. When managing long-term innovation areas, periodically review technical milestones along the way to monitor progress. Prioritize the importance of each technical problem to solve, then chip away one at a time.

Bet on the industry, not the technology. GE can't predict better than anyone else about when, or even if, game-changing technologies will take off. But by focusing on an industry such as energy, it can place big bets within it in an effort to stay in the lead.

Questions for Discussion

1. What in the culture of GE encourages and supports change and innovation?

2. Since GE is so large, why didn't the OLED project get lost in the array of projects?

3. The case states that the OLEDs project still faces a long road. What does this mean?

Source: Adapted from Ryan Underwood, "Lighting the GE Way," *FastCompany*, August 2004, pp. 73–75; *General Electric SWOT Analysis*, November 2004, pp. 1–7; and Kate Maddox, "General Electric Co," *B to B*, pp. 20–21.

Internet Exercise

A number of major companies, including McDonald's, Accenture, and Motorola have established their own corporate universities. These internal learning centers provide a wide range of courses, training activities, and programs. Explore the increase of corporate universities by examining the Internet.

1. Prepare a brief report on your findings.

2. Identify a major non-U.S. firm that has a corporate university. Determine whether it is similar to the corporate universities of U.S. firms.

3. Why will many firms resist the trend toward creating their own corporate university?

Experiential Exercise

Paper Plane Corporation

Purpose: To work on a task and use the functions of planning, organizing, leading, and controlling.

Setting Up the Exercise: Unlimited groups of six participants each are used in this exercise. These groups may be directed simultaneously in the same room. Approximately a full class period is needed to complete the exercise. Each person should have assembly instructions and a summary sheet, which are shown below, and ample stacks of paper (81/2 x 11 inches). The physical setting should be a room large enough so that the individual groups of six can work without interference from the other groups. A working space should be provided for each group.

- The participants are doing an exercise in production methodology.

- Each group must work independently of the other groups.

- Each group will choose a manager and an inspector, and the remaining participants will be employees.

- The objective is to make paper airplanes in the most profitable manner possible.

- The facilitator will give the signal to start. This is a ten-minute, timed event utilizing competition among the groups.

- After the first round, each six-member group should report their production and profits to the entire group. They also should note the effect, if any, of the manager in terms of the performance of the group.

- This same procedure is followed for as many rounds as there is time.

Data Sheet

Your group is the complete workforce for Paper Plane Corporation. Established in 1943, Paper Plane has led the market in paper plane production. Currently under new management, the company is contracting to make aircraft for the U.S. Air Force. You must establish an efficient production plant to produce these aircraft. You must make your contract with the Air Force under the following conditions:

1. The Air Force will pay $20,000 per airplane.

2. The aircraft must pass a strict inspection made by the facilitator.

3. A penalty of $25,000 per airplane will be subtracted for failure to meet the production requirements.

4. Labor and other overhead will be computed at $300,000.

5. Cost of materials will be $3,000 per bid plane. If you bid for ten but only make eight, you must pay the cost of materials for those you failed to make or that did not pass inspection.

Summary Sheet

Round 1:

Bid: _____ Aircraft @ $20,000 per aircraft = _____

Results: _____ Aircraft @ $20,000 per aircraft = _____

Less: $300,000 overhead _____ x $3,000 cost of raw materials _____ x $25,000 penalty

Profit: _____

Round 2:

Bid: _____ Aircraft @ $20,000 per aircraft = _____

Results: _____ Aircraft @ $20,000 per aircraft = _____

Less: $300,000 overhead _____ x $3,000 cost of raw materials _____ x $25,000 penalty

Profit: _____

Round 3:

Bid: _____ Aircraft @ $20,000 per aircraft = _____

Results: _____ Aircraft @ $20,000 per aircraft = _____

Less: $300,000 overhead _____ x $3,000 cost of raw materials _____ x $25,000 penalty

Profit: _____

Endnotes

Chapter 1

1. George Kahn, "Global Economic Integration: Opportunities and Challenges," *Economic Review,* Fourth Quarter 2000, pp. 5–15.

2. Peter Drucker, *Management: Tasks, Responsibilities, Practices* (New York: Harper & Row, 1973), p. 17.

3. Drucker, *Management: Tasks, Responsibilities, Practices,* p. 41.

4. Carole Schweitzer, "Professional Development Forums— Fast," *Association Management,* February 2001, pp. 77–82.

5. Frederick W. Taylor, *Principles of Scientific Management* (New York: Harper & Row, 1911).

6. Charles D. Wrege and Richard M. Hodgetts, "Frederick W. Taylor's 1899 Pig Iron Observations: Examining Fact, Fiction, and Lessons for the New Millennium," *Academy of Management Journal,* December 2000, pp. 1283–1291.

7. Frank B. Gilbreth, *Motion Study* (New York: D. Van Nostrand, 1911); Frank B. Gilbreth and Lillian M. Gilbreth, *Fatigue Study* (New York: Sturgis and Walton, Co., 1916).

8. Max Weber, *The Theory of Social and Economic Organizations* (New York: Free Press, 1947).

9. Robert Schwartz and John Mayne, *Quality Matters: Seeking Confidence in Evaluating, Auditing, and Performance Reporting* (New Brunswick, NJ: Transaction Publishers, 2004).

10. Henri Fayol, *Industrial and General Administration* (Paris: Dunod, 1916).

11. Henri Fayol, "Managing in the 21st Century," *British Journal of Administrative Management,* January–February 2000, pp. 8–10.

12. Geoffrey R. Marczyk, David De Matteo, and David Festinger, *Essentials of Behavioral Sciences* (New York: John Wiley, 2005).

13. Mary Parker Follett, *The New State: Group Organization, the Solution of Popular Government* (London: Longmans, Green, 1918).

14. Elton Mayo, *The Human Problems of an Industrial Civilization* (New York: MacMillan, 1933).

15. Bradley J. Rieger, "Lessons in Productivity and People," *Training & Development,* October 1995, pp. 56–58.

16. Shamsud D. Chowdhury and Michael J. Geringer, "Institutional Ownership, Strategic Choices and Corporate Efficiency: Evidence from Japan," *Journal of Management Studies,* March 2001, pp. 271–291.

17. Gary Yukl and Richard Lepsinger, *Flexible Leadership: Creating Value by Balancing Multiple Challenges and Choices* (San Francisco, CA: Pfeiffer, 2004).

18. Paul Hersey, *The Situational Leader* (New York: Warner Books, 1984).

19. Anthony J. Berry, Jane Broadbent, and David Otley, *Management Control: Theories, Issues, and Practices* (New York: Palgrave Macmillan, 2005).

Chapter 2

1. D. Scott Sink, Thomas C. Tuttle, and Sandra J. DeVries, "Productivity Measurement and Evaluation: "What Is Available?" *National Productivity Review,* Summer 1984, p. 265.

2. Donna K. McNeese-Smith, "Staff Nurse Views of Their Productivity and Nonproductivity," *Health Care Management Review,* Spring 2001, pp. 7–19.

3. Catherine Dixon-Kheir, "Supervisors Are Key to Keeping Young Talent," *HRMagazine,* January 2001, pp. 139–142.

4. Frank Shipper and John E. Dillard, Jr., "A Study of Impending Derailment and Recovery of Middle Managers Across Career Stages," *Human Resource Management,* Winter 2000, pp. 331–345.

5. Robert Bruce, "The Middle Ground," *Accountancy,* July 1997, p. 41.

6. Paul C. Nutt, "Half of the Decisions We Make Are Wrong. Why?" *Across the Board,* March/April 2001, pp. 63–66.

7. Gerald R. Ferris, Pamela L. Perrewe, William P. Anthony, and David C. Gilmore, "Political Skill at Work," *Organizational Dynamics,* Spring 2000, pp. 25–37.

8. Janna P. Vice and Lana W. Carnes, "Developing Communication and Professional Skills Through Analytical Reports," *Business Communication Quarterly,* March 2001, pp. 84–98.

9. James Collins and Jerry Porras, *Built to Last: Successful Habits of Visionary Companies* (New York: Harperbusiness, 1997).

10. Gerry Miles and Richard H. Koonce, "Multi-Level Visioning," *Training & Development,* March 2001, pp. 31–39.

11. Henry Mintzberg, *The Nature of Managerial Work* (Englewood Cliffs, NJ: Prentice-Hall, 1980).

12. Ibid.

13. Peter Garber and Peter R. Garber, *Giving and Receiving Performance Feedback* (Human Resource Development Press, 2004).

14. Arthur M. Langer, *IT and Organizational Learning: Managing Change Through Technology and Education* (New York: Routledge, 2004).

15. Gary Yukl and Richard Lepsinger, *Flexible Leadership: Creating Value by Balancing Multiple Challenges and Choices* (San Francisco, CA: Pfeiffer, 2004).

16. Langer, op. cit.

17. Rob Flickenger, *Building Wireless Community Networks* (New York: O'Reilly, 2003).

18. Adam Jolly and Jeremy Philpott, *A Handbook of Intellectual Property Management: Protecting, Developing, and Exploiting Your IP Assets* (New York: Kogan Page, 2005).

19. Ibid.

20. Bernard Marr, *Perspective on Intellectual Capital: Multidisciplinary Insights into Management, Measurement, and Reporting* (New York: Butterworth-Heinemann, 2005).

21. Ibid.

22. Ibid.

Chapter 3

1. John E. Richardson, *Annual Editions: Business Ethics* (New York: McGraw-Hill/Dushkin, 2005).

2. *No Longer Business as Usual: Fighting Bribery and Corruption* (Paris: OECD, 2001).

3. *U.S. Sentencing Commission Guidelines Manual* (New York: Diane Publishing, 2004).

4. Suggested by S. Prakash Sethi, "A Conceptual Framework for Environmental Analysis of Social Issues and Evaluation of Business Response Patterns," *Academy of Management Review,* January 1979, pp. 63–74.

5. Milton Friedman, *Capitalism and Freedom* (Chicago: University of Chicago Press, 1962).

6. Milton Friedman, "The Social Responsibility of Business Is to Increase Its Profits," *New York Times Magazine,* September 1970, pp. 33, 122–126.

7. Doug Bandow, "What Business Owes to Cure Society's Woes," *Business & Society Review,* Spring 1992, pp. 94–96.

8. Sethi, "A Conceptual Framework," p. 66.

9. Josef Wieland, *Standards and Audits for Ethics Management Systems: The European Perspective* (New York: Springer-Verlag, 2003).

10. Ibid.

11. Peter Arlow and Martin J. Gannon, "Social Responsiveness, Corporate Structure, and Economic Performance," *Academy of Management Review,* April 1982, p. 235.

12. Aniysa S. Thomas and Roy L. Simerly, "Internal Determinants of Corporate Social Performance: The Role of Top Managers," *Academy of Management Journal, Best Papers Proceedings,* 1995, pp. 411–415.

13. Stephen B. Knouse and Robert A. Giacalone, "The Six Components of Successful Ethics Training," *Business & Society Review,* 1997, pp. 10–13.

14. Doris Rubenstein, *The Good Corporate Citizen: A Practical Guide* (New York: John Wiley, 2004).

15. Ibid.

16. "How Businesses Are Helping Nonprofits," *Nonprofit World,* January/February 1997, p.54.

17. Thomas W. Stallings, "Learning to Love Compliance," *Life Association News,* October 1997, pp. 140–144.

18. Boyd Alison, "Employee Traps—Corruption in the Workplace," *Management Review,* September 1997, p. 9.

19. Veronica J. Schmidt and Norman A. Scott, "Work and Family Life: A Delicate Balance," *Personnel Administrator,* August 1987, pp. 40–46.

20. Sheila Rothwell, "Human Resources Management: Flexible Firm Strategies," *Manager Update,* Spring 1997, pp. 22–33.

21. Fern Schumer Chapman, "Executive Guilt: Who's Taking Care of the Children?" *Fortune,* February 16, 1987, pp. 30–37.

22. Ronald Buckley, Danielle Ben, Dwight Funk, Jack Howard, Howard Berkson, Tommie Mobbs, and Gerald Ferris, "Ethical Issues in Human Resource Systems," *Human Resource Management,* Spring/Summer 2001, pp. 130–136.

23. Sara A. Morris, "Internal Effects of Stakeholder Management Devices," *Journal of Business Ethics,* March 1997, pp. 413–424.

24. C. I. Barnard, *The Functions of the Executive* (Cambridge, MA: Harvard University Press, 1938).

25. Evan M. Dudik, *Strategic Renaissance* (New York: AMACOM, 2000).

26. Anne T. Lawrence, James Weber, and James E. Post, *Business and Society: Stakeholders, Ethics, Public Policy* (New York: McGraw-Hill/Irwin, 2004).

27. Ibid.

28. Thomas A. Hemphill, "Legislating Corporate Social Responsibility," *Business Horizons,* March/April 1997, pp. 53–58.

29. Justin Fox, "The Amazing Stock Option Sleight of Hand," *Fortune,* June 25, 2001, pp. 86–92.

30. Ken Cottrill, "Another Audit in Your Future?" *Journal of Business Strategy,* May/June 1996, p. 57.

31. Mike Drumond, "Thinking Outside the Box," *Business 2.0,* July 10, 2001, pp. 64–73.

32. www.nw3c.org/sixnonth-trendsreport.htm, July1, 2001.

33. James Butler and Jennifer Dunn, "Safety Fight Brings Ford, Firestone to End of the Road," *Detroit Free Press,* May 22, 2001.

34. "What the Companies Say," *St. Petersburg Times,* May 20, 2001.

35. Cyndee Miller, "Marketers Weigh Effects of Sweatshop Crackdown," *Marketing News,* May 12, 1997, pp. 1, 19; and Annabelle Perez, "Sports Apparel Goes to Washington: New Sweatshop Code Enlists Vendor Support," *Sporting Goods Business,* May 12, 1997.

36. Dawn-Marie Driscoll and W. Michael Hoffman, *Ethics Matters: How to Implement Values-Driven Management* (Waltham, MA: Bentley College, 2000).

37. Ibid.

38. Jeffrey M. Kaplan, "Hoffman-LaRoche Case: A Sentencing Guidelines Milestone," *Ethics and Corporate Conduct Quarterly,* July/August, 1999, pp. 1–11.

39. Laura P. Hartman, *Perspectives in Business Ethics* (Burr Ridge, IL: McGraw-Hill Irwin, 2002).

40. Business Week/Harris Poll: How Business Rates: By the Numbers (September 11, 2000), *Business Week Online,* www.businessweek.com/2000/00_37/b3698004.htm.

Chapter 4

1. Fred Harmon, *Business 2001* (Washington, DC: Kiplinger Books, 2001).

2. "The World View of Multinationals," *The Economist,* January 29, 2000, p. 24.

3. R. A. Pitts and D. Lei, *Strategic Management: Building and Sustaining Competitive Advantage* (Cincinnati: South-Western, 2000).

4. Michael W. Peng, *Business Strategies in Transition Economies* (Thousand Oaks, CA: Sage, 2000).

5. Jackie Kraft, *The Process of Competition* (Northampton, MA: Edward Edgar, 2000).

6. Klaus Menrad, "Market and Marketing Function of Functional Food in Europe," *Journal of Food Engineering,* February 2003, pp. 181–188.

7. John Thacker, "Much Ado About Marketing," *Across the Board,* April 1985, pp. 38–46; Vernon R. Alden, "Who Says You Can't Crack Japanese Markets?" *Harvard Business Review,* January–February 1987, pp. 53–56; and John S. Hill and Richard R. Hill, "Adapting Products to LDC Tastes," *Harvard Business Review,* March/April 1984, pp. 92–101.

8. "U.S. Trade," *The World Almanac* (Mahwah, NJ: World Almanac Books, 2000); and Nick K. Nanto and Vivian C. Jones, *U.S. International Trade: Data and Forecasts,* May 18, 2001, pp. 1–13.

9. "Economic Trends in Economic Trade," *Economic and Business Outlook,* June 2000.

10. Peng, *Business Strategies.*

11. J. Carlos Fernandez-Molina, "Licensing Agreements for Information Resources and Copyright Limitations and Exceptions, *Journal of Information Science,* Winter 2004, pp. 337–346.

12. Christopher A. Bartlett and Sumantra Goshal, "Going Global: Lessons from Late Movers," *Harvard Business Review,* March/April 2000, pp. 132–142.

13. Kathryn R. Harrigan, "Joint Ventures That Endure," *Industry Week,* April 20, 1987, p. 14. Also see L. G. Franko, *Joint Venture Survival in Multinational Corporations* (New York: Praeger, 1971).

14. Sherif Mohamed, "Performance in International Construction Joint Ventures: Modeling Perspective, *Journal of Construction Engineering & Management,* December 2003, pp. 619–626.

15. John S. McClenahen, "Alliances for Competitive Advantage," *Industry Week,* August 24, 1987, pp. 33–36; and J. Peter Killing, "How to Make Joint a Venture Work," *Harvard Business Review,* May/June 1982, pp. 120–127.

16. United Nations Conference on Trade and Development, *World Investment Report 2004.*

17. Robert Grosse and Duane Kujawa, *International Business: Theory and Managerial Applications* (Homewood, IL: Richard D. Irwin, 1988), pp. 91–93.

18. T. Sugiura and A. Pirola-Merlo, "The Effect of Cross-Cultural Adjustment on Performance and Turnover Intention of Expatriate Managers," *Australian Journal of Psychology,* 2003 Supplement, p. 63.

19. John B. Cullen, *Multinational Management: A Strategic Approach* (Cincinnati: South-Western, 2001).

20. Linda B. Catlen and Thomas F. White, *International Business: Cultural Sourcebook and Case Studies* (Cincinnati: South-Western, 2001).

21. Carl Rodrigues, *International Management: A Cultural Approach* (Cincinnati: South-Western, 2001).

22. Rosalie E. Tung and Rosalie Lam, *The Handbook of International Business* (Boston: International Thomson Business Press, 2000).

23. Cullen, *Multinational Management,* pp. 100–120.

24. Ibid.

25. Robert Weigand, "International Investments: Weighing the Incentives," *Harvard Business Review,* July/August 1983, pp.146–152.

26. *International Trade and Labor Statistics* (Paris, France: OECD, 2000). (www.oecd.org).

27. Carl A. Nelson, *Import/Export: How to Get Started in International Trade* (New York: McGraw-Hill, 2000).

28. Ibid.

29. John M. Ivancevich, *Human Resource Management* (New York: McGraw-Hill, 2000).

30. Claude B. Erb, Campbell R. Harvey, and Tadas E. Viskanta, "Political Risk, Economic Risk, and Financial Risk," *Financial Analysts Journal,* November/December 1996.

31. John C. Leontiades, *Managing the Global Enterprise: Competing in the Information Age* (London: Financial Times, 2001).

32. Terri Morrison, Wayne A. Conaway, and Joseph J. Dourees, *Dun & Bradstreet's Guide to Doing Business Around the World* (Englewood Cliff, NJ: Prentice-Hall, 2000).

33. Gary Clyde Hufbauer, Daniel C. Esty, Diann Orejas, Luis Rubio, and Jeffrey J. Schott (eds.), *NAFTA and the Environment* (New York: Institute for International Economics, 2000).

34. Ibid.

35. Ibid.

36. "Facts and Figures," *European Union Report* (Washington, DC: June 2001).

37. Arvind V. Pratak, *International Management* (Cincinnati: South-Western, 1997), p. 60.

38. Rick L. Click and Thomas N. Duening, *Business Process Outsourcing: The Competitive Advantage* (Hoboken, NJ: John Wiley & Sons, 2004).

39. William Spain and Andrea Coombes, "Worked Over: Job Exports Seen Constraining U.S. Recovery," *CBS Marketwatch,* August 29, 2003.

40. "Users of BPO Report High Satisfaction with Existing Relationships," *Gartner, Inc.,* October 7, 2002, p. 1.

41. Benjamin Beasley-Murray, "Business Process Outsourcing Gains Ground," *Global Finance,* September 2003, pp. 54–56.

42. Ahmed Riahi-Belakaoul, *The Role of Corporate Reputation for Multinational Firms* (Westport, CT: Quorum, 2001).

Chapter 5

1. Gudela Grote, "Uncertainty Management at the Core of System Design," *Annual Review in Control,* December 2004, pp. 267–274.

2. Peter H. Antoniu and Igor H. Ansoff, Strategic Management for Difficult Times, *Technology,* June 2004, pp. 275–291.

3. Ibid.

4. George Lakoff, "Our Moral Values," *Nation,* December 6, 2004, pp. 6–7.

5. Ahmad Diba and Lisa Munoz, "American's Mot Admired Companies," *Fortune,* February 19, 2001, pp. 64–69.

6. "Toyota," *Forbes,* January 13, 1997, p. S19.

7. Michael Foley, "The Lager Connection," *Chief Executive,* May 1997, pp. 12–13.

8. R. Silkos and C. Yang, "Welcome to the 21st Century," *Business Week,* January 24, 2000, pp. 36–44.

9. Burt Nanus, *Visionary Leadership* (San Francisco, CA: Jossey-Bass, 1992), p. 8.

10. R. A. Burgleman, *Strategy Is Destiny: How Strategy-Making Shapes a Company's Future* (New York: Free Press, 2000).

11. Ibid.

12. Charles A. O'Reilly, III, and Jeffrey Pfeffer, *Hidden Value: How Companies Achieve Extraordinary Results with Ordinary People* (Boston: Harvard Business School Publishing, 2000).

13. Jason K. Phillips, "An Application of the Balance Scorecard to Public Transit System Performance Assessment," *Transportation Journal,* Winter 2004, pp. 26–55.

14. Dieter Roller, Oliver Eck, and Stavros Dalakakis, "Knowledge-Based Support of Rapid Product Development," *Journal of Engineering Design,* August 2004, pp. 367–388.

15. Michael A. Verespej, "A Dearth of Good Managers," *Industry Week,* April 2, 2001, pp. 38–39.

16. Steven Van Yoder, "Beware the Coming Corporate Backlash," *Industry Week,* April 2, 2001, pp. 68–71.

17. R. Boucher Ferguson, "SAP Turns to Pattern Development," *eWeek,* August 9, 2004, pp. 9–10.

18. R. J. Grossman, "Measuring Up," *HR Magazine,* February 2000, pp. 28–35.

19. Roberto C. Goizueta, "Essence of Business," *Executive Excellence,* May 1997, pp. 4–5.

20. Victoria Hanna and Kathryn Walsh, "How to Co-Operate for Competitive Advantage," *Engineering Management,* August–September 2004, pp. 28–31.

21. Rainer Feurer and Kazem Chaharbaghi, "Defining Competitiveness: A Holistic Approach," *Management Decision,* 1994, pp. 49–58.

22. Francis J. Quinn, "Team Up for Supply Chain Success," *Logistics Management,* October 1997, pp. 39–41.

23. Fred Harmon, *Business 2010* (Washington, DC: Kiplinger Books, 2001).

24. Miles H. Overholt, "Flexible Organizations: Using Organizational Design as a Competitive Advantage," *Human Resource Planning,* 1997, pp. 22–32.

25. David A. Garvin, "Competing on the Eight Dimensions of Quality," *Harvard Business Review,* November–December 1987, pp. 101–109.

26. J. M. Liedtka, "Strategic Planning as Contributor to Strategic Change: A Generative Model," *European Management Journal,* May 2000, pp. 195–206.

27. Kirsten Murphy, "Alternative Scenarios," *News Media & The Law,* Winter 2004, pp. 20–21.

28. J. V. Crosby, *Cycles, Trends, and Turning Points: Practical Marketing and Sales Forecasting* (Chicago: NTC, 2000).

29. C. P. Stickney and R. L. Welch, *Financial Accounting* (Ft. Worth, TX: Dryden, 2000).

30. Ibid.

31. Carol M. Lehman and Debbie D. Dufrene, *Business Communication* (Cincinnati: South-Western, 1999).

32. Richard Baskerville and Jan Pries-Heje, "Short Cycle-Time Systems Development," *Information Systems Journal,* July 2004, pp. 237–264.

33. R. Neff, "A New Japan," *Business Week,* October 25, 1999, pp. 69–78.

34. Ibid., p. 268.

35. Joseph D. Blackburn, "The Time Factor," in *Time-Based Competition: The Next Battleground in American Manufacturing,* ed. Joseph D. Blackburn (Homewood, IL: Business One Irwin, 1991), p. 19.

36. Ibid.

Chapter 6

1. Kathleen M. Eisenhardt and Donald N. Sull, "Strategy as Simple Rules," *Harvard Business Review,* January 2001, pp.16–116.

2. Clayton M. Christensen, "Making Strategy: Learning by Doing," *Harvard Business Review,* November/December 1997, pp. 141–156.

3. Tor Tonnessen and Torger Gjefsen, "The Enterprise Development: Direct Employee Participation in Strategic Planning," *Total Quality Management,* July 1999, pp. 739–744.

4. Steven Weinstein, "Listening to the Consumers' Voices," *Progressive Grocer,* July 1997, pp. 49–52.

5. Massimo Piliucci, "Chaos and Complexity," *Skeptic,* Fall 2000, pp. 62–70.

6. Henk W. Volberda and Tom Elfring, *Rethinking Strategy* (Thousand Oaks, CA: Sage, 2001).

7. Rick Dove, "An Ear for Strategy," *Production,* January 1997, pp. 30–32.

8. Rosabeth Moss Kanter, "The Best of Both Worlds," *Harvard Business Review,* November/December 1992, pp. 9–10.

9. Robert L. Lattimer, "The New Age of Competitiveness," *Competitiveness Review,* 2003, pp. 1–14.

10. "Strategic Planning," *Quality Progress,* July 1997, pp. 83–84.

11. Anne S. Huff, James O. Huff, and Pamela S. Barr. *When Firms Change Direction* (New York: Oxford University Press, 2000).

12. Andrew Dolbeck, "M&A In the U.S. and Europe," *Weekly Corporate Growth Report,* August 16, 2004, pp. 1–3.

13. Marc Gunther, "What Does AOL Want? Growth, Growth, and More Growth," *Fortune,* July 23, 2001, pp. 84–94.

14. J. Scott Armstrong and Roderick J. Brodie, "Effects of Portfolio Planning Methods on Decision Making: Experimental Results," *International Journal of Research in Marketing,* January 1994, pp. 73–84. For a critique of this research, see Robin Wensley, "Making Better Decisions," *International Journal of Research in Marketing,* January 1994, pp. 85–90. For Armstrong and Brodie's reply, see "Portfolio Planning Methods," *International Journal of Research in Marketing,* January 1994, pp. 91–93.

15. Al Achenbaum and Pete Bogda, "Fifteen Years Later, The Return of Strategy," *Brandweek,* February 24, 1997, p. 18.

16. Tony McCann, "The Rule of the 2x2," *Long Range Planning,* February 1995, pp. 112–115.

17. Andrew S. Grove, "Navigating Strategic Inflection Points," *Business Strategy Review,* Autumn 1997, pp. 11–18.

18. John H. Sheridan, "Now It's a Job for the CEO," *Industry Week,* March 20, 2000, pp. 22–27.

19. Elizabeth Corcoran, "Making Over Motorola," *Forbes,* December 13, 2004, pp. 103–107.

20. I. M. Jawahar and Gary L. McLaughlin, "Toward a Descriptive Stakeholder Theory: An Organizational Life Cycle Approach," *Academy of Management Review,* July 2001, pp. 397–414.

21. P. J. H. Shoemaker, "How to Link Strategic Vision to Core Capabilities," *Sloan Management Review,* Fall 1992, pp. 67–81.

22. Myra Faye Black, "How Does Your Company Measure Up?," *Black Enterprise,* November 2001, p. 52.

23. Andy Hines, "Applying Integral Futures to Environmental Scanning," *Futures Research Quarterly,* Winter 2004, pp. 49–62.

24. T. J. Tetenbaum, "Shifting Paradigms: From Newton to Chaos," *Organizational Dynamics,* Spring 1998, pp. 21–32.

25. William Drohan, "Principles of Strategic Planning," *Association Management,* January 1997, pp. 85–87.

26. Tony Jaques, "Issue Definition: The Neglected Foundation of Effective Issue Management," *Journal of Public Affairs,* May 2004, pp. 191–200.

27. John F. Mahon, Pursey P.M.A.R. Huegens, and Kai Lamertz, "Social Networks and Non-Market Strategy," *Public Affairs,* May 2004, pp. 170–189.

28. Ethel Auster and Chun Wei Choo, "How Senior Managers Acquire and Receive Information in Environmental Scanning," *Information Processing and Management,* September/October 1994, pp. 607–618.

29. John M. Ivancevich and Thomas N. Duening, *Managing Einsteins: Leading High-Tech Workers in the Digital Age* (New York: McGraw-Hill, 2001, pp. 202–215).

30. Peter Fingar, "Real Time Reality," *eWeek,* November 8, 2004, p. 46.

31. Glenn Rifkin, "GM's Internet Overhaul," *Technology Review,* October 2002, pp. 62–66.

32. Kevin Kelly, "New Rules for the New Economy," *Wired,* September 1997, pp. 140–145, 186–197.

33. Ibid.

34. "Automakers Eye Overseas Cake," *China Business Weekly,* June 28, 2004.

35. Rob Spiegel, "E-Spend Dilemma," *Line 56,* July/August 2001, pp. 40–45.

36. W. Edwards Deming, *Out of the Crisis* (Cambridge, MA: MIT Center for Advanced Engineering Study, 1986), p. 175.

37. Mark L. McConkie and R. Wayne Boss, "Using Stories as an Aid to Consultation," *Public Administration Quarterly,* Winter 1994.

38. Philip B. Crosby, *Running Things: The Art of Making Things Happen* (New York: McGraw-Hill, 1986), pp. 78–80.

39. "This Month's Focus: The Mission Statement," *Manager's Magazine,* February 1995, pp. 30–31.

40. Charles A. Rarick and John Vitton, "Missions Statements Make Cents," *Journal of Business Strategy,* January/February 1995, pp. 11–12.

41. Morris A. Cohen, Carl Cull, Haus L. Lee, and Don Willen, "Saturn's Supply-Chain Innovation: High Value in After-Sales Service," *Sloan Management Review,* Summer 2000, pp. 93–101.

42. Karen Bemowski, "To Boldly Go Where So Many Have Gone Before," *Quality Progress,* February 1995, pp. 29–33.

43. Michael E. Porter, "What Is Strategy?" *Harvard Business Review,* November/December 1996, pp. 61–78.

44. See, for example, Thomas A. Stewart, *Intellectual Capital* (New York: Currency, 1997).

45. Ian Buick and Muthu Ganesan, "An Investigation of the Current Practices of In-House Employee Training and Development Within Hotels in Scotland," *Service Industries Journal,* October 1997, pp. 652–668.

46. Arno Penzias, "New Paths to Success," *Fortune,* June 12, 1995, pp. 90–93; George Stalk and Thomas M. Hout, *Competing Against Time* (New York: Free Press, 1990).

47. Alfie Morgan, *Strategic Leadership: Managing the Firm in a Turbulent World* (Dubuque, IA: Kendall/Hunt, 2001).

Chapter 7

1. Mehdi Dastani, Joris Hulstijn, and Leendert Van der Torre, "How to Decide What to Do," *European Journal of Operational Resarch,* February 2005, pp. 762–784.

2. Victor H. Vroom, "Reflections on Leadership and Decision Making," *Journal of General Management,* Spring 1984, pp. 18–36.

3. Sara Kiesler and Lee Sproull, "Managerial Response to Changing Environments," *Administrative Science Quarterly,* December 1982, pp. 548–570.

4. Errol R. Iselin, "Individual Versus Group Decision Making Performance," *Journal of Business Finance & Accounting,* January 1991, pp. 191–208.

5. John B. Bloniarz, "Weighing the Evidence," *Intelligent Enterprise,* April 7, 2001, pp. 54–55.

6. Mark Casson, "Economics and Anthropology—Reluctant Partners," *Human Relations,* September 1996, pp. 1151–1180.

7. Tilmann Betsch, Susanne Haberstroh, Beate Molter, and Andreas Glockner, "Oops, I Did It Again—Relapse Errors in Routine Decision Making," *Organizational Behavior and Human Decision Processes,* January 2004, pp. 62–74.

8. James C. Anderson and James B. L. Thomson, "Combining Value and Price to Make Purchase Decisions in Business Markets," *International Journal of Research in Marketing,* December 2000, pp. 307–329.

9. Eugen Tarnow, "A Recipe for Mission and Vision Statements," *IEEE Transactions on Professional Communication,* June 2001, pp. 138–141.

10. Robert Gandossy, "The Need for Speed," *Journal of Business Strategy,* January/February 2003, pp. 29–33.

11. Erik Dane and Michael Pratt, "Intuition: Its Boundaries and Roles in Organizational Decision Making," *Academy of Management Proceedings,* 2004, pp. A1–A5.

12. Lisl Klein, "Rigour and Intuition in Professional Life," *Ergonomics,* May 20, 2001, pp. 579–587.

13. Eugene Sadler-Smith and Erella Shefy, "The Intuitive Executive: Understanding and Applying 'Gut Feel' In Decision Making," *Academy of Management Executive,* November 2004, pp. 76–91.

14. Henry Mintzberg and Frances Westley, "Decision Making: It's Not What You Think," *MIT Sloan Management Review,* Spring 2001, pp. 89–93.

15. Dennis J. Moberg, "Managers as Judges in Employee Disputes: An Occasion for Moral Imagination," *Business Ethics Quarterly,* October 2003, pp. 453–477.

16. "What Are Mental Models?" *Sloan Management Review,* Spring 1997, p. 13.

17. Steve Harmon, "Venture Capital Pours into Internet," *Upside,* December 1997, p. 176.

18. William P. Densmore, "Surf's Up, and VCs Are Riding the Wave," *Computerworld,* September 29, 1997, pp. C6–C7.

19. Anya Sacharow, "Capital Crunch?" *Mediaweek,* October 6, 1997, pp. 50–52.

20. P. N. Rastogi, "Sustaining Enterprise Competitiveness: Is Human Capital the Answer?," *Human Systems Management,* 2000, pp. 193–203.

21. Gerard Puccio, "Creative Problem Solving Preferences: Their Identification and Implications," *Creativity & Innovation Management,* September 1999, pp. 171–178.

22. R. A. Cozier and C. R. Schwenk, "Agreement and Thinking Alike: Ingredients for Poor Decisions," *Academy of Management Executive,* February 1990, pp. 69–74.

23. Peter M. Todd and Gerd Gigerenzer, "Bounding Rationality to the World," *Journal of Economic Psychology,* April 2003, pp. 143–165.

24. Katsuhito Iwai, "A Contribution to the Evolutionary Theory of Innovation, Imitation, and Growth," *Journal of Economic Behavior & Organization,* October 2000, pp. 167–198.

25. Sheila Murray Bethel, "Productive Delegating," *Executive Excellence,* January 2000, p. 16.

26. Robert L. Schalock and Gordon S. Bonham, "Measuring Outcomes and Managing for Results," *Evaluation and Program Planning,* August 2003, pp. 229–235.

27. For a related discussion, see Charles R. Schwenk, "Information, Cognitive Biases, and Commitment to a Course of Action," *Academy of Management Review,* April 1986, pp. 298–310.

28. Robert J. Baum and Stefan Wally, "Strategic Decision Speed and Firm Performance," *Strategic Management Journal,* November 2003, pp. 1107–1129.

29. Rob Lebow and William L. Simon, "Making Decisions," *Executive Excellence,* November 1997, p. 13.

30. Craig W. Kirkwood, "Approximating Risk Aversion in Decision Analysis Applications," *Decision Analysis,* March 2004, pp. 51–67.

31. William Umiker, "Risk Taking: A Supervisory Imperative," *Health Care Supervisor,* December 1997, pp. 1–8.

32. Tony Elkins, "Virtual Teams," *IIE Solutions,* April 2000, pp. 26–31.

33. John P. Wanous and Margaret A. Youtz, "Solutions Diversity and the Quality of Group Decisions," *Academy of Management Journal,* March 1986, pp. 149–158.

34. For some examples of research on group decision making, see Charles Holloman and Harold Henrick, "Adequacy of Group Decisions as a Function of the Decision-Making Process," *Academy of Management Journal,* June 1972, pp. 175–184; Andrew H. Van de Ven and Andre Delbecq, "Nominal Versus Interacting Group Processes for Committee Decision-Making Effectiveness," *Academy of Management Journal,* June 1972, pp. 203–212; B. M. Staw, "The Escalation of Commitment to a Course of Action," *Academy of Management Review,* October 1981, pp. 577–588; and David M. Schweiger, William R. Sandburg, and James W. Ragan, "Group Approaches for Improving Strategic Decision Making," *Academy of Management Journal,* March 1986, pp. 51–71.

35. James Surwiecki, "Mass Intelligence," *Forbes,* May 24, 2004, p. 48.

36. Alan R. Dennis, "Information Exchange and Use in Group Decision Making: You Can Lead a Group to Information, But You Can't Make It Think," *MIS Quarterly,* December 1996, pp. 433–457.

37. For examples, see Solomon Asch, "Studies of Independence and Conformity," *Psychological Monographs,* 1956, pp. 68–70; Normal Dalkey and Olaf Helmer, "An Experimental Application of Delphi Method to Use of Experts," *Management Science,* April 1963, pp. 458–467; E. M. Bridges, W. J. Doyle, and D. J. Mahan, "Effects of Hierarchical Differentiation on Group Productivity, Efficiency, and Risk-Taking," *Administrative Science Quarterly,* Fall 1968, pp. 305–339; Victor Vroom, Lester Grant, and Timothy Cotten, "The Consequences of Social Interaction in Group Problem-Solving," *Organizational Behavior and Human Performance,* February 1969, pp. 77–95; P. A. Collaras and L. R. Anderson, "Effect of Perceived Expertise upon Creativity of Members of Brainstorming Groups, *Journal of Applied Psychology,* April 1969, pp. 159–163; Richard A. Guzzo and James A. Waters, "The Expression of Affect and the Performance of Decision-Making Groups, *Journal of Applied Psychology,* February 1982, pp. 67–74; and D. Tjosvold and R. H. G. Field, "Effects of Social Context on Consensus and Majority Vote Decision Making," *Academy of Management Journal,* September 1983, pp. 500–506.

38. "People Networking," *British Journal of Administrative Management,* November/December 2001, pp. 24–25.

39. James G. March and Michael D. Cohen, *Leadership and Ambiguity* (Burr Ridge, IL: McGraw-Hill, 1974).

40. Norman Dalkey, *The Delphi Method: An Experimental Study of Group Opinion* (Santa Monica, CA: Rand Corporation, 1969). This is the classic work on the Delphi method.

41. Chitu Okoli and Suzanne D. Pawlowski, "The Delphi Method as a Research Tool: An Example, Design Considerations, and Applications," *Information & Management*, December 2004, pp. 15–29.

42. See Andre L. Delbecq, Andrew H. Van de Ven, and David H. Gustafson, *Group Techniques for Program Planning* (Glenview, IL: Scott, Foresman, 1975) for an outstanding work devoted entirely to NGT and other group decision-making methods. The discussion here is based on this work.

43. Ibid., p. 18.

44. Sally Redman, Sue Carrick, Jill Cockburn, and Sheila Hurst, "Consulting About Priorities for the NHMRC National Breast Cancer Centre: How Good Is the Nominal Group Technique?," *Australian & New Zealand Journal of Public Health*, June 1997, pp. 250–256.

45. Daniel Bell, *The Coming of Post Industrial Society* (New York: Basic Books, 1973).

46. Roger Eberlin, "Data Warehousing Breaking Out on the Web," *National Underwriter*, December 8, 1997, pp. 16–17.

47. F. Ozden Gur Ali and William A. Wallace, "Bridging the Gap Between Business Objectives and Parameters and Data Mining Algorithms," *Decision Support Systems*, September 1997, pp. 3–15.

48. Karen Spinner, "Going Down to the Data Mart," *CFO: The Magazine for Chief Financial Officers*, December 1997, pp. 81–86.

49. Justin Hibbard, "Straight Line to Relevant Data," *Informationweek*, November 17, 1997, pp. 21S–25S.

50. V. Thomas Dock and James C. Wetherbe, *Computer Information Systems for Business* (St. Paul, MN: West, 1988), p. 36.

51. Nikos I. Karacapilidis and Costas P. Pappis, "A Framework for Group Decision Support Systems: Combining AI Tools and OR Techniques," *European Journal of Operational Research*, December 1, 1997, pp. 373–388.

52. Sukumar Rantham and Michael V. Mannino, "Tools for Building the Human-Computer Interface of a Decision Support System," *Decision Support Systems*, January 1995, pp. 35–59.

53. Tom Bridge and Yuri Y. Lin, "Expert Systems in Banking," *Canadian Banker*, July/August 1992, pp. 20–35.

Chapter 8

1. David Holman, Toby D. Wall, Chris W. Clegg, Paul Sparrow, and Ann Howard (eds.), *The Essentials of the New Workplace: A Guide to the Human Impact of Modern Working Practices* (New York: John Wiley & Sons, 2004).

2. Michael T. Brannick and Edward L. Levin, *Job Analysis: Methods, Research, and Applications for Human Resource Management in the New Millennium* (Thousand Oaks, CA: Sage, 2002).

3. Ibid.

4. *Job Analysis: An Important Employment Tool* (Washington, DC: Department of Labor, 2002).

5. Ibid.

6. Nadene Peterson and Roberto Cortez Gonzalez, *The Role of Work in Lives: Applied Career Counseling and Psychology* (Cincinnati, OH: Wadsworth Publishing, 2004).

7. Thomas W. Malone, *The Future of Work: How the New Order of Business Will Shape Your Organization, Your Management Style, and Your Life* (Boston: Harvard Business School Press, 2004).

8. Ibid.

9. Peter F. Drucker, *On the Profession of Management* (Boston: Harvard Business School Press, 2003).

10. Kevin Ford and Joel Cutcher-Gershenfeld, *Valuable Disconnects in Organizational Learning Systems* (New York: Oxford Press, 2004).

11. Ibid.

12. Jay A. Block and Michael Betrus, *Great Answers! Great Questions! For Your Job Interview* (New York: McGraw-Hill, 2004).

13. Sigvaled J. Harryson, "How Canon and Sony Drive Product Innovation Through Networking and Application-Focused R&D," *Journal of Product Innovation Management*, July 1997, pp. 288–295.

14. Leigh Ann Klaus, "Small Companies Finish First," *Quality Progress*, November 1997, pp. 12–13.

15. Arthur N. Turner and Paul R. Lawrence, *Industrial Jobs and the Worker: An Investigation of Response to Task Attributes* (Cambridge, MA: Harvard University Press, 1965).

16. Kae H. Chung and Monica F. Ross, "Differences in Motivational Properties Between Job Enlargement and Job Enrichment," *Academy of Management Review*, January 1977, pp. 114–15.

17. Frederick Herzberg, "The Wise Old Turk," *Harvard Business Review*, September/October 1974, pp. 70–80.

18. Morten T. Hansen and Bolko von Oetinger, "Introducing T-Shaped Managers: Knowledge Management's Next Generation," *Harvard Business Review*, March 2001, pp. 106–117.

19. Ronald L. Jacobs, *Structured On-The-Job Training: Unleashing Employee Expertise in the Workplace* (San Francisco: Berrett-Koehler, 2003).

20. D. C. D'Angelo, "Lifestyles," *Pennsylvania CPA Journal*, Spring 1999, pp. 16, 18.

21. Leigh Ann Klaus, "Small Companies Finish First," *Quality Progress*, November 1997, pp. 12–13.

22. David E. Bowen and Edward E. Lawler, "Total Quality-Oriented Human Resources Management," *Organizational Dynamics*, Spring 1992, pp. 29–41.

23. Joan E. Ridgon, "Talk Isn't Cheap," *The Wall Street Journal*, February 27, 1995, p. R13.

24. "UCI Gets Creative with Work Schedules," http://www.communications.uci.edu/99ucinews/990414d.html.

25. Keri E. Pearlson and Carol S. Saudners, "There's No Place Like Home: Managing Telecommuting Paradoxes," *Academy of Management Executive*, May 2001, pp.117–128.

26. Estimates received from U.S. Department of Labor Statistics Division, November 22, 2004.

27. www.officeteam.com, February 8, 2001.

28. "Telecommuting Grows with New Economy, Helping Fuel Productivity Gains," *Wall Street Journal*, February 6, 2001, p. A1.

29. K. Rose, "Work/Live Flexibility: A Key to Maximizing Productivity," *Compensation and Benefits Management*, Autumn 1998, pp. 27–32.

30. K. Kiser, "Working on World Time," *Training*, April 1999, pp. 28–35.

31. Gerald R. Ferris and David C. Gilmore, "The Moderating Role of Work Context in Job Design Research: A Test of Competing Models," *Academy of Management Journal*, December 1984, pp. 885–892; and Edwin A. Locke and Richard L. Somers, "The Effects of Goal Emphasis on Performance on a Complex Task," *Journal of Management Studies*, July 1987, pp. 405–412.

32. Adrian Gostick and Chester Elton, *A Carrot a Day! A Daily Dose of Recognition For Your Employees* (New York: Gibbs Smith, 2004).

33. Ibid.

34. Leslie P. Willcocks and Robert Plant, "Getting from Bricks to Clicks," *MIT Sloan Management Review*, Spring 2001, pp. 50–59.

35. Ridgon, "Talk Isn't Cheap," p. R13.

36. Jacobs, *op.cit.*

Chapter 9

1. Jeffrey F. Rayport and Bernard J. Jaworski, "Best Face Forward," *Harvard Business Review*, December 2004, pp. 47–57.

2. Rachael Green, "Change Management: How to Teach It, How to Control It," *Journal of Organizational Excellence*, Winter 2004, pp. 84–85.

3. John Kavanagh, "Level of Professionalism in Firm Affects IT Performance Standards," *Computer Weekly*, December 2, 2003, p. 46.

4. J. Keith Louden, "The Board World, According to Louden," *Directors & Boards*, Fall 1997, p. 123.

5. Frances Hill and Rozana Huq, "Employee Empowerment: Conceptualizations, Aims, and Outcomes," *Total Quality Management & Business Excellence*, October 2004, pp. 1025–1041.

6. Trevor Merriden, "It's Big to Think Small," *Management Today*, December 1997, pp. 83–84.

7. Charles M. Parks, "Instill Lean Thinking," *Industrial Management*, September/October 2002, pp. 14–18.

8. Karin Breu, Christopher J. Hemingway, Mark Strathern, and David Bridger, "Workforce Agility: The New Employee Strategy for the Knowledge Economy," *Journal of Information Technology*, March 2002, pp. 21–31.

9. Ron Ashkenas, David Ulrich, Todd Jick, and Steve Kerr, *The Boundaryless Organization: Breaking the Chains of Organizational Structure* (San Francisco: Jossey-Bass, 2002).

10. Ajay Menon, Bernard J. Jaworksi, and Ajay K. Kohli, "Product Quality: Impact of Interdepartmental Interactions," *Journal of*

the *Academy of Marketing Science*, Summer 1997, pp. 187–200.

11. Peggy Leatt and Rodney Schneck, "Criteria for Grouping Nursing Subunits in Hospitals," *Academy of Management Journal*, March 1984, pp. 150–164.

12. Henry Tosi, *Theories of Organization* (New York: John Wiley & Sons, 1984).

13. Dennis J. Patterson and Kent A. Thompson, "Product-Line Management: Organization Makes the Difference," *Healthcare Financial Management*, February 1987, pp. 66–77.

14. Ron Sanchez and Joseph T. Mahoney, "Modularity, Flexibility, and Knowledge Management in Product and Organization Design," *Strategic Management Journal*, Winter 1996, pp. 63–76.

15. Richard B. Chase and David A. Tansik, "The Customer Contact Model for Organization Design," *Management Science*, September 1983, pp. 1037–1050.

16. William G. Ouchi and John B. Dowling, "Defining the Span of Control," *Administrative Science Quarterly*, September 1974, pp. 357–365.

17. Robert D. Dewar and Donald P. Simet, "A Level-Specific Prediction of Spans of Control Examining the Effects of Size, Technology, and Specialization," *Academy of Management Journal*, March 1981, pp. 5–24.

18. David D. Van Fleet, "Span of Management Research and Issues," *Academy of Management Journal*, September 1983, pp. 546–552.

19. Kenneth J. Meier and John Bohte, "Ode to Luther Gulick," *Administration & Society*, May 2000, pp. 115–137.

20. James Brian Quinn and Frederick G. Hilmer, "Strategic Outsourcing," *Sloan Management Review*, Summer 1994, pp. 43–55.

21. Ravi Venkatesan, "Strategic Sourcing," *Harvard Business Review*, November/December 1992, pp. 98–107.

22. "Nike in China: Selling the Swoosh," *Crossborder Monitor*, December 18, 1998, p. 8.

23. Richard Normann and Rafael Ramirez, "From Value Chain to Value Constellation: Designing Interactive Strategy," *Harvard Business Review*, July/August 1993, pp. 65–77.

24. Thomas N. Duening and Rick L. Click, *Essentials of Business Process Outsourcing* (Hoboken, NJ: John Wiley & Sons, 2005).

25. Nelson D. Schwartz, "Down and Out in White-Collar America," *Fortune*, June 23, 2003, pp. 79–86.

26. William Spain and Andrea Coombes, "Worked Over: Job Exports Seen Constraining U.S. Recovery," *CBS Marketwatch*, August 29, 2003.

27. Richard S. Blackburn, "Dimensions of Structure: A Review and Reappraisal," *Academy of Management Review*, January 1982, pp. 59–66.

28. See Peter H. Grinyer and Masoud Yasai-Ardekani, "Dimensions of Organizational Structure: A Critical Replication," *Academy of Management Journal*, September 1980, pp. 405–421, for discussion of formalization in relation to centralization.

29. Eric J. Walton, "The Comparison of Measures of Organization Structure," *Academy of Management Review*, January 1981, pp. 155–160.

30. Rick Delbridge and James Lowe, "Manufacturing Control: Supervisory Systems on the 'New' Shopfloor," *Sociology*, August 1997, pp. 409–426.

31. Jeffrey D. Ford, "Institutional Versus Questionnaire Measures of Organizational Structure," *Academy of Management Journal*, September 1979, pp. 601–610.

32. Richard L. Daft and Patricia J. Bradshaw, "The Process of Horizontal Differentiation: Two Models," *Administrative Science Quarterly*, September 1980, pp. 441–456.

33. Dennis S. Mileti, Doug A. Timmer, and David F. Gillespie, "Intra- and Interorganizational Determinants of Decentralization," *Pacific Sociological Review*, April 1982, pp. 163–183.

34. Gregory S. Whitney, "Organizational Analysis: Its Application to Performance Improvement," *National Productivity Review*, Spring 1987, pp. 168–176.

35. Georgiy M. Levchuk, Yuri N. Levchuk, Luo Jie, Krishma R. Pattipati, and David L. Kleinman, "Normative Design of Organizations. Part II: Organized Structure," *IEEE Transactions on Systems, Man, and Cybernetics*, May 2002, pp. 360–375.

36. Tom Burns and G. M. Stalker, *The Management of Innovation* (London: Tavistock, 1961).

37. C. R. Gullet, "Mechanistic vs. Organic Organizations: What Does the Future Hold?" *Personnel Administration*, 1975, p. 17.

38. Rensis Likert, *The Human Organization* (New York: McGraw-Hill, 1967).

39. Jay R. Galbraith and Robert K. Kazanjian, "Organizing to Implement Strategies of Diversity and Globalization: The Role of Matrix Organizations," *Human Resource Management*, Spring 1986, pp. 37–54; Diane Krusko and Robert R. Cangemi, "The Utilization of Project Management in the Pharmaceutical Industry," *Journal of the Society of Research Administrators*, Summer 1987, pp. 17–24.

40. Kenneth Knight, "Matrix Organization: A Review," *Journal of Management Studies*, May 1976, p. 111.

41. Ibid., p. 114.

42. Paul R. Lawrence, Harvey F. Kolodny, and Stanley M. Davis, "The Human Side of the Matrix," *Organizational Dynamics*, September 1977, p. 47.

43. The following discussion is based on Knight, "Matrix Organization," pp. 109–121.

44. Richard Lally and Jacklyn Kostner, "Learn to Be a Distance Manager," *Getting Results… For the Hands-On Manager*, July 1997, pp. 6–7.

45. William G. Ouchi, *The M-Form Society* (Reading, MA: Addison-Wesley, 1987), pp. 23–25.

46. Charles C. Snow, Raymond E. Miles, and Henry J. Coleman, "Managing the 21st Century Network Organization," *Organizational Dynamics*, Winter 1992, pp. 5–19.

Chapter 10

1. John M. Ivancevich, *Human Resource Management* (Burr Ridge, IL.: McGraw-Hill/Irwin, 2004).

2. Stephen P. Robbins and David A. Decenzo, *Fundamentals of Management* (Upper Saddle River, NJ: Prentice-Hall, 2004).

3. Allison K. Verderber Herriott, "Toward an Understanding of the Dialectical Tensions Inherent in CEO and Key Retention Plans During Bankruptcy," *Northwestern Law Review*, Winter 2004, pp. 579–622.

4. Daniel H. Pink, *Free Agent Nation: How America's New Independent Workers Are Transforming the Way We Live* (New York: Warner Books, 2001).

5. Alan L. Sklover, *Fired, Downsized, or Laid Off* (Ontario, Canada: Owl Books, 2000).

6. Peter Bradley, "A Passion for Service," *Logistics Management*, May 1997, pp. 49–51.

7. Michele Pepe, "Midsize Firms Showcase Opportunities," *Computer Reseller News*, November 11, 1996, p. 69A.

8. Richard C. Busse, *Employees' Rights: Your Practical Handbook to Workplace Law* (New York: Spinx, 2004).

9. Tayla N. Bauer, Donald M. Truxillo, Matthew E. Paronto, and Jeff A. Weekley, "Applicant Reactions to Different Selection Technology: Face-to-Face Interactive Voice Response and Computer-Assisted Telephone Screening Interviews," *International Journal of Selection Assessment*, May 2004, pp. 135–148.

10. "Testing Measures Up for Quality Control," *HR Focus*, October 1997, p. 2.

11. Steven Bates, "Science Fiction," *HR Magazine*, July 2001, pp. 34–44.

12. Bently Baranabus, "What Did the Supreme Court Really Say?" *Personnel Administrator*, July/August 1971, pp. 22–25.

13. Bates, "Science Fiction," pp. 34–44.

14. Nancy C. Ahlrichs, *Competing for Talent: Key Recruitment and Retention Strategies for Becoming an Employer of Choice* (New York: Davies-Black Publishing, 2000).

15. Stephen J. Hirschfeld, "The Danger of Employment References," *Chronicle of Higher Education*, June 25, 2004, p. B11.

16. Jonathan A. Segal, "An Offer They Couldn't Refuse," *HR Magazine*, April 2001, pp. 131–144.

17. Linda Wilson, "Know Your Surroundings," *Computerworld*, June 1997, p. 31.

18. Jeanne C. Meister, *Corporate Universities* (New York: McGraw-Hill, 2001).

19. Associated Press, "Dilbert Creator Dupes Executives with Spiel," *Houston Chronicle*, November 17, 1997, p. 2A.

20. Neil M. Boyd and Ken Kyle, "Expanding the View of Performance Appraisal by Introducing Social Justice Concerns," *Administrative Theory & Praxis*, September 2004, pp. 249–277.

21. Carla Joinson, "Making Sure Employees Measure Up," *HR Magazine*, March 2001, pp. 36–41.

22. Peter C. Honebein, "Improving Performance," *Marketing News*, November 10, 1997, p. 11.

23. Jon R. Katzenbach, *Peak Performance: Aligning the Hearts and Minds of Your Employees* (Boston: Harvard Business School Press, 2000).

24. Jorgen Sandberg, "Understanding Human Competence at Work: An Interpretive Approach," *Academy of Management Journal*, February 2000, pp. 9–25.

25. Brian Flannigan, "Turnaround from Feedback," *HR Focus*, October 1997, p. 3; Katherine A. Karl, "The Art and Science

of 360-Degree Feedback," *Academy of Management Executive,* August 1997, pp. 100–101.

26. Mary F. Sully de Luque and Steven M. Sommer, "The Impact of Culture on Feedback-Seeking Behavior: An Integrated Model and Propositions," *Academy of Management Review,* October 2000, pp. 829–849.

27. Michael C. Clayton and Linda Hayes, "Using Performance Feedback to Increase the Billable Hours of Social Workers: A Multiple Baseline Evaluation," *Behavior Analyst Today,* April 2004, pp. 91–100.

28. Fred Luthans and Alexander D. Stajkovic, "Reinforce for Performance: The Need to Go Beyond Pay and Even Rewards," *Academy of Management Executive,* May 1999, pp. 49–57.

29. Jeffrey Pfeffer, *The Human Equation: Building Profits by Putting People First* (Cambridge, MA: Harvard Business School Press, 1998).

30. David Kiley and Del Jones, "Ford Alters Worker Evaluation Process," *USA Today,* July 11, 2001, p. 31.

31. J. M. Smither, *Performance Appraisal: State of the Art in Practice* (San Francisco: Jossey-Bass, 1998).

32. P. C. Smith and L. M. Kendall, "Retranslation of Expectations: An Approach to the Construction of Unambiguous Anchors for Rating Scales," *Journal of Applied Psychology,* April 1963, pp. 149–155.

33. Cohen and Jenkins, *Abolishing Performance Appraisals.*

34. James S. Russell and Dorothy L. Goode, "An Analysis of Manager's Reactions to Their Own Performance Appraisal Feedback," *Journal of Applied Psychology,* February 1988, pp. 63–67.

35. Smither, *Performance Appraisal.*

36. Timothy L. Ross, Larry Hatcher, and Ruth Ann Ross, "The Incentive Switch," *Management Review,* May 1989, pp. 22–26.

37. Ivancevich, *Human Resource Management,* pp. 328–333.

38. Ibid.

39. Ibid.

40. Ibid.

41. Ibid.

42. Arthur H. Kroll, "Exploring Options," *HR Magazine,* October 1997, pp. 96–100.

43. "Employment and Earnings," Bureau of Labor Statistics, U.S. Department of Labor, Tables 73, 79, October 1994.

44. "If Women Don't Ask: Implications for Bargaining Encounters, The Equal Pay Act and Title VII," *Michigan Law Review,* May 2004, pp. 1104–1129.

45. Ibid.

46. Michael E. Cohen and James G. March, *Leadership and Ambiguity* (Boston, MA: Harvard Business School Press, 1974).

47. Jackie Jones, "Current Developments, Tackling an Old Problems Afresh: The Equal Opportunities Commission's New Code of Practice on Equal Pay," *Journal of Social Welfare and Family Law,* February 2004, pp. 99–109.

48. Ibid.

49. "Women in Sales Are Closing the Earnings Gap," *Personnel Journal,* July 1995, p. 28.

50. "Controlling the Costs of Employee Benefits," *The Conference Board,* 1992, p. 8.

51. J. E. Santora, "Employee Team Designs Flexible Benefits Program," *Personnel Journal,* April 1994, pp. 30–39.

52. Susan J. Wells, "The Elder Care Gap," *HR Magazine,* May 2000, pp. 38–49.

53. Jeffrey P. Englander, "Handling Sexual Harassment in the Workplace," *The CPA Journal,* February 1992, p. 14.

54. Kathryn Gravdal, "Screening for Harassment," *HR Magazine,* May 2000, pp. 114–124.

55. "Drug and Alcohol Testing Rules: An Overview," http://www.fmcsa.dot.gov/rulesregs/fmcsr/regs/382menu.htm.

56. Joel B. Bennett and E. K. Wayne (eds.), *Preventing Workplace Substance Abuse: Beyond Drug Testing to Wellness* (Washington, DC: American Psychological Association, 2003).

57. Ibid.

58. Dawn Anfuso, "It Makes Devastating Moments in Life Easier," *Workforce,* March 1999, p. 112.

Chapter 11

1. John P. Kotter, *The Leadership Factor* (New York: The Free Press, 1988).

2. Keith Davis, *Human Relations at Work* (New York: McGraw-Hill, 1967), pp. 96–97.

3. Bill Leonard, "Leaders Are Not Just Limited to Managers in Corporate America," *HR Magazine,* August 2001, pp. 27–28.

4. "Defining Leadership," *Leadership for the Front Lines,* November 1, 2000, p. 2.

5. J. Clifton Williams, "Self-Control," *Baylor Business Review,* Fall 1997, pp. 9, 32.

6. David Kipnis, Stuart M. Schmidt, Chris Swaffin-Smith, and Ian Wilkinson, "Patterns of Managerial Influence: Shotgun Managers, Tacticians, and Bystanders," *Organizational Dynamics,* Winter 1984, pp. 58–67.

7. Ibid.

8. Cited in Vivian Pospisil, "Nurturing Leaders," *Industry Week,* November 17, 1997, p. 35.

9. "AMA News," *Management Review,* January 1999, pp. 62–63.

10. Einar J. Westerlund, "What It Means to Lead," *HR Professional,* October/Novemeber 2004, p. 26.

11. Abraham Zaleznick, "Leaders and Managers: Are They Different?" *Harvard Business Review,* 1977, pp. 31–42.

12. Lynda Radosevich et al., "Leaders of the Information Age," *CIO,* September 15, 1997, pp. 137–181.

13. Michelle Marchetti, "Dell Computer," *Sales & Marketing Management,* October 1997, pp. 50–53.

14. E. L. Zimmerman, "What's Under the Hood? The Mechanics of Leadership Versus Management," *Supervision,* August 2001, pp. 10–12.

15. Jim Collins, *Good to Great: Why Some Companies Make the Leap and Others Don't* (New York: HarperBusiness, 2001).

16. Richard A. Baker, "How Can We Train Leaders If We Do Not Know What Leadership Is?" *Human Relations,* April 1997, pp. 343–362.

17. Ronald K. Mitchell, Lowell Busenitz, Theresa Lant, Patricia P. McDougall, Eric A. Morse, and J. Brock Smith, "Toward a Theory of Entrepreneurial Cognition: Rethinking the People

Side of Entrepreneurship Research," *Entrepreneurship: Theory & Practice,* Winter 2002, pp. 93–104.

18. Ralph Stogdill, "Personal Factors Associated with Leadership," *Journal of Applied Psychology,* January 1948, pp. 35–71.

19. Jim Loehr, "The Making of a Corporate Athlete," *Harvard Business Review,* January 2001, pp. 120–128.

20. Edwin E. Ghiselli, "Managerial Talent," *American Psychologist,* October 1963, pp. 631–641.

21. E. Kirby Warren, "Dealing with Change," *The CPA Journal,* August 1997, pp. 68–69.

22. Max DePree, "Attributes of Leaders," *Executive Excellence,* April 1997, p. 8.

23. Timothy F. Bednarz, "Where Have All the Leaders Gone?" *Executive Excellence,* November 2004, p. 5.

24. Stogdill, "Personal Factors," pp. 40–42.

25. Ghiselli, "Managerial Talent," pp. 633–635.

26. Jane Pickard, "Future Organizations Will Need Higher IQs," *People Management,* December 4, 1997, p. 15.

27. Daniel Goleman, Annie McKee, and Richard Boyatzis, *Primal Leadership: Realizing the Power of Emotional Intelligence* (Cambridge, MA: Harvard Business School Press, March 15, 2002).

28. Daniel Goleman, Richard Boyatzis, and Annie McKee, "Primal Leadership: The Hidden Driver of Great Performance, *Harvard Business Review,* December 2001, pp. 42–51.

29. Edwin E. Ghiselli, *Explorations in Management Talent* (Pacific Palisades, CA: Goodyear Publishing, 1971).

30. Robert J. House, "Research Contrasting the Behavior and the Effect of Reputed Charismatic Visions Reported by Non-Charismatic Leaders." Paper presented at the annual meeting of the Administrative Science Association of Canada, Montreal, 1985.

31. Kimberly B. Boal and John M. Bryson, "Charismatic Leadership: A Phenomenological and Structural Approach," in *Energy Leadership Vistas,* ed. J. G. Hunt, B. R. Billiga, H. P. Dachler, and C. A. Schriesheim (Lexington, MA: Lexington Books, 1988), pp. 11–28.

32. J. M. Howell, "A Laboratory Study of Charismatic Leadership." Paper presented at the annual meeting of The Academy of Management, San Diego, 1985.

33. B. M. Bass, *Leadership and Performance: Beyond Expectations* (New York: The Free Press, 1985).

34. W. G. Bennis and B. Nanns, *Leaders* (New York: Harper & Row, 1985); and M. Sashkin, *Trainer Guide: Leader Behavior Questionnaire* (Bryn Mawr, PA: Organizational Design and Development, 1985).

35. Jay A. Conger, Rabindra N. Kanugo, et al., "Measuring Charisma: Dimensionality and Validity of the Conger-Kanugo Scale of Charismatic Leadership," *Canadian Journal of Administrative Sciences,* September 1997, pp. 290–302.

36. Jay A. Conger and Rabindra N. Kanungo, "Toward a Behavioral Theory of Charismatic Leadership in Organizational Settings," *Academy of Management Review,* October 1987, pp. 637–647.

37. Frederick W. Taylor, *Scientific Management* (New York: Harper & Row, 1911), p. 39.

38. Rensis Likert, "Management Styles and the Human Component," *Management Review,* October 1977, pp. 23–28, 43–45.

39. Edwin A. Fleishman and James G. Hunt, eds., *Current Developments in the Study of Leadership* (Carbondale: Southern Illinois University Press, 1973), pp. 1–37.

40. Robert S. Blake and Jane S. Mouton, *The Managerial Grid* (Houston: Gulf Publishing, 1964).

41. Henry P. Sims, Jr. and Charles C. Manz, "Observing Leader Verbal Behavior: Toward Reciprocal Determinism in Leadership Theory," *Journal of Applied Psychology,* May 1984, pp. 222–232.

42. Robert Tannenbaum and Warren H. Schmidt, "How to Choose a Leadership Pattern," *Harvard Business Review,* May/June 1973, pp. 162 100.

43. Victor Vroom and Arthur Jago, "Decision Making as a Social Process: Normative and Descriptive Models of Leader Behavior," *Decision Sciences,* 1974, pp. 743–770.

44. Richard L. Priem, "Executive Judgment, Organizational Congruence, and Firm Performance," *Organizational Science,* August 1994, pp. 421–437.

45. Paul Hersey and Kenneth H. Blanchard, *Management of Organizational Behavior* (Englewood Cliffs, NJ: Prentice-Hall, 1979).

46. Fred E. Fiedler and Martin M. Chemers, *Leadership and Effective Management* (Glenview, IL: Scott, Foresman, 1974).

47. Fred E. Fiedler and Joseph E. Garcia, *New Approaches to Effective Leadership* (New York: John Wiley & Sons, 1987).

48. Terence R. Mitchell and James R. Larson, Jr., *People in Organizations* (New York: McGraw-Hill, 1987), p. 452.

49. Robert J. House and Terrence Mitchell, "Path-Goal Theory of Leadership," *Journal of Contemporary Business,* Autumn 1974, pp. 81–97.

50. Stephen R. Covey, *The Seven Habits of Highly Effective People* (New York: Simon & Schuster, 1989).

51. Stephen R. Covey, *The Eighth Habit: From Effectiveness to Greatness* (New York: Free Press, 2004).

52. Warren Bennis, *On Becoming a Leader* (Reading, MA: Addison-Wesley, 1989).

53. Michael D. Cohen and James G. March, *Leadership and Ambiguity* (Boston, MA: Harvard Business School Press, 1974).

Chapter 12

1. Richard M. Steers, Richard Mowday, and Debra L. Shapiro, "The Future of Work Motivation Theory," *Academy of Management Review,* July 2004, pp. 379–387.

2. Jennifer J. Laabs, "Aristotle's Advice for Business Success," *Workforce,* October 1997, pp. 75–79.

3. Amy Wrzeniewski and Jane Dutton, "Crafting a Job: Revisioning Employees as Active Crafters of Work," *Academy of Management Review,* April 2001, pp. 179–201.

4. Stephen Reiss, "Multifaceted Nature of Intrinsic Motivation: The Theory of 16 Basic Desires," *Review of General Psychology,* September 2004, pp. 179–193.

5. Kenneth W. Thomas, "Intrinsic Motivation and How It Works," *Training,* October 2000, pp. 130–135.

6. Shari Caudron, "The Myth of Job Happiness," *Workforce,* February 2001.

7. Ibid.

8. Bob Nelson, "How to Keep Incentives from Becoming Entitlements," *Manage,* February 1997, pp. 11–12; Abraham H. Maslow, *Motivation and Personality* (New York: Harper & Row, 1954), pp. 93–98.

9. Judy Cameron and W. David Pierce, *Rewards and Intrinsic Motivation: Resolving the Controversy* (Westport, CT: Bergin and Garvey, 2003).

10. Maslow, *Motivation and Personality,* pp. 93–98.

11. Ibid., p. 82.

12. Ibid., p. 92.

13. Michael N. Bazigos and W. Warner Burke, "Theory Orientations of Organizational Development Practitioners," *Group & Organization Management,* September 1997, pp. 384–408.

14. D. C. McClelland, "Some Social Consequences of Achievement Motivation," in *Nebraska Symposium on Motivation,* ed. M. R. Jones (Lincoln: University of Nebraska Press); and D. C. McClelland, *The Achievement Society* (Princeton, NJ: Van Nostrand, 1975).

15. D. C. McClelland, *Motivational Trends in Society* (Morristown, NJ: General Learning Press, 1971), p. 5.

16. D. C. McClelland, "Motive Dispositions: The Merits of Operant and Respondent Measures," in *Review of Personality and Journal Psychology,* ed. L. Wheeler (Beverly Hills, CA: Sage, 1980), pp. 10–41.

17. Debbie Schachter, "How to Set Performance Goals," *Information Outlook,* September 2004, pp. 26–29.

18. Dinesh D'Souza, "Stairway to Heaven," *Business 2.0,* April 17, 2001, pp. 79–82.

19. D. C. McClelland and D. H. Burnham, "Power Is the Great Motivator," *Harvard Business Review,* January–February 1995, pp. 126–139; and Lee Tom Perry, "Two Virtues of Competition," *Executive Excellence,* August 1990, pp. 15–16, March/April 1976, pp. 100–110.

20. See Frederick Herzberg, B. Mausner, and B. Snyderman, *The Motivation to Work* (New York: John Wiley, 1959).

21. Frederick Herzberg, *Work and the Nature of Man* (Cleveland: World Publishing, 1966).

22. Frederick Herzberg, "Workers Needs: The Same Around the World," *Industry Week,* September 21, 1987, pp. 29–32.

23. R. House and L. Wigdor, "Herzberg's Dual Factor Theory of Job Satisfaction and Motivation," *Personnel Psychology,* Winter 1967, pp. 369–389.

24. See, for example, Ebrahim A. Maidani, "Comparative Study of Herzberg's Two-Factor Theory of Job Satisfaction Among Public and Private Sectors," *Public Personnel Management,* Winter 1991, pp. 441–448.

25. L. K. Waters and C. W. Waters, "An Empirical Test of Five Versions of the Two-Factor Theory of Job Satisfaction," *Organizational Behavior and Human Performance,* February 1972, pp. 18–24.

26. Victor H. Vroom, *Work and Motivation* (New York: John Wiley, 1964).

27. Robert E. Allen, Margaret A. Lucero, and Kathleen L. Van Norman, "An Examination of the Individual's Decision to Participate in an Employee Involvement Program," *Group & Organization Management,* March 1997, pp. 117–143.

28. Hugh J. Arnold, "A Test of the Multiplicative Hypothesis of Expectancy-Valence Theories of Work Motivation," *Academy of Management Journal,* March 1981, pp. 128–141.

29. Wendelien Van Eerde and Henk Thierry, "Vroom's Expectancy Models and Work-Related Criteria: A Meta-Analysis," *Journal of Applied Psychology,* October 1996, pp. 575–586.

30. Ibid.

31. J. Stacy Adams, "Toward an Understanding of Inequity," *Journal of Abnormal and Social Psychology,* November 1963, pp. 442–436.

32. T. D. Schellerhardt, "Rookie Gains in Pay Wars Rile Veterans," *Wall Street Journal,* June 4, 1998, pp. B1, B7.

33. Suzanne S. Masterson, Kyle Lewis, Barry M. Goldman, and M. Susan Taylor, "Integrating Justice and Social Exchange: The Differing Effects of Fair Procedures and Treatment on Work Relationships," *Academy of Management Journal,* August 2001, pp. 738–748.

34. Robert Folger and R. Cropanzano, *Organizational Justice and Human Resource Management* (Thousand Oaks, CA: Sage, 1998).

35. E. L. Thorndike, *Animal Intelligence* (New York: Macmillan, 1911), p. 244.

36. B. F. Skinner, *Science and Human Behavior* (New York: Macmillan, 1953); and B. F. Skinner, *Contingencies of Reinforcement* (New York: Appleton-Century-Crofts, 1969).

37. Edward E. Lawler, III, *Rewarding Excellence* (San Francisco: Jossey-Bass, 2000).

38. Robert Rodin, *Free, Perfect, and Now* (New York: Simon & Schuster, 1999).

39. "From Quality Circles to TQM," *Government Executive,* July 1997, pp. 60–62.

40. Neil D. Opfer, "Creating Effective Construction Quality Circles," *Cost Engineering,* April 1997, pp. 42–46.

41. Michel Wensing, Bjorn Broge, Petra Kaufmann-Kolle, Edith Andres, and Joachim Szecsenyi, "Quality Circles to Improve Prescribing Patterns in Primary Medical Care: What Is Their Actual Impact?" *Journal of Evaluation in Clinical Practice,* August 2004, pp. 457–466.

42. J. Lawrence French, "Employee Perspective on Stock Ownership: Financial Investment or Mechanism of Control?" *Academy of Management Review,* July 1987, pp. 427–435.

43. www.mystockoptions.com/home/home.cfm, August 20, 2001.

44. Ibid.

45. Ibid.

46. Leah Carlson, "Flextime Elevated to National Issue," *Employee Benefits New,* September 15, 2004, pp. 1–3.

47. Liz Hughes, "Make the Case for Flextime," *Office Pro,* April 2004, p. 7.

48. Franklin Becker and Tom Kelley, *Offices at Work: Uncommon Work Strategies That Add Value and Improve Performance* (San Francisco: Jossey-Bass, 2004).

49. Alfie Kohn, *Punished by Rewards* (Boston: Houghton Mifflin, 1999).

50. T. Kanni, "Why We Work," *Training,* August 1998, pp. 34–39.

Chapter 13

1. Derek Burn, "Heading Up HR's Agenda," *People Management,* October 23, 1997, pp. 32–34.

2. Angela Sinickas, "Communicating Is Not Optional," *Harvard Management Communication Letter,* June 2001, pp. 1–3.

3. Henry Mintzberg, *The Nature of Managerial Work* (New York: Harper & Row, 1973).

4. Walter Kiechel III, "The Big Presentation," *Fortune,* July 26, 1982, pp. 98–100; and Henry Mintzberg, "The Manager's Job: Folklore and Fact," *Harvard Business Review,* July/August 1975, pp. 49–61.

5. Lura K. Romei, "Busy Isn't the Same Thing as Productive," *Managing Office Technology,* September 1997, p. 7.

6. "Marshall McLuhan," *MacLean's,* September 4, 2000, p. 29; David Skinner, "McLuhan's World—And Ours," *Public Interest,* Winter 2000, pp. 52–64.

7. Sim B. Sitkin, Kathleen M. Sutcliffe, and John R. Barrios-Choplin, "A Dual-Capacity Model of Communication Choice in Organizations," *Human Communications Research,* June 1993, pp. 563–598.

8. Ojelanki K. Ngwenyama and Allen S. Lee, "Communication Richness in Electronic Mail: Critical Social Theory and the Contextuality of Meaning," *MIS Quarterly,* June 1997, pp. 145–167.

9. Hilkka Yli-Jokipii, "Cross Talk: Communicating in a Multicultural Workplace," *International Journal of Commerce & Management,* 1997, pp. 111–113.

10. Bruce Harriman, "Up and Down the Communications Ladder," *Harvard Business Review,* September/October 1974, pp. 143–151.

11. Allen D. Frank, "Trends in Communication: Who Talks to Whom?" *Personnel,* December 1985, pp. 41–47.

12. Chee W. Chow, Richard Hwang, and Woody Liao, "Motivating Truthful Upward Communication of Private Information: An Experimental Study," *Abacus,* June 2000, pp. 160–179.

13. Frank, "Trends in Communication," p. 42.

14. Sheri Rosen, "Shared Knowledge Is Power," *Communication World,* June/July 1997, p. 52.

15. K. M. Watson, "An Analysis of Communication Patterns: A Method for Discriminating Leader and Subordinate Roles," *Academy of Management Journal,* June 1982, pp. 107–122.

16. Randall H. Lucius and Karl W. Kuhnert, "Using Sociometry to Predict Team Performance in the Organization," *Journal of Psychology,* January 1997, pp. 21–32.

17. E. M. Rogers and R. Agarwala-Rogers, *Communication in Organizations* (New York: The Free Press, 1976).

18. Malcolm Groat, "The Informal Organization: Ride the Headless Monster," *Management Accounting—London,* April 1997, pp. 40–42.

19. Debbie Therrien, "Rid Your Office of Backstabbers," *Canadian Business,* November 22, 2004, pp. 109–110.

20. Keith Davis, *Human Behavior at Work: Organizational Behavior* (New York: McGraw-Hill, 1981); O. W. Baskin and C. E. Aronoff, *Interpersonal Communication in Organizations* (Santa Monica, CA: Goodyear Publishing, 1980).

21. Margaret Boles and Brenda Paik Sunoo, "Talk to Your Shiftworkers," *Workforce,* November 1997, p. 13.

22. Robert Levy, "Tilting at the Rumor Mill," *Dun's Review,* December 1981, pp. 52–54.

23. R. L. Rosnow, "Psychology in Rumor Reconsidered," *Psychological Bulletin,* May 1980, pp. 578–591.

24. Frederick Koenig, *Rumor in the Marketplace* (Dover, MA: Auburn House Publishing, 1985).

25. Roy Rowan, "Where Did That Rumor Come From?" *Fortune,* August 13, 1979, pp. 130ff.

26. Mildred Culp, "Making Rumor Work for You in the Workplace," *San Diego Business Journal,* March 15, 1999, p. 41.

27. Fred Luthans and Janet K. Larsen, "How Managers Really Communicate," *Human Relations,* 39, no. 2 (1986), pp. 161–178.

28. This discussion is based on Jay Hall, "Communications Revisited," *California Management Review,* Fall 1973, pp. 56–67.

29. "Interpersonal Communication and Relations," *Communication Abstracts,* August 2000, pp. 454–459.

30. Lisa Aldisert, "What Is Your Communication Style?" *Bank Marketing,* October 2000, p. 46.

31. John Mullen, "Graduates Deficient in 'Soft' Skills," *People Management,* November 6, 1997, p. 18.

32. Patricia A. Merrier and Ruthann Dirks, "Student Attitudes Toward Written, Oral, and E-Mail Communication," *Business Communication Quarterly,* June 1997, pp. 89–99.

33. Dale A. Level, Jr. and William P. Galle, Jr. *Managerial Communications* (Plano, TX: Business Publications, 1988).

34. Morey Stettner, "Body of Evidence," *Successful Meetings,* October 1997, p. 128.

35. Albert Mehrabian, *Silent Messages* (Belmont, CA: Wadsworth, 1971).

36. John Keltner, *Interpersonal Speech—Communication* (Belmont, CA: Wadsworth, 1970).

37. Paul Ekman and W. V. Friesen, *Unmasking the Face* (Englewood Cliffs, NJ: Prentice-Hall, 1975).

38. Level and Galle, *Managerial Communications,* p. 66.

39. Michael B. McCaskey, "The Hidden Messages Managers Send," *Harvard Business Review,* November/December 1979, pp. 135–148.

40. Anne Warfield, "Do You Speak Body Language?" *Training & Development,* April 2001, pp. 60–61.

41. Edward Hall, *The Hidden Dimension* (Garden City, NY: Doubleday, 1966).

42. Phillip L. Hunsaker, "Communicating Better: There's No Proxy for Proxemics," *Business,* March/April 1980, pp. 41–48.

43. Thomas Kuhn, *The Structure of Scientific Revolutions* (Chicago, IL: University of Chicago Press, 1996).

44. Frank, "Trends in Communication," p. 45.

45. Sheperd Walker, "Listening Skills for Managers," in *The Handbook of Executive Communication,* ed. John Louis DeGaetani (Homewood, IL: Dow Jones-Irwin, 1986), p. 651.

46. Cynthia Hamilton and Brian H. Kleiner, "Steps to Better Listening," *Personnel Journal,* February 1987, pp. 20–21.

47. Walter Kiechel III, "Learn How to Listen," *Fortune,* August 17, 1987, pp. 107–108.

48. Christine Kelly and Michele Zak, "Narrativity and Professional Communication," *Journal of Business and Technical Communication,* July 1999, pp. 297–317.

Chapter 14

1. Rosabeth Moss Kanter, Douglas Raymond, and Lyn Baranowski, "Driving Change at Seagate," *Harvard Business School Cases,* September 1, 2003, pp. 1–19.

2. Marie Reid and Richard Hammersley, *Communicating Successfully in Groups: A Practical Guide for the Workplace* (Philadelphia: Routledge, 2000).

3. Daniel Pilone, "Making Enterprise Process Stick," *Intelligent Enterprise,* December 5, 2002, pp. 44–45.

4. Howard Risher, "Eyes on the Prize," *Government Executive,* September 1997, pp. 25–29.

5. Vanessa Urch Drisket and Steven B. Wolff, "Building the Emotional Intelligence of Groups," *Harvard Business Review,* March 2001, pp. 80–91.

6. Barbara Pate Glacel, "Teamwork's Top Ten Lead to Quality," *Journal for Quality & Participation,* January/February 1997, pp. 12–16.

7. Erika Rasmusson, "Brief Case: Wild Ideas at Work," *Sales & Marketing Management,* July 1999, pp. 22–23.

8. Philip M. Podsakoff, Michael Ahearne, and Scott B. MacKenzie, "Organizational Citizenship Behavior and the Quantity and Quality of Work Group Performance," *Journal of Applied Psychology,* April 1997, pp. 262–270.

9. George Homans, *The Human Group* (New York: Harcourt Brace, 1950).

10. Robert L. Kahn, D. M. Wolfe, Robert P. Quinn, J. D. Snock, and R. A. Rosenthal, *Organizational Stress: Studies in Role Conflict and Role Ambiguity* (New York: John Wiley & Sons, 1964).

11. Holly B. Thompson and Jon M. Werner, "The Impact of Role Conflict/Facilitation on Core and Discretionary Behaviors: Testing a Mediated Model," *Journal of Management,* 1997, pp. 583–601.

12. Ruth C. King and Vikram Sethi, "The Moderating Effect of Organizational Commitment on Burnout in Information Systems Professionals," *European Journal of Information Systems,* June 1997, pp. 86–96.

13. Jill Hecht, "Fourteen Heads—and Budgets—Are Better Than One," *Inside Technology Training,* March 1999, p. 37.

14. Janice R.W. Joplin and Catherine S. Daus, "Challenges of Leading a Diverse Workforce," *Academy of Management Executive,* August 1997, pp. 32–47.

15. Claudia Kampmeier and Bernd Simon, "Individuality and Group Formation: The Role of Independence and Differentiation," *Journal of Personality & Social Psychology,* September 2001, pp. 448–462.

16. Robert C. Ford, John W. Newstrom, and Frank S. McLaughlin, "Making Workplace Fun, More Functional," *Industrial & Commercial Training,* 2004, pp. 117–120.

17. This definition is based on the group cohesiveness concept presented by Stanley E. Seashore, *Group Cohesiveness in the Industrial Work Group* (Ann Arbor: University of Michigan, Institute for Social Research, 1954).

18. Marvin E. Shaw, *Group Dynamics—The Psychology of Small Group Behavior* (New York: McGraw-Hill, 1981), p. 64.

19. Kenneth R. Bartkus, Roy D. Howell, R. Michael Parent, and Cathy L. Hartman, "Managerial Antecedents and Individual Consequences of Group Cohesiveness in Travel Service Selling," *Journal of Travel Research,* Spring 1997, pp. 56–63.

20. Fred Luthans and Alexander D. Stajkovic, "Reinforce for Performance: A Need to Go Beyond Pay and Even Rewards," *Academy of Management Executive,* May 1999, pp. 49–57.

21. Jeff Cowell and Jery Michaelson, "Flawless Teams," *Executive Excellence,* March 2000, p. 11.

22. Anthony M. Townsend, Samuel M. DeMarie, and Anthony R. Hendrickson, "Virtual Teams, Technology, and the Workplace of the Future," *Academy of Management Executive,* August 1998.

23. K. Kiser, "Working on World Time," *Training,* March 1999, pp. 29–30.

24. Amy Helen Johnson, "Teamwork Made Simple," *CIO Magazine,* November 1, 1999, p. 20.

25. "Communicating with Virtual Project Teams," *Harvard Management Communication,* Summer 2000, p. 3.

26. Gina Imperato, "Real Tools for Virtual Teams," *Fast Company,* July 2000, pp. 378–379.

27. Charlene Marmer Solomon, "Managing Virtual Teams," *Workforce,* June 2001, pp. 60–64.

28. Irving L. Janis, *Victims of Groupthink: A Psychological Study of Foreign Policy Decisions and Fiascos* (Boston: Houghton Mifflin, 1972); and Irving L. Janis and Leon Mann, *Decision Making: A Psychological Analysis of Conflict, Choice, and Commitment* (New York: Macmillan, 1977).

29. Bob Donath, "In-House Groupthink Undermines Strategy," *Marketing News,* September 1, 2004, p. 8.

30. Clarence W. VonBergen, Jr., and Raymond J. Kirk, "Groupthink: When Too Many Heads Spoil the Decision," *Management Review,* March 1978, pp. 44–49.

31. Sally Bell, "Companies Lack Crisis Plans," *Dallas Times Herald,* August 5, 1984, p. 8.

32. Charlan Jeanne Nemeth, Joanie B. Connell, John D. Rogers, and Keith S. Brown, "Improving Decision Making by Means of Dissent," *Journal of Applied Social Psychology,* January 2001, pp. 48–58.

33. Kenwyn K. Smith and David N. Barg, *Paradoxes of Group Life* (San Francisco: Jossey-Bass, 1987).

34. "Over the Rainbow," *Economist,* November 22, 1997, p. 76.

35. Daan van Knippenberg, Carsten K. DeDreu, and Astrid C. Homan, "Work Group Diversity and Group Performance: An Integrative Model and Research Agenda," *Journal of Applied Psychology,* December 2004, pp. 1008–1022.

36. Warren E. Watson, Kumar Kamalesh, and Larry K. Michaelson, "Cultural Diversity's Impact on Interaction Process and Performance: Comparing Homogeneous and Diverse Task Groups," *Academy of Management Journal,* June 1993, pp. 590–602.

37. Audrey K. Charlton and Jerry D. Huey, "Breaking Cultural Barriers," *Quality Progress,* September 1992, pp. 47–49.

38. James B. Strenski, "Stress Diversity in Employee Communications," *Public Relations Journal,* August/September 1994, pp. 47–49.

39. Leonie Huddy, "Contrasting Theoretical Approaches to Intergroup Relations," *Political Psychology,* December 2004, pp. 947–967.

40. Louis R. Pondy, "Organization Conflict: Concepts and Models," *Administrative Science Quarterly,* September 1967, pp. 296–320.

41. Martin W. Rempel and Ronald J. Fisher, "Perceived Threat, Cohesion, and Group Problem Solving in Intergroup Conflict," *International Journal of Conflict Management,* July 1997, pp. 216–234.

42. Suzy Wetlaufer, "Common Sense and Conflict," *Harvard Business Review,* January/February 2000, pp. 114–124.

43. Joseph E. McCann and Diane L. Ferry, "An Approach for Assessing and Managing Inter-Unit Interdependence," *Academy of Management Review,* January 1979, pp. 113–119.

44. Michael M. Byerlein, ed., *Work Teams: Past, Present, and Future* (Boston: Kluwer, 2000).

45. Christine Avery and Diane Zabel, *The Flexible Workplace: A Sourcebook of Information and Research* (Westport, CT: Quorum, 2001).

46. Pat McMillan, *The Performance Factor* (Nashville, TN: Broadman & Holman, 2002).

Chapter 15

1. Karen R. Adler and Paul M. Swiercz, "Taming the Performance Bell Curve," *Training & Development,* October 1997, pp. 33–38.

2. Mike Bourne, Monica Franco, and John Wilkes, "Corporate Performance Management," *Measuring Business Excellence,* 2003, pp. 15–21.

3. Larry Pavey, "Raybestos Brakes Has a Commitment to Quality," *Aftermarket Business,* July 2001, p. 62.

4. Jeffrey S. Kane and Kimberly A. Freeman, "A Theory of Equitable Performance Standards," *Journal of Management,* 1997, pp. 37–58.

5. Mike Kennerly, Andy Neely, and Chris Adams, "Survival of the Fittest: Measuring Performance in a Changing Business Environment," *Measuring Business Excellence,* 2003, pp. 79–86.

6. Clyde Kofman, "How Measurement Can Undercut Performance," *Banking Strategies,* July/August 1997, p. 44.

7. Bert Mills, "Getting Comfortable with Disciplining Employees," *Journal of Business,* January 25, 2001, pp. B10–B11.

8. Johna Till Johnson, "Put the 'Service' Back in Service Provider," *Network World,* April 5, 2004, p. 34.

9. "Rethinking Strategic HR: HR's Role in Creating a Performance Culture," *HRProfessional,* December 2004/January 2005, p. 44.

10. Lawrence L. Steinmetz and H. Ralph Todd, Jr., *First-Line Management,* 3d ed. (Plano, TX: Business Publications, 1986).

11. Gary Klein, "Why Won't They Follow Simple Directions?" *Across the Board,* February 2000, pp. 14–19.

12. Cortland Cammann and David Nadler, "Fit Control Systems to Your Managerial Style," *Harvard Business Review,* January/February 1976, pp. 65–72.

13. Avi Rushinek and Sara F. Rushinek, "Using Financial Ratios to Predict Insolvency," *Journal of Business Research,* February 1987, pp. 74–77.

14. Richard Barrett, "Why There Are No Longer Valid Excuses to Avoid ABC," *Journal of Corporate Accounting & Finance,* March/April 2004, pp. 29–35.

15. David A. Garvin, "Competing on the Eight Dimensions of Quality," *Harvard Business Review,* November/December 1987, pp. 101–109.

16. Ibid., p. 107.

17. Everette E. Adam, Jr., James C. Hershauer, and William A. Ruch, *Productivity and Quality* (Englewood Cliffs, NJ: Prentice-Hall, 1981).

18. Jack Campanella and Frank J. Corcoran, "Principles of Quality Costs," *Quality Progress,* April 1983, pp. 16–22.

19. R. Les Tubb, "Exposing Hidden Costs in Purchased Parts," *Furniture Design & Manufacturing,* November 1997, pp. 108–113.

20. Quality cost estimates are from A. V. Feigenbaum, *Total Quality Control* (New York: McGraw-Hill, 1983), pp. 112–113.

21. Russell Paine, "Paine's Recycling and Rubbish Removal: The 'Three S' Policy," *World Wastes,* November 1997, pp. 19–20.

22. Leigh Ann Klaus, "Benchmarking Is Still a Useful Quality Tool," *Quality Progress,* November 1997, p. 13.

23. Kamar J. Singh and John W. Lewis, "Concurrent Engineering: Institution, Infrastructure, and Implementation," *International Journal of Technology Management,* 1997, pp. 727–738.

24. Lynne B. Hare, Roger W. Hoerl, John D. Hromi, and Ronald D. Snee, "The Role of Statistical Thinking in Management, *Quality Progress,* February 1995, pp. 53–60.

25. Iain Caville, "The Case for SPC," *Metalworking Production,* September 2004, pp. 55–56.

26. Gabriel L. Paul, *Quality Process Management* (Englewood Cliffs, NJ: Prentice-Hall, 1987), p. 94.

27. Robert Nix, "A Hunger for Quality," *Quality Progress,* November 2004, pp. 53–54.

28. Chuen-Sheng, "A Multi-Layer Neural Network Model for Detecting Changes in the Process," *Computers and Industrial Engineering,* January 1995, pp. 51–61.

29. Mark Weiner, "Six Sigma," *Communication World,* January/February 2004, pp. 26–29.

30. Sunil Thawani, "Six Sigma: Strategy for Organizational Excellence," *Total Quality Management & Business Excellence,* July/August 2004, pp. 655–664.

31. Mike Carnell, "The Six Sigma Mambo," *Quality Progress,* January 2004, pp. 87–89.

32. Thomas J. Peters and Robert H. Waterman, *In Search of Excellence* (New York: Harper & Row, 1982).

33. W. Edwards Deming, *Out of the Crisis* (Cambridge, MA: Center for Advanced Engineering Study, Massachusetts Institute of Technology, 1986), Chapter 9.

34. Joseph Juran, *Juran on Leadership for Quality: An Executive Handbook* (New York: Free Press, 1989), Chapter 5.

35. Ibid., pp. 147–148.

36. Ibid., pp. 148–150.

37. Armand Feigenbaum, *Total Quality Control* (New York: McGraw-Hill, 1991), pp. 204–209.

38. See George E. Wollner, "The Law of Producing Quality," *Quality Progress,* January 1992, pp. 35–40.

39. Many books are available on quality control and approaches to quality improvement. Especially noteworthy are W. Edwards Deming, *Quality, Productivity, and Competitive Position* (Cambridge, MA: MIT Press, 1982); J. M. Juran, Frank M. Gryna, Jr., and R. S. Bingham, Jr., eds., *Quality Control Handbook* (New York: McGraw-Hill, 1974); A. V. Feigenbaum, *Total Quality Control* (New York: McGraw-Hill, 1983); and Richard J. Schonberger, *World Class Manufacturing: The Lessons of Simplicity Applied* (New York: The Free Press, 1986), pp. 123–143.

40. For some interesting examples of quality improvement efforts by U.S. businesses, see Otis Port, "The Push for Quality," *Business Week,* June 8, 1987, pp. 130ff.

Chapter 16

1. "Nice Work" *Precision Marketing,* April 4, 2003, p. 43.

2. Peter Gill, "Save Money and Time with Cellular Manufacturing," *Furniture Design & Manufacturing,* October 1997, pp. 126–128.

3. Ronald G. Askin, Hassan M. Selim, and Asoo J. Vakharia, "A Methodology for Designing Flexible Cellular Manufacturing Systems," *IIE Transactions,* July 1997, pp. 599–610.

4. "Cellular Manufacturing How-To Handbook," *IIE Solutions,* April 2001, p. 11.

5. Roger Morton, "Labor Looms Large in Site Selection," *Transportation & Distribution,* September 2001, pp. 43–44.

6. Tom Andel, "Be Hip to Hype," *Transportation & Distribution,* October 1997, pp. 59–62.

7. Li Zhaoxi, Michael Anson, and Li Guangming, "A Procedure for Quantitatively Evaluating Site Layout Alternatives," *Construction Management & Economics,* September 2001, pp. 459–457.

8. C. M. Tam, Thomas K. L. Tong, Arthur W. Leung, and Gerald W. C. Chiu, "Site Layout Planning Using Nonstructural Fuzzy Decision Support System," *Journal of Construction Engineering & Management,* May/June 2002, pp. 220–231.

9. "How Big Can It Grow?" *Economist,* April 17, 2004, pp. 67–69.

10. James Aaron Cooke, "Steering Through the Storm," *Logistics Management & Distribution Report,* July 2001, pp. 51–53.

11. Lee Copeland, "Automakers Reap Gains from E-Locator," *Computerworld,* January 15, 2001, p. 10.

12. Tim Minahan, "Toyota Continues Quest for True JIT Excellence," *Purchasing,* September 4, 1997, pp. 42–43.

13. Ron McLachlin, "Management Initiatives and Just-In-Time Manufacturing," *Journal of Operations Management,* November 1997, pp. 271–292.

14. Richard J. Schonberger, *Japanese Manufacturing Techniques: Nine Hidden Lessons in Simplicity* (New York: The Free Press, 1982).

15. For an excellent comparative discussion of JIT and other systems designed to boost manufacturing efficiency, see Sumer C. Aggarwal, "MRP, JIT, OPT, FMS?" *Harvard Business Review,* September/October 1985, pp. 8ff; also see Sadao Sakakibara et al., "The Impact of Just-In-Time Manufacturing and Its Infrastructure on Manufacturing Performance," *Management Science,* September 1997, pp. 1246–1257.

16. Schonberger, *Japanese Manufacturing Techniques,* p. 20; and Harris Jack Shapiro and Teresa Cosenza, *Reviving Industry in America: Japanese Influences on Manufacturing and the Service Sector* (Cambridge, MA: Ballinger, 1987).

17. Greg Ip, "As Security Worries Intensify, Companies See Efficiencies Erode," *Wall Street Journal,* October 24, 2001, pp. A1, A14.

18. Michael Fredericks, "MRP into the Next Century," *Logistics Focus,* June 1995, pp. 36–37.

19. "Small Manufacturer Solution," *Industrial Engineer,* June 2004, p. 63.

20. Brian Albright, "Assessing ERP Software," *Frontline Solutions,* August 2004, pp. 18–23.

21. Christopher Koch, Derek Slater, and E. Baatz, "The ABCs of ERP," *CIO Online,* www.cio.com/research/erp.

22. Jim Romeo, "ERP on the Rise Again," *Network Computing,* September 17, 2001, pp. 42–46.

23. Dexter Johnson, "Taking a Byte Out of the Supply Chain," *Chemical Market Reporter,* December 1, 1997, pp. FR24–FR25.

24. Julekha Dash, "Buying Off the Shelf Apps," *Software Magazine,* November 1997, p. 50.

25. J. R. Tony Arnold, *Introduction to Materials Management,* (New York, NY: Prentice-Hall, 2001).

26. Miryam Williamson, "From SAP to 'Nuts,'" *Computerworld,* November 10, 1997, pp. 68–69.

Chapter 17

1. Robert Tie, "Managing Change," *Journal of Accountancy,* November 2004, pp. 27–29.

2. Michael A. West, Giles Hirst, Andreas Richter, and Helen Shipton, "Twelve Steps to Heaven: Successfully Managing Change Through Developing Innovative Teams," *European Journal of Work & Organizational Psychology,* June 2004, pp. 269–299.

3. A. M. Webber, "Learning for a Change," *Fast Company,* May 1999, p. 180.

4. Peter M. Senge and Goran Carstedt, "Innovating Our Way to the Next Industrial Revolution," *MIT Sloan Management Review,* Winter 2001, pp. 24–38.

5. Amy Wrzesniewski and Jane E. Dutton, "Crafting a Job: Revisioning Employees as Active Crafters of Their Work," *Academy of Management Review,* April 2001, pp. 179–201.

6. Laura B. Cardinal, "Technological Innovations in the Pharmaceutical Industry: The Use of Organizational Control in Managing Research and Development," *Organization Science,* January/February 2001, pp. 19–36.

7. Fernando Alvarez and Urban J. Jermann, "Using Asset Prices to Measure the Cost of Business Cycles," *Journal of Political Economy,* December 2004, pp. 1223–1255.

8. Guntram F. A. Werther, "Doing Business in the New World Disorder: Assessing, Understanding, and Effectively Responding to the Challenges of Social and Political Instability Within Emerging Markets," *Competitive Intelligence Review,* Winter 1997, pp. 12–18.

9. Michele Williams, "In Whom We Trust: Group Membership As an Affective Context for Trust Development," *Academy of Management Review,* July 2001, pp. 377–396.

10. Jeanenne LaMarsh, "The Resilient Worker: Employees Who Can Cope with Change," *Hospital Material Management Quarterly,* November 1997, pp. 54–58.

11. "The Most Dangerous Game?" *Nation's Business,* September 1995, p. 20.

12. Robert N. Lussier, "Startup Business Advice from Business Owners to Would-Be Entrepreneurs," *Sam Advanced Management Journal,* Winter 1995, pp. 10–13.

13. Anne S. Huff, James O. Huff, and Pamela S. Barr, *When Firms Change Direction* (New York: Oxford University Press, 2000).

14. Todd Lapidus, *High-Impact Training* (San Francisco: Jossey-Bass, 2000).

15. Cirum B. Eriksson, "The Effects of Change Programs on Employees' Emotions," *Personnel Review,* 2004, pp. 110–126.

16. Tony Grundy, "Human Resource Management—A Strategic Approach," *Long Range Planning,* August 1997, pp. 507–517.

17. Rick Maurer, "Transforming Resistance: Using Resistance to Make Change Happen," *Human Resources Professional,* November/December 1997, pp. 3–6.

18. Susan Staring and Catherine Taylor, "A Guide to Managing Workforce Transitions," *Nursing Management,* December 1997, pp. 31–32.

19. Landon Thomas, Jr., "Citigroup Job Changes May Be Dress Rehearsal for the Top Post in Future," *New York Times,* September 28, pp. C1–C2.

20. W. Lynne Markus, Brook Manville, and Carole E. Agres, "What Makes Virtual Organizations Work?" *MIT Sloan Management Review,* Fall 2000, pp. 13–26.

21. Bob Stewart and Sarah Powell, "Team Building and Team Working," *Team Performance Management,* 2004, pp. 35–38.

22. Rick W. Weymeir, "Eliminating Office Politics Through Team Building," *Physician Executive,* January–February 2004, pp. 64–66.

23. Jane Pickard, "Team Building," *People Management,* September 2, 2004, pp. 40–41.

24. Peter White, "Team Building Is No Picnic," *Employee Benefits,* April 2004, pp. 27–28.

25. Michelle A. Marks, John E. Mathieu, and Stephen J. Zaccaro, "A Temporarily Based Framework and Taxonomy of Team Processes," *Academy of Management Review,* July 2001, pp. 356–376.

26. Ibid.

27. Rick Tallarigo, Sr., "Managing Diversity: The Courage to Lead," *Personal Psychology,* Summer 2001, pp. 531–534.

28. Carolyn Weethoff, "Motivation to Learn and Diversity Training: Application of the Theory of Planned Behavior," *Human Resource Development Quarterly,* Fall 2004, pp. 27–28.

29. Richard G. Kipsey, "Total Factor Productivity and the Measurement of Technological Change," *Canadian Journal of Economics,* November 2004, pp. 1118–1150.

30. Lidia L. Lourenco and Margarida Vaz Pato, "An Improved Genetic Heuristic to Support the Design of Flexible Manufacturing Systems," *Computers & Industrial Engineering,* March 2004, pp. 141–157.

31. H. Kevin Steensma and Kevin G. Corley, "Organizational Context as a Moderator of Theories on Firm Boundaries for Technology Sourcing," *Academy of Management Journal,* April 2001, pp. 271–291.

32. Richard E. Walton and Gerald I. Susman, "People Policies for the New Machines," *Harvard Business Review,* March/April 1987, pp. 98–106.

33. Quy Nguyen Huy, "In Praise of Middle Managers," *Harvard Business Review,* September 2001, pp. 72–81.

34. Wayne F. Cascio and Peg Wynn, "Managing a Downsizing Process," *Human Resource Management,* Winter 2004, pp. 425–436.

35. Jennifer Netherby and Susanne Ault, "Suppliers Bemoaning Toys 'R' Us Downsizing," *Video Business,* August 23, 2004, pp. 6–7.

36. Craig R. Luther, "The Paradox of Managerial Downsizing," *Organizational Studies,* 2004, pp. 1159–1184.

37. Spence Laschinger and Joan E. Finegan, "Empowerment, Interactional Justice, Trust, and Respect: A Nursing Recruitment and Retention Strategy," *Academy of Management Proceedngs,* 2004, pp. C1–C5.

38. Jay F. Stright, Jr., "Five Levers of Effective Change in HR," *Employment Relations Today,* Spring 1997, pp. 59–73.

39. Henrich R. Greve and Alva Taylor, "Innovations as Catalysts for Organizational Change: Shifts in Organizational Cognition and Search," *Administrative Science Quarterly,* March 2000, pp. 54–80.

40. E. B. Dent and S.G. Goldberg, "Challenging Resistance to Change," *Journal of Applied Behavioral Science,* March 1999, pp. 25–41.

41. Wendel L. French and C. H. Bell, *Organizational Development: Behavioral Science Interventions for Organizational Improvement* (Upper Saddle River, NJ: Prentice-Hall, 1999).

42. Peter M. Senge, *The Fifth Discipline* (New York: Doubleday, 1990).

43. Dvora Yanow, "Organizational Learning and the Learning Organization: Developments in Theory and Practice," *Management Learning,* June 2001, pp. 267–273.

44. B. Moingeon and A. Edmondson, *Organizational Learning and Competitive Advantage* (Thousand Oaks, CA: Sage, 1996).

45. Dale G. Lake, "Making Change Happen One Person at a Time," *Human Resource Management,* Spring 2001, p. 87.

46. Jeffrey Pfeffer and Robert I. Sutton, *The Knowing-Doing Gap: How Smart Companies Turn Knowledge into Action* (Boston: Harvard Business School, 2000).

Glossary

360-degree feedback   A form of performance evaluation that involves gathering information about a person's behavior from a boss or bosses, direct reports, colleagues, team members, internal and external customers, and suppliers.

A

accounts receivable turnover   The ratio of credit sales to average accounts receivable that indicates how rapidly credit sales are being turned to cash.

acid-test ratio   A test of liquidity that relates only cash and near-cash items to current liabilities.

acquisition phase   A step in human resources management that involves recruiting, screening, selecting, and properly placing personnel.

actions   Specified, prescribed means to achieve objectives.

activity   The work necessary to complete a particular event in a PERT network that consumes time, which is the paramount variable in a PERT system. In PERT networks, three time estimates are used for each activity: an optimistic time, a pessimistic time, and a most likely time.

activity-based costing (ABC)   Activity-based costing is a system of cost accounting based on actual processes (activities) rather than labor and materials.

adapters   Physical expressions used to adjust psychologically to the interpersonal climate of a particular situation; frequently used to deal with stress (e.g., drumming fingers on a table); a form of body language.

affect displays   Usually subconscious expressions that directly communicate an individual's emotions (e.g., a "closed posture" that communicates defensiveness); a form of body language.

affective attitude   The part of attitude that involves a person's emotions or feelings.

affirmative action   A company program that requires the firm to take steps to guarantee equal employment opportunities for people within protected classes.

altruism   An ethical standard that places highest value on behavior that is pleasurable and rewarding to society.

analytical skills   The abilities to identify key factors, to understand how they interrelate, and to understand the roles they play in a situation as well as to diagnose and evaluate.

applicant form   A document used to obtain information from a job applicant that will be helpful in reaching an employment decision.

applicant screening   The use of preliminary interviews to screen out unqualified applicants.

appraisal costs   All expenses involved in directly evaluating quality.

arena   The theoretical "best place" for communication where each party knows each other's positions and motivations well. This is the most effective domain for interpersonal communications.

artificial intelligence   A computer program that allows computers to solve problems using imagination, abstract reasoning, and common sense.

attitude   A mental state of readiness to feel and behave toward some object in some way.

attribution   An inference a person makes about his or her feelings or another person's feelings based on observed behavior.

authority   The legitimate right to use assigned resources to accomplish a delegated task or objective; the right to give orders and to exact obedience.

B

balanced scorecard   An approach to establishing appropriate objectives and priorities by presenting a balanced picture of current operating performance and the drivers of future performance.

balance sheet   The balance sheet provides managers with a "snapshot" of the firm's financial condition at a specific point in time. The firm's assets are matched against its liabilities and owner's equity.

bandwidth   The amount of data that can be squeezed through an electronic medium.

behavior   Any observable response given by a person.

behavior modification   An approach to motivation that uses principles of operant conditioning. Operant behavior is learned on the basis of consequences. If a behavior causes a desired outcome (for managers) it is reinforced (positively rewarded), and because of its consequences it is likely to be repeated. Thus, behavior is conditioned by adjusting its consequences.

behavior motivation   The term used to describe techniques for applying the principles of operant conditioning to the control of individual behavior.

behavioral approach to management   A management approach that emphasizes people and how the structure of an organization affects their behavior and performance. The advocates of a behavioral orientation to management believe that the classical approach suppresses personal development because it is so rigid and restrictive.

behavioral change techniques   Attempts to change employees' behavior to redirect and increase their motivation, skills, and knowledge bases.

behavioral theory of leadership   A theory that attributes performance differences to the behaviors and style of leaders.

behaviorally anchored rating scales (BARS)   Rating scales developed by raters and/or ratees that use critical behavioral incidents as interval anchors on each scale; uses about six to ten scales with behavioral incidents to derive the evaluation.

benchmarking   A popular approach to identifying and studying firms that are leaders in a given area of business.

biofeedback   A technique, usually involving the use of some kind of instrumentation, in which the user attempts to learn to control various bodily functions such as heart rate and blood pressure.

blind spot   When relevant information is known to others but not to a particular individual. In this context, the individual is at a disadvantage when communicating with others because he or she cannot know the others' feelings, sentiments, and perceptions.

bona fide occupational qualification (BFOQ)   A qualification that is reasonably necessary for the normal operation of the particular business.

Boston Consulting Group (BCG) matrix   An approach developed by the Boston Consulting Group that evaluates strategic business units with regard to the firm's growth rate and market share.

boundaryless organization   An organization in which the formal structure characteristics such as spans of control, departmentalization, and a rigid chain of command are minimized or eliminated.

brainstorming   A technique for stimulating creativity by using a rigorous set of rules that promote the generation of ideas while avoiding the inhibitions that many people feel in group settings.

brand-switching model   A model that provides the manager with some idea of the behavior of consumers in terms of their loyalty to brands and their switches from one brand to another.

budget   A predetermined amount of resources linked to an activity.

buffer   A term used by the scholar James Thompson to describe the departments or units that are created to deal with environmental uncertainty and complexity.

bureaucracy   An organization design that relies on specialization of labor, a specific authority hierarchy, a formal set of rules and procedures, and rigid promotion and selection criteria.

business plan   A written report that provides an overview and analysis of a proposed business; includes description of the prospective product or service, a thorough market analysis, the firms' strategic objectives, plans for each of the business's functional areas, a profile of the management team, and the venture's projected financial position and funding needs.

buyout   Entering a business by acquiring an existing company in the selected business and market.

C

career   An individually perceived sequence of attitudes and behaviors associated with work-related experiences and activities over the span of a person's life.

career path   The sequence of jobs associated with a particular initial job that leads to promotion and advancement.

career planning   The process of systematically matching an individual's career aspirations with opportunities for achieving them.

career stages   Distinct, but interrelated, steps or phases of a career, including the prework stage, the initial work stage, the stable work stage, and the retirement stage.

carrying costs   The costs incurred by carrying raw materials and finished goods in inventory.

cash flow statement   The cash flow statement provides managers with a view of the firm's cash position.

categorical imperative   An ethical standard that judges behavior in terms of its consistency with the principle to "act as if the maxim of your action were to become a general law binding on everyone."

cellular organization   An organization structured around units that complete entire assembly processes rather than a continuous line or linear production process.

central tendency error   The tendency to rate all ratees around an average score.

centralization   Describes the location of decision-making authority in the organization's hierarchy; refers to the delegation of authority among the organization's jobs.

chain of command   The formal channel that defines authority, responsibility, and communication relationships from top to bottom.

change agent   An individual who is appointed or hired to promote and facilitate change.

changing external environment   One in which there are rather frequent and expected changes in the actions of competitors, market demands, technology, and so on.

charismatic leadership   Charismatic leaders generate excitement and increase the expectations of followers through their visions of the future.

classical approach to management   An approach that places reliance on such management principles as unity of command, a balance between authority and responsibility, division of labor, and delegation to establish relationships between managers and subordinates.

classical organization theory   A body of ideas that focused on the problems faced by top managers of large organizations; its two major purposes were to develop basic principles that guide the design, creation, and maintenance of large organizations and to identify the basic functions of managing organizations.

clinical method   An approach to analyzing application form responses in which the interviewer carefully analyzes answers and attempts to gain a sense of the applicant's attitudes, personality, and career goals.

cliques   Groups within an organization that tend to communicate internally on a regular basis.

closed system   An approach that generally ignores environmental forces and conditions.

code of ethics   A written statement of an organization's values, beliefs, and norms of ethical behavior.

coercive power   The power of a leader derived from fear because the follower perceives the leader as a person who can punish deviant behavior and actions.

cognitive attitude   The part of attitude that involves a person's perceptions, beliefs, and ideas.

cognitive dissonance   A state in which there is a discrepancy between a person's attitude and behavior.

command group   The group shown on an organization chart that reports to a single manager.

commission   A compensation plan that is the equivalent of straight piecework and typically a percentage of the item's price.

common cause variation   The random variation in a system that typically can't be completely eliminated.

communication   The transmission of mutual understanding through the use of symbols.

communication overload   The inability to absorb or adequately respond to messages directed to a person because of the excessive amount of information and data they must absorb.

comparable worth   A compensation concept that attempts to prove and remedy the allegation that employers systematically discriminate by paying women employees less than their work is intrinsically worth, relative to what they pay men who work in comparable professions; sometimes called *pay equity*.

compensation system   An organization's established procedure that specifies pay levels, benefits packages, and other rights, privileges, and perks according to job classification.

competitive benchmarking   Careful examination of a competitor's product to determine its costs and quality.

complexity   Difference among jobs as the direct outgrowth of dividing work and creating departments.

conceptual skills   The ability to coordinate and integrate ideas, concepts, and practices. Such skill is most important to top-level managers.

concurrent control   The techniques and methods that focus on the actual, ongoing activity of the organization.

conditions of certainty   A situation in which a person facing a decision has enough information to know what the outcome of each alternative will be.

conditions of risk   A situation in which a person facing a decision can estimate the likelihood (probability) of a particular outcome.

conditions of uncertainty   A situation in which the decision maker has absolutely no idea of the probabilities associated with the various alternatives being considered. In such a situation, the decision maker's intuition, judgment, and personality can play an important role.

consideration   Behaviors by a leader that imply supportive concern for the followers in a group.

contingency approach   A management approach that considers an organization's objectives, organization and job design, human resources, environment, and managerial skills as interacting and affecting the type of management decisions made about planning, organizing, leading, and controlling.

contingency theory of leadership   A theory that attributes performance differences to the leader's behavior and style in combination with situational factors.

control chart   A record of an organization's targeted activity over time, with established upper and lower control limits.

controlling function   The actions and decisions that managers undertake to ensure that actual results are consistent with desired results.

core job dimensions   As proposed by Hackman and others, the five core job dimensions (variety, task identity, task significance, autonomy, and feedback) that, if present, provide enrichment for jobs.

corporate philanthropy   Financial donations by corporations to organizations for socially responsible purposes.

corporate social performance   Defined by D. J. Wood as "a business organization's configuration of principles of social responsibility, processes of social responsiveness, and policies, programs and observable outcomes as they relate to the firm's societal relationships."

corrective action   The actions a manager takes to bring a system back into conformance with performance standards.

cost-benefit analysis   A technique for evaluating individual projects and deciding among alternatives.

critical path   The longest path in a PERT network, from the network beginning event to the network ending event.

culture   A very complex environmental influence that includes knowledge, beliefs, laws, morals, art, customs, and any other habits and capabilities an individual acquires as a member of society. It is important to be aware that cultures are *learned*, cultures *vary*, and cultures *influence behavior*.

current ratio   The ratio of a firm's current assets to its current liabilities.

customer-perceived value   The need and value of customers identified through the use of techniques such as conjoint analysis and focus groups.

D

data mart   A subset of a data warehouse that is easier for people to search for the data and information they need.

data mining   The use of software to search through the warehouse of stored information for relevant bits.

data warehousing   The storage of pieces of knowledge, often in the form of stories, for easy access for those who have future need of it.

debt ratios   Measures of the amount of financing being provided by creditors.

debt to asset ratio   An expression of the relationship of the firm's total debts to its total assets.

debt to equity ratio A measure of the amount of assets financed by debt compared to the amount financed by profits retained by the firm and equity investments.

decentralization The process of pushing downward the appropriate amount of decision-making authority. All organizations practice a certain degree of decentralization.

decision A conscious choice among alternatives followed by action to implement the choice.

decision support systems (DSS) Interactive information systems that enable managers to gain instant access to information in a less-structured format than a traditional management information system database.

decisional roles A manager's most important duties as entrepreneur, disturbance handler, resource allocator, and negotiator.

decoding The process by which receivers translate a message into terms meaningful to them.

defensive behavior Behavior such as aggression, withdrawal, and repression that an individual resorts to when blocked in attempts to satisfy needs.

delegation The process by which authority is distributed downward in an organization.

Delphi Technique A technique for stimulating creativity that involves soliciting and comparing anonymous judgments on the topic of interest through a set of sequential questionnaires that are interspersed with summarized information and feedback of opinions from earlier responses.

departmentalization The process of grouping jobs together on the basis of some common characteristic, such as product, client, location, or function.

descriptive statistics Computed measures of some property of a set of data, making possible a statement about its meaning.

developed country (DC) A nation in which most workers are employed in the industrial or service economy; has a significant middle class.

developmental purpose A performance evaluation policy of informing employees of their strengths and weaknesses and ways to improve their skills and abilities in an effort to improve performance through self-learning and personal growth.

devil's advocate A person playing devil's advocate will intentionally attempt to argue against the prevailing wishes of the group.

diagnosis The use of data collected by interviews, surveys, observations, or records to learn about people or organizations.

differential piece rate A compensation plan in which an employer pays one rate per piece up to a certain standard number and then a higher rate per piece.

differentiation The degree of differences in the knowledge and emotional orientations of managers in different departments of an organization.

differentiation strategy An organization's policy to offer a higher-priced product with more product-enhancing features than those of its competitors.

digital skills Managerial skills comprising the conceptual understanding of and ability to use computers, telecommunications, and digital technology.

direct financial compensation Consists of pay an employee receives in the form of wages, salary, bonuses, and commissions.

direct investment entry strategy A policy to begin producing a firm's products in a foreign country without the association with a host country investor. The strongest commitment to becoming an MNE, it enables the firm to maintain full control over production, marketing, and other key functions.

direction A method of concurrent control that refers to the manager's act of interpreting orders to a subordinate.

discounted rate of return The rate of return that equates future cash proceeds with the initial cost of an investment.

discriminatory requirement The requirement that a performance evaluation standard must recognize the difference between good, average, and poor performers.

disseminator role A manager's role that involves providing important or privileged information to subordinates.

distinctive competence A factor that gives the organization an advantage over similar organizations; what the organization does well.

distributive justice The concept that different rewards to individuals should not be based on arbitrary criteria.

disturbance handler role A manager's role to make decisions or take corrective action in response to pressure from circumstances beyond the manager's control.

diversity training A training technique that stresses the process rather than the content of training and emotional rather than conceptual training.

downsizing An organizational response to declining revenues and increasing costs that involves reducing the workforce and often closing and/or consolidating operations.

downward communication Communication that flows from individuals at higher levels. The most common type of downward communication is job instructions that are transmitted from the superior to the subordinate.

dual careers Situations in which both the husband and the wife are pursuing careers.

E

egoism An ethical standard that places highest value on behavior that is pleasurable and rewarding to the individual.

emblems Nonverbal communication that resembles sign language; examples include a "thumbs up" gesture indicating approval.

emergent leader A person from within the group who comes to lead or influence its members.

empathy The ability to put oneself in another person's role and to assume that person's role and to assume that person's viewpoints and emotions.

employee empowerment The management practice of pushing decision-making authority down the chain of command to the individuals or groups responsible for carrying out tasks.

employee stock option plans (ESOP) A program that awards company stock to employees as a form of compensation; usually employees are allowed to purchase shares of company stock at a discount from the market prices after a specified performance standard has been surpassed.

empowerment The practice of delegating authority and responsibility to employees.

enacted role The manner in which the received role is expressed or redefined by the individual assuming the role.

encoding The translating of a communication into an understandable message by a communicator.

enterprise resource planning (ERP) Software that attempts to integrate all departments and functions across a company into a single computer system.

entrepreneur An individual who establishes and manages a business.

entrepreneurial role A manager's role to change the unit for the better.

environmental scanning A technique that organizations use to stay in touch with developments in the sociocultural milieu.

EOQ model The economic order quantity model, which is used to resolve problems regarding the size of orders. A manager concerned with minimizing inventory costs could utilize the model to study the relationships between carrying costs, ordering costs, and usage.

equal employment opportunity Employment opportunity must be equal for all persons, no matter what their race, color, religion, gender, or national origin.

equity theory A theory of motivation that explains how employees respond to situations in which they feel they have received less (or more) than they deserve based on their contributions to the job.

esteem needs The awareness of the importance of others and of the regard accorded by others.

ethics A code of moral principles and values that provides guidance for a person or group in doing what is right.

event An accomplishment at a particular point in time in a PERT network; consumes no time.

exception principle of management Theory that states that only significant deviations from policies and procedures should be brought to the attention of managers.

executive information system (EIS) A user-friendly DSS designed specifically for executives; doesn't require prior knowledge of computers or databases but provides analysis by interpreting it in terms of the organization's strategic goals and presenting the results in an easily understandable format.

expatriate An MNE employee transferred to a host country from the MNE's home base or from an MNE facility in another country.

expectancy theory of motivation A theory that defines motivation, or the force to perform, as expectancy times instrumentality times valence,

$$M = E \times I \times V.$$

expected time (t_e) A time estimate for each activity that is calculated by using the formula

$$t_e = \frac{+4m + b}{6}$$

where a = optimistic time, m = most likely time, and b = pessimistic time.

expected value The average return of a particular decision in the long run if the decision maker makes the same decision in the same situation over and over again; found by taking the value of an outcome if it should occur and multiplying that value by the probability that the outcome will occur.

expert power The power that individuals possess because followers perceive them to have special skills, special knowledge, or a special expertise.

expert systems Computer systems that can make decisions without human interaction.

explicit knowledge Knowledge within an organization that is codified and stored in manuals, databases, or handbooks.

export entry strategy The simplest way for a firm to enter a foreign market. This strategy involves little or no change in the organization's basic mission, objectives, and strategies since it continues to produce all of its products at home. The firm usually secures an *agent* in the particular foreign market who facilitates the transactions with foreign buyers.

exposure The process that the self uses to increase information known to others.

expropriation Seizure of an MNE's property in a host country without compensation.

external change forces Forces for change outside the organization, such as the pricing strategies of competitors, the available supply of resources, and government regulations.

external communications Information that flows outward from the organization to the various components of its external operating environment. Whatever the type of organization, the content of this information flow is controlled by the organization (e.g., advertising in business organizations).

F

façade When information is known to an individual but unknown to others, the individual may resort to superficial communications; that is, he or she may present a false front.

failure costs The costs incurred by a defective product or service.

feedback The component of a system whereby the effects of the system on its environment influence the future functioning of the system.

feedback control The techniques and methods that analyze historical data to correct future events.

Fiedler's LPC theory A leadership theory that fits the leader to the situation; uses an instrument to identify the leader's least preferred coworker (LPC).

figurehead role The symbolic or ceremonial role preformed by managers.

final performance review The last step in the MBO process, a final meeting between the manager and the subordinate that focuses on performance over an entire period. The final performance review must accomplish two important purposes: (1) evaluation of the objectives achieved and relating these accomplishments to rewards such as salary increments and promotion and (2) evaluation of performance that is intended to aid the subordinate in self-development and to set the stage for the next period.

financial pro forma Documents in which the entrepreneur shows how the business will pay its bills and make a profit; includes sales forecast, income statement, cash flow statement, and balance sheet.

first-line management The lowest level of the hierarchy; a manager at this level coordinates the work of nonmanagers but also reports to a manager. Those involved in front-line management are often called supervisors, office managers, or foremen.

flat rates A pay scale established by collective bargaining.

flexible manufacturing systems Production systems that manufacture a part of product entirely by automation.

flextime A job arrangement that permits employees the option of selecting their starting and quitting times, provided that they work a certain number of hours per week.

force field analysis The process of identifying the forces that drive and the forces that resist a proposed behavioral, technological, or structural change.

forecasting An important element of the planning function that must make two basic determinations: (1) what level of activity can be expected during the planning period and (2) what level of resources will be available to support the projected activity. In a business organization, the critical forecast is the sales forecast.

foreign subsidiary entry strategy An approach to entry in a foreign market that involves joining with nationals in the foreign country to establish product and/or marketing facilities.

formal groups The departments, units, and project teams that an organization forms to do the work.

formal leaders Individuals who lead their assigned groups, divisions, or departments by virtue of their position and title.

formal organization The organization as it is drawn on the organization chart and as its titles and authority structure are designed.

formalization The degree to which an organization's expectations as to the means and ends of work are specified and written.

formative feedback Feedback on job performance *while the job is being performed.*

franchise A business in which the entrepreneur (franchisee) provides a product or service under a legal contract with the franchise owner (franchisor). The *franchisor* provides the distinctive elements of the business (i.e., name, image, signs, facility design).

friendship groups An informal group that evolves because of some common characteristic, such as age, political sentiment, or background.

fringe benefits Indirect financial compensation consisting of all financial rewards not included in direct financial compensation.

functional-design structure The assignment by an MNE of global responsibilities for functions such as production, marketing, and financing to managers at corporate headquarters.

functional management As the management process becomes horizontally specialized, a functional manager is responsible for a particular activity rather than a department or division.

funnel principle This principle states that the earlier in the production process quality problems are detected, the less is their cost to the organization.

G

gain-sharing plan A group incentive compensation plan whose purpose is, through a financial formula, distributing organizationwide gains.

garbage can phenomenon A commonplace occurrence in group decision making where individuals bring their favorite problems or solutions to each group meeting.

generativity An individual's concern for actions and achievements that will benefit future generations.

geographic-design structure The grouping by an MNE of all functional and operational responsibilities into specific geographic areas.

globalization The ability and freedom to connect to almost anyone, anytime, anywhere.

goal participation The amount of involvement a person has in setting task and personal development goals.

grapevine An informal communication network in organizations that short-circuits the formal channels.

grid training A leadership development method proposed by Blake and Mouton that emphasizes the necessary balance between production orientation and person orientation.

group assets The advantages derived from the increase in knowledge that is brought to bear on a problem when a group examines it.

group cohesiveness The attraction of individual members to a group in terms of the strength of the forces that impel them to remain active in the group and to resist leaving it.

group development The phases or sequences through which a group passes, such as mutual acceptance, decision making, motivation, and control.

group liabilities The negative features of groups, such as the group pressure that is expected to bring dissident members into line, the takeover of a dominant member, and the reduced creativity that results from the embarrassment of members about expressing themselves.

group norm Explicit or implicit agreement among a group's members about how they should behave.

group (panel) interview An interview in which a job candidate meets with an entire work group to discuss job requirements.

group politics The use of self-serving tactics to improve a group's position relative to that of other groups.

groupthink A phenomenon that occurs when a group believes that it is invincible, turns off criticism, attempts to bring noncomplying members into line, and feels that everyone is in agreement.

H

halo effects The forming of impressions (positive or negative) about a person based on an impression formed from performance in one area.

halo error A positive or negative aura around a ratee that influences a rater's evaluation.

Hawthorne Effect The tendency of people who are being observed or involved in a research effort to react differently than they would otherwise.

Hawthorne Studies Management studies involving teams of researchers studying working conditions and pay plans conducted at the Western Electric Hawthorne plant in a suburb of Chicago; the most famous studies conducted in the field of management.

hidden costs Costs of operating that don't appear on a firm's income statement but affect the profitability of the firm.

hierarchy of needs Maslow's framework of five core needs to explain human motivation.

horizontal communication Communication that occurs when the communicator and the receiver are at the same level in the organization.

human relations The manner in which managers interact with subordinates.

human relations skills The ability to work with, motivate, and counsel people who need help and guidance; most important to middle-level managers.

human resource management The process of accomplishing an organization's objectives by acquiring, retaining, developing, and properly using its human resources.

human resource planning Estimating the size and makeup of the future workforce.

human rights audit A process for evaluating how well a company protects employee rights.

hurdle rate The standard established by a company for financial performance of an investment or capital expenditure.

I

illustrators Physical gestures that illustrate what is being said (e.g., extended hands to indicate the size of an object); a form of body language.

immediate performance measures Measures of results that are monitored over short periods of time, such as a day, a week, a month, or a year. These include measures of output, quality, time, cost, and profits. Immediate performance measures are not always easy to obtain.

income statement A statement (also called the "profit and loss statement") that tells a manager whether the firm is able to make a profit from operations. This statement is divided into three parts: revenues, cost of goods sold, and expenses.

indirect financial compensation Consists of all the rewards, such as vacation time and insurance coverage, not included in direct compensation.

individual incentive plan A compensation plan that pays the employee for units produced; includes piecework, production bonuses, and commissions.

inferential statistics Computations done on a set of data, or among several sets of data, designed to facilitate prediction of future events or to guide decisions and actions.

informal group Natural grouping of people based on common interests or needs.

informal leaders People who lead their groups, divisions, or departments based on their leadership skills, and not on formal authority or titles.

information Derived from data; essentially, data that are organized for a specific purpose.

information age The period characterized by the abundance of newspapers, journals, magazines, television and radio programs, seminars, and the explosive increase in the use of computers and especially the Internet.

information revolution A term used to describe a shift in the focus of Western economies from heavy industry to information and services.

information richness The ability of information to change understanding within a time interval.

informational role A manager's duties involved in being the point central for receiving and sending nonroutine information.

initiating structure Leadership acts that develop job tasks and responsibilities for followers.

integration The degree to which members of various departments work together effectively.

intellectual capital The concept that the principal assets of many modern organizations lie in the heads of their workers rather than in machinery, bricks, and mortar.

intelligence information Data on such elements of the organization's operating environment as clients, competitors, suppliers, creditors, and the government for use in short-run planning; data on developments in the economic environment, such as consumer income trends and spending patterns; and in the social and cultural environment for use in long-run strategic planning.

interest group An informal group formed to achieve some job-related, but personal, objective.

intergroup conflict The disagreements, hostile emotions, and problems that exist among groups as a result of limited resources, communication problems, differences in perceptions and attitudes, and lack of clarity.

intermediate performance reviews In the MBO process, periodic reviews of performance that monitor progress toward achieving the objectives that have been established and the action plans that have been developed; important elements of control in management by objectives.

internal change forces Forces for change that occur within the organization, such as communication problems, morale problems, and decision-making breakdowns.

interpersonal communications Communications that comprise the full range of direct verbal and nonverbal signals that pass between and among individuals in the workplace.

interpersonal roles A manager's interpersonal roles include being a figurehead, providing leadership, and being a liaison both within the company and to stakeholders outside the company.

interpersonal style The way in which an individual prefers to relate to others.

intertype competition Occurs between different types of institutions. Kellogg competes with Procter & Gamble for shelf space in supermarkets, and hospitals compete with private clinics for medical practitioners.

intrapreneur An individual inside an organization who pursues innovation and champions it for a period of time.

intratype competition Occurs between institutions engaged in the same basic activity. Ford competes with General Motors for automobile customers.

intuitive decision making Basing decisions on the use of estimates, guesses, or hunches to decide among alternative courses of action.

inventory models A type of production control model that answers two questions relating to inventory management: "How much?" and "When?" An inventory model tells the manager when goods should be reordered and what quantity should be purchased.

inventory turnover A measure of the composition of current assets by comparing cost of goods sold to average inventory.

inventory turnover ratio A comparison of cost of goods sold to average inventory.

investment decisions Commitments of present funds in exchange for potential future funds; controlled through a capital budget.

isolates Individuals or small groups within an organization that tend not to communicate with other individuals and/or groups.

issues management A technique used by many firms that focuses on gathering information about a single issue and analyzing it.

J

job analysis A process of determining what tasks make up the job and what skills, abilities, and responsibilities are required of an individual to successfully accomplish the job.

job depth The relative freedom that a jobholder has in the performance of assigned duties.

job design The result of job analysis that specifies job range, depth, and relationships.

job enlargement A job strategy that focuses on despecialization, or increasing the number of tasks that an employee performs.

job enrichment A strategy that seeks to improve performance and satisfaction by building more responsibility, more challenge, and a greater sense of achievement into jobs.

job range The number of tasks assigned to a particular job.

job rotation Rotating an individual from one job to another to enable the individual to complete more job activities because each job includes different tasks.

job satisfaction A jobholder's satisfaction based on levels of intrinsic and extrinsic outcomes and the way the jobholder views those outcomes.

job sharing A job arrangement in which two part-time employees perform the job duties and tasks that otherwise would be completed by one full-time employee.

joint venture When foreign investors form a group with local investors to begin a local business with each group sharing ownership.

judgmental purposes The use of performance evaluation results as bases for salary, promotion, and transfer decisions.

just-in-time (JIT) manufacturing An approach to inventory management designed to minimize inventory and boost plant productivity and improve product quality.

K

knowledge management Refers to the many techniques managers can employ to capture and use the knowledge that is generated within the organization.

knowledge worker A modern employee who spends more work time using his or her brain than muscles.

L

leader-member relations A factor in the Fiedler situational model of leadership that refers to the degree of confidence, trust, and respect that followers have in the leader.

leadership In the context of management theory, a person's ability to influence the activities of followers in an organizational setting. Management theory emphasizes that the leader must interact with his or her followers to be influential.

leadership climate The nature of the work environment that results from the leadership style and the administrative practices of managers.

leadership role A manager's duties that involve directing and coordinating subordinates' activities.

learning organization An organization in which employees are engaged in problem solving, learning, and education so that continuous improvement in effectiveness is the result.

legitimate power The power given to a leader in the managerial hierarchy based on the rank held.

less-developed country (LDC) Has a very low gross national product, very little industry, or an unequal distribution of income with a very large number of poor.

Level Five Leadership Level Five leaders are individuals who usually have risen up within a particular industry and who lead primarily by example.

level of detail The amount of specificity in a plan.

liaison The role played by individuals or small groups in an organization to facilitate communication among isolates and cliques.

liaison role A manager's duties that involve interpersonal relationships outside the manager's area of command.

licensing The granting by a firm to an outside firm the right to produce and/or market the firm's product in another country.

life cycle theory A theory of leadership that suggests that leaders must adjust their leadership style based on the maturity of those being led. In this case, "maturity" refers to the followers' ability to perform the assigned tasks.

line functions Activities that contribute directly to the creation of the organization's output. In manufacturing, the line functions are production, marketing, and finance.

listening skills The ability to focus on the communicator, block our distractions, and comprehend the communicator's message.

M

macro-organizational design The design of an organization or a department.

management The process undertaken by one or more persons to coordinate the activities of other persons to achieve results not attainable by any one person acting alone.

management by objectives (MBO) A planning and controlling method that comprises two meetings between the superior and the subordinate (1) first to discus goals and to jointly establish attainable goals for the subordinate and (2) later to evaluate the subordinate's performance in terms of the goals that have been set.

management development The process of educating and developing selected employees so that they have the knowledge, skills, attitudes, and understanding needed to manage in future positions.

management functions The activities that a manager must perform as a result of the position held in the organization. The text identifies planning, organizing, leading, and controlling as the management functions.

management information system An organized, structured complex of individuals, machines, and procedures for providing management with pertinent information from both external and internal sources and for supporting the planning, control, and operations functions of an organization by providing uniform information that serves as the basis for decision making.

management of change The concept of organizational development in its broadest sense.

management science approach Formerly known as the operations research approach; involves mixed teams of specialists from fields required to address a specific problem.

managerial grid A highly publicized leadership behavior model developed by Blank and Mouton that considers leaders as most effective when they achieve a high and balanced concern for both people and task.

managerial roles The organized sets of behavior that belong to the manager's job. The three main types of managerial roles discovered by such researchers such as Mintzberg are interpersonal, informational, and decisional roles.

manufacturing The physical process of producing goods.

materials requirements planning (MRP) A computer-driven system for analyzing and projecting material needs and then scheduling their arrival at the right worksite at the right time in the right quantities.

matrix organization A design in which a project-type structure is imposed on a functional structure.

mechanistic model An organization design in which there is differentiation of job task, rigid rules, and a reliance on top-management objectives.

media richness The capacity of a medium to convey data.

micro-organizational design The design of a job.

midcareer plateau The point or stage of a career at which the individual has no opportunity for further promotion or advancement.

middle management The middle level of an administrative hierarchy. Managers at this level coordinate the work of managers but also report to a manager.

mission A long-term vision of what an organization is trying to become; the unique aim that differentiates one organization from similar organizations. The basic questions that must be answered to determine an organization's mission are "What is our business? What should it be?"

mission critical knowledge Knowledge that is vital to the firm's survival.

monitor role The aspect of a manager's role that involves examining the environment to gather information or to detect changes, opportunities, and problems that may affect the unit.

motivation The inner strivings that initiate a person's actions.

multidivisional (M-form) organization A high-performance organization form that allows highly interdependent operating units or divisions.

multinational enterprise (MNE) A firm doing business in two or more countries.

N

nationalization A process that occurs when a host country government forces an MNE to sell its facility to local buyers.

need hierarchy A model that presents five levels of individual needs—physiological, safety, social, esteem, and self-actualization. According to Maslow, if a person's needs are unsatisfied, the most basic levels of needs will be more pressing than the other levels.

negative reinforcement An increase in the frequency of a response that is brought about by removing a disliked event immediately after the response occurs.

negotiator role A manager's role that involves bargaining with other units and individuals in obtaining advantages for the unit.

network organization A flexible, usually temporary set of alliances among disparate companies that have come together for a specific, single purpose.

niche strategy When a firm provides a product or service in a special area.

noise Any element or condition that disturbs or interferes with sending and receiving effective communication.

nominal group technique (NGT) A technique for generating ideas that involves the anonymous contribution of ideas in a group setting.

nonprogrammed decision A decision for novel and unstructured problems or for complex or extremely important problems; deserves special attention of top management.

nonverbal communication The transmission and receipt of messages by some medium other than verbal or written.

normal curve A statistical representation that applies to a wide range of phenomena that can be measured on a two-by-two scale. No matter the data being collected, the results tend to align according to the normal curve with most data tending toward the mean or average, and increasingly fewer data above and below the mean.

O

open system An organization that interacts with its environment and uses the feedback received to make changes and modifications.

operating cycle The set of activities, including their costs, that are involved in the conversion of raw materials into finished goods ready for sale.

operating management Manages the implementation of programs and projects in each area of performance, measures and evaluates results, and compares results with objectives.

operating strategy A broad plan for action for pursuing and achieving a firm's goals and satisfying its mission.

operational planning Translates the broad concepts of a strategic plan into clear numbers, specific steps, and measurable objectives for the short term.

operations The functions needed to keep a company producing and delivering.

opportunity cost The cost of using cash or other resources for a particular purpose to the exclusion of other potential uses (opportunities).

oral communication The transmission and receipt of messages that occurs when the spoken word is used to transmit a message.

ordering cost An element in inventory control models that comprises clerical, administrative, and labor costs.

organic organization An organization with a behavioral orientation, participation from all employees, and communication flowing in all directions.

organizational change The intentional attempt by management to improve the overall performance of individuals, groups, and the organization as a whole by altering the organization's structure, behavior, and technology.

organizational communications Information that flows outward from the organization to the various components of its external operating environment. Whatever the type of organization, the content of this information flow is controlled by the organization (e.g., advertising in business organizations).

organizational culture   The impact of group norms and values and informal activities on the organizational environment.

organizational design   The process by which managers develop an organization's structure.

organizational objectives   The broad continuing aims that serve as guides for action and as the starting point for more specific and detailed operating objectives at lower levels in the organization. This book classifies organizational objectives into four categories: profitability, competitiveness, efficiency, and flexibility.

organizational performance   The extent to which an organization achieves the results that society expects of it. Organizational performance is affected in part by managerial performance.

organizational strategy   The general approaches the organization uses to achieve its organizational objectives. These approaches include market penetration, market development, product development, and diversification strategies.

organizational structure   The formally defined framework of task and authority relationships. The organizational structure is analogous to the biological concept of the skeleton.

organizing function   All managerial activity that results in the design of a formal structure of task and authority.

orientation   A process of providing new employees specific information about their organization.

outcomes   The tangible consequences of a group's existence.

outsourcing   The practice of one company contracting with another to provide products or services that are not part of the first company's core activities.

P

paradigm   A frame of reference used to understand the world.

path-goal leadership theory   House and Mitchell's theory of leadership based on the theory of motivation that defines a twofold role of the leader: to clarify for the follower the path that will lead to the achievement of personal goals and organizational outcomes and to rewards that the follower values.

payback method   The payback method calculates the number of years needed for the proposed capital acquisition to repay (payback) its original cost out of future cash earnings.

payback period   The length of time that it takes for an investment to pay for itself out of future funds.

perceived job content   The aspects of a job that define its general nature as perceived by the jobholder and as influenced by the social setting.

perceived value   The value customers place on a good or service as opposed to its cost or price.

perception   The process by which individuals organize and interpret their impressions of the environment around them.

performance evaluation   A postcontrol technique that focuses on the extent to which employees have achieved expected levels of work during a specified time period.

performance review   The formal meeting between the manager and the subordinate that occurs once or twice per year.

performance standards   Standards that form the basis for appraising an individual employee's effectiveness during the performance evaluation.

personal-behavioral leadership theories   A group of theories that are based primarily on the personal and behavioral characteristics of leaders. These theories focus on *what* leaders do and/or *how* leaders behave in carrying out the leadership function.

personality   The sum of an individual's traits or characteristics. These traits interact to create personality patterns.

personnel development   Training, educating, appraising, and generally preparing personnel for present or future jobs.

person-oriented leadership   Attempts to build effective teamwork through supportive, considerate, and nonpunitive employee-centered behavior.

persuasion   A process of selling a plan to those who must implement it and communicating relevant information so individuals understand all implications.

phased internationalization   Designing a product or service for international expansion based on product-market research in the prospective host country and identified needs of host-country consumers.

physiological (basic) needs   Needs of the human body, such as food, water, and air.

piecework   A compensation plan that bases pay rate on the number of pieces produced; a type of individual incentive plan.

planning function   All managerial activities that lead to the definition of objectives and to the determination of appropriate means to achieve those objectives.

planning values   The underlying decision priorities that determine planning objectives and decisions.

policy   Guidelines for managerial action that must be adhered to at all times. Policymaking is an important management-planning element for ensuring that action is oriented toward objectives. The purpose of policies is to achieve consistency and direction and to protect an organization's reputation.

political risk   Unanticipated changes in the host country's political environment that affect MNE operations; can be macro (affecting all MNEs in a host country) or micro (affecting only certain industries or firms).

political risk analysis   Identification and assessment of the sources of political risk and the probabilities that adverse political change will occur in a particular location.

position power   A factor in the Fiedler situational model of leadership that refers to the power inherent in the leadership position.

positive reinforcement   An increase in the frequency of a response that results when the response is followed by a positive reinforcer.

power   The ability to influence another person's behavior.

practical requirement   An evaluation standard that must have meaning to the evaluator and the person evaluated.

preliminary control   The methods that focus on the acquisition of resources.

prescriptive management   Discovering and reporting how managers should perform their functions.

prestart-up stage   The stage in which the potential of a product or service is analyzed.

prevention costs   The costs of preventing product or service defects.

principle of management   A generally accepted tenet that guides the thinking and on-the-job practices of managers.

private sector organizations   Profit-making organizations in the U.S. economy.

proactive decision A decision made in anticipation of an external change or other condition.

problem The realization that a discrepancy exists between a desired state and current reality.

procedural justice The concept that a reward should be clearly stated and impartially provided.

process manufacturing A manufacturing approach that focuses on repetitive and mass production of goods.

product-design structure The assignment by an MNE of operational responsibilities for a product or product line of a single unit.

production The total process by which a company produces finished goods and/or services.

production bonus systems A system that pays an employee an hourly rate. Then a bonus is paid when the employee exceeds the standard, typically 50 percent of labor savings.

productivity The relationship between real inputs and real outputs; a measure of how well resources are combined and utilized to produce a result desired by management.

profitability measure A meaningful standard appropriate to a particular firm; includes the ratio of net profit to capital, to total assets, and to sales.

program evaluation and review technique (PERT) A network management model that enables managers to focus on all necessary project tasks.

programmed decision Response to repetitive and routine problems, which is handled by a standard procedure that has been developed by management.

project manufacturing A manufacturing approach that focuses on major projects, such as bridges, dams, or buildings.

project organizational design A design in which a project manager temporarily directs a group of employees who have been brought together from various functional units until a specific job is completed.

projection The tendency of people to attribute to others traits that they feel are negative aspects of their own personality.

proper use of people An understanding of both individual and organizational needs so that the full potential of human resources can be employed.

proxemics An individual's use of space when communicating with others.

public sector organizations Federal, state, and local governmental bodies.

punishment The introduction of something disliked or the removal of something liked following a particular response in order to decrease the frequency of that response.

Q

quality audit A study of every factor that affects quality in an activity or process.

quality circles Small groups of workers who meet regularly with their supervisor as their leader to solve work-related problems.

quality of work life A formal program that attempts to integrate employee needs and well-being to improve productivity, increase work involvement, and provide higher levels of job satisfaction.

R

ranking methods The ranking of ratees on the basis of relevant performance dimensions.

rate of return on investment The ratio of the annual returns to the initial cost of the investment.

reactive decision A decision made in response to changes that have already occurred.

realistic job previews (RJP) The practice of providing realistic information to new employees. The recruiter tells it like it is to avoid creating expectations that cannot be realized.

received role The role recipient's understanding of what the sent role means.

recency of events error The tendency to make biased ratings because of the excessive influence of recent events.

recycling The process by which one MBO cycle gives way to another. The final performance evaluation session of one MBO leads directly into the establishment of objectives for the next cycle. Divisional or departmental objectives are established, individual objective-setting sessions are conducted, and the MBO process recycles.

reference ratio The ratio comparing a person's input to outcome.

referent power The power of a leader that is based on the leader's attractiveness. The leader is admired because of certain personal qualities, and the follower identifies closely with those qualities.

regulators Physical movements that regulate a conversation (e.g., nodding the head to indicate understanding); a form of body language.

reinforcement theory Theory of motivation that considers the use of positive or negative reinforcers to motivate or create an environment of motivation.

relevant requirement A measure used as a performance standard must be determined to have a significant and determinable necessity (relevance) to the individual and the organization.

resource allocator role A manager's role that requires allocating resources.

resources An organization's financial, physical, human, time, or other assets.

retention An employer's ability to hold employees.

reward power The power generated by the perception of followers that compliance with the wishes of leaders can lead to positive rewards (e.g., promotion).

role A set of shared expectations regarding a member's attitude and task behavior within the group.

role ambiguity The situation existing when role requirements are unclear.

role conflict The incompatibility between the role's requirements and the individual's own beliefs or expectations.

role overload A condition that occurs when a task's demands overwhelm the role occupant's ability to perform the task.

rumors Unverified beliefs that circulate in an organization or into its external environment; comprises the *target* (the rumor's object), the *source* (the rumor's communicator), and the *allegation* (the rumor's point about the target).

S

safety needs   Needs include protection from physical harm, ill health, economic disaster, and the unexpected.

satisficer   A decision maker who accepts a reasonable alternative course of action that isn't necessarily the optimum course.

scalar chain   The graded chain of authority through which all organizational communications flow.

school of management   A body of knowledge, concepts, and procedures used by managers. The authors discuss three schools of management. The *classical* school, the *behavioral* school, and the *management science* school.

scientific management   The practices introduced by Frederick W. Taylor to accomplish the management job. Taylor advocated the use of scientific procedures to find the "one best way" to do a job.

scope   The range of activities that a plan covers.

search engines   Internet services that locate information on the World Wide Web using key words or phrases.

security needs   Human needs such as protection from harm, ill health, and economic disaster and the need for job security.

selection of personnel   The hiring process that depends largely on an organization's needs and compliance with legal requirements.

selection tests   Commonly used tests used to screen applicants.

selective perception The process of blocking out new information, especially if it conflicts with what the receiver believes.

self-actualization needs   The human need to fully realize one's potential.

semistructured interview   An interview for which the interviewer prepares some questions in advance but has flexibility in the questions to ask.

sensitivity training   An organizational change approach that focuses on the emotions and processes of interacting with people.

sent role Group member agreement about the role to be performed.

service level agreements (SLAs)   The fine-grained details about performance expectations and potential remedies if performance falls short of those expectations.

short-circuiting   The failure of the formally prescribed communication system, often as the result of time pressures.

shot-in-the-dark method   Method of choosing a product or service for international expansion by selecting a product that is successful in the home country market and introducing it abroad.

single-use plans   Plans with a clear time frame for their usefulness; includes detailed goals and objectives concerning quality, primary markets, rollout schedule, and so on.

situation analysis   An attempt to understand the environment in which the organizations' efforts will be expended; an important phase of the strategic planning process.

situationalist theory of leadership   An approach that advocates that leaders understand their own behavior, the behavior of their subordinates, and the situation before they utilize a particular leadership style.

skill   An ability or proficiency that a person possesses that permits him or her to perform a particular task.

small business   An organization that is privately owned, not dominant in its market, maintains local operations, and generally employs fewer than 100 people.

social harmony   A factor in departmentalization. Managers must be attuned to the social relationships in an organization and be careful not to create a departmental structure that creates disharmonies.

social needs   Needs for social interaction and companionship.

social obligation   The theory that business must repay society by making profits for allowing the business to exist.

social reaction   A theory that views actions that exceed legal requirements as being socially responsible.

social responsibility   Behavior directed exclusively (but legally) in pursuit of profit.

social responsiveness   A theory that refers to actions that exceed social obligation and social reaction.

sociogram   A graphical presentation of pathways used for communication; shows who is communicating with whom.

software agents   Software tools that will perform services for an individual on the World Wide Web. For example, a person may request than an agent find the lowest price for a new computer.

solvency   A firm's ability to meet its long-term (fixed) obligations.

source credibility   The trust, confidence, and faith that the receiver has in the words and actions of the communicator.

span of control   The number of subordinates who report to a superior. The span of control is a factor that affects the shape and height of an organization structure.

special cause variation   A variation due to some external influence on a system.

spokesperson role   A manager's role in representing the unit to other people.

stable external environment   An environment in which there is little unpredictable change.

stable requirement   The requirement that a performance evaluation standard must be reliable; that is, different evaluations performed at different times should be in agreement.

stable system   A system that has eliminated special cause variation and is subject only to the unavoidable (yet reducible) common cause variation.

staff functions   Activities that contribute indirectly to the operation of the organization's output. Ordinarily, staff personnel advise line personnel.

staffing   A process that includes the forecasting of personnel needs and the recruitment, selection, placement, and training and development of employees.

stakeholder management devices (SMDs)   Relatively new mechanisms through which organizations respond to the concerns of individuals with an interest in the organizations.

standard cost system   A system that provides information that allows managers to compare actual costs to budgeted or predetermined costs.

standard operating procedures (SOPs)   Specific, written instructions about how to perform a certain task.

standards   Conditions for control derived from objectives.

standing plan   A plan that has ongoing meaning and applications for an organization.

start-up planning   Planning activities that occur before a firm opens for business; involves determining the product or service the business will provide, the business's market, and how the business will be established, operated, and financed.

statistical process control (SPC) A control process based on two assumptions: nature is imperfect and variability exists everywhere in systems; uses probability and statistics to understand and control complex systems.

statistics "That branch of applied mathematics which describes and analyzes empirical observations for the purpose of predicting certain events as a basis for decision making in the face of uncertainty," according to Gabriel Pall.

status consensus Agreement as to the relative status of all group members.

status differences The differences between communicators that often hinder the communication.

status incongruity A behavioral factor in group decision making where lower-status individuals are inhibited by higher-status individuals in the group.

stereotyping The attribution of a whole set of traits to persons on the basis of their membership in particular groups.

strategic business units (SBUs) Divisions within an organization by product or service to establish goals and objectives that are in harmony with the firm's overall mission and to assign responsibility for profits and losses.

strategic management Develops the mission objectives and strategies of the entire organization; the top-level decision makers in the organization.

strategic planning The activities that lead to the definition of objectives for the entire organization and to the determination of appropriate strategies for achieving those objectives.

strategic thinking The determination of basic long-term goals and objectives of an enterprise and the adoption of courses of action and the allocation of resources necessary for carrying out these goals.

strategy A process that results in an outcome, which is the basis for organizational decisions and actions.

strictness or leniency rater errors Mistakes in ratings that are lower or higher than the average ratings usually given because of the strictness or the leniency of the rater.

structural change A planned change of the formally prescribed task and authority relationships in an organization's design.

structured interview An interview for which the interviewer prepares questions in advance and asks these specific questions of all interviewees.

summative feedback Used at the end of the implementation process to provide a "bottom-line" assessment of the effectiveness of a decision by comparing the results to company and industry standards.

supply chain management (SCM) A company's efforts to organize and control its acquisition and handling of raw materials and other supplies needed for operations.

supportive relations The consideration and interest displayed by a manager toward subordinates.

SWOT analysis A systematic, thorough analysis that requires attention to internal *strengths*, internal *weaknesses*, internal *opportunities*, and *threats*.

System 4 Likert's people-oriented organizational design, which emphasized open communication, supportiveness, inputs from employees to managers, and general supervision. The opposite extreme of System 4 is System 1 organizational design.

systematic decision making An organized exacting, data-driven decision-making process that requires a clear set of objectives, a relevant information base, and a sharing of ideas among key managers and other employees.

systems approach A way to think about organizations and management problems; views an organization as interrelated parts with a unified purpose: surviving and thriving in its environment.

T

tacit knowledge Knowledge within an organization that is stored in the minds of workers.

tactical planning Planning that deals more with issues of efficiency than with long-term effectiveness.

task group A formal group put together temporarily to complete a specific job or project.

task structure Refers to the degree of routineness found in a job; a highly routine job is said to have high task structure.

team A group of individuals who are experienced and understand the work and who interact and coordinate their work to accomplish goals.

team cohesiveness The degree to which team members are attracted to the team and are motivated to remain as members.

technical skill The skill of working with the resources and having knowledge in a specific area. Such skill is most important to first-level managers.

technological change A planned change in the machinery, equipment, or techniques used to accomplish organizational goals.

telecommuting Telecommuting means workers either stay at home or travel short distances to "telecenters" to link to the workplace via IT.

termination Ending an employee's employment.

terrorism The use or threat of use of violence for political purposes.

the unknown If neither party in a communication pattern knows the relevant feelings, sentiments, and information, each party is functioning in the unknown region.

theory X-theory Y McGregor's theory that behind every management decision is a set of assumptions that a manger makes about human behavior. The Theory X manager assumes that people are lazy, dislike work, want no responsibility, and prefer to be closely directed. The Theory Y manager assumes that people seek responsibility, like to work, and are committed to doing good work if rewards are received for achievement.

time and motion study The process of analyzing work to determine the most efficient motions for performing tasks and to determine the appropriate elapsed time for the completion of a task or job.

time frame The period considered by a plan, ranging from short term to long term.

time pressures Communication problems caused by inadequate time.

time value of money Money can be invested and earn interest over time. Its value in the present is a function of its ability to earn such interest.

Tobin's Q A measure developed by Nobel Prize–winning economist James Tobin that compares an asset's market value with its replacement cost.

top management   The top level of an administrative hierarchy. Managers at this level coordinate the work of other managers but do not report to a manager.

total quality control (TQC)   An approach to quality in organizations that seeks to achieve continual quality improvement in all aspects of the organization and to involve employees substantially in the improvement effort.

total quality management (TQM)   The generic name given to the approach to quality-based management developed by W. Edwards Deming that is heavily oriented toward treating the *system* as the primary source of error or defects in manufacturing or service work.

trait theory of leadership   A theory that attempts to specify which personal characteristics (physical, personality, mental) are associated with leadership effectiveness. Trait theory relies on research that relates various traits to effectiveness criteria.

transactional analysis   A behavioral change approach that is designed to give individuals insight into their impact on others and their interpersonal communication style.

transactional leadership   A leadership style in which the leader appeals to workers' rational exchange motives, clarifying for the worker the path from effort to reward.

transformational leadership   A leadership style in which inspirational leader behavior is based on modifying followers' beliefs, values, and behavior.

turbulent external environment   An environment in which changes are unexpected and unpredictable.

two-factor theory of motivation   The theory, popularized by the work of Frederick Herzberg, that the absence of some job conditions dissatisfies employees but that the presence of those conditions doesn't build employee motivation and that the absence of other job conditions doesn't dissatisfy employees but that their presence builds employee motivation.

U

unity of command   A management principle that states that each subordinate should report to only one superior.

unity of direction   The process of grouping all related activities under one superior.

unstructured interview   An interview for which the interviewer has the freedom to discuss whatever information is considered important.

upward communication   Communication that flows from individuals at lower levels of an organization structure to those at higher levels.

V

value chain   All activities undertaken by an organization to create value for the customer.

value judgments   The assignment by a receiver of an overall worth to a message before the receiver receives the entire communication.

value set   A lasting set of convictions that are held by a person, an accompanying mode of conduct, and the importance of the convictions to the person.

values-based decision making   A methodical decision-making approach that ensures organizational values enter into all major decisions.

verbal communication   Communication by talking or writing.

virtual organization   A collection of individuals and other factors of production that have no central, physical locations but use electronic technologies to facilitate work and interaction.

W

weighted application method   An approach to analyzing application form responses in which some elements in a person's background are identified as being more important than others.

weighted checklist   A rating system consisting of statements that describe various types and levels of behavior for a particular job. Each of the statements is weighted according to its importance.

work group   A collection of interacting employees (managerial or nonmanagerial) who share certain norms and are striving toward member need satisfaction through the attainment of group goals.

work overload   There are two types of overload: *quantitative*—when a person has too many different things to do or an insufficient amount of time to do the job; *qualitative*—when a person feels a lack of ability to do a part of the job.

work team   A special type of organizational work group; teams are self-managing and have a great deal more decision autonomy than work groups.

written communication   The transmission and receipt of messages through the written word.

Name Index

Author names are referenced to the pages where their works are cited. An italic *n* following a page number (e.g., 241*n*) indicates that the reference citation appears on that page; an italic *n* and number following a page number (e.g., 241*n*13) indicate the page on which the author is cited and the note number of the citation.

Subject Index

Page numbers in italics identify illustrations. An italic *t* next to a page number (e.g., 241*t*) indicates information that appears in a table. An italic *n* and number following a page number (e.g., 241*n*13) indicate information that appears in an end-of-chapter note and the number of the note where the material can be found. A page number followed by an italic *n* with no note number (e.g., 241*n*) indicates an on-page note reference.

Company Index